The Sociology of Mental Health and Illness

Allen Furr
Auburn University

Los Angeles | London | New Delhi
Singapore | Washington DC | Melbourne

FOR INFORMATION:

SAGE Publications, Inc.
2455 Teller Road
Thousand Oaks, California 91320
E-mail: order@sagepub.com

SAGE Publications Ltd.
1 Oliver's Yard
55 City Road
London, EC1Y 1SP
United Kingdom

SAGE Publications India Pvt. Ltd.
B 1/I 1 Mohan Cooperative Industrial Area
Mathura Road, New Delhi 110 044
India

SAGE Publications Asia-Pacific Pte. Ltd.
18 Cross Street #10-10/11/12
China Square Central
Singapore 048423

Acquisitions Editor: Jeff Lasser
Product Associate: Kat Wallace
Production Editor: Vijayakumar
Copy Editor: Christobel Colleen Hopman
Typesetter: TNQ Technologies
Proofreader: Benny Willy Stephen
Indexer: TNQ Technologies
Cover Designer: Candice Harman
Marketing Manager: Jennifer Haldeman

Copyright © 2023 by SAGE Publications, Inc.

All rights reserved. Except as permitted by U.S. copyright law, no part of this work may be reproduced or distributed in any form or by any means, or stored in a database or retrieval system, without permission in writing from the publisher.

All third-party trademarks referenced or depicted herein are included solely for the purpose of illustration and are the property of their respective owners. Reference to these trademarks in no way indicates any relationship with, or endorsement by, the trademark owner.

Printed in the United States of America

Library of Congress Cataloging-in-Publication Data

Names: Furr, Allen, author.

Title: The sociology of mental health and illness / Allen Furr.

Identifiers: LCCN 2022007512 | ISBN 9781071815533 (paperback; acid-free paper) | ISBN 9781071815502 (adobe pdf) | ISBN 9781071815526 (epub) | ISBN 9781071815519 (epub)

Subjects: LCSH: Social psychiatry. | Mental health–Social aspects. | Mental illness–Social aspects. | Psychology, Pathological–Etiology.

Classification: LCC RC455 .F85 2023 | DDC 616.89/14–dc23/eng/20220316

LC record available at https://lccn.loc.gov/2022007512

This book is printed on acid-free paper.

22 23 24 25 26 10 9 8 7 6 5 4 3 2 1

Brief Contents

Preface		xi
About the Author		xv
1	Introduction to the Sociology of Mental Illness	1
2	Mental Illness in History	20
3	Sociology's Theories of Mental Illness	48
4	Prevalence and Costs of Mental Illness	73
5	Social Class and Mental Illness	96
6	Race and Ethnicity	118
7	Mental Health and Gender	140
8	Mental Health Over the Life Course	164
9	Communities and Organizations	194
10	Social Problems and Disasters	214

11	The Career of Mental Health Patients	245
12	The Medicalization of Social and Psychological Problems	270
13	International Mental Health	296
14	Mental Health Policy and the Law	323

Epilogue	348
Appendix 1: Glossary of Diagnostic Categories	352
Appendix 2: Glossary of Key Terms	359
Bibliography	370
Index	417

Detailed Contents

Preface — xi
About the Author — xv

1 Introduction to the Sociology of Mental Illness — 1

Learning Objectives	1	Cultural Factors	14
Introduction	1	Social Structural Factors	15
Sociology and the Study of Mental Illness	2	Interaction Factors	16
What Is Mental Illness?	3	The Search for Meaning	17
A Sociological Definition of Mental Disorder	8	About the Quote	18
Social Construction of Psychiatric Illness	10	Discussion Questions	19
Social Forces and Mental Illness	12	Key Terms	19

2 Mental Illness in History — 20

Learning Objectives	20	Key Intellectual Developments of the Nineteenth Century	42
Introduction	20	The Twentieth Century	43
Prehistory	21	Talk Therapies	44
Early Civilizations	23	The Rise of Pharmaceuticals and the Fall of Institutions	45
The Classical Era	24	About the Quote	46
The Middle Ages	29	Discussion Questions	47
The Renaissance and the Enlightenment	33	Key Terms	47
Mental Illness in American History	38		
Reform and the Beginnings of Modern Psychiatry	40		

3 Sociology's Theories of Mental Illness — 48

Learning Objectives — 48
Introduction — 48
Lay Theories of Mental Health — 49
  Lay Beliefs of Causality — 50
Sociological Approaches — 52
  Labeling Theory (Aka Social Reaction Theory) — 53
    Modified Labeling Theory — 54
      Step 1: Beliefs — 54
      Step 2: Internalization — 54
      Step 3: Response — 54
      Step 4: Consequences — 54
      Step 5: Vulnerability — 55
  Labeling Theory and Power — 55
  Labeling Theory Criticisms — 55
Structural Strain Theory — 55
Stress Theory — 58
  The Biology Side of Stress Theory — 59
  Sociology and Stress Theory — 61
    Daily Hassles — 61
    Ambient Stressors — 63
    Catastrophes and Traumas — 63
    Acute and Chronic Stressors — 64
  Responding to Stressors — 65
Critical Theory — 65
Social Constructionism — 68
About the Quote — 71
Discussion Questions — 71
Key Terms — 72

4 Prevalence and Costs of Mental Illness — 73

Learning Objectives — 73
Introduction — 73
Epidemiology — 74
Measurement Issues — 80
Social Patterns in the Distribution of Mental Illness — 88
The Social Costs of Mental Illness — 92
About the Quote — 94
Discussion Questions — 95
Key Terms — 95

5 Social Class and Mental Illness — 96

Learning Objectives — 96
Introduction — 96
Stratification and Social Class — 97
  Caste and Class — 97
  What Is Social Class? — 100
How Does Social Class Impact Mental Health? — 102
  The Question of Causality — 103
  Social Selection and Social Drift Theories — 104
  The Social Causation Model — 105
  Which Is Right? — 105
Social Class and Stress — 106
Subjective Aspects of Social Class — 108
  Relative Deprivation Hypothesis — 110
  Status-Based Identity — 111
  Fatalism — 111
What About the Upper-Class? — 112

Social Class, Parenting, and Personality	113
Linking Class Position and Psychological Distress	115
About the Quote	116
Discussion Questions	117
Key Terms	117

6   Race and Ethnicity — 118

Learning Objectives	118
Introduction	119
Understanding Race and Ethnicity	120
Differences in Mental Health Among Ethnoracial Groups	124
Discrimination and Mental Health	126
Special Circumstances Within Groups	128
American Indians and Native Alaskans	129
African Americans	130
Hispanics	133
Asian Americans	135
About the Quote	138
Discussion Questions	139
Key Terms	139

7   Mental Health and Gender — 140

Learning Objectives	140
Introduction	140
Essentialism	142
Gender and Mental Illness Prevalence	144
Gender Bias in Diagnosing	145
Stereotyping and Interpretation of Symptoms	147
Are Women More Emotional than Men?	148
The Sociology of Gender and Emotions	149
Mental Health and Social Roles	151
How Roles Affect Mental Health for Women	152
How Roles Affect Mental Health for Men	153
Men's Vulnerability to Alcohol Abuse	155
Vulnerability Factors of Depression	156
Parental Loss	156
Lack of a Confiding Relationship	157
Caring for Children	158
Unemployment	159
Childhood Abuse	160
About the Quote	160
Discussion Questions	163
Key Terms	163

8   Mental Health Over the Life Course — 164

Learning Objectives	164
Introduction	164
Lives are Embedded in and Shaped by Historical Context	164
Individuals Make Choices About Their Lives, but Those Decisions Are Constrained by Historical Events and Social Circumstances	165

Our Lives Are Intertwined Through Social Relationships	165	Children and Adolescents	180
		Helicopter Parents	183
The Meaning and Impact of a Life Transition Is Contingent on When It Occurs	166	Bullying	184
		Social Media and Mental Health	185
Socialization	167	Adulthood	186
Disruptions of Mental Health During Childhood	172	Early Adulthood	186
		Middle Adulthood	187
Loss of Parenting	173	Late Adulthood	188
Exposure to Family Violence	174	*Dementia*	188
Sexual Abuse	175	*Depression*	189
Physical Abuse	176	*Suicide*	190
Material Deprivation	177	*Alcohol Abuse*	191
Summary of Childhood Disruptions on Development	177	*Elder Abuse*	191
		About the Quote	192
Early Traumas	177	Discussion Questions	193
Life Transition Timing and Sequencing	178	Key Terms	193
Life Course Disruptions	178		

9 Communities and Organizations 194

Learning Objectives	194	Neighborhoods and Social Diversity	202
Introduction	194	Where We Work	205
Where We Live	195	Voluntary Organizations	209
Urban and Rural Residence	195	Religion and Mental Health	209
Rural and Urban Differences in Mental Health	196	About the Quote	212
Farmer Suicide	196	Discussion Questions	213
Rural Mental Health Care Services	197	Key Terms	213
Neighborhoods	198		

10 Social Problems and Disasters 214

Learning Objectives	214	Dependency and Addiction	222
Introduction	214	Prevalence	222
Homelessness	216	Substance Abuse Disorder	225
Homelessness and Mental Illness	217	Intimate Partner Violence	228
Homeless Adolescents	218	Causes of Intimate Partner Violence	229
Cause and Effect	219	*Sociocultural Factors*	229
Drugs and Alcohol	219	*Social Structural Factors*	230
Drug Use	221	*Family Factors*	230
Drug Abuse	221	*Individual Factors*	230
		Victimization	231

Terrorism and Mental Health	232	Pandemics	239
Terroristic Actors	232	About the Quote	242
Victims of Terrorism	236	Discussion Question	244
Natural and Human-Made Disasters	237	Key Terms	244
Disasters	238		

11 The Career of Mental Health Patients 245

Learning Objectives	245	Demographic Effects on Mental Health Care Utilization	256
Introduction	245	Gender	256
The Career of a Mental Health Patient	246	Sexual Minorities	257
The Pathway of the Moral Career	246	Ethnorace	258
Inchoate Feelings	247	Social Class	260
Feeling That Something Is Really Wrong	247	Stigma	260
Crisis Stage	248	Stigma in Everyday Life	262
Coming to Terms	248	How Stigmatization Affects People With Mental Illness	263
Variations in Karp's Model	248	Status Loss	263
The Decision to Take Psychiatric Medications	249	Individual Discrimination	264
Desperation	249	Interactional Discrimination	264
Experimentation	250	Structural Discrimination	264
Engagement	250	Self-Labeling	267
Marriage	251	About the Quote	268
The Decision to Seek Help	251	Discussion Questions	269
The Health Beliefs Model	252	Key Terms	269
The Socio-Behavioral Model	253		
Network-Episode Model	253		

12 The Medicalization of Social and Psychological Problems 270

Learning Objectives	270	The DSM	278
Introduction	270	Hospitalization	283
The Medical Model	271	Medicalization	287
Brain Studies	272	Medicalization Occurs in Degrees	289
Neurotransmitters	272	Levels of Medicalization	290
Genetics	274	Demedicalization	293
The Intersection of Sociology and Biology	275	About the Quote	294
		Discussion Questions	295
Psychiatry as a Medical Specialty	276	Key Terms	295

13 International Mental Health 296

Learning Objectives 296
Introduction 296
Global Prevalence 297
   Collecting International Data 298
   Key Findings of the World Mental Health Surveys 301
      The Burden of Psychiatric Disorders 303
      What Accounts for the Differences Among Income Groups? 304
Social Change and Mental Health in Developing Countries 305
   Problems in Developing Countries 308
      Urbanization and Poverty 308
      Women's Health in Developing Countries 310
      Children's Health in Developing Countries 311
      War 312
Perceptions of Mental Health Around the Globe 313
   Culture-Bound Syndromes 314
   Cultural Diversity in Treatments 316
About the Quote 320
Discussion Questions 321
Key Terms 322

14 Mental Health Policy and the Law 323

Learning Objectives 323
Introduction 324
Mental Health Policy in the United States 324
   Public-Based Mental Health Programs 325
      Veterans Administration Hospitals 325
      State Hospitals 326
      Community Mental Health 327
   Funding for Mental Health Services and Research 329
      Research Funding 333
      Parity 334
Mental Health and the Law 336
   What Is Insanity? 337
      Four Types of Insanity Defense 337
         The M'Naghten Rule 337
         Impulse Insanity Defense 338
         Substantial Capacity Test 338
         The Durham Rule 339
      Implications of Insanity Verdicts 339
   Civil Commitment 340
   Criminalization of the Mentally Ill 343
      Illness Only Group 345
      No-Place-to-Go Group 345
      Survival Group 345
      Substance Abuse Group 345
      Criminal Thinking Group 345
About the Quote 346
Discussion Questions 346
Key Terms 347

Epilogue 348
Appendix 1: Glossary of Diagnostic Categories 352
Appendix 2: Glossary of Key Terms 359
Bibliography 370
Index 417

Preface

I became interested in sociology as a young person because in reflecting on my own life, I realized that it was not psychological factors but historical and social forces that were dictating my life's circumstances. In my mind, I saw a causal path in which my behaviors, thoughts, and emotions stemmed from my sociological context. My class, ethnicity, religion, family history of migration, and living during the Civil Rights and Women's Movements and the Viet Nam era accounted for how I saw the world and, more importantly, how I reacted to it. My social background and environment also accounted for how I understood myself.

Little did I know at the time, I was practicing C. Wright Mills' sociological imagination, so when I eventually read his seminal book in graduate school, along with other classics such as Sennett and Cobb's *The Hidden Injuries of Class*, Gerth and Mills' *Character and Social Structure*, and Berger and Luckmann's *The Social Construction of Reality*, I developed richer insights into how my social milieu had worked to shape and influence me to fit a model of conformity that was based on the expectations of other people, not my own aspirations. The problem was that I had difficulty conforming, not because my psychological tools such as coping skills were inadequate, but because society was not always working in my best interest. The great sociological thinkers told me how and why that was happening.

This text is an extension of the curiosity that I developed as a teenager in high school and college. Its primary aim is to give readers a sense of how social conditions and relationships create life pathways toward mental health and psychological struggles. I've long believed that most learning should take place outside the classroom through students' own inquisitiveness, and this text is intended to give them the platform on which to grow the desire to discover more about the linkages between individuals and the world around them.

Therein lies the goal of this book: to foster the sociological imagination as it pertains to mental well-being. Macro social forces, such as structural inequality, discrimination, neighborhood characteristics, economic conditions, and social organization, are central to any discussion of mental health because they can cause or exacerbate psychological ill-health and are as fundamental to understanding mental illness as genes, neurotransmitters, and individual temperament.

Three learning objectives guide our journey to the sociological imagination. First, the text shows the subjective nature of mental illness and systems of diagnostics and treatment. I pose the idea that current perspectives on diagnostics are reifications of a medical approach to mental illness because confirmatory medical evidence to support diagnoses is not necessarily convincing. Labeling mental disorders is a subjective and interactive phenomenon rather than an empirically or evidentiary-based mechanical system that corresponds to medical or physiological conditions and diagnoses. Definitions of mental illness are largely social constructions. Individuals' emotional pain is real, but how we collectively label psychological troubles are subject to social, not medical, factors. We must also keep in mind that many people who "society" says are mentally ill believe that nothing is wrong with them. This situation is quite uncommon among real medical disorders. There are few better examples of the social construction of reality than attempts to explain mental illness.

The second objective of the text is to demonstrate that material conditions, including social relationships, cause physiological and psychological stress that can contribute to and even cause mental illness. Utilizing the idea of Fundamental Cause, emphasis is given to topics such as the relationships between political-economic forces and the distribution of mental illness. A particular focus is given to the ways health disparities, structural inequalities, and discrimination are related to stress. The strategy assumed in this text integrates biological and psychological factors associated with mental health and illness within the context of the sociocultural forces, such as individualism, narcissism, disenchantment, deprivation, and medicalization, in which they are embedded.

The third learning objective is to provide students the opportunity to understand the concept of "patient career" to orient discussions on how consumers of mental health services interact with mental health professionals and treatment centers. I have relied on research on help-seeking behavior that shows how people diagnosed with depression come to understand and define their emotions and thoughts and being labeled as "disordered." Understanding and reconciling a psychiatric diagnosis is quite different than a "med-surg" condition because the psychiatric label is more interactive and has different consequences for one's sense of self and identity. Having a sound grasp of this dynamic is key to a successful course on the sociology of mental health and central to the sociological imagination.

In the spirit of these objectives, this textbook is designed to serve as a foundation upon which to build classroom lectures, assignments, and activities, while providing students a basic understanding of the main concepts in the field and a reference for key terms and theories. Keeping in line with the current directions of the discipline, I have relied upon and presented the most current literature from sociologists who study mental illness and psychological distress.

More importantly, instead of being overly encyclopedic, the text is written in a generally conversational style and is grounded in critical thinking. Readers are given the tools to challenge existing dominant beliefs about mental illness and broaden their understanding of people's emotional and behavioral troubles. I have encouraged students to look beyond individual-level explanations of individual problems and expand their conceptual repertoire. They are also pointed toward asking difficult questions about the sociological roots of psychological distress. Many people are uncomfortable talking about the origins and consequences of racism, inequality, and sexism. Therefore, a less formal writing approach is used to help readers see the relevance of those social forces on health and to begin incorporating the notion that social structural conditions affect personal well-being into their own analyses of psychological health.

To facilitate learning, several tools are included in each chapter. Chapters have "Boxes" that present information that is interesting but parenthetical to the more scholarly oriented text. For example, Chapter 6, which is concerned with racial and ethnic dynamics in mental health, includes a box on the Tuskegee Syphilis Study. This discussion is not about research ethics, which is usually the context in which Tuskegee is taught to students, but on the scientists' prejudiced motivations in designing the decades-long study and their racist perceptions of the mental capacity of African Americans that provided the intellectual basis of the research. Other examples of boxes include a somewhat comical look at the idea of bureaucrat as a disorder and a failed attempt to make motorcycle riding a mental illness.

Chapters include other pedagogical features. Each chapter begins with a set of learning objectives that represent the primary topics found in the unit and ends with discussion questions. These questions are designed to help students use critical thinking skills to solve a problem or develop their own ideas based on information given in the text. Many of them can be used for group discussions and presentations, while others are better suited for personal reflection.

A unique feature is the section in each chapter called "About the Quote." It is common for authors, writing either scholarly and fictional books, to start chapters with a quote from someone else that has some intellectual or philosophical connection to the central point of the chapter. Authors, however, rarely, if ever, reference the quote, leaving it to the reader's own devices to make the connection between it and the narrative's theme. In the present text, however, the quotes are turned into "learning moments." Each chapter concludes with a discussion of the relevance of the quote to its themes and what can be learned from it. These were fun to write, and it was hard to resist writing long essays about each one.

The book also contains two glossaries. One is a list of key terms from sociology and the behavioral sciences. These concepts are identified in boldface throughout the chapters. The second is a description of the disorders that are mentioned in the text. While there are problems with thinking of psychiatric disorders as discrete categories of illness, as is discussed in the book, having a common language to discuss symptoms that often cluster together is helpful, though the boundaries between those groupings are not always as tidy as many would desire. This glossary is meant to share that vocabulary so that we all understand what we are talking about despite the reality that the terms themselves are often suspect and subject to criticism.

Textbook writing can be a lonely enterprise, and authors often forget how important their social context is for developing the ideas and putting them to paper in a meaningful and satisfactorily pedagogical way. Most of this book was written during the COVID-19 pandemic, which means that my social world was just as upside down as everyone else's. Still, folks came to the rescue to help me complete this project. I would like to thank Katie Perkins for reading drafts of the chapters and seeing if they pass the "does it make sense" test. Cynthia Negrey, Professor Emeritus from the University of Louisville, for reading Chapter 5 and fact-checking my approach on stratification. Thanks to Auburn University's Greg Weaver and Heather Rosen, my former star student now at the University of Georgia, for talking me through some of the ideas in Chapter 10. I also appreciate the help from the wonderful librarians at Auburn University's Ralph Brown Draughon Library. You are the best.

I received valuable help from both old friends and new. Thanks go to David Friedman for calculating the possible combinations of depression symptoms presented in Chapter 12. Junior high math for me is long forgotten, so David, I hope you're right. And thanks to my new friend, Sofia Tartaglia, a student at Emory University, for her paper and discussions about the drugs routinely given to post–World War II women in the United States.

Very special appreciation goes to Devin Walsh and all the good folks at Daymoon Coffeebar in Asheville, NC, for letting me take up too much space for too much time working on this text. Much of the book, including this preface, was researched and written at my favorite table at my favorite coffee shop.

None of this would have happened without the support of my dear family. Abby Shapiro, my wife and best friend, read every word and provided the first line of defense against bad writing and ill-formed paragraphs. Her authority as resident grammarian was often imposed, but rarely resisted. As a retired clinical psychologist, she also made sure I got the psychology right, which, to my surprise, I did more often than I expected. To our daughter Anna Furr, thanks and appreciation for her discussions on Chapter 7 and the time she took to help me check the bibliography. The text has about 900 citations, and not being skilled in the art of detail, I needed considerable help inspecting their accuracy at the conclusion of the first draft. She and I examined each reference, one by one, and despite thinking I had a sound system to create an error-free bibliography, we found many mistakes, duplications, and consequences of occasional lapses in attentiveness on my part. My love to you both.

Sincerest appreciation goes to the editorial staff at Sage Publishing. Jeff Lasser, thank you. After we first met at the Southern Sociological Association's meetings in Atlanta, I hoped we would work together on this project, despite cheering for different baseball teams. I appreciate you accepting the original prospectus, and your advice along the way proved most valuable. It has a been a pleasure working with you. Finally, every writer, no matter how accomplished, needs a good editing team. A thousands thanks go to Tiara Beatty, Vijayakumar, and Olivia Weber-Stenis who provided expert editing and project management skills in putting this book together. I am in your debt. Finally, my sincere appreciation is extended to my anonymous peers in sociology who read the manuscript and provided much appreciated feedback. Thank you, all.

About the Author

Allen Furr is Emeritus Professor of Sociology at Auburn University. Professor Furr's research focuses on the sociology of health, with a particular interest in mental health. Much of his work has investigated the psychosocial dynamics of facial disfigurement and face transplantation. He was part of the University of Louisville's research team that pioneered facial transplantation, and his most recent work investigates the stigma experienced by facially disfigured women in India. His book *Women, Violence, and Social Stigma: A Sociology of Burn Attacks* was printed by Rawat Publishers in India in 2017. In addition, Furr and his colleagues wrote the first academic reviews of the new concept of head transplantation. His work crosses disciplinary lines and can be found in journals in psychiatry, medicine, nursing, social work, as well as sociology. He received a PhD in sociology from the Louisiana State University and later a master's in social work with a concentration in mental health from the University of Louisville. In 2005, he was awarded a Fulbright Scholarship to teach at Punjabi University in India where he often returns to lecture, conduct research, and lead study abroad trips. A retired drummer and percussionist, he now lives a less rhythmic life on a mountainside in Asheville, NC.

To the memory of my mother, Margaret Gale Furr, who taught me that *milieux* have context.

CHAPTER 1

Introduction to the Sociology of Mental Illness

> It takes two to make a psychotic—an actor and an observer.
>
> —Morris Rosenberg (1984)

Learning Objectives

After reading this chapter, students will be able to:

1. Paraphrase sociology's approach to studying mental health and mental illness.
2. Explain the variations and difficulties in defining mental illness.
3. Interpret how sociology defines mental illness.
4. List the social forces that impact individual mental health.
5. Demonstrate how the tension between psychosocial needs and the social environment has resulted in a new search for meaning in everyday life.

Introduction

We have all used words like "crazy," "insane," and "nutty" to describe a person or incident that struck us as unusual, bizarre, or undesirable. If an otherwise "sane" friend, for example, were about to buy an automobile that you saw as a heap and a really bad idea, you might say, "You're crazy if you buy that car!" to emphasize that your friend is about to do something without your approval or, in your opinion, in bad judgment. Typically, we use such language to identify things that do not match our expectations of what should happen or fit our sense of good judgment. We also use these words to label people with psychological and psychiatric problems.

Terms describing physical illnesses, however, do not carry a similar dual purpose. For instance, we would never say, "You would have to be sick with a cold to buy that car." This simple linguistic exercise is quite telling. It may suggest that we diminish mental illness, or it could mean that anything we disagree with or is different from our own expectations is, in fact, "crazy." Using the same words to describe someone with mental illness and making a bad life decision or behaving in a way we think is improper may give clues to how we understand what mental illness is. It may also represent a hierarchy in perceptions of illness where physical medical conditions are viewed more sympathetically, and psychiatric and psychological problems are suspect.

All societies have a vocabulary for defining and responding to mental illness and emotional distress; however, there is no cross-cultural agreement on what mental illness actually is. Nor is there agreement within societies. Regardless of how people define mental illness, they all believe that they have *the* truth and *the* explanation of mental problems. Even though these "truths" and explanations change greatly over time and that no one approach has any more supportive evidence than another, we tend to have passionate beliefs about the origins of mental illness and who is mentally ill.

The main point here is that we do not yet have a definitive causal explanation for psychological distress and mental illness, and that means there is no exact definition of mental illness that everyone agrees on. Different socio-cultural groups and academic disciplines, including sociology, have strong opinions about mental illness, and conversations about what constitutes psychological problems are broad and sometimes even a bit contentious. We will begin our foray into this debate by exploring sociology's approach to the study of mental illness.

Sociology and the Study of Mental Illness

The sociological approach to understanding psychological well-being differs from those offered by psychologists and psychiatrists. Rather than focusing on individual pathologies and coping abilities, sociologists working in health and medicine are generally interested in asking two different types of questions. First, sociologists are curious about how society understands and responds to health problems. These studies, known as the **sociology of medicine** (Straus 1957), help us understand how the medical system works and how we define what is health and what is ill-health. Sociologists asking these questions may explore how a society labels behavior as mental illness and the behavior of health care providers. Here the focus is health and medicine as a social institution and the social and psychological consequences and experiences of someone being labeled mentally ill.

Sociologists working within this approach might ask questions regarding the ways a therapist interacts with patients from a different culture or ethnic group, or they may investigate governmental policies affecting funding of community mental health services or the ethics of certain types of psychotherapies. Other sociologists may ask what is it like to be a psychiatric patient? It is often the case that receiving mental health services places people in a different and stigmatized social category; that is, they are treated differently than before they received those services. How do people respond to this? Do they accept or resist this new identity? Do people labeled mentally ill believe they are mentally ill?

A second type of sociological studies focuses on **sociology in medicine** (Straus 1957), which is employing sociological theory and method to help solve the puzzle of who is more or less likely to experience mental health problems and what may cause social patterns in mental illness. Examples here are studies on the relationship between poverty and mental health or the impact of economic development on mental health in a poor, pre-industrial country.

A major focus of sociology *in* medicine is **health disparities**, which refers to differences in the distribution of preventable ill health and opportunities for good health that are caused by social inequality. Does everyone have the same likelihood of experiencing a psychological problem or getting treatment? While many health problems occur randomly in a population, many others, especially psychological distress, happen in predictable social patterns. Psychological problems are often related to structural inequalities, which can cause persistent hardships and limit access to health promoting resources. The impact of chronic deprivation, exposure to discrimination, and the lack of mental health services are central to explaining why some groups are more likely to experience a higher burden of the psychological problems found in a population.

Using the sociology *of* medicine and sociology *in* medicine as a guide, this book centers on two themes. We will look at how mental health is defined and how societies decide which behavior is "normal" and which is "abnormal." Sociology's perspective envisions mental illness not as a purely individual pathology, but as a consequence of social forces that produce conditions that create psychological distress. Our focus on health disparities will lead us to discuss the distribution of mental health in the United States. Who is more exposed to the risk factors of mental distress? Who is more likely to develop psychological problems? How do wealth, poverty, and discrimination contribute to the likelihood of distress?

What Is Mental Illness?

What do we mean when we say someone is mentally ill or has a psychological disorder? It's not always clear. Mental illness is one of the most difficult terms to define in the social and behavioral sciences. While definitions and conceptual schemes have been around for decades, none is completely convincing as a single definition of mental illness. Many are broad in scope, while others are narrow (Goldman and Grob 2006), and all reflect the culture in which they were written (Watson 2012).

However, none of these definitions is particularly wrong, nor do they necessarily prevent us from understanding mental illness despite their seemingly contradictory nature. As sociologist Howard B. Kaplan (1975) wrote many years ago, while there may be no true definition of mental illness, each attempt to define it has its own value in terms of explaining psychological problems.

It is not difficult to see the great variation in definitions. In many Asian cultures, for example, mental illness is defined quite differently than in the West. In China, for example, depressive symptoms are often perceived as physical complaints rather than as emotional or cognitive (Lee et al. 2007). Tsai and colleagues (2007) contend that Chinese people typically somaticize their emotional experiences because they use more somatic and social words than Americans do. To somaticize means to express psychological issues as physical complaints. Because Chinese culture views mind and body as intertwined and essentially indistinguishable, they cannot be separated (Xur 2016). If a problem exists in one area of the body, the other is equally affected.

In the West, definitions of mental illness are more formal and usually treat mind and body separately. These definitions vary, however, in orientation and focus.

Some definitions prefer to focus on mental wellness, rather than illness. The World Health Organization (WHO) (2004), for example, defines mental health as "a state of well-being in which the individual realizes his or her own abilities, can cope with the normal stresses of life, can work productively and fruitfully, and is able to make a contribution to his or her community."

Such characterizations, however, do not account for conditions in which well-being, as described in the definition, does not exist. It may not be true that the failure of individuals' ability to reach self-fulfillment or cope with stressors is the consequence of their lack of emotional fortitude or feeble physical constitution. If someone does not achieve these life accomplishments because of life circumstances, social barriers, or personal choice, is that person necessarily mentally ill?

Definitions of mental illness, on the other hand, typically attempt to specify deviations from what is thought to be usual human psychological well-being and functioning, but agreement on what this looks like is hard to reach. Schinnar and associates (1990) uncovered 17 dissimilar definitions in the scholarly literature between 1980 and 1990 alone.

The National Institute of Mental Health defines mental disorder in terms of functional impairment. In this view, mental illness is a cognitive, behavioral, or emotional condition that limits a person's major life activities (2022).

The ***Diagnostic and Statistical Manual*** (DSM) is a handbook published by the American Psychiatric Association (APA) that lists and describes all the psychiatric and psychological disorders recognized by the APA. It is a guide that clinicians use to diagnose individuals, and its current edition is known as the DSM-V. The APA's definition, however, is fluid. Prior to the DSM-III, the APA defined mental illnesses as existing along a continuum of problems in cognition, emotion, and behavior. Psychological complaints were the result of environmental conditions that produced difficult life problems. As Mayes and Horwitz (2005: 249) stated, until the 1980s, symptoms were "reflections of broad underlying dynamic conditions."

In the 1980s, however, a radical shift occurred in how formal psychiatry perceived disorders. Mental illnesses were reconfigured to be categorical diagnoses akin to nonpsychiatric, medical-surgery illness. Although there were no new studies to substantiate the paradigm shift, it reflected tendencies to standardized patients' complaints and to make problems amenable to insurance companies' needs to bureaucratize the process of covering mental health treatment.

There were relatively few "illnesses" in the first two editions of the DSM. Beginning with DSM-III, the number of diagnoses greatly expanded, and the definition of mental illness changed accordingly. In the DSM-IV

> *A mental disorder is a clinically significant behavioral or psychological syndrome or pattern that occurs in an individual and that is associated*

with present distress or disability or with a significantly increased risk of suffering death, pain, disability, or an important loss of freedom.

But just a few years later, the APA created a quite different definition in its DSM-V, clearly making the claim that mental illness has biological origins:

A mental disorder is a syndrome characterized by clinically significant disturbance in an individual's cognition, emotion regulation, or behavior that reflects a dysfunction in the psychological, biological, or developmental processes underlying mental functioning.

The change was resisted by many outside psychiatry. As psychologist Eric Maisel wrote in *Psychology Today* (2013), "the very idea that you can radically change the definition of something without anything in the real world changing and with no new increases in knowledge or understanding is remarkable."

The point here is that defining mental illness is daunting. Some definitions treat mental disorders as categorical and discrete medical entities, while others avoid medical language altogether. One school of psychiatry, the so-called anti-psychiatry movement, along with some sociologists, denies the existence of mental illness, stating that mental illness is merely the creation of the psychiatric industry to justify its treatments and theories. Most sociologists, however, generally agree that odd, distressing, or even bizarre behavior exists, but the argument is over how to understand and define them (Eaton 2001).

To add to the confusion, we can certainly observe behavior that is strange and unusual, but the people eliciting the behavior do not necessarily see themselves as mentally ill. Their friends and family may not think of them as mentally ill either (Aneshensel et al. 2013).

The problem, as Horwitz (2002) states, is that we notice behavior that is different from what is expected, which means behavior that is considered normal. Social values and behavioral norms constitute the basis of "normal" by specifying the standards of right and wrong, good and bad, desirable, and undesirable. Norms and values, of course, are subjective and vary by social group and place in time.

Therefore, how mental illness is defined in society is a target of sociological investigation. Indeed, many sociologists working in this area focus on how mental health and illness are defined, exploring patterns of which social groups promote a particular definition and how people understand behaviors, thoughts, and emotions contradict what they consider "normal."

Outside sociology, definitions of mental illness typically fall into three categories: (1) a statistical deviation from behavioral norms; (2) any condition treated by a mental health professional; or (3) conditions associated with biological disadvantages (Houts 2001). Each of these definitions, however, has significant problems that limit their utility in helping us understand mental health.

First, let's look at mental illness as statistical deviation from the norm. As Houts states, this approach has a great deal of appeal because it is relatively simple and straightforward: a statistical range defines normality, and those falling out of that range are identified as abnormal. In other words, what people usually do is considered normal and therefore healthy.

There are significant limitations in defining mental illness this way. First, what is the standard for tolerated deviation? At what point does the behavior change from normal to abnormal? Such thinking implies that normalcy is a matter of degree, but the exact point that a behavior crosses a statistical line to become abnormal is arbitrary. A second problem with this perspective is that there is no reason to believe that all statistical variations are bad. From your high school days, you may remember classmates who excelled academically and some who performed well under the class average. Both sets of students were deviating from the statistical norm set by all students in the class. Most likely only one group, the poor performers, was judged to be a problem. But what about those who are below the norm in one area yet excel in another? Perhaps the academically underperforming student is a brilliant musician. Plus, there are times when we all feel "not normal," not our usual selves. Most people, at some point in time, have intervals in their lives when they would meet the criteria of a disorder. Statistics and bell curves are of little use in these situations.

What is normal and abnormal, therefore, implies a judgment based on the values of the groups rendering the judgments (see Box 1.1 for an example). In societies with cultural diversity, people in minority groups may be considered "crazy" because their cultural practices deviate from the dominant cultural standards of the society. When conceptualized in this way, mental health is often equated with conformity.

Box 1.1 The Teachings of Don Juan

In his famous book, *The Teachings of Don Juan* (1968), anthropologist Carlos Castañeda discusses his relationship with Don Juan, a priest in a traditional culture of northern Mexico. Though not necessarily portrayed accurately by Castañeda, the teachings of the traditional Yaqui religion center on the practice of ingesting hallucinogenic plants such as peyote and jimsonweed. Once a person can tolerate the chemicals in these plants, the practitioner then learns to experience the mind-altering effects of the plant in religious and spiritual terms. When Don Juan consumed one of the hallucinogenic plants in a ritual, he believed he literally transformed into a crow and could fly and "see" an otherwise hidden view of the spiritual world that heightened his insights into understanding himself and human nature. Traditional western cultural standards, on the other hand, would lead many to label the priest as a drug addict or psychotic. In Yaqui culture, however, Don Juan was held in high esteem, and the visions he had while under the influence of peyote or jimsonweed were treated as having great spiritual value. During his apprenticeship, Carlos consumed jimsonweed and had the experience of flying, but he challenged Don Juan about his actual physical metamorphosis into a bird and flying above the ground. Carlos persisted, asking: "if I had tied myself to a rock with a heavy chain" would I have flown? Don Juan, increasingly frustrated with Carlos' questions, replied, "The trouble with you is that you understand things in only one way" (1968: 147–8). Don Juan insisted that Carlos "flew" and that the difference in flying physically or metaphysically does not matter. What is important is the experience. The point of the fictionalized story is that reality and truth are relative to one's socio-cultural sensibilities and interpretations.

The second way mental illness is commonly defined considers anything treated by mental health professionals to be a disorder. Mental illness in this case is based on what defines people called "patients" (Houts 2001). The problem with this definition is that it lacks objectivity and consistency. Decisions to seek care can be voluntary or involuntary, arbitrary, and costly. Those who enter psychological or psychiatric care, as we shall see later, are largely a self-selecting group, a process rife with bias. Clients, furthermore, bring a wide array of problems to mental health professionals, so virtually anything can become a disorder. Spouses who are upset because their partner had an affair or a person has developed chronic anxiety because they recently received a serious medical diagnosis, for example, are "mentally ill" the same as someone suffering from chronic, debilitating schizophrenia. This definition of mental illness lacks sufficient objective diagnostic criteria and puts nonparallel types of conditions and problems into one category of mental illness.

Third-party payment plans reinforce this approach. For a practitioner or patient to file for insurance to cover therapy sessions and treatments, the insurance company requires a diagnosis recognized in the DSM and represented by a code number. Because insurance companies will not pay without a code, the practitioner must enter a diagnosis. The patient now "has" a psychiatric disorder.

One surgeon-general's report (New Freedom Commission 2003: 4–5) exemplifies this category of definition:

Mental illness is the term that refers collectively to all diagnosable mental disorders. Mental disorders are health conditions that are characterized by alterations in thinking, mood, or behavior (or some combination therefore) associated with distress and/or impaired functioning.

Third, mental illness has been defined as an outcome of biological disadvantage. In recent times, many studies on mental illness have searched for damaged physiologic functions that lead to distressing thoughts, emotions, and behaviors. These theories and definitions have gained interest because they are assumed to be value-free, organic, and objective and contend that people with psychological and psychiatric problems have a discrete naturalistic disadvantage that hinders their ability to engage in normal activities.

This approach, known as the **medical model**, remains the dominant approach in psychiatry. Comparable to nonpsychiatric medicine in form, the medical model organizes psychological complaints into discrete categories. These clusters of symptoms are then classified as disorders that are presumed to have a physical cause. Another way to say it is that psychological problems are symptoms of an underlying bio-medical disorder. For example, depressive symptoms such as prolonged sadness, feelings of hopelessness and guilt, and thoughts of suicide are the expression or consequence of brain chemistry or perhaps genetic inheritance. Once a diagnosis is made, a disorder is treated with drugs prescribed by a physician.

This definition falls short of providing the definitive explanation of mental illness. First, as Houts suggests, any time human activity is compared to a model of "normalcy," the question of what constitutes normalcy arises. As in the case of the Yaqui, as shown in Box 1.1, "normal" may be a function of social and cultural conformity, being in the right social group at the right time, or judgments of what is right and wrong. Despite the organic approach's claims to scientific objectivity, saying that deviation from normalcy is a "disease" that causes deficiencies in functioning efficiency is a value-laden position.

Second, there is the problem of lack of evidence. Despite considerable public and professional opinion, there is little solid, science-based evidence to connect biological dysfunctions with mental illness in a direct and causal way. While there is some indication that biology may play a part in some cases, biological correlates of mental illness are not necessarily predictive. In addition, the range of conditions that fall into the category of mental illness is quite broad, making a singular explanation of all of them unlikely.

A Sociological Definition of Mental Disorder

Sociology provides a fourth way to approach mental illness. In attempting to avoid the pitfalls of the other definitions discussed, many sociologists classify mental illness as a type of deviant behavior in which people behave in ways social standards define as inappropriate (Horwitz and Scheid 1999). Horwitz' definition of mental disorder, for example, states that psychological disorders are "internal dysfunctions" that social standards label as inappropriate (2002: 35). These dysfunctions are emotions, thoughts, motivations, and behavior that are not as they should be, according to social conventional norms and values. As Horwitz says, only those internal dysfunctions that are also seen as deviant are considered mental disorder.

Rather than studying intra-psychic or physical pathology, these sociologists focus on the social processes that create social expectations, define who or what violates those rules, and under which conditions deviance from those rules is labeled illness. Symptoms of distress, such as feelings of depression and anxiety, and nonconforming behaviors, in this view, are interactive and connected to a social environment that promotes them, not indicators that something biological is "broken."

In the sociological approach, mental illness is an **ascribed status**, which implies that it is a status bestowed by a social agent, such as a mental health professional, on individuals. This social agent has reassigned the meaning of the behavior from simple rule-breaking to illness. But which dysfunctions are labeled an illness varies from one psychiatrist or psychologist to another. Many, and perhaps most, mental health professionals do not rush to give a diagnosis to everyone who enters their doors; others, however, claim to the ability to identify a disorder in virtually everyone within a few minutes of an assessment interview.

From this perspective, mental illness is a complex, multidimensional concept. Individuals can be ascribed mental illness status unwillingly via the judgment of others who are distressed or threatened by a person's behavior, thoughts, or emotions. Or individuals can accept the label because their internal feelings of discomfort lead them to believe something is wrong. The second category includes distressed individuals who subjectively see themselves as ill or disordered, or at least make themselves available for diagnosis and treatment. The sufferer may contend that the deviance occurs as abnormal or undesirable behavior, thoughts, or emotions, and there is usually agreement from a mental health care worker to validate the mental illness status.

Despite the attractiveness of this approach, it, too, has certain limitations. First is the problem separating causality from association. Establishing direct causal links in the social sciences is a risky exercise. Because human behavior is neither linear nor mechanical, many socio-cultural, individual, and biological factors impact what people do and how they think. Sociological research often reveals patterns of association, two or more things happening together in a meaningful, logical way. Does this mean one factor directly acts upon the other forcing a change in its previous state? For example, we know that people with higher levels of educational achievement have better overall mental health compared to people with lower levels of schooling. Mental health is not directly taught in school, and psychological therapy is not a requirement for a college degree. Educational success, however, often translates into economic success, which in turn makes life more comfortable and less stressful. Education also facilitates self-awareness and the ability for insight. Despite this pattern, it is not a strict one-to-one relationship. Many people with very high academic attainment have severe mental health problems, while many with low levels of education are free from psychological distress. Nonetheless, we can say with certainty that education and mental health are associated because people with higher levels of educational achievement have a far lower probability of mental illness than people with lower levels of education. But is it a causal relationship in the same sense that natural phenomena are causally connected? Finding the answer is not easy.

Sociology, as a science, is based on the calculation of probabilities rather than linear determinism. We look for the chances of a particular outcome given the presence of certain predicting or causal conditions. We usually cannot say if or when a particular event will happen, but we can calculate the likelihood of the event occurring. Because of the complexities of human behavior, we devise theories to explain the relationships that we observe. Theories argue for causal relationships, but typically do so in terms of explaining patterns of probabilities rather than specific, linear causal effects.

Second, the definition ignores the role biology may play in explaining differences in human behavior. There is no question that biological factors account for some individual differences between people. If you've been around newborns and young babies, you probably observed that they already have a temperamental style about them. In just the first few weeks and months of life, infants begin to act in ways unique to their own character. Some are quiet and calm from the beginning, while others are more vocal and active. As you follow the children into adulthood, you may begin to notice consistency in those styles that were first seen in infancy. Biology likely accounts for these styles of temperament that form a baseline or foundation of personality by providing basic predispositions of taste and certain talents. But do inheritable factors account for mental illness? The answer right now is that we don't know. There are measurable characteristics in brain and neurological functioning among some categories of mental illness that differ from "nonill" groups; however, these biological markers of disorder are not consistent, and it is not known which came first—the so-called ill behavior or the biological condition. Biologists are now exploring ways that stimuli from the social environment affect brain structure and function. This research demonstrates the value of biologists and sociologists working together.

A third criticism of this approach is the discipline's traditional reliance on the study of behavior. Much psychological distress is experienced as disturbing thoughts and emotions, but the sufferer can cope behaviorally. Many can put on such strong public faces that emotional and cognitive unease are masked from others. Intra-personal dynamics are not necessarily expressed in outward, observable behavior, but can nonetheless be very distressing. In response to this criticism, however, we could argue that distressing thoughts and emotions constitute deviance because of the way they are presented in clinical settings. Usually someone with such intra-personal stress will frame upsetting emotions or thoughts as not normal or wrong, as if they were deviant behavior. These "abnormalities" are just as real to sufferers as externalized behavior.

Social Construction of Psychiatric Illness

One of the main problems in creating definitions of mental illness has been establishing validity; that is, does the definition match the actual phenomenon being defined? It would be a mistake to presume that all people who are labeled mentally ill believe they are ill. They may neither feel that their behavior is an indication of a mental problem nor seek treatment voluntarily. Still, some authority in society such as parents, teachers, health care workers, or the police, has defined that person as psychiatrically disordered partly because they have control over what is and what is not termed "sick" behavior and because they have the social power to enforce the label on the person. An interesting example from the former Soviet Union comes to mind. The leaders and ideologues of the Soviet Union contended that the soviet socialist system was the idyllic form of social organization. The ideals of this society proclaimed that all people in the Union of Soviet Socialist Republics (USSR) lived equally, received what they needed to flourish as human beings, and were free from the wrongs committed by all other types of society. One would have to be crazy to find fault in this system, and that is what Soviet psychiatry believed! Many people who were critical of the Soviet state were labeled insane and sent to psychiatric facilities to "re-cover." The only symptoms these patients had were political opinions.

In this sense, we can say that mental illness is socially constructed. Social interactions shape the concepts of mental health and illness and set the boundaries of what is and what is not a disorder. The categories of disorders are determined more by social rules than biologic conditions (Busfield 2000). The **social construction** view of psychiatric disorders also contributes to our understanding of the biases inherent in the various concepts and definitions in health and illness (Brown 1995). A social constructionist perspective furthers a richer understanding of cultural differences in mental illness patterns. Socio-cultural systems produce diagnoses and treatments unique to their particular norms and values. What mental illness is and how symptoms are perceived may dramatically differ from culture to another.

While it is not uncommon for different cultures to recognize clusters of symptoms as co-occurring, western and nonwestern cultures often offer quite different explanations for the same set of symptoms. The symptoms of what we call depression, for example, are recognized similarly across cultural lines, yet where westerners might view depression as an illness or maladaptive response to something in the social environment, others, such as the Jiri people in Nepal, are likely to claim that persons with those symptoms are suffering because they ate the wrong foods or are possessed by a demon (Tausig et al. 2000). The Jiris' explanations are just as valid to them as bio-psycho-social explanations are real to many westerners. Differences in cultural history and knowledge patterns accounts for the difference. The social construction concept, therefore, gives us insight into the social processes that provide definitions of behavior as illness.

While social construction provides insights into how we define certain behaviors, thoughts, and emotions, this perspective does not explicate the sources of distress. As stated earlier, many people indeed feel psychological distress and emotional pain and relate to them as a problem in carrying out their everyday lives or just trying to enjoy their lives. In the absence of definitive theories of causality, in this book we will assume an interactive approach to studying mental illness. We will approach mental disorder sociologically, yet also make note of neurological and other biological mechanisms when they apply. The direction many contemporary biologists and sociologists are taking is to show that social conditions may trigger certain biological responses and lead to structural changes in the body. The basic question then is: How do the social environment, psychological well-being, and biology interact with each other?

I'm sure by now the age-old "nature versus nurture" debate has come to mind. Scholars and laypersons alike have argued forever over whether personality is made (nurture) or in-born (nature). The argument has been between two discrete, nonoverlapping choices: either human personality was totally inherited and was established at birth or was the sum of the individual's contact with the world. Now we know that this debate is moot, a throwback to old ways of thinking, and factually in error. The processes of nature and nurture are reciprocal not discrete and oppositional (Eisenberg 1995). The key question today is how the social environment and biology intersect. In short, it is not "nature versus nurture," but "nature *and* nurture."

Let's look at a couple of examples that show the advantages of integrating biology and sociology. When acquired immunodeficiency syndrome (AIDS) was first identified as a discrete disease, many theories to account for its origins were posed. Eventually, the human immunodeficiency virus (HIV) was discovered and linked to AIDS as the direct causal mechanism. If a person had the virus, its actions would eventually destroy the immune system and lead to AIDS. After several years had passed, researchers noticed social patterns in the distribution of HIV/AIDS. Higher AIDS rates were associated with certain social problems such as poverty, intravenous drug use, and sex work. Poor countries in Africa, for example, began to develop such high rates of AIDS that the disease threatened their demographic and economic stability. With this knowledge, questions of what caused AIDS began to change. Yes, the virus is the mechanical trigger of biological AIDS, but the psychosocial conditions of deprivation, exclusion, and alienation play a causal role too. To have the full picture of AIDS means more than understanding the biochemistry of the virus that causes AIDS; it also requires understanding the nonrandom, social climate that organizes the way HIV is transmitted.

Lead poisoning in children is another situation in which the value of integrating biological and social factors is evident. The element lead is considered a cumulative toxicant, which means that its toxicity accumulates over time. It affects several organs, particularly the brain, and is stored in teeth and bones. Children are especially harmed by lead because they absorb the element four to five times as much as adults and are more likely to ingest it. Mass lead poisonings resulting in many deaths have occurred in western Africa due to lead-contaminated soil, dust from battery recycling, and mining.

Lead poisonings are not relegated to developing countries; in 2017 over 500,000 US children are believed to have toxic concentrations of lead in their blood (Mayans 2019). As an important side note, there is no safe level of lead in the body.

After lead was banned from gasoline and paints in the 1970s, ingesting the element has become less common; however, there is reason to believe it has increased recently. Today, about 70 percent of exposure in children comes from old paint and house dust comprised of old paint and lead-contaminated soil. The remaining 30 percent comes from lead-based water pipes used for drinking water and imported goods including candies, pottery, and herbal remedies. Most of the toxicity found in children originates from old houses in disrepair. The lead in the paint has a sweet taste and the dust gets on children's fingers, which often go into their mouths.

Exposure to lead is linked to several negative mental health outcomes such as phobias, depression, mania, and schizophrenia, in addition to developmental disorders and behavioral problems.

The distribution of lead contamination is not equally distributed in the US population. Poor families and children are more likely to live in old houses that are not properly maintained or updated. These houses may still have lead paint and pipes. Researchers in Wisconsin (Christensen et al. 2019), found that children enrolled in Medicaid were three times the risk of lead poisoning than children not registered with Medicaid. In addition, because lead is more easily absorbed when other nutrients such as calcium and iron are deficient, malnourished children are more susceptible to the effects of lead. Since these health outcomes have connections to social interactions and a person's location in society, poverty can be considered a causal factor in lead poisoning, and consequently mental illness.

Social Forces and Mental Illness

How society influences mental health is another major area of interest of sociologists of mental health.

In his famous book, *The Sociological Imagination*, C. Wright Mills asked readers to look beyond their individual life spaces to think about and analyze their lives in the context of broader society. The secret to understanding much of what happens to us, according to Mills, is connecting our lives to what is happening in the larger society, a process known as the **sociological imagination**. For example, Mills recognized that divorce feels like a personal trouble because it is often accompanied by emotions such sadness, guilt, grief, fear, and shame. If only one couple divorced each year, then it would indeed be a problem, likely a psychological one, in one or both partners of the couple that made it hard for them to live together. However, roughly half of all marriages in the United States end in divorce, and that means it is a little harder to argue that half of married people have a psychological problem unique to themselves. Instead, Mills proposed that a better explanation is that social conditions have made it challenging for people to live together as a married couple. Indeed, in the last 50 years expectations of marriage have changed from a focus on following social expectations of tradition-based status and a gendered division of labor, to expectations of emotional fulfillment, which are much tougher to maintain over time. Also, increased educational and economic opportunities for women have made marriage less critical for women's identity and life satisfaction. Though it may have psychological outcomes, divorce is actually a social issue, a problem that is rooted in social, not psychological, dynamics.

While some sociologists who work in the mental health and illness area focus on how society defines mental illness, others explore patterns of psychological distress in society. Many decades ago, we learned that psychological problems do not occur randomly in society, and studies consistently report predictable patterns in the distribution of distress. These patterns mean that something sociological is happening and that sociological theories and research can offer insight into understanding them.

Sociologists use the term **social forces** to describe external patterns of behavior, emotions, and thinking typical to a society or group that coerce or direct individuals to act in certain ways. Outside the scope of individual people, social forces take the form of social structures and cultural norms and values that influence action and thinking. Social forces are the activities of the social environment that act upon individuals and to which individuals must respond. That response can be conscious or unconscious. The patterned activities of the education system, a group's morality code, and a family's household rules are among the countless examples of social forces that constantly envelope and shape us.

Social forces exert strong influence in the onset, maintenance, and diagnosing of mental illness. In this regard, the sociological approach to the study of mental illness in a population, in general, asks two types of questions. First, what is the role of social forces in the etiology or cause of mental disorder? And second, how do social forces influence who is at higher or lower risk of psychological problems in a given population? We will address these questions as we go along, but let's look at a couple of ideas now that will "set the table" for discussions in later chapters.

Social forces are those social things that act upon individuals, and many have been empirically linked to the incidence and prevalence of mental illness in populations. Many sociologists propose that mental distress is largely a consequence of social forces that conflict with individuals' psychosocial needs and interfere with psychological development and well-being. The volumes of data on this question seem to support this proposition, and recent changes in social patterns may explain observations that rates of mental illness are increasing (Nikelly 2001).

Meaningful human associations and close satisfying relationships are essential for mental health and are barriers to psychological and psychiatric problems. Social integration, attachments to community, voluntary participation in civic and religious organizations have been shown to reduce anxiety (Bergeman and Wallace 1999). Research further indicates that improvement in the symptoms of severe and persistent mental illness and depression is facilitated largely by sufferers' enhanced social environment, active participation in the community, healthy living conditions, satisfying and meaningful employment, and the therapist's interpersonal style and personal characteristics that demonstrate warmth, hope, and acceptance (Nikelly 2001: 306).

Sociologists have identified three sets of broad social forces that include both antecedents to mental health problems and facilitators to recovery from them. These forces are culture, social structure, and the dynamics of social interaction.

Cultural Factors

Several social critics see contemporary culture as rife with chaotic and confusing references and changing in ways that make the development of psychological health difficult. The intrusion of rationality into everyday life, rampant materialism and consumerism, individual gratification, bureaucratized labor, surveillance technologies, and the commodification of sacred culture are examples of socio-cultural forces that have led individuals to withdraw from a broader social life and to a narrow social milieu. Individualism and the mentality of "if it feels good, do it," furthermore, sends signals that life primarily centers on individual gratification and that social obligations and responsibilities are in some way negotiable. A retreat from the social arena, which can be seen in studies that report we are less involved in voluntary groups, know less about politics, and know fewer of our neighbors than ever before, may offer protection from the perceived threatening world around us, but may have injurious consequences for psychological health.

Cultures socialize their individual members in their own particular way. The values of a culture provide the contextual basis upon which individuals interpret their experiences, objects, and social roles. Culture is like a perceptual lens that people use to understand the world around them, and the interpretations an individual makes of the social environment have considerable implications for mental health (Simon 2002).

Although self-actualization seems the ultimate humanistic achievement, it comes with a price. According to Christopher Lasch (1979), contemporary western culture has become a culture of narcissism. A culture that rewards individualism and self-gratification, de-values intrinsic meaning, stresses "feel good" activities and products, and equates success with individual achievement, force us to retreat from society and dive more deeply into ourselves. A culture organized around the glorification of the individual creates psychological distress because individuals also face demands to conform, follow rules, and care for others. Narcissism and social obligations, to a large extent, are antagonistic forces. One cannot fully attend to the responsibilities of raising a child, for example, when the needs of the parent compete with the needs of the child. These pressures toward isolation and individualism make forming attachments with others difficult. Consequently, unstable marriages and children who are disconnected from their parents are commonplace.

Retrenching to our individual private worlds, and being alienated from society, disenchanted with its institutions, and cynical about its intentions, hinders the ability to ground one's sense of self. Communities are often viewed with suspicion where once they were seen as the foundation of social life and the primary provider of identity. These cultural forces contribute to problems of depression and anxiety, and existential dilemmas over our places in society and our identities.

Social Structural Factors

Social structure, which refers to the organization of societies and groups and the ways wealth and social resources are distributed, has a dramatic impact on psychological health. As Carol Aneshensel (1992) argues, psychosocial stress is an inevitable consequence of social organization because social systems create tensions between the needs of individuals and needs of the system. Ordinary people often experience stressful, yet normal and usual social practices with distressing emotional consequences (Aneshensel 1992).

Society is organized in such a way that individuals and groups have different levels of vulnerability to the risks of mental health problems and varying access to the social resources needed to ameliorate those problems. The harmful effects of poverty on mental health in particular are among the most established hypotheses in all mental health studies (Perry 1996). Economic marginality (as well as comfort) infiltrates all aspects of personal and family life. Because money is tight and opportunities are poor, life can be very stressful for those on the economic edges. For those who are economically disadvantaged or in working class jobs, work is not only more repetitive and meaningless but also less reliable as well. Seasonal, temporary employment and greater vulnerability to layoffs are common among lower income strata. The small social networks, marital discord, and economic dependence that frequently evolve out of living on the economic fringe magnify the stress of having little income. Repeated exposure to these stressors through one's life increases dramatically one's risk for mental illness, depression, and anxiety (Wandersman and Nation 1998) and to behavioral expressions of these conditions such as crime, divorce, and alcoholism, among many others (Nikelly 2001).

In addition to social class, other arenas of social structure have influence on mental health. Family, work, and peer environments where conflict and tension are present and poorly handled promote chronic stress. Violent and abusive families, racism, sexism, and struggles for valuable necessities create stressful environments and have negative implications for psychological health.

These social forces impact individuals' psychological well-being in several ways. Mirowsky and Ross (2012) contend that seven social factors contribute to depression in the US population: economic hardship, education, gender, age, personal control, social support, and mistrust. Their research found that half of all symptoms of depression are caused by these social factors in large part because of inequities in wealth, power, and access to important resources.

Most people who are exposed to stressful life events and conditions, however, fail to develop psychological and psychiatric problems (Kessler et al. 1985). Having a supportive social support system of friends, family, and community resources, few conflicts, and confrontations at work, can ameliorate and vary the severity of stress (Kessler et al. 1985; Pearlin 1989). Therefore, social structure can also provide barriers to and relief from psychological distress.

Interaction Factors

Concurrent with the socio-cultural forces and changes described previously are changes in the rules of personal, day-to-day interactions. Wheaton (2001) argues that recently measured increases in mental illness may reflect the consequence of social changes that have altered the basic meaning of social life at the interpersonal level.

The first of these social changes, according to Wheaton, is an increase in the rate of regulation of daily interaction. With the emergence of bureaucratization as the dominant form of social organization, regulation occurs at virtually all levels of social life. Many sociologists contend that the bureaucratic rationalization of social institutions has spread to the regulation of interpersonal relations. As traditional family functions are replaced by nonfamily agencies and as communication technologies have penetrated most aspects of personal activity, private life has become increasingly public. Daily living, which is often organized around informal social rules, is becoming formalized. One important example is Arlie Hochschild's (1985) concept of **emotional labor,** a term that describes the management of emotions to create a publicly observable facial and bodily display within the context of employment. The goal of emotional labor is to produce the proper state of mind in others. Whereas traditional physical labor in industrial societies required the coordination of mind and body, which is working with one's hands to run a machine, make a product, or perform some other manual task, emotional labor requires the coordination of mind and feelings. Emotional labor involves dividing the self, whereupon one must create a sense of "emotional elation" on the job despite one's true emotional condition at the time. Workers that Hochschild studied talked about the smiles *on* them, not *of* them. They were required to be cheerful continuously and to disguise fatigue and irritation. Hochschild concluded that emotional labor demands lead workers to feel detached from their own emotions in order to present the emotions demanded by their employers in interactions with customers. Cynicism and the depersonalization of others were also consequences of emotional labor. An important trend in contemporary society is to present a certain "public face" when interacting with others; this false presentation of self is often out of sync with the intentions of the social actor (Wheaton 2001).

A second social force having an impact on mental illness is the spread of mistrust of others, which has become a regular feature of daily interpersonal interaction (Wheaton 2001). The anxiety of managing risk, the erosion of tradition authority, and the increase in perception of interpersonal betrayal, have contributed to a culture of mistrust that has bred social disengagement and hostility. For an example, see Box 1.2.

Box 1.2 Understanding Society through Self-Reflection

We become uncomfortably aware of the integration of this "culture" into our psyche when we travel to other countries where this sense of distrust is absent. I have personally experienced this intra-personal conflict during my travels in Nepal, an Asian country where I have conducted research and traveled for pleasure. As a rule, the people of Nepal are uncompromisingly friendly; many will do things for you out of feelings of simple kindness and an obligation to help others that we have learned not to expect in our own country. During my research work in the former Hindu Kingdom, I relied upon Nepalis for various services ranging from transportation to typing to translating. Many of these services were offered to me without charge. I contended that this activity was work, not pleasure, and that the assistants should be compensated. Still many refused payments, saying they were honored to help. The first few times this occurred, I admit, with guilty feelings, my first reaction to myself was, "OK, what is this guy going to want from me later? What's the catch?" I soon realized what was happening. I was exporting a conditioned cultural sense of distrust on to people who had no intention of conning or taking advantage of me. Their culture is based upon trust and social cooperation, especially to strangers. I felt ashamed, but it was a strong lesson in how cultural processes affect the mind and the meanings of action with other people.

Third, Wheaton describes an increase in the negative labeling of others in day-to-day life. Changes in the nature of interaction patterns have resulted in more rejection, condemnation, and avoidance of others. As Wheaton says, in interpersonal interaction people often judge others as guilty until proven innocent. These judgments are made without evidence to substantiate them. Interaction based on negative projections makes engaging with other people difficult and can lead to a retreat into the self.

The Search for Meaning

The tension between psychosocial needs and the social environment has generated a desperate revolution in the search for meaning. "Bottom-line" economic practices and scandals by political, religious, and economic leaders have undermined traditional institutions that historically provided emotional succor and guidance for personal living. Much of the meaning revolution is not fought in mainstream religious houses or the halls of science, but on the vanguard of alternative thought and practices. Eastern religions and disciplines, notably Buddhism and yoga, so-called new age health practices, and therapeutic pseudo-psychologies not concerned with data-based conclusions (George 2006), are the directions many people are turning in their quest for the meaning of life. Similarly fanatical and extremist religious and hate groups are increasingly attractive because they preach a message of acceptance, belongingness, and identity in an age of ambiguity. These unconventional strategies are mechanisms in which people are utilizing to fight the existential battles brought on by changes in the social order.

We also seem to know less about ourselves, so we seek the guidance of psychologists, psychiatrists, social workers, gurus, and psychics; we sleep on crystals, attend "harmonic convergences," and chant mantras in languages we don't understand, all in an attempt to "find ourselves" within a social environment that is perceived as disenchanting and aimless.

Society has created new challenges for people in recent years. Few resources, however, have been presented that are adequate to cope with them, and the result has been a rise of existential and psychological complaints. The social "ocean" in which we "fish" swim and live has radically changed. New social forces have altered the rules of behavior and the definitions of what is expected and what is sane.

Despite the strong evidence that social factors have a considerable impact on mental health, sociological explanations of mental health problems have largely been underestimated (Nikelly 2001) and biological explanations remain popular and receive the lion's share of funding and media attention.

In our culture of individualism, we assume individuals are responsible for their own lot in life. This ideology presumes that personality and personal achievement are the result of rational-based decision-making and that we choose, without influence from the outside world, everything we are and will become. If something is wrong, therefore, it is not due to the social environment, but to bad morals or choices or biological impairment. Biological reductionism fits extant cultural norms and values well.

Biological reductionism also fits current industrial demands. The pharmaceutical industry has invested heavily in this ideology and has developed medications that, as some critics say tongue-in-cheek, are looking for a disease to cure. Despite the lack support that drugs are a panacea for psychological problems, the research and development and marketing of these treatments continue not only to be a multibillion-dollar industry, but a power in reinforcing the ideology that mental illness is a function of physiopathology. From a sociological viewpoint, biological reductionism itself is a social force that influences thought and behavior and facilitates the creation of mental illness.

About the Quote

Rosenberg's twelve words sum up sociology's perspective on mental health and illness. In our discipline, mental well-being is viewed as the result of an interactive, or social, process that evolves over time amid a sea of dynamic interpersonal relationships, institutional practices, and ideologies about authority and power. His quote reminds us that normality is not inherent: someone else has to tell people they are mentally ill or healthy. We are neither until a social "something" gives us the label and the label has social meaning.

A sociological study of mental health and illness essentially lies in two points. First, there is no agreement on what constitutes mental illness. Definitions change over time and vary by culture, and the criteria for defining a condition as a discrete mental illness are fluid and subject to interpretation. Therefore, the processes that are exercised to define a condition as a disorder or an illness are social constructions. In the absence of concrete biological evidence that, as shall be seen later, predicts and explains mental illness conditions, the void is often filled by ideology, mysticism, theories, and various other explanations of why people behave and feel the way they do. The very act of labeling behaviors and emotions as illness is a sociological phenomenon and subject to social theory.

Second, the distribution of cases of mental illness is not randomly dispersed in any population—there are predictable social patterns in the distribution of psychological distress. Social forces at the cultural, structural, and interactive levels have been linked to these trends and may either intersect with biological conditions or serve as separate causes of mental ill-health. Because disorders and treatments follow social patterns, sociological theories are applicable and relevant to discussions on the causes of these mental illness.

In sum, social forces can make us psychologically distressed and determine that we are mentally ill—one of us has to behave in a way that someone else thinks is psychotic. In other words, there is no mental illness unless another person says so.

DISCUSSION QUESTIONS

1. What have you learned about the definition of mental illness after having read this chapter? Why is mental illness so difficult to difficult to define?

2. Think about the social forces that impact your own life. Using your sociological imagination, how have these forces shaped your emotions, thinking, and behaviors? What social forces have been positive or negative emotionally for you?

KEY TERMS

Ascribed Status 8
Diagnostic and Statistical Manual 4
Emotional Labor 16

Health Disparities 3
Medical Model 7
Social Construction 10
Social Forces 13

Sociological Imagination 12
Sociology in Medicine 3
Sociology of Medicine 2

CHAPTER 2

Mental Illness in History

Learning Objectives

After reading this chapter, students will be able to:

1. Provide examples of how prehistoric peoples may have understood mental illness.
2. Describe the emerging theories of physical causes of mental illness and how they related to religious views.
3. Summarize the components and significance of humors theory and other contributions of the classical civilizations of Greece and Rome.
4. Analyze the relationship between social organization and its understanding of mental illness.
5. Explain how social changes affected views on mental illness during the Renaissance and Enlightenment.
6. Describe the evolution of how early American society approached mental illness.
7. Outline the evolution of competing approaches and main theoretical streams of thought that accelerated the rise of psychiatry in the nineteenth century.
8. Discuss the wide range of changes in treating mental illness that occurred in the twentieth century.

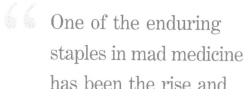

One of the enduring staples in mad medicine has been the rise and fall of cures.

—Robert Whitaker (2002)

Introduction

Because of its revelation of bizarre treatments and theories, the history of mental illness has long held the fascination of scholars and the public alike. How societies have responded to mental illness over the centuries is not always a pleasant reality to accept. Cruel punishments, inhumane confinements, and weird medical interventions largely characterized the treatment of the mentally ill well into the twentieth century.

Accumulating "factoids" recounting the strange practices of times past does not constitute a study of the history of mental illness treatments, however. We need context, and history provides that for us. What we will see by studying the history of mental illness is that people have wrestled with the same questions about sanity for centuries, and treatments and societal responses to mental illness have improved but remain distanced from the "grand solution." We are no closer to a cure than we have ever been.

We learn two major lessons by looking at this history. First, current thought and practice do not lie in a cultural vacuum. How we see mental illness today is the result of the evolution of ideas that have taken millennia to develop. Second, history provides examples of how we socially construct ideas about psychological illness. As mentioned in Chapter 1, definitions of mental disorders are fluid, and societies of different types produce unique definitions and responses to mental illness. For example, a society that commands strict religious conformity usually has a religious explanation for insanity, whereas an advanced technological society relies on technical explanations and highly bureaucratized treatment methods.

Also important is that every historical explanation of mental illness was assumed to be correct by the members of society at that time, which means that given mental health's inexact definitions and treatments, a historical perspective can provide insights into understanding why and how people are labeled mentally ill. Mental illness, evidence suggests, is found in every human population in all places and times. The great variations in which peoples have dealt with these conditions are most interesting, and history reminds us that context determines whether a behavior is considered normal or abnormal (Farreras 2022). Perhaps José Bertolote (2008) best summarized the importance of studying the history of mental illness by stating that because mental health has a number of meanings and possesses poorly defined borders, a historical perspective provides insights into understanding our emotional troubles and coming to firm conclusions about what illness actually means.

Over time, beliefs about the origins of mental illness have fallen into three categories: **supernaturalism**, **somatogenic**, and **psychogenic** (Farreras 2022). Supernatural theories contend that mental illness is caused by demons, evil spirits, gods, or magic in the form of possession, temptation, or curses. Astrological explanations fall into this category—eclipses, lunar phases, and planetary alignments are believed in some cultures to account for unusual behavior.

Somatogenic theories argue that mental illnesses fare rooted in physiological dysfunctions. Brain injuries, "chemical imbalances," and genetics are frequently cited as causes of abnormal behavior. Lastly, psychogenic theories posit that traumatic or stressful experiences, poor social learning and development, and distorted perceptions lead to mental disorders (Farreras 2022).

These three groups of theories have been found, in one form or another, from the earliest of times. They typically co-occur; that is, we often find elements of two or three of these approaches at any one time and place. A society's theory or belief system drives its responses to abnormal behavior, and the theory is grounded in the type of society that produces it. As we will see in this and later chapters, social status also influences perception of mental illness. This process has been true throughout history and still is today.

Prehistory

Prior to the ancient Greeks and Romans, there is scant evidence of how people thought about mental illness. Judging from remains and artifacts uncovered by archeologists and anthropologists, early cultures likely assigned supernatural causes to unusual behavior. Demonic influence or possession led individuals to act weirdly; therefore, shamans performed religious rituals to exorcise devils and free the troubled souls from the evil spirit that haunted them.

In addition to archeological data, prehistoric supernaturalism is also supported by encounters with nonwestern peoples who have minimal exposure to other cultures and continued to live somewhat uninterrupted or uncontaminated by outside influences. These traditional cultures' views of mental illness also rested on evil spirits, curses, or demonic possession. In many traditional sub-Saharan African cultures, for example, mental illness was the result of curses by enemies, sorcery, or supernatural beings that bewitched innocent victims (Akyeampong 2015; Patel 1995). In traditional Arab cultures, mental distress could be caused by the evil eye, satanic temptations to think or act improperly, or punishment by God (Bener and Ghuloum 2011)

Magic and rituals, however, may not have been prehistoric people's only remedies. It is possible that some attempted to relieve mental illness through a surgical technique called **trepanation**, a procedure of perforating the skull by drilling a hole or scraping off bone to reach the brain. Trepanation was perhaps conducted to relieve head pain caused perhaps by pressure from the build-up of blood after a head trauma. As improbable as it sounds, trepanation was likely successful on occasion in alleviating potentially fatal hematomas.

Archeological finds in Europe and Iran show that trepanation dates back 7,000 years to Neolithic times and was practiced in coastal Peru as early as 2,400 years ago, continuing in some areas of Africa into the twentieth century (Rawlings and Rossitch 1994). Trepanation was the world's first brain surgery; in addition to relieving blood build up, some believe it was conducted for magical purposes to create an exit for evil spirits to escape the body they possessed, thus relieving possessed victims of the disease or mental illness the spirit caused (Arani et al. 2012; Woods and Woods 2014).

Supernaturalism would continue for centuries and was more complicated than a simplistic "demons enter body" model. From their research on ancient Egypt, Okasha and Okasha (2000: 414–15) outlined the basic principles of magical practice in health and medicine. Through these precepts, magicians, "witch-doctors," and shamans created a system of belief that appeared rational in their culture—shamans' practices had to be consistent with the sensibilities of their culture to be accepted by their people. These principles are:

1. The belief in an "immaterial and impersonal force" that pervades the entire universe. This force holds all things together, and magicians can invoke or control this power to suit their needs.

2. In magic, logic and inferences are based on analogy and similarity. This means that two things are related and connected because they resemble one another in form or by name. The Oshakas give the example of a plant shaped like a body organ having healing powers over that organ.

3. The law of solidarity states that a body remains connected to any fragment separated from it. Based on this belief, it is possible to act on beings through locks of hair, nail clippings, used clothes, and so forth.

4. The last principle of magical healing is the notion that death is "protracted sleep." Deceased people continue to live, albeit in an altered state, and can revisit people they knew, descendants, or even strangers. These "ghosts," to use a popular term for these beings, can influence the mental health of the living, usually for the worse.

Though based on their study of ancient Egypt, the Okashas' guidelines for understanding magical thought are universally relevant. These qualities in "magic medicine" have persisted to modern times.

Early Civilizations

Most ancient peoples, such as the Hebrews, Egyptians, and Mesopotamians, believed that supernatural forces caused mental distress. If offended, gods or ghosts of deceased ancestors could curse the sinner with various afflictions. In ancient India, mental illness was thought to be caused by sinful behavior in a present or previous life.

Egypt, the dominant culture of the ancient Mediterranean world, produced great advances in architecture, arts, religion, and science, and became the leading producer and warehouse of knowledge prior to the Greeks. These advances in knowledge inspired Egyptian and Mesopotamian physicians to create a different mode of thinking about psychological disorders. While supernatural explanations for unusual behavior were most common, educated and literate thinkers began to explore somatogenic theories. Vestiges of one Egyptian theory remain with us. An Egyptian papyrus written around 1900 BCE describes a particular condition suffered uniquely by women in which the uterus wanders around the abdomen bumping into other organs and causing both bodily and emotional misery. The Greeks would later learn of the "roaming uterus" and incorporate it into their theories. Although the Greeks would eventually reject the notion that the uterus moves about the body, they would claim that the organ was the center of strong emotions in women and caused a condition called **hysteria**, a term derived from *hystera*, the old Greek word for uterus. Men were not thought to suffer from hysteria or histrionics until the nineteenth and early twentieth centuries when research showed that hysteria was not a female-only disorder (Tasca et al. 2012). The term "hysteria" remains in use to describe uncontrolled emotions and sudden excitability, and "histrionics" refers to an exaggerated need to be noticed and a self-esteem that requires external validation.

An interesting quality of ancient Egyptian thought is that Egyptian physicians distinguished between the causes and symptoms of mental illness (Okasha and Okasha 2000). While causes were attributed to the supernatural, symptoms were organic. For example, while delirium was due to feces in the heart and dementia was caused by certain poisons, it was supernatural forces that moved the feces and applied the poisons. Similarly, forgetfulness and "perishing of the mind" originated from inhaling the breath of a priest, which would confuse the mind. Treatments, therefore, followed the theory. Magical and religious treatments were aimed at the causes, and practical treatments, such as prescriptions of minerals, animal fats, alcoholic beverages, and drugs made from various plants, targeted the symptoms (Okasha and Okasha 2000).

The Classical Era

The ancient Greeks would continue the intellectual school initiated by the Egyptians and begin to search for somatogenic causes of psychological distress. The great philosopher Plato (c. 429–348), for example, wrote that diseases of the soul were consequences of bodily dysfunctions (Sassi 2013). He defined immoral behavior as contrary to nature, but not necessarily a medical condition. For Plato, the soul needed to be kept in balance, just like the body needs balance to avoid illness (Seeskin 2008). Plato divided mental problems into two categories: mania and ignorance, both of which were due to an excess or deficiency of one of the primary elements of the body. Rejecting supernatural explanations, Greeks physicians, particularly Hippocrates (c. 460–370 BCE) developed the **Four Humors Theory**, perhaps the first coherent theory of both physical and mental illness. The four humors—blood, yellow bile, black bile, and phlegm—were thought to represent the four elements that composed all earthly matter, including the human body, and had qualities that affected mental well-being. For health, both physical and mental, the four humors needed to exist in a balanced state. Table 2.1 shows the humors, their qualities, and their relationship to human temperament.

According to Hippocrates' theory, each humor's physical quality corresponded to a different emotional characteristic, and the correct balance of the four fluids, all of which are found in the bloodstream, is necessary for health and well-being. Too much or too little of one of the fluids caused disease and mental illness. Excessive black bile led to melancholia, too much phlegm caused apathy, and yellow bile was associated with aggression. Mania was due to disproportionate amounts of blood or yellow bile (Smith 2008).

TABLE 2.1 The Four Humors

Humor	Element	Quality	Emotion	Temperament
Blood	Air	Hot and Wet	Sanguine	Courageous, Hopeful, Amorous
Phlegm	Water	Cold and Wet	Phlegmatic	Calm, Cool, Unemotional
Yellow Bile	Fire	Hot and Dry	Choleric	Bad-tempered
Black Bile	Earth	Cold and Dry	Melancholic	Despondent, Gloomy

The cause of nightmares provided another curious explanation. Humors theory presumed that too much blood made the body hot and wet. Therefore, a person suffering nightmares had excessive blood that heated the brain and caused frightening dreams during sleep. Treatments, therefore, involved relieving the body of the excessive blood. Bloodletting, a treatment that would last into the nineteenth century, was frequently recommended for treating psychological distress (and many diseases as well).

The Greeks prescribed a wide array of treatments of mental problems. Inducing elimination through the bowels using laxatives was a common remedy. But not all Grecian treatments were of such severity. More humane treatments, such as aromatherapies or vapors (steam, naturally occurring and intoxicating ethylene, and various pleasant fragrances), baths, and dietary changes, were advanced to balance the humors.

Humor theory was complex and included effects of the seasons and temperature, all acting in concert with the natural elements and the body. It would continue as a dominant paradigm for centuries and spread to other parts of the world including such faraway places as India. While humors theory sounds ridiculous to twenty-first century sensibilities, it was an important step in the history of mental illness. Humors theory was a wholly naturalistic framework for explaining and treating diseases and directed physicians away from supernatural explanations of earthly phenomena (Scull 2015). The Hippocratics, as Hippocrates and his theory's adherents were called, also introduced to western civilization the notion of balance, keeping our lives centered, and thinking holistically. Because of the Hippocratics, we still focus on having a balanced diet, living a balanced lifestyle, and engaging all things in moderation (Smith 2008).

Roman Era physicians and philosophers continued Greek intellectual traditions but expanded upon Hippocratic thinking. Several, particularly Asclepiades, Cicero, Soranus, Celsus, and Galen, made important contributions to western thinking on mental health. Asclepiades (171–110 BCE), although an ethnic Greek, rejected the Hipporcatics' humors theory and created a unified theory of health and mental illness rooted in systematic process and a rationalism that we would understand today as the scientific method. This theory centered on the notion that the body included networks of conduits (blood vessels and nerves) that, if clogged, would irritate the brain and cause mental problems. Various substances, including alcohol and opium, could congest the nervous system, leading to psychological disorders. Asclepiades was the first to distinguish between hallucinations, illusions, and delusions (Millon 2004). See Box 2.1 to learn about these terms.

Box 2.1 Delusions, Illusions, and Hallucinations

Asclepiades was the first to make the distinction between delusions, illusions, and hallucinations. In clinical settings, it is essential to know the difference because they refer to quite different phenomena and indicate different disorders and conditions. Therapists often find it difficult to decipher the differences

(Continued)

Box 2.1 Delusions, Illusions, and Hallucinations *(Continued)*

when their clients and patients present their experiences, but it is clinically important to sort them out.

Delusions are incorrect beliefs that do not match facts. People will maintain their delusional beliefs even when confronted by irrefutable and unassailable evidence, and they are not open to logical explanations. An example is paranoia such as when people arrive at the conclusion that they are being secretly stalked by covert government agents. These people *know* the world is threatening and that they are being persecuted.

Illusions are about perceptions rather than beliefs. Rather, they are misperceptions of real things. Modern magicians, who of course do not perform real magic, are masters of illusions. They trick our eyes. A person suffering from illusionary problems misreads actual stimuli. We all have had experiences with illusions such as when you saw a shadow that looked like someone was sneaking up on you or if you misjudge water depth because it appeared deeper that it really was.

Hallucinations are also about perceptions but imply perceiving things that are not real or present. They are false sensory perceptions. Hearing voices that no one else hears is perhaps the most common hallucination. Hallucinations are defining symptoms of schizophrenia but can occur with drug and alcohol abuse and other disorders.

From these basic definitions, it is easy to see why clinicians must sort out their patients' experiences.

The sociological aspects of these three concepts, however, are not so clear. There are times and places in which delusions and seeing and hearing things that others do not is not considered weird or pathological. Religious visions are often considered divine. Moses and Mohammed both said they spoke directly or indirectly to God. The French war hero of 1429, Saint Joan of Arc, claimed that she saw, heard, felt, and smelled deceased saints (Sackville-West 1936/1992). Other religions, including Hinduism and Buddhism, similarly incorporate divine experiences in the foundations of their faiths (Hastings 1991). Many who had divine guidance were and remain revered individuals who were chosen by their god to lead, inspire, or simply live good lives.

By medieval times, religious visions were so common that they were practically expected, forcing clerics and scholars to devise ways to separate the genuine from the false (Kemp 2019). By the late fifteenth Century, spiritual encounters were no longer accepted in the Christian world. The *Malleus Maleficarum*, the infamous "hammer of witches" written in 1486, served as the guidebook to witch-hunting and prosecution and attributed hallucinations to witchcraft and satanic influences (Liester 1998).

In today's time, differences in understanding hallucinations continue to exist. In many cultures, having visions and anomalous experiences, the term for benign hallucinations, lucid dreaming, past life experiences, dream reality, and the feeling of foreseeing the future are not considered troublesome behaviors. You may recall the conflict between Don Juan and Carlos Castenada from Chapter 1 in which one perceived to have turned into a crow and flown, and the other in disbelief. What is the difference?

One proposed idea is the cultural source hypothesis (Maraldi and Krippner 2019). In this theory, these unusual experiences are legitimated because they are rooted in the belief in the existence of extraordinary phenomena that allow for and explain those experiences. There is no physiological basis to them, as westerners would typically understand hallucinations. Instead, there are cultural beliefs and expectations that the experience is real, which is why Carlos had such a difficult time believing that Don Juan turned himself into a crow. The interpretation of the peyote-derived hallucination was rooted in cultural beliefs in what is true.

The son of a wealthy Roman, Cicero (c. 106-43 BCE) established himself as a highly respected politician, lawyer, writer, and philosopher who addressed numerous subjects including health. Cicero's writings were influential on other scholars and elites, and intellectuals would read his ideas on mental health for centuries. He was among the first to argue that mental distress had **psychogenic causes** such as environmental conditions, unbridled emotions, and undisciplined thinking. Consequently, Cicero proposed treatments to teach disturbed individuals to think more clearly and rationally and to control emotions. Cicero's two other major contributions were to discover that emotional distress can lead to body pain and disease, a group of medical conditions now known as psychosomatic disorders, and he created perhaps the first questionnaire to identify psychosocial problems in individuals. His clinical instrument was widely used in its time and looks remarkably similar to current clinical assessment protocols (Millon 2004).

Soranus, who was ethnically Greek but practiced medicine in Rome, was born in the late first century of the Common Era. Soranus wrote several important texts including *On Acute and Chronic Diseases* in which he classified three types of madness: phrenitis, mania, and melancholy. Phrenitis was characterized by delirium due to fever and accompanied by a high pulse rate and convulsive movements. In phrenitis, he most likely was describing the psychological effects of various viral or bacterial infections or other health problems. Like today's use of the term, mania was characterized by chaotic thoughts, intense emotional expressions, and agitation. Melancholy presented like today's depression with feelings of sadness, fear, and dependency and social withdrawal.

Celsus (c. 25 BCE–50) was a prolific writer and encyclopedist who wrote extensively on medical theory and practice. He is regarded as among the first to instruct physicians on conducting plastic surgery on human faces using skin grafts, washing and sterilizing wounds with vinegar and thyme oil, which are mildly antiseptic, and identifying tissue inflammation. His works on mental illness, however, were less progressive. Celsus countered many of his fellow Roman physicians and philosophers by preserving humors theory, albeit with some modifications, and maintaining belief in the "wandering uterus." Celsus also firmly held that mental illness was of divine consequence, and his recommended treatments, notably starvation, intimidation, and bloodletting, are inhumane by modern standards (Millon 2004). Largely unknown during his lifetime, Celsus' theories on mental illness would become influential after the fall of Rome and into the Middle Ages.

Galen (129–210) was the most important physician of his time. A leader of intellectual thought throughout the Roman Empire, Galen's work, perhaps more than anyone else's, would reverberate throughout his civilization and have lasting influence on future physicians.

The concept of mental illness did not exist in ancient times, but Galen's theories moved us closer to conceptualizing unique fields in psychology and psychiatry. His concept of psychic pathology was based on a dysfunction in the physiology of the central nervous system, and pathological symptoms could be caused by toxins, humoral imbalances, emotions, and other internal conditions (Millon 2004). Galen also created a classification system to articulate distinctions among mental disorders. This taxonomy of disorders identified many types of depression, psychosis, and hysteria. Most importantly, Galen brought all mental symptoms together into one medical rubric, linking them theoretically and physiologically unlike anyone in the ancient world (Ahonen 2019).

While these scholars and practitioners left complex writings on medicine and mental health and served emperors, senators, and generals in the field of battle, their work had scant influence in the homes and villages of everyday people with no wealth or who lived outside the major cities of the empire. Families provided care for individuals experiencing mental problems. When troubles became particularly stressful, families sought the advice of local priests or healers, whose knowledge was trusted but provincial. These healers generally defined problems in religious and supernatural terms, which made sense to villagers, and would prescribe various ritualistic treatments or plant-based remedies derived from local flora. Most individuals acting in bizarre or unusual ways were inhumanely treated during Roman times. Beatings, deprivations, bloodletting, and harsh physical restraints were common interventions throughout the Roman world. It was primarily the elites and "cultured classes" who received medical treatments based on civil and rational approaches. A few elites such as Asclepiades sought to end cruel treatments, but his reach was limited and had virtually no impact on the everyday life of Roman subjects.

Greek and Roman societies marked the beginning of western social organization and worldviews. The Greeks organized themselves into city-states that adopted democratic principles. They invested in education, and the Greek intelligentsia developed scientific methods and complex philosophical systems of thought that emphasized the notion that all things were composed of smaller parts, each having its own discrete properties and functions.

In comparison, Eastern philosophers, notably the Taoists and Confucians, saw everything as composed of a single substance. The world existed as a holistic mass in which harmony with nature and other people was central to mental health and overall well-being. In an East-Asian worldview, all things are connected and interdependent.

To illustrate this point, Nisbett wrote, "The Chinese philosopher would see a family with interrelated members where the Greek saw a collection of persons with attributes that were independent of any connections with others" (2003: 19). Because of the Greeks' curiosity and focus on categories of individual objects, western intellectuals would eventually discover atoms, genes, DNA, and bacteria and viruses, and their characteristics. They would also direct us to dissect mental processes into separate categories of thoughts, emotions, and behaviors, each with its own unique character and discrete meaning.

The theories and practices of the Greek and Roman physicians, though complex and rigorous for their time, were largely incorrect. Nevertheless, we continue to study them because they set the questions to ask about mental and psychological problems and helped form the boundaries of the study and treatment of mental illness. In the Classical Era, we see the beginning of contemporary perspective. Because people then faced the same basic life issues that confront us today, the Greeks and Romans started searching for causes and resolutions to those difficulties, setting in motion the way we think, reason, and solve problems. Modern scholarship is derived from classical rationality and builds off the successes and failures of its thinkers.

The Middle Ages

The period of European history called the Middle Ages was a critical time not only for Europeans, but for global history. During the millennium between roughly 500 and 1500, Europe floundered socially, economically, and technologically compared to other cultures in Africa, the Middle East, and Asia. After the fall of Rome and the Western Empire in 476 CE, most of Europe collapsed into political and social disorganization, and this lack of social cohesion had an injurious impact on every aspect of society and culture. The population declined, trade waned, and wars were seemingly constant. The downfall of the Roman Empire created a stark political void, leaving swaths of Europe without central governance and swamped with regional fiefdoms and "lords of the manor" who fought each other for control of lands, wealth, and strategic advantages.

As political institutions teetered, the Roman Catholic Church emerged as the one entity that transcended the national and ethnic boundaries of Europe. Except for parts of the Balkans, far north and eastern Europe, and Moorish Spain, virtually all of Europe had been Christianized by the year 1000. By 1200, Northern Europe was converted to Christianity, and the Moors would be driven out of Iberia later that century. Religious minorities, such as Jews, were ruthlessly persecuted, especially at the onset of the Inquisition in the 1490s, and were forced to convert, leave, or suffer brutal deaths as heretics. During the Middle Ages, the Church had become a unitary political and social voice that directed intellectual affairs, controlled great wealth, and held political influence over royal heads of state throughout the continent.

With images of chivalry, knights, and "damsels in distress," medieval life is often romanticized. In actuality, living during this time was hard, filthy, and violent. Only clerics and some aristocrats were literate (King John who signed the Magna Carta could neither read nor write). Most people were uneducated serfs, bound to their lords to work the fields, while a few were village or urban skilled workers and shopkeepers. These conditions produced poor health outcomes. Infant mortality was extraordinarily high, perhaps 30 percent, and life expectancy was in the 40s. Escaping childhood bode well for a long life, but childhood deaths were common, and males were often conscripted to fight wars in which women and children were too frequently unfortunate victims.

Public health was essentially nonexistent. Human and animal waste covered the streets and contaminated the water supplies of towns and feudal estates, and the floors of ordinary houses, usually made of grasses, were breeding grounds for various harmful viruses and bacteria and vermin. Infectious diseases were common and often fatal. Epidemics, such as the plagues that struck in the fourteenth and seventeenth centuries that killed 40 percent and 30 percent of the European population, respectively, decimated the social landscape and caused severe social despair and long-lasting problems that would require centuries to repair.

The health of the people during the Middle Ages reflected the times, and people commonly lived with both acute and chronic health problems including bad teeth and skin diseases, diarrhea and countless other infections, poorly treated injuries, and mental illness.

There is a temptation to say that because of these gloomy health conditions and the ascendancy of the Church in intellectual matters, the Middle Ages were a time of stagnation, the so-called Dark Ages. While that might be true of the Early Middle Ages, from 500 to about 1000 when Europeans produced very little new knowledge and art, especially compared to the Islamic world and the Chinese, the High (the middle period) and Late Middle Ages were centuries of grand advancement in architecture, art, music, and many technologies. The great universities of Italy, France, Germany, and Britain opened between 1000 and 1500 and fostered innovations in medicine such as the development of eyeglasses, expanded knowledge of anatomy and physiology, improved surgery and disinfectants, and created techniques for safer Caesarian births. Hospitals for the sick and infirm began to be erected in the Byzantine Empire and spread into the Christian world. Almost from the beginning, rooms dedicated for the insane were included in the construction.

Despite these advances, virtually no systematic study of medicine existed during the Middle Ages, and medicine remained a poorly developed field of knowledge and practice. Examinations of urine, for example, were a typical clinical assessment. Observable qualities in urine were associated with particular diseases. One diagnosis was that among elderly patients, white urine was considered a sign of frailty or childishness.

People who called themselves physicians were rarely trained and frequently ineffective. The cure rates of physicians who were educated, however, were not much better. Unsanitary conditions plus no conception of the causes of diseases led to physicians having low social status during this time. Barbers competed with physicians and often conducted surgeries, which led to the famed red, white, and blue striped poles still found outside barbershops today. The poles, which were later placed outside the shop as an advertising device, were originally positioned for patients to grab to remain still and help endure pain when barbers applied leeches for bloodletting, extracted a tooth, or conducted some other surgery, all without anesthesia (the pole's red stripe indicated blood and leeching, the white represented bandages, and the blue separated barbers from physicians, telling men they could also get a shave there!)

Few advancements in mental health were made during the Middle Ages in large part because the Church held an intellectual hegemony over affairs of the mind and heart. Consequently, it is also tempting to conclude that everyone believed that people who acted in nonconforming ways were tempted by the devil, possessed by demons, or being punished for their sins. Indeed, demon possession did exist as an explanation for erratic behaviors and conditions that we now label psychoses, personality disorders, and epilepsy, and exorcisms were occasionally performed (Espí Forcén et al. 2014).

Demons and magic, however, were not the only proposed causes of mental illness in the Middle Ages. In the eleventh and twelfth centuries, humors theory and Galenic ideas were still used by intellectual elites to account for eccentric behavior and bizarre thoughts (Høyersten 2007). Medieval cognitive psychology was based on an intersecting dualism of mind and body. The mind, the ephemeral and immortal intellect and soul, was distinguished from the material and mortal body, specifically the brain. The mind comprised peoples' thoughts, reasoning, and motives, which were believed to be processed by the front and rear areas of the brain (Kemp 2019). Since thoughts and values—the stuff of the soul—were the province of the church and God-given, the mind could not be damaged. The ability to process the soul, however, relied on a healthy brain; therefore, a troubled soul was considered the result of a body dysfunction, environmental circumstances, bad habits, or temptations of the flesh by Satan.

Surviving records suggest that numerous causes of mental health problems were proposed in the Middle Ages. Eleventh-century writings from the Italian physician Constantine of Africa show worldly psychogenic origins of mental distress. He wrote that financial ruin and the loss of a child could lead to melancholia and that love-sickness was a disorder best treated by sex. Franciscan friar Bartholomeus Angelicus (c. 1203–1272) stated that poor dietary habits, overwork, and alcohol consumption caused melancholy and recommend listening to music to overcome it. Kroll and Bachrach (1984) studied 57 accounts of psychological impairments written during the Middle Ages and found that only nine attributed mental illness to sin or supernatural origins. They concluded that the literate elite of the time, most of whom were clerics, were aware of rational and earthly causes of mental distress. Nevertheless, uneducated ordinary people, along with many literate and knowledgeable elites, were more likely to hold religious and superstitious opinions about the origins of mental distress.

European and Islamic scholars and physicians engaged in academic and clinical exchanges throughout much of the latter Middle Ages, and the Europeans found that treatment of the mentally ill in Arabic and Islamic cultures, though similar in many respects, differed from their own. Europeans saw that Turks and Arabs held a more secular and tolerant perspective toward mental distress. Several factors may explain these differences. Unlike the Europeans, Islamic culture placed medicine atop the hierarchy of secular knowledge and considered the health and well-being of others a religious duty. As evidence of their more secular approach, Islamic physicians believed mental illness to have both physical and psychological causes and attributes (Amad and Thomas 2011; Sarhan 2018) and prescribed gentle treatments such as music and talk therapies, possibly inventing psychotherapy (Sarhan 2018), and therapeutic baths. Unlike in Europe where families tended to their mentally disturbed relatives, Islamic communities often provided care to those afflicted with more severe mental problems. Hospitals flourished in the Islamic world and by the late twelfth century, every town of any size had one. These hospitals, or *maristans* (meaning "place for the sick"), were secular organizations funded by donations and charitable contributions. They were well-ordered facilities with systematic medical practices featuring primarily humane treatments. Practitioners in the *maristans* separated sin from moral defects and illness and were optimistic about recovery and a return to health (Pérez et al. 2012).

Maristans, however, were not consistent, and treatments ranged from advanced clinical interventions to violence. Records show that treatments often followed Galen's recommendations and included diets, special baths with chamomile and various oils and ointments, and washing the head with milk to cool and moisten the body to neutralize the heating and drying effects of excessive blood or bile (Scull 2015). Other, more abusive treatments were also employed. Bleedings and induced emesis and purging of the bowels, similar to European treatments, were sometimes recommended. Also, as in Europe, beatings were common to "beat sense" into patients thought to be deluded or confused (Scull 2015), and those patients who were hopelessly mad and out of control were chained to hospital walls.

As in Europe, Islamic peoples, particularly those in lower classes without access to centers of advanced knowledge, usually relied on supernatural explanations of nonconforming behavior. Different types of spirits, demons, and curses were commonly blamed. Religious rituals and trips to graves of saints to pray for interventions and cures, again as occurred in Europe, were common practices. Many insane persons were abandoned to roam the towns and countryside begging for their living.

The relationship between social and cultural conditions and the treatment of mentally ill persons is particularly visible in the Middle Ages in both Arab and European regions.

In the Middle East, treatment of mentally ill persons would not always remain progressive, as Amad and Thomas (2011) discovered. They found that in the Islamic sphere, when socioeconomic times were good, persons with mental distress were well-treated. When times were hard, that was not necessarily the case. The Mongol invasion into the Middle East in the thirteenth century, for example, disrupted social cohesion throughout the region and destroyed institutions, which led to a decline in care for people with mental illness. During these times, ill people were more likely kept in isolated detention, and social supports for their care diminished. In addition, when society entered a state of turmoil, beliefs in divine punishment as a cause of mental problems expanded and replaced medical approaches in many places (Amad and Thomas 2011).

Social life in Europe was often tumultuous during the Middle Ages. Wars, the Crusades, the Inquisition, epidemics, famines, and a hardscrabble daily life, plus the gradual transition from a rural agricultural economy to one of urban industry, migration to cities, and tensions between traditional aristocratic rule and liberal republican governance kept European social organization in a constant state of flux.

Consequently, the Middle Ages produced little toward improving the lot of the mentally ill in Europe. Mental hospitals operated differently and generally less humanely than their Arab counterparts. Run by religious groups, European hospitals evolved into warehouses to rid families, villages, and cities of people considered unwanted nuisances or were too difficult to handle. Treatments were repressive and punishing and reinforced the belief that mental illness was due to sin. Throughout the Middle Ages and into the Renaissance, attitudes toward persons with mental illness were, in general, hostile, and by the late Middle Ages and the Renaissance, mass confinements and lynchings of "lunatics" and witches, many of whom were mentally ill, began (Kroll 1973). One belief about the treatment of the mentally ill has been questioned, however. As Box 2.2 shows, the notion that mentally ill persons were put on ships and taken away to unknown places, the infamous Ships of Fools, may be false.

Box 2.2 Ship of Fools

In his important book *Madness and Civilization* (1965), Foucault described a tactic that communities commonly used in Europe during the fourteenth and fifteenth centuries to segregate themselves from mentally ill people. He wrote, quite elaborately in fact, that towns across Europe, especially in Germany, collected insane persons and loaded them onto ships, sending them to wander the seas and waterways on endless voyages never to return. Because of the influence of *Madness and Civilization*, many psychologists and psychiatrists included these ships of fools in their textbooks and other writings to illustrate attitudes toward mental illness during the Middle Ages.

The ships of fools, however, never happened, and their descriptions are imaginary. According to Maher and Maher (1982), there are no ship logs, diaries, marine records, sightings, or departure records (which were kept in detail for taxation purposes) to suggest that such ships with human cargos ever existed. So why would Foucault and others over the next 15–20 years perpetuate and even embellish the myth that the ships of fools were real?

The ship of fool was a common allegorical image of the Medieval Period. There are several paintings, woodcuttings, and books with references to the concept. Foucault may have inferred the literal ships of the insane from a book called *Das Narrenschiff*, written in 1494 by Sebastian Brant, a Dutch author, and a late fifteenth-century painting called the *Ship of Fools* by Hieronymus Bosch, who also was Dutch. Both are allegorical criticisms of un-Christian behavior. Brant's book is a collection of 112 poems that satirize human folly and the sinfulness of such behaviors as vanity, self-indulgence, deception, and immorality. Insanity is neither mentioned by Brant (Maher and Maher 1982) nor symbolized by Bosch.

So why did modern writers propagate this tale despite the absence of evidence? Maher and Maher argued that these accounts perpetuated beliefs that scholars had about madness in the Middle Ages, and their theories needed evidence. Structuralism, Foucault's theoretical orientation in this book, contends that ideas about culture and social things are best understood by their relationship to broad, overarching social organization, or structure. Foucault and others thought that with the beginnings of rationalism, medieval peoples cast their insane aboard ships and sent them to remote places or to just wander aimlessly to maintain and protect the new society based on reason and logic. Because they subscribed to the theory, these scholars assumed Foucault was correct in his depiction of the imagined popular image of the mentally ill. As Maher and Maher state, "The image of the storm-tossed soul cast adrift from rational society fills the bill [of the theories] perfectly. Since real ships of fools did not exist, it was necessary to invent them" (1982: 760).

The Renaissance and the Enlightenment

The Renaissance, roughly the 1400s and 1500s, followed by the Enlightenment period (seventeenth and eighteenth centuries) were transitions bridging the Middle Ages and the Modern Era. For scholars and their wealthy patrons, it was a time of adventurism and discovery. Many famous names that we equate with the origins of modern European civilization date to the Renaissance—da Vinci, Galileo, Hobbes, Chaucer, Michelangelo, and Descartes, among many others.

The Renaissance was fueled in large measure by the end of the Eastern Roman Empire, the Byzantine Empire, when Constantinople fell to the Ottoman Turks in 1453. Eastern scholars fled the invasion and moved westward into Europe, taking their classical training and libraries with them. They revitalized Greek and Roman scholarship in Europe, which was facilitated by the Gutenberg printing press that allowed them to disperse classical knowledge throughout the continent. One of the rediscovered theories was the Hippocratics' approaches in medicine and mental health, which restored beliefs in bodily origins of insanity and rejected the supernatural.

Perhaps most critically for our story, the Renaissance, in addition to its resurgence in art and science, produced humanism, the philosophical belief that humans are the center of their world and that the human spirit is boundless and destined to master nature. The Renaissance scholars did not challenge the Church's authority over spiritual matters or abandon their own belief in the Christian god, but they did call for a revision of the image of the human self to possess the intellect to perceive and comprehend themselves, nature, and the essence of all things. The Renaissance writers contended that reason, mathematics, and logic were the central features of human consciousness, and that people were not simple beings acting on reflexes like the lower animals (Porter 2002). The humanist movement of the Renaissance is perhaps best summed up by Descartes famous argument, "*cognito, ergo sum*" or "I think, therefore I am."

From this new way of thinking, consciousness was the mind's natural proclivity toward rationality and sound reasoning. Insanity, it follows, is irrationality caused by some illness in the body that disrupts the mind's physical ability to reason. This formula made mental illness a valid topic for medical research and practice (Porter 2002).

Despite these advances, madness remained largely explained by mystical forces during the Renaissance. Satan was a literal and ever-present being roaming the earth looking for weak souls to tempt and inhabit. The Renaissance also produced, as Scull aptly stated, "a veritable epidemic of trials" (2015: 86), such as the infamous witch trials that occurred throughout Europe and spread to the North American colonies. The "witches," who were disproportionately marginalized or nonconforming women, were usually scapegoated for community troubles such as crop failures, diseases, bad weather, or other unusual and unfortunate events. In many cases, victims were people known or suspected to be mentally ill, but for the most part, they were ordinary people who were socially powerless and unprotected and easy marks for false accusations. The witch trials, of course, matched well with the beliefs that insanity was supernatural.

There were occasional public debates over specific cases of individuals charged with witchcraft where some learned person argued that a defendant was sick of body rather than in league with the devil. Johann Weyer (1515–1588), a Dutch physician, is often considered the first physician to specialize in mental illness, focused on melancholia. Weyer, who despite his own religious convictions that included a literal and material devil, fought against the witch trials. He frequently testified on behalf of those whom he knew to be melancholic and wrote books that criticized witch-hunting. Weyer made logic-based arguments that confessions of heresy, virtually always made under duress and torture, were not reliable representations of the truth. He and those like him, however, were often publicly challenged. On one such occasion, Jean Bodin, a famous sixteenth-century scholar and counselor to the king of France, rebuked Weyer by saying that he (Weyer) should "stick to examining urine rather than intruding lofty territories of theology and jurisprudence" (Cavanaugh 2015). The Inquisition banned books written by Weyer and other like-minded progressive thinkers (Farreras 2022).

By the time of the Enlightenment (seventeenth and eighteenth centuries), changes in European society were increasingly rapid and dramatic. Whereas the Renaissance focused on human's artistic nature and creativity and introduced rationalism and individualism, the Enlightenment centered on the application of rationality in science, mathematics, and technology. Everything, including art and music, was rationally assessed and examined. One might say that the Enlightenment was the implementation of the Renaissance.

The Enlightenment, also called the Age of Reason, had its own worldview that centered on science, logic, and human rights (at least as they were defined then). Its ideals produced the American and French Revolutions and technological innovations that would change the world. The Age of Reason entrenched individualism as a cornerstone of western thought, but also led European nations to conquer much of the world outside the continent. They institutionalized slavery and indentured servitude to exploit the riches of their colonies and submitted indigenous peoples to barbaric imperial control, sowing the seeds of modern racism, segregation, and the systematic denial of certain peoples to the civil liberties and opportunities that the Enlightenment produced. This new ordering of peoples into a social hierarchy would have implications for psychological well-being that would last to the present time.

Three key ideas on mental illness arose from the Enlightenment. First, eighteenth-century physicians and scholars gradually won the freedom to investigate human nature without oversight or censorship by the state and the church (Weiner 2008). With the Enlightenment's concentration on rationality, reason, and individualism, intellectuals argued that individuals with psychological impairments had the same rights as healthy or "normal" people. Second, a theory that mental illness was a disease of the nerves and brain emerged, and that meant that physicians could devise a cure and return a deranged, alienated, or confused person back to sanity (Weiner 2008).

Third, with the rise of urban manufacturing and the Protestant Reformation taking hold in various areas and challenging the hegemony of the Roman Church, work became a moral duty, and idleness "the devil's workshop." The new economy was based on increasingly rational industrialization and trade, and as more people flocked to the cities, pressure increased to provide them with work and places to live. Those lucky enough to get jobs in the new manufacturing centers, however, faced horrible working conditions and unsafe machinery. Many workers suffered severe injuries, and unlike today where insurance and government support programs aid those who experienced work-related injuries, seventeenth- and eighteenth-century workers who were injured or permanently maimed at work were simply fired and quickly replaced with another person desperate to work.

The mores of the 1700s emphasized the morality of work and sinfulness of dependency. To handle the surplus of nonproductive people in the cities, many areas of Europe created institutions, sometimes called poorhouses, to imprison indigents to punish them for their poverty and teach them the discipline to regain their productivity. The poor who were locked up were a diverse lot. Unproductive people included not only the poor, but also vision-impaired and maimed people, criminals, disreputable women including sex workers, and the insane. They were all treated essentially indistinguishably.

Madhouses proliferated in the Enlightenment period, and there is an image of them as dreadful places where patients were abandoned and treated horrifically. Some, such as Salpetriere founded in 1656 in Paris and London's Bethlem (1247), both of which still exist, were notorious for cruel treatment. Bethlem even charged admission for tourists to see the "exhibits" as if they were visiting a zoo. Though many of them were called hospitals, the large majority neither were headed by a physician nor provided medical care, such as it was then. Some were for-profit and catered to the genteel classes, while others were funded by the Crown. One asylum in Amsterdam was subsidized by a lottery!

The worst of the lunatic asylums were dreary places in which recovery to health was not likely. Considered to be more animal-like than human, patients were kept in dank cells with straw floors and without heat. At Bicêtre in France, patients were fed only a pound of bread in the morning, leaving them mad with hunger the rest of the day (Whitaker 2002). Patients were denied routine health care and exposure to the sun and were often beaten for any type of real or perceived offense.

The madhouses of the eighteenth century became the subject of many books and articles after philosopher Michel Foucault first wrote about them in the 1960s. Foucault (1965) championed the notion that throughout Europe in the 1700s, massive numbers of insane people were locked up involuntarily and subjected to harsh inhumane treatment. This so-called "Great Confinement," Foucault argued, was a deliberate strategy to reduce the political threats and social disruptions posed by the large numbers of unemployed and hungry urban dwellers. In addition, the idleness of the poor threatened the rational values of work championed by elites, and the best way to control a threat is to segregate people who were thought dangerous to the social order from those who conformed and followed the rules and contributed to the new economy of industrialization.

There are several criticisms of Foucault's work that cause us to rethink the notion of the Great Confinement. First, it is possible that the conditions of the asylums and the number of people actually held in them have been overstated. During and after the Enlightenment, authors, especially playwrights, frequently set their plays and other writings in asylums or wrote about people who had been placed in one. These plays are often cited as the main sources on asylum life. Nonfictional reports from the time, however, suggest that the asylums only locked up a relatively small percentage of people with mental illness. Second, there are several accounts written by people who were committed to an asylum, and these narratives indicate that their treatment was not insufferable, but therapeutic and humane. From these reports, we can conclude that some hospitals were better than others, a conclusion that counters the assumptions of the Great Confinement assertion. A third criticism of the Great Confinement concept is that if patients were confined because they had lost their way and were unable to work, then one might expect that patients would be subjected to work programs in the hospitals. This might not be the case. According to Porter (2002), many of the asylums were for-profit enterprises that marketed (literally advertised) their services to wealthy families and patients. Rich patients would not be expected to toil in common conditions or be exposed to harsh treatments. There are also few records that indicated organized work programs at any madhouses.

As Porter contends, it would be too simplistic and perhaps even conspiratorial to say that these institutions arose as a tool of control to enforce the new norms of the nascent industrial society. People more likely entered the madhouses via their families in negotiations with the community and local officials and the directors of the asylums. Locking up the insane, especially when they became unmanageable, was not new to Medieval Europe or the seventeenth century. Families had long kept their insane kin in basements, barns, and pig pens. Wealthier families hid their mentally ill relatives under the charge of a servant (Porter 2002). The rise of asylums was in line with the rest of society—it was a more formal, bureaucratic, and rational approach to solving the family and community distress that an unproductive and burdensome individual posed. Box 2.3 tells the story of Nathaniel Lee and how he entered an asylum.

Box 2.3 Nathaniel Lee

Among their many contributions, scholars during the Renaissance also produced individualism, a way of thinking that centers on the moral value of each individual person. In individualism, people are autonomous, and their main objective is to discover and pursue their own interests and life goals. With individualism comes questioning society if the goals of the individual do not match society's or if society impedes progress toward one's ambitions. When people perceive society as a barrier to their personal interests, which often leads to feelings of helplessness, sadness, and hopelessness, common symptoms of depression, they will often criticize society as "crazy" for acting in a way that keeps people from freely living their lives and being happy. While this sounds like a twenty-first-century thought, the idea of blaming society for "being crazy" may have started in the 1600s.

Nathaniel Lee (c. 1653–1692), the son of a Presbyterian minister, was a successful Cambridge educated playwright who began to hang around with free-thinking members of the literati set, most notably John Wilmot, the 2nd Earl of Rochester, a highly regarded (and often censured) poet and war hero, who lived lavishly and decadently before dying from a sexually transmitted disease at the young age of 33. Nathaniel coveted and engaged in Wilmot's indulgent and licentious lifestyle, which tarnished his reputation and contributed to his excessive alcohol consumption and eventual psychological demise. He was then evaluated and sent to Bethlem Hospital for five years. Acting in his own defense, he famously questioned whether it was society that was mad for judging his behavior as wrong: "They called me mad, and I called them mad, and damn them, they outvoted me." Lee died young and in a drunken state on a street in London.

Mental Illness in American History

Records of mental illness date to the seventeenth century in the British colonies of North America. Data, however, are sparse and mostly come from court records, diaries, and personal correspondence (Eldridge 1996). Eldridge analyzed these chronicles and found enough cases and accounts of mental illness to give us a general idea of how the colonists dealt with these problems. He found that mental health issues were generally believed to be the result of supernatural or physical conditions. Cases of head trauma leading to behavioral changes were noted, but Satan's influence was also known to cause bizarre behavior.

In the colonial and early republic years, unrequited passions and one's basic disposition were also thought to bring on insanity. Madness, however, was also largely gendered and racialized. For example, environmental factors such as failed business ventures could release passions that drove White males to madness. For African Americans and women, on the other hand, their bodies were the source of uncontrollable emotions (Holland 2019). Benjamin Rush, though an abolitionist and student of the Enlightenment, was a man of his times and wrote in 1812: "in consequence of their bodies by menstruation, pregnancy, and parturition, and to their minds, by living so much alone with their families, [women] are more predisposed to madness than men" (quoted in Holland 2019).

Physicians, especially in the US South, often believed that African Americans as slaves rarely experienced mental illness. Blacks supposedly possessed an undeveloped nervous system and were not suited for independence and competing in a "civilized" society. As slaves, according to the belief, they lived a life of simple dependence, which better suited their biological constitution.

After emancipation, however, ideas changed, and by 1900, mental illness was "alarmingly common" among former slaves and their descendants (Hughes 1992). Following the Civil War, Blacks were disproportionately locked away in institutions where they were more likely to become malnourished and physically ill compared to institutionalized Whites, who received better care. In 1890, almost half of hospitalized African Americans died in the institution, compared to only 22 percent of Whites (Hughes 1992).

Many different behaviors were suspected of being illness in the colonies. Most any bizarre or irrational behavior or thinking implied mental illness, but so too was not conforming to mainstream religion and lisping.

Early American treatments for mental health problems are particularly telling of the state of knowledge. In addition to the conventional treatments of the day—prayer, fasting, bloodletting, and purging—Eldridge (1996) uncovered several rather unusual prescriptions:

1. An elixir of blood from a male cat's ear and milk from a woman suckling a male child.

2. Suppositories made of seeds from plants.

3. Pills of exact portions of castoria (which has a laxative effect), women's hair, and pine resin.

4. A living swallow halved and placed atop the shaved head of the patient.

Another treatment was Rush's tranquilizing chair. Physicians strapped patients into a chair, with a toilet bowl attached underneath, and a box covering their heads to deprive them of sensations. The theory was that brain inflammation caused madness, and the chair produced tranquility, thus reducing inflammation.

While the logic of these "cures" is not intuitive to twenty-first-century sensibilities, it would be reasonable to start with the Okashas' blueprint for magical logic outlined earlier in the chapter to understand them. Apparently, these plants, animals, and other substances had qualities that looked like something related to health or had religious significance. Perhaps some treatments, like the tranquillizing chair, were derived from humors theory. Regardless of their origins, they were probably ineffective.

Colonial and early republic White families cared for their ill relatives in consultation with the local physician. When individuals' health debilitated to the point that they were not manageable, colonial law required that communities build a facility for their care, though few of these places were constructed before independence. Psychologically distressed African Americans and American Indians were largely ignored or maltreated.

Religion and region also played a role in care provision. The Puritans of the northern colonies were averse to cruelty and tended to be more sympathetic than other religious groups. Northerners were more likely to live in towns and small communities, which facilitated community care. Conversely in the rural South, people were more spread out and lived on farms and plantations. Consequently, communities in the South provided less care for mentally ill persons (Eldridge 1996).

Beginning in 1820, asylums began to expand across the country, and eventually became the preferred course of action for families who could no longer care for their mentally ill relative. The asylums of nineteenth-century America had dual goals: to rehabilitate patients and set an example of how to behave and think rationally. Poor patients were taught to follow the behavioral examples of "proper" wealthy people. The notion that patients could improve their psychological health by changing their lifestyles suggests the belief that social conditions were thought to contribute to mental illness. Contemporary reports do cite that social factors, like loss of property, excessive study, and political excitement, contributed to mental distress.

The asylum movement failed in reaching these goals (Rothman 1971). They became unpleasant places, and little actual care or rehabilitation existed. Dorothea Dix, a nineteenth-century social worker and activist spoke and wrote on life within the asylums. She made a compassionate presentation to Massachusetts lawmakers attesting to those conditions saying, "I proceed, Gentlemen, briefly to call your attention to the present state of insane persons confined within this Commonwealth, in cages, closets, cellars, stalls, pens! Chained, naked, beaten with rods, and lashed into obedience!" (1843). In time, her advocacy led asylum officials to separate mentally ill persons from criminals and improve patient care.

The general mood of the first generation of American psychiatrists was one of optimism. For those that believed that social factors were the root of mental illness, the asylums would reform them. Those subscribing to medical causes were hopeful that finding the physiological problems that plagued their patients would lead them to an effective treatment. Autopsies to locate brain lesions and inflammation were common prior to the Civil War. The American scientific community in the 1800s shared Americans' optimism of technical and industrial growth, national expansion, and "Yankee know-how." This optimism was not held by all Americans, however. The industrial and agricultural poor, most minorities, and poor women who had few resources and no political empowerment were often subject to the worst care. There was little hope for them.

Reform and the Beginnings of Modern Psychiatry

The American and French Revolutions ushered in a new philosophy of applied humanism. Ideals such as the rule of law, personal liberties, and authority through consent were central to political movements in North America and western Europe. While these new principles did not apply equally to slaves, all ethnic groups, and women, they did have an impact on the way asylum patients were treated. By the late eighteenth century and early 1800s, asylum physicians and administrators slowly began to remove the chains that bound many patients. Led by reformers such as Philippe Pinel (1745–1826) in France, England's William Tuke (1732–1822), and America's Benjamin Rush (1745–1813) and Dorothea Dix (1802–1887), asylums embarked on a new course of treatment in which patients would be treated less like animals and more like human beings. These reformers believed that mental illnesses were due to either a physiological condition or psychological circumstances and stress. They unleashed patients and sought to provide basic human needs, including respect.

Moral treatment, as the new movement was known, differed from the usual treatment in madhouses. In the old system, the asylums themselves were the treatment (Spain 2018). It was a one-size-fits-all model. Under moral treatment, asylums were relatively more flexible and tried to provide the tools for relieving insanity. In the moral treatment model, curative care was more personalized and more humane.

Moral treatment began with Tuke, a well-respected Quaker merchant and philanthropist, who proposed a revision of asylum care after learning of the death of a mentally ill Quaker at the York Asylum and then witnessing patients in chains and manacles. As an alternative to the nearby brutal madhouse, he created the York Retreat. The Retreat was modeled on the family life of the wealthy and the peaceful precepts of the Quakers' faith.

Life and treatment at the York Retreat were unlike anything seen in the care of the mentally ill. Community life was emphasized: patients and staff lived together on the grounds and shared meals. The staff emphasized patients learning self-control with methods centered on love, sympathy, and esteem (Charland 2002). Violence and restraints were infrequent. When residents became rowdy or hard to manage, they were secluded in a dark quiet room. Apparently, there was little cause to do that. It was rare that two residents needed to be segregated from the others at the same time (Whitaker 2002).

The York Retreat, according to their records, had an excellent success rate. Using relapsing to operationalize success and failure, 70 percent of York patients who had been ill for less than a year recovered, never again to develop symptoms, and 25 percent of chronically ill patients, those previously considered incurable, became symptom-free (Whitaker 2002).

Moral treatment spread throughout Europe and to the United States. While there were different approaches to moral treatment (Spain 2018), all had as centerpieces John Locke's sense of human rights and Tuke's insistence on humane care. Though York Retreat had a religious foundation, the leaders of the moral treatment movement used the word "moral" as we use "psychology" today (Charland 2002). Moral treatment physicians later became known as alienists, those who treat the "mentally alienated," and provided psychological care as opposed to the oppressive and ineffective tactics of typical madhouses (Frances 2016).

Pinel's theories and practices were inspired by the French Revolution's ideals of liberty, equality, and fraternity. Although it is often assumed that Pinel personally removed the chains of madhouse inmates, it is more likely that his theories inspired freeing mentally ill people from the neglect, custodial incarceration, and punishment that were the madhouses' primary curative strategies (Porter 2002, Scull 2015). Pinel became highly influential. He embraced the progressiveness of the Enlightenment, which led him to conclude that mental problems had to be handled psychologically. For Pinel and other advocates of moral treatment, madness was a breakdown of a person's rational self-control, and their psychological abilities and sensibilities had to be restored. Inner self-restraint replaced external coercion (Porter 2002). This modality, as Porter notes, meshed neatly with the social and political optimism of the American and French Revolutionary era.

The peaceful, gentle handling of mentally ill persons in the care of moral treatment physicians, however, should not be sentimentalized. While at the beginning, these asylums were somewhat idyllic, especially in comparison to the madhouses, they were considered hospitals, and patients were subjected to medical interventions (Frances 2016). As physicians gained more control of the asylums, moral treatment quickly morphed into a new form of asylums that increased in number and in census. The period beginning in the early 1800s and ending in the 1950s may be more accurately described as the real Great Confinement because admissions to mental hospitals skyrocketed to levels far exceeding any previous period (Scull 2005). Tuke's vision of moral treatment did not last long.

Why did moral treatment fail? After all, it was humane, kind, and according to accounts from the time, successful in preventing future symptoms. Why would the movement only last a couple of decades before transforming into a different mode of care? Moral treatment ended because physicians trained in the new biological sciences took over and rested control of the asylums from moral care administrators and physicians (Rothman 1971). Some consider the nineteenth-century asylum physicians as ushering in modern psychiatry because the mad doctors, as they were sometimes called, were working within a new medical paradigm based on systematic observations and taxonomies of disorders. Physicians strove to classify patients into categories such as melancholia, mania (insanity), dementia, and idiotism. The mad doctors initiated the idea that alcohol abuse was a medical, not a moral, condition (Nathan et al. 2016).

In the nineteenth century, after the end of the moral treatment movement, asylums rather families were considered the best place for the insane, depressed, and disturbed. Patients were subjected to ineffectual medical interventions and were often abused. The alienists essentially ruled over warehouses of unwanted and unproductive people who were seen as threats to their families and communities. It was best, in physicians' eyes, to separate the mad from civilized society and use them as subjects to test their treatments.

Key Intellectual Developments of the Nineteenth Century

Three intellectual developments in the nineteenth century—Darwin's theory of evolution, **germ theory**, and **Social Darwinism**—moved mental health care toward a medical model that emphasized physiology over environmental causes. This new approach ended humors theory and supernaturalism as causes of madness, but it did not necessarily improve the lot of mentally ill persons.

Charles Darwin's observations of species evolving to adapt to their environment revolutionized the biological sciences. Though Darwin himself had little interest in human social dynamics, his rudimentary theories of genetics were adopted by other scholars attempting to explain mental illness. Their theory was straightforward: it is all genetics. Physicians and biologists believed that madness was due to a degenerate family trait passed from one generation to the next. More highly evolved individuals were free of mental illness, but others were genetically regressed and unable to cope physiologically or psychologically. These traits had physical indicators, such as particular facial features or skull shapes. **Degeneracy theory**, as this perspective was known, would linger until just after World War II and contribute to twentieth-century **eugenics** practices in Germany and the United States (Arboleda-Florez and Stuart 2012). Eugenics was an attempt to alter a population's genetic base by involuntarily sterilizing or killing persons with mental illness.

Germ theory was the second major intellectual stream of the nineteenth century. Infectious diseases such as cholera, typhoid fever, and influenza ravaged human populations and were the primary causes of deaths throughout the world. Anthrax, a persistently troublesome disease, terrorized ranchers because it could easily decimate herds of cattle and sheep. Identifying the bacteria and viruses that caused these and other diseases enacted profound changes on not only human health, but on social conditions. Localizing these pathogens gave solid evidence for public health and sanitation programs to provide clean water, remove human and animal waste, and create treatments and inoculations. Because of these achievements, biology emerged as the most successful scientific discipline in the 1800s. Since these discoveries reduced suffering and lengthened life expectancy to unprecedented levels, physicians began to associate microorganisms with all human health problems, including mental health. The theory here was simple too: germs caused mental illness.

The bulk of early research on microorganisms rightfully focused on pressing life and death diseases such as cholera and anthrax and the benefits of sanitation, wound cleansings, and surgical sterilizations. Overall, germ theory had relatively little impact on our knowledge of mental illness, though it did inspire a few related discoveries. For example, untreated syphilis was linked to insanity, and vitamin deficiencies were connected to mental health troubles. Research continues in this area, however. Recent studies implicate infections in some cases of schizophrenia, bipolar disorder, and depression (Prusty et al. 2018).

The third important theme to emerge from the nineteenth century was Social Darwinism. Social Darwinism is an ideological framework that is not derived from Charles Darwin, who disapproved of it, but from Herbert Spencer, the English civil engineer turned philosopher. The term "survival of the fittest" was coined by Spencer in application of Darwin's idea of natural selection to humans and society. Darwin himself adamantly stated that survival of the fittest was an incorrect derivative of his theories of biology.

Nonetheless, Spencer maintained his position that society evolved similarly to Darwin's model of species and that what separates the rich and powerful from the poor and defenseless is genetic fitness. This position, therefore, justified policy decisions that sought to deny assistance to individuals and social groups that were not doing well socially. This framework was soon applied to mentally ill people.

Social Darwinism assumed that mental illness was organic and had no connection to psychological and social environmental factors. Because the environment had no influence on one's health, assistance, care, and education were considered unnatural interference (Albee 1996). The term *laissez-faire* originated from this perspective and means "hands off," that is, do not get involved in the affairs of the disadvantaged and upset the progression of natural evolution. Since recovery was hopeless, there was no need to help those who suffered from mental illness. Instead, nature should run its course and allow these people to simply die out and fade away.

Social Darwinism became a highly influential political force in the United States. It was used to justify withholding care and assistance to people in need, and in the twentieth century, it too was part of the rationale of the American eugenics movement.

The Twentieth Century

The twentieth century was unlike any other period in the history of mental illness. Theories of mental illness exploded into a cascade of diverse approaches and treatment modalities. The twentieth century, often called the "Age of Therapies," produced some 200 different psychotherapy models ranging from communing with nature to brain surgery. Doctors and patients relied heavily on pharmaceuticals to control symptoms of many severe disorders, and for the first time in over two centuries, the number of institutionalized people fell dramatically. The disciplines of psychology and sociology became influential disciplines and contributed deeply to our understanding of mental illness. In addition, the twentieth century slowly democratized mental health treatments. The Civil Rights and Women's movements and the Cultural Revolution of the 1960s brought access to mental health services to disadvantaged people, and theories were developed to understand the mental health consequences of being socially and economically unfortunate. Access for the poor was and remains insufficient, but for the first time in history, attempts were made to understand the psychology of poverty and oppression.

Although much of the proliferation of twentieth century research and development will be discussed in later chapters, four important and interrelated trends should be mentioned here: the rise of talk therapies, increase in medications, **de-institutionalization**, and a new focus on the social environment, which will be discussed throughout this text.

Talk Therapies

The merits of talking about one's troubles appear sporadically in the history of mental illness, but as a modality of treatment, talk therapy, the method of intervention we most commonly attach to clinical psychology, social work, and related fields, had its true beginnings in the 1850s. English psychiatrist Walter Dendy introduced the term "psycho-therapeia" to describe the process in which patients and their physicians would try to sort through their difficulties in getting through life (Haggerty 2020). Psycho-therapeia, however, would not become a widely accepted method until the works of Austrian neurologist Sigmund Freud's first important work was published in 1900. Freud's theories were complex and comprehensive and would dominate clinical psychology, psychiatry, and other clinical disciplines for six decades.

In a nutshell, Freud believed that mental illness symptoms, as well as other behaviors such as smoking, overindulgence in food and drink, and misspeaking ("Freudian slips"), to be indicators and consequences of repressed and unresolved emotional conflicts. In Freud's view, psychologically distressed patients were unaware of these conflicts—they were stored in the subconscious mind. If analysands, those undergoing therapy, tapped into their unconscious thoughts and memories, the conflicts could be analyzed and resolved. To do this, Freud designed a complex technique called psychoanalysis. Unlike anything in history, psychoanalysis allowed patients to actively participate in their own treatment. They could choose to engage in self-discovery, or they could resist treatment by throwing up defenses to unlocking their inner-most memories and anxieties. Psychoanalysis was seen as liberating and revolutionary, and for over half a century, a clinician in training was likely studying Freudian techniques.

Freud's hegemony over psychiatry, psychology, and social work began to fade in the 1960s, and by the end of the century there were relatively few pure psychoanalysts remaining. A handful of clinical and research centers dedicated to traditional psychoanalysis remain in the United States and Europe, but for the most part, those working in the Freudian school, the neo-Freudians, practice new versions of the technique.

Of Freud's many contributions, none perhaps has been more lasting than institutionalizing talk therapy as the main intervention modality of nonmedical clinical treatments. All major psychological schools of thought, including behaviorism, cognitive, and gestalt, as well as other disciplines like social work and pastoral counseling have produced scores of talk therapy systems, each with an underlying theoretical foundation and treatment protocol.

The Rise of Pharmaceuticals and the Fall of Institutions

The asylum movement began in the Middle Ages, accelerated in the nineteenth century, and escalated deep into the twentieth century. In 1955, the peak admissions year, 560,000 people in the United States, or 385 per every 100,000 in the population, were admitted to public and private psychiatric institutions for long-term stays of two to three months or longer (Deas-Nesmith andMcLeod-Bryant 1992). By 2014, this number would fall to 170,000 (Lutterman et al. 2017). The latter number is somewhat misleading in that there were over 5.6 million hospitalizations for mental health diagnoses and another 1.5 million for substance use disorders in 2012. Note that stays in psychiatric wards and drug and alcohol units averaged less than seven days that year (Heslin et al. 2015). Long-term institutionalization had essentially come to an end by 2000.

How did this happen, and what were the consequences? People with many types of mental distress were admitted to long-term institutional stays for treatment and protection. Those who were institutionalized the longest had late-stage debilitating psychotic disorders such as schizophrenia or severe bipolar disorder. Most of these individuals were no longer capable of self-care and often posed a danger to themselves or others, or at least they were perceived as such. Their symptoms burdened their families to the point that their kin could no longer cope or provide for them.

Three factors caused de-institutionalization. First, the movement to release patients from long-term inpatient care began with the 1954 invention of **Thorazine** (chlorpromazine), the first successful antipsychotic drug for treating schizophrenia and the manic phase of bipolar disorder. Thorazine, though not a cure, allowed patients to control their symptoms, providing they took the medicine, and avoid institutional care. Second, 10 years after Thorazine was introduced, changes in funding policies shifted financial responsibility for mental health from the states to the federal government with the introduction of Medicare, Medicaid, and Social Security Disability insurance programs. These programs, however, did not pay for residential psychiatric institutions.

Lastly, de-institutionalization represented an ideological turn regarding patients' rights (Markowitz 2011). Along with civil rights activism on behalf of racial and ethnic groups and women came movements for patients and persons with disabilities that challenged involuntary and long-term confinements on civil liberties grounds. Several twentieth-century lawsuits led states to toughen their standards for involuntary confinement from almost any reason to strictly in cases of imminent endangerment to self or others.

The consequences of de-institutionalization have been profound. The rate of severe disorders has not changed significantly since 1955, so where did people with severe mental illness go? Despite economic incapacities due to their illness, many were able to live on their own and take care of themselves. Most, however, were less fortunate. Prisons now house a disproportionately large population of people with mental illness, and others contributed to the rise in homelessness in the 1980s, living on the streets barely eking out their subsistence.

About the Quote

Whitaker's quote at the beginning of this chapter, "One of the enduring staples in mad medicine has been the rise and fall of cures," clearly illustrates the history of understanding mental health, as well as today's approaches. "Cures" come and go. None has yet been the answer, though the advocates of each theory were certain they were right. A so-called cure will catch on and get attention for a while before it is shown to be ineffective or even dangerous to patients.

Cures rise and fall, and so do diagnoses. Every few years there seems to be an ascendency of "fad diagnoses," or what some clinicians anecdotally call "diagnoses *du jour*." This phenomenon occurs when a particular disorder becomes popular, and clinicians begin to "see" it in everyone. The repressed memory movement of the 1980s is a good example. Repressed memories are a real but rare phenomenon in which an individual's memories of a traumatic experience are so painful that they are repressed or stored in the unconscious mind. In the 1980s, extracting repressed memories became a common therapeutic technique to help people in therapy identify the true cause of their emotional troubles. Many of these therapies assumed that adult problems were caused by repressed memories of childhood abuse. Through clinical practices designed to elicit these memories, individuals began to remember having been abused and many filed criminal charges against their alleged offenders. These charges usually came many years after the alleged abuse occurred, and many were imprisoned for child abuse. The trouble was these "memories" were usually false and in some cases even planted by therapists, leading judges to overturn many of the convictions.

Another "diagnosis *du jour*" was multiple personality disorder (MPD), an extraordinarily rare condition that became popular in the latter twentieth century. MPD is a condition in which people disassociate from themselves and fragment into two or more distinct personalities. The condition was popularized by the hit movie *The Three Faces of Eve* in 1957, the popular book *The Minds of Billy Milligan* (1981), and the book and Emmy award-winning TV miniseries *Sybil* (1973). In psychology and psychiatry, training workshops were taught nationwide, and an institute was founded in Kentucky to train psychiatrists to treat MPD. MPD is quite rare, but because of the training and the popularity, clinicians in droves began to see patients' "others." Eventually, it was shown that the surge in MPD cases were either based on inaccurate repressed memories, simply incorrect diagnoses, or, as in the case of "Sybil," allegedly manipulating patients into believing that "others" existed inside them (Nathan 2012). The social pressure brought on by the critics of MPD was so strong that the American Psychiatric Association removed it from the DSM and replaced it with dissociative identity disorder.

DISCUSSION QUESTIONS

1. Elaborate on Whitaker's quote that opened this chapter. What did he mean, and was he correct?

2. In his rebuke of Johann Weyer, what was Jean Bodin really saying about the study and public response to mental illness? What role did power and ideology play in his statement? Do you see any parallels in today's responses to mental health issues?

3. Most of the history of mental illness tells us that people with mental illness have been treated harshly and cruelly. Do you see vestiges of that history today?

4. In what ways can we trace our current thinking about mental illness through history?

KEY TERMS

Degeneracy theory 42
De-institutionalization 44
Eugenics 42
Germ theory 42
Four Humors Theory 24

Hysteria 23
Moral treatment 40
Psychogenic causes 27
Social Darwinism 42
Somatogenic theories 21

Supernaturalism 21
Thorazine 45
Trepanation 22

CHAPTER 3

Sociology's Theories of Mental Illness

Learning Objectives

After reading this chapter, students will be able to:

1. Describe various lay theories of mental illness.
2. Compare and contrast the major theories within sociology: labeling theory, structural strain theory, stress theory, critical theory, and social constructionism.

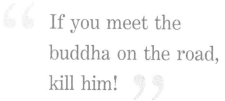

"If you meet the buddha on the road, kill him!"

—Sheldon Kopp (1974)

Introduction

Sociology is a field of theories. The primary contribution of sociology to general knowledge is its unique way of collecting and interpreting data to see what lies underneath the veneer, the obvious, and the official explanations of social things. As sociologists, our job is to uncover the hidden realities of social life, all while remembering that conducting sociological research, as with all sciences, is a social act itself. The very act of creating and using a theory is a sociological phenomenon. The theories we adopt or apply to a particular subject are a function of our basic orientation to the world. Sometimes, however, our data take us in a different direction from our expectations, and we must engage theories that challenge what we thought we already knew.

By employing the scientific method and following the rules of logical theory construction, sociological knowledge differs from lay knowledge. Lay thought is often based on information not grounded in systematically collected evidence and rooted in subjective experience. Whereas sociology tries to minimize the intrusion of personal values and opinion, lay thought is steeped in subjective bias. The notion that "you see what you want to see" is not far from true. People tend to read and subscribe to views that are consistent with their already formed attitudes and social positions.

Individuals often rely on their own experiences and values to determine what is true; however, personal experience as a source of knowledge fails to allow for other possibilities and cuts off the contributions of alternative sources of knowledge. Individual experience is too narrow to generalize to all things, and we need insights from science-based techniques to give us a complete understanding of the nature of the world around us.

Sociological theory and methods strive to minimize the biases inherent in relying on personal experience to create knowledge. The sociological approach expands our senses so that we can see beyond what is familiar to us and identify and explain patterns not readily visible.

This chapter presents different views on mental health, some of which may be new to you. We will highlight the major approaches sociologists use to explain mental illness, an exercise intended to broaden our thinking about mental illness and show other ways to look at things.

Far too often we latch onto a particular perspective and use it religiously to explain everything. This approach to knowing, however, is an error in logic known as **reductionism**, reducing everything down to one explanatory factor. The problem with reductionist thinking is that it excludes key facts or insights. For example, some physicians and biologists believe that all aspects of mental health are due to a person's physiology and that social experiences tell us nothing. This is bio-reductionism. On the other side, sociologists are sometimes guilty of socio-reductionism. That is, biology is unimportant, and individuals' environments exclusively account for their mental well-being.

Both reductionistic assumptions are wrong. As the cliché says, the truth lies somewhere in the middle. All established and legitimate theories contribute something.

So, for this chapter we will review the assumptions of sociology's theories that contribute to our knowledge of mental health and illness. The basic tenets of the medical approach will be discussed in later chapters.

Let's explore the different ways sociologists study mental illness, and by the end of the chapter, you will have a more complete set of theoretical tools for building a stronger perspective on behaviors we call mental illness. As a point of comparison, let's first look at how people in the general public understand mental illness.

Lay Theories of Mental Health

As Chapter 2 suggested, there were at least two major threads of knowledge about mental health in a society at any given time. There were the ideas of intellectuals who were thinking and theorizing about mental health and lay beliefs and traditional ideas generally held by the general public. As we saw, the ideas of the educated classes did not always trickle to uneducated and often illiterate people.

That began to change after World War II as education expanded and people became increasingly aware of mental health and insightful into their own well-being. The 1960s witnessed the beginnings of a strong mental health awareness movement that publicized information about mental illness and promoted seeking help for depression, anxiety, or anything that seemed troublesome in peoples' lives.

In addition to these social trends, the media influenced attitudes. Countless websites and computer and smartphone applications help people recognize symptoms, recommend professionals for care, and even serve as virtual therapists. Pharmaceutical companies spend millions of dollars developing and advertising medications that target emotional complaints.

Mental health signposts are everywhere: bulletin board signs for 24-hour crisis hotlines, TV and radio "reality" shows addressing guests' emotional or relationship problems, advertisements for stress relief gadgets and mental health "get-aways," and so on. Addressing student mental health has become an important objective in all levels of education, and some workplaces offer programs to help their workers "decompress" from stress and anxiety.

All of this has impacted public opinion on mental illness, which has become complex and multifaceted. For now, let's focus on lay thought about the causes of psychological distress. Public attitudes about mentally ill people and seeking help will be covered in later chapters.

Lay Beliefs of Causality

Public beliefs about the causes of mental illness reveal how a society makes sense of and defines deviance. As Jason Schnittker (2013: 75) contends, lay beliefs "reflect longstanding cultural legacies." By this he means that we can see what the culture is doing by looking at historical trends in the people's thinking and behavior.

Studies have sought to identify lay theories of mental illness in a wide range of places and have found a great variation in mental health literacy. Ideas vary by religion, social class, ethnicity, education, and residency (urban or rural); there is no homogeneity in thought in most places.

Here is a sample of public theories about the etiology of mental illness across the globe. In Nigeria, among rural and less educated people, supernatural beliefs remain prevalent. Among the urban and highly educated, however, biomedical and psychosocial causes are common (Adewuga and Makanjuola 2008). Among the Swiss, about 57 percent think that family issues are the main cause of depression, followed by occupational and other stresses (53%), and trauma (18%). Because a third also see biomedical conditions as causal indicates that in Switzerland, people tend to see an intersection of bio–psycho–social factors contributing to mental illness (Lauber et al. 2003). Malaysians are similarly varied in their thoughts, but Khan and colleagues (2011) found a preponderance of supernatural thinking in that population. Hindus in India often see mental illness as a natural part of suffering that is predestined for them (Choudhry et al. 2016), and Pacific rim peoples often connect depression and anxiety to family conflicts (Douglas and Fujimoto 1995). In Haiti, believers in Vodou attribute psychiatric problems to spells, hexes, or curses (McShane 2011). Among Orthodox Jews, mental distress is framed as an opportunity to receive divine messages and improve one's soul through acts of forgiveness (Choudhry et al. 2016; Selekman 2012).

People in the United States support a complex causal model that does not emphasize any one approach (Schnittker et al. 2000). Acceptance of biomedical causes is high, especially for severe disorders. Bernice Pescosolido and her colleagues (2010) found that 86 percent believe schizophrenia is biological and about two-thirds say major depression is also has a biological underpinning. At the same time, 67 percent say that depression is a result of daily life annoyances, and another 41 percent agree that depression is a consequence of family upbringing. Nature and nurture are not inconsistent among North Americans who seem to accept that biological and environmental factors contribute to mental illness (Link et al. 1999; Schnittker 2013).

As in other societies, subgroups in the United States endorse different ideas. The biomedical perspective is not equally accepted. African Americans, for example, while not ruling out biomedical factors, are less likely than Whites to say that physiological factors cause mental illness. African Americans tend to be more skeptical of genetic explanations of health and behavioral matters because American medicine has historically used genetics arguments against them, leaving Blacks with a deep-seated mistrust of medical theories that suggest humans differ in DNA in significant ways (Furr 2002; Schnittker 2013).

In the United States, lay views on the causes of mental illness are complicated and reflect contradictions in thinking. Schnittker (2013) summarizes lay theory in these two conflicting positions.

- Americans tend to hold biomedical views, but their fear of mentally ill people is higher than in the past.

- Mentally ill people are not responsible for their behavior, but we still use derogatory words in labeling them.

It seems reasonable to conclude that if mental illness is endemic to the body and renders people in less control of themselves, there would be more sympathy for mentally ill people. The exposure to so many and often contradictory messages about mental illness may leave people in the United States somewhat ambivalent about its causes.

Disconnects between lay thought and professional theories often affect the welfare of mental health patients. Some people may be reluctant to discuss some of their beliefs about their symptoms because they think their care provider will reject them. For example, a study in Europe found that just over three percent of interviewees believed their problems were due to evil spirits. Another 10 percent thought their symptoms were of obscure or mysterious origins such as foreboding horoscopes, environmental pollution, or demonic possession (Spence 1992). In another European study, Pfeifer (1994) found that among Protestant patients at an out-patient clinic, over half believed schizophrenia came from evil spirits and 48 percent said the same for anxiety, and 33 percent for mood disorders such as depression. The rates were higher among Christians who belonged to nonmainstream churches. These people may be hesitant to reveal their beliefs because they counter their society's prevailing ideas.

Lay theory is important to listen to and understand because it captures individuals' sensibilities toward those exhibiting symptoms of mental illness or understanding of their own problems. If a consumer of mental health services disagrees with a provider's recommendations, the probability of treatment compliance and recovery is reduced. Conversely if care providers and their clients agree on the cause of their symptoms, chances of improvement are higher.

Sociological Approaches

Theorizing about psychological well-being dates to the beginnings of the discipline.

Although the intellectual founders of the field, except perhaps for Emile Durkheim, would not say they were writing about mental health, their work is largely about society's influence on peoples' psychological frame of mind, contentment, and stability. If you took an introductory sociology class or a theory course, you probably learned about the contributions made by Karl Marx, Durkheim, and Max Weber to social thought. Their works remain the foundations of most social theory, and they all addressed psychological well-being. Marx' concept of alienation, Durkheim's anomie, and Weber's disenchantment can be framed as troubling social-psychological conditions brought on by social organization, conflict, and tension. Alienation refers to feelings of powerlessness originating from social conflicts and the unequitable distribution of wealth and power. Durkheim's anomie is the state of mind of not knowing how to act when social rules break down and social surroundings become confusing, chaotic, or normless. Disenchantment was Weber's term to describe feelings of disillusionment at the loss of belief in social institutions and ideologies as they are challenged and replaced by different ways of thinking and living.

We may not use these terms directly in studies of psychological well-being, but they are the basis of the general sociological approach, which is to study how the social environment affects our emotions, ability to think, and behavior.

While sociology has produced divergent theories related to mental health, certain themes run through them all. First, sociology does not always see DSM disorders as discrete and separate entities. Studies of the symptoms of schizophrenia, alcoholism, depression, and anxiety have found that they do reliably cluster together, but that the symptoms overlap more like a spectrum than discrete and unique constellations (Dohrenwend et al. 1980; Mirowsky and Ross 2012). Contrary to DSM conceptualization of disorders, no real boundary separates them.

A second theme in sociology contends that mental illness disorders, as outlined in the DSM, are socially constructed artifacts of psychiatry as an industry. The idea is that since the symptoms do not cluster in naturally occurring ways, as nonpsychiatric medical conditions do, conceptualizations of the disorders are only as real as their social meanings and usages. The main benefit of creating categories of disorders is to provide a framework for psychiatry as a medical practice. Third, material conditions of life affect people's subjective well-being. Wealth, power, access to resources and being in control of one's life are powerful social forces that exert great influence on mental well-being.

A fourth theme is that material conditions and social dynamics influence labeling psychiatric disorders. The adage, "rich people are eccentric and poor people are crazy," tells us something: the social status of the "patient" influences the diagnosis.

As mentioned in Chapter 1, sociologists look at mental health from distinctive angles and ask different questions than medicine and psychology, which focuses on individual development and reaction to environmental stimuli. Sociology not only attempts to identify social patterns in mental health but also how some behaviors are defined as mental illness, while others are not.

The remainder of this chapter will review five major sociological perspectives: labeling theory, structural theory, stress theory, critical theory, and social constructionism.

Labeling Theory (Aka Social Reaction Theory)

Labeling Theory is a multidimensional approach to the sociology of mental illness. It seeks to understand why some people are identified as deviants and the consequences of that social designation. The perspective has a long and influential history in the discipline and played a role in the deinstitutionalization movement of the 1960s and 1970s (Thoits 2017).

Labeling Theory, as Peggy Thoits states, is grounded on one major assumption: "people who are labeled as deviant and treated as deviant become deviant" (2017: 139). Labeling assumes that mental illness is behavior that violates social expectations of correct behavior. Mental illness, in this view, is deviant behavior. When norms are broken, society reacts by labeling deviants with some label to identify and make sense of them. Those assigned a label, in turn, respond to their ascribed social status. In our case, that marker is mental illness.

Classic Labeling Theory contends that people do not start life intending to be deviant, but at some point, everyone will eventually break the rules. You have committed acts of deviance: you have probably exceeded the speed limit while driving, been late for class, did not study for an exam, or had a naughty thought now and again. We all have broken norms, but most of us have not been called a deviant. These acts of initial deviance are called primary deviance, and are often ignored, denied, or explained away. They are typically singular acts caused by social strains like peer pressure, heavy role burdens, poverty, competitiveness, psychological stressors such as loneliness, or physiological reasons like genetics.

A person is usually not identified as deviant until these behaviors are repeated or publicly noticeable and come to the attention of social authority agents such as parents, teachers, judges, and doctors. Once labeled, rule violators are treated differently than before their deviance was known, and usually for the worse. Most importantly, society merges the person's actions with their identities, and at that point, the behavior is now labeled secondary deviance.

Once people enter secondary deviance, they are forced to react to the label, and what usually happens is that they internalize the identity of their new deviant status and act consistently with the expectations of that status. Someone labeled as "bad," for instance, will continue to act in a socially defined "bad" way (Lemert 1967). It is an illustration of sociologist Robert Merton's (1948) concept "self-fulfilling prophecy."

Mental illness, therefore, is a product of a particular process of labeling individuals who break rules in certain ways. But does the label cause symptoms? Labeling Theory was not designed to address the causes of primary deviance, but it does give us ideas about how people are labeled and the consequences of being identified as mentally ill.

Modified Labeling Theory

A more recent approach to Labeling Theory, known as **Modified Labeling Theory** (MLT), provides detailed insights into how labeling affects mental health. Proposed by Link and colleagues (1989), MLT illustrates a series of five steps in the labeling process that detail how a deviant label reinforces and continues psychiatric symptoms.

Step 1: Beliefs. Society generally holds negative attitudes and beliefs toward people with mental illness. These beliefs usually stereotype mentally ill people as violent, dangerous, and unpredictable sorts whose trustworthiness is uncertain. Mentally ill people are devalued and dehumanized to some extent (Hunter et al. 2017). These negative perceptions of mental illness are pervasive in society and easily encountered and learned.

Step 2: Internalization. Individuals enter Step 2 when they recognize their behavior, thoughts, or emotions match society's labels of mental illness. Now they must reconcile the stereotyped social image of mental illness with their own behavior. If individuals internalize the stereotyped image as "who I am," meaning they connect the public belief to their sense of self, they are more likely to experience declines in quality of life and increases in their symptoms (Livingston and Boyd 2010; Hunter et al. 2017).

Step 3: Response. In Step 3, MLT posits that labeled individuals will attempt to cope with the label and the social behaviors that are expected of people labeled mentally ill. They may attempt to conceal their symptoms in secrecy, withdraw, or avoid social encounters in which they may be rejected. They may also try to distance themselves from other people with the same label as not to "be like them" or deflect others away by saying "That's not me" (Thoits 2011a; Link and Phelan 2013). Step 3 is primarily about coping with being labeled mentally ill.

Step 4: Consequences. Step 4 in MLT involves the consequences of the label and focuses on coping strategies. The more the deviant image is internalized and becomes central to the person's identity, the more likely an individual will cope in self-destructive ways. Research by Kroska and Harkness (2011) shows that negative self-labeling increases individuals' tendency to withdraw socially, especially among people with affective disorders. Poor coping practices tend to alienate others, which leads to less social support and attention to self-care.

Step 5: Vulnerability. In Step 5, with diminished social supports, the labeled person becomes at increased risk for continuing and often worsening symptoms. Those holding negative self-perceptions, for example, tend to have lower self-esteem and diminished confidence in their ability to accomplish tasks and reach goals (Pasman 2011). Link and colleagues (1989) argue that labeling may or may not produce a mental disorder, but it can lead to negative psychological outcomes. If someone accepts how most people feel about mental patients, these beliefs take on new significance for individuals who enter psychological or psychiatric treatment. In short, the more individuals labeled mentally ill feel discounted and rejected, the more threatened they feel when encountering other people, which can lead to more troubled emotions, behaviors, and thoughts.

Labeling Theory and Power

Power is an important dimension of Labeling Theory. Differences in power means that not everyone has an equal chance of receiving the same label, even for the same behavior. Labels are usually made by people in higher status positions and attached to those in lower positions of the social ladder. Behaviors of marginalized people are often attributed different causes than people from dominant groups. Kutchins and Kirk (1997), for example, discovered that severe psychological symptoms among minority members are often ignored or criminalized. Cultural stereotypes are known to influence perceptions of clients' behaviors, especially if the clinician is a member of the dominant social group and is fearful of a minority.

Labeling Theory Criticisms

Despite its insights, Labeling Theory has a couple of distractions and limitations. First, it does not explain the onset of primary deviance, in this case, the symptoms of mental illness. The theory "begins" as a person is ascribed a label. A second shortcoming is that in some cases, people are happy to receive a label. Attaching a name to their troubles may help people find relief and relocate blame for their difficulties (Young et al. 2008). An example is Alcoholics Anonymous, whose participants often attribute alcoholism to a medical disease that is only treatable by discontinuing consumption. Blame for their behavior is assigned to their bodies, like any disease, and it is not an indication of poor character or social environmental factors.

Box 3.1 provides an example in which labels of mental illness can be manipulated to shape an image or public persona.

Structural Strain Theory

Structural Strain Theory is perhaps the oldest approach in sociology for studying mental health and contends that macro social forces create pressures or barriers for psychological well-being. The theory posits that mental health problems

Box 3.1 Self-Labeling: The Case of Ariel Castro

People sometimes resist the labels assigned to them by agents of authority. Research usually finds that people oppose medical labels, but that is not always the case. Take Ariel Castro, for instance. In the early 2000s, Castro kidnapped and imprisoned three young women, two of whom were teenagers, and for over a decade, committed horrible and degrading acts of cruelty against them. While holding them at his home and in chains, Castro pursued a nondescript and somewhat normal appearing life outside his house. His atrocities remained secret until one of the women bravely escaped and notified authorities.

In 2013, a Cleveland, Ohio, grand jury indicted Castro on 977 counts of kidnapping, endangerment of a minor, rape, and other assault charges; he pled guilty to 937 of them to avoid a trial. He was sentenced to life plus 1,000 years with no possibility of parole and forfeiture of his property (his house was torn down). He also had to waive his right to an appeal and pay a fine. About a month after sentencing, Castro took his own life in a detention cell.

At his sentencing hearing, Castro made a 20-minute statement about his life and the charges against him. It is on the internet and makes for a most interesting study in labeling theory. In his account of himself, Castro attempted to reframe his behavior by saying that he was the "best daddy" (he had grown children and fathered a child with one of his captives) and "not a violent person." "I simply kept them without letting them leave," he said to the court to minimize his actions. He also said, "I'm not violent. I am a musician." He claimed that sex with the enslaved women was consensual and denied his culpability by blaming the victims themselves and his ex-wife for his behavior.

He furthered denied responsibility for his actions by attempting to label himself as having a disease. At one point, he said, "These people are trying to paint me as a monster. I am not a monster. I'm sick." He then proceeded to talk about having an addiction to sex and pornography and an impulse control disorder. "It is the same as alcoholic addiction," he claimed. By deflecting his heinous crimes to an organic illness, he sought to deny moral responsibility, minimize the consequences of his behavior, and manipulate the social judgements people had of him. He wanted to be labeled as mentally ill because he thought society would judge him more sympathetically. In short, his statement to the court was an attempt to manage his public image and social identity, not to atone for his crimes or genuinely apologize to the people he viciously brutalized.

You can see video of his court statement posted by the *Wall Street Journal* on YouTube. Caution: his statement may be distressing to watch.

---

evolve from macro-level forces that impede healthy emotional and cognitive development. These barriers block opportunities and stymie individuals' aspirations, creating feelings of frustration, loneliness, and disappointment. Also important in Structural Theory are feelings of deprivation related to social and economic differences in wealth and power.

This approach looks at social aggregates, emphasizing structural conditions and rates of mental problems in a society or group. The key question for structural theorists, therefore, is how do large scale social forces impact individual-level emotional states.

A famous example of structural analysis is Durkheim's 1897 study of suicide. In *Suicide*, one of the first empirical case studies in the discipline, Durkheim sought to show that social forces beyond individual thoughts and emotions could cause suicidal behavior. He argued that norms and values guide behavior in social situations and control or regulate emotions. Rules of appropriateness in expressing emotions, he believed, help people keep their emotions in check. Therefore, the degree to which an individual is integrated into a social community that provides those controls is central to emotional well-being. People who are inadequately integrated into a group are more likely to become overly passionate, distraught, or depressed, and they will be more suicidal.

Durkheim's research uncovered several social patterns that were associated with suicide. Because of their lack of normative social attachments, people who were unmarried, childless, male (except for older women who were childless), Protestant (compared to Catholics and Jews), and soldiers were more likely to take their own lives. He contended that these groups faced social pressures that prevented them from fully integrating into a social community that provided emotional stability, guidance, and safety. From his data, Durkheim created a typology of three types of suicide: **egoistic**, **anomic**, and **altruistic**. His three types of suicide are based on integration into society and are illustrated in Chart 3.1.

Structural Theory is particularly helpful in understanding the social patterns of mental health and illness. Underlying structural factors such as inequality, discrimination, war, social opportunities, working conditions, disenfranchisement, and violence are so strong that they are considered "fundamental causes" of mental illness.

Economic inequality is particularly important in structural research due to the strains it places on people. Neighborhood characteristics in particular have been shown to affect emotional well-being. Residents in neighborhoods that are in physical decay (vacant buildings, vandalism, graffiti) or social disorder (drug

CHART 3.1 Durkheim's Three Types of Suicide

Type	Integration Context	Causal Mechanisms	Examples
Egoistic	Feeling like one does not belong Detached from meaningful social groups Feeling disconnected	Less guidance from stable social norms Poor socialization	"Loner" suicide–homicides People who do not "fit in"
Anomic	Moral confusion and lack of direction due to social changes	Social breakdowns that make rules unclear	Economic ruin Death of spouse
Altruistic	Overwhelmed by group's expectations of conformity Individual interests are not important	Suicide protects the group	Suicide bombers Kamikazes Heroes

dealing, few services, noisy, prostitution) have a higher risk of depression (Diez Roux and Mair 2010) and anxiety about safety (Austin et al. 2002). Neighborhood quality is also associated with children's aggressiveness, defiance, and antisocial mentality (Li et al. 2017).

The main limitation of Structural Theory is that it addresses health outcomes only in aggregate forms. All these macro conditions are associated with higher rates of mental health problems, but we cannot necessarily determine how they impact individuals who do or do not develop problems. This weakness of Structural Theory constitutes an ecological fallacy, an error in logic attempting to predict or specify individual behavior from aggregated data. That impoverished people tend to have more symptoms than wealthy persons is a statistical generalization of the groups. We cannot deduce from aggregated data alone the individual characteristics of a poor person having a mental illness.

Stress Theory

Stress Theory, currently one of the major theoretical paradigms used in sociological research on mental health, is often employed to connect structural conditions to individual responses. As Pearlin and colleagues stated, "[Stress] presents an excellent opportunity to observe how deeply well-being is affected by the structural arrangements of people's lives and the repeated experiences that stem from these arrangements" (1989: 241). The intent of stress theory is to explain how a person's social location creates stress that can translate into psychological symptoms.

Stress Theory is perhaps the most widely employed sociological theory in research today, and Thoits (2017) summarized its advantages. First, Stress Theory emphasizes individuals' social situation and context. Biology and psychology tend to avoid the impact of social forces on individual behavior. Second, Stress Theory connects the relationship between social location and rates of psychopathology. Sociology has long demonstrated that where people are situated in the social hierarchy influences the likelihood of mental health problems. In particular, lower status groups, whose lives are more stressful, show more symptoms of mental distress. Third, the components of Stress Theory are easily quantified and studied. Sociologists can measure stressful relationships and situations, support resources, and individual coping abilities. Lastly, there is extensive empirical support for the assumptions of stress theory: certain conditions of **stress** do indeed predict psychological problems.

It's also a theory that can join sociology to biology, providing insights into how our social environment affects our bodies. In that regard, Stress Theory over the last few decades has proven to have high validity and reliability for connecting social context to individual pathology.

Let's begin by defining **stressor**, **distress**, and stress. Stressors are "conditions of threat, challenge, demands, or structural constraints that, by the very fact of their occurrence or existence, call into question the operating integrity of the organism" (Wheaton and Montazer 2010: 173). Stressors are those external events or conditions that place pressure on mental and physiological well-being and usual functioning. Examples of stressors are unemployment, persistent threat of violence, and conflicted relationships. Distress is the subjective state that results from having difficulty coping with a stressor. Distress refers to a dysfunctional or destructive cognitive, behavioral, or emotional response to stress and stressors.

In sociology, the word "stress" has two meanings. First, stress can refer to a force enacted against a person. Much like engineering's use of the term, stress refers to pressure. Nonhuman examples are the weight of a heavy snowfall that causes a roof to collapse or a dam that breaks because of too much water pressing against it. In this usage, "stress" and "stressor" are roughly equivalent. In sociology, such pressure is caused by a discrete environmental event or change that is perceived as a threat and requires a social or psychological adjustment in an individual (Wheaton et al. 2013). One example is the reported rise in domestic violence cases during the coronavirus crisis of 2020. The "weight" of the shutdown forced a change in everyday behavior and economic well-being that resulted in a prolonged emotional reaction. For some, the stress was expressed through violence or drug and alcohol use.

A second meaning of stress is the physiological response to a threat or socio-environmental demand that taxes a person's usual coping ability (Aneshensel 1992). It is a generalized physiological alert to an external stressor.

Since Stress Theory allows for a biology–sociology connection, let's explore both sides of that equation.

The Biology Side of Stress Theory

Stress Theory has its beginnings in the 1930s when Hans Selye, an endocrinologist, first discovered and enunciated the physiological stress process. His writings in the 1950s further promoted his discovery, but his ideas were not fully accepted until the 1970s. Since that time, thousands of articles and books have been written on stress and coping with it.

It's hard to imagine that someone had to discover stress. It seems so ubiquitous—everybody has experienced the stress response. Think of a time when something seemed threatening or challenging to you. It may have been a shadowy figure lurking in a dark alleyway or a near-miss auto collision. After the threat ended, you may have detected your sweaty palms, racing heart, and heavy breathing. You probably did not notice that your gastrointestinal tract had slowed, and your sexual responses were nil.

Those physical changes are called **"fight or flight,"** which is our body's way of preparing itself to handle a threatening situation. Our breath speeds to get more oxygen in the body and the heart beats faster to get that oxygen to our muscles. We sweat to keep our bodies from overheating while we "do battle."

Evolution gives us fight or flight. Millenia ago, the biggest threats to humans were mainly singular, one-off, concrete events like sudden animal attacks or fights with other people. Our bodies developed fight or flight responses to prepare us for these trials, which is a good thing. In contemporary social life, however, most of the stress we encounter is chronic, not acute. Most people today do not have many short, unexpected, and life-threatening menaces relative to the many daily or on-going problems characteristic of modern life. Here's the bad thing: our bodies only know how to respond to acute stress. Modern stress is chronic, continuous, and part of everyday life, but our bodies continue to react in a primitive, fight or flight way.

The primary stress system in our bodies is the **hypothalamic–pituitary–adrenal axis**, or HPA. As our central stress response mechanism, the HPA axis is a neuro-endocrine system that alters the functioning of various tissues to mobilize the body to respond to a stressor.

When the brain recognizes a serious threat, the hypothalamus produces CRF, corticotropin-releasing hormone, which binds to receptors in the pituitary gland, which in turn stimulates adrenocorticotropic hormones (ACTH) that bind to the adrenal cortex, which, finally, produces adrenaline and **cortisol** (natural steroids). Along the way, epinephrine in the body and norepinephrine in the brain are also released to alert the body to action. These hormones divert the body from its normal functioning to a state of arousal and excitability.

Cortisol levels, which are widely studied as a reliable indicator of stress, fluctuate normally throughout the day. Persistent high levels of cortisol, however, signal that the body is in constant fight or flight. The body can handle this stimulation for a short duration, but if extended, negative consequences are likely. For example, long exposure to stress and cortisol affects the immune system and increase the risk for heart disease, hypertension, and, indirectly, cancer as stress increases the likelihood of smoking, overeating, and alcohol consumption.

Elevated cortisol is also associated with psychological distress. Numerous studies over the last several years point to a strong relationship between the hormone and psychological troubles. One area of interest is family conflict, especially in relation to children's mental health. Most adolescents have the psychosocial resources to cope with familial problems, but many do not. Those teens either externalize their anger or become withdrawn and emotionally troubled. Both response patterns are paired with elevated cortisol levels and are associated with symptoms of general anger and depression (Koss et al. 2017).

Cortisol and psychological distress are closely linked in other areas as well. Elevated cortisol is common among those with post-traumatic stress, and when paired with obesity and depression can lead to metabolic syndrome (hypertension, waistline body fat, high blood sugar, and high cholesterol) and an increased risk of cardiovascular disease (Aaseth et al. 2019).

Another study found that interpersonal relationships can raise cortisol levels. Meyer and colleagues (2019), in a study of heterosexual relationships, found that women's poor health, relationship dissatisfaction, and high depression scores correlated with elevated cortisol in their male partners. However, the reverse was not true. On these three variables, men had no impact on women's cortisol.

Elevated cortisol may also contribute to health disparities by shaping physiological responses to social stressors (Doyle and Molix 2017). Bi-racial and bi-cultural individuals are often refused membership in the groups with which they identify, a process known as **identity denial**. When identity denial occurs, individuals typically have strong emotional responses and experience elevated cortisol (Albuja et al. 2019). Doyle and Molix' (2017) research uncovered similar findings. They learned that **stigma consciousness**, a concept referring to expectations of being devalued, discriminated against, or stereotyped, also produces heighten cortisol. Jackson's group (2017) found elevated cortisol connected to perceived racial and gender bias and discrimination among African American women.

Sociological factors underlie the stressful conditions that stimulate the HPA axis and cortisol production. Family functioning, gender norms, and social stratification, all features of social structure, have physiological consequences that are associated with distress.

Sociology and Stress Theory

Soon after Selye's research on stress was published, social and behavioral scientists began to look for social stressors that might stimulate the HPA axis. Among the first were psychiatrists Holmes and Rahe (1967) who created the Social Readjustment Rating Scale (see Figure 3.1) in an attempt to measure stress-inducing life events that significantly changed people's lives and perhaps caused illness. The "Life change units" were derived by asking people to rate on a scale of 0–100 how much readjustment is required for each event.

The Holmes and Rahe index was an important early step in linking stressors to health. There are several problems with this technique, however. First, the list of stressors is not culturally sensitive. The stressors on the list are most likely to impact the lives of White, Christian, middle class, heterosexual males. Stressors stemming from workplace discrimination, sexism, and revealing minority sexual orientations are not listed (Thoits 2010). Item 34, "changes in church activities" and 42, "Christmas," implies Christian-centricity. Second, these events are highly subjective. People are likely to experience them in vastly different ways. What is stressful for one person, may be liberating for another. Leaving an abusive or grossly unsatisfying marriage, for example, is not necessarily a negative stress event; it may be an act of defiance, liberation, and self-empowerment. Lastly, these stressors are not unidimensional in nature; they have variability in duration and severity. The longer a stress-producing event lasts and the more harm it causes, the more likely it will result in health problems (Brown and Harris 2012). Research relying on life-changing events has offered little to our present understanding of stress and mental health. Events are too variable to explain distress; therefore, greater specification is needed.

Refinements in stress research have improved on simple events studies. Research now centers on identifying how the severity, duration, and timing of stressors connect to stress reactions. The result: now we know that childhood traumas, early adult events, recent events, **chronic stressors**, and daily **hassles** are most likely to lead to psychological distress (Wheaton and Montazer 2017).

We can conceptualize stressors that are associated with distress into several categories, keeping in mind they are not necessarily mutually exclusive.

Daily Hassles. Daily hassles are routine day-to-day stressors that disturb a person's everyday routines. They are relatively minor events that emerge from the habits of daily life at home, work, school, and neighborhoods. Daily hassles may be registering for classes, handling a parking ticket, encounters with angry customers at work, or dealing with a grouchy neighbor. Hassles are life's "little" conflicts and

FIGURE 3.1 Holmes and Rahe (1967) Social Readjustment Rating Scale

Rank	Life Event	Life Change Unit
1.	Death of a spouse	100
2.	Divorce	73
3.	Marital separation	65
4.	Jail term	63
5.	Death of a close family member	63
6.	Personal injury or illness	53
7.	Marriage	50
8.	Fired at work	47
9.	Marital reconciliation	45
10.	Retirement	45
11.	Change in health of family member	44
12.	Pregnancy	40
13.	Sexual difficulties	39
14.	Gain a new family member	39
15.	Business readjustment	39
16.	Change in financial state	38
17.	Death of a close friend	37
18.	Change to different line of work	36
19.	Change in number of arguments with spouse	35
20.	Major mortgage	32
21.	Foreclosure of mortgage or loan	30
22.	Change in responsibilities at work	29
23.	Son or daughter leaving home	29
24.	Trouble with in-laws	29
25.	Outstanding personal achievement	28
26.	Wife starts or stops work	26
27.	Beginning or end of school	26
28.	Change in living conditions	25
29.	Revision of personal habits	24
30.	Trouble with boss	23
31.	Change in working hours or conditions	20
32.	Change in residence	20
33.	Change in schools	20
34.	Change in recreation	19
35.	Change in church activities	19
36.	Change in social activities	18
37.	Minor mortgage or loan	17
38.	Change in sleeping habits	16
39.	Change in number of family reunions	15
40.	Change in eating habits	15
41.	Vacation	13
42.	Major Holiday	12
43.	Minor violation of law	11

Scale
Score of 300+: At risk of illness.
Score of 150-299: Risk of illness is moderate (reduced by 30% from the above risk).
Score <150: Only have a slight risk of illness.

Source: Holmes and Rahe (1967). Copyright © 1967 Published by Elsevier Inc.

problems. The emotional consequences are usually low to moderate and typically dissipate (Serido et al. 2004).

These seemingly insignificant annoyances, however, can accumulate and be detrimental to mental health. Several studies have found that daily hassles can have an independent impact on well-being or exacerbate the effect of other stressors such as physical abuse (Campbell et al. 1997).

Hassles also have differential effects among people in diverse social statuses. In a study of college students, Jung and Khalsa (1989) learned that African American students, compared to Whites, reported more daily hassles that accumulated into more severe outcomes. While the severity of the hassles predicted depression in both groups, the effects were stronger for African American students since they had more severe stressors. Family support, however, was particularly important for Black students to mediate stress and lower the risk of depression.

In a similar study, Grzywacz and colleagues (2004) found that education influenced the effect of hassles. While people with higher education levels reported more hassles, they also had more resources to cope with them, which meant fewer psychological symptoms and distress. Individuals with less education, however, had more severe daily hassles and subsequently more distress.

The perception of the severity of hassles, not necessarily their frequency, is the key (Crnic and Booth 1991). The more someone perceives daily hassles to be disruptive and aggravating, the greater their effect on well-being.

Ambient Stressors. **Ambient stressors** are chronic, unpleasant, uncontrollable, and unmanageable environmental conditions such as overcrowding, noise, odors, and pollution (Campbell 1983). These conditions often exist in the background, and people usually think they can ignore or adapt to them. Ambient conditions, however, are known to raise stress levels (Oiamo et al. 2015).

Research has found that ambient exposures vary in a population. Low-income earners lacking the resources to escape ambient stressors have a lower psychological quality of life (Bickerstaff and Walker 2001). Low income older African Americans are particularly over-exposed to this form of stressor (Cornwell 2014). Ambient stress appears to accumulate over time as the effects of early and prolonged exposure mounts and negatively affects individuals' ability to cope with other stressors (Evans et al. 1987; Wheaton and Clarke 2003).

Catastrophes and Traumas. Wheaton and Montazer define traumatic stressors as "fundamental and comprehensive challenges to the personal foundational meanings that guide and support social life and personal identity" (2017: 191). Natural disasters such as tornados and earthquakes and traumatic events like sexual and physical assaults, human trafficking, and combat can trigger devastating lifelong emotional outcomes. These events are overwhelming and can change one's life even if they appear to have successfully coped with it. As Wheaton and Montazer say, these stressors cannot be put aside or dismissed. Traumas become an enduring part of a person's identity and a signpost for when people's lives changed.

Psychological distress can often be traced to a profound, catastrophic event. An assault, parents' divorce, physical abuse, witnessing a horrific scene, or a destructive weather event or terrorist attack can leave everlasting emotional scars that appear as anxiety, depression, fear of the event repeating, self-blame, identity crises, problems trusting others and forming relationships, and suicide. It is typical for catastrophic events to generate chronic and sometimes life-long stress, especially if the exposure occurs at a young age and is repeated. Increased severity of a stressor also impacts the degree of psychological harm.

The psychological effects of traumas and catastrophes, which will be discussed in more detail in Chapters 8 and 10, often intersect with physical health. Studies have shown that traumatic exposure is connected to substance abuse, overeating, gastrointestinal and neuroendocrine disorders, and cognitive impairments. There are likely two pathways into subsequent health problems. First, conscious and unconscious reactions to reminders of the trauma elicit stress responses, and second, when individuals try to cope by suppressing their emotions, their bodies will initiate HPA axis responses (D'Andrea et al. 2011).

Experiencing an early childhood stressor can have a long-lasting effect on the HPA axis. Unless the problem gets resolved through psychotherapy or other means, heightened HPA activation can extend into adulthood and can lead to depression, anxiety, panic disorders, and phobias (Juruena et al. 2020).

In addition, the effects of stress exposure can be multigenerational, even affecting babies *in utero*. Cowan and associates (2015) reviewed several stress events that produced multigenerational distress. The children of women who were pregnant during the Dutch famine of 1944–1945, which was caused by the Nazi occupation of the Netherlands, experienced higher rates of schizophrenia and depression than Dutch children whose mothers were not exposed to the food shortages. Another example of prenatal exposure to stress is the Tanshen, China, earthquake of 1976. Bu age 18, these children had higher likelihoods of depression than those not exposed to the stress of the quake. A last example of multigenerational stress is of already-born children of parents who experienced severe stressors such as combat or children born to Holocaust survivors after they left Europe and were safe, also have higher rates of depression and anxiety disorders (Cowan et al. 2015).

How do multigenerational effects of stress exposure happen? It is likely that parenting styles are impacted by a parent's stress exposure. Research shows that after an earlier severe and high-impact stressor, parents often develop atypical styles of relating to their children. They may engage in role reversal, where parents use their children to meet their own emotional needs, violence, emotional abuse, or over-protectiveness (Cowan et al. 2015). Some parents may become withdrawn or have trouble forming stable attachments with their children and other adults.

Acute and Chronic Stressors. **Acute stressors** are short in duration, whereas chronic stressors longer lasting. However, they are not really different. Acute stress is the initial impact of a stressor event. For example, stressful events such as losing one's job, divorcing, or suffering economic loss may cause an initial shock, but the more serious effect occurs if the stress becomes a chronic condition as it temporally extends beyond the actual event (House 2002). Stress becomes chronic when it persists over an extended period of time. The effects of a stressful event, such as losing a job, can last for months or even years. Therefore, the differences between acute and chronic do not matter significantly. Research repeatedly shows that chronic stressors have the most impact on mental health. For example, getting a divorce, a relative short or acute situation, does not produce the same psychological distress as feeling trapped in a marriage wrought with persistent tension and conflict.

Responding to Stressors

Life events are not equally stressful to all people; the characteristics of an individual and the conditions of the stressor impact how a person responds (Pearlin and Bierman 2013; Wheaton 1983). In addition, stressors have more impact when they are perceived as taxing one's ability to cope and threatening or challenging (Lazarus and Folkman 1984). The more we believe a stressor will harm us, the greater the stress reaction will be.

Dealing with stress generally relies on two factors: personality strengths and social support. Personal resiliency, insight, and problem-solving skills go far in avoiding or minimizing the impact of a stressful event. Social support, in the form of having confidants with whom to discuss problems, friends or relatives to help resolve problems such as day care or transportation, financial resources, health care, and relaxation opportunities (vacations, leisure time, babysitters), can mediate the effects of stress and reduce the likelihood of depression and other mental health problems.

Brown and Ciciurkaite (2017: 221–222) have summarized the research on the effects of social support on managing stress.

- The perception of social support is vitally important in the effectiveness of support. As Brown and Ciciurkaite say, the love of others does not protect against distress if it is "kept a secret." A person in stress needs to know that social support is present.

- Social support relieves distress regardless of stress level. It is especially effective when stress exposure is high.

- Perceived social support varies with social status. People who are married and in higher social class positions report the highest levels of perceived support.

Critical Theory

The next perspective to review is **Critical Theory**, which is more philosophical in nature with roots in the works of a group known as The Frankfurt School. The Frankfurt scholars included several famous theorists including Herbert Marcuse, Theodor Adorno, Erich Fromm, Wilhelm Reich, and Max Horkheimer, among others who were based at Goethe University in Frankfort, Germany. These scholars were trained in different disciplines but came together to create a school of thought based on integrating the ideas of Karl Marx, Sigmund Freud, and, to a lesser extent, Max Weber. The primary thrust of the Frankfurt School was to critique contemporary society, pointing out the ways in which society restricts people from developing their full human potential and self-realization. While not a theory of mental illness *per se*, their approach questioned whether mental illness was a real illness. As Fromm wrote, symptomatic behavior was a rational approach to an irrational society. If one could sum up the Frankfurt School in a short oversimplification, it would be "there are no sick people, only sick societies."

Critical Theory attempted to explain how social structures and processes prohibited people from exercising their true humanness. According to this perspective, society's rules, which are not designed to protect people as much as they are to protect wealth, property, and privileged groups, are restrictive and cause people to repress their true aspirations, emotions, and sexuality. Fromm described social organizations as creating a state of "normalcy" that is incompatible with human fulfillment and self-realization. Society, through its demands for conformity, oppressive social controls, and restrictions on expression, essentially prohibits people from living a happy and meaningful, and, therefore, "healthy" life (Fromm 2010; Harris 2019).

Because of the Nazi's ban on free thought and academic speech, the Frankfurt School scholars fled Germany in the late 1930s to seek refuge elsewhere. Most settled in New York and continued their work at Columbia University. During and after the War, several of them turned their gaze toward Nazi Germany to try to explain many Germans' blind devotion to a philosophy and regime that started a horrific war and enslaved and slaughtered millions of innocent men, women, and children. The most well-known of these works is Adorno's *Authoritarian Personality* (1950/2019).

Attempting to explain Nazis and their behavior, Adorno and his colleagues created the concept of the **authoritarian personality** as one that compensates for personal insecurities and anxieties by blindly relying on other people and an external dogma to define what is real and provide a sense of order. These people have difficulty coping and managing their own lives, so external ideologies and authorities provide a sense of purpose and meaning to offset their uncertainties.

Seemingly contradictory, authoritarians succumb to a broader authority, such as leaders of political party, a restrictive religion, or a set of political doctrine like Nazism but impose themselves on weaker social groups. Anyone who is believed to challenge or threaten the authorities and their ideologies are stereotyped and deemed dangerous. It is not just a political challenge; it is a personal threat since the sense of self and the ideology have merged. Authoritarians, therefore, are both submissive and dominating. Adorno argued that authoritarian relations arise when they are bureaucratized and competition for wealth is valued, as they were in Nazi Germany.

The authoritarian personality can be summarized by the following qualities:

- Dominant and submissive relationship to authority. Defers to authority, but aggressive toward weaker groups.

- Intellectually dependent and obedient on the ideology of powerful leaders, yet willing to violate rules of conventional behavior to obey authorities and control others.

- Strong sense of self-righteousness and indignation.
- Sees the world as hierarchies of power.

In authoritarian social organization, the mind is conditioned to conform to the demands of the bureaucracy and the rules of competitiveness set by the authorities. Authoritarians strongly support traditional values and conventionality and are fearful of a world that appears to threaten that authority structure (Altemeyer 1998; Whitley 1999).

This "perfect storm" of anxiety, social organization, and appealing ideology impacts personality orientation and allows powerful leaders to control public and social narratives on a wide array of subjects. People who are authoritarian are more likely to follow social scripts of prejudice against GLBTQ communities (Haddock et al. 1993), people with disabilities (Noonan et al. 1970), and even mental health services (Furr et al. 2003). They tend to be hostile toward feminism and gender equality and are more likely to commit a sexual assault (Duncan 2006; Walker et al. 1993).

A second study in the tradition of the Frankfurt School is Christopher Lasch's famous book, *The Culture of Narcissism* (1979). According to Lasch, the primary pathology of our time is narcissism, a personality style in which a person whose underlying emotional foundation is grounded in anger and self-doubts creates a grandiose self-conception. The classical definition describes a narcissist as one who manipulates other people for self-gratification, while desperately yearning for others' love and approval.

Lasch believed that the conventional social world was harder to comprehend, and dangerous. Challenges to and flaws in established social institutions made them less attractive as a grounding for identity and personal satisfaction. For example, unlike generations before us, we now marry for emotional fulfillment rather than economic cooperativeness, gendered social expectations, and to reproduce, and we participate less in the practices of organized religions. Finding little meaning in the broader social world, Lasch thought we turn inward to emotionally survive society's trials and find gratification. For people who are angry and insecure, having no secure social foundation creates difficulties in finding a meaningful existence.

Lasch saw several social forces working against individual fulfillment. Lower skilled, routinized, and meaningless work, dependencies on large bureaucracies such as corporations and the government for subsistence, impending nuclear or environmental disasters, and a dominant individualistic ideology all contributed to forcing a retreat from social life and withdrawal into self-absorption. Indications of this disillusionment can be seen by shallow personal relationships that often dominate people's lives, a fascination with the lives of celebrities as escapist illusion, more people seeking therapy, high marital dissatisfaction, and an attraction to foreign religions and "new age" beliefs and practices. Lasch contended that these seemingly personal behaviors were in fact consequences of a society that failed to provide a meaningful sense of purpose and allow individuals to live harmoniously and authentically.

Social Constructionism

The last theory to discuss is Social Constructionism, a perspective that assumes that reality only exists as humans assign meanings to things, name them, and develops a narrative about them. Through society's rules and values, we construct what reality is. If society does not accept something as real, then it truly does not exist. The earlier discussion of lay theories about mental illness is a demonstration of social constructionism. Each cultural group constructs a different social definition and understanding of mental symptoms. Depressive symptoms are recognized in most cultures, but there is great difference in how those cultures understand them. Some construct a reality that mental illness is spiritual, some as psycho–social, and so on. The key questions for social constructionism are how social forces create these definitions and what makes something real.

An example of a social construction concerns how post-traumatic stress disorder (PTSD) is understood. PTSD is a mental health problem that occurs to many people who have experienced or witnessed a terrifying event such as a hurricane, sexual assault, or combat. Those who develop PTSD frequently have flashbacks to the traumatic event, experience nightmares and reactivity symptoms such as being easily startled, feel tense anger, and cognitive disturbances like negative thoughts and a distorted sense of guilt or blame.

What we now call PTSD has undergone a long history of social constructions. The first written records of what we call PTSD were recorded in 440 BCE following the Battle of Marathon in ancient Greece, but probably was not labeled as a condition until the late 1600s when a physician recognized symptoms among Swiss soldiers following a battle. He called the condition "nostalgia." During the United States' Civil War, nostalgia was seen as a personal failing due to mental feebleness. To snap nostalgic soldiers back to a correct, and manly, state of mind, doctors, officers, and fellow soldiers ridiculed and abused them. After the Civil War, the condition was redefined as a medical condition called "soldier's heart" because the emotions of combat were believed to overstimulate the heart. During World War I, the condition was reconstructed as "shell shock," and yet again in WW II as "battle fatigue." By 1952, it was reconstituted as "gross stress reaction" by the APA, and in DSM II it was known as an "adjustment reaction to adult life" (Crocq and Crocq 2000). The term PTSD did not evolve until studies of Vietnam veterans and Holocaust survivors led to the current classification, which is strictly medicalized and treated in hospitals and clinics as a pathology.

Not everyone accepts the medical model construction of PTSD. In a study of minority veterans in New York City, Elliot and colleagues (2018) found that these PTSD sufferers rejected the medical view of their troubles, opting instead to address their symptoms in their own way. Rather than accepting they have a disorder, and the stigma that attends it, these former soldiers preferred to normalize their symptoms as part of the experience of going to war. In a sense, they adopted a Frankfurt School perspective to understand their experiences. To them, symptoms were not a result of having a disorder, but a more normative human response to a horrible experience. These veterans constructed their symptoms in a way that made more sense to them.

Social constructionism states that knowledge and perceptions are social in origin. It assumes there is no natural order of knowledge, but what is real is made so because of human representations. There is no inherent true or false. Reality, instead, emerges from social interactions. What makes society possible is that these meanings are shared through language, socialization, and a process called **typification**. Typification refers to the creation of social types or entities that have their own identity and role expectations. We are expected to conform to the types placed before us. Everyday life is taken for granted, in the constructionist perspective, which means we do not often think about everyday occurrences until someone deviates from the expected, from their "type." When this happens, we must construct new meanings to make sense of this unexpected behavior.

Thompson's (2010) study illustrates this phenomenon. She was curious about what predicts judges' decisions to order psychiatric evaluations for people charged with a crime and who may demonstrate psychiatric symptoms. It would seem logical that everyone needing an evaluation would receive one, but that was not the case. Thompson found that psychiatric status was only one factor judges use. Demographic, family, and criminal characteristics influenced the decision as well. Thompson, for example, discovered that men were more likely to receive an evaluation, but that women were more likely to be viewed as "mad rather than bad" (2010: 116). Women who conformed to gender-stereotypical roles, the traditional female "type," were less likely to receive an evaluation and deemed "mad."

We must construct a new "reality" when the taken-for-granted social types are violated. Sometimes we construct a definition of that deviance by simply writing it off as odd or quirky, but sometimes we construct it as mental illness. The social forces guiding a particular situation will determine which way that construction goes. Box 3.2 describes the Motorcycle Syndrome, a psychiatrist's attempt in the 1970s to construct a mental disorder out of a nonconforming behavior—riding a motorcycle. This case provides a good example of how social forces construct meaning out of a behavior that does not match a socially approved type.

Box 3.2 Motorcycle Syndrome

Not every proposed disorder makes its way into the DSM. Sometimes someone "invents" a condition of psychological distress, but it simply does not catch on. One such proposal is Armand Nicholi's Motorcycle Syndrome published in 1970 in the prestigious *American Journal of Psychiatry*. Nicholi, apparently, was concerned that people spent too much time on their bikes, and that, he decided, was pathological. Here are the characteristics of the Motorcycle Syndrome.

- Unusual preoccupation with the motorcycle.
- A history of being accident prone, extending to early childhood.
- A persistent fear of bodily injury.
- A distant, conflict-ridden relationship with one's father and strong identification with one's mother.
- Extreme passivity and inability to compete.
- A defective self-image.

(Continued)

Box 3.2 Motorcycle Syndrome *(Continued)*

- Poor impulse control.
- Fear of and counterphobic involvement with aggressive girls. (Counterphobia means to intentionally seek out feared objects or situations.)
- Impotence and intense homosexual concerns.

In addition, Nicholi warned clinicians about their motorcycle-riding patients' anxieties, which must be "carefully regulated" because of their "tendency to use the motorcycle for sudden departure to other parts of the country."

To quote columnist and humorist Dave Barry, I am not making this up.

There are several lessons to be learned here. First, we get a hint at some of the criticisms of Freudian thinking. Excessive motorcycle riding seems intricately connected to sexuality and the inability to separate from parents, especially one's mother, and stand as a self-assured, competent adult. Plus, there is the latent homosexuality that must be present if one is having trouble relating to "girls," especially aggressive ones, whatever that means. This is a common Freudian equation to explain people who act in certain ways. Being accident prone is another Freudian sign of neurotic behavior. Having accidents means that a person is distressed by something that distracts the mind from carefulness, but it is unclear what "accident proneness" means. These hypotheses have little merit and are inherently untestable and illustrate what I call the "bad Freud." There is a "good Freud," in my opinion, which provides a sound approach for explaining some instances of psychological distress. But the motorcycle syndrome is not it.

Second, there is little data (or common sense) to support the claims. As a motorcycle rider myself, I can attest that clumsy, fearful, and passive people are not inclined to ride motorcycles. Without concentration and coordination, bikes can be dangerous, and a certain degree of fearlessness and adventurism is mandatory. Plus, in other countries such as India, motorcycles are a primary means of transportation. So, if there were such a thing as motorcycle syndrome, it would have to be culture specific.

Nicholi based his conclusions on interviews with nine supposedly accident-prone motorcyclists. He states that he was trying to find psychological causes of the rising number of motorcycle accidents happening at that time.

What was this really about? Nicholi wrote this article in 1970, a time when motorcycles had a negative social connotation. Largely because of movie images, many people thought that motorcycle riders were gang members, thugs, and hooligans wearing leather jackets and committing crime and mayhem—all undesirable in a "polite society." Bike riding was believed to indicate a rejection of society and an inability or unwillingness to conform, which could be considered pathological under some circumstances if it were true. But it wasn't. Nicholi was attempting to medicalize a mode of transportation and a hobby because he did not like it or was afraid of it. His conclusion was that only a mentally ill person would do something that was so nonconforming and incongruent with society.

Fortunately, the motorcycle syndrome was not accepted, but the social construction of disorders is clearly evident in this case. There was insufficient social support for this proposal to create a disorder, thus the "type" did not become official.

About the Quote

The chapter started with the quote from psychologist Sheldon Kopp whose book of the same title discussed what it means to be in psychotherapy. His point was that the answers to the question of life were to be found by looking inward. You must be your own Buddha, the guide of your own life's journey. He said that advice that comes from outside ourselves is not real. Living life according to the expectations of others equates with dependency and bounds you to an identity defined by others. Reliance on one way of living, according to Kopp, limits people's ability to find their true and authentic selves.

In this age of uncertainty and unprecedented risks, as Lasch discussed, many people flutter from one guru, health trend, or guiding philosophy to another. Many people seem to be searching and hoping that the "next big thing" will provide all the answers and liberate them from their pains.

Although Kopp is writing about one's personal journey through life, the quote is an appropriate metaphor for theorizing about mental illness. No one approach has all the answers, and there is something to learn from all of them. Putting all the theoretical pieces together gives us a sense of sociological Buddha-hood, to coin a phrase. We should resist attaching ourselves to a single theory that purports to explain everything. The Motorcycle Syndrome is an excellent case in point. The author of that study clearly was forcing a Freudian solution to a problem that was probably more sociological than psychological. If he was trying to explain a rise in motorcycle accidents, he needed to consider social factors. Perhaps there were more bikes on the road (there were), car drivers were not accustomed to watching for motorcycles (they weren't), and bikes were not as visible as they are today (they were not).

Instead, theories are best approached on an "as needed basis" where we pick the theory that helps us best understand a problem or data that we have collected. A multi-theoretical position creates a holistic picture of mental health. Once that is accomplished, you no longer need a Buddha, a theoretical crutch to lean on. You can stand on your own as your own Buddha.

DISCUSSION QUESTIONS

1. Recall the difference between sociology *of* and sociology *in* medicine? Consider the social theories you have just learned and think of ways that they can be used in both areas of inquiry. Select one and try to create a few research questions using it in each domain of study. For example, what questions can stress theory ask in a sociology *of* and a sociology *in* medicine?

2. Sociology and biology are often at odds with each other, but they need not be. What can sociology and biology teach each other? What is important for biology to know about sociology's contribution to the study of mental health and illness?

KEY TERMS

Acute Stressors 64
Altruistic Suicide 57
Ambient Stressors 63
Anomic Suicide 57
Authoritarian Personality 66
Chronic Stressors 61
Cortisol 60
Critical Theory 65

Distress 58
Egoistic Suicide 57
"Fight or Flight," 59
Hassles 61
Hypothalamic–pituitary–adrenal axis 60
Identity Denial 60
Labeling Theory 53

Modified Labeling Theory 54
Reductionism 49
Stigma Consciousness 60
Stress Theory 58
Stressor 58
Structural Strain Theory 55
Typification 69

CHAPTER 4

Prevalence and Costs of Mental Illness

> Whether or not the individual is healthy, is primarily not an individual matter, but depends on the structure of…society.
>
> —Erich Fromm (1955: 71)

Learning Objectives

After reading this chapter, students will be able to:

1. Differentiate and utilize the key concepts of epidemiology.
2. Explain the sources of error in measuring mental illness in a population.
3. Describe many of the social costs of mental illness.

Introduction

Thus far we have focused on the debate about what mental illness is and how it is defined. We have touched on the origins of the concept of mental illness and how our perceptions vary across time and disciplines. Now let's shift gears from the abstract to the specific and try to determine how much mental illness actually exists. On the surface, this would seem a simple task; however, establishing accurate figures on the distribution of mental illness is elusive owing to the disagreements on what mental illness is and how to measure it.

In this chapter, we will explore how socially mapping the distribution of mental illness is done. As we review the studies that attempt to specify a population's health, we should understand that while these studies are quite sophisticated, they all contain a degree of error due to conflicting definitions and the actuality that mental illness categories, as we saw in the last chapter, are not sufficiently delineated by boundaries.

Epidemiology

As the name implies, **epidemiology** originated as the study of epidemics. Since the 1940s, the field has evolved into a more comprehensive area of research that investigates the origins and social patterns in the distribution of diseases and other health conditions in human populations. Now epidemiology includes contributions from several disciplines including sociology, geography, anthropology, public health, statistics, and medicine to study both communicable and noncommunicable conditions. Though a late addition to the field, mental health epidemiology has recently become increasingly important and has made significant contributions to our understanding of population health and well-being.

Epidemiology is basically the study of four concepts: **risk, prevalence, incidence**, and **disability-adjusted life years** (DALYs).

Risk is the likelihood of acquiring or developing a disease or disorder. By observing the precursors to a condition in established cases, the probability of an outcome in another case can be calculated. For example, stress studies are often designed as risk analyses. Because people who have experienced certain stressors such as early childhood trauma or abuse are more likely to develop depression or anxiety later in life, we can calculate the risk of future mental health conditions with that information along with severity and duration of the stressor. Risk is important to assess because it predicts future quality of life and the demands for services and treatments.

Prevalence is the number of cases of a disorder in a specified population and time. It is *all* people with a disorder at any given time. Two timeframes for prevalence are common: over a person's lifetime (ever had symptoms or a diagnosis) and the number of people with symptoms or diagnoses in the last year. Prevalence is reported as a total number or as a rate, that is, the proportion of the population experiencing the condition. Using schizophrenia as an example, studies estimate the total number of cases in the United States range from 1.6 to 2.2 million or a rate of approximately 0.5–0.64 per 1,000 people in the population (Desai et al. 2013; Kessler et al. 2005; Wu et al. 2006). Globally, these rates are consistent across national borders, and prevalence is about 20 million cases.

Incidence is the number of *new* cases in a specific time, usually within the last year or 30 days. New cases are important to count because they indicate trends and changes in existing patterns in the occurrence of a disorder and can help determine factors that may cause a particular condition. Staying with schizophrenia as an illustration, one study estimated an incidence rate of 15.2 per 100,000 people, which projects to over 50,000 new cases each year in the United States (McGrath et al. 2008).

CHAPTER 4 Prevalence and Costs of Mental Illness

Global incidence of schizophrenia is about 1.13 million new cases each year (He et al. 2020).

DALY is a more complicated calculation. Created by Christopher Murray and Alan Lopez (1996), a DALY is one lost year of "healthy" life, and when summed, represents the years of life lost (YLL) due to premature mortality and years lost to disability (YLD) caused by a health problem in a population. DALYs constitute a good indicator of the burden of ill health. It is the difference between actual health and ideal health conditions where everyone lives into their senior years free of disease and disability (WHO 2020). The basic formula for calculating DALYs is found in Box 4.1.

DALYs teach us a great deal about the health of a population. Review Tables 4.1 and 4.2 from the World Health Organization (Mathers et al. 2008) and note the psychosocial conditions that rank among the top causes of health burdens across the globe. The first column of numbers is the number of quality years lost to the

Box 4.1 Calculating DALYs

The World Health Organization (2020) created the DALY measure to study the impact and burden of health conditions on populations. The full operationalization of the variable is highly complex because hundreds of health conditions are considered in the formula and weights are added in some cases to normalize the statistics. Nevertheless, the basic equation sheds light on the central concept. DALYs measure the gap between a populations' actual health and what its health would be without health problems. DALYs are the sum of YLL due to premature mortality and YLD or experiencing a degree of disability but are living with the health condition or its consequences. Therefore, the first equation is

$$DALY = YLL + YLD$$

But how are YLLs and YLDs calculated? That's the hard part. YLLs are essentially the number of deaths multiplied by the standard life expectancy at the age at which death occurs. The basic formula for YLL is the following for a given cause, age, and sex:

$$YLL = N \times L$$

where:

N = number of deaths
L = standard life expectancy at age of death in years

YLL takes into consideration the age of the deceased in relation to how long that person would normally be expected to live if the condition had not caused death.

To calculate YLD for specific condition, the number of cases is multiplied by the average duration of the disease or condition. The condition is weighted by its severity on a scale of 0 (perfect health) to 10 (death). Therefore, the equation for YLD is

$$YLD = I \times DW \times L$$

where:

I = number of incident cases
DW = disability weight
L = average duration of the case until remission or death (years)

As you can see, a great deal of information is needed to calculate DALYs. Consequently, studies on DALYs are not common and are usually only undertaken by large well-funded organizations such as the World Health Organization.

TABLE 4.1 Leading Causes of Burden of Disease (DALYs), All Ages, 2004

	Disease or Injury	DALYs (Millions)	Per Cent of Total DALYs
1	Lower respiratory infections	94.5	6.2
2	Diarrheal diseases	72.8	4.8
3	Unipolar depression disorders	65.5	4.3
4	Ischemic heart disease	62.6	4.1
5	HIV/AIDS	58.5	3.8
6	Cerebrovascular disease	46.6	3.1
7	Prematurity and low birth rate	44.3	2.9
8	Birth asphyxia and birth trauma	41.7	2.7
9	Road traffic accidents	41.2	2.7
10	Neonatal infections	40.4	2.7
11	Tuberculosis	34.2	2.2
12	Malaria	34.0	2.2
13	COPD	30.2	2.0
14	Refractive errors	27.7	1.8
15	Hearing loss, adult onset	27.4	1.8
16	Congenital anomalies	25.3	1.7
17	Alcohol use disorders	23.7	1.6
18	Violence	21.7	1.4
19	Diabetes mellitus	19.7	1.3
20	Self-inflicted injuries	19.6	1.3

Source: Mathers et al. 2008. Reprinted with permission of World Health Organization.

condition, and the second is the percentage of total DALYs contributed by each condition. In Table 4.1, we see that depression is the third leading cause of DALYs internationally, alcohol use disorders are 17th, and self-inflected injuries and suicide are 20th. Adding the percentages of those three conditions equals 7.2 percent of all life years lost, making psychosocial problems the leading cause of DALYs in the world.

Table 4.2 compares countries in different income levels. In middle- and high-income countries, depressive disorders are the leading cause of life years lost. In low-income countries where infectious diseases dominate the health landscape,

TABLE 4.2 Leading Causes of Burden of Disease (DALYs) countries grouped by income, 2004

	Disease or Injury	DALYs (Millions)	Percent Total DALYs		Disease or Injury	DALYs (Millions)	Percent Total DALYs
World				*Low-Income Countries*			
1	Lower respiratory infections	94.5	6.2	1	Lower respiratory infections	76.9	9.3
2	Diarrheal diseases	72.8	4.8	2	Diarrheal diseases	59.2	7.2
3	Unipolar depression	65.5	4.3	3	HIV/AIDS	42.9	5.2
4	Ischemic heart disease	62.6	4.1	4	Malaria	32.8	4.0
5	HIV/AIDS	58.5	3.8	5	Prematurity and low birth weight	32.1	3.9
6	Cerebrovascular disease	46.6	3.1	6	Neonatal infection	31.4	3.8
7	COPD	44.3	2.9	7	Birth asphyxia and birth trauma	29.8	3.6
8	Prematurity and low birth weight	41.7	2.7	8	Unipolar depression	26.5	3.2
9	Road accidents	41.2	2.7	9	Ischemic heart disease	26.0	3.1
10	Neonatal infection	40.4	2.7	10	Tuberculosis	22.4	2.7
Middle-Income Countries				*High-Income Countries*			
1	Unipolar depression	29.0	5.1	1	Unipolar depression	10.0	8.2
2	Ischemic heart disease	28.9	5.0	2	Ischemic heart disease	7.7	6.3
3	Cerebrovascular disease	27.5	4.8	3	Cerebrovascular disease	4.8	3.9
4	Road accidents	21.4	3.7	4	Alzheimer's disease	4.4	3.6
5	Lower respiratory infections	16.3	2.8	5	Alcohol abuse	4.2	3.4

(Continued)

TABLE 4.2 Leading Causes of Burden of Disease (DALYs) countries grouped by income, 2004 *(Continued)*

	Disease or Injury	DALYs (Millions)	Percent Total DALYs		Disease or Injury	DALYs (Millions)	Percent Total DALYs
6	COPD	16.1	2.8	6	Adult hearing loss	4.2	3.4
7	HIV/AIDS	15.0	2.6	7	COPD	3.7	3.0
8	Alcohol abuse	14.9	2.6	8	Diabetes	3.6	3.0
9	Refractive errors	13.7	2.4	9	Trachea and lung cancers	3.6	3.0
10	Diarrheal diseases	13.1	2.3	10	Road accidents	3.1	2.6

Source: Mathers et al. 2008. Reprinted with permission of World Health Organization.

depression is still among the top ten. Alcohol abuse is also among the top 10 in middle- and high-income societies.

Clearly mental health problems are causing considerable losses for individuals with the conditions, for their families, and for societies at large. Given current trends, it will only get worse. Kyu and associates (2018) demonstrated that DALYs for depression have risen dramatically in recent years. In low-income countries, DALYs for men rose 26 percent and 79 percent for women from 1990 to 2017. Men and women in high-income countries, the increase is 22 percent for men and 20 percent for women. The WHO predicts that by 2030, as shown in Table 4.3, mental health problems will leap over infectious disease and heart disease and become the leading cause of DALYs internationally (Mathers et al. 2008).

In their initial study, Murray and Lopez (1996) found that psychiatric disorders accounted for 28 percent of all YLDs. Five of the ten leading causes of YLDs worldwide were psychiatric and behavioral disorders. Unipolar depression was ranked as the leading cause of YLDs and was responsible for about 11 percent of all YLDs. Alcohol use (3.4 percent) was ranked fourth, bipolar disorder was sixth (3 percent), schizophrenia ninth with 2.6 percent, and obsessive-compulsive disorders were the tenth leading cause of YLDs, accounting for 2.2 percent of all YLDs. The remaining five health contributors to the top 10 causes of YLDs globally were iron-deficiency anemia, falls, lung disease, congenital anomalies, and osteoarthritis. These figures are similar when comparing developed and developing countries. The only difference is that obsessive-compulsive disorders are not among the top 10 in developing societies (Murray and Lopez, 1996).

Comparing men and women on disabilities, Murray and Lopez found that depression and alcohol use caused 13.6 percent of all YLDs among men, but that depression alone accounted for 13.8 percent of DALYs among women. Also in the

TABLE 4.3 Ten Leading Global Causes of Burden of Disease, 2004–2030 (Projection)

2004

Rank	Disease/Injury	DALYs as % of Total
1.	Lower respiratory infection	6.2
2.	Diarrheal diseases	4.8
3.	Depression disorders	4.3
4.	ischemic heart disease	4.1
5.	HIV/AIDS	3.8
6.	Cerebrovascular disease	3.1
7.	Premature/low birth weight	2.9
8.	Birth asphyxia and trauma	2.7
9.	Road accidents	2.7
10.	Neonatal infections	2.7
11.	COPD	2.0
12.	Refractive errors	1.8
13.	Adult hearing loss	1.8
14.	Diabetes	1.3

Projection for 2030

Rank	Disease/Injury	DALYs as % of Total
1.	Depression disorders	6.2
2.	Ischemic heart disease	5.5
3.	Road accidents	4.9
4.	Cerebrovascular disease	4.3
5.	COPD	3.8
6.	Respiratory infection	3.2
7.	Adult hearing loss	2.9
8.	Refractive errors	2.7
9.	HIV/AIDS	2.5
10.	Diabetes	2.3

(Continued)

TABLE 4.3 Ten Leading Global Causes of Burden of Disease, 2004–2030 (Projection) *(Continued)*

Projection for 2030		
Rank	Disease/Injury	DALYs as % of Total
11.	Neonatal infections	1.9
12.	Premature/low birth weight	1.9
15.	Birth asphyxia and trauma	1.9
18.	Diarrheal diseases	1.6

Source: Mathers et al. 2008. Reprinted with permission of World Health Organization.

top 10 for men were bipolar disorder and schizophrenia. For women, depression, bipolar disorder, schizophrenia, and obsessive-compulsive disorders were among the ten highest sources for YLDs.

Psychiatric illnesses typically are not major direct causes of mortality or believed to affect directly premature loss of life, at least as can be directly measured. If we assume that depression is linked to most suicides, then depression could be among the leading causes of YLLs in richer countries. Self-inflicted injuries were the fifth leading cause of years lost to premature death in North America and western Europe (Murray and Lopez, 1996).

Two studies have shown patterns of DALYs within the United States. The first, presented in Table 4.4, compares men and women (McKenna et al. 2005). Heart disease is the leading cause of DALYs for both groups, but the difference in psychosocial conditions is noteworthy. Depression is the second leading source of DALYs for women, but 11th for men; however, for men, self-inflicted injuries and drug abuse are ninth and 14th respectively but are not among the top 15 among women.

A second study reports on DALYs in the state of Rhode Island (Jiang and Hesser 2012). Their findings are reported in Table 4.5 and show that depression is the second leading source of DALYs, and drug use is eighth. Looking solely at YLDs, which excludes mortality, depression surpasses all other conditions by a large margin. Summing depression with other psychosocial conditions in the top 10—drug use, bipolar disorder, alcohol abuse, and schizophrenia—results in over 25 percent of years lost by disabilities in Rhode Island being due to psychosocial and psychiatric conditions.

Measurement Issues

How much mental illness exists in a group or population is at best a rough estimate. In the absence of objective and measurable indicators of psychological problems, inconsistencies in defining mental illness generate reliability and validity problems in tabulating the number of people who experience symptoms. Therefore, rates of mental illness are influenced by the definition used to measure disorders. In an

TABLE 4.4 Leading Causes of DALYs Among US Men and Women

Men Rank	Condition	Percent	Women Rank	Condition	Percent
1	Heart disease	11.0	1	Heart disease	7.7
2	Road-traffic accidents	5.2	2	Depression	5.9
3	Lung cancer	4.6	3	Cerebrovascular disease	5.5
4	HIV/AIDS	4.3	4	COPD	4.0
5	Alcohol use	4.1	5	Lung cancer	3.6
6	Cerebrovascular disease	3.8	6	Breast cancer	3.4
7	COPD	3.6	7	Osteoarthritis	3.3
8	Homicide and violence	3.2	8	Alzheimer's disease	3.3
9	Self-inflicted injury	3.0	9	Diabetes	3.3
10	Depression	2.6	10	Road-traffic accidents	3.0
11	Diabetes	2.4	11	Alcohol use	2.7
12	Osteoarthritis	2.4	12	Asthma	2.4
13	Drug use	2.3	13	Congenital abnormality	1.5
14	Congenital abnormality	2.3	14	Colon cancer	1.5
15	Alzheimer's disease	2.1	15	Perinatal problems	1.4

Source: McKenna et al. (2005).

interesting study published by the *American Journal of Psychiatry*, Schinnar and associates (1990) combed the psychiatric literature and found 17 different definitions of severe and persistent mental illness. The definitions varied on several dimensions such as duration of symptoms, problems in daily functioning, and which symptoms to include. After applying each definition to information on a representative sample of over 200 people from the same Philadelphia neighborhood, Schinnar calculated rates of mental illness for the population from which the sample was drawn. The results were fascinating. The researchers found that rates of serious mental illness ranged from four percent to 88 percent, depending on the definition applied. This study, along with similar work in Europe (Ruggeri et al. 2000), shows how the lack of agreement among scholars and mental health providers leads to gross disparities in the estimation of the scale and scope of mental illness in society.

Problems measuring prevalence is a consequence of the socially constructed nature of mental illness, as discussed in earlier chapters. Deciding what is and what is not mental illness is a subjective exercise. Therefore, the process of placing

TABLE 4.5 Ten Leading Causes of DALYs and YLDs in Rhode Island

DALYs			YLDs		
Rank	Condition	Percent	Rank	Condition	Percent
1	Heart disease	11.8	1	Depression	12.5
2	Depression	6.3	2	Osteoarthritis	8.8
3	Cerebrovascular disease	5.9	3	Cerebrovascular disease	7.6
4	Alzheimer's disease	5.7	4	Drug use	4.9
5	Lung cancer	4.8	5	Alzheimer's disease	7.4
6	COPD	4.5	6	COPD	4.6
7	Osteoarthritis	4.4	7	Asthma	4.6
8	Drug use	2.6	8	Bipolar disorder	3.1
9	Road-traffic accidents	2.4	9	Alcohol abuse	2.8
10	Diabetes	2.4	10	Schizophrenia	2.8

Source: Jiang and Hesser (2012).

individuals in diagnostic categories for statistical and counting purposes lacks precision, and results should be considered rough estimations.

Studies that assess mental illness prevalence and incidence in populations are typically very expensive because of the numerous disorders to include in the screening and the large samples necessary to make accurate projections. Furthermore, psychiatric and psychological conditions cannot be measured by asking one or two questions. Diagnoses require a substantial number of survey or interview questions to assess the presence and severity of the disorder. This requirement lengthens the research or clinical instrument, thereby increasing the cost of collecting the information.

Another reason for the relative scarcity of mental health data compared to data on the prevalence of physical health morbidity has been the low priority of mental health needs both in the United States and across the globe. Compared to the immediate risks posed by life-threatening health problems such as infectious diseases, mental health concerns are usually deemed less important to the welfare of a people.

Although no "gold standard" exists for assessing prevalence or incidence (Wakefield and Schmitz 2010), we can estimate incidence and prevalence of psychological problems to a reasonable degree of accuracy using three primary methods. The first assesses clinical prevalence, which is the number of people in psychiatric institutions, treated by a physician or other mental health professional, or under the control of authorities (in prison, for example). Clinical prevalence informs mental health professions of demands for services and helps to plan what types of services are most utilized. This technique reports how many people are in treatment or "in the system" at a given point in time, but it does not tell us the **true prevalence**, which includes people with symptoms who are not seeking help.

A second data source is meta-analysis, which is a study of studies. Meta-analysis organizes the literature on a specific topic and reports on trends in those studies' findings. There may be many studies on one subject, but they may cover various populations and social settings. Meta-analysis is a particularly effective tool for bringing studies together and determining social patterns in disorders.

One example of a meta-analysis study is on the risk of psychological distress among internationally adopted children (Juffer and van IJzendoorn 2005). Before a suitable adoptive family is found, these children are often subjected to poor health care, malnutrition, parental separation, and neglect and abuse in orphanages. Hence the question: are children who are adopted from other countries more vulnerable to psychological distress as they get older?

There are many studies on international adoption and mental health, but they are diverse, focusing on different countries of birth and types of mental health questions, making conclusions hard to draw. Juffer and van IJzendoorn (2005) analyzed this research and found two important patterns. First, most international adoptees are well-adjusted, but in later years are more likely to be referred to mental health services than nonadopted individuals. Second, international adoptees, however, present fewer behavior problems and are less likely to need mental health services than domestic adoptees.

The third source of data comes from surveys in which a sample of people are asked about symptoms they may have at a particular point in time. Epidemiological surveys are the best techniques for getting the most information from the most people. With surveys, a large and geographically diverse population can be sampled to get the best estimation of the whole population's mental health. Survey data yield the best estimates of the "true prevalence" of disorders.

Survey methods include a set of questions in the form of a questionnaire or a structured interview. Since psychiatric conditions, as specified in the DSM, are usually specified as a checklist of symptoms, surveys are excellent tools for identifying the symptoms that correspond to a disorder.

Despite the straightforwardness of this approach, problems linger. First, the operationalization of disorders (how they are measured), just like definitions, are not consistent across studies, and these differences produce different rates of occurrence. Table 4.5 shows various measures of unipolar depression that are frequently used in prevalence research, and Box 4.2 compares two of the more popular measures, the BDI and the CESD long version. There are many others, but these are among the most employed in survey research.

Notice in Table 4.6 that the indexes have different numbers of items and ranges in scores. Having different scores means that samples using different measures are not comparable and that interpretations are inconsistent. Now we can see why different indexes produce different rates of prevalence and may result in over-estimated rates (Wakefield and Schmitz 2010).

A second limitation with survey techniques in estimating prevalence and incidence is that virtually every psychiatric symptom listed in DSM can occur under some conditions in people who do not meet the full criteria of a diagnosis (Wakefield and Schmitz 2010). Consequently, a high score on a particular day may reflect normal responses to life stressors such as family death, problem at work, or the coronavirus quarantine, rather than a clinically valid syndrome or illness. Therefore, because categorical psychiatric conditions are defined as a collection of symptoms, which can be met in the course of normal life, the chances increase that a person will satisfy the criteria of a diagnosis and create the appearance that conditions such as depression exist in "epidemic proportions" (Jauho and Helén 2018).

Third, the cut-off scores for determining a diagnosis in survey-based measures are arbitrary. Notice in Box 4.2 that the BDI has a continuum scoring system of six categories ranging from 1–10 indicating "normal ups and downs" to "over 40" which suggests "extreme depression." The CESD, however, takes a more discrete approach. A score of 16 or greater indicates "clinical depression." There is no psychological or physiological reason to explain the score that separates depression from nondepression.

Fourth, measures rooted in the United States and Europe and DSM diagnostic categories are not always reliable in nonwestern cultures. One important study found that DSM criteria are not consistent with how other cultures experience depression. Haroz' study learned that clinical descriptions of depression in nonwestern societies, notably social isolation, loneliness, crying, anger, and physical pain, are not mentioned in the DSM. In addition, two DSM criteria, difficulties in

Box 4.2 Comparing the BDI and CESD Measures of Unipolar Depression

This box includes two of the most used measures of depression, the Beck Depression Inventory (BDI) and the Center of Epidemiologic Studies—Depression (CESD), from the National Institute of Mental Health. Scholars and mental health professionals have used both for decades. Let's compare them.

First, note that they have a different number of items. Second, they are scaled differently. The BDI has scaled responses that fit each item, but the CES-D uses the same responses for all, and since the BDI has more items, the scores are not comparative with those gained from the CES-D. Third, the scores indicating clinical depression are not the same, again indicating inconsistency in the measures. Fourth, and most importantly, the two indexes operationalize depression differently. While there is direct overlap with items about sleep, crying, appetite, and feeling sad, there are several indicators unique to each. In the BDI, queries about feeling guilty, suicidal thoughts, weight, and sex are not found on the CES-D. Reversely, asking if people "dislike me" and feeling lonely and fearful are not on the BDI. If we look at the other measures listed in Table 4.6, we can see similar discordant operational definitions.

Both the BDI and CES-D have newer or shorter versions, which adds to the statistical and theoretical confusion.

The BDI and CES-D are easily found on the internet for self-assessment. However, it is important to realize that these measures are not the same as a clinical assessment by a trained mental health professional. Diagnoses are more complex than simple checklists and require more information than a 15-minute questionnaire provides.

The Beck Depression Inventory

The scoring scale is at the end of the questionnaire.

1.
   - 0   I do not feel sad.
   - 1   I feel sad
   - 2   I am sad all the time and I can't snap out of it.
   - 3   I am so sad and unhappy that I can't stand it.

2.
   - 0   I am not particularly discouraged about the future.
   - 1   I feel discouraged about the future.
   - 2   I feel I have nothing to look forward to.
   - 3   I feel the future is hopeless and that things cannot improve.

3.
   - 0   I do not feel like a failure.
   - 1   I feel I have failed more than the average person.
   - 2   As I look back on my life, all I can see is a lot of failures.
   - 3   I feel I am a complete failure as a person.

4.
   - 0   I get as much satisfaction out of things as I used to.
   - 1   I don't enjoy things the way I used to.
   - 2   I don't get real satisfaction out of anything anymore.
   - 3   I am dissatisfied or bored with everything.

5.
   - 0   I don't feel particularly guilty
   - 1   I feel guilty a good part of the time.
   - 2   I feel quite guilty most of the time.
   - 3   I feel guilty all of the time.

6.
   - 0   I don't feel I am being punished.
   - 1   I feel I may be punished.
   - 2   I expect to be punished.
   - 3   I feel I am being punished.

7.
   - 0   I don't feel disappointed in myself.
   - 1   I am disappointed in myself.
   - 2   I am disgusted with myself.
   - 3   I hate myself.

8.
   - 0   I don't feel I am any worse than anybody else.
   - 1   I am critical of myself for my weaknesses or mistakes.
   - 2   I blame myself all the time for my faults.
   - 3   I blame myself for everything bad that happens.

9.
   - 0   I don't have any thoughts of killing myself.
   - 1   I have thoughts of killing myself, but I would not carry them out.
   - 2   I would like to kill myself.
   - 3   I would kill myself if I had the chance.

10.
    - 0   I don't cry any more than usual.
    - 1   I cry more now than I used to.
    - 2   I cry all the time now.
    - 3   I used to be able to cry, but now I can't cry even though I want to.

11.
    - 0   I am no more irritated by things than I ever was.
    - 1   I am slightly more irritated now than usual.
    - 2   I am quite annoyed or irritated a good deal of the time.
    - 3   I feel irritated all the time.

12.
    - 0   I have not lost interest in other people.

(Continued)

Box 4.2 Comparing the BDI and CESD Measures of Unipolar Depression *(Continued)*

	1	I am less interested in other people than I used to be.
	2	I have lost most of my interest in other people.
	3	I have lost all of my interest in other people.
13.	0	I make decisions about as well as I ever could.
	1	I put off making decisions more than I used to.
	2	I have greater difficulty in making decisions more than I used to.
	3	I can't make decisions at all anymore.
14.	0	I don't feel that I look any worse than I used to.
	1	I am worried that I am looking old or unattractive.
	2	I feel there are permanent changes in my appearance that make me look unattractive
	3	I believe that I look ugly.
15.	0	I can work about as well as before.
	1	It takes an extra effort to get started at doing something.
	2	I have to push myself very hard to do anything.
	3	I can't do any work at all.
16.	0	I can sleep as well as usual.
	1	I don't sleep as well as I used to.
	2	I wake up 1–2 hours earlier than usual and find it hard to get back to sleep.
	3	I wake up several hours earlier than I used to and cannot get back to sleep.

17.	0	I don't get more tired than usual.
	1	I get tired more easily than I used to.
	2	I get tired from doing almost anything.
	3	I am too tired to do anything.
18.	0	My appetite is no worse than usual.
	1	My appetite is not as good as it used to be.
	2	My appetite is much worse now.
	3	I have no appetite at all anymore.
19.	0	I haven't lost much weight, if any, lately.
	1	I have lost more than five pounds.
	2	I have lost more than ten pounds.
	3	I have lost more than fifteen pounds.
20.	0	I am no more worried about my health than usual.
	1	I am worried about physical problems like aches, pains, upset stomach, or constipation.
	2	I am very worried about physical problems and it's hard to think of much else.
	3	I am so worried about my physical problems that I cannot think of anything else.
21.	0	I have not noticed any recent change in my interest in sex.
	1	I am less interested in sex than I used to be.
	2	I have almost no interest in sex.
	3	I have lost interest in sex completely.

Source: Center for Epidemiologic Studies, National Institute of Mental Health. Center for Epidemiologic Studies Depression Scale (CES-D).

Interpreting the Beck Depression Inventory

To interpret the responses, the scores, which range from 0 to 63, are summed and rated on the following table:

1–10 = Normal ups and downs	17–20 = Borderline clinical depression	31–40 = Severe depression
11–16 = Mild mood disturbance	21–30 = Moderate depression	Over 40 = Extreme depression

Center for CES-D from the National Institute of Mental Health

Here is a list of the ways you might have felt or behaved. Please tell me how often you have felt this way during the past week.

- Rarely or none of the time (less than 1 day)
- Some or a little of the time (1–2 days)
- Occasionally or a moderate amount of time (3–4 days)
- Most or all of the time (5–7 days)

- I was bothered by things that usually don't bother me.
- I did not feel like eating; my appetite was poor.
- I felt that I could not shake off the blues even with help from my family or friends.
- I felt I was just as good as other people.
- I had trouble keeping my mind on what I was doing.
- I felt depressed.
- I felt that everything I did was an effort.
- I felt hopeful about the future.
- I thought my life had been a failure.
- I felt fearful.
- My sleep was restless.
- I was happy.
- I talked less than usual.
- I felt lonely.
- People were unfriendly.
- I enjoyed life.
- I had crying spells.
- I felt sad.
- I felt that people dislike me.
- I could not get "going."

The conventional cutoff score for clinical depression is ≥16.

concentrating and psychomotor agitation or slowing, were rarely mentioned internationally in identifying depression (Haroz et al. 2017). While we have long known that psychological measures often fail to translate culturally outside the western world, Haroz' group identified with greater specificity where the "mismatch" lies. Box 4.3 describes another example of the problems inherent in cross-cultural research.

TABLE 4.6 Comparing Different Measures of Depression

Measure	Items	Range of Scores	Author(s)
BDI and BDI-II	21	0–63	Beck 1961; Beck et al. 1996
CESD	20	0–60	Radloff 1977
CESD-Short Form	10	0–30	
CESD-Other Versions	4–16	varies	
DASS (depression section only)	14	0–42	Lovibond & Lovibond 1995
GDS	30	0–30	Yesavage et al. 2011
GDS-Short Form	15	0–15	
HADS	10	0–60	Zigmond & Snaith 1983
PHQ	9	0–27	Kroenke et al. 2001
Hamilton Scale	17	0–50	Hamilton 1986
MADRS	9	0–54	Montgomery & Åsberg 1979
Zung Depression Scale	20	20–80	Zung 1965

Source: BDI, Beck Depression Inventory; CESD, Center for Epidemiologic Studies Depression Scale; DASS, Depression Anxiety Stress Scales; GDS, Geriatric Depression Scale; HADS, Hospital Anxiety and Depression Scale; MADRS, Montgomery and Asberg Depression Rating Scale; PHQ, Patient Health Questionnaire.

Ideally, a clinical assessment of everyone in a large and randomly selected sample would best determine true prevalence. Extreme costs and time demands, however, make such a study impossible. Plus, research and forensic testimony have shown that psychiatrists and psychologists often disagree on diagnoses, even in cases of possible schizophrenia. Therefore, if we had all the money in the world to hire all the psychiatrists to conduct a clinical assessment of everyone, we would still have incongruence and error in our findings.

Even with these limitations, survey methods stand as the best tools for assessing prevalence and incidence of psychological problems in a particular group or population. While the results of these studies, as we now know, are estimates, they are all we have for determining the extent of psychiatric problems in a large social group. Survey methods provide additional benefits. They help us (a) understand linkages between symptoms and social factors to which individuals and groups may be exposed, (b) acquire insights into the patterns of the distribution of symptoms, and (c) calculate the costs of mental illness to individuals, families, and the society at large.

Social Patterns in the Distribution of Mental Illness

What do prevalence studies tell us? The National Institute for Mental Health (NIMH) (2017b) compiles and reports epidemiologic data on prevalence and

Box 4.3 Using Measures in Cross-Cultural Settings

Several years ago, I conducted a study in Nepal on the effects of westernization on psychological well-being (Furr 2005). The country was undergoing dramatic social and cultural changes, and I was curious if they made people feel anxious or depressed. At the time, I knew of no measure of depression or anxiety specific to Nepalese cultures, so I used basic, though western oriented, measures to identify those affective conditions.

I selected the Costello-Comrey Depression and Anxiety Scales (Costello and Comrey 1967), tried-and-true measures, which include a 14-item depression measure and nine statements aimed at detecting anxiety. A Nepali translator was moving along without much trouble, finding suitable wording that matched the intent of each statement in English, until she reached this one: "I am a 'high-strung' person." The literal translation in Nepali was something to the effect of "I am a string that is wound too tightly"! That statement obviously made no sense. We worked hard to find a good translation, but the English idiom was too difficult to decipher linguistically into Nepali, and there was no equivalent phrase. So, we simply rephrased the item into a more straightforward form knowing that it slightly changed the measurement.

Not only are there cultural differences in the definition and experience of psychological and psychiatric conditions, but there are also problems in relying on words to measure them. Since mental illnesses have no reliable physical markers of identification, we use words to determine if symptoms are present and, if they are, to rate their severity. But words have different meanings among social groups. Not only do language groups have unique linguistic traditions, so do social classes and race and ethnic groups. Even the most conventional of words are sometimes heard differently than intended. This is especially true with idioms.

Idioms, such as the one just discussed, are often pointless to translate because they represent a meaning separate from their literal words. Phrases such as "runs in the family," "sick and tired of," and "feel on top of the world," when translated, do not make sense in other languages.

All languages have idioms that refer to moods and emotions. An idiom in French telling a person not to sulk—*ne fais pas la tete*—literally translates into English as "don't make the head." Sometimes you wake up in a bad mood because you get up "on the wrong side of the bed," but in France, you *te lever du pied gauche*—get up "on your left foot"!

The point is that using words as measurements can create bias and error in determining prevalence of a disorder. We must choose words very carefully, eliminating all words or phrases that could have double or unclear meanings. That is why all questionnaire and interview items should be constructed at the middle-school reading level and then pretested to ensure that the meanings are clear to everyone who is likely to participate in the study.

---

incidence in the United States. Using data from the National Survey on Drug Use and Health (NIMH 2017b), the NIMH reports on two categories: "any mental illness" (AMI) and "serious mental illness" (SMI). AMI refers to any cognitive, behavioral, or emotional disorder of any severity. SMI is defined as a disorder that results in a serious functional impairment that hinders or limits major life activities such as work, school, self-care, or social interactions and relationships.

The NIMH indicates that almost one in five adults (about 47 million people) in the United States live with a mental illness (AMI) and that the rate is higher among women (22.3%) than men (15.1%) (see Table 4.7). Young adults (18–25 years) have

TABLE 4.7 Overall Last-Year Prevalence of Any Mental Illness Among US Adults

Overall	18.9
Women	22.3
Men	15.1
Age	
18–25	25.8
26–49	22.2
50 and over	13.8
Race/Ethnicity	
Hispanics	15.2
Non-Hispanic Whites	20.4
African Americans	16.2
Asian Americans	14.5
Native Hawaiians	19.4
American Indians	18.9
Mixed Race	28.6

Source: National Institute of Mental Health (2019).

the highest rates compared to other age groups. Race and ethnic breakdowns show that non-Hispanic Whites and people identifying as mixed race have the highest prevalence. Asian Americans and Hispanics report the lowest rates of mental disorder.

Table 4.8 specifically addresses depression in adults and adolescents. Girls and women and younger age groups, ages 15–25 have particularly high prevalence as do Whites, American Indians, and those identifying as mixed race.

Another way to assess prevalence is the rate of serious mental illness. According to the NIMH (2019), SMIs affect about 4.5 percent of the US population. Rates for women, people aged 18–25, Whites, Native Hawaiians, American Indians, and mixed-race identifiers exceed the general population's prevalence. Of people who report any mental illness, the conditions of approximately 22 percent are rated as "serious," 37 percent are "moderate," and 40 percent as "mild" (Kessler et al. 2005).

These numbers are general, aggregated figures that do not specify subgroup variations or social context dynamics. A number of a factors, most of which will be discussed in the next four chapters, differentiate mental health within groups.

There is a lot of variation within race and ethnic groups. Despite lower lifetime and past-year rates of mental disorder among Americans of Asian, Hispanic, and African origins, compared to Whites, evidence shows that mental disorders are more *persistent* among minorities. Persistence refers to how long symptoms are present. This means

CHAPTER 4 Prevalence and Costs of Mental Illness

TABLE 4.8 Rates of Depression Among Adults and Adolescents in the United States in the Last Year

Adults		Adolescents	
Overall	7.1	Overall	13.3
Female	8.7	Female	20.0
Male	5.3	Male	6.8
Age		Age	
18–25	13.1	12	4.8
26–49	7.7	13	8.8
50+	4.7	14	11.8
18–29	–	15	17.2
30–44	–	16	16.9
45–59	–	17	18.5
60+	–		
Race/Ethnicity		Race/Ethnicity	
Hispanics	5.4	Hispanics	13.8
Non-Hispanic Whites	7.9	Non-Hispanic Whites	14.0
African Americans	5.4	African Americans	9.5
Asian Americans	4.4	Asian Americans	11.3
Native Hawaiians	4.7	Native Hawaiians	n.a.
American Indians	8.0	American Indians	16.3
Mixed-Race	11.3	Mixed-Race	16.9

Source: National Institute of Mental Health (2019).

that these groups experience symptoms over a longer period. Education and nativity (where people were born) may account for some of this (Vilsaint et al. 2019). Non-Hispanic Whites without college, and African Americans without high school have comparatively high risks for chronic mood and substance abuse disorders, Whites who were born in the United States were at higher risk of distress than Whites born outside of the country or in the United States with two foreign-born parents.

The relationship between education and mental illness is complex, and not always a simple expectation that more education lowers the risk of distress. There are also variations within education levels, especially when paired with developmental changes and external stressors. Colleges and universities in the United States now are deeply concerned about the psychological well-being of their students. Most, if not all, provide mental health services to students (and faculty) because of the recognition of the seemingly increased stress that occurs during this developmental lifetime change. Major depression is perhaps the most common mental disorder among college students, maybe as high as 7 percent of all first-year students, many of whom have suicidal ideations (Ebert et al. 2019). According to Ebert's research, three factors signal potential major depressive disorder among students: a previous depressive episode, a history of childhood trauma, or stressful experiences in the last 12 months (such as death of a parent, parents' divorce, or unemployment).

Despite the errors in measurements, studies are consistent in their findings. Women consistently demonstrate higher rates of depression than men. Impoverished people have higher rates of most all disorders than middle- and upper-class individuals. The question concerns the degree or magnitude of the number of people experiencing symptoms or are clinically diagnosable. Social patterns in the distribution of mental illness in a population are clear, reliably identified in research, and are maintained over time. The real questions are why these social patterns occur and how they are perpetuated over the years.

The Social Costs of Mental Illness

With psychological disorders affecting such a large segment of the population, it is important to have an idea of the effects of mental illness on society. The social costs of psychological and psychiatric disorders can be conceptualized in several ways.

Economic consequences in the form of lost wages and productivity are often the first to come to mind, and they are dramatic. In the United States, it is likely that five to six million workers between the ages 15 and 54 lose, fail to seek or cannot find employment because of mental illness (Marcotte and Wilcox-Gök 2001). A longitudinal study that followed participants for 40 years demonstrated that childhood psychological problems had a large impact on adult work and earnings. Childhood problems created risks for education achievement and an income reduction of about 20 percent, compared to people without childhood problems (Smith and Smith 2010). Mental distress can increase absenteeism and reduce effective productivity.

Many employers have become keen to improve the psychological well-being of their employees and include mental health services and programs in their employees' benefits package and insurance. The need is real, as the total loss of wages due to mental illness surpasses the costs of treatment and insurance coverage. Programs aimed at workers' emotional welfare have shown to enhance performance while on the job (Berndt et al. 1998) and, therefore, proven to be a good investment for employers.

When psychiatric conditions reach a point where individuals are incapable of supporting themselves, economic safety nets in the form of financial assistance are often engaged. Psychiatric causes account for 35.4% of all Social Security disability beneficiaries, roughly 4.5 million Americans (Social Security Administration 2018). About 40 percent receive Supplemental Security Income (SSI), which is a Social Security program based on financial need, and one in three receive Social Security Disability Insurance, which provides income to people unable to work and who qualify for Social Security. Medicare and Medicaid expenditures account another $47 billion a year, and the Veterans Administration and Department of Defense spend an additional $10 billion (Jaffe 2017). The benefits that go to psychiatrically disabled people and to those in treatment total in the billions of dollars each month.

One economic problem is the lack of employment support for people with psychiatric disabilities. Research confirms that over half want to work but need assistance; however, that support is either not available or adequate in most areas. A strong jobs training and vocational support program tailored to meet the needs of psychiatric disability would save millions in public costs (Drake et al. 2009).

Economic matters are indeed important among the costs of mental illness. They are not the sole considerations, however. Expanding the costs of mental illness to include social factors adds a human element to costs, rather than a simple "bottom line" dimension, to the face of mental illness.

As the tenth leading cause of death in the United States, suicide's costs are dramatic. Suicide, which rose from 44,965 cases in 2016 to 47,173 in 2017, has a domino effect on the pain and suffering it causes (Heron 2019). In addition to the tragic loss of life of the deceased, the emotional pain can continue among relatives and friends for years. Lingering emotions of guilt and shame can exert a toll on family members and ruin relationships. Suicide also affects health care workers' and first responders' caseloads, resources, and emotions. A single suicide can also spur copycat events, especially among teenagers.

Mental illness increases homelessness. While most homelessness is a result of economic and housing policies (no jobs, low wages, a lack of affordable housing), many people are without homes because of their mental conditions. Since deinstitutionalization began in the 1960s, many severely mentally ill people have no place to live. Family and friends have either turned them away or lack the resources to take care of them. Many are left to roam the streets, while others end up in prison and become a burden on the judicial system. To be clear, *homelessness is not caused by mental illness* but rather by policies that do not allow for the care of people with psychological problems. The reverse also can be true: homelessness very often leads to psychological distress. Stress created by concerns for personal safety, food insecurity, and no or low income can accumulate to a psychological breaking point and lead to symptoms of depression, anxiety, or other mental and behavioral health problems.

Parents with psychological problems have greater difficulty meeting their children's developmental needs, thereby increasing the risk of their children developing emotional and psychological distress. Parents facing their own mental health problems may be less available to their children, dysfunctionally over- or under-protective, engage in role reversal, or abusive, thereby increasing the odds of reproducing their distress in their children.

Because stressful social environments such as poverty tend to foment fatalism, depression, and anxiety, realizing personal ambitions and dreams of fulfillment for society's most disadvantaged members often becomes untenable. Society's loss may lie in the failure to develop the minds of great people who could have made important contributions to the common good and led happy, satisfying lives.

Lastly, mental illness can have an impact on individuals' immune systems, making individuals more vulnerable to stress-related physical disorders and even some infectious diseases, which adds an additional burden to the health care system.

About the Quote

Despite its long and storied history, mental health has maintained a relatively low priority among public health issues. In many places mental health is seen as a private matter rather than a public trouble, but now having seen the prevalence and costs of mental illness on society, we should perhaps reconsider the priority rating of psychological distress and recognize it as a social problem.

As Chapter 14 will discuss, billions of dollars are spent by the states and federal government on mental health treatment and research each year, but little of these resources are dedicated to resolving the social conditions that produce higher rates of disorders. Prevention is rarely addressed, and many people in need are priced-out of the best care. People are increasingly distressed and alienated, and the fragility of the collective psyche was exposed during the COVID-19 pandemic both in the United States and around the world. If 19 percent of the population had an infectious disease instead of a mental illness, authorities would be quick to label the condition a severe epidemic. In comparison, by January 2022, roughly 20 percent of the US population had acquired COVID-19, a figure quite similar to the rate of mental illness on any given day.

Mental health treatment is reactive; people seek help when they feel something is wrong or they are having trouble coping or enjoying life. Public health works similarly. Little effort is made to prevent the fundamental causes of mental illness. By looking at the tables in this chapter, it is clear that mental health follows social patterns. Some groups are more vulnerable to mental illness than others. The argument that differences in the psychosocial constitutions of individuals vary between groups is untenable; therefore, the organization of society becomes an important contributor to poor mental health.

This theoretical argument is the point of Fromm's quote. Fromm, working from the framework of critical theory, argued quite elegantly in *The Sane Society* (1955) how the structure of society creates conditions that make life difficult and emotional stability hard to maintain. A "sane" society is one that provides for the objective, or material, needs of its people without bias or prejudice. In such a society the basic needs of nutritious food, affordable and proper housing, clean water and air, education, and health care are satisfied, and so are the needs of social justice, freedom from inequality, and an opportunity to maximize one's human potential. By eliminating social stressors, the sane society would create sane people.

One of the key themes in the sociology of mental health and illness is that there are multiple pathways to psychological distress and mental disorders. Some people may develop problems because of a biological or organic factor while others' mental distress stems from stress produced by micro-level dynamics such as poor parenting or interpersonal difficulties such as a stressful intimate relationship. A third course to mental distress and disorders are sociological, or macro-level, factors grounded in the organization of society. The social structure that governs the distribution of wealth and power and the rules for how groups treat each other are responsible for considerable stress, which, if unattended, can accumulate and evolve into a full-blown disorder.

Thus, can we say that mental health is a public issue? Very often, that answer is yes. The 2020 COVID-19 quarantine, for example, served as a great experiment to study the relationship between social structure and mental health. The quarantine afforded us the opportunity to see what happens when social structure is fundamentally altered, unstable, and stressful. The outcome was that for many people, the effects were devastating. Changes in social organization created by the quarantine and other public health provisions exposed emotional vulnerabilities of many people and required maximum coping skills from almost everyone. COVID-19 will be discussed in more detail in Chapter 10, but for now, we can say that the social changes that came from the pandemic were devasting for the mental health of many people throughout the world. Hostile social environments work in much the same way.

People rely on a stable social structure to nurture sound mental health, but it is a double-edged sword. Stable social environments are beneficial for mental health but subjectively that environment must be conducive to emotional, cognitive, and behavioral development. It must be "sane." Too many or drastic social changes or chronic hostility in the environment are likely to fail to foster good mental health.

DISCUSSION QUESTIONS

1. How might the Sociological Imagination make sense of the relatively high rates of mental distress in our society? Would you say mental health is a personal problem or a public issue, as Mills defined the terms? Explain your answer.

2. Mental health studies prevalence studies have flaws even before they start. What causes those errors? What decisions should we make in light of those errors?

3. In epidemiology, how can we tell if anyone really has a mental disorder as specified in the DSM?

4. How can social forces be considered necessary or sufficient causes for psychological distress? Think about epidemics and quarantines here. Under what circumstances could a prolonged quarantine be considered necessary or sufficient to cause somewhat to experience psychological symptoms?

KEY TERMS

Disability-Adjusted Life Years 74
Epidemiology 74
Incidence 74
Prevalence 74
Risk 74
True prevalence 83

CHAPTER 5

Social Class and Mental Illness

Learning Objectives

After reading this chapter, students will be able to:

1. Articulate a theory of stratification that shows how social class position is a fundamental cause of mental health problems in a population.
2. Analyze the two major theories that propose causality between social class and mental distress.
3. Compare the opportunities for mental health among individuals in different social class positions.
4. Give original examples of how the characteristics of stratification impact mental health.

> "The despair…people feel is deeply personal. Their problems are deeply social. More than that, it is the despair that identifies the social facts as social problems."
>
> —John Mirowsky and Catherine E. Ross (2003)

Introduction

Stratification, the process by which people are organized into a hierarchical system of classes, is a universal characteristic of human societies. Where people are located in this hierarchy has considerable influence on their quality of life and physical and psychological well-being. Being situated in the lower ranks means a likelihood of faring poorly on virtually every indicator of healthfulness: shorter life expectancy, higher overall mortality, higher mortality in the top causes of death, and greater risk of infant mortality. Added to that burden is generally poorer psychological health. Sociologists have long researched the connections between mental health and socioeconomic standing and have consistently found that the poorer and less powerful people are, the more likely they are to experience mental health problems (Eaton and Muntaner 2017). This chapter will explore this relationship and provide an understanding of why psychological distress is much more prevalent among lower income people.

Stratification and Social Class

To understand how class impacts mental health, we need to review how stratification systems work. Stratification systems distribute individuals and groups in social hierarchies within which power, prestige, and material resources are allocated. A person's or group's location within social hierarchies is based on characteristics that are shared and identifiable and differentiated such as race and ethnicity, sex and gender, religion, ideology, age, and marital status, among others. This chapter focuses on **social classes**, which are social divisions rooted in economic factors such as occupation, education, income, and authority.

The characteristics used to rank people and groups are intersecting not mutually exclusive. The intersectionality of statuses leads to people having different life experiences based on possessing two or more relevant status positions. For example, a White person in a lower-class position has a different life experience than a Black person in a similar economic situation. They both share the stressors of having a low income, but differences in their racial status mean that they are subject to society's rules on how these groups are treated.

Social class position is relevant to understanding mental health because the economics of class exert tremendous influence over our identity and how we engage others around us, all of which translates into differential burdens on psychological well-being. Because of the strength of this influence, a review of the dynamics of stratification is needed to illustrate the mechanisms by which the socioeconomic hierarchy creates barriers to mental distress for some but may lead to problems for others.

Because social class can be a difficult term to define, let us start with a review on the nature of class and ways to operationalize it.

Caste and Class

Examining stratification usually begins by separating the two broadest types or systems of distributing wealth and power: caste and class. In a caste, or closed system, a person's station in the hierarchy is determined at birth and is based on the class position of parents. A person born to a poor family would always be poor, and a child born to a rich and powerful family could look forward to a life of wealth and privilege. The traditional culture of India is often the first caste system that comes to mind, but it could be argued that the United States has had strong caste characteristics, especially during slavery and the era of Jim Crow segregation. During those times, Black people rarely rose above their low station, and poor Whites fared little better than their parents. The relationships among castes are fixed and rigid, and **social mobility**, moving from one socioeconomic position to another, seldom occurs.

Caste systems are guided by an ideology that explains and justifies the inflexible unequal distribution of wealth and power. In traditional India, the principles of the Hindu religion, notably karma and the transmigration of souls, explained that caste placement was based on how one lived in past lives. Being in a high caste was a reward for righteous living in a previous life, but being poor indicated past lives of sinfulness and wrong-doing. In the United States, caste, embodied by slavery and segregation, was justified by racist beliefs in the biological inferiority of the peoples of Africa. Some Whites accepted slavery as ordained by religious precepts. Box 5.1 presents additional information about the caste system in India and introduces an interesting way of connecting caste and perceptions of mental illness.

Box 5.1 Is Stratification Ideology a Delusion?

The ideologies that are invoked to justify inequality are very powerful both in terms of words and actual force to back them up. Social norms and values are invented to reinforce differences in social rank and to maintain boundaries between them. Rules of etiquette, clothing, property values, legacy admissions to colleges, redlining in the banking and insurance industries, and even how the rich and poor talk to each other are ways in which we are reminded of class differences. But what about the underlying ideas behind these behaviors? Stereotyping the poor is one social force that lies at the heart of class differences and keeping them separated. Poor people are often perceived as threatening, unmotivated, uninterested in education, dependent, bad parents, and of "poor breeding." The stereotype wraps around the idea that the poor are simply "not good people."

This is also true in India, where social organization remains dominated by its ancient caste system. According to India law, caste is illegal, but the reality is that interpersonal relationships and macro-level social organizational structure are still subject to beliefs about the inherent differences among the social ranks. The origins of the caste system in India are debated, but they were probably started as divisions of labor and the logic of generations of kinfolk keeping the same line of work as their forebears. At some point over two thousand years ago, Hinduism was used to legitimate social inequality, and that led to the near absence of anyone resisting or challenging the caste system. In Hinduism, souls are immortal and are reincarnated as another person. If one lives a righteous life, the next life will be more comfortable, and if a moral and religious life continues, eventually the soul will reach heaven and not return to a material form. These are powerful beliefs for controlling behavior.

One group of people known as Dalits or "untouchables" are actually beneath the traditional caste structure. They are so low that they are barely recognized as people because the horrible life they are forced to live in the present indicates what terrible people they were in previous lives. The *Manusmriti*, sometimes called the Hindu Code of Conduct, was written about 2,200 years ago and spells out how the castes are to relate to each other. Here are a few rules about how Dalits should be treated:

1. They should eat left-over foods and only on broken plates
2. They should wear the "clothes of the dead," which implies "hand-me-downs" from deceased people
3. Their furniture is limited to broken throw-away pieces from families of higher castes
4. Their houses can only be built from sheets of materials, which means without a frame
5. They must reside outside the village
6. Their wealth is limited to donkeys and dogs.

The Untouchables were restricted to only the filthiest jobs and scavenging for their living. They handled dead bodies and collected animal dung to use for fuel and building materials.

Today, their lot is not much better. They are easily visible in the cities working jobs that are physically hard and extremely low paying and living in slums. Dalits are subject to random acts of physical violence and mob attacks and remain the least educated and most unhealthy group in the country. As G. C. Pal (2015) wrote, social exclusion is widely embedded in the Indian societal structure, and one cost of being denied access to the life chances that society offers is poor mental health.

Here is an interesting "spin" on the question of the effects of caste on mental health. Ramaiah (2007) contends that the real mental health problem concerning caste is belief in the ideology that justifies it, which Ramaiah calls "caste delusion." As we learned in Chapter 2, a delusion is a belief that lacks any empirical or logical truth. People holding delusional beliefs resist or defy logical explanations that refute the belief. Socio-cultural forces can reinforce a delusion, reifying an untruth and making it acceptable.

Ramaiah argues that caste delusion is the root of the caste problem in India. Among the symptoms of this "mental illness" are fears of interacting with Dalits in all areas of life: sharing food, living near a Dalit family, sitting next to a Dalit, learning from a Dalit, being in a Dalit's shadow, having Dalit children in their children's school, or marrying a Dalit. Upper caste members often resent seeing Dalits in nice clothes or with any of life's amenities or even the most basic of luxuries. Traditional upper caste members, Brahmins in particular, "know" they are cursed if they have any contact with a Dalit person and must take a ritual bath to cleanse themselves of the impurities contracted by being exposed to a Dalit.

Ramaiah states that these beliefs, because they have no empirical or tangible evidence to support the notion of Dalits' inherent inferiority, are unfounded. Is it a delusion? Can an ideology be a clinically significant delusion? It is an interesting question not just in the case of India, but for us too. Do the stereotypes of the poor, which are part of the justification of inequality in the United States, constitute a delusion? These are indeed interesting questions.

Contrary to castes, a class system is dynamic and open; moving up or down in class standing is possible and encouraged by the society's rhetoric and ideology. Opportunities exist for children from lower class positions to achieve levels of education, income, and status beyond the class in which they were born. As with caste, class systems also have ideologies to justify why some people fare better than others. In the United States, the prevailing idea is the notion of the meritocracy, the belief that wealth and power go to the most talented and the smartest. In this ideology, everyone begins on equal footing, and then education "sorts them out." Those who do well in school, which is often called the "great equalizer" because of the assumption that all students have the same chance to excel, get the best jobs that yield the greatest financial returns.

In an ideal world, society would provide the foundation for all children to have the chance to realize their potential. Unfortunately, this is not the case. Social mobility has become more attainable since the mid-twentieth century, but the rules for achieving wealth, power, and prestige make moving up difficult to achieve. Our social narrative may declare that everyone has a chance to succeed, but the reality is that most people stay in or very near the class position of their parents (Beller and Hout 2006). Stratification in the United States is certainly a class system, yet vestiges of caste characteristics linger. "Rags to riches" stories, while they happen occasionally, are not common.

The problem with the idea of meritocracy is that people do not start life as equals and that schools are also stratified, making some better than others. Poorer children have fewer intellectually stimulating life experiences and likely attend underfunded schools, and children of rich families usually have access to more learning resources and better teachers. In addition, moving up is connected to the structure of opportunity. Jobs must be available. Social forces such as the "gig economy," automation, changing market conditions, international politics, and public health restrictions in the era of COVID-19 cause the job market to fluctuate and opportunities to open or close. The opportunity structure is often out of the control of individual people. A good education and marketable skills cannot pay off if jobs are not present.

What Is Social Class?

The term "class" is perhaps the most debated and confused concept in the social sciences (Wodtke 2016; Wright 1979), and for good reason. Conceptualizing class is quite complicated because inequality is produced by a complex of norms, values, customs, and ideologies that are hard to untangle. Because their discipline is a multiparadigmatic field, there are many ways to approach the same problem. Sociologists have formed several, often conflicting, theories that define and operationalize social class. Some theories, for example, use individual characteristics such as occupation, educational achievement, and income to identify class position, and others look at stratification as a dynamic system of relationships among groups. For our purposes, a social relational approach to understanding how stratification works is best to see how the class hierarchy affects mental health.

Taking a relational stance on stratification pulls together the factors of socioeconomics that affect mental health under one coherent theoretical umbrella. This theory holds that a person's position within the authority structures of society is the primary determinant of income, material resources, and life chances (Dahrendorf 1959). In contemporary society, most people work in bureaucracies where ownership of the means of production (places where money is made) is diffused by numerous stockholders or controlled by the government, but the amount of control each person has over the organization's resources is clearly articulated. Socioeconomic position, then, is based on a person's relationship to the authority structure of that organization.

Everyone is familiar with terms like "the rich," "the middle-class," and the "top one percent" because they have a conventional meaning for the classes in everyday language (Wodtke 2016). However, they lack specificity in that they fail to imply how a position was attained and its relationship to others. The terms of **authority relations theory** provide a better description of the dynamics of social inequality in contemporary society because it reflects the socioeconomic relationships most people have with each other.

The relational approach to stratification states there are four classes, each with a specific relationship to the other. The criteria for specifying classes have little to do with individuals' social capital (income, wealth, power, and social networks), but rather their position in the bureaucracy in relation to controlling the organization's resources and authority relations with other people in the organization. Figure 5.1 shows how these classes are constructed.

The proprietor class, what many think of as the "upper class," includes people who own the means of production. Their money comes more from wealth (investments) than income (earned wages). People in this position control the resources of the organization and the labor of others.

Managers do not have ownership, but they plan the use of resources and give orders to other workers. While they are supervised themselves by boards of directors, proprietors, or higher managers, they engage in some degree of self-directed labor and have control over their own work.

Workers control neither resources nor labor. Since their relationship to authority is that of order-taker, their labor is other-directed. Because they are always supervised, workers exercise little discretion at work. Jobs in this class are often low paying, precarious, and nonstandard.

Independent producers own and operate their own businesses. They have few if any employees except perhaps family members.

Each of the classes is structurally antagonistic to one another because they occupy different positions of authority and develop interests related to their place in the hierarchy. Positions of authority have an interest in maintaining that authority and its benefits; positions of lower authority have interests in increasing their control over their social and work environments and receiving more benefits.

FIGURE 5.1 Wright's Authority Relations Theory and Social Class

Class	Owns Means of Production	Controls Resources	Controls Activities of Others
Proprietors	Yes	Yes	Yes
Managers	No	Yes	Yes
Workers	No	No	No
Independent Producers	Yes	Yes	---

The structure of social classes, therefore, rests on the relationship among people in different levels of authority. These relationships are not limited to socioeconomic status, but intersect with race, ethnic, and gender relations as well. For now, the focus is on social class and life conditions. Relationship to authority greatly influences economic and political awards and life chances to receive a good education, life in a safe place, have good health care, and to be relatively free from stressful social environments.

One way to see the complications of social class constructs is a situation where people have high social capital—education, income, and prestige—but do not control their labor. For example, for the first time in US history, more physicians in the United States work for medical practices they do not own. That means they graduated from medical school and then looked for a job. As of 2019, 47.4 percent of practicing physicians worked for someone else, compared to almost 46 percent who owned their practices (Henry 2019). From a sociological point of view, while these physicians have high social capital, they must compete in the labor market and follow the orders of those who employ them. They may have independence in their professional decision-making about the practice of medicine and can give orders to nurses and technicians, but in terms of their relationship to authority, they are mid-level managers who are paid a wage and can be dismissed from their jobs.

Two concepts, **exploitation** and **alienation**, are central to this approach and have relevance for mental health. Exploitation refers to some groups' exclusionary control over others' behavior and the authority to appropriate the wealth generated by the people who produce it (Wright 1979; 2002). It means that workers must work harder and longer to produce wealth beyond what they earn in wages to pay those who have the most authority and do not produce the product or service. Alienation is present in situations where a group is denied power over their own labor activities and the rewards of their labor. Alienation is a material and emotional condition of powerlessness.

While this is not the time to explore this theory in depth, this review of its major concepts is necessary because of their implications for mental health. As shall be seen, individuals who lack authority and control over their labor generally receive a lower income, have less access to good health care, and feel powerless in their social environments, all of which are tied to stress and a greater likelihood of psychological problems especially depression and anxiety.

As a point of order, to make the discussion easier to follow, the conventional terms "upper," "middle," and "working" classes will substitute for, respectively, proprietors, managers, and workers. The term "lower-class" will also be used to refer to a subset of the working class that includes the chronically poor whose work is often seasonal and poorly paid and who experience high levels of unemployment and on occasion must rely on government safety net programs for subsistence. Please keep in mind that these terms imply real social relations of authority and power, which translate to opportunities for health and well-being.

How Does Social Class Impact Mental Health?

Research consistently finds that social class divisions and inequality are major predictors of the distribution of mental health in a population. Perhaps this finding is due to social inequality having the most basic and primary impact on social relationships (Wilkinson and Pickett 2017). Social class groups are, in many ways, sub-cultures, each with its own tastes in food, music and art, clothing, and manner of speaking, which translate into class-specific life experiences (Bourdieu 2002; Kraus et al. 2013). As with other cultural distinctions, social classes have different expectations of behavior, including health related behavior, and subjective, or phenomenological, experience of life. Perhaps the most important part of class cultures is the difference in exposure to chronic stress, which, along with a lack of resources, is responsible for those in lower social strata being more likely to engage in unhealthy behaviors such as tobacco use, eating a less nutritious diet, and, since they are more likely to engage in manual and physical labor, getting less exercise.

The interplay between class and mental health has been known for a century in sociology. Early important studies by sociologists established that neighborhood conditions and social economic position exerted strong influences on mental health. Two of these studies are particularly important in this history.

Faris and Dunham (1939) were curious about where mental health patients originated in Chicago. Studying almost 35,000 people in treatment facilities in the 1920s and early 1930s, they uncovered strong social patterns in two important conditions: "manic depressive insanity" (now known as bi-polar disorder) and schizophrenia. Bi-polar disorder cases were randomly distributed throughout Chicago, suggesting that the condition had a genetic cause, but people with schizophrenia were highly likely to reside in the city's poorer areas. In studying the history of each case, Faris and Dunham found that people with schizophrenia lived in these areas before their symptoms began, forcing them to conclude that the conditions of disorganized neighborhoods and institutions played a causal role in the onset of schizophrenia by creating negative community and family affiliations and social isolation. Faris and Dunham were among the first to present evidence that not all schizophrenia could be traced to biological origins, a fact later supported with more sophisticated research techniques (Busfield 2000).

A second study of historical significance is the work by sociologist August Hollingshead and psychiatrist Frederick Redlich (1958). Their seminal study focused on social class, finding a strong relationship between economic situation and both type and severity of mental illness. People from the lowest socioeconomic positions had higher rates of severe disorders and were more likely ordered into treatment by courts or other official agencies. Once in treatment, the poorer a person was, the greater likelihood a biological or medical treatment was prescribed. Higher status people were typically treated with talk and psychological therapies.

These studies, among many others, contributed pivotal discoveries for both sociology and the behavioral sciences, and proved to be the foundations of our understanding of how class and mental health intersect.

The Question of Causality

The relationship between class and mental health, though empirically strong and irrefutable, poses an interesting question about causality. Which comes first? Are poor people more prone to mental distress or do psychological problems make people poor? When we seek to determine if any two variables are causally related, their temporal ordering must be specified. The cause must precede the effect. Condition X cannot cause condition Y if Y occurs before X. Usually, it is not difficult to assess the temporal ordering of social variables, but in this case, the time element is murky and not always easily identified. Since there are two possibilities in the causal path between class and mental health, there are two aligning theories. One approach, called social selection or social drift theory, contends that mental well-being causes class position, and the other, social causation theory, argues, that class affects mental health.

Social Selection and Social Drift Theories

The **social selection-drift hypothesis** suggests that mental distress affects people's participation in the economic system. According to this view, psychological impairment is an impediment to economic behavior and hinders a person's ability to perform at a sufficiently high level to achieve the social capital necessary to compete in the job market.

The terms selection and drift are often used interchangeably, but they denote slightly different phenomena (Eaton and Muntaner 2017). Drift refers to situations in which a mental condition causes a person to "drift" downward in status, or intragenerational mobility. In this context, a person reaches a certain socioeconomic level but cannot maintain it because of an impairment. Consider this hypothetical scenario. John is a person with schizophrenia. He graduates from college with a degree in business and gets a job in marketing with a company. To this point, his symptoms are manageable, and he is doing well and making a good entry-level salary. After a couple of years, however, his symptoms become increasingly severe and he begins to miss work. Plus, he starts having difficulty relating to and communicating with co-workers and clients. In time, his boss dismisses him because of poor performance and disrupting the office work environment. John gets another job but cannot stay focused on his duties, and his behavior becomes increasingly erratic. He is soon fired from this position too. Eventually he is unable to find work in an office setting and must settle for low-paying menial jobs. John has now "drifted" down in class status.

Social selection refers to intergenerational mobility, where an impairment impedes individuals' ability to maintain or surpass their parents' class position. In the previous example had John come from a middle- or upper-class family, his experience would be called "social selection" because he fell into a lower social position because of his impairment. As John's situation suggests, the two concepts are not necessarily mutually exclusive.

The commonality of the drift and selection models is that a person cannot attain or sustain a higher class standing because of a psychological problem and drops downward in status. In the social selection-drift perspective, psychological well-being contributes to the separation of the classes. Many people are poor because they are burdened by mental health problems that prevent them from doing well in obtaining the education and social skills necessary to reach middle- and upper-class jobs.

The Social Causation Model

The **social causation model** reverses the causal sequencing of the two variables. In this view, the social conditions of class create hardships for those in lower social strata, causing a greater burden of mental health problems. The life struggles that are often attached to low authority positions become barriers for doing well in school, achieving higher education, and getting a good job. The stressful conditions of deprivations brought on by living in disadvantaged and under-resourced families and neighborhoods cause the higher rates of psychological impairments found in lower social class positions.

Consider this hypothetical example. Mary is a single mother of two who works as a salesclerk in a "big box" hardware store. She did well in high school and was generally a happy teenager. Two years after graduating high school, she married her high school sweetheart, who had been a star athlete in school, and by age 25 both her children were born. A year later, however, she was divorced. Her ex-husband pays no child support and has little contact with the children. By age 35, life has become exceedingly hard for Mary. Paying rent, maintaining her car, and the everyday costs of children's school supplies, clothes, entertainment, utilities, and insurance mean that she lives paycheck to paycheck. After several years of this lifestyle, Mary finds herself constantly tired and increasingly irritable. She becomes short-tempered with the kids, finds sleeping difficult, and gains weight. She often feels guilty that she cannot provide for her children and that her life has not worked out as she had hoped. She does not want to do anything pleasurable except watch TV. Mary is depressed.

Which Is Right?

On the surface, both selection/drift and social causation seem to satisfy common sense logic. By employing advanced research and statistical techniques, however, sociologists have begun to sort out the viability of the two theories. They have discovered that there is considerable empirical evidence that the downward drift and selection hypotheses have limited applicability and power in explaining higher rates of both incidence and prevalence of mental distress among people in lower levels of the hierarchy (Fox 1990; Perry 1996). Conversely, research shows that the social causation approach explains most of the dynamics between class and mental health. Social selection research has established a time ordering pattern of causality that is so robust that socioeconomic position is considered a "fundamental cause" of mental illness in a population (Link and Phelan 1996).

As in the case of Mary described earlier, the stress of constantly fragile economic circumstances, a lack of social resources, limited access to agencies of authority takes its toll over time. Known as **allostatic load**, the accumulation of wear and tear on the body caused by the inefficient switching on-and-off of physiological responses to stress is believed responsible for the emotional and cognitive distress disproportionately found among the poor and working classes (McEwen and Seeman 1999). As Dowd and colleagues (2009) have shown, the greater the stress load, the more likely maladaptive biopsychosocial stress responses will occur. People in lower class positions have disproportionately high blood pressure, blood sugars, obesity, cholesterol, cardiovascular disease, and other organ problems. They are also more likely to have feelings of helplessness and symptoms of depression (Cohen et al. 2006), and the more time spent in poverty, and the resultant exposure to stress-induced cortisol, the greater the cumulative effect of the disadvantaged social conditions and the higher probability of pervasive and serious expressions of disorder (Evans and English 2002; Evans and Kim 2007).

More recent research shows that the effects of poverty run deeper than symptomatic expressions of stress. These studies have identified measurable and significant changes in the brain structure of children chronically exposed to the stressors of poverty. Brody and associates (2017), for example, have confirmed the association between childhood poverty and diminished volume of the limbic regions of adults. Brody's research also found that supportive parenting and parenting-focused intervention programs can offset the persistent effects of stress due to poverty on brain structure.

Social Class and Stress

If we look at the effects of stratification over the life cycle, it is theorized that stress accumulates over one's lifetime (Eaton and Muntaner 2017). Childhood disorders are neither common nor differentiated by social class. By the teenage and early adulthood years, however, the classes begin to chart separate psychological paths. These are the times when symptoms indicating "full-blown" disorders emerge and become more pronounced. The stress that people face over their lifetimes has been organized by Eaton and Muntaner's authoritative review of sociological research into five categories of risk for developing a mental illness (2017: 245–248).

The first of Eaton and Muntaner's life course risk categories is the possibility of disturbances during pregnancy and birth, which are known to lead to mental health problems in later life. While adverse prenatal environments can affect the mental health of people across the socioeconomic spectrum, they are more common for children in low-income families with less educational achievement because of their increased rates of maternal smoking and gestational hypertension (Tearne et al. 2015).

Second, environmental pollutants are found in higher concentrations in low-income neighborhoods. In cities, poor people live in greater proximity to industrial waste and high automotive traffic, which leads to greater exposure to polluted air and heavy metals such as lead. In rural areas, exposure to the chemicals used in fertilizers and pesticides, and found in abandoned factories, similarly create risk for poorer people. Middle- and upper-class neighborhoods and residences, on the other hand, are typically situated farther from industrial zones, brownfields, and landfills. In addition, occupational differences place people in different risk categories. Factory and construction workers and migrant agricultural workers have greater exposure to chemicals, putting them at exceedingly high risk. Exposure to these pollutants is more widely recognized as causes of a number of physical health problems, but they are also associated with mental deficiencies.

Third, children in lower socioeconomic positions have a higher chance of experiencing an adverse childhood experience (ACE) such as physical and sexual abuse, neglect, and household substance abuse and criminality. They are more likely to witness or have reason to fear violence and are more likely targets of bullying behavior. Years ago, it was believed that child abuse and family violence were more or less equally spread out in the population, but now we know that is not true. Since the 1970s, strong evidence exists to substantiate the negative relationship between class and child abuse and family violence: the lower the class position, the more likely violence and neglect will occur. Experiencing an ACE dramatically raises the risk of developing mental health problems, especially among the poor who in addition to greater exposure, have fewer resources to resolve them (Mersky et al. 2018).

Fourth, Eaton and Muntaner report that the social and psychological conditions of work play an important role in class differences in mental health. Middle- and upper-class jobs allow generally safer work environments in addition to better remunerations. Holders of these positions, while certainly not free from stress, generally do not have to fear personal safety or take physical risks as do people holding blue-collar positions. Fear for safety can be a strong source of stress that can accumulate over time. Construction workers, for example, face countless risks in their work, and the stress can build, especially if safety is not handled well by their employer (Leung et al. 2012). Effective safety equipment and proper safety training moderates some of the stress encountered by these workers.

Front-line workers who have the most contact with the general public also face considerable stress and report psychological and sleep complaints. Workers in call centers, for example, report anxiety and emotional exhaustion stemming from dealing with abusive and difficult customers (Deery et al. 2010), and prison guards also develop stress responses from their work (Rutter and Fielding 1988). Police officers experience high rates of clinically significant symptoms of PTSD, depression, relationship stress, and alcohol abuse (Ballenger et al. 2011; Kirschman et al. 2014; Wang et al. 2010).

One concern is the growing incidence of violence committed by retail customers, which is known to contribute to psychological distress (Boyd 2002). During the coronavirus crisis, the media reported many cases of violence against hourly wage earners in retail outlets and fast food restaurants. The stress of dealing with an often angry public while worrying about getting sick, accumulated quickly, and by mid-April of 2020, only four weeks after the national emergency was declared in the United States, hourly wage employees in grocery stores and pharmacies were showing signs of anxiety and depression and in need of mental health attention (Repko 2020).

Lastly, people in lower socioeconomic positions have less access to resources that can serve as a barrier to psychological distress or help relieve it. As Eaton and Muntaner state, the problem extends beyond the ability to afford psychotherapy, hospitalizations, or drug and alcohol rehab, which of course are often unavailable to low-income people who cannot afford those services or have no insurance. But because the poor often do not receive medical care for conditions like diabetes, cardiovascular problems, hypertension, among many others, their mental health may deteriorate as a consequence of simply being chronically sick. In addition, cultural differences may hinder many poor people from seeking mental health services. Language differences or the belief that mental illness is a family matter or would bring shame to the family if the problem were made public may keep some people from getting help. For others, asking someone for psychological care is act of personal failure or an admission that one is "not right."

Perhaps the most important key to accessing social benefits for enhancing mental health is education (Mirowsky and Ross 2012). Education is largely connected to one's socioeconomic position and provides both material and subjective advantages that facilitate mental health. At each level of education achieved, depression symptoms decline dramatically; women in particular reap benefits from increasing their education. Men with less than a high-school diploma feel depressed about 80 percent more often than men with college degrees. Women who have not graduated high school feel depressed about 170 percent more often than college educated women (Mirowsky and Ross 2012). Income and control over one's work and social environment rises with formal education, but education also gives people a sense of mastery over their lives and increased personal awareness.

The social causation model, however, does not explain all the relationship between class and mental health. Social drift and selection theory has supporting data in some areas, though they are not conclusive. Unlike depression, anxiety disorders, and substance abuse problems, social selection theory may be more important for understanding the social class standing of people with schizophrenia (Dohrenwend et al. 1992). Symptoms of schizophrenia, usually marked by a person's first psychotic break, typically begin between the ages of 18 and 30. The usual trajectory of schizophrenia's course makes keeping a job, especially one that requires concentration and relating to other people, hard to maintain. Work skills often diminish, and absenteeism can increase as symptoms worsen, which they typically do over time.

The drift and selection hypothesis, as it pertains to schizophrenia, is not necessarily decisive. Studies are mixed on this problem (Muntaner 2004). We do know that schizophrenia and other psychotic disorders occur where social inequality is greater. In fact, the larger the gap between rich and poor, the greater is the prevalence of schizophrenia in a society, which brings the social causation theory into play (Burns et al. 2014). It is possible that greater exposure to chronic stress enables or triggers biological predispositions to schizophrenia. These seemingly contradictory data suggest that perhaps there are different pathways into schizophrenia.

Subjective Aspects of Social Class

Material restraints are not the only conditions that account for the stress burden experienced among people in lower positions in the hierarchy. Inequality manifests itself beyond the material tangibles of money, wealth, housing, insurance, and possessions. The **subjective aspects of class** are the affective reactions people have to their material deprivations or affluence (McLeod and Kessler 1990). As demonstrated in Box 5.2, for example, in addition to skills and knowledge, education provides valuable intangible emotional and cognitive returns to people with higher levels of achievement. Educational success instills confidence, self-efficacy, and a refinement that prepares them to work with other people at a high level of social intercourse. Individuals who do not receive a good education are less likely to develop those qualities.

Box 5.2 Education and Mental Health

There is no question that education has a positive effect on mental health, and that's interesting because I suspect that you have never had a class that solely focused on your psychological well-being, was devoted to raising your self-awareness and personal insights, or engaged you in therapy. Because education is not directly about students' mental health, it must create other benefits that serve as barriers to mental distress, some of which are material and others are more subjective in nature.

Analyzing how education affects mental health offers an opportunity to learn a lesson about causality. Specifically, we can see the differences between direct and indirect effects in the relationship between a cause and an outcome.

A direct effect occurs when event X has a direct impact on event Y, which means that no other conditions are needed to explain the relationship between X and Y. Direct effects are drawn as:

$$X \to Y$$

For example, one way that class position has a direct effect on mental health is that the lack of resources generally inherent in the definition of class restricts access to mental health services such as psychotherapy. So, we can say:

$$\text{Income} \to \text{Mental health}$$

An indirect effect occurs when other variables are needed to elaborate the causal relationship between an X and a Y. Under this condition, X produces other outcomes (Z) that lead to changes in Y. X, therefore, needs a Z to connect it to Y. Indirect effects, where X indirectly causes Y, are drawn as

$$X \to Z \to Y$$

Education is a good example of an indirect effect. As mentioned earlier, education itself does not provide mental health services, brain enhancements, or psychotropic medications, but schooling does influence mental health because it creates other social and psychological benefits that reduce the likelihood of developing problems later in life.

Think about this for a minute and make a list of the psychosocial benefits education provides.

Here is my list. Education:

- Serves as a gatekeeper to jobs higher up the authority structure that provide more financial rewards, control, and resources to mitigate stress
- Improves self-efficacy and confidence
- Facilitates self-awareness and personal insights
- Increases communication skills and the ability to express personal problems
- Improves a person's vocabulary and abstract reasoning, making it easier to confront problems.

Did you think of more psychosocial benefits to education?

The factors on this list have a direct impact on mental health, but they often are dependent on education:

(Continued)

Box 5.2 Education and Mental Health *(Continued)*

education increases the likelihood that a person will have these qualities and opportunities.

These "Z" variables connect education to mental health. Without them, education might not have much impact. These patterns are graphically visually conceptualized as:

The subjective components of inequality, social comparisons, class-based identities, and feeling in control, can be as stressful as material deprivations.

Relative Deprivation Hypothesis

One subjective facet of social class is known as the **relative deprivation hypothesis**, which is when individuals evaluate themselves along class lines. The realities of inequality appear in various forms of social comparisons as people without money reference their life situations against wealthier individuals (Mishra and Carleton 2015).

And people do think in comparative terms—we all do it. Think of a time when you compared yourself to someone in terms of what you were wearing or how you were acting in a social situation such as a party. You may have also compared yourself to friends or classmates in terms of the house they lived in or the kind of car they or their parents drove. This process represents the fundamental sociological concept of **reference grouping**. Individuals use reference groups as standards for evaluating themselves and their behavior. We compare ourselves to a particular group to evaluate ourselves and see if we "measure up."

But when people compare themselves to those who are higher up the social hierarchy, especially those who are in geographic proximity to themselves, and appear to be failing in this comparison, are often left with feelings of personal inadequacy that lead to psychological injuries and negative mental health outcomes. Feelings of defeat, low self-worth, and even depression often occur.

Status-Based Identity

Status-based identity refers to the subjective meanings and values people attach to understanding their own socioeconomic position and incorporating them into their social identity (Destin and Debrosse 2017). How do people understand and interpret being in a certain social class position? What does it mean to be poor or rich? How do people mediate the limitations and opportunities that a class position presents? The way that a person works out these questions is how class affects identity.

Sennett and Cobb (1972), writing in *The Hidden Injuries of Class*, saw that working-class individuals typically experience intense anxieties due to feeling out of control of their lives. They also frequently feel a strong sense of self-defeat. Sennett and Cobb concluded that the trappings of class—housing, clothing, occupation—were "badges of ability," signs of the amount of social respect they were likely to receive. Because our society values wealth, prestigious occupations, and authority, those without them often feel inadequate and self-doubt. For example, have you ever heard anyone try to conceal their job or make it sound better than it really is, or qualify their jobs by saying, "I'm only a …"? These anxieties are psychological wounds and can have a real and lasting impact on emotional well-being.

Status-based identity joins together the story of one's life, one's identity as a member of social group (class in this case), and one's future identity, which refers to the kind of person one expects to be by being transformed by education, occupation, aging, and the various relationships we encounter (e.g., marriage, clubs, or religious communities). A self-defeating identity can hinder future accomplishments and leave goals unattained. Unfilled life dreams can be a source of depression and anxiety.

The concept of status-based identity helps us understand the experience of unemployment and the often harsh psychosocial outcomes of losing a job (Griep et al. 2016; Simandan 2018). When people are laid-off, they are saddled with a two-fold external stressor. First, they experience downward social mobility, even if the unemployment is short-lived. Second, because the lay-off happened outside their personal control, they are often left feeling powerless. If the period of unemployment lasts longer than expected, causes economic stress, and strains social relationships, clinical levels of depression, anxiety, psychosomatic symptoms, and self-esteem are common. Changes in wealth are detrimental to the psychological well-being of everyone (D'Ambrosio et al. 2020), but people in the working class experience the most negative psychological effects of unemployment because they have fewer personal and social resources to weather the storm (Paul and Moser 2009).

Fatalism

Fatalism is another subjective aspect of social class that contributes to the psychological burden of holding lower positions in the authority structure. Fatalism is the belief that life circumstances are out of one's control and in the hands of external forces such as fate, destiny, or a deity. The opposite of fatalism is **agency**.

Where fatalistic thinking is often believed to be irrational and passive, agency represents taking action to control one's life. Agency is based on **self-efficacy**, the belief in one's ability to control their own behavior to fulfill goals and complete tasks and overseeing one's life situation; fatalism is acquiescing, passively accepting things as they are and letting life happen *to* them (Drew and Shoenberg 2011).

You may have already assumed that individuals in lower class positions tend toward fatalism and the upper classes toward agency. And while that is generally the pattern, it is easy to conclude that fatalism is an act of surrender or a self-acceptance of failure and weakness. This belief is an unfortunate stereotype of the poor and working class. A different way of understanding fatalism is to see it as a rational response to structural powerlessness. Because their jobs are low paying, often seasonal, without benefits, and are other-directed (they take orders), the poor and working class, due to the uncertainty and stress of their social positions, need a way to understand their life circumstances and avoid self-blame (Keeley et al. 2009). In many ways their lives are out of their control, especially the economic and political aspects, so fatalism becomes crucial to making sense of their world. Fatalism is akin to karma in the sense that the prevailing attitude is resignation, a concession to the reality that forces outside themselves shape their futures.

Blair Wheaton contends that people assign attributes and biases to explain the causes of their social situations and buffer the stress (1980; 1983). According to **attribution theory**, higher class people, who by social measures are successful, see their prosperity as a result of their own efforts. They trend toward greater self-efficacy and optimism, which affords them the confidence to believe they are successful and better equipped to handle stress.

Lower class individuals, however, develop the habit of attributing their position, which is relatively less successful or even a failure by social standards, to external forces. External events frequently engulf poor and working-class individuals, and their attempts to overcome them often fail because of the lack of material and personal resources (social capital and authority). Fatalism, therefore, increases individual susceptibility to psychological disorders. Ceding control of one's life circumstances to external forces appears similar to clinical depression: feelings of worthlessness and low self-efficacy, fatigue, and trouble concentrating (Eaton and Muntaner 2017). Reducing fatalistic beliefs and engaging personal agency, on the other hand, improve coping and reduce the impact of environmental stressors (Wheaton 1983).

What About the Upper-Class?

The discussion thus far has focused on the poor and working-class and their greater vulnerability to psychological distress because of the weight of the stressors that stem from their position in the hierarchy. But what of people in higher standing? The question is: does money make you happy? And the answer is, predictably, yes.

Money and wealth matter for happiness in both absolute and relative ways: rich people enjoy being rich, and they enjoy being richer than other people (Clark and Oswald 1996). Poor people, conversely, are frustrated at their poverty and living in the margins (D'Ambrosio et al. 2020). Relatedly, people in great debt, relative to their wealth have more psychological health problems than those who do not (Keese and Schmitz 2014). The formula is fairly clear: life satisfaction is related to household net wealth (Headey and Wooden 2004). Stable household wealth and having greater control over one's social environment produce the best outcomes for mental health.

Having a materially comfortable life may make people happy, but it does not guarantee psychological health. Just as not all poor people have psychological problems, not everyone in the upper echelons of the hierarchy is free from distress. There are other stressors, such as conflicted family dynamics, that have little connection to social class but can impact mental health.

While occupants of the upper-class are less likely to experience class-based anxiety and clinical depression, they are more likely to develop narcissistic disorders. Higher status people often act the narrative of their class; that is, they assert their social superiority over weaker and more vulnerable groups, especially if they feel humiliated, challenged, or inconvenienced (Wilkinson 2005). When feeling vulnerable, many in upper-class positions engage in behaviors that reinforce the hierarchy and their position in it (Napoletano et al. 2016). Just as those in poverty may suffer from the burdens of social disadvantages, higher status people often have a strong desire for wealth and acquisitions, tools which can be used to influence or manipulate other people (Cisek et al. 2008). They may act in an ingenuine and unethical way to get what they want and have feelings of entitlement while paying less attention to the consequences of their own actions toward others. One seemingly mundane example of this behavior comes from a study that found that higher status people were more likely to cut off pedestrians at a crosswalk. Another and more cogent example: higher status children and adults were more likely to engage in bullying behavior (Napoletano et al. 2016). With depression and anxiety, people feel bad about themselves. People with narcissistic disorders, however, typically do not feel emotional distress. Instead, they make those around them miserable.

As a side note, the higher class' relative freedom from psychological distress is not cross-culturally consistent. An interesting study conducted by Kohn and colleagues in 1990 found that different types of socioeconomic systems produce a distribution of psychological distress different from that in the United States. In Poland, which at that time was organized in a more socialist fashion, managers bore the burden of poor psychological ill-health while workers were relatively happier and distress-free. Workers in industrial and socialist Poland enjoyed job and social protections that comparable blue-collar workers in the United States did not have. Managers, however, bore the stress of meeting production goals, thereby making their positions and security less tenable.

Social Class, Parenting, and Personality

The material realities of inequality have a direct effect on psychological well-being via financial stress and instability. Deprivations also exert an indirect effect via their strong influence on parenting behaviors, which, in turn, impact children's mental health. Parenting dynamics have considerable influence in children developing depression and anxiety disorders in later life; they also influence personality orientation, which has implications for mental health.

Parents prepare their children to survive in the world with which they are familiar, a world largely shaped by social status. Because parents can only teach what they know, parenting behaviors are deeply divided by class and act as a mechanism for reinforcing and reproducing parents' class position (Ishizuka 2019; Sherman and Harris 2012). Parents teach their children to survive within the boundaries of their own social class.

Srole and colleagues (1963) and Kohn and Schooler (1983) were among the first to demonstrate class differences in parenting. Parents in the middle- and upper-classes prepare their children for a world in which they are expected to attain higher education, gain professional positions, and make decisions that affect the development and allocation of resources, become planners of the works of others, and set and implement organizational policies and guidelines. To prepare their children for these assumed eventualities, parents high in the hierarchy teach their children to be intellectually flexible, work independently, and be self-motivated. Higher status children are taught to control their emotions and impulses to focus on delayed gratification and engaging in intellectual, or mental, labor. This parenting orientation serves as a barrier to depression and anxiety in adulthood.

On the other end of the spectrum in the world of working-class parents, following orders is essential for economic survival, given that their jobs are usually characterized as order-takers. Since they do not control their own labor, successfully executing the work planned by others is essential for keeping that job and income. Free thinking and questioning "the system" while on the job are not usually tolerated by holders of authority positions. Therefore, working-class kids are taught to control themselves to tolerate following orders and conforming to the demands of managers and supervisors.

Merging these differences in family environments and varying levels of material conditions and exposure to stressors, it is of little surprise that classes produce different types of disorders. Low positions in the hierarchy produce more depression, but types of personality disorders are distributed differently among classes (Ullrich et al. 2007). Wealthy and high-status people were more likely to report traits consistent with three personality disorders: obsessive-compulsive, narcissistic, and avoidant. While scoring high on the avoidant measure is not easily explained, obsessiveness and narcissism, traits that are often interpreted as ambition and capability, are rewarded by the class system. Narcissistic people in particular come across as competent and confident in job interviews and work meetings. These impressions, however, mask the psychological motivations hidden behind narcissism: an exaggerated sense of their own importance, a need for attention and admiration from other people, and a lack of empathy for the emotions and life circumstances of other people.

Lower status individuals, however, scored higher on measures of dependent, schizotypal, schizoid, and antisocial (sociopathy) personality disorders. These conditions, though they manifest as distinct personality styles, have several threads of commonality—all involve difficulty relating to other people, seeing the world as a mean and confusing place, and feeling out of control of their lives. Having no preparation to develop trust in other people because they are controlled by them makes lower- and working-class individuals vulnerable to these kinds of psychological maladaptation.

Personality disorders, which are neither especially common nor easily diagnosed, are not the primary ways that class position lead to different clinical paths. They are, however, the principal disorders that vary by social class. Most all other disorders occur more often among lower status individuals and groups. Poverty, blue-collar job status, and lower educational attainment pose greater risks for a number of disorders such as depression, agoraphobia, panic disorders, social phobias, generalized anxiety, all phobias, and conduct disorders (Eaton 2001; Muntaner 2004). This group experiences these disorders at about two times the rate of higher status individuals, and in cases of depression, the persistence of the symptoms lasts for longer periods of time (Muntaner 2004).

Linking Class Position and Psychological Distress

This chapter began with a review of the authority relations theory of social class to show how class is relevant for understanding how mental health is not equally distributed in a population. The connection between stratification and mental health outcomes is not necessarily a direct, linear relationship as the association between them is mediated by several conditions of the class structure. Low socioeconomic status does directly cause depression and anxiety, but the characteristics of the class structure can contribute to mental distress.

Authority relations set the table for social patterns of distress. As Mirowsky and Ross state, people in different structural authority positions develop "beliefs, interpretations, and assumptions about the nature of society, human relations, themselves, and their relationship to others and to society; the level of distress depends on the nature of these beliefs" (2012: 129). These beliefs regulate access to the class system's advantages and disadvantages and are the basis of alienation, authoritarianism, and inequality.

For people with lower class status whose relationship to authority affords them little autonomy and self-direction over their lives, class position can illicit emotions of powerlessness and self-estrangement, isolation, and a sense of meaninglessness about life. Collectively these emotional and cognitive states are known as alienation. Alienation is a structural social dynamic that has psychological consequences.

Two other structural features of authority relations—authoritarianism and inequality—further contribute to differences in a population's access to mental health. People who are subject to authority that is inflexible, controlling, and mistrustful are vulnerable to feeling isolated and out of control. A system that is exploitive and victimizes people by taking advantage of them with low wages and benefits, unsafe and hostile workplaces, and being inconsiderate of workers' personal lives and contributes to the structural origins of mental illness. Material inequality combined with workplace conditions of alienation and authoritarianism creates higher risks of experiencing depression and anxiety (Mirowsky and Ross 2012).

The main takeaway of this discussion of social class is that a sense of controlling one's life is a foundation for mental health. Variances in authority and material deprivations make achieving control extremely difficult. If subjected to a strict authoritarian regimen organized by class divisions, discriminatory racial and ethnic relations, or traditional gender role assignments and expectation, people's lives can metaphorically feel like being trapped in a small closet. Feelings of powerlessness and meaninglessness that often accompany the material realities of inequality can be devastating to self-esteem, motivation, and self-efficacy and can easily devolve into full-blown depression, anxiety, and other disorders. If people lose control over their social selves, they can easily lose control over their psychological selves.

About the Quote

Lower income people and their problems are often invisible to those residing in the higher ranks. Their problems are generally ignored by policymakers and government and those in higher class positions who are free from worries about affordable housing, providing nutritious food and good health care for their families, and job security. The origins of psychological pain for poor and working-class individuals are not existential but structural, which means it is their place in the social hierarchy that is the fundamental cause of their psychological selves.

The poor are stereotypically assumed to lead happy and carefree lives, and the rich are sometimes accused of being detached from the realities of people whose jobs are not steady and pay little. These stereotyped images of the poor have serious consequences: they cause us to overlook how poverty and low income affect personality, emotions, and behavior. The United States has not had a comprehensive policy to lower poverty since President Lyndon Johnson's "War on Poverty" programs in the early 1960s. That initiative resulted in reduced infant mortality, overall better health, and improved economic standing for poor families. More recently, national policy has largely pressured the poor by limiting social supports, reducing the inventory of affordable housing, lowering the real value of low incomes (we must remember that the large majority of poor people are employed), underfunding public education, and cutting financial support of community mental health programs.

The conditions in which socially disadvantaged individuals and families live are very stressful and, as Mirowsky and Ross aptly state, are at the core of the feelings of despair that low-income people often experience. This quote describes a sociological "smoking gun"—where there is despair, there is a social problem.

DISCUSSION QUESTIONS

1. How would you describe the differences in the type of stressors most experienced by poor and wealthy individuals? Make a list of five to 10 stressors each group is likely to face and compare them. What conceptual terms would you use to characterize each set of stressors?

2. Reflect on how social class has influenced your own biography. What subjective characteristics have you experienced? How might they differ for someone in a different social class than yourself?

KEY TERMS

Agency 111
Alienation 102
Allostatic Load 105
Attribution Theory 112
Authority Relations theory 101
Caste 98
Exploitation 102

Fatalism 111
Reference Grouping 110
Relative Deprivation Hypothesis 110
Self-efficacy 112
Social Causation Model 105
Social Classes 97

Social Selection-Drift Hypothesis 104
Social Mobility 98
Social Selection 104
Status-Based Identity 111
Stratification 96
Subjective Aspects of Class 108

CHAPTER 6

Race and Ethnicity

Learning Objectives

After reading this chapter, students will be able to:

1. Explain what the terms "race" and "ethnicity" mean and how they are relevant to understanding the distribution of mental health in the United States.
2. Illustrate how social relationships among ethnic and racial groups have caused these groups to have unique psychosocial experiences.

❝ A Kentucky master owns a negro child. He brings that child up in a state of moral and mental blindness—in consequence of that blindness, the child commits many blunders and is guilty of many crimes. Can the child be held accountable for the crimes, which resulted from the control which his master exerted over him? ...[T]hose vices and crimes perpetuated by the slave that are directly, clearly

> and only traceable to the power exerted over him by the master, must be charged to the master.
>
> —Frederick Douglass

Introduction

Some have argued that understanding the history of the United States requires knowing the history of **race** and ethnic relations in the country. There may be a degree of truth to that statement because how racial and ethnic groups have interacted over the centuries mirrors the flow of the nation's history. Slavery, the American Civil War, Jim Crow segregation, Exclusion Laws, the Civil Rights Movement, and the upswell of protest against social injustices in 2020 have anchored many of the major periods of American social history, and much of what concerns us today is a legacy of those past times. Debates on equity in education, voting rights, employment, and housing are often directly connected to race and **ethnicity**. Racialized events involving police activity, terroristic violence, racist images and rhetoric in the media and internet, and micro-aggressions in social interactions frequent our conversations and emphasize our difficulties in living together as a multicultural and multiethnic nation. Racial and ethnic tensions seem ubiquitous and consume a large share of our public resources and emotional energy.

The social profile of racial and ethnic minorities shows considerable inequality among the various groups that make up the American "melting pot." The effects of slavery and persistent segregation continue to show in contemporary society. For example, most race and ethnic minorities earn far less than White European Americans. According to the US Census, in 2017 10.7% of the total population had household incomes under $15,000; however, Blacks (19 percent) and Hispanics (12 percent) carry a heavier burden of families with low income compared to non-Hispanic Whites (8.8 percent). Black households earn about half of Whites', and African Americans are about two times more likely to be poor. More severe patterns hold for wealth. White families are 13 times more wealthy than Black Americans' households, a gap that has grown since the Great Recession of 2008 (Pew Charitable Trust 2016).

Education, important for reducing stress and mental health problems, fails to be attainable for many people in racial and ethnic minorities. Whites and Asians are much more likely to graduate from college at 34.5 percent and 52.7 percent, respectively. Among African Americans, however, 20.6 percent have degrees, and 15.2 percent of Hispanics and 14.3 percent of Native Americans and Native Alaskans have completed a four-year degree. Education, however, does not pay the same dividends for all race and ethnic groups. Even with college degrees, African

Americans and Hispanics earn less money than Whites and Asians who finished college.

These differences in resources are consequences of power and authority inequalities that have plagued American history. European Americans have long held positions of power in all levels of government, education, and business, and, consequently, have benefitted socially and economically. One of those benefits is better health.

As we saw in Chapter 5, people with fewer resources and greater social distance from authority and power experience more negative consequences of stress. Owing to a history of social and economic exploitation and being targets of prejudice and discrimination, some race and ethnic groups carry a heavy and disproportionate load of poverty and poor mental health. Health disparity among race and ethnic groups, like income and education gaps, is a serious social problem that hinders productivity, causes needless pain and suffering, and limits the ability to attain fulfillment and life satisfaction.

One goal of the US Government's health initiatives of both 2010 and 2020 was to "achieve health equity, eliminate disparities, and improve the overall health of all groups" (CDC 2020a). Has this goal been reached? Not really. Gaps in physical health remain, and as shall be seen in this chapter, many racial and ethnic minorities have disproportionate mental health problems when compared to more affluent and powerful groups.

The goal of this chapter is to describe how race and ethnicity are relevant for mental health variations in our population.

Understanding Race and Ethnicity

The terms race and ethnicity are often emotionally charged concepts, and they elicit many different definitions and theories about the relationships among these groups. Let's review what these concepts mean and how they relate to health.

The term "ethnicity" refers to a cultural group, people who share a distinct language, customs and rituals, national origins, and cultural identity. The United States is a composite of scores of diverse cultural groups that are readily visible in the ethnic enclaves found in most American towns and cities (Chinatown in San Francisco, Boston's North End Little Italy, Little Havana in Miami, and the Vietnamese community in Bayou La Batre, Alabama, for example) and in simply observing the distinctly American social landscape. Surnames in the United States are perhaps the most diverse in the world, and every family has its own ethnic stories, most of which are blends of the many ethnicities of Europe, Africa, Asia, and the indigenous peoples of North and South America.

Race is a controversial term that emerged during the colonial era of the seventeenth and eighteenth centuries to represent biological classes or categories within the human species. For centuries, European and American researchers sought to validate and reify these divisions by conducting studies attempting to demonstrate that racial categories were real and like different breeds of dogs or even constituted sub-species. These studies, collectively called scientific racism, were largely politicized and though they were conducted by scientists and scholars, by today's standards they would be considered pseudo-science in method and theory. Many famous and influential writers, including Americans Samuel George Morton, the influential nineteenth-century physician and scholar who is often credited as the founder of American scientific racism, and Benjamin Rush, among many others, developed theories bidding to prove that the so-called races were distinct peoples, if not disparate species. These theories, for instance, made varying contentions about the origins of skin color. Rush, a physician and founder of American psychiatry and a slave-owning abolitionist, wrote in 1799 that blackness was caused by a skin disease like leprosy, and while Black people could be cured and become White again, Blacks and Whites should not marry to minimize the contagion.

Other famous scholars and physicians, including philosophers like Voltaire and David Hume, supported a polygenism ideology, the belief that categories of humans have separate origins. This view, which Morton and others claimed to have Biblical support, explained that racial variations in humans represented different species or at best sub-species. As a side note, some believed that human races were similar to donkeys and horses. While they could reproduce, their offspring would be sterile just like the mule, the issue of donkeys and horses mating. Hence the Spanish-origin term *mullato* that was long used to describe the children of Black and White parents.

Not all the writings were theoretical. Empirical studies were also conducted to "prove" the apparent divisions were meaningful and substantive. One such study by the eighteenth-century Dutch scholar Petrus Camper, measured the slope of the faces of Greco-Roman statues (seen as the ideal face), a European, a person from Asia, an African from Angola, and an orangutan. The slope of the skull was thought to be an indicator of cranial capacity, and hence, brain size and intelligence. The measurements from the incisor teeth to the prominent point of the forehead followed a hierarchy: the slope of the statues ranged from 85° to 100°, the European's 80°, the Asian's and Angolan's slopes were about 70°, and the orangutan's was 58°. While there is debate as to whether Camper meant his research to prove racial differences, readers of his work interpreted the findings as evidence of distinct racial sub-species (Meijer 1999).

The theories that divisions among humans were more significant than they really are varied widely. But all agreed that whiteness was a sign of biological advantage that entitled Europeans to positions of superiority.

The intent of this pseudo-research, or what today may be called "fake" research, was to justify the colonization of territories outside Europe and to reconcile enslavement during the period of the Enlightenment when the establishment of human rights as a core social value began. An ideology was needed to legitimate the contradiction between slavery and indentured servitude and the creation of the new European democracies, and science contributed by trying to prove that non-Europeans were biologically less than human, another species in fact, and could, therefore, be legally defined as chattel and treated inhumanely.

This research, which continued into the twentieth century (Box 6.1 provides an example of twentieth century racialized research), produced no proof that race was real apart from superficial differences such as skin tone, facial features, and hair

Box 6.1 Syphilis and Insanity

If you have taken a research methods class in sociology, or most any social or behavioral science, you probably learned about the Tuskegee Syphilis Study when discussing research ethics. This long-running research project, which lasted from 1932 to 1972 in Tuskegee, Alabama, is often cited as an example of scientists conducting studies on people without their consent and without providing remedies to the participants who were harmed by the study. What is less known, however, are the theoretical underpinnings of the infamous project and what the scientists were studying.

Syphilis is a common sexually transmitted bacterium that if untreated leads to grave, irreversible problems such as brain injury, cardiovascular damage, blindness, and death. If not treated, syphilis typically develops into two types—cardiac syphilis or neurosyphilis. Essentially the difference is where the bacterium settles. For some, it will land in the neurological system and cause brain and nerve damage, and for others, arteries and the heart are impaired.

Untreated neurosyphilis causes a wide range of psychiatric symptoms including cognitive impairment, personality disorders, delirium, hostility, confusion, disruption of their sleep–wake cycle, dysphoria, paranoia, hallucinations, expansive mood, and mania (Lin et al. 2014). As Lin stated, neurosyphilis "mimics almost all psychiatric disorders" (2014: 233).

Prior to the application of penicillin to treat the syphilis bacterium in the late 1940s, the disease was widespread throughout the world. Easily transmitted and often undiagnosed, syphilis was a major global health problem that was portrayed in western countries as an "unclean" disease common to the "lower classes" that often led to madness. Medical literature in early twentieth-century America reflected that image and portrayed African Americans as innately prone to the disease because of their supposed immoral and sexually iniquitous behavior.

The Tuskegee Study sought to follow the course of untreated syphilis in African American men to test the hypothesis that syphilis followed different courses in Blacks than Whites. Blacks were believed to be vulnerable to cardiac syphilis, whereas Whites were thought more likely to develop neurosyphilis. The reasoning behind this hypothesis, although sounding scientific, was derived from racist beliefs that Blacks were simple and lacked mental sophistication. Whites, on the other hand, were mentally sophisticated and carried the burden of creating and maintaining complex social, political, and financial institutions, making their neurological system, paradoxically, vulnerable to invasion of the disease. Having to handle the stress of modern life took its toll on the nervous system, so the reasoning went, and compromised Whites' resistance to the bacterium (Crenner 2012).

The Tuskegee Study, therefore, tested this theory by allowing African American men to enter the late stages of syphilis. If the test hypothesis were proven true that Blacks were more likely to develop cardiac syphilis, then it could be argued that Blacks were biologically incapable of participating in advanced "White society." The racist beginnings of the theory, not surprisingly, were linked to the exploitative treatment of people whom the scientists considered inferior. The study did not support the hypothesis but does raise another question regarding "caste delusion." Is racist ideology about the mental capabilities of racial and ethnic groups a delusion?

texture. These traits, we now know, are due to adaptations to climate and terrain, not taxonomic categories. Humans have a monogenic origin (we all have African beginnings), and the brain and other organs have no variability from one group to another, making us all equally human, thus contradicting and debunking racialized thinking.

The conclusion that all people are of one biological species, however, has not deterred many from perpetuating the belief that race is real. While race is not particularly meaningful biologically, except in some biomedical situations (e.g., Europeans are more susceptible to cystic fibrosis and sickle-cell anemia is more common among sub-Saharan Africans), the term is socially quite concrete. As the classical sociologist Thomas and Thomas stated in 1928, if people define situations as real, they are real in their consequences. This means that if people act on an idea (the actions are the consequences), then that idea becomes what is considered reality or the truth. This famous theorem suggests that reality is subjective and socially constructed. The concept of race is an excellent application of the Thomas theorem. Despite the biological vagaries of race, race is "real" because people act on the *notion* of race, and those actions have tangible consequences. Sociologist W. E. B. Du Bois argued over 100 years ago that race as a biological concept is often used to explain differences in people that are social and cultural.

Therefore, we can say that race is a biological term that has a sociological definition. Race is not a set of discrete categories of human groupings, but a continuum of traits, most of which are not important for understanding the capabilities or health of groups.

To close this discussion on race and ethnicity, we can conclude that the difference between race and ethnicity is not necessarily important. It is difficult to distinguish what is a racial or an ethnic group. People of the same race may have many different cultures, while people of the same ethnicity may have a wide range of physical qualities, including skin color. There are several Asian and Hispanic ethnicities, and the experiences of one group differ from another. Hispanic Americans from Cuba have different lives than those from Guatemala or Argentina. Hispanics can share racial qualities with and identify as Black or White, and mixed-race individuals have characteristics of two or more groups. European Whites have great ethnic variety and very noticeable physical differences, and there are many dark-skinned "Caucasoid" peoples in south and west Asia and north Africa.

Since race and ethnicity concepts do not necessarily constitute valid biological or cultural divisions, let's think of the terms in another way. Rather than the characteristics they possess, race and ethnicity are more about the relations between and among people (Smaje 2000). They are social markers and ways that we identify ourselves and others and frame our lived experiences. They are also the foundations of social hierarchies and authority structures. People with certain racial and ethnic characteristics are classified as "us," while others are deemed "them." Whenever we create an "other" or "them" or "outsider," we are assuming that out-group members are inherently different and perhaps inferior in some way. By definition, this is racism, an unsympathetic belief that human groups vary in physical, intellectual, and emotional constitution, and that these differences are detectable in behaviors, values, and the display of emotions. Racism is often accompanied by hostile discriminatory behavior.

Because the terms "race" and "ethnicity" are often vague and imprecise, we will use the term **ethnorace** to refer to groups that are socially recognized as possessing a distinct ethnic-specific identity and/or may share certain phenotype characteristics such as skin color that are socially relevant for identity and lived experience.

In addition, the word "minority" refers not to numerical population size but to a group's subordinate relationship to power. In sociology, there are many categories of minority group status, but in everyday usage, the term is usually directed toward ethnoracial groups. An ethnoracial group can be a minority and constitute over 50 percent of a population, as was the case in apartheid South Africa and many places in the US south.

This brief discussion of race and ethnicity is critical in understanding the sociology of mental health. The measurable differences in the mental health of race and ethnic groups are not attributed to intrinsic characteristics of the group. Instead, mental health disparities reflect inequalities in the relationships among the groups. As Smedley and Smedley (2012) state, the United States is a race-based society, and its social hierarchy is largely defined by race and ethnicity as it intersects with social class. People falling into the different ethnoracial categories are usually stereotyped and have differential access to adequate housing, education, wealth, power, and good health.

Differences in Mental Health Among Ethnoracial Groups

Establishing the differences in prevalence rates of psychological distress has proven to be a difficult task in sociological research. At first glance, it would seem that because many ethnoracial minorities are overrepresented in poverty, rates of mental illness would be higher than the White dominant authority ethnoracial group. Contrary to expectations, that is not generally the case; however, there are important dynamics that affect the circumstances of psychological distress among minority group members and differentiate their experiences from those of Whites.

Historically the study of the mental health of minority groups has yielded mixed results. Inadequate theories, definitions, and research techniques did not allow for consistency or accuracy in measuring mental health across ethnoracial group boundaries. Plus, ideology and racism often interfered with the work, making results further questionable. In the last several decades, however, bias has been reduced (but not necessarily eliminated) and methods have improved to the point that we now have a fairly clear picture on the mental well-being of most ethnoracial groups in the country.

Research now reliably finds that minority groups, despite their high rates of poverty, have about the same or in some cases lower rates of mental illness than Whites, with the exception of Puerto Ricans and American Indians. Chart 6.1 shows that rates for African Americans, Asian Americans, and Hispanics are lower than their White counterparts. Two groups, American Indians and Alaska Natives and individuals identifying as two or more races have particularly high rates, approaching one in four experiencing a psychological disorder in the past year. Of the three largest ethnoracial groups—Whites, Blacks, and Hispanics—Whites have the highest rate of serious mental disorders. For Whites, 4.3 percent reported a serious mental illness compared to 3.1 for African Americans and Hispanics (SAMHSA 2015). Hispanic adolescents, however, report the highest rates of depression symptoms and aggressive behavior (CDC 2017).

CHAPTER 6 Race and Ethnicity

CHART 6.1 Any Mental Illness in the Past Year Among Adults, by Race/Ethnicity, 2008–2012

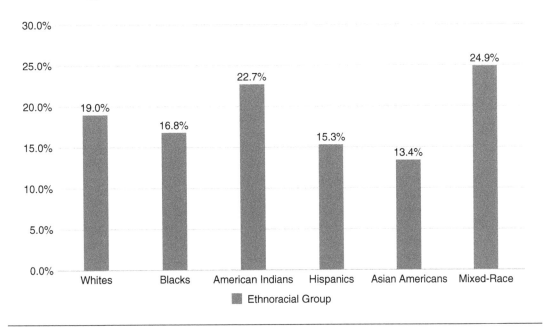

Source: Substance Abuse and Mental Health Services Administration (SAMHSA). 2015.

The aggregated statistics for all mental conditions appear to show a better picture than expected for minorities given their overrepresentation in poverty; the details, on the other hand, reveal hidden realities of the effects of a social hierarchy based on race and ethnicity.

Overall, over their lifetimes, African Americans are less likely to develop clinical levels of mood and anxiety disorders and substance abuse problems (Breslau et al. 2005). Their rates of depression in the last 12 months, however, are about the same as that of Whites (Ojeda and McGuire 2006). This is an important difference. It means that depression symptoms last longer for African Americans than for White Americans, and that is what the research has found. Disadvantaged ethnoracial groups have more persistent symptoms—their depressive episodes last longer than those experienced by Whites (Breslau et al. 2005; Ojeda and McGuire 2006).

Mental health statistics, as we saw in Chapter 4, often count cases that meet the clinical definitions of disorders specified in the DSM. These so-called "full-blown" cases satisfy the standards of the DSM but using DSM definitions as discreet categories does not allow for counting symptoms, just sets of symptoms. If we look solely at symptoms, African Americans report more than Whites (McGuire and Miranda 2008). These situations are known as **"sub-threshold"** conditions, which mean that indicators of the disorders are present but not at the level necessary to be assigned a DSM diagnosis. Despite not meeting DSM standards, the symptoms are of such severity that daily functioning is impaired.

In general, ethnoracial minorities are not at greater risk for psychiatric disorders but they have more persistent mental health problems. Because of the extended duration of psychological problems among disadvantaged minorities, the effects are often more severe (Williams et al. 2007).

Some research suggests that the diagnoses that mental health professionals assign to people presenting with psychological symptoms vary by ethnoracial groups. Whites are reported to have higher rates of depression, anxiety, panic disorder, and bipolar and mood disorders than African Americans and Hispanic groups. African Americans receive more diagnoses of conduct disorders, schizophrenia, psychotic disorders, behavioral disorders, and schizoaffective disorder, which are, in general, very serious. Compared to non-Hispanic Whites, Hispanics are more likely to receive diagnoses of "other" as well as behavioral and psychotic disorders (Bao et al. 2008; Hamilton et al. 2018; Maura and Weisman de Mamani 2017).

The veracity of these variations in diagnostic patterns is questionable. They may be an artifact of ethnoracial and social class bias in diagnosing rather than actual differences in how psychological distress is expressed (Blow et al. 2004). Unconscious bias may influence diagnosticians' interpretation of an out-group member's behavior, leading them to assign a more severe diagnosis or medicalize behavior that might be a normal response to prolonged stress. Differences in diagnoses could also be attributed to diagnostic tools that are insensitive to cultural differences (Peltier et al. 2017). Even with schizophrenia it is possible that African Americans are often over-diagnosed because of bias in interpreting their behavior (Blow et al. 2004). On the other hand, it may also be the case that symptoms presented by ethnoracial minorities are in fact more severe because of the additional stress burdens stemming from their minority position in society.

Discrimination and Mental Health

Racism has often been described as a public health problem and for good reason. Social inequality along ethnoracial lines foments physical and mental illnesses and restricts access to treatments to relieve them. Creating and maintaining unfair social organization exposes groups to numerous types of noxious conditions that increases the burden of both acute and chronic stress. The psychological distress brought on by discrimination takes the form of general unhappiness in life, lower self-esteem, and an erosion in people's mastery of their social environment (Williams et al. 2003). Taking into account the effect of discrimination likely explains the higher occurrence of distress of ethnoracial minorities.

Experiencing discrimination based on ethnoracial identity is a stressor that Whites do not face and explains why poor Blacks have greater psychological distress than poor Whites. Discriminatory, hostile acts are deeply personal, demeaning, and degrading, and they can have a lasting imprint on the minds of victims. Research is clear that discrimination based on ethnic and racial group membership damages mental well-being (Kessler et al. 1999).

Discriminatory events do not affect all victims the same. While anger is a common response to discrimination, some people do not react with that emotion. Older victims, for example, experience less anger perhaps because they are more likely to use religious support to manage their affective responses to hostile behavior (Head and Thompson 2017). For others, angry reactions to discrimination can lead to depression as internalized anger (Bridewell and Chang 1997), and the more episodes of discrimination people face, the more likely they are to react emotionally (Gayman and Barragan 2013; Grollman 2012). The depth of the psychological effects of discrimination is dependent upon a people's mastery over their lives and social environment. For people who have less such control, notably people in poverty, acts of discrimination have a larger effect, causing more psychological distress and elevated risks of depression (Miller et al. 2013).

Psychological responses to acts of discrimination generally take two usually intersecting symptomatic forms: **avoidance** and **intrusion** (Sanders Thompson 1996). After an event of ethnoracial hostility, victims often develop avoidance tendencies and try to avoid interactions that cause anxiety. Avoidance often includes feelings of numbness, blunted sensations, and a denial of the impact and meaning of the event. Intrusion describes how much the event "gets into one's head." Nightmares, repetitious behavior, and intrusive thoughts and images are typical of the effects of racist encounters. The type of racial experience is related to the level of intrusion symptoms: minor incidents have less effect than those rated as moderate or severe, and symptoms tended to decrease over time. Avoidance symptoms, however, increase with time. It bears mentioning that avoidance and intrusion are comparable to the symptoms of PTSD.

Ethnoracial discrimination among adolescent peers is particularly harmful. Taunting, racial slurs, physical assaults, and social exclusion are some of the ways in which children hurt minority peers. Childhood episodes of bias and hostility affect important developmental areas such as identity, peer acceptance, self-concept, and emerging abstract reasoning (Hughes et al. 2016).

Observing the experiences of immigrants is another way to see the effects of discrimination on the mental health of ethnoracial minorities. Cultural diversity is largely derived from historical and continued immigration into the country, and the mental health of new arrivals to the country is often affected by three factors: stressful conditions in their home country, stress conditions during travel and entry into the United States, and their experiences after being in the country. For the most part, foreign-born Americans have lower rates of mental disorders than people who are born in the United States (Gee et al. 2006). Despite whatever conditions pushed them to leave their native lands, they arrive here appearing mentally healthy. Unfortunately, as immigrants spend more time in the country, their psychological troubles mount and the more their mental health profile begins to look like that of the general population, especially for people of African origin (Gee et al. 2006).

Discrimination likely causes the gradual erosion of immigrants' mental health. Initially new Black immigrants may be treated better than their US born peers, but those benefits diminish over time (Read and Emerson 2005). Gee and associates (2006) studied immigrants from Africa and several Latin American countries and found that the mental health of African émigrés eroded faster than that of Hispanic immigrants because they experienced more episodes of discrimination. The longer they lived in the United States, the more symptomatic they were. This effect was found among Somali immigrants even when controlling for any trauma they encountered in their home country or in their voyage to reach the United States (Ellis et al. 2008).

A similar effect was found among Korean immigrants. Overt racial discrimination such as being hit or insulted was tied to negative affect, but more subtle expressions of racial hostility caused the most psychological damage (Noh et al. 2007). Subtle acts of racism, such as being ignored or denied service, are highly intimidating and often lead to feelings of powerlessness and helplessness. When treated this way, people often become confused and commence to questioning whether they belong in their new home. It is no surprise then that repeated episodes of subtle discrimination are associated with depressive symptoms and frustration.

Special Circumstances Within Groups

The discussion thus far has focused on general issues influencing the mental health patterns of ethnoracial minorities and how they relate to social practices of discrimination and authority. While the mental health dynamics of several groups have been mentioned, we have not yet discussed those groups in detail. This section reviews how these processes have affected four major ethnoracial minority groups. The discussion will center on the **minority stress model**, which contends that social disadvantages translate into health disparities.

The main idea of the minority stress theory is that lower and stigmatized social status exposes minority groups to more stressful life circumstances and fewer social and economic resources to manage them (Schwartz and Meyer 2010). Review Chart 6.2 which compares three ethnoracial groups, poverty status, and depression

CHART 6.2 **Percent of Persons Aged 12 and Over With Depression, by Poverty Status and Race and Hispanic Origin**

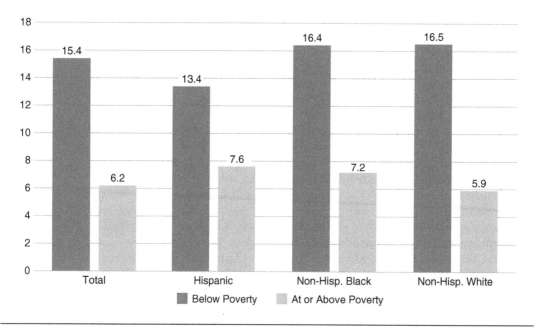

Source: Pratt and Brody (2014).

rates. It is easy to see that poverty has a strong impact on the likelihood of becoming depressed in all three groups. Notice, however, that being at or above the poverty line has a more injurious effect on ethnoracial minorities than on non-Hispanic Whites, which suggests that economic stability does not offset the social stresses ethnoracial minorities experience.

American Indians and Native Alaskans

The indigenous peoples of the western hemisphere migrated to North and South American 16,000 to 20,000 years ago. American Indians and Native Alaskans (AINA) are the original peoples of the present United States and comprise scores of ethnicities and national or tribal identities. They have great linguistic and cultural diversity, and prior to the arrival of Europeans in the late fifteenth century, were organized as independent and sovereign nations, with sophisticated social institutions. Many developed great empires with advanced cities and sciences.

All the indigenous nations fell to the invading Europeans. It is generally believed that most AINA peoples died in battle trying to defend themselves against the colonizers, but the large majority perished because of the lack of "herd immunity" against diseases such as influenza, pneumonic plague, and smallpox that the Europeans carried to the "new world." Contacting these diseases almost always resulted in death. Advanced military weaponry, disease, and a governmental policy of genocide brought on the destruction of native peoples and their cultures. In time, the government relocated most survivors to reservations that were often lands with little economic value and void of spiritual significance.

AINA peoples have continued to be subject to forced erosions of their traditional cultures and languages. Living in places that are so remote that economic viability is unlikely (some still lack necessities such as electricity) and jobs are scarce, AINA carry a high load of extreme poverty. Western education is often forced on their children, erasing their language and traditional beliefs and practices, and leading them to question or reject their culture's values and lifestyle. Social forces working against native cultures fuel social disintegration and tribal disunity. They also promote psychological fragmentation.

Nicholas Guittar aptly stated that "one of the major inhibitors of social, physical, and mental well-being for all Native Americans is the extensive discrimination that the different indigenous nations have encountered over the past 500 years" (2012: 238). The evidence supports his statement. Based on the continuing history of bias and structured disadvantages, American Indians and Native Alaskans are more likely than any other ethnoracial group in the United States to experience mental distress (Barnes et al. 2010). Early childhood disorders do not differ from the population at large, but beginning at ages 10 to 20, studies report extraordinarily high rates of emotional difficulties, delinquency, and drug and alcohol abuse, which are consequences of the accumulation of stress over time.

AINA have disproportionately high rates of psychological distress and depression in particular. Over one in four AINA experience psychological distress, and they have the highest rate of depression within the last year (12.1 percent). AINA adolescents have an estimated lifetime depression prevalence of 13.3 percent, and their rate within the last year is 9.3 percent (SAMHSA 2007). Depressive symptoms and aggressive behavior among American Indians are strongly associated with perceived discrimination and anger stemming from disadvantaged social conditions (Hartshorn et al. 2012; Whitbeck et al. 2002).

American Indian and Native Alaskan communities also witness a very high rate of suicide. In fact, AINA have the highest suicide rate of all ethnoracial groups in the United States. Using data from the CDC, the National Indian Council on Aging (2019) reports that since 1999, the suicide rate has increased by 139 percent for American Indians and 71 percent among Alaska Natives, compared to 33 percent for the US population at large. Suicide is the second leading cause of death for Native youths aged 10 to 24 and is 2.5 times higher than the overall national average. Suicide attempts are about the same for those living on and off reservations, but successful suicides are higher on reservations (Freedenthal and Stiffman 2004).

For all American Indians, alcohol use occurs at about the same rate as Whites and Hispanics; however, among some tribal communities, alcohol use and abuse are particularly high (Cheadle and Whitbeck 2011). In their study of native peoples living on eight somewhat remote and impoverished American and Canadian reservations, Cheadle and Whitbeck found that adolescents began drinking earlier than the population in general and progressed more rapidly to regular alcohol use. About 20 percent began drinking at ages 11 and 12. Another 20 percent began shortly thereafter. About 17 percent of youths who abstained from drinking before age 15 later showed signs of problem drinking. The authors of this study concluded that problem drinking stems from perceived discrimination and parents' own depression, both of which were also associated with persistent anger and negative attitudes about school.

Other problems that AINA peoples face at higher rates than other groups are alcohol related accidents, domestic and intimate partner violence, and homicide. These problems are the result of the anger, depression, and frustration caused by isolation, economic futility, political disenfranchisement, and the degradation of traditional culture. That last factor, cultural degradation, is critical in understanding the mental health of American Indians. Depression is more likely for those who as children attended boarding schools, which were designed to force acculturation and assimilation on native children, and for those who think about their loss of traditions, language, and religion (Walls and Whitbeck 2011). A remedy for depression and other psychosocial problems among American Indians may lie in reviving their traditional culture to develop a strong sense of ethnic identity.

African Americans

If the protests against institutional racism that occurred during the turbulent year 2020 taught us anything, they provided a lesson about the psychological costs of persistent and excessive discrimination on the collective psyche of a people. The public heard heartfelt messages of African Americans' fears of walking in their neighborhoods and of being killed by police officers or by rogue community "enforcers" of some rule or law. Suddenly the anxieties caused by simply being African Americans in a racist place became one of the main subjects of political and social discourse.

The novel coronavirus of 2020 further exposed African Americans' disproportional vulnerability to national emergencies. There is a saying that "when America gets a cold, African Americans get the flu," and COVID-19 is a case in point. African Americans were diagnosed with and died from COVID-19 at almost twice the rate of Whites and disproportional to their share of the population. The increased probability for COVID-19 was not related to anything inherent in biology; rather, it was a function of inequality. African Americans

- hold disproportionately more low paying jobs, such as bus drivers, janitors, food service workers, and cashiers that put them in greater contact with the general public;
- are more likely to live in poverty, which puts them at risk for other health problems that can increase the severity of COVID-19;
- are less likely than Whites to have health insurance;
- are more likely to live in neighborhoods that have more pollution and fewer adequate social services.

We have long known about the hazards of "driving while Black" or "talking while Black," but in 2020, we began to see the cumulative psychological effects of being reported to police for taking a nap on a university campus couch, having police called on a birdwatcher in a city park, and a restaurant owner calling police to remove a woman whom she claimed was harassing her child, which video evidence did not confirm. For African Americans, the list goes on and on.

The year 2020 will also be remembered as the year in which symbolic reminders of White entitlement began to be removed from public places. Monuments started falling, and even the state flag of Mississippi, the last official state emblem endorsing Confederate sympathies, was approved for redesign.

Attempts to control African Americans through intimidation, violence, and poverty are as old as the country itself. Today's violence against African Americans is a continuation of the institution of slavery and its aftermath of Jim Crow segregation. Perhaps with the exception of Jews, no other people in history have been victim of persistent injustice and violence for more centuries than people of African descent. African Americans have long known the psychological distress derived from slavery, segregation, discrimination, and violence. Only now does mainstream society seem to be awakening to the psychological impact this history has had.

Whites' thoughts on the mental health of African Americans date to slavery times. Prior to 1865, many White physicians associated Black mental illness with slavery. John Galt, director of the Eastern Lunatic Asylum in Virginia, contended in 1848 that Blacks were immune to mental illness because they did not engage in the rigors of western society—owning property, plying in commerce, or participating in civic duties such as voting or holding political office. Slaves were believed to be free from stress and had no reason to become depressed or anxious or insane (Umeh 2019).

Other nineteenth-century physicians, however, disagreed and saw people of African descent as capable of mental illness, but were subject to only three disorders. One was a general insanity, which was either a developmental disorder or schizophrenia in today's terms. The other two conditions, however, were uniquely applied to Black slaves. The first was drapetomania, an attempt to medicalize the desire to escape involuntary servitude. The word was derived from Greek roots roughly meaning "runaway slave" and "crazy." In creating drapetomania—"the disease causing Negroes to run away"—a southern physician named Samuel Cartwright sought to identify a rational explanation for Blacks attempting to flee the insanity of slavery. Here is the first paragraph of his 1851 article:

The cause in the most of cases, that induces the negro to run away from service, is as much a disease of the mind as any other species of mental alienation, and much more curable, as a general rule. With the advantages of proper medical advice, strictly followed, this troublesome practice that many negroes have of running away, can be almost entirely prevented, although the slaves be located on the borders of a free state, within a stone's throw of the abolitionists.

The medical advice he recommended was "whipping the devil out of them."

The second paragraph of the short article articulated the ideology behind the racial hierarchy and described Whites' religious duty to keep Africans and their descendants in their Biblically ordained place of forced servitude. Freeing slaves, he said, violated God's will.

A second "disorder" assigned to slaves was *dysaethesia aethiopica* which was also "discovered" by Cartwright (1851) who described it as follows:

It differs from every other species of mental disease, as it is accompanied with physical signs or lesions of the body discoverable to the medical observer, which are always present and sufficient to account for the symptoms. It is much more prevalent among free negroes living in clusters by themselves, than among slaves on our plantations, and attacks only such slaves as live like free negroes in regard to diet, drinks, exercise, etc. It is not my purpose to treat of the complaint as it prevails among free negroes, nearly all of whom are more or less afflicted with it, that have not got some white person to direct and to take care of them.

Two clarifications of Cartwright's description of this so-called disorder are needed. First, the "physical lesions" he refers to as markers of the condition were scars caused by vicious lashings. Second, the primary "presentation" of *dysaethesia aethiopica* was a state of dullness, lethargy, and an unwillingness to work. In reality he most likely was diagnosing either depression associated with their past or present social standing as slaves or passive resistance to slavery. It never occurred to him or other similar thinkers that running away or being "work shy" were normative responses to the brutality and indignity of slavery.

After slavery ended, a Dr. T. O. Powell, the head of an asylum in Georgia in 1895, saw (in his mind) an alarmingly high rate of insanity among Blacks which he attributed to Blacks' prolonged freedom. He believed that Blacks could not handle the rigors of White society. Slavery forced Blacks to control their passions and appetites, which were assumed licentious and generally immoral. With freedom, these passions were also unbound and led former slaves to various vices and excesses that, in turn, caused insanity (Umeh 2019).

Finally, African Americans were more likely to be subjects of the American eugenics movement, which began in earnest in the 1920s and continued until the 1970s. Eugenics programs are attempts to control the genetic makeup of a population by sterilizing or even murdering people who are believed unfit to reproduce. In many states, Black women were more likely sterilized without consent than women or men of any other group. In California in the 1930s, African Americans comprised only one percent of the population, but made up four percent of sterilizations, and in the 1960s in North Carolina, 85% of sterilized women were Black (Umeh 2019).

The accumulation of stressors due to persistent discrimination account for African Americans having more symptoms, a condition often referred to as racial trauma. During the 2020 protests, news media reported that African American psychotherapists were inundated with calls from people seeking treatment for heightened anxiety due to racism. Racial trauma appears similar to PTSD, and signs include irritability, low self-esteem, difficulty concentrating, hopelessness, anxiety, and depression (Murray 2020). The ubiquity of racist encounters is extraordinary. English and colleagues (2020) found that Black adolescents encountered just over five experiences of racial discrimination every day.

Hispanics

The Hispanic population of the United States is a rich amalgam of nationally distinct cultures from Spain, Mexico, the Caribbean, and Central and South America. Hispanic peoples have immigrated to the United States for hundreds of years. Though most Hispanics and their ancestors settled in the United States after World War II, many Spanish-speaking people were living "north of the border" before the United States was founded. Parts of the country, including Texas, the southwest, California, and Puerto Rico, were part of the Spanish Empire, but started joining the United States when the Republic of Texas was annexed in 1845.

Hispanic groups have been subject to intense discriminatory practices for over a century. Some of the worst ethnoracial violence has taken place along the southern border in Texas as vigilante groups, the military, and Texas law enforcement officers routinely engaged in terroristic attacks against Mexican Americans. The most telling event was the destruction of the Texas village Porvenir, which was burned to the ground in 1918 after the Texas Rangers, ranchers, and US cavalry soldiers rounded up all the men, some as young as 16 and as old as 72, and massacred them in cold blood. The women and younger children fled to Mexico. A century later in 2019, anti-Hispanic rhetoric led to the killing of 23 innocent shoppers in an El Paso store. Twenty-three others were wounded. Violence, derogatory images, exclusion, and denial of access to social advantages (employment, education, and housing) have confronted Hispanics for decades so that now, Hispanics tend to live in poor housing and in neighborhoods with inadequate public services and high crime.

Hispanic peoples constitute the second largest ethnoracial group in the United States, but the largest group proportionally with limited English proficiency. Compared to other immigrants, Hispanics retain their native language and cultural traditions longer than most other groups. This group's cultural retention has both positive and injurious implications for mental health—in some ways maintaining native culture provides psychological benefits, but in others, doing so can marginalize and estrange people from mainstream societal opportunities.

As stated earlier, given their over-representation in poverty, Hispanics have lower than expected rates of psychological disorders. Several protective features may account for lower rates of distress. Perhaps the most important is the strong personal relationships most Hispanic cultures emphasize among family and friends. Family remains the central social organization in the lives of most Latinos and Latinas, and the deep sense of connectedness to kinfolk offsets social forces such as poverty that may push people toward depression and anxiety. Second, many Hispanics have maintained a strong attachment to the Catholic Church and its emphasis on collective worship and rituals, which work to provide a sense of belongingness and social support that facilitate coping with hard times. Because of their connectedness to their cultures, the mental health of Hispanic immigrants appears to be stronger than native-born Hispanics and non-Hispanics.

Despite these generally good indicators, the incidence of psychological problems may be rising, especially among Hispanic youth (Piña-Watson et al. 2019), and the mental health of immigrants, as we saw earlier, does not necessarily remain high once they have been in the country for a few years.

As mentioned, the mental health of Hispanics is believed to benefit from the community's strong orientation toward family or **familism**. Being embedded in family relationships provides the social support necessary to cope with life's difficulties, find a sense of identity and purpose, and, simply, to love and feel loved. However, familism may not contribute to Hispanic mental health as much as previously thought (Diaz and Niño 2019). There are many ways to be attached to family, and some are more beneficial than others. Among Hispanic families, according to Diaz and Niño's study, when people think that they should strictly follow their family's expectations, a process known as referent familism, their mental health is likely to suffer. Feeling pressure to conform to family rules limits self-expression and causes conflict between individual desires and family demands.

Much of the mental health problems experienced by Latinas and Latinos in the United States stems from their status as a minority group. Hispanics are confronted by "**double jeopardy**," a situation in which a person is a target of discrimination based on two statuses. In the case of Hispanics, being darker skinned and Spanish-speaking makes them targets them of discriminatory behavior. The effects of persistent exposure to unequal education and employment, unequal treatment by the judicial system, and interpersonal microaggressions build over time and result in perceived powerlessness or feeling out of control of their social environments

(Mirowsky and Ross 2012). Depression and anxiety symptoms for many Hispanics, especially people of Mexican descent, often follow.

This process is also applicable to Hispanic immigrants. Ornelas and Perreira (2011) classify three categories of stress for Hispanic newcomers to the United States. First, pre-migration experiences can be predictors of psychological distress. The decision to leave one's home country is usually based on economic hardships, political turmoil, or the desire to reunite with one's family already in the United States. Those migrants who in their home countries experienced trauma or were impoverished with low education are susceptible to depressive symptoms in the United States. Second, the experience of migration can be extraordinarily stressful. The trip to the United States exposes emigres to risks of assault, robbery, sexual abuse, arrest, and exploitation, all of which are stress inducing. Those who endured a more stressful trek to the United States are five times more likely to develop symptoms of depression than those who had a relatively easier trip. Third, post-migration experiences of discrimination, economic hardships, and the absence of family are further sources of stress. These stressors build up and increase with residency, leading to more symptoms of depression, which are exacerbated by the unavailability of Spanish-speaking mental health professionals.

The precarious position in which many Hispanics live exposes them to other stressors that negatively impact mental health. For example, the enforcement of immigration policies is a source of stress that affects Latinos and Latinas and their families (Vargas et al. 2019). Deportation affects personal safety and stokes anxiety and fear among Hispanics from Mexico and Central America and creates chronic stress within the community. Most Hispanics in the United States know an undocumented immigrant, and many know someone who has been detained or deported. As Vargas and associates found, simply knowing a deportee leads to mental health problems.

Finally, one key question regarding the mental well-being of Hispanics concerns acculturation, which refers to the process of assimilating into and adopting a culture different than one's own. Are Hispanic immigrants better off psychologically if they assimilate into the dominant Anglo culture? Research suggests that neither full assimilation nor cultural marginalization promote mental health. Instead, biculturalism appears to be the best barrier to psychological problems. Understanding the dominant culture and English proficiency translate into being able to better negotiate school and work environments and increase accessibility to medical and mental health care services (Gonzalez et al. 2001). Biculturalism also provides a social and ethnoracial identity and an attachment to a person's ethno-history and cultural rituals, celebrations, and cultural tastes.

Asian Americans

While realizing it is not a particularly valid descriptor, the term "Asian Americans" is one that sociologists are sometimes forced to use for statistical purposes. The social and cultural diversity within this category is broad and includes South Asians from India and Sri Lanka, East Asians from China, Japan, and Korea, and Laotians, Vietnamese, and Cambodians from Southeast Asia, among many others.

These ethnic groups have great differences in both the cultures of their ancestral homes and their experiences in the United States. Plus, many people of Asian origin can trace their American lineage to the early and mid-1800s, longer than many Americans of European ancestry.

Like other ethnoracial groups, since their arrival in the United States, Asian Americans have experienced often violent discrimination. Two historical examples typify Asians' relationship to dominant culture: the Chinese Exclusion Act of 1882, which barred immigration from China, and the internment of Japanese Americans during World War II because the government assumed, and incorrectly so, that these American citizens would be loyal to their ethnic origins rather than the United States. Parenthetically, the loyalty of Americans of German descent was not similarly questioned. During the COVID-19 pandemic, incidences of discrimination and violence targeting Asian Americans skyrocketed as members of this community were scapegoated and blamed for the disease.

Asian Americans are subject to minority-related stress, though it sometimes works differently than among other ethnoracial minorities. Stacey Lee (2009) theorizes that Asians, even those who are fifth generation Americans, are often viewed as "perpetual foreigners." Lee, an Asian American who was born in California to parents born in Massachusetts and Mississippi, is often asked "where do you come from?" When she says California, the question then becomes "where do you *really* come from?" Asians are often seen as outsiders living in the margins but stereotyped as coming from strong families and good cultures (Lee 2009).

Because of the educational and economic success of several Asian ethnic groups, the homogenous identity of Asian Americans is often saluted as the so-called "**model minority**." This label began in the 1960s and targeted Chinese and Japanese who were singled out as good citizens. In reality, these two groups probably were lauded because they were seen as "quiet, uncomplaining, and hard-working who achieved success without depending on the government" (Lee 2009: 12).

The idea of the model minority, however, has proven to be a destructive concept because it conceals real social problems among some of the groups included under the Asian American umbrella. While some "model minorities" may appear to be doing well, their experiences prove otherwise. For example, as groups, Asian Indians, Japanese, Chinese, and Koreans have succeeded economically and educationally in the United States. Other groups have not fared as well, as noted in Table 6.1.

Asian immigrants who came to the United States after World War II were mostly highly educated professionals, but subsequent immigrants, particularly those coming from Southeast Asia following the conclusion of the Vietnam War, were poorer, not well educated, and had primarily worked as farmers in their home countries. The assumption of high achievement conceals the broad spectrum of social and psychological experiences these groups have faced since arriving in the United States and masks chronic racism and discrimination.

The model minority image suggests a Pan-Asian ethnic identity, but mental health differences illustrate the dangers of the myth because problems often go unnoticed. Korean and Vietnamese Americans experience considerably more depression and anxiety than their Chinese and Japanese peers. Southeast Asians,

TABLE 6.1 Southeast Asian Americans and Education and Poverty, 25 Years of Age and Older

	No High School	In Poverty
Cambodians	53%	30%
Hmong	60%	38%
Laotians	50%	19%

Source: Lee (2009).

notably the Hmong and Lao, have high rates of PTSD (Africa and Carrasco 2011), and Filipinos have a higher likelihood of depression than the general US population (David 2008).

Feelings of perpetual foreignness may account for some of the variation. Identity conflicts and a loss of their ethnoracial character are associated with depression and problematic behaviors among Asian Americans (Vaghela and Uemo 2017). This conflict may explain Asian American youths having more mental health problems, more suicidal thoughts and attempts, and lower self-esteem than White youths (Africa and Carrasco 2011; Bachman et al. 2011).

A second area of concern is parents' rigorous expectations of educational achievements and occupational success, which is often associated with children's mental health problems. Chinese and Vietnamese young adults, as Lee and Zhou (2015) show, find their parents' "success frame" of having to be the best at everything very stressful. In addition to school and work performance, in her study of Korean, Chinese, and Taiwanese Americans, Chung (2017) found that second-generation young adults often struggle with their familial expectations on marriage, family, and culture, which conflict with their personal aspirations. The tension is particularly strong for young women who publicly may act in traditional ways, but privately pursue conflicting personal goals. Chung cited the example of women who are expected to hold in their emotions, marry within the ethnic group, carry on the family name, and devote themselves to a caretaking role often at the expense of their personal aspirations. Cognitive and emotional dissonance often follow, causing feelings of guilt, regret, and inner turmoil.

Warikoo and colleagues (2020), however, warn not to rely on simplistic explanations of Asian American families. Although some studies find that intensive pressure on children to excel causes psychological distress, Warikoo's study compared Asian and White families on parenting style in addition to parental expectations and found that "intensive parenting" has the same impact on children in both ethnoracial groups. In families where the bonds between parents and children are emotionally strong and unconflicted, children are less affected by the intensive success demands. Where there is conflict between parents and their children, the children have more stress-related emotional and behavioral complications, though the two groups responded slightly differently. Asian girls tend to internalize symptoms (become anxious or depressed) at about the same rate as White girls but externalize (engage in rule-breaking or aggressive behavior) them less. Asian boys, on the other hand, became anxious or depressed more than their White peers, but exhibit troublesome behavior about the same as Whites.

Differences in psychological distress also differ among the elderly. Because of seemingly constant losses in their lives, depression is not uncommon for people over 70. However, depression among the elderly varies by social group. Elder Chinese and Japanese Americans are less likely to become depressed than non-Hispanic Whites, but Asian Indian Americans have high rates of geriatric depression, second only to American Indians and Pacific Islanders (Hooker et al. 2019). Depression among elderly Asian Indians, especially immigrant women, is likely due to assimilation and adjustment troubles and the loss of family and kin networks that makes life lonely and unrewarding.

About the Quote

Over the last several years, several well-known actors and sports figures were caught on video making atrociously overt racist statements. Their behavior was highly publicized, and their employers and the public responded with great indignation. For some, the incidences shortened their careers, and as labeling theory would predict, their names became connected to their deviant acts. Of the more famous cases, the athletes were ordered to undergo psychotherapy and two of the actors publicly announced they would seek psychiatric care to learn the origins of their beliefs and ways to improve themselves. Is this an attempt to redefine racism as psychopathology?

As this chapter shows, dominate scientific views during the nineteenth and twentieth centuries argued that racism against Blacks, Jews, and other minorities were common. Scientists largely accepted it as fact that these groups were in a powerless position because they were biologically inferior and vulnerable to mental illness because they could not cope with the rigors of modern society. But as Gilman and Thomas (2016: 225) wrote, "the shift from seeing *race* through the lens of medical science to seeing *racism* through the lens of medical science was and remains a contested one."

Racism (and classism, sexism, ageism, and all other forms of prejudice) is not rooted in individual psychopathologies but in the social conditions of power, competition, and historically devaluing and dehumanizing the "other." Racism implies the social transmission of a set of beliefs that some groups are inferior while others are superior. But with science now confirming that a biological basis of racist ideologies is false, it could be argued that acceptance of those beliefs constitutes a delusion. Chapter 5 introduced the idea of caste delusion. Is racism different?

This is an important question, but it should not be confused with *the* question about the origins of racism.

Racism, like caste-ism and classism, is a macro-level social dynamic with psychological consequences for both perpetrator and victim. For perpetrators, racist beliefs are indicators of a state of mind characterized by anger, insecurity, and the need to control and manipulate others. For victims, persistent discrimination creates a psychological hole in people. It represents the damage done by fear, unfairness, and a lack of opportunity. That African Americans have more and more persistent symptoms of depression and anxiety but less clinical depression than non-Hispanic Whites is not surprising. One theory is that because the forces that cause so much of their stress are imposed on them economically and politically, African Americans externalize their anger rather turning it inwards as White Americans do, since Whites cannot blame "society" for their problems.

The psychological aspects of racism are excellent examples of the relationship between social organization and processes and their impact on individual well-being, and Frederick Douglass realized that fact well over a century ago.

DISCUSSION QUESTIONS

1. The idea that racism constitutes a culturally conditioned delusion in intriguing. Do delusions have to be ideographic or unique to an individual or can they be collectively shared? If racist beliefs fit the definition of a delusion, it would radically change definitions of mental illness. What do you think?

2. How would you design a study to explore the relationship between experienced discrimination and mental health? What variables would you include, and how would you measure them? What methodological steps are necessary to connect being a victim of discriminatory acts and emotional, cognitive, and behavioral outcomes?

KEY TERMS

Avoidance 127
Double Jeopardy 134
Ethnicity 119
Ethnorace 123

Familism 134
Intrusion 127
Minority Stress Model 128
Model Minority 136

Race 119
Sub-threshold Symptoms 125

CHAPTER 7

Mental Health and Gender

Learning Objectives

After reading this chapter, students will be able to:

1. Summarize the concept of essentialism as a social process that underlies gender patterns in the distribution of mental illness.
2. Outline and analyze gender patterns in the presentation of mental illness.
3. Compare the two theories of gender and emotions.
4. Contrast gendered role expectations and how they influence mental health among men and women.
5. Recognize social factors that increase an individual's vulnerability of developing depression.

Many suburban housewives were taking tranquilizers like cough drops.

—Betty Friedan (1963)

Introduction

Not that long ago, the concepts of **sex** and **gender** were uncomplicated. Sex referred to biological differences in human males and females, and gender represented the social, psychological, political, and economic implications of those differences. Each term was binary: male and female, masculine and feminine. While we have long known that gender operates as a continuum, it was still largely thought that femininity generally was contained *within* the boundaries of the female category and masculinity within the male.

Now we know otherwise. Neither sex nor gender is a stagnant, dualistic concept. Our society has moved dramatically fast in recent years to accept the idea that gender and sex are as socially defined as they are biologically, and, therefore, relative to perspective. Traditional beliefs have attempted to medicalize deviations from the binary, as in the case of homosexuality's placement in the earliest versions of the DSM, but that movement is challenged by opposing paradigms. Pronouns are now self-proclaimed rather than imposed by a binary-thinking society. Women's athletics have never been more popular, and beauty pageants are dismissed by many as crass objectification. Same-sex legal and common law marriages are recognized in 30 countries, and transgendered people have argued that even biological sex itself is a construction of meaning, self-identity, and choice. Clearly the old binary rules and perceptions of sex and gender are evolving. We are realizing that gender is a social construction, and that sexuality and gender are fluctuating, fluid, and continuous rather than discrete (Lorber 1994).

Physical differences in sex, except for reproductive systems, are not discrete, but occur *on average*. Men are only slightly better at spatial reasoning and worse at impulse control and are bigger, faster, and stronger only on average. Women are, on average, better at emotional intelligence, verbal ability, perceptual speed, and fine-motor coordination (Goldman 2017), while boys and men demonstrate better gross motor performance because of their bone density and muscle mass advantages (e.g., they can throw a ball farther and harder). Men and women are far more alike than different physiologically. Where there are differences, they exist along a bell curve, and the greatest variations are found only on the ends of those curves.

Psychological differences between sexes are also non-existent or minor. As Janet Shibley Hyde (2005) found, variations *within* gender groups are greater than differences *between* gender groups. On variables such as aggression, facial expression processing, leadership, consciousness, and self-esteem, among others, differences between genders are either nil or of small significance (Hyde 2005).

Physiological and psychological differences, however, are often exaggerated to explain seemingly everything about sex and gender. Men and women do tend to express psychological distress differently. Women trend toward affective disorders and men toward behavioral disorders. But again, only on average: men become depressed and experience anxiety disorders, and women develop chemical dependency and personality disorders.

Here we must distinguish between brain and mind. We cannot yet confirm a biological hypothesis of women's vulnerability to depression. Hormones may account for situational conditions such as postnatal depression (the "baby blues"), but they and other physiological factors have not been determined as a cause of full-blown affective disorders such as major depression, and arguments for physiological causes for alcoholism or drug addiction are not fully convincing (Pescosolido et al. 2008). Nonetheless, expressions of depression tend to cluster by sex, but currently it is difficult to determine if biological factors represent the origins of depression, its consequences, or function in an interaction with social conditions.

What we know for certain is that the thoughts that run through people's minds are a result of psychosocial experiences, which usually chart different paths for males and females. Our focus is on the gendered experiences of men and women and how they affect mental health. The evidence here is strong, and as Angst (2010) says, biological psychiatric knowledge on sex differences is of little significance clinically for early recognition or treatment of depression.

Our focus in this chapter is how the social environment contributes to the gendered nature of mental illness. Symptoms of mental illness are not randomly distributed in the population. The gendered patterns of symptoms and diagnoses are stark, and research has identified several psychosocial conditions in which these patterns are likely to emerge. As we did in the last two chapters, let's first do some sociological table-setting to see the social forces that may play a role in the gendered social patterns of mental illness.

Essentialism

Gender inequality pervades all levels of social interaction. National policies, institutional practices, group dynamics, and interpersonal relationships and interactions all are influenced by the sexual composition of the group and the norms that govern how people relate to one other. Gender is a strong social force and sexism, discrimination based on perceived sex or gender, is evident throughout society. Here are a few pertinent examples.

Women are more likely than men to:

- receive less pay for doing the same job and face the "glass ceiling" of economic opportunity;
- become the victim of domestic violence and abuse;
- be minimized or dismissed in group settings;
- receive unsolicited or unwanted sexual advances and comments about their appearance;
- deal with a "double standard" as people interpret their assertiveness and sexuality;
- be subject to violent but normative expectations such as genital mutilation, honor killing, female infanticide, and sex-selective abortion;
- become spoils of war where rape is used as a strategic weapon against an enemy.

Discrimination against women is pervasive and often blatantly open. There are many theories addressing the origins and perpetuation of gender inequality, some are biological, and others come from psychological and sociological perspectives. This is not the time to address them, but there is one thread of commonality that seems to run through all the theories and has relevance for mental health—**essentialism**.

The core notion of essentialism is that foundational, physiological differences between males and females guide and direct the psychological and behavioral orientation of individuals and the gendered structure of the social order. Essentialism, therefore, suggests the presence of a metaphorical "gender gene" that implies a biological determinism to temperament, ability, values, emotions, and social position. Essentialism proposes universal claims about all women and men—that each group possesses its own qualities, reactions, and experiences.

Essentialism may best be thought of as a verb: to essentialize the "other." It means to create and impose the idea that men and women have unique and intrinsic physiological characteristics that imply and influence social and psychological traits, aptitudes, propensities, and capabilities. Despite the absence of biological evidence that would account for such essentialist conclusions, some segments of virtually all societies will define males and females *as if* they are substantially disparate and even contradictory to one another in their humanness.

Therefore, essentialism exists as a socially defining ideology that differentially and externally guides the life chances and behavioral expectations of males and females. Present evidence contradicts inherent "femaleness" or "maleness" in humans, and that implies that essentialism is a socially constructed artifact of a power structure that enables men but restricts opportunities for women. Too emotional, too ignorant, or too unreliable, women subjected to essentialist beliefs are defined as inapt in the "man's world." In this ideology, women do not have the wherewithal to compete or meet the physical and intellectual demands asked of males. Essentialist qualities may or may not be inherent, but they are certainly imposed.

Ultimately essentialism focuses on perceptions of the natural body, and perceptions of gendered bodies become the basis of gender inequality (Shilling 2012). More to the point, Foucault argued that the body, or physical self, is an unfixed, malleable object in which power is invested; power controls individuals through the conception of the human body. The very idea of "the body" is produced by social forces that identify bodies as having certain social meanings, regardless of any biological constitution, limitation, or proclivity. The body, therefore, is a biological phenomenon that has a sociological definition, and, as a social object, it is endowed with social meaning, complete with definitions of social opportunities and limits.

As "society" identifies the biological sex, it simultaneously recognizes the limits of acceptable behavior for that sex. The female body is therefore defined as inherently different socially and politically from the male body. Hence gender is socially constructed, and cultural values and social precepts bind men and women into demands of conformity, aided by law, religion, and customs that allow a tolerated range of acceptability that differs for men and women. These gender positions, subsequently, are stratified and ranked, implying a perception of unequal value and worth and are loci of dominance and subordinance.

Essentialism channels men and women into different life courses with varying emotional and behavioral expectations. These pathways are structured by the rules of how males and females relate to one another and translate into varying opportunities of lifestyles, occupations, social roles, identities, and emotional management.

Essentialism is also relevant for mental health. Let's frame four points as questions. First, do perceptions of the body affect how a person's symptoms are interpreted and diagnosed? Two, are women and men expected to process emotions differently? Three, does essentialism affect opportunities for self-expression and self-fulfillment? Finally, since many social roles are gendered, how does that affect stress and stress management?

Gender and Mental Illness Prevalence

Until the early 1990s, scholars and clinicians believed that women had more psychological problems than men (Rieker and Bird 2000). They may have drawn this conclusion because women tend to be more expressive about their emotions and willing to discuss the difficulties in their lives, which make it appear that they experience more psychological trouble than men. In addition, due to essentialist beliefs women were often thought of as histrionic in nature and unable to handle stress without becoming overly emotional or fainting. Prevalence studies, outside those on severe mental illness such as schizophrenia, generally limited their definition of psychological problems to two mental health conditions, depression and anxiety, which are more prevalent among women (Rieker and Bird 2000). Beginning with The Epidemiological Catchment Area study in 1991, studies have included other patterns of mental health distress, drug and alcohol abuse for instance, and have changed our understanding of the distribution of psychological problems by sex.

Research on prevalence now demonstrates that women and men show no overall differences in the likelihood of developing a mental illness (Rieker and Bird 2000; WHO 2002). The patterns and symptoms of mental health problems, however, do differ by gender. Boys' and girls' symptoms begin to bifurcate during the adolescent years as girls start to develop their symptoms emotionally and boys behaviorally, and these patterns continue into adulthood. Table 7.1 shows diagnostic troubles that girls and boys tend to demonstrate.

One of the most consistent findings in epidemiological, psychological, and sociological research is that adult women are more likely diagnosed with affective disorders and men are more often assigned diagnoses such as personality disorders and substance abuse disorders. Charts 7.1 and 7.2 show rates of several disorders by lifetime and past-year prevalence, respectively. Lifetime prevalence rates of depression, anxiety, and PTSD are clearly higher among women, and women are more likely to develop symptoms of bipolar disorder, but that margin is not as large. Adult men present with very different symptoms and are more apt to be diagnosed with impulse control disorders and twice as likely diagnosed with lifetime substance abuse disorders (Richards and Sayres Van Niel 2017; National Institute of Mental

TABLE 7.1 Adolescent Differences in Patterns of Mental Distress by Gender

Boys	Girls
Anger problems	Depression
Risky behavior	Eating disorders
More successful suicides	Suicide attempts
Behavioral symptoms	Inward-directed symptoms

Source: World Health Organization (2002).

CHART 7.1 Rates of Disorders—Lifetime Prevalence Among Women and Men, by Percent

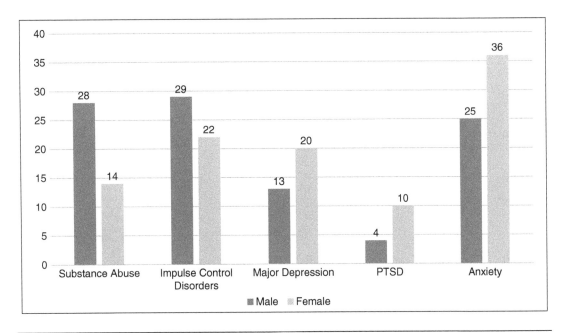

Source: Richards and Sayres Van Niel (2017), data from the National Comorbidity Study Replication.

Health 2017). In other research, a prevalence ratio of 3:1 of men versus women with anti-social personality disorder diagnoses has been reported (Alegria et al. 2013).

These findings are persistent along cross-cultural lines, making them seem universal. Does this mean that women are inherently more prone to depression than men? The data would say no. There are many factors that influence the onset of depression and behavioral problems, and they may concern the common social experience of women and men rather any common biological state specific to sex.

Let's review three areas that may affect the interpretations of symptoms: bias in diagnosing, stereotyping, and gender and emotions. Then we will turn to understanding how the social experiences that men and women typically share as status groups may lead to different psychological outcomes.

Gender Bias in Diagnosing

Research on the distribution of depression and other disorders that follow gender patterns has been analyzed for gender bias in how the research was conducted and the measurements of the disorders. Depression measures, such as those reviewed in an earlier chapter, have been studied for such bias, and are not thought to account for women's higher rates of depression (Mirowsky and Ross 1995).

CHART 7.2 Rates of Disorders—Past Year Prevalence Among Adult Men and Women, by Percent

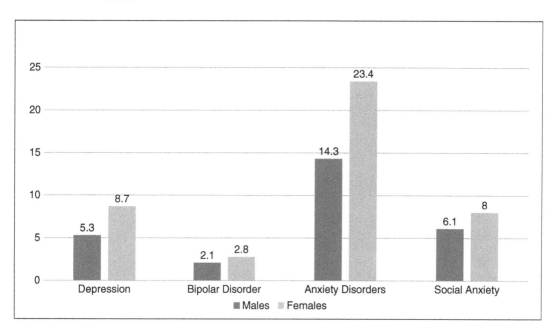

Source: National Institute of Mental Health (2017), data from the National Survey on Drug Abuse and Health.

Clinical settings, however, are a different matter. Psychiatric and psychological diagnostics, which are often described as much an art as a science, are based on interpreting the information presented to the clinician through psychological testing and assessing clients' affect, nonverbal communication, and descriptions of their life situations. While research often employs standardized research instruments to identify patterns of distress, clinicians must rely on their experience and insight to make sense of their clients' complaints. Diagnosing is a more subjective and interpretive skill and involves clinicians' personal understanding of symptoms and their feelings about their clients. Therefore, we can say that diagnosing clinical patients is neither a value-free nor purely evidence-based endeavor.

The social characteristics of people undergoing psychotherapy or psychiatric care can also influence a diagnosis and their treatment. Mental health professionals, like everyone else, are subject to their culture's values and stereotypes, biases that influence their own conceptualization of mental health (Skopp 2018). Gender bias has been identified with respect to the sex of both the client and the clinician and affects the diagnosis that a person receives (Becker and Lamb 1994).

Several disorders, according to Becker (2000), have essentially become "women's diagnoses." Depression, borderline personality disorder, and posttraumatic stress are often twice as likely, if not more, assigned to women. According to Judith

Norman (2004), depression in particular has been "feminized." In one study, women with serious mental illness were over-diagnosed with affective disorders and underdiagnosed with substance abuse disorders (Eriksen and Kress 2008). Compared to men, women were more likely assigned labels such as histrionic, borderline, or dependent personality disorders, labels that reflect emotional distress rather than cognitive and behavioral problems.

Stereotyping and Interpretation of Symptoms

One way to see how women are more likely diagnosed with an affective disorder is by analyzing gender stereotypes, and to do this, let's play a game. Stop reading here and go to Box 7.1 for instructions. Once you finish the game, continue reading the next paragraph.

You probably concluded that the qualities listed as feminine stereotypes appear pathological. Research would confirm your deduction. The presentation of depression and stereotypes of women are indeed similar (Landrine 1988). A far back as 1970, research has found that stereotypically masculine traits are perceived by clinicians as more socially desirable than traditional feminine traits and that therapists' views of a healthy adult generally coincide with masculine traits (Broverman et al. 1970). Depressed people are often described as dependent with poor self-confidence and emotionally frail, terms that are similar to the feminine stereotype. "Healthy" people, on the other hand, are often described as possessing qualities associated with masculinity.

Gender has been demonstrated to affect clinicians' decisions. One example comes from Fuss and associates' (2018) study on mental health professionals' assessment of atypical sexual behavior (exhibitionism and frotteurism, among others). The researchers presented several vignettes portraying characters

Box 7.1 Gender Stereotypes: Pathologizing the Script

Take a piece of paper and make two columns, one labeled Women and the other labeled Men. Now, list traditional sex role stereotypes that are associated with femininity or women. When you are finished, do the same for masculinity and men.

Now, look at your lists. I'm guessing that for women, you recorded stereotypes such as dependent, emotional, nurturing, weak, passive, family-centered, and focused on appearance. Your men's list probably looks quite different (remember these are *traditional* sex role stereotypes). Here you have qualities such as self-reliance, strong, independent, confident, unemotional, active, assertive, and best suited for jobs that involve leadership or command.

In the last step of the game, cover the words "Women" and "Men" and study your collection of traits again but without thinking of them as stereotypes. Consider them as psychological profiles. Does one look more pathological to you? You do not need to be a trained mental health professional to see the pattern.

exhibiting various forms of sexual behavior to mental health professionals and asked them which were considered a mental disorder. Fuss found that mental health professionals rated the vignettes' female characters that engaged in atypical sexual behavior significantly less pathological, yet they stigmatized them more than the male characters who engaged in the same behaviors, with one exception. Women engaged in masochism were highly pathologized, but men involved in masochism were not. Masochism was defined as a masculine behavior, rather than a feminine one. The study's authors concluded that mental health professionals tend to ignore or downplay paraphilic interests in women, which, they assumed, meant that sex norms for women and men are different and impact their evaluation of the behavior presented in the vignettes.

Stereotyping may also account for other biases identified in clinical settings. Owen and colleagues (2010) found that women clients' perceptions of microaggressions during treatment can influence the process and outcome of therapy, and recent studies have identified such bias against women with disabilities and obesity (Kinavey and Cool 2019; Olkin et al. 2019). Perhaps microaggressions related to physical appearance stem from views that women face more pressure to live up to social expectations of attractiveness.

Are Women More Emotional than Men?

Women are universally judged as more emotional than men. Images in public media and entertainment and beliefs in everyday life demonstrate the notion that women display emotions more quickly and sometimes more irrationally than men. Most studies concur and show that women express emotions more frequently than men. For example, women, on average, cry more and for longer durations than men (Kring and Gordon 1998; Madison and Dutton 2020). Women have also been found to smile and laugh more and use head and hand gestures with more emotionality than men (Brody and Hall 2008). These gender patterns in expressiveness may begin by age four. Brody and Hall (2008) found that little girls are more likely to express sadness and anxiety than boys of the same ages.

Despite evidence showing that women are more emotionally expressive, other studies have drawn conflicting conclusions. Ansfield (2007) found that in certain situations, men smiled more than women, and Greenwald and colleagues (1989) and Barrett and Bliss-Moreau (2009) reported that men use more facial muscles in response to affective stimuli.

The bulk of the research, however, indicates that girls and women are more emotionally expressive. But does this also mean that women are more emotional? Perhaps not. It may be a case of "we see what we want to see," and a concept called **correspondence bias** may help us understand this. Correspondence bias suggests that people believe that behavior reflects a deep-seated and unique attribute. For women, one of those essential and inherent features is thought to be emotionality; therefore, women act emotionally not because they really are, but because people assume they are emotional. Men's emotionality, on the other hand, is considered limited to situational contexts. Men display emotions when emotions are necessary to manage a situation (Barrett and Bliss-Moreau 2009). Research supports this hypothesis. Barrett and Bliss-Moreau (2009) found that people believe that women express emotions because they are emotional beings whereas men are not.

Correspondence bias can also influence clinicians' perceptions of their clients. Mizock and Brubaker (2019) have written that women sometimes feel they are not taken seriously or feel their symptoms are dismissed by their therapists. The women they studied believed that mental health providers misattributed their symptoms to other factors such as their families or their gender rather than taking their symptoms, including their emotions, seriously as part of a mental health problem.

Consequently, correspondence bias may lead clinicians to minimize women's emotional distress and mental health complaints because such emotions come "naturally" to women and may not necessarily be a problem when, in fact, they are.

A related idea, **restrictive emotionality**, concerns men's emotional expressiveness. Restrictive emotionality indicates the tendency to inhibit the expression of emotions and unwillingness to express intimate feelings (Jansz 2000). The concept assumes that men and women experience emotions similarly but that women appear to express them more because men express them less. Emotional displays are regulated by social rules, which differ for men and women. Social norms govern how, when, and where emotions can be expressed. For example, men are not expected to cry publicly because suppressing emotions that might indicate frailty or vulnerability is necessary to maintain western conceptions of masculinity (Brody 2000). For women, showing anger is stereotypically nonfeminine and is often judged in a derogatory manner. The idea here is that men and women experience emotions similarly, but the rules dictate how they are shown. For men, the rules are generally more restrictive and confining.

Clinicians, therefore, may interpret men's emotions in a stereotypical way. An overly emotional man may be subjectively judged rather than treated objectively, or symptoms of a stoic, unexpressive man may be misunderstood and considered "normal" when in fact the absence of signs of emotion may be part of the person's problems. Either way, a clinician holding such biases can misdiagnose a client.

The Sociology of Gender and Emotions

Emotions are complex reactions to environmental stimuli. They involve physiological responses and psychological conditioning as well as social contextual factors. Since emotions have social meanings and relevance, sociologists' interest in emotions lies in linking them to social patterns that extend beyond an individual's personal experience. Social situations influence emotional experiences and expressiveness, and two approaches have been devised to explain the relationship (Simon and Nath 2004).

First is **normative theory** (Hochschild 1975). This theory contends that cultural beliefs in the form of feeling rules, or cultural norms, specify the appropriate type, intensity, duration, and target of subjective feelings (Simon and Nath 2004). These norms govern emotions just as other cultural folkways and mores guide behavior. They tell us what we should and should not feel and express in a given situation and time (Simon and Nath 2004).

Regarding gender, this theory suggests that gender norms intersect with emotion norms to produce a set of rules that guide normative masculine and feminine emotions. Examples of gendered emotional norms include "boys don't cry" and "to man up" as emotional strategies to cope with troubling or potentially challenging circumstances. Anger is often believed a male emotion, and cultural rules usually give boys and men more leeway in expressing that emotion. Eder and colleagues (1995) concluded that boys' aggressiveness is directly related to male socialization and part of preparing boys for a future of competitiveness and conflict. Conversely, girls' social environments typically provide fewer outlets for expressing that emotion and in some social situations girls and women who show anger are labeled in a derogatory way and their femininity is questioned.

For girls, the rules focus on being "proper" and "ladylike" in emotional demeanor. Women are taught to be warm and gentle. Playing with dolls, as young girls are often encouraged to do, is emotional training in rules promoting nurturance and kindness. In another example, social expectations direct women to pay more attention to romantic emotions and feelings of love more so than men (Simon et al. 1992; Hochschild 1981).

The second theory often used in the sociology of emotions is the **structural theory of emotions** proposed by Kemper (1978). Kemper thought that status and social power have a strong influence on subjective feelings and provoke different emotions during social interactions. During an interaction, people holding a higher status in a relationship are in a different emotional position than those who have less. Having "the upper hand" leads a person to more positive feelings like happiness, comfort, and contentment. Those with less power, however, experience more negative emotions such as fear, sadness, and anger (Kemper 1978; Simon and Nath 2004). Having more influence in an interaction increases the chances of a satisfactory and gratifying outcome in that interaction—you are simply more likely to get what you want.

This theory's relationship to gender is fairly clear. Since women have less social power and generally hold lower status positions in the social hierarchy, the theory holds that women should experience more negative feelings than men (Simon and Nath 2004).

Both approaches are compelling, but which best explains gender emotional differences? Simon and Nath sought to compare the two theories, and their findings largely support the structural approach. Their data showed that the frequency of emotional experiences of women and men were similar; however, men reported more positive emotions and women more negative ones. Men were more likely to say they feel calm and excited (in a positive way), and women felt more anxious and sadness than men. Furthermore, while men and women did not appear to differ in anger, women held on to their anger longer and were more likely than men to view their anger as justified.

Two important factors accounted for differences in men's and women's emotional expressions. Women's greater probability of negative emotions was associated with lower status position, especially lower household income, and anxiety was explained by living with small children, a factor that did not hold with men (Simon and Nath 2004).

Similarly, Mirowsky and Ross' (1995) findings oppose traditional thinking on gender and emotions. Their study also found that in comparison to men, women feel more anger and irritation toward others. Comparing depressed men and women, the women in their study were angrier and more anxious. In all, Mirowsky and Ross concluded that women feel about 30 percent more psychological distress than men.

Normative rules learned during the early years of life do play a role in the emotional development of children and will continue into adulthood, as we will see shortly. Among adults, however, having more status and power creates an advantage in the opportunity to feel happy and satisfied with life. The emotional realities of holding lower status and power are often experienced as frustrating, sad, worrisome, and depressing, all emotions more likely felt and expressed by women.

Let's consider a couple of scenarios. The first is easy and perhaps more familiar than the second. This has probably never happened to you so imagine (rather than remember) missing a deadline for a term paper in a class. You politely ask your professor for more time to complete the assignment, but the professor says no and seems uninterested in your reason for being late. What are the emotions of the two social actors? The professor probably shrugs it off with little emotional response. Your emotional reaction is likely some combination of anger, disappointment, or frustration. The sole differences between the two actors are status and authority, and that authority-based relationship produced the two emotional outcomes.

Now for the second and more unpleasant example. A woman works as an administrative assistant to a male corporate executive. They enjoy a good working relationship, and the emotional climate of the office is relaxed but professional. Both enjoy coming to work and are generally happy with their jobs. One Friday afternoon, however, the executive makes a sexual advance toward the woman, who rejects him. On Monday, other employees notice a cold, less pleasant relationship between the executive and his assistant. The office environment has lost its comfortable emotional tenor. Friends try to engage the assistant to find out what is wrong but find her reluctant to talk, deeply troubled, and unlike her usual self. What are the emotions at play here? For the assistant, fear, resentment, and anger are likely. Other than a wounded ego, the boss may have responded indifferently or perhaps feel vindictive and want to punish her for rejecting his overtures. Those emotions would likely remain until either the boss or the assistant left their job.

There are many examples of structural situations that promote negative emotions among women. Glass ceiling effects, sexual harassment, being minimized or excluded during critical situations or everyday life, and lower incomes are just a few of the disadvantages women face that generate the higher likelihood of negative emotions. The conditions of essentialism, as discussed at the beginning of the chapter, provoke anger, anxiety, or depression because they are persistent features of contemporary society.

Mental Health and Social Roles

If women have more negative emotions and those emotions are connected to their status in the hierarchy, what is the nature of that status that produces stress and increased anger in relation to men? And what about men? As a class of people, men enjoy a number of social advantages, but they experience mental illness at the same rate as women. Why are their disorders more likely to be behavioral and women's emotional? Let's investigate these questions further and begin by first looking at social roles.

Sociologists are interested in gender role differentiation for several reasons. First, roles are typically the vehicles through which resources, particularly wealth, power, and social privilege, are distributed. Second, roles affect the levels of stress people encounter, and third, roles affect how we interpret our life situations and assign meanings to stressful events, supportive resources, and the actions of other people (Rieker and Bird 2000). Roles organize our lives and provide a sense of order and meaning, but because they also expose us to stress, they have a significant influence on psychological well-being. One feature of this role structure is that it is typically organized into gendered spheres of behavior and perceptions.

Even today as we see a narrowing in gendered behavior among men and women, society's institutions of gender create and maintain socially significant differences between them (Lorber 1994). The world often seems separated into "spheres" of feminine and masculine orientations (Rosenfield et al. 2017). Women are directed to identify with the private sphere of relationships, emotions, home, and family, while men identify with their work roles.

The division of the world into masculine and feminine was once considered functional, desirable, ordained, and inflexible. While we cannot look too far into the past to see if gender roles affected psychological well-being, we know that in contemporary society these structural differences in gender-related activities do indeed affect men's and women's mental health (Gove 1984).

How Roles Affect Mental Health for Women

Women's role placement is best described by two themes: role strain and loss of control. Contrary to men, women often find themselves in social situations in which they carry multiple roles. While multiple roles alone are not necessarily predictive of women's higher rates of depression, the quality of the roles and the support they receive to perform their roles are important in the onset of affective problems (Piechowski 1992).

Women hold a dissimilar place in the social hierarchy than men. For those in the paid labor force, their jobs are often lower in status and pay. Women are more likely found in jobs that have less discretion in decision-making, which implies their work is more likely other-directed rather than self-directed, making them less in control of their environment. As in the earlier scenario, they are more likely to be the administrative assistant than the administrator. In this case, their relationship to the authority structure is similar to that of workers, as discussed in Chapter 5, often with the same results of higher risk for psychological distress.

Women's lives often include an added role burden. Social expectations that women take on more household chores and child-rearing responsibilities remain central throughout much of society (Lachance-Grzela and Bouchard 2010). Compared to their male partners, women, even those working outside the home, devote more hours to household tasks. Entering the paid labor force does not mean that women necessarily relinquished their caretaking responsibilities. The paid work is additive to those duties; in a sense they are working two jobs (Auerbach and Figert 1995; Thoits 1991).

Women are also more likely to serve as primary caregivers. Not only do they do more of the day-to-day care of their own children, they also monitor the health and manage the care of family members who are ill or elderly. Since women are more likely to have lower paying jobs, they are more likely to miss work to care for children and other family members (Auerbach 1988).

Women's roles are wrought with more limitations and less personal discretion. They are frequently pressured for time and often feel unappreciated and under-valued. Consequently, women often feel overwhelmed and overburdened by the demands of their roles. All these conditions are linked to depression among women.

Compared to men, women have more social networks and supports, and they are also comparatively more highly focused on and invested in those relationships. These social connections can place women at an emotional disadvantage and become a source of stress leading to affective disorders (Rosenfield et al. 2017). Some have called this dynamic the "cost of caring." The traditional feminine socialization process emphasizes that girls and women should value others over themselves, putting others' needs ahead of their own. Having stronger social networks but a self-sacrificing self-identity can be a source of significant stress and increase women's risk for anxiety and depression (Elliott 2013).

How Roles Affect Mental Health for Men

In the masculine sphere, roles affect men's mental health, but differently than among women. Men's socialization experiences are less likely to provide the opportunities to develop skills to become aware of their immediate emotional environment or feel responsible for managing the emotions in others. Instead, male socialization prepares them for competition and conflict, not intimacy and caretaking, and part of that preparation is emotional control and repression (Nolen-Hoeksema and Hilt 2006; Simon 2002). Consequently, men are more likely to define themselves in relation to public life, especially work (Elliott 2013).

Unlike women whose work and household expectations often conflict, the roles of partner, parent, and earner overlap for men. For many men, being a good parent and partner means being a good provider and reliable breadwinner. Therefore, men are less likely to feel guilty for working or being away from home to conduct their business. Their sense of self and self-esteem are closely connected to providing for their family, and status markers related to job performance, promotion, and salary become important in self-identity. Being in control of their social environment, therefore, is a criterion of success as a person. Showing real emotions or managing the emotions of others are of little importance and can possibly hinder workplace success.

Since employment and public success are central for men's identity and reaching masculine ideals, having a job is a barrier to mental health problems; however, because work is critically important for men's self-esteem, they are more vulnerable to work stress than women (Elliott 2013).

Mental health problems in men, alcohol abuse in particular, are more likely to stem from psychological injuries related to their relationship to external social locations such as work or other competitive environments (Elliott 2013). Men are emotionally vulnerable to losses in work status, financial hardships, and failure to achieve social expectations of success, a core component of the masculine persona. Men who are less prepared to handle disappointment, anger, and resentment have the most trouble coping with these types of losses.

Unlike women who tend to internalize emotional distress and risk depression, men typically act out their emotional discord behaviorally in part because they have not been taught how to process negative emotions. As these emotions escalate, however, men often find it increasingly hard to suppress them. (See Box 7.2 for a metaphor for repressing anger.) Since men usually have smaller social support networks and less practice identifying and talking about emotions, alcohol and drugs become effective means for emotional repression (Rosenfield et al. 2017). Drugs help them escape, forget, and find relief from social stress.

Box 7.2 The Beach Ball Metaphor

Unlike many sociologists, I also have training in clinical social work and conducted psychotherapy for a couple of years. I mostly worked in a clinic whose clientele was charged on a sliding scale based on their income, and many were ordered by a judge to undergo therapy. The latter group, needless to say, often did not want to be in therapy. Because there were only a few male clinicians in this practice, much of my caseload consisted of men with serious problems, including some who had been accused of sexual misconduct or had alcohol abuse problems.

Most of the men I worked with had trouble with emotions. Many of them seemed to have only two emotional states: anger and not anger. At least that's what they showed me. They often were confused by their emotions. For some, if they felt angry, they thought it was sexual arousal. For others, if they felt depressed, they thought they were hungry and would eat excessively. It was clear that many of these men had no idea what they were feeling or how to handle the emotions. Often the first clinical task was to help them identify their emotions. Unlike my women clients who knew exactly what they were feeling and could label each emotion, the men seemed lost in emotional chaos. Many had no vocabulary to express the emotions once they "found" them, and they certainly did not know how to manage them.

Their futile attempts to organize their emotionalism reminded me that their problems were not necessarily of their own doing. While exploring their personal histories, it was always the case that they had never been given the chance to express their emotions in a genuine or authentic way. In some cases, they recalled times when there were punished for expressing themselves emotionally, especially when their expressions did not conform to the expectations, gendered or otherwise, of their parents or other authorities.

Not only did their parents hinder their emotional growth, but these messages were often reinforced by cultural images of the stoic male. The idea of the emotionally controlled male is virtually culturally iconic—think Mr. Spock and Data from *Star Trek*, Severus Snape, Dr. House, and Sheldon Cooper. They are strong male characters that either avoid emotions or struggle with them. These characters are widely popular because they are familiar in theme and, probably, reality. The Stoic Trope, as these character types are often called, are aloof and sometimes effective problem solvers. They use their emotionless stoicism to fight injustice or to solve problems.

Interestingly we usually recognize these characters as somewhat normal males, not "bad guys." What these characters have in common is that they are presented in positive, heroic ways, and boys often want to emulate them. In real life, however, the stoic male is often more troubled than glorious.

One of the ways that I helped my clients free themselves from their emotional entanglements was my beach ball metaphor. I suspect you have done this in a swimming pool or at the beach: hold an inflated beach ball under the water. What does the ball do? It tries to reach the surface. What do you do? You struggle to keep it down, and the lower you push it below the surface, the greater the pressure you must exert to keep it there. The ball continues to fight you, and the more resistance it gives, the harder you push and try to control its movements.

What happens when you let it go? It shoots upward in a violent rush to the surface and an equalized pressure environment. In fact, the lower you hold it, the higher it will go.

Repressed emotions act the same way as the beach ball. The more we hold them down, the more explosive they are when we express them. For men, holding the ball under the water is hard and painful, and sometimes they need help, so they turn to alcohol or have outbursts of anger or become violent.

The beach ball metaphor was a particularly valuable device to help men understand that their coping strategies of emotional repression were failing them. They could see that their troubles, such as excessive drinking or sexual offenses, were connected to their lack of emotional management skills. I asked one man, who had been convicted of rape, a question he said no one had asked him before then: "What were you feeling just before committing the assault?" His response was "severe loneliness." How did he confuse loneliness with anger and express it as sexual aggression? Why did loneliness produce a need to control a woman with horrible violence? Why was he lonely?

Of course, effective therapy requires more insight than a simple metaphor. But once they understood that their emotions were like beach balls under water and were motivated to make changes in their lives, a new world opened for them. We could then explore how their emotions became so confused and begin their path to recovery.

Men's Vulnerability to Alcohol Abuse

According to the Center for Behavioral Health Statistics and Quality (2017), men are more likely than women to develop an alcohol abuse disorder. Women, parenthetically, are equally likely to develop a drug abuse disorder (National Institute on Drug Abuse 2020). Some have argued that women's depression and men's alcohol abuse are different expressions of the same underlying emotional distress (Horwitz et al. 1996; Rosenfield et al. 2005), and data show similarities in the predictors of women's depression and men's alcohol abuse. For example, women in low level jobs are at higher risk of depression and men in similar statuses are more likely to abuse alcohol (Rosenfield et al. 2017). Because of the gender rules governing emotional expression, men tend to suppress their culturally inappropriate feelings of depression with alcohol and drugs to avoid being labeled weak or unmanly (Simon 2014).

Why men are more likely to abuse alcohol has both sociological and psychological roots. Sociologically, men's alcohol disorders are an expression of their tendency to externalize their reactions to stressors (Horwitz and White 1987). As discussed earlier, gender socialization provides males with fewer opportunities to learn how to handle emotions, especially negative ones. Alcoholic behavior can be seen as "acting out" the stress that they have difficulty managing.

Psychologically, men who avoid their emotions, especially the negative ones, are more likely to abuse alcohol because drinking becomes perceived as an acceptable coping strategy. In addition, men who hold strong expectations that alcohol will be effective in managing stress and relieving tensions, anxiety, and other stress-related negative emotions are more likely to over-consume (Cooper et al. 1992).

Vulnerability Factors of Depression

As discussed in Chapter 3, risk factors are characteristics, behaviors, and conditions that increase people's risk for a negative health outcome. The conditions of inequality and the nature of gendered social roles are not the sole social environmental sources of stress that predict or cause depression in women. Other factors disrupt affective health as well, and while they are believed to cause, or at least be correlated with depression in both women and men, we will discuss them in the context of women's depression because they are more likely to happen to girls and women than males.

We will frame this review around George Brown and Tirril Harris' influential book entitled *The Social Origins of Depression* (1978/2012) in which the authors identified four "vulnerability" factors that preceded the onset of depression in a sample of adult women. The study has been richly debated since its initial publication and some studies have failed to replicate their findings, though methodological issues may account for some of these inconsistencies (Patten 1991). Nevertheless, their basic findings have largely survived continuous scrutiny and remain relevant over 40 years after their initial publication. The four sources of stress that make women vulnerable to depression are: parental loss, lack of fulfilling intimate relationship, unemployment, and caring for young children.

Parental Loss

Harris and Brown found that girls who lost a parent because of death or divorce before age 11 were at risk for adult depression. Studies since then have confirmed this relationship, though their findings have not necessarily replicated the age 11 threshold. To confirm Brown and Harris' study, Patten (1991) found that women who lost a parent during childhood were about two times more likely to develop depression in adulthood than women who did not lose a parent. McLeod (1991) also confirmed this pattern and found that losing a parent affects both men and women, but depression was much more likely among women than men. McLeod also found that parental divorce may not always have a direct effect on depression. For many women, their parents divorcing affects their socioeconomic status as indicated by lower educational attainment and income. In addition, when parents divorce, their children often develop difficulty in their own intimate relationships. Children of divorced parents marry younger, have more conflict, have troubles establishing trust, and eventually are more likely to get divorced themselves, all of which are stress inducing. The effects of these conditions are all stronger on women in terms of depression risk.

Death and divorce are not the only ways to experience parental loss. Studies have also looked at the effects of losing a parent to incarceration. Foster and Hagan (2013) discovered that parental incarceration has a strong impact on the psychological health of children and that the effects are different based on which parent is imprisoned. Maternal incarceration is associated with depression, but when fathers are jailed, their children have a high probability of substance abuse.

Losing a parent can be psychologically catastrophic for youngsters, but it is tragic for children of any age, including adult children. Parental absence affects identity and can create a sense of loss in emotional support, guidance, and the emotional and material security that parents provide (Umberson and Chen 1994).

That said, it is important to note that divorce and death of a parent do not always lead to psychological distress or full-blown depression. In some cases, it may also bring relief. For children who had a strained relationship with their parents or painful memories, parental loss can bring an end to a distressing chapter of family history (Wheaton 1990). The loss of parents who were abusive, manipulative, or unloving rather than supportive causes less psychological harm for children. Still, not resolving conflicts children may have had with their difficult parents can fester into psychological problems later. Residual anger may be present and unresolved conflicts may linger.

Lack of a Confiding Relationship

Close, emotionally intimate, and mutually satisfying relationships are a potent barrier to psychological distress. Marriage, as one of several types of confiding relationships, has been studied extensively and researchers have found it to have social and psychological benefits for both men and women, but more for men. Conversely, a poor relationship, one that is plagued with conflict and mistrust, can have the opposite effect and is often an antecedent of depression, especially among women.

Emotionally strong relationships have many social and psychological benefits that defend against stress. Having a confidant to share one's inner-most thoughts, solve problems, offer emotional and material support, and provide acceptance and a sense of belongingness enable people to minimize risks of depression. A loving relationship minimizes loneliness, and the existential crisis of having to confront the world alone and without support is reduced if not eliminated by having a supportive and caring partner. Distressed marriages, or other intimate relationships, depletes one's sense of purpose and meaning in life (Choi and Marks 2008). They can lead to feelings of guilt and shame and a loss of social status, as being married is still considered an important status position in many social contexts.

A lack of marital trust has a strong impact on depression risks for women, especially when paired with a serious marital or family problem (McLeod 1991). Research by McGrath and associates (1990) and Patten (1991) found women in unhappy marriages were 3 and 3.7 times, respectively, more likely to develop depression than men.

Divorce has a stronger negative impact on women than men (Kessler and McLeod 1984). Women experience financial setbacks, since they typically hold lower paying jobs than their ex-husbands. Judges grant mothers custody of their children more than fathers, which causes a financial strain on women, even when child support payments are made. The emotional effect of divorce may also impact women more given that women generally have greater emotional involvement in relationships with other people, especially spouses, which makes women more vulnerable to undesirable events in close relationships (Kessler and McLeod 1984).

Caring for Children

Brown and Harris found that caring for three young children increases women's vulnerability for depression. Patten corroborated this by finding that women with this childrearing situation were about twice as likely to develop depression. Given that women now give birth to fewer children, it is increasingly difficult to study the effect of multiple small children on maternal depression and anxiety. Researchers now primarily study the affective consequences of caring for young children, regardless of how many are in the family. The results are not that dissimilar to Brown and Harris' original finding and Patten's replication.

Numerous studies have confirmed what parents already know—parenting is stressful. Having young children interrupts sleep, and parents must make adjustments to their previous child-free lives. Work schedules, finances, and household division of labor become sources of tension and conflict that perhaps did not exist before the arrival of the baby. Of course, parental stress is not always a direct cause of eventual maternal depression. Most mothers (and fathers, too) do not develop psychological disorders from being primary caregivers of young children. Nevertheless, the occurrence of parental stress is such that it is a risk factor for depression (Nam et al. 2015).

Wang and colleagues (2011) studied psychological distress among mothers with young children and found that about a third of women developed depressive symptoms within six months of giving birth. Just over seven percent experienced symptoms when their children reached two years of age. More alarmingly, over 13 percent of new mothers experienced what Wang called "chronic symptoms." The symptoms started before their child reached six months and lasted at least until the child became a two-year-old. Parenting stress, as Williford and associates (2007) found, can cause long-lasting maternal depression.

Not all mothers have an equal chance of developing depression. Maternal depression related to childrearing is connected to several social conditions. Parental stress is highest among Hispanics and African American mothers primarily because of their overrepresentation in poverty and lower access to resources and social supports (Wang et al. 2011; Nam et al. 2015). Giving birth at a younger age, being unemployed, and raising children on their own are also predictors of parental stress and depression among mothers.

Children's temperaments can also influence parental stress. Children who are more prone to expressing anger, develop emotional controls more slowly, and have behavioral or conduct problems cause more psychological distress for their parents

(Williford et al. 2007). But these conditions are in many cases connected to poorly educated parents in lower socioeconomic status who may have less knowledge of child development (Bornstein et al. 2015). Families in lower socioeconomic strata are less able to provide stable home environments, which are important for raising emotionally secure children. Because of disruptions in employment, higher rates of divorce or short-term relationships, and residential changes, children have more difficulty grounding their identities and learning to control their emotions. The more parents, especially mothers, are vulnerable to the forces of the stratification system, the more parental stress they and their children are likely to experience.

Unemployment

Brown and Harris identified unemployment as a risk for depression among women, and Patten (1991) found that women who were not working outside the home had about twice the probability of depression of women who were working. Employment, however, is a difficult variable to assess in terms of predicting psychological problems for women. The link between unemployment and depression or anxiety is not unique to women. In fact, the impact of not having a job when one is desired impacts men's well-being more than women's (Mossakowski 2009). Nevertheless, the cost of involuntary unemployment on women's psychological health is high (Pavalko and Smith 1999).

One issue regarding women's employment concerns women's level of contentment with staying at home to care for the family and focus on domestic tasks. For many women, being a full-time homemaker and stay-at-home mom is fulfilling and enriching, and research has confirmed that employed women and housewives do not differ in depressive symptoms (Brown and Gary 1988). But when women are unhappy being full-time homemakers and would prefer to work, depressive symptoms may well appear.

Both housework and paid labor have positive and negative potentials for women. Homemaking offers autonomy, little time pressure, and less physically demanding activity. On the other hand, it also means more social isolation and interruptions. Paid labor offers social recognition for work and economic rewards, but it often comes with role overload as women try to balance work and household responsibilities (Riley and Keith 2004). Riley and Keith compared the rate of depressive symptoms among three groups of employed married women—those in professional, sales-clerical, and service-blue collar positions—and full-time homemakers. They found that professional women reported the fewest symptoms primarily because they enjoyed the most advantaged economic outcomes to their work and experienced the least financial strain. Homemakers and employed women demonstrated fewer symptoms if others showed appreciation for their work and if they had sufficient autonomy over the conditions of their work and daily activities. Clerical and service blue collar workers reported more depressive symptoms, which Riley and Keith concluded were due to the taxing combination of managing both work and family responsibilities on a more limited income.

Childhood Abuse

Child abuse is a fifth vulnerability factor that should be added to Brown and Harris' basic model. Because girls are more likely to be sexually abused than boys and the effects of abuse are long-lasting, the experience of childhood trauma is now considered an important risk for adult depression among women. This topic will be discussed in more depth in a later chapter, but for now, it is important to recognize abuse as a significant causal factor for women's depression.

To conclude this section on vulnerability factors, a caveat about these conditions should be mentioned. These factors are indeed linked to depression, but their causal nature remains uncertain. Perhaps they are effects rather than causes. In the case of a lack of marital intimacy, depression may cause the relationship stress, rather than the intimacy issues causing the depression. As we saw with McLeod's (1991) research, the vulnerability factors may also be mitigated by other conditions such as education and income. Nevertheless, subsequent research has continued to find that Brown and Harris' vulnerability factors are predictive of depression among women. Women's experiences expose them to risk conditions that differ from men's and when they intersect with cultural feeling norms and women's general orientation to relationships with others, they are more likely to lead to depression. Box 7.3 illustrates one situation in which women are faced with a stress burden not experienced by men.

About the Quote

The 1950s witnessed a "perfect storm" of a return to social conservatism in the aftermath of the Great Depression and World War II paired with the rise of psychopharmaceuticals. Following the war, which saw an unprecedented mobilization of

Box 7.3 North Korean Refugees' Mental Health

North Korea, by all western accounts, is a stressful place to live. People, other than elites, enjoy few pleasures in daily living and are subjected to severe political repression, have no civil liberties as we understand them, suffer from frequent famines and shortages, and wallow in constant fear of violent government reprisals for minor digressions. Life is hard for most North Koreans, and many of them risk their lives to escape to the south.

The trek to South Korea, officially known as the Republic of Korea (ROK), is wrought with dangers. The borders with China and the ROK are heavily guarded, and the coasts are patrolled and monitored for vessels of any size leaving the shores. Those who are not killed while escaping, risk a violent capture, torture, "reeducation," and prison under the harshest conditions not only for themselves but their family members as well. Though the stakes for fleeing the repressive state are high, each year over a 1,000 make it out alive.

Not all is well once the refugees reach South Korea, however. Resettlement often comes uneasily as refugees must acculturate to new and foreign social, economic, and political values and systems. Interpersonal relationships are quite different, and the refugees must deal with discrimination by South Koreans, many of whom see them as outsiders and backwards.

North Korean refugees frequently suffer from several affective disorders including depression and anxiety. Many also develop symptoms of paranoia. They live with immense guilt for leaving their families, loneliness, and the symptoms of PTSD. They also have existential worries of identity, as they try to reconcile who they are in the midst of social chaos and change (Jeon et al. 2009). These problems are far worse among the women who make it to South Korea.

Contrary to expectations, most North Korean refugees living in the ROK, about 71 percent, are women (Shin and Yoon 2018). Women have greater freedom of movement in North Korea and receive more legal safeguards in China and Thailand, the usual countries of transit, as they make their way to South Korea. They have more opportunities to escape successfully than North Korean men; however, they pay a price in more severe mental health problems once they reach the ROK.

Among refugee women, the prevalence of depression is about seven times that of native South Koreans and is believed due to the absence of supportive family relationships, hardships in adjusting to their new lives, and poor personal coping skills (Kim 2006). North Korean women are typically less educated than men and once in South Korea, they have trouble getting a job. In addition, their migration experiences differ significant from men's: 80–90 percent of North Korean refugee women were victims of sex trafficking, sexual abuse, or forced marriage in China or Thailand before reaching the ROK (Emery et al. 2015). Many are forced into prostitution to support themselves and their children. As their stress accumulates, their mental health falters even after living in South Korea for three to five years (Cho et al. 2005).

Female North Korean refugees' experience of greater psychological problems can be argued from a structural theory perspective. Powerless to protect themselves from sexual exploitation, uneducated, poor, and often raising a child on their own, refugee women have a greater opportunity to feel depressed and anxiety than their male counterparts. They receive little psychological care in the ROK, so their PTSD and depression build until they start to feel suicidal. About one-quarter of refugee women have suicidal ideations, and the longer they live in South Korea without psychological care, the more likely they are to become suicidal (Noh et al. 2017).

women into manufacturing (think "Rosie the Riveter") and war-time deployment in the military, the country retreated to a conservative social ambience in which women were expected to become devoted housewives and mothers. Many early popular TV shows, such as *Leave it to Beaver, Father Knows Best,* and *The Adventures of Ozzie and Harriet*, depicted women as well-dressed but home-bound stereotypes of the essentialized middle class White woman. These shows were intended as models of "reality," but actually they were ideals representing calmness after the upheavals of the Depression and the war. If these female characters were truly real portrayals, chances were good that they were taking Valium, Librium, or some other tranquilizer.

The discovery of medications in the 1950s that reduced psychotic breaks in people with schizophrenia opened the door to research on drugs to treat other psychiatric conditions. Pharmaceutical competition became fervent, and we saw the first mass market advertising campaigns for psychotropic drugs, and these ads largely targeted women.

Here are a few examples of the texts of these ads.

- "Now she can cook breakfast again…When you prescribe new Mornidine" - G. D. Searle & Co. of Canada Ltd., undated
  The ad features a photo of a happy, well-dressed White woman cooking. Mornidine was introduced in 1959 to control morning sickness and vomiting and later prescribed as an antipsychotic, except that it did not work well for that purpose. The drug was suspended because it caused severe liver damage.

- "Now she can cope—Thanks to Butisol, daytime sedative for everyday situational stress" - McNeil Laboratories, Inc., undated
  Butisol is a barbiturate originally used for sedation before surgery and as an anti-anxiety treatment. It has potentially dangerous side effects but is still available in some countries.

- "When she *overreacts* to any situation" (Emphasis is original) - Winthrop Laboratories, undated
  This is an advertisement for Mebaral, which is another barbiturate designed to treat convulsion and epileptic seizures. It is addictive and has several serious side effects including harm to fetuses.

- "Pregnancy can be made a happier experience. Miltown relieves *both* mental and muscular tension" (Emphasis is original) - Wallace Laboratories, undated
  Miltown was prescribed short term for treating anxiety symptoms and was the best-selling tranquilizer for several years. It caused physical and psychological dependency and had many side effects, some of which were quite serious.

There were many such ads for these and other drugs that primarily targeted middle- and upper-class women. Later, ads for Valium and Librium, both strong sedatives, not only targeted housewives but also women college students.

Millions of prescriptions for these drugs were written to women. In 1978 alone, 2.33 billion Valium pills were sold in the United States; so many that Valium became known as "mother's little helpers."

Why were these drugs prescribed to women?

Betty Friedan described the complaints of post-World War II women as "the problem with no name." Their "symptoms" were feelings of emptiness and a sense of unfulfillment, which made it difficult for women to get through their humdrum daily routines with any joy and life satisfaction. The medical establishment, and indeed most of society, interpreted these "states" in psychiatric, reductionistic terms. Consequently, the collective decision was made to sedate women; after all, science had the answer to everything.

The postwar era engaged the essentialized female trope in high gear, and many women were left existentially confused, frustrated, and trapped because of the lack of opportunity that was presented them.

Women were not fulfilling their domestic roles because they were depressed or ridden with anxiety. Ironically, they were depressed and anxious *because* of their domestic roles. The problem rested in the social structural restrictions placed on women which resisted women who attempted to have a life outside their families. Instead of listening to their frustrations, they were, as a class of people, tranquilized.

DISCUSSION QUESTIONS

1. Essentialism is an interesting concept on which to ground discussions about gendered mental health problems. Think about a novel or movie in which women and/or men are defined by essentialist qualities and expectations, and then think about how their mental health is affected. One that comes to mind is Margaret Atwood's *The Handmaid's Tale*, a disturbing story in which the social structure quickly changes to dis-accommodate women and advance the status of men. While not necessarily a story of mental health, the book (and TV show) provides an opportunity to consider how such a social order could affect the well-being of the female characters, especially when the social order devolves and causes a loss of status.

2. Think about the structural origins of psychological distress for both men and women. How should society respond to these conditions? What policy and cultural changes would be required to relieve gendered stress?

KEY TERMS

Correspondence Bias 148
Essentialism 142
Gender 140

Normative Theory 149
Restrictive Emotionality 149
Sex 140

Structural Theory of
  Emotions 150

CHAPTER 8

Mental Health Over the Life Course

Learning Objectives

After reading this chapter, students will be able to:

1. Classify the major disruptions of childhood development that affect mental health.
2. Give examples of the primary mental health problems during childhood and adolescence.
3. Describe how the stress process impacts mental health during adulthood.

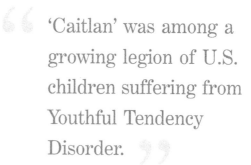

'Caitlan' was among a growing legion of U.S. children suffering from Youthful Tendency Disorder.

—The Onion (2000)

Introduction

Life course studies in sociology strive to understand how people's lives evolve over time. Researchers who focus on the life course want to know how institutional rules and social structural conditions, including history, affect human development from birth until death. When people are born and the socio-historical times in which they live are social forces beyond individual control and impact psychological well-being.

Deborah Carr (2011) summarized the life course approach as resting on four assumptions.

Lives are Embedded in and Shaped by Historical Context

Imagine the stressors growing up during the Great Depression and then living through World

War II in the mid-twentieth century or finishing school and going on the job market during the Great Recession of 2008–2010. Or visualize being a child in a segregated society where ethnoracial boundaries were maintained by force. Historical events and eras such as these exert great influence over how we see the world and ourselves. We are not always aware of the connection between history and our own biographies, to use C. Wright Mills' phrasing, but global events are part of the social environment that shape our identities and cause or reduce stress. These events, both those long in duration like the Great Recession and the COVID-19 pandemic and shorter occurrences like the terror attacks of September 11, 2001, affect our psychological "balance."

The 9/11 attacks on New York City, for example, had a particularly strong impact on psychological well-being there and in neighboring New Jersey. Depression, anxiety, post-traumatic stress symptoms, suicidal ideation, and in-patient and out-patient treatment visits rose immediately and persisted for some time. Although psychological symptoms gradually diminished for most groups in the metropolitan area, the impact of the attacks hit minority populations especially hard. Suicidal thoughts and workdays missed because of 9/11-related health problems had increased four years after 9/11 for low-income minority group members (Neria et al. 2013).

Individuals Make Choices About Their Lives, but Those Decisions Are Constrained by Historical Events and Social Circumstances

The presence of the novel coronavirus-2 and COVID-19 disrupted life around the globe. The virus caused large-scale physical suffering and death, near catastrophic global economic decline, political rancor, and unprecedented social restrictions. Because of the social changes adapting to COVID-19 required, the disease has also indirectly caused depression and anxiety. One early study in Spain, an area hit hard in the first months of the pandemic, found that 65 percent of the approximately 4,500 adults studied reported symptoms of anxiety or depression, many of which were described as moderate to severe (Fullana et al. 2020). During the pandemic, many people lost loved ones, livelihoods, and homes, and everyone had to adjust to restrictions in their daily lives.

While it is true that we make choices about our lives, our "free will" has limits imposed by social and historical realities such as racism and sexism. People cannot always do what they want or have the liberty to make decisions that are their best interests.

Our Lives Are Intertwined Through Social Relationships

It is axiomatic in sociology that positive and supportive social relationships are central in forming a healthy sense of self and protecting against psychological problems. The opposite is true as well: negative, harmful social relationships can increase the likelihood of poor self-esteem, low **self-efficacy**, and emotional, cognitive, and behavioral problems. Early adverse childhood events such as neglect and physical and sexual abuse have strong associations with future psychological health, and the quality of our relationships affect how good we feel.

Existentialist philosopher Jean–Paul Sartre, in his play *No Exit*, famously wrote "Hell is other people." Many have falsely taken that declaration to mean all relationships with people are punishing, repressive, or undesirable. What was tortuous, Sartre contended, was having to live with other people who created emotional climates rife with guilt, shame, or anger that caused us to have a poor sense of self. Writing in *Being and Nothingness* (1943: 222), Sartre clarified:

> *By the mere appearance of the Other, I am put in the position of passing judgement on myself as on an object, for it is an object that I appear to the Other…. I recognize that I am as the other sees me.*

When other people hold negative judgments of us, that is, when they see us as a problem or unwanted, we are forced to consider that assessment about ourselves as we think about who we are and develop our own personality. Some children whose parents divorce, for example, blame themselves for their parents' separation and unhappiness. If parental support or counseling fail to address these thoughts, serious and long-lasting injuries to the children's well-being could result.

We cannot escape the fact that we are subject to the emotional and behavioral climate created by others. We must deal with the judgments of others, whether it is within the family or in the society at large.

The Meaning and Impact of a Life Transition Is Contingent on When It Occurs

Psychotherapists are often trained to look for problems during changes in the life cycle. In US culture, beginning school at age six, going through puberty as young teenager, finishing high school, and entering early adulthood are important life transitions. Problems are often more serious when they occur during these periods and interrupt or interfere with the transitions. When young people reach 18 or 19 years of age, for instance, they are expected to make decisions about how they want to enter adulthood. This stage of life is often called "**launching**," as in launching the child into the adult world. People usually choose some combination of getting a job, marrying, going to college, or joining the military. These more normative options would ordinarily be considered a "successful launch," which often indicates a healthy sense of identity and confidence.

Sometimes, however, the launch is not smooth or healthy. The young person may elect a normative life choice but does so with emotional difficulty or for the wrong reason, such as marrying to escape abusive parents. Others may flounder and seem unable "to get it together" and take additional time to "find themselves." For some, it simply takes a little longer to "blossom." But a launch failure, where the young adult cannot transition to adult roles or take care of themselves and acts irresponsibly, indicates chronic sadness or anger. A troubled launch usually is an indication of a disturbed or anxious sense of identity and psychological distress that makes a person unprepared to assume the responsibilities of independence. Launch failures are almost always grounded in the stress of their emotional environment. They are, as many therapists say, "acting out" the emotional setting of their social milieu.

The significance of studying the life course lies beyond describing stress that occurs at different times of life. While important, the key point in the sociology of mental health over the life cycle is the proliferation of stress *over* the life cycle. Stress accumulates over time, which may explain why there are relatively few disorders among young children. It takes time for stressors to affect health. Single stress events are not likely to produce negative health outcomes; but chronic exposure to stress will (Pearlin et al. 2005).

Socialization

At the heart of life course studies is **socialization**, the process by which we learn how to function in society. Socialization occurs throughout life. We are constantly learning and adjusting to new social expectations and assessing our lives in the context of others. The earliest socialization experiences, often called primary socialization, occur during infancy and childhood. During this time, families and later teachers have the most influence in shaping not only our ideas of right and wrong but also our emotions and behaviors. They also should provide a sense of security and safety so that infants and children can learn to trust others, develop the confidence to perform tasks competently, and express themselves. Undue criticism, inattention, or abusive punishment can interrupt children's sense of security and confidence, which can impair their schooling and work futures and harm their ability to form stable relationships.

As we prepare to leave home and become adults, we engage in secondary socialization where we learn about life outside our families and schools. To effectively interact with others we do not know, employers, co-workers, and the general public, for example, we must learn not only what to do, but how to control our impulses and emotions. Delayed gratification, for instance, is a psychic conflict that many people have when social expectations conflict with internal motivations. As you read this text, for instance, you are studying for your sociology class. Would it not be more fun to go out with friends or exercise at the gym? But you are studying because you know that doing well in school has benefits down the road—a better job, a higher income, or achieving a personal goal, not to mention increasing your knowledge.

The social environment has responsibilities too. It must create an atmosphere in which individuals can develop confidence, self-efficacy, and expressiveness. To do that, it must provide safety, security, and a climate that does not induce feelings of anger, guilt, shame, or low self-esteem.

Socialization is about learning what is expected and adjusting to those expectations. We internalize the rules of other people and social institutions and shape ourselves to fit them. Social institutions and dynamics have a powerful impact on personal identity. To see it in yourself, go to Box 8.1 and take the 20 Statements Test.

There is more to socialization than accepting the rules and then conforming to them. We are not pawns of the social order obeying everything we are expected to do. Instead, we think about and negotiate social expectations. If the rules cause pain, for example, we may attempt to flee or mediate the situations in which they occur. Socialization can be highly emotional and conflicting. One person may undergo a

Box 8.1 Twenty Statements Test (TST)

Number a sheet of paper or a word processing page from 1 to 20. Now, write twenty answers to the question—Who am I?—in each blank. Give 20 different answers to the question as if you were giving the answers to yourself, not someone else. Write them in the order they occur to you (Baumann et al. 1989).

Now look at your answers. Who are you? I'm guessing that you first described yourself in terms of the social roles you hold and as members of social groups. Your identity, how you define yourself, is based on your spatial and emotional proximity to groups, which means that the more engaged you are to your status positions and social connections, the more they are core to your sense of self. Following your answers connecting you to social groups, you probably then began to list personal attributes. I am also guessing that you found those harder to identify.

The TST is a good way to see the concept "oversocialization," as opposed to total free will, in how you have become who you are. We like to think we are unique individuals, but really, we spend most of our time and energy reacting to those around us by either trying to conform to their expectations or negotiating how we want to perform the roles others assign to us. Our culture says it is ok "to walk to the beat of our own drum;" however, most of us march in a drum line, a row of drummers marching in step and playing the same rhythm in unison.

The role of culture is very important in self-identity. In addition to what I learned in Nepal that was reported in Box 1.2, I made an interesting miscalculation when I asked a sample of over 200 Nepali teachers to complete the TST. The teachers had noticeably clear difficulty in completing this exercise, and in the end, their responses were unusable because almost everyone answered with only three or four usually vague entries. You probably did not get to 20 yourself. The average number of responses is typically 13 or 14, but these folks provided so few valid responses that there was nothing to analyze. To make it worse, most everyone gave identical responses. Why did this happen?

Your social roles and positions impact you in powerful ways, and culture underlies everything. In an individualistic culture such as ours, identity is formed in a dynamic exchange between oneself and others where individuals can negotiate the norms and values of the social contexts in which we are embedded. While we usually conform, it is not necessarily a blind or robotic conformity.

In a collective society like Nepal, the individual is not the basic unit of culture, the family is. People think of themselves less as unique individuals and more as part of a collective. Their aspirations, goals, and emotional focus are centered on performing their duties as a member of their family or other social groups such as schools in the case of the teachers. So, the Nepalese people in my sample could not respond to the TST because it did not make sense to them. "Who am I" is not a relevant question in a collective culture.

socialization process that instills a sense of security, identity, and confidence, but another's experience may cause emotional pain and developmental interruptions.

Rather than a sterile one-way interaction where people internalize and follow the group's norms and values, socialization is a dynamic process of influence where context is important for understanding how people develop a sense of self, which in turn affects the likelihood of future psychological stability. Socialization has a powerful role in shaping personality, identity, and well-being, but people have some degree of choice to negotiate or even reject the norms and values that structure the conditions of their lives.

One way to see how socialization has implications for mental health is through the ideas of Charles Cooley who devised the idea that a sense of self emerges from social interaction (see Box 8.2). Theorists such as Cooley and his contemporary George Herbert Mead focused on the interplay between individuals and other people and stressed that individuals' sense of self and self-esteem are reflections of how other people treat them. We learn about ourselves by interpreting how others act around us. In other words, our selfhood is reflected to us in the "social mirror," and how we interpret that reflection is, in essence, our self-identity and perception of self-worth.

Cooley was an important early twentieth-century sociologist whose work has long served as a baseline for understanding the development of the self and provides a basis for understanding how some instances of mental illness can begin. Cooley's most famous concept, the "**looking-glass self**," was based on the then novel idea that a person's sense of self develops through social interaction. According to Cooley, interacting with others is like looking into a mirror and interpreting what is seen.

Box 8.2 The Looking-Glass Self

Cooley's looking-glass self is an important tool in the sociology toolbox. To facilitate learning how the idea works, someone years ago devised a poetic way to remember it. Authorship is unknown, or at least not agreed upon, but virtually every sociologist knows this poem.

Here is the looking-glass self, the poetic version:

I am not who I think I am.
I am not who you think I am.
I am who I think you think I am.

And here is what it means.
I am not who I think I am.—Self-perception is not a solitary or internal process. It requires social interaction.

I am not who you think I am.—I don't know what you think of me. I cannot read your mind.

I am who I think you think I am.—But I can interpret what you show me and draw conclusions from how you act towards me.

If you act nicely towards me, I'm likely to believe that I am a good person and someone of value. If you act with hostility and anger, I might believe that something is wrong with me that makes you act that way.

Individuals base their understanding of themselves on how they interpret the "reflection" of their appearance; that is, how people act toward them. Our self-concept, therefore, is generated or modified by how we are perceived (or think we are perceived) by others.

The looking-glass self is essentially a three-step process. First, people imagine how they appear to others. Second, they envision the other's judgment of that appearance. And third, they develop feelings in response to their perception of that judgment. These self-feelings, as Cooley called them, are the result of interpreting how others act toward us and are the core of self-identity.

To see how the looking-glass metaphor works, let's begin with this easy thought experiment. Visualize walking into a room containing 10 people. As soon as they see you, they collect their belongings and leave the room. They say nothing, just look at you and exit out the door. What would you think? It is likely that you would interpret their nonverbal behavior with hurt feelings. You might feel unwanted or out of place, angry, embarrassed, or under-valued. You may not have a good feeling about yourself. It could be a one-time coincidence, but what if this happened to you all the time?

Let's change the scenario. Now you walk into the room with 10 people, but this time they surround you with smiles on their faces. They are happy to see you and greet you warmly. Now how do you feel? Much better, right? You feel good about yourself and conclude that you are a good person who belongs to this group. What if *this* happened all the time?

Cooley's notion of the looking-glass self is well over 100 years old but continues to serve us well as a starting point to understanding the interplay between social interactions and how an individual's sense of self and identity develops. The context in which the "reflection" occurs is important. Stable, positive, and respectful interactions promote a strong sense of self identity and awareness, self-confidence, and healthy self-esteem. The opposite is true too: chaotic, threatening, and demeaning interactions often lead to unstable self-identities and psychological distress.

Now let's consider a more serious example of the looking-glass self. Children of neglectful parents are more likely to develop psychological problems than children who are not so abused. Penner and colleagues (2019) found that children who are emotionally and physically neglected are particularly at risk for **identity diffusion**, which refers to the "loss of capacity for self-definition and commitment to values, goals, or relationships and painful sense of incoherence" (Goth et al. 2012: 3). **Identity integration**, on the other hand, is an unfragmented sense of self where all aspects of personality and ability are consolidated into a solitary whole. Identity diffusion is more likely when children interpret parental neglect in personal terms; that is, the reflection of themselves they see in Cooley's looking-glass is one of an uncertain and deeply flawed person.

When children are neglected emotionally and physically, they try to make sense of their parents' behavior toward them. The tendency for children is to feel responsible and then guilty. They may also begin to see themselves as having little or no value to their parents while at the same time, children, especially young children, are dependent upon their parents for their care.

Cooley's idea establishes the importance of positive parental communication with children. For example, when a child misbehaves, there is a difference between telling the child that "you are a bad kid" versus "you did a bad thing." The former implies that there is something inherently wrong with you as a person, while the latter suggests that the child made a mistake.

If a child, or adult for that matter, is frequently confronted with a hostile demeaning social environment, it is difficult to resist interpreting that environment as a "reflection" of oneself. That environment becomes the frame of reference for developing identity and emotional, cognitive, and behavioral competence. As Cooley said, "we can scarcely rid ourselves of the impression that the way of life we are used to is normal" (1902: 36).

The importance of the looking-glass self is not limited to child development. Other characteristics, such as ethnorace, age, class, and gender, are reflected by the "social mirror." If the reflected image of social markers is interpreted as devalued, the effect can be devastating for mental health and lead people to feel shame, guilt, and low self-esteem because of their social status. Society can tell a group "You are bad" just as parents can tell a child.

Another example of how social reflections affect psychological well-being can be seen in African Americans' self-esteem and feelings of self-efficacy. Historically, African Americans have been cast as a low-status group and subject to hostile prejudicial attitudes, demeaning public images, defaming rhetoric, and violence from social institutions and in interpersonal interactions with members of other ethnoracial groups. Given the power of the other people in society to create ethnoracial inequality and influence the sense of selfhood in people, theoretically if African Americans accepted the attitudes of others, that is, they accepted the low status image that society "reflected" back to them, they should score lower on measures of self-esteem and self-efficacy.

Usually, self-esteem and self-efficacy scores parallel one another. People who score high on one, generally score high on the other. African Americans, however, often do not follow that pattern, scoring high on self-esteem but low on self-efficacy. Hughes and Demo (1989) studied this question and found that self-esteem for African American teenagers was based on relationships with their family members, friends, and their ethnoracial community. The rules among the African American community were more powerful than the rules and feedback from the larger society dominated by people outside their community. Strong and supportive relationships with people close to them and an affirming community insulated the teenagers from the larger society's messages of rejection and unimportance. Accepting the positive perspective of their immediate social relationships gave them the psychological tools to develop a healthy self-esteem and reject messages of racial inequality.

Self-efficacy, however, is a different matter. Historically, African Americans' low scores on this measure indicate a different relationship with generalized others. Self-efficacy refers to beliefs in one's ability to meet challenges, complete tasks successfully, and feel confident. For African Americans, their generally low self-efficacy may represent a psychological reflection of the perspectives of those "others" who place them in positions of inequality. Low status deprives Blacks of opportunities to experience themselves as efficacious or autonomous (Hughes and Demo 1989). Taking the role of the other in this instance means facing the other's belief in their incapacity, a perspective that is reinforced with fewer opportunities to prove themselves competent. In short, not having equal access to avenues for success means that African Americans are more likely to conclude that they are not competent or successful. Perhaps Leonard Pearlin and his colleagues (2005: 208) best described this relationship when they wrote,

> *Objectively, there is a difference between being in an inferior status and being an inferior person, but the difference may be lost in the translation to self-image; disadvantaged statuses may come to be mirrored in disadvantaged selves.*

Of course, not all African Americans have low self-efficacy. But to gain it, many African Americans must find ways to counteract the messages of inequality, and for that, they also rely on their community.

Self-efficacy has implications beyond feeling competent. It is related to suicidal behavior. In a study of Black teenagers, Valois and colleagues (2015) found that low self-efficacy was strongly related to suicidal ideation among adolescent Black boys. The self-object that is constructed from messages of incompetence delivered by "the other" can be life-threatening.

Cooley intended for the looking-glass concept to remind people to examine the effects of their actions on others. He was aware of the psychological impact that people have on others. In many ways, the looking-glass self-embodies Sartre's notion of "hell is other people."

Disruptions of Mental Health During Childhood

The discussion on socialization focuses on the dynamic relationship between the developing sense of self of individuals and their social environments. Children learn the basic rules and mores associated with their immediate social world as well as society in general, which also includes the norms and values related to their social class, ethnoracial membership, and gender. In addition, individuals must learn how to regulate their bodies, emotions, and behavior to fit the context of their social groups and environment. Nonconformity, as discussed in Chapter 1, is a criterion of mental illness in the sociological sense.

On some occasions, however, a healthy socialization process is derailed and developmental goals, as outlined in Box 8.3, are unmet. Children whose intellectual capacity to perform social roles, for example, may have difficulties establishing confidence and self-efficacy. Nelson and Harwood's (2011a; 2011b) review of studies on children with learning disabilities (LD) found that children with an LD were more likely to experience symptoms of both anxiety and depression than children without an LD. These symptoms were primarily in the moderate range, yet they posed added stress on children and may cause other people to have a negative evaluation of them.

There are several problems in childhood that make young people more susceptible to mental health problems. Some of these problems may create visible symptoms during childhood, while others manifest in later years. Let's look at five significant disruptions to socialization: loss of parenting, exposure to domestic violence, sexual abuse, physical abuse, and material deprivation.

Loss of Parenting

We discussed in Chapter 7 some of the impact of parental loss on emotional well-being. Let's look further into this relationship and focus more on divorce.

Since the publication of Wallerstein and Kelly's well-known book, *Surviving the Breakup* (1980), considerable attention has been paid to understanding how parents' divorcing affected their children. When their parents separate, children are likely to feel isolated, rejected, and powerless, and they become preoccupied with fantasizing their parents' reconciliation and returning to their "normal" family and household.

Children do not respond to their parents' divorce in uniform ways, and their reaction can vary by age and gender. Children aged roughly seven to eight often respond with sadness and feelings of grief and guilt, whereas slightly older children tend to be angry, embarrassed, and lonely (Wallerstein and Kelly 1976; 1980). Although it was earlier thought than young children in the seven to eight-year-old age range were not subject to anxiety and depression, Hoyt and colleagues (2010) found evidence to the contrary. Their study discovered that young children of divorced parents were at high risk for significantly serious symptoms of both disorders. Adolescents often become depressed and withdraw socially when their parents divorce (Hoyt et al. 1990).

Regarding gender, perhaps because most divorced mothers are awarded primary custodial rights, young girls adjust better than boys, who are prone to react to divorce by externalizing or "acting out" their emotions. Girls, however, generally have more emotional difficulty when their parents remarry (Peterson and Zill 1986).

Parental divorce can impact a wide array of life areas (Amato and Keith 1991; Reifman et al. 2001). Compared to children in intact families, children whose parents divorce experience:

- Lower school achievement
- More conduct problems
- Trouble making social and psychological adjustments to people and situations
- A lower self-concept
- Conflicted or emotionally distressed relationships with both mother and father

While these problems mostly dissipate within two years or so, many are not resolved by the end of childhood and persist into the adult years. Wallerstein (1984) found that five years after divorce, one-third of her sample of children remained seriously disturbed, and another third had emotional or behavioral difficulties. Ten years later, many remained troubled. By one estimate, parental divorce increases the probability of adult depression by 20 percent (Mirowsky and Ross 2003/2017).

Parental divorce does not cause problems for all children. An environment of constant fighting and bickering may be worse for children than parents living apart, and divorce may resolve the problems of protracted family conflict and tension. In addition, children who have positive supports in place and are involved in conventional activities (such as sports, music, or art), may direct their energies there rather than focusing on their parents' problems. Possessing high personal coping abilities also lessens long-term consequences. For example, Aseltine (1996) found that family conflict may predict distress for adolescents who can detach themselves from their parents to some degree to avoid the arguments and turmoil and who have peers and other adults for support and emotional attachments.

The economic hardships that follow parental divorce may have the most psychological impact on children in the long-term (Aseltine 1996). Economic privations can set off a chain reaction of negative events that can impact children for a longer period and underlie children's self-esteem, school performance, friendships, and perceptions of safety.

While the loss of parenting through death, divorce, or incarceration implies a physical separation, residential but emotionally absent and disengaged parents who show little love, support, or guidance are equally unavailable to attend to the needs of their children in ways that can cause more harm than death or divorce. Depressed parents may not show the love and affection necessary to make children feel secure and safe. In another condition of parental loss, parents who have addiction problems often fail to provide the security and affection necessary to stem off psychological distress. Oftentimes children of alcoholics begin to show psychological indicators of problems before they begin school. Infants as young as 12 months of age have shown more stubbornness and by 18 months, many have already developed emotional problems, compared to their peers whose parents were not alcoholic (Peterson Edwards et al. 2001). By school age, many of these children struggle with self-regulation, which means they have difficulty controlling their impulses and behavior (Adkison et al. 2013). A summary report prepared by the American Academy of Child and Adolescent Psychiatry (2019) shows that as these children get older, they increasingly have trouble with their emotions, often feeling guilty, confused, anxious, embarrassed, angry, and depressed. They often find forming positive relationships stressful as well, and these problems can continue into the adult years.

Exposure to Family Violence

Witnessing family violence, especially when parents hit each other, can disrupt childhood development and create conditions in which mental health problems are more likely to occur. About 20 percent of children under age 18 and younger have directly observed family violence, and over 10 percent have witnessed family assaults within the past year (Finkelhor et al. 2009).

Anger and fear encircle family violence and create a tremendous stress burden on children, which can be seen by their elevated levels of cortisol and higher heart rates (Costello and Klein 2019). Family violence generates a psychosocial environment in which children have difficulty learning to regulate their emotions and forming safe and trusting attachments with other people.

These children are prone to adjustment problems across a wide range of developmental areas. Academic, cognitive, and social deficits are common to children exposed to violence. They are likely to develop internalized conditions such as depression and social withdrawal and externalized symptoms including aggression and delinquency (O'Keefe 1994). In addition, these children are at high risk for trauma symptoms and PTSD (Evans et al. 2008; Costello and Klein 2019).

The psychological consequences of violence encountered during childhood are long-lasting, often extending into adulthood (Costello and Klein 2019). Childhood problems may impact adult achievement and wellness, and these children are more likely to become aggressive and violent during adulthood.

Sexual Abuse

The sexual abuse of a child perhaps causes more severe and enduring psychological harm than any other trauma or psychosocial condition. Childhood sexual abuse is related to multiple psychological pathologies in adulthood and high rates of psychiatric hospitalization (Finkelhor 1984).

Child sexual abuse creates a significant public health burden because of its prevalence and mental health sequelae. According to Pereda and colleagues' (2009) comprehensive meta-analysis, about 25 percent of girls and one in 13 boys experience some form of sexual abuse before reaching adulthood. Over 90 percent of abuse is perpetrated by someone known to the child or the child's family. About 187,100 sex offenses against juveniles are reported to police annually, constituting 66 percent of sex crimes against victims of all ages. Of victims, 19 percent are under age six, 26 percent are aged 6–11, and 54 percent are 12–17 years of age (Finkelhor and Shattuck 2012).

Sexual abuse, especially if committed by a family member or trusted adult, has a profound and virulently destructive effect throughout a person's life. The dynamics of sexual abuse are complicated, usually leaving child victims feeling out of control of both themselves (their minds and their bodies) and their social world. They can feel trapped and confused by people who may on some occasions provide love and security but at other times cause pain and humiliation.

The dynamics of childhood sexual abuse are associated with several injurious behavioral and emotional outcomes. Victims are often diagnosed with multiple disorders including PTSD, depression, anxiety, and sleep disorders. They are prone to obesity, eating disorders, and inappropriate sexual behavior (Keeshin et al. 2014). Compared to nonvictims, individuals exposed to sex abuse are 10 times more likely to attempt suicide after reaching adulthood (Pérez-Fuentes et al. 2013; Kaplan et al. 2016).

Sexual abuse also has a strong negative effect on self-esteem. Victims often feel dirty and singled out by the abuser for things they do not understand, and they usually interpret these feelings as believing that something is wrong with them. Sexual abuse is shrouded in secrecy, and many clinicians contend that maintaining the secret often causes much of the psychological damage associate with this type of assault. Abusers usually threaten their victims with physical harm or hurting someone close to them if they report the abuse. Victims, consequently, live in constant fear, upending the foundation necessary to build a strong sense of self-worth and identity.

One adult pathology often connected to childhood sexual abuse is borderline personality disorder (BPD), a serious condition marked by continuing patterns of mood changes, distortions in self-image, and contentious rage. People characterized by BPD have trouble managing their behavior and often find themselves in unstable and insecure relationships. One study estimated that victims of sex abuse are five times more like to develop BPD than nonabused children, and another found that as abuse severity increased, so did the BPD-connected impairment (Winsper et al. 2016; Zanarini et al. 2002).

Disorders associated with sexual abuse lead to more and longer hospital stays than other psychological conditions. In addition, victims are prescribed more psychotropic medications than other patients; however, treatment typically has poorer outcomes for abuse victims than patients who were not maltreated sexually (Keeshin et al. 2014).

Feelings of entrapment, anxiety, fear, being punished for unclear reasons, and low self-esteem affect sexually abused children and usually persist into adulthood, leading survivors to either withdraw from the social environment or to act out their distress behaviorally or sexually.

Physical Abuse

As with sexual abuse, physically maltreating a child causes severe damage to social-psychological development and is associated with a wide array of psychological and somatic disorders. Compared to nonabused children, a child who experiences physical abuse is twice as likely to develop PTSD and to experience symptoms of depression and anxiety, eating disorders, and persistent anger (Keeshin et al. 2014; Springer et al. 2007). As adults, physical abuse victims also develop somatic problems such as headaches and heart disease that last into adulthood (Springer et al. 2007).

Physical abuse threatens a child's sense of safety and security, making relationships difficult to manage out of fear of being assaulted or emotionally hurt. Child victims of abuse often interpret their assaults as caused by not being "good enough" or a disappointment to adults. Consequently, subsequent feelings of low self-esteem, guilt, and fear of abandonment are common among victims.

One question that often arises is whether spanking has a negative psychological effect on children. Spankings and other forms of corporal punishments have long been considered a normative method for parents to condition their children to act correctly. But are spanking and illicit violence against children different in terms of their psychological effects? Afifi and colleagues (2006) sought to answer this question by studying over 5,800 adults who were divided into three groups: those who were never physically punished or abused; those who spanked but not abused; and lastly, victims of abuse. As adults, the physically punished group, when compared to the neither punished nor abused group were significantly more likely to develop depression, alcohol dependency, and behavioral problems, all other things being equal. They were also more likely to have clinical symptoms of one or more DSM disorders. Both the punished and abused groups expressed commonalities in their relationships with their parents: neither had warm and loving relationships. In fact, the more violence they experienced (punishment and abuse), the less loving and protected they felt their parents were (Afifi et al. 2006).

Material Deprivation

As discussed in Chapter 5, material deprivation has a negative impact on adult well-being. Deprivation also has an effect on children. Children and adolescents in poverty and lower socioeconomic standing are three times more likely to have mental health problems than their peers in higher strata (Reiss 2013). How long a child lives in poverty matters: the more time spent in poverty, the greater its effect on children's psychological health. There is good news, however. Children whose families rise from poverty see their mental health improve, especially for externalized disorders (behavioral and conduct problems) (Reiss 2013).

Several factors may account for poor children's risks for psychological distress. Material deprivation may cause embarrassment or shame when children compare themselves to their peers, which may lead to low self-esteem and self-efficacy. Poverty may cause stress because of the lack of access to food and housing security, living with higher risks of crime and violence, and not having the opportunities of wealthier children. In addition, poor children are more likely to live in families, and often with psychologically burdened parents or guardians, that experience more instability because of the lack of resources. Impoverished parents are heavily stressed, which makes their risks for depression higher and effective parenting lower, both of which can make them less available to their children.

Summary of Childhood Disruptions on Development

In sum, hardships in early life have a profound impact on the mental health of children as well as adults. Pearlin and colleagues (2005) summarized disruptions of normative childhood development into three situations: early traumas, the timing and sequencing of life transitions, and the disruption of roles and statuses. The effects of traumatic events accumulate over time and are associated with psychological distress and disorders later in life (Turner and Lloyd 1995).

Early Traumas

The more a child is exposed to traumatic events, the greater the likelihood that child will develop a psychological pathology during both childhood and adulthood. Traumas, especially for those children in lower social strata, who are more likely to experience them, cause a proliferation of stress because they also lead to additional life stressors. After a traumatic experience, children often experience poor school performance, form less supportive relationships, develop poor decision-making skills, and have an eroded self-concept. Each can become a source of stress on its own; the combination of them makes recovery from trauma especially difficult.

Life Transition Timing and Sequencing

It is long known that unwanted and involuntary life transitions have a negative effect on mental health (Thoits 1983). While some may be reversible, such as a person who was forced into retirement but finds new and rewarding work, others are not. Pearlin and associates provide two examples: having to transition out of formal education to go to work, and a teenager who prematurely transitions into parenthood. The enduring consequences of these situations cannot easily be reversed. They interrupt efforts to achieve and carry out other roles, and they may cause regrets that can emotionally burden a person for many years (Pearlin et al. 2005).

Life Course Disruptions

Interrupting life situations can further proliferate stress and have lasting effects over the life course. While disruptions themselves are stressful, they often multiply and spread into other areas of life. These disruptions involve losing one's usual social environment and having to take on additional but unwanted roles or statuses. Again, to use Pearlin's examples, taking care of a life partner with Alzheimer's disease requires a change in most every avenue of life. It can be frustrating, tiresome, expensive, and isolating. Caretaking sometimes introduces conflict where previously there was none. All these conditions are stressful add-ons to the pain of the loved one's declining health and gradually impaired psychosocial functioning (Pearlin et al. 2005).

Box 8.3 Erikson's Stages of Development

Though Erik Erikson was a psychologist, his theory of psychosocial development has been popular with many sociologists because it focuses on the intersection between the social environment and psychological growth. Erikson contended that there are eight stages of development that extend through the life course, and that these stages are centered on a "crisis" or a developmental problem that must be resolved. The conflicts must be settled with support from the social environment and in order; failure to achieve success at one stage means subsequent stages will be unsettled. For Erikson, mental health stems from solving the crisis at each stage. People who successfully work out each conflict will likely feel confident and become a capable person who is able to navigate life's challenges.

Social environments, however, often interfere with individual psychosocial development. When the environment fails to nurture individuals and prevents them from solving the conflicts at each stage, mental health problems are likely to occur. For example, the main issues to resolve in early childhood are safety and learning to trust others (trust vs. mistrust). For a long period of time, children are completely dependent on others for their basic needs, and when the environment fosters security and trust by providing those needs, children are likely to feel a sense of security and comfort. If children feel safe with other people, they are psychologically able to progress to the next stage. For children whose needs are not met, however, they learn to mistrust others and feel anxious during social interactions. Children who have difficulty with trust are likely to struggle establishing confidence in the next stage (autonomy vs. shame) and have trouble in relationships. Shame and anxiety may become dominant emotions.

Erikson's developmental stages are summarized here. Each stage is listed along with what should happen and what can go wrong. When things do go wrong, usually the social environment has failed the individual and the potential for mental health problems increases.

Age	Psychosocial Crisis	What Should Happen	What Can Go Wrong
Infancy	Trust vs. Mistrust	Form attachments with caregivers Develop trust that others will meet basic needs	Lack of confidence in others Anxiety regarding basic needs being met Insecurity
Early Childhood 18 Months–3 Years	Autonomy vs. Shame	Development of gross and fine motor skills Successful potty training	Lack confidence in ability Mistrust, fear, anxiety if others fail to support or shame child's efforts toward personal control
Preschool 3–5 Years	Initiative vs. Guilt	Become assertive in play Enact roles in make believe play Feel secure in decision-making	If overly criticized and controlled, feel insecure in decisions Feel guilty if creativity is inhibited
School Age 5–12 Years	Industry vs. Inferiority	Learn academic skills Healthy peer relations Win approval through competence Feel pride in accomplishments	Feel inferior or low self-esteem if overly criticized or not encouraged
Adolescence 12–18 Years	Identity vs. Role Confusion	Explore personal values and goals Transition to adult roles Look toward the future Sexual identity formation	Confused about the future Feel shame about one's body if humiliated or shamed Inability to integrate the "whole self"
Young Adulthood 18–40 Years	Intimacy vs. Isolation	Form intimate relationships Establish strong sense of identity	Fail to form stable identity relationships Avoid intimacy Isolation Fear commitment Economic insecurity

(Continued)

Box 8.3 Erikson's Stages of Development *(Continued)*

Middle Adulthood 40–65 Years	Generativity vs. Stagnation	Peak creativity and productivity Nurturing others Make social contribution Feel useful and accomplished	Little interest in being productive or contributing to society Feel disconnected, restless
Maturity 65+ Years	Integrity vs. Despair	Contemplate accomplishments See self as having led a successful life Feel comfort with and accept life choices Feel good about a "life well lived"	Look back with regret Feel bitter or despair over life decisions Feel irritable, hopeless, guilty over the past

Children and Adolescents

Traumas and life course disruptions, in addition to other stressors children encounter, interfere with the healthy promotion of mental health during childhood and can extend over the course of the life cycle. Some conditions such as intellectual and autism spectrum disorders are identifiable from infancy, and bipolar and schizophrenia emerge in late adolescence or early adulthood, likely have a biological underpinning, and would occur with or without trauma or chronic environmental stress, though these may be exacerbated by environmental stressors.

While pre-pubescent mental health is not often studied, we know that for children, adolescents, and young adults, mental health and substance abuse disorders cause their single greatest health burden and rank sixth in DALYs globally (Erskine et al. 2015).

As Erikson explained, to minimize psychological problems, childhood requires the social environment to provide safety and security. Because human offspring have a long period of dependency, they rely on others for physical survival. If basic needs are not met or are paired with emotional tension, then children will have trouble forming a sense of trust in others, which can interfere with forming healthy relationships later in life.

Trust development is not limited to material needs. Children need to be encouraged to master their bodies and develop a sense of work and accomplishment.

They need to have initiative and opportunities to be creative. If these needs are squelched through criticism, humiliation, punishment, or disinterest, it is likely that these children will have difficulty performing adult roles well.

Typically, clinicians are hesitant to assign a DSM diagnosis to children because of the consequences of labeling, which can affect self-esteem, others' perceptions of them as "damaged," and the possibility that a child's problem is a temporary response to family stress or to situational troubles. An example of the latter is a six-year-old who is feeling anxious or withdrawn following the death of loved pet.

Young children do experience symptoms, but not all are necessarily pathological. Throughout the younger ages, children go through phases and periods in which they are overly emotional or aggressive or seem to lack confidence. This variability in behavior can usually be explained as reacting to a particular stressor, peer pressure, or perhaps hormonal changes within the body. Parents must keep in mind that children are learning and experimenting as they get older. Their bodies are changing, and their identities are a work in progress, which means that temporary fluctuations in behavior and affect are normal.

Large-scale studies on prevalence of disorders among children usually begin including them around the age of puberty, and over time, several important findings have been discovered. First, between 1960 and 1975, epidemiological data detected a shift to earlier onset of depression among children (Klerman and Weissman 1989) and, second, the occurrence of depressive episodes for American teens is steadily rising. Review Chart 8.1. You will see that between 2004 and 2017, the incidence of a depressive episode in the last 12 months has increased for all three age groups, especially 16- and 17-year-olds. Of that group, almost 18 percent reported at least one episode, a dramatic increase over the 2004 rate of just over 12 percent. The middle group, ages 14 and 15, saw a rise of well over 50 percent, and the younger group (12 and 13 years) saw about a 30 percent increase between 2005 and 2015, but followed by a decline the next two years. Still, the 2017 rate is much higher than reported in 2004.

Chart 8.2 compares teenage boys and girls. Boys' depression has risen slightly since 2004, but girls have seen a dramatic upsurge in episodes of clinical depression. For girls, the rate has increased from about 13 percent to 20 percent in only 13 years.

The historical period in which children are born and raised influences identity and mental health. Studies show that birth cohorts (children born within 10–15 years of each other) have similar psychosocial characteristics because they have had to face similar events, challenges, and overall social–economic–political conditions. Think of the labels given to cohorts. the Great Generation that experienced two world wars and the Great Depression. Baby Boomers, born between 1946 and 1960 experienced the Civil Rights and Women's movements, the Vietnam War, and unprecedented national wealth and demographic competition (there were many of them). Gen X and Gen Y came later and lived through the decadence of the 1980s, industrial decline, and the communications technology revolution.

CHART 8.1 Adolescent Depression: Percentage of Youths Who Had at Least One Major Depressive Episode in the Past Year

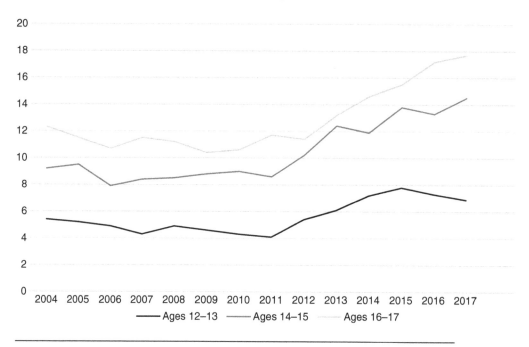

Source: Substance Abuse and Mental Health Services Administration (2019a).

During these periods, political and social values and cultural tastes and preferences changed. But so did mental health. Looking at the extreme ends, the Great Generation and post-Boomers, changes in mental health are dramatic. Gen X'ers, those born between 1965 and 1980, were teenagers and young adults in the 1990s. During that time, there was a dramatic increase in depression and anxiety. In the 1990s, the lifetime rate of a depressive episode was 10 times greater than among the Great Generation born between 1915 and 1940 (Twenge 2011). Studies from the 1990s and early 2000s show other psychological concerns among adolescents and young adults. For example, 29 percent of college students feel overwhelmed by their studies, 40 percent experienced hypomania, a mood state that is elevated above normal but not causing significant impairment, which would be a state of mania. Numerous reports of greater emotional fragility among students have been noted, and one study found that girls feel a stronger need to be perfect than in times past (Twenge 2011).

The group born after them, the Millennials, reached the teens and early 20s in the 2010s. Depressive episodes again increased, as shown in Charts 8.1 and 8.2.

What socio-historical changes may explain those differences? Theories abound. Perhaps it is because of the influence of social media, which exposes young people to more pressures and criticism. Worries about future job opportunities, debt loads,

CHART 8.2 Adolescent Depression by Sex: Percentage of Youths With a Major Depression Episode in the Last Year

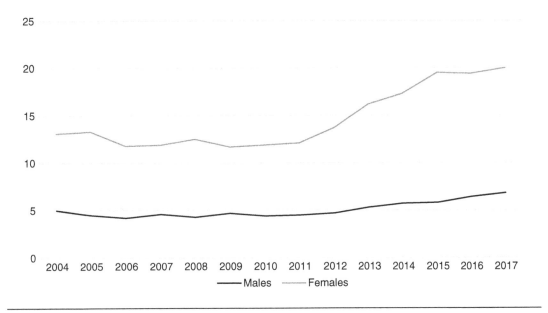

Source: Substance Abuse and Mental Health Services Administration (2019a).

and more children in single-parent families that have financial problems may account for some of the generational differences. Existential crises concerning a foreboding global climate catastrophe may also contribute to declining mental health, and fears of random shootings have turned formerly safe places into potential targets of extreme violence. Children today live more scripted lives and are seemingly constantly shuffled from place to place, which leaves them little time for unscripted play or meaningful social interactions. Moreover, parents seem to fail to teach their children strong skills to cope with stress.

Three present-day sources of children and adolescent stress are associated with psychological consequences and may account for some of the increase in adolescent depression. These are helicopter parenting, bullying, and social media use.

Helicopter Parents

One source of stress often connected to psychological troubles, especially among middle class families, is the style of parenting commonly known as **helicoptering**. Helicopter parenting describes parents who are over-involved in their children's lives and who intrusively and manipulatively control their children's behaviors (Padilla-Walker 2012).

Parental over-involvement in the lives of emerging adult children may have psychological benefits for the parents but is not necessarily good for their offspring.

Helicoptering impinges on children's emerging independence and ability to solve problems. Exerting parental control, especially during early adulthood, has negative effects on self-efficacy, life satisfaction, and managing emotions (more anxiety and depression). It is also associated with the inability to adapt to and solve problems at the workplace (Cui et al. 2019; Bradley-Geist and Olson-Buchanan 2014).

Helicoptering stems from two sources of anxiety, according to Rousseau and Scharf (2018). First, these parents tend to regret past mistakes and are focused, if not obsessed, with not wanting their children to repeat these mistakes. Second, helicopter parenting is grounded in anxiety over previous losses and negative outcomes. These parents are oriented to security and safety. Avoiding failure is a prime motivator because any sort of trouble or difficulty is perceived as a sign of incompetence rather than as an opportunity to learn.

The tragedy of helicoptering parents is children remaining dependent on their parents to make decisions for them and to rescue them from dilemmas and conflicts.

Bullying

In the past, bullying was perceived as a rite of passage during childhood and necessary to prepare youngsters for the trials of adulthood. Now, however, bullying is defined as a social problem that creates severe stress and serious mental health consequences for children.

Bullying has shown to be common. Studies on bullying prevalence have found anywhere from 10 percent to 70 percent of adolescents have experienced bullying victimization. A CDC report based on the Youth Risk Surveillance Studies, which uses a national random sample, found that 20 percent of 12- to 18-year-old students were subjected to bullying in the last year (US Dept. of Health and Human Services 2020).

Bullying victimization can be severe for children. Whether it is face-to-face or online, harassment and intimidation cause feelings of powerlessness, and the stress from being bullied is usually internalized as depression and anxiety, loneliness, low self-esteem and self-worth, and hopelessness (Baiden and Tadeo 2020). In addition, several studies have identified bullying as a cause of suicidal ideation. The risk is particularly high if an adolescent is victim to both cyber and physical bullying and intimidation (Baiden and Tadeo 2020; Ellis and Brass 2018).

The effects of childhood bullying victimization often extend beyond adolescence and decades into adulthood (Takizawa et al. 2014). Adults who were bullied as children find themselves having difficulty trusting others and feel their mental well-being is worse because of victimization. Some of the adults in deLara's (2019) study reported eating disorders that were attributed to being bullied as a child.

Bullying has probably always existed, but cyberbullying has expanded its landscape beyond physical intimidation. Information technology and social media have made it easy to ostracize others and to disseminate falsehoods and deceptions without ever directly confronting the victim. Compared to physical intimidation, cyberbullying is faster, constantly accessible, and has a larger audience. Cyber messages are permanent and can be anonymous, and intervention is not likely

(Kim et al 2018). Modecki's group (2014) estimated that about 15 percent of adolescents have been bullied online.

There is no question that cyberbullying is associated with depression and anxiety, but one question lingers: What comes first? It could be that depressed adolescents spend more time on the internet and act in ways that make them vulnerable to bullying (Rose and Tynes 2015). In a longitudinal study designed to answer this question, Rose and Tynes studied adolescents at three different points in time and found that the relationship between depressive and anxiety symptoms and cyberbullying is reciprocal, which means that each can affect the other. Adolescents who experience depressive and anxious symptoms are more susceptible to cyber victimization. But victimization can also lead to psychological distress.

Social Media and Mental Health

In the last few years, parents and teachers have expressed concern about children's engagement in the various media platforms that allow them to interact and share photos, videos, and the comments of other people. The apprehensions are that social media users spend too much time on their devices instead of interacting interpersonally or wasting time that could be used for study, healthy play, or work. A second concern is that social media affects users' mental health.

Researchers have asked these questions too, but the evidence on the effects of social media use (SMU) on mental health is mixed and often contradictory. Some data indicate that excessive SMU increases the likelihood of depressive symptoms, but other studies find no relationship or even that SMU is good for some individuals. The weight of the evidence, however, leans toward an association between extensive SMU and symptoms of depression and anxiety although the nature of that relationship is not necessarily clear.

SMU itself is not the issue. The problem is when SMU becomes habitual. The DSM does not provide a categorical definition for excessive SMU, but researchers have coined the term **problematic social media use** (PSMU) to describe a person who is excessively motivated to social media, demonstrates excessive concern about social media, and is so devoted to it that other relationships, studies, or work are negatively affected (Andreassen et al. 2014). People experiencing PSMU are preoccupied with social media and become anxious if they do not access their machines.

One indicator of PSMU is FoMO, or "fear of missing out." FoMO is defined as "a pervasive apprehension that others might be having rewarding experiences from which one is absent. FoMO is characterized by the desire to stay continually connected with what others are doing" (Przybylski et al. 2013: 1841). Worrying that other people are enjoying themselves without you can be a significant source of stress for adolescents and young adults. For many, this anxiety is associated with symptoms of mood disorders in young adults (Rosen et al. 2013).

At issue is whether PSMU causes psychological distress or is symptomatic of an underlying mental health problem. Barry and colleagues (2017) measured PSMU by the number of accounts a person has and frequency of checking those accounts. People with more accounts and who check them more often are prone to FoMO anxiety and loneliness. Parents' accounts of the impact of social media on their children who are high users include inattentiveness and hyperactivity, greater impulsivity, and anxiety and depression symptoms (Barry et al. 2017). Shensa's study (2017) found similar results but also that PSMU is associated with physical inactivity, fewer direct social interactions, and less sleep, all of which can affect mental health.

Findings such as these, however, do not establish clear causality. Shensa and associates (2017) argue that the relationship between PSMU and psychological distress is reciprocal. SMU may be functional for young people who are temperamentally shy or socially inhibited, for example. Going online gives them an outlet to expressive themselves and interacts in ways they may find difficult in "real life." Providing a sense of connectedness may be an important motivator for SMU for adolescents, especially since peer interactions are increasingly important for their psychosocial development. Therefore, it can be argued that SMU is very attractive to individuals who may already feel depressed or anxious, and the more rewarding SMU becomes, the more these individuals will use it.

Adulthood

Because adulthood is not a singular or one-dimension time of life, it is socially divided into three areas: young adulthood, mid-life, and older adulthood. These divisions are largely marked by differences in people's orientation to most everything in life.

Psychological distress follows a U-shape curve during adulthood (Mirowsky and Ross 2012). Young adults often carry a heavy burden of mental illness, but their symptoms begin to wane during the mid-life years until age 65 or so when distress re-emerge. As Mirowsky and Ross say, from a mental health perspective, the mid-adult years are the best time of life. Depression rates drop to their lowest level at age 40 before beginning to rise again in late adulthood and the senior years.

Early Adulthood

The ages 18 to 30 are the "launching" years when people leave their families of origin and form intimate relationships, establish families of their own, and find their place in the community. Problems during the early adult years are largely centered around three focal points: a continuation of childhood stressors, difficulties leaving their families of origin, and the stress that is associated with starting a career and establishing stable adult relationships and a family. Young people in their 20s are often wrought with symptoms of depression and anxiety as they sort out their lives and make the choices that will bear on their futures. Decisions on the right job, college major, and love and family are increasingly stressful, and many young adults are not equipped to handle them, especially during difficult economic and social times.

Despite legal adulthood beginning at age 18 in most places, the actual beginning of adulthood in the sociological sense is less clear. Adulthood is more social than biological. Socially we are grown when we maintain economic independence and participate in community affairs and civic activities at what is considered a mature level. We become adults when we engage in activities that society says are appropriate for and expected of adults. The roles and behaviors of a socially constructed adulthood include self-reliance, taking life's circumstances seriously, transitioning from one's family of origin to family of destination, having a stable position in the labor market, and possessing the wherewithal to provide responsible guidance to younger people (Pitti 2017).

In industrial and post-industrial cultures, adolescent dependency has become longer, lasting into the 20s and for some even the 30s. This incongruency leads to psychological and social conflict for young adults: the body has matured and is ready for independence, but social factors extend dependency. Think of this conflict as the body telling the mind it's time to exert itself and become independent, but the social environment is directing the mind toward dependency. The "person" is caught in the middle. As can be imagined, extended adolescence generally has a negative effect on the psychological health of young adults.

Adolescence has lengthened for several reasons. First, the need (and cost) for more education in the modern economy stretches out a person's dependence on parents or other sources of assistance. Second, the job market has shrunk in many key and often high-paying sectors. Robotization, downsizing, and relocating production and services to other countries have forced many young adults into longer periods of unemployment, underemployment, and wages that do not allow them to live independently and securely. Third, families have fewer children but invest in them more, which often entails keeping them close to home and protected. Fourth, longer life expectancies have contributed to young people launching later than in times past. If people expect to live into their 70s and 80s, rather than 40 or 50, there is less urgency to end childhood and begin adult social roles.

In many cases, young adults must live with and maintain dependency on their parents until they establish themselves financially. Rooted in the prevailing political-economic conditions, increased dependency becomes a stressor that can interfere with a young adult individuating, which means fully separating as an autonomous person, and becoming competent and secure in creating a career and family.

For most young adults, psychological distress stems from transitioning to adult expectations and social roles. Finding a good job and life partners with whom to share their lives are becoming increasing stressful in the current social climate. Many young adults start their careers saddled with heavy debt. Consumer debt is especially detrimental to mental and physical health, serving as a significant predictor of depressive symptoms, anxiety, and low life satisfaction (Sweet et al. 2013).

Middle Adulthood

For most people, these are halcyon days of mental well-being (Mirowsky and Ross 2003). By the late 30s and through the 40s and 50s, individuals have reached places where they can be productive and develop a sense of well-being and satisfaction. Usually relationships are stable, and many people are busy raising their children. Incomes are generally secure for most, and individuals tend to feel well-established. They have a life routine that brings comfort and security, and they feel enjoyment through their children, their work, and their leisure activities.

Parenting is not always a source of happiness and bliss, of course. Children are often stressful, especially if they are difficult infants (trouble sleeping or "colicky"), are chronically ill, have trouble adjusting to and performing in school, or develop behavioral problems. Mothers tend to be more distressed by children because child-tending more likely falls to them, even for those who work outside the home.

Unstable working conditions are another potential pitfall for middle-aged adults. For example, involuntary lay-offs, downsizing, or mergers create economic stress among middle-class adults as does seasonal employment for working class families and the poor.

Late Adulthood

During the last stage of the life course, Erikson believed that individuals begin to contemplate their lives and assess the decisions they made. They may ask: Did I go into the right job? Why did I not study music instead of business? Why did I waste so many years? It is a time of reflection for people to decide if they have lived successful lives. For seniors who are comfortable with their life's decisions, Erikson said they become wise and feel a sense of integrity about who they are as people. Otherwise, they are likely to feel a sense of despair and perhaps angry, despondent, or even depressed.

A traditional belief about aging is that a decline in mental health is inevitable with advancing years. Because of greater stressors, loss of significant people, lost roles, and declining physical ability, the elderly have been stereotyped as a depressed and senile lot who have little interest in life. For most people, however, life after 65 is filled with activity and learning, and for many, mental health improves with age (Markides 1986). Depression is not a predetermined part of aging; however, late adulthood is a time of increased risk of mental health problems.

Let's review five of those of those risks: dementia, depression, suicide, substance abuse, and elder abuse.

Dementia

Dementia refers to cognitive deficits caused by physiological changes in the brain and impaired nerve fibers. Of the several types of age-related dementias, Alzheimer's' disease (AD), is the most common and is caused by the build-up of proteins around and within brain cells. Dementia disorders impair memory, cognitive functioning, emotional expressions, intellect, and orientation. Symptoms cascade to debilitation and death, and no cures for any form of organic dementia are known at present.

Although Alzheimer's has a genetic component, the precise cause of the disease is not clearly understood. Researchers have identified genes that cause most cases that begin before age 65. Mutations in the *APP* gene, among others, that encode proteins lie at the heart of forming AD symptoms (Bertram and Tanzi 2008). In a study of 8,000 pairs of twins, Breitner's team (1990) found that Alzheimer's disease was not common, affecting only about 1 percent of the study group. Among fraternal twins, whose genetic make-up is no different than between other siblings, there were no cases of a person diagnosed with AD having a twin with AD. Incidence of Alzheimer's disease among identical twins, however, provides strong evidence of a genetic component to the disease: 35 percent of persons with an identical twin had a twin who was also diagnosed.

Studies such as this do not conclusively prove a genetics etiology of AD. If 35 percent of the identical twins' siblings also had AD, it also means that 65 percent did not. Furthermore, late-onset Alzheimer's disease (beginning after age 65) has a variable and inconsistent genetic foundation. Environmental factors, such as air pollution and exposure to heavy metals including lead and aluminum, may trigger the physiological chain that results in AD. Psychosocial factors may also contribute to dementia and AD. Higher education and staying mentally active improve cognitive functioning in late adulthood, and keeping physically energetic, which is often associated with social class, may play a role in preventing dementia disorders.

Depression

The incidence of depression rises during late adulthood, especially among 70–79-year-olds, but incidence numbers provided by the CDC (2017) report that major depression among older adults is not common, which betrays a stereotype many have of the elderly. As the CDC and other researchers make clear: Depression is not a normal part of aging. The prevalence of depression among older adults ranges from about 1 percent to 5 percent. The rate rises to over 13 percent of those who require home health care and 11.5 percent of older hospital patients, however (CDC 2017).

Several factors account for most of the increase in depression among older people. Whereas mid-adulthood is characterized by role stability—stable employment and family and friend relationships—the loss of key roles becomes a feature of the later years. The death of spouses, partners, and other relatives and friends changes social networks and sources of comfort and support. Retirement means not only losing income and benefits but also social identity and a sense of feeling relevant and productive. And for some, the loss of physical ability may lead to dependency after a lifetime of independence and self-reliance.

Mental health history is also important in understanding depression in late adulthood. Valiant and Valiant (1990) learned that a stable, cohesive childhood, and a history of emotional well-being predicted healthy self-esteem and ability for self-care among the elderly.

Depression among the elderly often presents similarly to depression in other age groups. Themes of loss and hopelessness are common, though these symptoms may be more reality-based among the aged who have fewer opportunities to replace or restore lost relationships, homes, and independent living (Riley 1994). Other indicators of depression among the elderly are apathy, lack of pleasure and interest in activities, withdrawal, and self-deprecating behavior.

In addition to "traditionally presented" depression, depression can take two other forms among the elderly. First, many depressed older adults mask their depressive symptoms (Riley 1994). In this form of depression, which is called **somatic depression**, older adults will complain of changes in sleep patterns, appetite, weight, energy levels, and sexual functioning rather than communicating their feelings of sadness or hopelessness. Somatic depression is more common among individuals who have their first depressive episode after age 65 and may be triggered by death or illness of a close loved one, changes in quality of living, or retirement.

A second form of depression found among the elderly is called **pseudo-depression**, which describes older adults who do not complain of melancholia, hopelessness, or somatic symptoms, but present with cognitive and memory deficits. Most often these individuals, as will those with the somatic type, are likely to go first to their family physician rather than a mental health professional, thinking that their problem is medical not psychological. This scenario can lead to inaccurate diagnoses of a dementia disorder (Riley 1994).

Bodies change in several ways with age. For example, coordination is poorer, movements are weaker and slower, and reactions to stimuli begin to slow, among other changes. Age-related changes to the brain (loss of cells) and nerve fibers are often to blame. Sometimes these changes are mistaken as a loss of cognitive ability or emotional stability. The mental well-being of the elderly is often judged by these unrelated physical changes and confused with dementia or depression, which promotes the stereotype.

It would be a fair deduction to suggest that elderly women are more prone to depression than elderly men; however, that is not necessarily the case. Elderly men who live alone are more prone to depression than women who live alone (Girgus et al. 2017; Russell and Taylor 2009).

Suicide

In most countries, suicide rates tend to rise for both men and women as they get older. (There is some variability in this pattern; suicide rates in Canada, for instance, peak at mid-life and decline thereafter.) In the United States, the suicide rate for people 75 and over is about four times the national average. This general statistic conceals important sex and ethnoracial differences. Suicide rates for Black and White women rise through mid-life before falling as they get into late adulthood. Black men's rates have two peaks, one during early adulthood and a second between ages 74 and 80. Suicide by White men, who have the highest suicide rates throughout the life course, rises to a peak between ages 44 and 55 (30 per 100,000 population) and again after age 75 to 45 per 100k population, which is the highest age-sex-ethnorace category of suicide (Conwell et al. 2011).

The rising size of the older population, powered by the aging of the baby Boomers cohort, which has a higher propensity to suicide than earlier or later birth cohorts, raises the possibility of more suicides among the elderly in the next 10–20 years (Conwell et al. 2011).

The higher rates of elderly suicide are likely conservative figures because older adults are known to commit "hidden" suicide by using unrecognizable methods. Their self-destructiveness may take the form of ignoring their physician's orders, failing to take medications, eating improperly, and abusing alcohol and other substances that result in death. Many elderly suicides, therefore, may be mislabeled as deaths due to other causes.

Suicide in late adulthood is largely attributed to the loss of social connectedness and control. Threats to health and functional impairment, bereavement, loss of social identity and social supports, and financial problems serve to disconnect individuals from social networks and meaningful relationships. Increasing social opportunities for older persons to feel useful and connected to others and therapy for depression and anxiety are critical for reducing suicidal behavior among older individuals.

Alcohol Abuse

Alcohol abuse is a particular problem among the elderly. Studies estimate that between 1 percent and 16 percent of people in late adulthood may have problems with alcohol consumption. Researchers typically divide alcohol abusers into two groups: early-onset and late-onset heavy drinkers who began abusing alcohol during late adulthood. The early-onset started drinking heavily relatively early in life and continued into old age. Their drinking problem is more severe, and they are likely to show signs of long-term effects of abusing alcohol. For example, early-onset alcohol abuse is associated liver disease, heart attacks, and stomach and intestinal ulcers, among other health complaints. In addition, early-onset drinkers have more depressive and anxiety symptoms, memory deficits, and lower self-esteem.

The two groups are similar in one important way. Prior to taking the first drink on days in which they consume alcohol, both groups report that they feel depressed and excessively lonely. According to Schonfeld and Dupree (1991), these emotional antecedents of drinking may indicate diminished social support. Small social networks common among early-onset drinkers may be due to others avoiding them and their persistent heavy drinking. For the late-onset group, heavy drinking may serve to assuage or cope with more recent losses. Retirement and the loss of loved ones may lead to depressive feelings which an individual may try to relieve by consuming alcohol.

Elder Abuse

Elder abuse has not received the attention that child abuse has in recent years, despite that fact about 10 percent of seniors 65 and over report incidence of physical abuse, psychological or verbal abuse, sexual abuse, financial exploitation, and neglect (Lachs and Pillemer 2015). For seniors in nursing homes, the risk for abuse may be as high at one in three because of their limited physical and cognitive abilities (Schiamberg et al. 2012).

As with other forms of abuse, elder maltreatment increases the risk for psychological problems, particularly depression, negatively emotional symptoms, and general distress. In some cases, abuse is predictive of suicidal ideations (Yunus et al. 2019). Abused seniors are often isolated and cut off from their social resources and support networks, making it more difficult for them to receive relief and services.

About the Quote

This chapter's lead-off quote comes from *The Onion*, a "newspaper" dedicated to satire and parody. Its stories are either completely fictional or based on real events but spoofed to make tongue-in-cheek social or political comments. The story, entitled "More U.S. Children Being Diagnosed with Youthful Tendency Disorder," is of the former type: a completely invented story about a made-up family having trouble understanding their child. That child, "Caitlan," is a preschooler who is worrying her parents because she often engages a "bizarre fantasy world" and pretends "to be people and things she was not." Caitlan bursts into nonsensical songs and runs aimlessly through her backyard giggling and squealing as she chases imaginary objects.

This weird behavior frightened her parents who failed to prevent her from acting in these strange ways. So, as any good parents would do, they placed Caitlan in therapy with a psychologist. After months of no improvement, they took her to a leading (still fictional) neurologist who finally diagnosed her with Youthful Tendency Disorder or YTD. The parents felt great relief at finally getting answers. They weren't bad parents; their daughter had a medical disorder. And they could live with that.

The story also reported on "Cameron," another child diagnosed with YTD. Cameron, age six, would sit on a swing set for long periods of time swaying back and forth in a way that seemed to comfort him. But then he would suddenly jump off the seat and start to run around the playground laughing and acting "crazy." His mom became really concerned when she discovered that young Cameron could name all the *Pokemon* characters, which are not real, but not one member of his hometown's city council.

Symptoms of YTD include long periods of "senseless and unproductive physical and mental exercises" and psychotic-like states of fantasy. It sounds horrible, and parents whose children show signs of this disorder must be panicked.

Did you get the joke? You probably figured it out immediately: both Caitlan and Cameron are normal children doing normal things. The story is a parody of the practice of diagnosing behavior that does not fit the script of expectations of what children, or anyone else for that matter, should be. Children's lives are heavily planned these days, and they stay so busy that they have little time to engage in free play and just being a kid. Is it parents or the children who want all these activities? It's probably the parents. Many parents engage in what's known as "hyper-parenting." They feel the need to prepare or market their children for a life course of their own choosing, not necessarily the child's. Micromanaging their children's lives out of fear that their child will not be competitive for admission into good schools or careers does not always result in the desired outcomes. Over-scheduled children often burn out or become bored. They also are susceptible to the effects of stress, and then they may actually qualify for a real diagnosis.

DISCUSSION QUESTIONS

1. Think about how Cooley's theory can be applied to physical and sexual abuse. In Cooley's approach, what image is "reflected" back from significant others who are committing the abuse? How might a child interpret the behavior of an abusive parent?

2. Here's another Cooley experiment. How could his theory be applied to ethnorace relations? It is well-known that retail workers are more likely to surveil African Americans customers than Whites. In Cooley's approach, what image is "reflected" back from store workers? How might African Americans interpret this behavior?

3. For the elderly, personal losses mount to the point that, for many, maintaining emotional strength becomes a burden. What can society do to relieve the stress that loss of family members, friends, employment, and physical ability creates?

4. Write your socio-biography that describes your life in relationship to macro-level social and historical events. For example, what were the economic and political influences that directed your family to where you live? How have ethnoracial relations and social class at the societal level impacted your sense of self and your well-being?

KEY TERMS

Identity Diffusion 170
Identity Integration 170
Helicoptering 183
Launching 166
Life Course Studies 164
Looking-glass Self 169
Problematic Social Media Use 185
Pseudo-Depression 190
Self-efficacy 165
Socialization 167
Somatic Depression 190

CHAPTER 9

Communities and Organizations

Learning Objectives

After reading this chapter, students will be able to:

1. Judge the effects of residential location on mental health.
2. Describe the effects of workplace conditions on psychological well-being.
3. Determine how participation in voluntary organizations promote or hinder mental health.

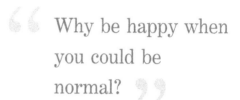

" Why be happy when you could be normal? "

—Jeanette Winterson (2011)

Introduction

The social forces that affect psychological well-being are not limited to broad macrolevel phenomena such as social class, ethnorace, or gender. Sometimes these forces are closer geographically and socially. Neighborhoods, workplaces, and voluntary organizations exert significant influence on mental health both in negative and positive ways. They can create stress or provide resources that help ease life's struggles.

At least once in our lives, most of us have will have a job or live in a neighborhood that we do not like, and stress is one of the ways our dislike of that job or residence is expressed. If we are lucky, we can move to a better situation, but for many people, there is no escaping unpleasant social environments.

This chapter focuses on the impact that social forces originating from neighborhoods, workplaces, and organizations can have on mental health.

Where We Live

Communities of place impact quality of life. Where we live affects the kinds of stress we encounter and the resources necessary to cope with and respond to that stress. In this section, the literature on place of residence's effect on mental health is reviewed. First, urban and rural locations will be compared, and then the focus will turn to neighborhood conditions and their relationship to mental health.

Urban and Rural Residence

The difference between urban and rural behavior and attitudes has been discussed for over a century. The famous German sociologist Ferdinand Tönnies (1887/1957), for example, sought to describe ideal versions of rural and urban lifestyles using the German words **gemeinschaft** and **gesellschaft**. *Gemeinschaft* societies and communities are those where residents live more communally and possess a universal sense of solidarity. The population tends to be less diverse socially and culturally. These communities are typically rural, follow traditional rules of conduct, and share core values. Relationships in *gemeinschaft* communities are simple but more direct, and personal social ties are based upon emotional connections governed by a sense of moral obligation to others.

Gesellschaft communities are urban and socially heterogeneous. They are characterized by rational self-interest and impersonal behavior. *Gesellschaft* emerges when many people live close together and are organized in governmental and industrial bureaucracies that stress efficiency and a complex division of labor that tend to erode the traditional bonds of family, kinship, and religion found in *gemeinschaft* communities. In a *gesellschaft* society, behavior is more calculated, indirect, and less personal and emotional.

Gemeinschaft and *gesellschaft* are not categories of classifications but ideal types and are most useful as conceptual tools when analyzing a society's organization and social behavior. There are elements of both types in rural and urban locales. Therefore, the point is made that in contemporary society, differences in rural and urban living are not separated by distinct boundaries. There are elements of *gesellschaft* in the most rural of places and *gemeinschaft* relationships occur in the largest of cities. As cities sprawl into rural areas and technology allows rural residents to participate in the global economy, uniquely urban and rural lifestyles are becoming less identifiable. Rural living does not presume a "little house on the prairie"; instead, rural homes have modern conveniences, and satellite TV and internet bring all aspects of modern culture into the most isolated of homes.

Following Tönnies' definitions, it was assumed in early sociology that living in a *gesellschaft* society increased the risk of mental illness. From the 1930s through the 1950s, studies found more depression in cities, which was attributed to the stress of city life: breakdown of communal cohesion, a hallmark of *gemeinschaft* communities, separation of family members, less familial support, and greater mobility (Wang 2004). The urban environment was believed to cause more social isolation and a greater chance of failure because of increased competition for housing, jobs, and education (Frissen et al. 2017).

By the 1980s, however, fewer studies were finding differences in urban and rural mental health. Today there is little evidence that living in a rural area provides mental health advantages for adults or protective barriers against mental illness for adolescents as was previously thought (Johnson et al. 2008; Wang 2004).

While there may be more opportunities of risk in urban areas, the rural-urban distinction itself does not contribute significantly to the development of psychiatric morbidity. The real problems are poverty, unemployment, social class position, family health, discrimination, and childhood abuse and trauma, regardless of where they occur (Judd et al. 2002).

Rural and Urban Differences in Mental Health

Despite the merging of urban and rural lifestyles and mental health, there are urban-rural differences in some aspects of mental health epidemiology. For example, rural teens are equally or more likely than their suburban and urban counterparts to report experiencing many indicators of violent behavior, victimization, suicidal behaviors, and drug use. Rural teens are more likely to hurt themselves in a suicide attempt and to be coerced into sex, both of which can have long-lasting mental health consequences (Johnson et al. 2008).

In addition to these trends, suicide and mental health care utilization follow unique patterns in rural areas and warrant special attention.

Farmer Suicide

The farm crisis of the 1980s was accompanied by a rash of suicides among farmers. Farmers killing themselves in large numbers was a new phenomenon, making the news and causing public disquiet about the state of agriculture in the United States.

The crisis was caused by a number of macrolevel forces. Prior to 1980, American farm products were highly desired commodities globally. Droughts around the world and a weak US dollar created both demand and favorable prices, and American agriculture reached new heights in production and profit. The price of US farmland soared, and farmers expanded their operations with offers of easy credit terms.

By the early 1980s, however, the dollar had risen in international money markets, which made American products more expensive to import. Following the former Soviet Union's invasion of Afghanistan, the US government imposed a grain embargo against the USSR, closing off an important market for American wheat. Because of high production and inventory, prices fell, and the value of land dropped by as much as 50 percent in many parts of the country while the cost of machinery, fuel, and fertilizer rose. Farmers entered into debt, and their resources for managing that debt dwindled.

During the crisis, farms began to dissolve by the tens of thousands. While government subsidies helped, most farmers were unable to weather this financial storm. None of these conditions was of their doing, and because their world was collapsing around them, many farmers committed suicide. According to government statistics, during the crisis, the farmer suicide rate peaked at 58 per 100,000 farmers in 1982.

Unfortunately, the farmer suicide rate has increased again, and has almost doubled the 1982 rate in the first two decades of the twenty-first century (McIntosh et al. 2016). Many studies have explored the causes of rural suicide, and Hirsch and Cukrowicz (2014) have deduced several predictive factors from this literature. While farmers and other rural residents are subject to many of the same psychosocial dynamics that are associated with suicide elsewhere (for example, interpersonal conflicts, family dysfunctions, and marginalization), several factors unique to farming cause an additional stress burden.

- Isolation. Because farmers often reside in remote places, access to other people and communities is difficult. Being away from urban centers distances farmers from services that could help them cope with negative emotions and suicidal ideation in more positive ways.

- Agricultural factors. Natural and social forces unique to farming, such as the weather, exposure to chemicals, market and finance issues, and debt, are out of the control of farmers and add to farmers' stress.

- Sociocultural factors. For many farmers, especially men, agricultural work rests on core values of honor and a rugged individualistic perception of masculinity. These values exert pressure to succeed and to develop a stoic persona to downplay or hide emotional pain from themselves and others.

To connect these conditions theoretically, Stark and colleagues (2011) applied the **Cry of Pain/Entrapment model** of suicide risk to farmers. This theory states that social isolation leads to feelings of defeat and entrapment, and when individuals are unable to cope with stress, they start to feel there is no safe exit or imminent rescue (Williams et al. 2001). In essence, the theory states that:

feelings of entrapment + no escape + no rescue → suicide

Stark and colleagues contended that because of "rural restructuring," which refers to the depopulation of rural areas, an aging rural population, less profitability for family farming, and the need to work a "regular" job while farming has made farmers feel more socially and politically cut-off and excluded. Rural social life has been dramatically disrupted, leading many farmers to feel helpless to deal with their problems.

Farmer suicide is a prime example of Durkheim's theory that suicide is not solely an existential or psychological behavior. Rather, it is rooted in social forces that are beyond the influence of individuals and their families but exert great control over them.

Rural Mental Health Care Services

In comparing the mental health landscape of rural and urban places, we find that the key questions are less about prevalence or distribution of disorders and more about treatment utilization. While need is proportionally similar in rural and urban areas, the gap between need and service in rural places is much greater. Two factors account for this difference. First, rural counties and towns have few mental health professionals. In Appalachia, for example, 75 percent of nonmetropolitan counties have severe shortages in providers (Hendryx 2008). This deficiency of professional services is particularly problematic for children with acute needs and suggests that a larger proportion of children living in rural areas have psychological problems, especially behavioral concerns, because their symptoms are receiving less attention when compared to urban children (Lenardson et al. 2010).

Because of the shortage of mental health providers in rural areas, distressed rural residents often rely on hospital emergency rooms (ERs) for care when their usual coping strategies fail. While urban residents similarly depend on ERs for treatment, urban-rural patterns differ. Compared to metropolitan ERs, rural emergency facilities are more likely to treat elderly patients, poor families, and those on Medicare and Medicaid for mental health problems. Rural women depend on ERs more than their urban counterparts. Overall, ER patients present, in rank order, with symptoms of anxiety and depression and suicidal thoughts. Rural ERs treat, again in order by frequency, anxiety, depression, and panic disorders (Schroeder and Peterson 2018). ERs only provide short-term services and try to stabilize patients. Care beyond the immediate crisis is not provided by emergency professionals, and in rural communities, continuing care is often not available.

Second, the large number of rural adults not receiving treatment suggests that stigma may also contribute to underutilization of services. Mental ill-health remains a highly discrediting condition among many rural residents. Compared to urban denizens, rural residents with psychological complaints are more subject to stereotyping and discrimination. Mental health problems are more likely to lead to status loss and are assigned a lower health priority among rural residents (Stewart et al. 2015). Research has found, for example, that older adults living in isolated rural communities hold negative attitudes toward receiving care for psychological problems even when controlling for education and income (Stewart et al. 2015). This research is consistent with Pescosolido and colleagues' (2015) work that found that developing countries having more *gemeinschaft* characteristics are more likely to stigmatize mental illness than societies and communities described as having *gesellschaft* qualities.

Neighborhoods

Neighborhoods constitute much of a person's social environment. As such, they are key social markers of class, occupation, and ethnorace and play a central role in identity formation, self-esteem, and psychological health. Because neighborhoods are intertwined with personal life space, their attributes, regardless of social class and ethnoracial make-up, can become independent sources of stress for residents.

Neighborhoods have a character or personality of their own, and families and individuals are embedded within them. In a sense, neighborhoods constitute the immediate material and emotional context of everyday life. For example, they provide our first contact with society outside our own homes. When we leave our residences each day, the first part of the social world we physically encounter is our neighborhood, which can stimulate emotions such as anxiety or comfort, pride or disappointment, or fear or safety. For many, neighborhoods are havens, safe places to escape the stresses of the broader society. For others, however, neighborhoods are frightening places where families feel safe only in their homes. Many people take pride in their neighborhoods and feel a sense of contentment where they live; others may feel ashamed of their neighborhoods because of social comparisons or because of the neighborhood's social and physical obstacles to happiness and life satisfaction.

Neighborhoods, like people, are not singular, one-dimensional entities. Conceptualizing neighborhoods as a dichotomy of "good" and "bad," therefore, is an empirical error. Because there are many facets to a sociological profile of neighborhoods, appearances can be deceiving. There are several qualities of neighborhoods that can impact mental health. Generally, when studying the effects of neighborhoods on psychological well-being, sociologists look at five characteristics: violence, economic resources, social order, social cohesion, and collective efficacy. See Chart 9.1 for definitions of these terms.

Hill, Ross, and Angel state that neighborhood qualities can have a profound effect on psychological well-being.

The stress of living in a neighborhood where the streets are dusty and dangerous; buildings are run-down, abandoned, and vandalized; and people hang out on the streets drinking and using drugs creates anxious fear and arousal followed by depressed lethargy and demoralization. Daily exposure to disadvantage, decay, and disorder in one's neighborhood is distressing. (2005: 170–171)

Troubled neighborhoods create an ambient threat that elicits perceptions of powerlessness, normlessness, mistrust, and isolation, conditions that can become antecedents to symptoms of anxiety and depression (Ross and Mirowsky 2009). The more economically disadvantaged or distressed a neighborhood is, the more likely residents will suffer psychologically. Depression, for instance, is associated with a breakdown in neighborhood social control and order (Ross 2000). Poverty, abandoned buildings, and crime prevent residents from feeling that they can rely on their neighbors to create social networks that provide social and emotional support. In short, residing in disordered neighborhoods is linked to depression and anxiety, and the longer a person lives in these neighborhoods, the poorer an individual's affective health is likely to be (Hill et al. 2005).

Generally, psychological outcomes associated with disadvantaged neighborhood features are thought to result from the cumulation effects of stress. In an innovative study using smartphone and GPS technology, York Cornwell and Goldman (2020) found that the moment that people are exposed to a disordered environment, both within and outside their own neighborhood, they have a physiological stress response. Spikes in physiological indicators of stress occurred whenever an individual encountered an abandoned building, broken windows, and litter. Data from this study also indicate how quickly and under what circumstances the fight or flight process commences.

CHART 9.1 Neighborhood Characteristics

Violence in a neighborhood refers to frequency of violent acts both within homes and in public areas. The more violence and crime occur in a neighborhood, the more fearful and anxious residents feel.

Economic advantage is a measure of neighborhood income, wealth, and collective material and social resources. Economic disadvantage is not necessarily a cause of neighborhood problems, but it increases stress on residents and reduces the resources necessary to solve problems.

Social cohesion refers to perceptions of trust, reciprocity, and shared values among neighbors.

Social order represents stability, cleanliness (no litter or trash), safety, well-maintained houses and yards and few vacant properties. Social order implies that people are law-abiding and conforming to local norms of cooperativeness.

Collective efficacy means neighbors' ability to solve neighborhood problems together. Much like self-efficacy, collective efficacy creates a sense of mastery over the environment and avoids feelings of helplessness. Examples are neighborhood watches, monitoring activities of youngsters, and preventing properties from becoming derelict or poorly maintained.

As we have already discussed, self-efficacy is central to mental health and arises from experiencing control of one's environment (Bandura 1997). Neighborhoods, being an important part of a person's milieu, play a key role in generating opportunities for residents, especially adolescents, to feel capable and confident to master both themselves and their surroundings. Neighborhoods shape residents' experiences of social control and facilitate, or hinder, feelings of predictability and safety. For example, in neighborhoods with low crime rates, well-maintained properties, and less communal stress, residents tend to feel more self-efficacious because they feel in control of their environment by contributing to those factors that enhance residential contentment. In neighborhoods plagued with violence and disorder, however, residents often feel helpless in that any action they may take to quell the disturbances will likely be for naught (Kim 2010; Rabinowitz et al. 2020).

Consequently, residents report lower self-efficacy where violence is high (Dupéré et al. 2012). Dupéré's research group uncovered three ways in which the association between neighborhood characteristics and low self-efficacy happens. First, neighborhood violence generates fear, especially for residents who are directly exposed to the violence, which can erode self-efficacy. Residents believe there is little they can do to protect themselves and others from violence and confrontations. Second, troubled neighborhoods negatively affect self-efficacy if problems restrict access to quality institutions. Schools, recreation centers, and parks that are safe and reliable can instill positive self-assessments in both children and adults. To prove themselves capable and gain confidence, people need the opportunities that good and affirming teachers, coaches, clerics, and relatives can provide. Challenging and high-quality extracurricular activities are essential to feel self-efficacious. And third, neighborhoods must exhibit high collective efficacy. Residents need to see that neighbors have the capacity to achieve common goals through collective action. Societal cohesion benefits residents' sense of belongingness and self-efficacy because they can see and experience how collective action brings about safe and resourceful environments. Collective self-efficacy enables individual feelings of safety and personal empowerment, both of which improve mental health. High levels of trust and expectations that control over public spaces will be maintained lowers the likelihood that social disorder will be experienced as a psychological stressor (Browning et al. 2013).

The effects of neighborhood distress on adolescents are particularly important because of the developmental tasks facing teenagers and the risk of future mental health problems should they fail to accomplish those tasks. If youths perceive their neighborhoods as cohesive through collective efficacy, they will have more positive interactions with other residents and stronger ties to their communities, which, in turn, provide them with protective, instrumental support when they experience hardships (Rabinowitz et al. 2020). Adolescents in economically disadvantaged neighborhoods and areas in which residential mobility is high, that is, people are frequently moving in and out of apartments and houses, are prone to more emotional distress than their peers in neighborhoods with few vacant sites, high employment rates, and high percentages of adults with college degrees (Snedker and Herting 2016). Compared to higher income neighborhoods, adolescents in low-income residential areas perceive more ambient stressors such as crime, violence, drug use, and graffiti. Teenagers in these neighborhoods who translate those stressors into perceived dangerousness are more likely to develop symptoms of depression, anxiety, oppositional defiant disorder, and conduct disorder (Aneshensel and Sucoff 1996).

If the evidence that disadvantaged neighborhoods are injurious for adolescent mental health is so strong, how is it that psychologically healthy individuals can emerge from this environment? Rabinowitz and colleagues (2020) created a typology of disadvantaged neighborhood profiles and their association with adolescent psychological distress (see Chart 9.2).

Of the four types of disadvantaged neighborhoods, the fourth subgroup, "Highest Cohesion and Lowest Disorder," would be expected to produce the lowest levels of psychological distress among resident adolescents. That, however, was not the case. Compared to youths from the other subgroups, teens from the "Highest Violence and Highest Disadvantaged" subgroup statistically demonstrated the best ability to cognitively reframe their neighborhood stressors into positive outcomes. They also exhibited higher levels of problem-solving coping skills by learning from their environmental hardships. Exposure to this level of stress facilitates adaptation to the adversities of life. Youths in this setting learn to think about the positives in their lives and develop skills to avoid the negatives. These skills, furthermore, promote self-efficacy and self-esteem and serve as buffers against future mental health problems (Rabinowitz et al. 2020).

CHART 9.2 Four Types of Disadvantaged Neighborhoods and Their Characteristics

Type	Description	
Highest Social Disorder	High social disorder	Low social cohesion
	High economic disadvantage	Low collective efficacy
Highest Violent and Highest Disadvantaged	Very violent	Low social cohesion
	Very disordered	High social disorder
	Low collective efficacy	Very economically disadvantaged
High Violence	High rates of violence	Average disorder
	High economic disadvantage	Average cohesion
Highest Cohesion and Lowest Disorder	Average collective efficacy	Highest collective efficacy
	High disadvantage	Lowest disorder

Source: Adapted from Rabinowitz et al. (2020).

Neighborhoods and Social Diversity

Residing in disordered neighborhoods is unevenly distributed by social status. Compared to their White counterparts, African American youths who live in low-income, single-parent households disproportionately reside in disordered neighborhoods and are more likely to experience psychological distress because of their neighborhoods' social problems (Turner et al. 2013). While African Americans and Whites are comparably affected by severe neighborhood social problems in terms of stress, anxiety, and depressive symptoms, a perception of community cohesion has more benefits for Whites (Gary et al. 2007).

The situation is similar for Hispanic teens. As shown in Chapter 6, cultural discrimination, based on characteristics of the group, can have a negative impact on psychological health. This tension, called cultural stress, is particularly harmful when parents perceive their neighborhood to have average or high levels of neighborhood problems. Lorenzo-Blanco and colleagues (2019) found that in Hispanic neighborhoods, the teenage children of parents who see their neighborhoods as relatively free from social problems such as crime, drug use, gangs, and graffiti are less vulnerable to cultural stress and not as likely to engage in aggressive or self-destructive behavior. A strong neighborhood fabric, we can conclude, protects against the impact of cultural discrimination in Hispanic communities.

One question that often rises among scholars, policymakers, and the lay public is whether segregated neighborhoods affect psychological health. Two hypotheses are derived from this question. The first is called the **ethnic density hypothesis** which states that living in ethnoracially homogeneous neighborhoods improves mental health and *lowers* the risk of depression when compared to persons living in neighborhoods with fewer people of their own ethnorace. This approach contends that good mental health is promoted by increases in social support, cultural cohesion, and better access to resources via social connections among members of the group (Halpern 1993). For example, immigrants in ethnic enclaves have greater social ties and support from kinship groups and community organizations. They share information about jobs, teach one another to negotiate a foreign culture, and celebrate and enjoy cultural events together (Mair et al. 2010).

The second, the **residential segregation hypothesis**, states that living in neighborhoods with a high proportion of residents from their own ethnoracial group *increases* the risk of psychological symptoms. The argument here is that mental health problems arise because of ethnoracial isolation. The institutional racism, forced segregation, restrictive housing markets, and fewer job opportunities often found in these neighborhoods compound cultural stress and increase the risk to emotional health. A primary example is the high concentration of poverty often found in urban ethnoracial communities. When impoverished people are segregated into a central city, crime and other factors that impact quality of life can become epidemic and cause stress to escalate (Mair et al. 2010).

Studies comparing these hypotheses are not conclusive; however, when controlling for other neighborhood characteristics, it appears that the effects of ethnoracial homogeneity vary by social groups. High rates of ethnoracial concentration are associated with depressive symptoms among African American men and to a lesser extent Hispanic women and men and Chinese women (Mair et al. 2010). This finding supports the residential segregation hypothesis. The failure to find this relationship among other groups, however, supports the ethnic density theory. The question becomes why ethnoracial segregation affects Black men more than men or women in other groups. It may be that ethnoracial concentration impacts these men because of the greater likelihood of confronting stressors related to economic disadvantage and the absence of conventional and health-strengthening social supports and activities. Mair and colleagues theorize that men in primarily Black neighborhoods may have more encounters with trauma via gang activity and incarceration in addition to a high stress burden from discrimination in employment and education and damaging stereotypes.

Similarities among neighbors' social and demographic characteristics in general are important for mental well-being and responding to stress. When people live in neighborhoods with people who are socially similar, they tend to share norms and values that provide a sense of meaning to life's conflicts and stressors. Young and Wheaton (2013) studied whether neighborhood composition affected how couples with children managed conflicts in balancing work and family obligations and found that neighbors who share social characteristics also share a common understanding of stressors caused by tension when work and family roles conflict. This shared worldview of work and family stress reduced the emotional toll of work-family conflict by increasing the likelihood of emotional and tangible support. The effect was stronger for women than for men.

Among the elderly, neighborhood cohesion has proven critical for psychological health. Individuals in late adulthood benefit from active engagement with neighbors, developing trusting relationships, reciprocity in interactions, and shared values. For older people, cohesive neighborhoods improve coping strategies such as seeking social support, sharing activities and hobbies, and enhance positive thinking, all of which promote mental health (Kim et al. 2020).

In addition to the effect of neighborhoods on mental health, the quality of housing and the physical home environment similarly promote or reduce stress and mental health. For example, women with young children who live in high-rise apartments are subject to emotional distress because the built-environment increases social isolation. Poor housing quality is strongly related to psychological symptoms in adults, especially in deteriorating neighborhoods, and the effects of overcrowding are worse in substandard housing. Poor housing quality increases stress due to hassles with maintenance, safety concerns, and increased hazards such as vermin and insect infestations. Housing problems diminish control and mastery and increase helplessness (Evans et al. 2003). Box 9.1 describes problems in public housing projects and how these developments are associated with behavior and mental health concerns.

Box 9.1 The Consequences of Demolishing Neighborhoods

In the 1950s and 1960s, federal and local governments in the US initiated plans to handle mental health problems and the social disorder that seemed to be caused by living in cities. As we mentioned in Chapter 5, sociologists in the first half of the twentieth century were finding and mapping mental illness cases concentrated in urban areas. They found that mental health problems were more likely to occur in poor and working-class neighborhoods where the housing was substandard, crime rates were higher, and, at least to middle class observers, social disorder was common. These neighborhoods came to be known as slums, and because of the way the data gleaned by the sociologists and scholars in other fields were interpreted, city planners and policy-makers came to believe that the slums were the cause of geographical variations in mental health in urban areas.

After World War II (though some of the programs began as early as 1942), the country's cities set on a plan to remove their slums in a social movement known as urban renewal. The champions of urban renewal sold the country on the idea that slum neighborhoods caused social and psychological problems and if the cities removed the slums, those problems would disappear. Massive demolitions occurred throughout the nation's cities, and thousands of families were displaced. Old established neighborhoods vanished in the blink of an eye.

To house the displaced families, many cities built publicly financed housing projects. Many of them were high-rise monstrosities or clusters of large buildings situated over several acres of land. Many of these projects are well-known. Cabrini-Green in Chicago, the Magnolia Projects in New Orleans, and Pruitt-Igoe in St. Louis are among the most infamous, and were, along with many others, demolished just two or three decades after their construction.

These projects were absolute failures in several ways. Their construction design was not people-centered; that is, they were not conducive to the way individuals and families live their daily lives. The buildings were isolating, which meant that families could not easily interact with each other, and they had countless "blind spots," places where the drug trade, prostitution, and other criminal activity could flourish. These projects did not consider children's normal activities and made it easy for children to act without supervision.

Another problem was that these projects destroyed cohesive, solid neighborhoods. Although their houses were not well kept and many were dilapidated, the residents of the neighborhoods were emotionally attached to their neighbors and communities. These neighborhoods were socially and culturally vibrant but because they were poor, they were presumed to be pathological environments for mental health. Planners did not see the informal social controls that had evolved through generations of residents who looked after each other and their children and who worked together to support their families and communities. Where the government only saw slums, developers saw opportunities for profit.

Boston's West End provides a telling example. A slum typical of post-war American cities, most houses and other structures in the West End were run down and ramshackle. Home to lower working-class Italians, Jews, Irish, and Poles, the neighborhood was described by the psychiatric "establishment" as places without social cohesion where mental illness was rampant (Ramsden and Smith 2018). That, however, was not the case. The West End was an active, engaging neighborhood of high social cohesion. West Enders were loyal to where they lived and to each other. The neighborhood provided them a sense of identity and belongingness.

Boston municipal government, however, determined that the West End was an unhealthy environment for residents' mental health, and in 1958, the city began to tear down the neighborhood, displacing over 2,700 families. Herbert Gans, a well-known sociologist, was brought in, along with other social and behavioral scientists, to study the displacement. He wrote that it was not the existing housing but the destruction of "socially and emotionally important social systems" that caused stress (quoted in Ramsden and Smith 2018). Though it was crowded, and the buildings were not in great condition, the community was healthy and stable. Gans concluded the families were better off in the slums than in the homes assigned for resettlement. What made the families' lives better was the cohesive neighborhood, which was demolished. The families were not able to recreate that cohesiveness later.

What replaced the neighborhood after demolition? High-rent apartments now occupy the land where people once lived in solid and ordered neighborhoods and in houses they could afford.

Where We Work

Apart from their homes, people with jobs spend more time at work than any other place. The work people do is an important contributor to their sense of identity, contentment, life satisfaction, and personal fulfillment. As John Mirowsky (2011: 85) states

> *Americans express themselves, develop themselves, and discover themselves through physical and mental effort and activity directed towards production or accomplishment of something.*

For Mirowsky, productive self-expression constitutes an elemental need in humans, and when that need is suppressed, frustrated, or neglected, psychological well-being is subverted. Work is important not only for meeting material needs, but for personal identity and happiness as well. For many people, the old saying "work to live and live to work" is more than a truism—it represents a foundation to their sense of self, and their psychic health rests on the social and psychological rewards received from work.

Employment is generally better for mental health than nonemployment (Llena-Nozal 2009). Earning the money to support oneself and one's family is a central measure of success in industrial and postindustrial societies. Economical self-reliance is a sign of emotional maturity in these societies, whereas dependency is an indicator of failure as well as mental illness. One example of the importance of work is the strategic way in which it improves the recovery of patients with mental health problems. Work has been found to facilitate improvements in well-being by offering a routine and structure to daily living, hopefulness, security, and social inclusion (Leamy et al. 2011). Indeed, work delivers more than a paycheck; it promotes identity and personal empowerment.

Having a job may be necessary for mental health for most people, but it is not sufficient. Workplace conditions and experiences exert a powerful influence over mental health and, according to Woods and colleagues (2019), a hostile work environment can psychologically disable individuals. As you know, there are good jobs and bad jobs (Box 9.2).

Bad jobs are easy to specify. Low pay plays a part, but perhaps more important in terms of mental health are interpersonal and environmental factors such as excessive pressures and demands, exposure to dangerous or toxic conditions, and unchallenging and monotonous tasks (Limonic and Lennon 2017). Highly routinized tasks that require little cognitive engagement and restrict workers' ability to have a say in their work have been shown to increase psychological distress (Reynolds 1997).

Box 9.2 Bureaucrat as Disorder?

The great classical sociologist Max Weber argued that western society was moving toward a social organization in which rationalization based on efficiency, specialization, and impersonality was becoming the dominant order of social life. He noticed that values and expectations of behavior were increasingly controlled by ever-growing organizations governed by a set of principles designed to maximize productivity. Weber called this process bureaucratization, and he foretold a future in which everything in social life would be organized, produced, and consumed within a bureaucratic hierarchy. He was not optimistic about such a future and predicted that a bureaucratically organized society would become an "iron cage of rationality" in which bureaucracies would entrap people into dehumanized social relations, demystify sacred things, and, to paraphrase his ideas loosely, simply take the pleasure out of life. Bureaucracies make life too formal, overly regulated, and passionless.

There is little argument that Weber's prophetic and somewhat dystopian projection of contemporary life holds a degree of truth. Sociologists and mental health professionals have voiced concern about the effects of the bureaucratic organization of work, government, religion, schools, and even leisure on psychological well-being. One psychiatrist (Powers 1994) even proposed a bureaucrat disorder as a DSM-recognized condition. Here are his diagnostic criteria for the bureaucrat disorder:

1. Employed over two years in a position that produces no clear product or service.
2. Must have met four of the following nine symptoms over the past year.

   a. Frequent complaints of low pay but rarely seeks better employment.
   b. Frequent complaints of being overworked, but rarely works over 38 hours per week.
   c. References everything in life to retirement.
   d. Attends two or more staff meetings, each lasting 45 minutes or more, per week.
   e. Produces or forwards one or more memos involving control issues, per week.
   f. Believes that others do not realize their importance.
   g. Believes their position is essential to public order, despite the absence of supportive evidence.
   h. Deals with conflict by procrastination, passive aggressiveness, or withdrawal.
   i. Maintains control through rules, guidelines, committees, and threats of administrative revenge.

Writing his short proposal as a Letter to the Editor of the prestigious *American Journal of Psychiatry*, Dr. Powers was having a bit of fun, but his point is well taken. Working in a bureaucracy is not always good for us. It not only adds a stress burden that affects mental health, but because of its strict adherence to formal rules and impersonality, it can create an existential crisis of "Who am I?"

Jerome Braun (1982) felt similarly. He believed that modern people are becoming more one-dimensional and lacking in personal depth because they are overly embedded in one-dimensional bureaucratic institutions that control and socialize them. These institutions are all-encompassing and orient our behaviors to the point that, according to Braun, we often feel more comfortable at work than we do with our families.

Most everything we do involves large bureaucracies with their own rules and procedures. Virtually all sectors of the economy, everything from groceries to fashion to entertainment to communication to news media, are dominated by large corporate entities. Even education has become excessively bureaucratic: registering for college classes is complicated and the number of compliance standards that regulate your college's activities is mind-numbing. Bureaucracies are ubiquitous in modern life.

Bureaucracies make countless demands on our personal behavior, yet we rarely realize how they influence us. (Years ago, I worked in a psychiatric hospital that instructed us to end every phone conversation with the word "goodbye." They even made quality control phone calls to see if we followed that policy.) They narrow our perspectives and force us to see other people as objects identified by a case number that need to be processed rather than human beings with names and emotions.

Bureaucracies, Braun contends, direct us to become task-oriented and consumed with completing assignments planned by someone with bureaucratic authority over us, conforming to rules and following a schedule, all of which we try to do as efficiently as possible. Free time, consequently, is often more about escapism (such as taking drugs, overeating, overinvolvement with gaming, too much TV, or passively following sports or celebrities) than truly relaxing or engaging in a meaningful leisurely activity. When people are amusing themselves, they are not engaging in creative hobbies, volunteering in their

(Continued)

Box 9.2 Bureaucrat as Disorder? *(Continued)*

community, reading books, or exercising, all of which are activities that foster good mental health.

While bureaucracies bring order and routine to social life and lower confusion and risk, they are also alienating and disenchanting. Bureaucracies can make us lose the ability to connect with people at a human level of genuineness, which, Braun says, drives us toward authoritarianism (because we are forced to conform to, identity with, and experience the institution as reality) and narcissism (among those who refuse to conform but need to protect themselves psychologically). Bureaucracies require us to act as the institution not as ourselves, and that level of alienation and detachment could be conceived as a pathology.

What makes for a good job? Compensation is certainly important. A job that pays so poorly that it prevents individuals from affording necessities and security creates significant stress. If high enough, material rewards can offset some of the negative social-psychological aspects of work and the workplace. What is important is the subjective connection between effort and rewards. If income, security, and career opportunities are not believed to match perceived effort, then emotional distress is more likely to occur (Siegrist 1996).

Other workplace factors help define a good job in relation to mental health. Control is one critical aspect of work associated with well-being. Controlling one's work brings greater satisfaction and psychological well-being. In the context of work, control implies setting the pace and schedule of work and having some degree of autonomy in decision-making. Jobs that allow individuals to plan their own tasks promote better mental health (Moen et al. 2011). Self-directed labor means enabling intellectual flexibility and personal competency and being free from over-supervision (Kohn and Schooler 1983).

Control over one's labor is especially significant for good mental health for workers who experience high levels of workplace stress: control helps negate the effects of conflicting and harsh workloads and demands for fast work speed (Karasek and Theorell 1999). Under such conditions, not having a say over one's labor is particularly harmful for mental health. As an example, several environmental workplace factors such as a seemingly endless patient caseload are associated with a relatively high burnout rate among psychiatrists (Kumar 2007).

As discussed in Chapter 5, labor expectations vary by social class. Managers and owners who control policies and workplace guidelines have a higher sense of mastery and consequently well-being. Managerial and professional jobs, however, are not totally safe from stressful workplace conditions because they are subject to micromanagement, high performance demands, and long work hours. In addition, managers experience emotional problems when they are forced to institute or enforce unpleasant policies or decisions, such as informing employees of impending layoffs (Moore et al. 2006).

Macrolevel economic issues, which refers to the broader economic conditions in which jobs are located, have also been shown to affect mental health. Economic stress in the form of uncertainty, recessions, high unemployment, fear of layoffs, and changes in work conditions (such as workplace policies, hours, or duties) are associated with psychological distress. These conditions are particularly harmful to middle-class workers who occupy more rewarding and complex jobs (Reynolds 1997). Lam and colleagues (2014) studied the impact of the Great Recession of 2008 and found that job insecurity had a negative impact on overall happiness and increased the number of days in which individuals experienced poor mental health. This study also found that middle-class employees were more affected psychologically than blue collar workers, which, the authors concluded, implied a growing insecurity of those people who are traditionally more advantaged. The middle class, men in particular, may be less prepared psychologically to cope with economic uncertainty and threatened job loss.

One of the ways in which some groups manage economic hard times is through positive group affiliations. Hughes, Kiecolt, and Keith (2014) found that a strong racial identity serves as an effective buffer against financial stress for African Americans. While it does not eliminate distress, strong ties to their ethnoracial community fortify their coping abilities and reduce the likelihood of depressive symptoms.

Voluntary Organizations

Not all encounters with social organizations occur in the context of employment or residence. While it is necessary to work and live among other people, many individuals engage in aspects of their communities voluntarily. Working without pay and in service to others is certainly a "feel good" endeavor and reinforces altruistic values. Thus, participating in volunteer activities has a positive effect on mental health.

Performing volunteer services without financial compensation has been shown to enhance mental health and protects individuals against symptoms (Wilson 2012). Most studies confirm that people who engage in volunteer activities report fewer indicators of depression; this effect is strongest among the elderly and women (Hong and Morrow-Howell 2010). While it is possible that people with good mental health are more likely to volunteer, longitudinal studies demonstrate that mental health improves following a stint of volunteer activity (Yuen et al. 2008). Volunteering enhances or provides several aspects of good mental health: feelings of empowerment, self-efficacy, and self-esteem (Cohen 2009; Fraser et al. 2009). Volunteerism is considered a buffer against stress because it helps people to "switch off" from work or other daily stressors, reduces social isolation, and creates positive social contacts (Wilson 2012).

Religion and Mental Health

Dating back to the late nineteenth century and Durkheim's seminal work, *The Elementary Forms of Religious Life* (1912/2001), participation in religion is perhaps the most studied voluntary behavior. Durkheim argued that religion functions to unite social groups by binding together their core values and expectations for behavior. Individuals who conform to the religious group's "collective effervescence" benefit psychologically by integrating into the social whole, feeling a sense of belongingness, and developing strong attachments. Religion, according to Durkheim, facilitates emotional comfort and security and creates a collectively shared understanding of the world and the universe. Since Durkheim's study, research has continued to demonstrate the psychological benefits of involvement in religious practice and communities. Data presented by Greenfield and colleagues (2009) showed two dimensions of religiosity had independent effects on mental health. First, being engaged in institutional religious participation (formal religious practice) was related to mental health. Second, intrapsychic spiritual perceptions, which were defined by Underwood and Teresi (2002) as a feeling of deep inner peace or harmony, a feeling of being deeply moved by the beauty of life, a strong connection to all life, and a deep appreciation and sense of caring for other people, had an even stronger correlation with psychological well-being than religious practice (Greenfield et al. 2009).

Though the world is moving toward a secular orientation, religion remains an integral part of the identity and social life of many people (Leavey and King 2007). Congregants rely on the clergy for personal spiritual and guidance, and this creates the opportunity for clerics to become the caretakers of their members' mental health. To meet that need, pastoral counseling has become a field of study in the curricula of many seminaries.

Religious communities provide many supportive and self-help services in addition to pastoral care (Leavey and King 2007). Many host AA meetings, for example, and others provide education to congregants about the nature of mental illness and support services such as discussion and support groups.

In addition, religion provides a group-based identity that instills a sense of belongingness and a meaningful, guided existence (Thoits 2003). These social assets of religion are generally beneficial psychologically as a buffer against stress. One study found that over a 10-year period, participating in religious practices had a long-term protective effect against depression, and self-identifying religious people had one-fourth the risk of depression than that of less-religious people (Rosmarin et al. 2013). Religiosity also lowers the risk of suicide attempts and suicide, though not necessarily suicidal ideation (Rasic et al. 2011).

Several factors may account for the psychological benefits of religion. Studies vary on the effects of social support and social attachments offered by the community; for many who emotionally benefit from religion, social support is less important than other benefits that religion may offer. For example, Sternthal and associates (2010) found that while weekly religious service attendance served as a buffer to depression and anxiety, a sense of purpose was the key predictor of emotional well-being. Participating in rituals, singing, or listening to music, and finding meaning and identity through them may offset stress or serve as a catharsis. In addition, the social regulation of thoughts and behaviors contribute to the link between religion and mental well-being. Although the effects of spirituality alone are less clear, the benefits of socially engaging a religious community are psychologically advantageous for those who say that religion is important for them (Miller et al. 2012).

Data that indicate the psychological advantages of religion should not be interpreted to mean that religion is necessary for mental health. Complete nonbelievers are not necessarily more prone to mental illness because they often gain benefits comparable to a religion by having a coherent worldview and social affiliations with other groups.

Other studies of religious involvement, however, contradict Durkheim's hypothesis. Rather than encouraging social integration, religion can generate conflict that translates into psychological dissonance. Research has discovered several areas in which religion has a deleterious effect on well-being. Spiritual struggles and chronic doubt in which people question the tenets of their faith have been linked with psychological distress. Also, negative interpersonal relationships or encounters with coreligionists, especially for a person who is criticized by other members of the faith, are harmful (Sternthal et al. 2010).

Many people turn to religion for support in coping with stress and difficult life events. This strategy, however, does not necessarily serve to buffer individuals from distress. DeAngelis and Ellison (2018), in their study on coping with aspiration strain, found that people who are caught up in the struggle to achieve personal goals often feel distress, loneliness, and less optimism. Religious involvement tempered that stress in individuals; however, they found that religion only proved helpful for those with high school or less education.

Because religion is intertwined with other factors including social class, ethnorace, and gender, it does not have an isolated or independent effect on psychological well-being (Pearce et al. 2019). The meaning of religion varies by context. For example, religion has less impact on the mental well-being of African American adolescents when compared to White youths perhaps because religious involvement is less voluntary in the Black community (Yonker et al. 2012). For Whites, religion may have a greater impact because attendance is more choice based; consequently, those who are prone to troubles may opt not to attend or participate in religious-based activities. The weight of other social forces such as stratification systems are too strong for religion to overcome, which may explain why religious participation does not predict achieving a college degree for Blacks but does for Whites (Pearce et al. 2019). Gender also plays a role in the impact of religion on mental health. Mirola (1999) found that religious meditation and prayer buffered the effects of chronic stress among women and was associated with less depression. For men, however, no measure of religious involvement had an impact on depression.

In some circumstances, religion creates an "us versus them" mentality when the congregation or faith holds prejudicial attitudes or engages in discriminatory behavior. Religious-based social discrimination is linked to psychological distress and a decline in well-being for targeted individuals. One example is the effect of religion on members of the LGBT community. If LGBT teens internalize their faith's antigay rhetoric and turn those beliefs inward, shame, anger, self-blame, and feeling humiliation are likely and can result in depression (Szymanski and Carretta 2020). Relatedly, in educational settings where antigay messages are core values of a school, LGBT students are vulnerable to depression and anxiety (Wolff et al. 2016; Heiden-Rootes et al. 2020).

About the Quote

Jeanette Winterson is a successful, award-winning novelist and professor of English at the University of Manchester in the United Kingdom. Her best-known works are *The Passion* and *Oranges Are Not the Only Fruit*, both written in the 1980s. When Jeanette was 16 years of age, she came out as lesbian to her mother, a conservative, highly religious woman who strongly disapproved. After her disclosure, her parents forced to leave home, which she did with little money or social support. According to Jeanette's autobiography, her mother, whom Jeanette calls "Mrs. Winterson" in the book, asked her why she would continue to see her girlfriend knowing it meant becoming homeless. Jeanette replied, "When I am with her I am happy." To this Mrs. Winterson responded, "why be happy when you could be normal?" (Winterson 2011: 114).

Sometimes society's demands for conformity come with a price. Freud believed, for example, that conforming to sexually oppressive norms that denied people their natural sexual expressiveness was responsible for much psychopathology in the western world. More recently, a study from South Korea found that women employees who worked in sales and customer service jobs for companies that mandated "emotional display rules," which required them to suppress their own emotions while on the job, were more likely to experience depression than women whose employers did not demand this level of emotional control (Chun et al. 2020). Another study reported that American teenage boys and young men who were of normal weight and height (i.e., a healthy body mass index) but viewed themselves as either underweight or overweight, were significantly more likely to report symptoms of depression compared to those who accurately viewed their weight as average (Blashill and Wilhelm 2014). Males' distorted body image was a function of cognitively and subjectively misinterpreting their own physiology in comparison to social images of the ideal body. The list of examples of how conformity to social expectations is associated with depression and anxiety goes on and on.

Many individuals have trouble adjusting to the world around them because that world does not provide them with a stable and secure environment in which it is clear what behavior and emotions are expected. But in other cases, the expectations are well defined but do not match the needs or desires of individuals. The disconnect between individual and social needs and expectations is the source of much of the stress people encounter in contemporary society.

The stresses caused by the world around us impact both our minds and our bodies. Disordered and violent neighborhoods, disingenuous or hostile work environments, and conflicts in religious beliefs happen *to* individuals, and they impact the physical and psychological health and happiness of ordinary people who want nothing more than to live their lives in contentment.

From the viewpoints of policymaking and research and development, an argument could easily be made that if we targeted social causes of mental health problems—improved wages, supported families, provided treatment for drug abusers instead of incarcerating them, created more relaxed workspaces, and developed tolerances for diversity in ideas—we could solve more cases of mental illness than by investing billions in testing and marketing pharmaceuticals. Such a policy strategy, however, requires a paradigm shift in collective action and a political willingness to address social problems and everyday life conditions rather than promote a pill to makes one's problems disappear.

DISCUSSION QUESTIONS

1. Refer to Chapter 3 and think about which of Durkheim's types of suicide best applies to farmers? Why did you select this type?

2. Weber was correct in predicting that bureaucracies would essentially take over as the dominant form of social organization. There is little in our lives today that is not touched by a bureaucracy. Think about the ways in which his idea of the "iron cage of rationality" affects mental health and adds to the stress burden of daily life. How many of life's hassles stem from bureaucracies?

KEY TERMS

Cry of Pain/Entrapment Model 197
Ethnic Density Hypothesis 202
Gemeinschaft 195
Gesellschaft 195
Residential Segregation Hypothesis 203

CHAPTER
10

Social Problems and Disasters

Learning Objectives

After reading this chapter, students will be able to:

1. Explain the relationship between mental illness and homelessness.
2. Differentiate between drug use, abuse, addiction, and dependency.
3. Assess the role of mental illness in intimate partner violence.
4. Determine if terrorism is an act of mental illness.
5. Give examples of how natural and human-made disasters affect mental well-being.

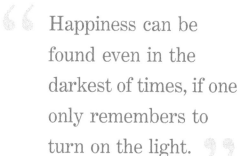

" Happiness can be found even in the darkest of times, if one only remembers to turn on the light. "

—Albus Dumbledore (J. K. Rowling 2000)

Introduction

A **social problem** refers to any social condition that interrupts or damages usual social functioning for large numbers of people and has negative consequences for the collective society. There are many kinds of social problems in the objective sense. Crime, drug abuse, violence, poverty, and pollution pose problems that only collective social action can resolve. Social problems such as these just listed can be classified as chronic conditions, while others, natural or human-made disasters and epidemics, for example, are acute, having distinct temporal boundaries.

Just because a social condition presents itself objectively as a problem does not imply that society accepts or recognizes it as such. According to the social constructionist perspective, a condition becomes a social problem when an influential group, authority agent, or the public's perception define it as a problem. For example, domestic violence did not become a "social problem" until the publication of *Behind Closed Doors* (1980) by sociologists Murray Straus, Richard Gelles, and Suzanne Steinmetz. This book was among the first voices to present the breadth of domestic violence and to treat family violence as an epidemiological or public health problem. By reporting how prevalent violence is in American homes, the authors' work changed public awareness from domestic violence as a "family matter" to an issue that concerns all society. The book coincided with the women's movement, and not long after its publication, new services such as shelters and supportive programs were provided by the society-at-large to support victims, the large majority of whom were women.

A similar process occurred with physical child abuse, which became a "problem" after Henry Kempe's 1962 study of x-rays of children's broken bones found that certain types of breaks could only result from violent behavior toward a child. Again, public perception previously held that parents' behavior toward their children was a private matter and not of public concern. After Kempe's research was published, public attitudes changed.

The pattern can go in the reverse direction as well. Poverty was viewed as a social problem in the 1960s during the administrations of Presidents Kennedy and Johnson. Their "war on poverty" placed social inequality in the national limelight, and their programs helped to ease the pains of being poor and reduced the number of people in poverty. By the late 1960s, however, the collective will retreated, and by the 1980s, political rhetoric and governmental programs concerning inequality shifted to benefit the middle class. Poverty is no longer a "social problem" in the subjective sense, and national policy has in recent years largely sought to restrict access to the social "safety net" (welfare and food stamps, for example).

When social problems are discussed, it is common to hear voices contending that people cause their own problems (a process known as "blaming the victim"). Psychological reductionism is often invoked to explain problems of the aggregate in the public and political sphere. This line of thinking would state that terrorism is the activity of sociopaths, people become homeless because they are failures or incompetent, women are responsible for domestic violence and sexual assaults, and that people are poor because they either like the lifestyle or are inferiors who deserve nothing better.

Akin to social problems are the social aftermaths of natural or human-made disasters. Disasters are specific calamitous events that expose people, communities, and social systems to severe disruption and hazards that normally do not occur. Disasters like hurricanes, tornados, and terror attacks are usually of short duration, but the problems they create can affect many people and last long after the event has ended.

When studying social problems and disasters, sociologists consider both objective and subjective aspects of the situation or condition. For example, following a severe tornado, the objective consequence of the storm includes the physical destruction of the built environment (houses, power lines, and blocked streets) that may impair social systems, the delivery of essential services, leadership, and reconstruction. The subjective element is the interpretative aftermath—how survivors make sense of the destruction, attach meanings to the storm, and respond emotionally and behaviorally to the objective conditions.

This chapter reviews how disasters and selected social problems affect millions of people and have mental health implications. The cause-and-effect relationships between these problems and mental health, however, are not always clear. In addition, public perceptions often contradict research findings. These problems will be approached sociologically to show how social conditions at the macro-level intersect with micro-level psychological pathologies. What is interesting is that the nature of this intersection is not the same with all the problems we will discuss:

- Some of these conditions, such as the COVID-19 pandemic, intimate partner violence, and catastrophes, have direct mental health outcomes.
- Drug abuse, on the other hand, is a social problem that is also defined as psychological disorder.
- Psychological problems can both cause and be caused by homelessness.
- The psychological dimensions of terrorism are still under study but seem to have little connection to pathology as we currently define it.

The goal of the chapter is to examine how disasters and social problems interconnect with mental health. We will attempt to parse out cause-and-effect where relevant, but the main task is to determine how large, macro-level phenomena impact and influence individual psychological welfare.

Homelessness

Although homelessness is not a new phenomenon, it seems to have emerged in different forms over the years. From the 1890s to the 1920s, the vagabond drifter reflects the image of homelessness of that period. Men who "didn't fit in" or were rootless would wander the country in search of a favorable climate, meal, or place to stay. Charlie Chaplin's cinematic "tramp" trope exemplified who and what homelessness was during that era.

The next wave of homelessness came during the Great Depression when markets collapsed, devaluing money and property and erasing families' accumulated wealth. During the 1930s, unmarried men and families seemingly overnight had lost their jobs and mortgages and then were evicted from their homes or farms. A severe drought hit the Midwest in the 1930s and furthered the miseries of people throughout the country. Many homeless people from the middle part of the United States traveled to California in search of a better life, making US Route 66 a national symbol of hope and opportunity.

After World War II, the next pattern of homelessness centered around "skid row bums" who were mostly single, White, older alcoholic men who floated from one flophouse to another to get a meal and a bed for the night (Lee et al. 2010).

The next period of homelessness, sometimes called the "New Homelessness" began in the 1980s and continues to the present day. The causes of the new homelessness are a complex of macro and micro circumstances. A housing "squeeze," a term that represents a condition in which the demand for affordable housing exceeds the supply, declining economic conditions and jobs for middle- and low-income workers, and shifts in housing policy (more gentrification and less low-cost housing) have contributed to the rise of people who cannot sustain adequate and permanent housing for themselves and their families (Lee et al. 2010). The lack of housing for economically and psychologically vulnerable people is at the root of the problem.

Surveys on homelessness estimate that over 500,000 people are without permanent housing in the United States on any given day. For most, homelessness is a temporary condition; but roughly 10 percent are chronically homeless, which means they are without sustainable housing for at least one year. In part because of their large number, homeless people now have fewer options for overnight accommodations than in times past and can be found sleeping on the streets or in their cars. The profile of today's homeless is different from that of the previous three periods. The homeless population now is more ethnoracially diverse, composed of people of all ages, and includes both single men and women (and girls and boys) and families. They are also highly likely to be suffering from mental distress or illness.

Homelessness and Mental Illness

A strong connection exists between homelessness and mental illness. In the early years of the New Homelessness era, policymakers and some researchers contended that deinstitutionalization caused the rise in homelessness (Jones 2015). Policy and funding changes and new medications, as we saw in Chapter 2, disincentivized institutions from providing long-term care for chronically and severely mentally ill persons, and former residents and others in need of in-patient services no longer could rely on institutional treatment and housing. Those who could not provide for themselves and whose families were unable or unwilling to house them had no place to live. Many enter the prison system after committing crimes while others live on the streets or drift from one inadequate housing situation to another. Deinstitutionalization, however, does not account for the mass of people who have experienced homelessness since the 1980s. Nonetheless, mental illness is a significant part of the New Homelessness but whether psychological health is a cause, or a consequence of homelessness, is not clear.

Studies vary in their reported prevalence rates, but they have consistently found that mental illness among homeless people far exceeds that of housed adults and adolescents. Two studies by Lee et al. 2010 and Lyons Reardon and colleagues (2003) estimated that 25 to 50 percent of homeless people manifest mental health problems. The most common problems are affective disorders, bipolar disorders, alcohol abuse disorders, and antisocial personality disorder. Studies have found that schizophrenia among homeless persons ranges from three percent to 11 percent, which significantly exceeds the rate of the general population of less than one percent (Ayano et al. 2019; Kessler et al. 2005; NIMH 2018; Wu et al. 2006).

Comorbidity, experiencing two or more diagnosable problems, is estimated in four to 26 percent among homeless persons (Lyons Reardon et al. 2003).

Homeless Adolescents

When teenagers lose their homes, they bring to the streets a myriad of affective, cognitive, and behavioral problems that are exacerbated by their homelessness (Kulik et al. 2011). Prior to losing their homes, teens likely experienced one or more of the following: lack of parental care, physical and/or sexual abuse, parental conflict, or a parent having a psychiatric disorder (Edidin et al. 2012). The lack of support after becoming homeless worsens the effects of these precipitating conditions, and the longer a teenager is without permanent housing, the worse the consequences on their mental health. In addition to the lack of adequate shelter, homelessness usually means having to drop out of school, witnessing or experiencing violence on the streets, being subjected to stigma of living in a shelter, and having little or no privacy, which is important for adolescent psychosocial development (Kulik et al. 2011). While most want to work regular jobs, homeless teenagers face many barriers to employment. Having no permanent address, little education, and few marketable work skills often deter employers from hiring homeless youths.

Given that their environment is wrought with problems that create excessive stress and interfere with developmental tasks as specified by Erikson (see Chapter 8), homeless adolescents experience high rates of both internalized and externalized disorders. Research has identified high rates of clinical depression (as high as 61 percent), bipolar disorders (41 percent), post-traumatic stress disorder (PTSD) (48 percent), suicidal ideation (40–80 percent), and suicide attempts (23–67 percent) (Edidin et al. 2012; Medlow et al. 2014). The effects of homelessness are particularly pernicious for LGBTQ youth who have high rates of depression and the highest probability of PTSD (Medlow et al. 2014).

Homeless youths often externalize their stress and exhibit behavioral problems at four times the rate of teens with permanent housing. Research estimates that 75 percent of homeless teenagers manifest behavior that could be classified as a conduct disorder (Edidin et al. 2012). Conduct disorder behaviors include fighting, especially starting fights, refusing to respect or obey authority, vandalism, and stealing.

Homeless teens also exhibit signs of substance abuse disorders at levels that far exceed national prevalence rates. Medlow and colleagues (2014) report that almost half of homeless adolescents met the criteria for a DSM substance use disorder. Another study of homeless and runaway youths identified two-thirds of their sample as meeting the lifetime criteria for at least three substance abuse disorders (alcohol abuse, alcohol dependency, and substance abuse), and about half were diagnosable for at least one disorder within the last 12 months (Johnson et al. 2005). Almost all the teens in Johnson's study (93 percent) with substance abuse disorders were comorbid with another clinically significant mental condition. Drugs of choice vary by primary diagnosis. Homeless youths diagnosed with PTSD were more likely to abuse heroin, and individuals with a bipolar disorder engaged in polysubstance abuse, taking mostly heroin and methamphetamine. Those who were not diagnosed with a primary condition were more likely to abuse alcohol (Merscham et al. 2009).

Cause and Effect

The cause-and-effect relationship between homelessness and mental illness is unclear. Some studies show that mental illness and substance abuse precede homelessness, while others show the reverse. These data are not necessarily contradictory. We should recognize that there are multiple pathways to homelessness, and it is worth remembering that homelessness is a function of the housing supply and economic conditions that provide individuals and families with the resources to secure reliable housing. In the past, people with severe mental illnesses did not have to resort to living on the streets or in shelters and prisons. They lived in institutions or with their families, and if they were able to work, they could afford even the most minimal permanent housing. Members of families who lost housing because of economic conditions often develop psychological problems because of the stress of homelessness. Because of the problems they are trying to escape, teenage runaways are vulnerable to mental health problems that are aggravated while on the streets.

Reducing homelessness to the characteristics of the people who are without fixed housing fails to recognize the psychosocial effects of childhood abuse, intimate partner violence, economic vulnerability, and untreated mental illness, conditions that often precede homelessness, on the ability of individuals to achieve developmental goals and attain independence and self-reliance. Homelessness aggravates the problems individuals bring to the streets, which suggests that homelessness and mental illness can be co-occurring and mutually reinforcing. Homelessness makes everything in life harder—getting a job, finding a safe place to sleep, obtaining health care, establishing a daily routine, and maintaining human dignity (Lyons Reardon et al. 2003). Both social drift and social selection theories are applicable in predicting homelessness.

Drugs and Alcohol

Anthropological evidence suggests that the use of drugs and alcohol dates back over ten millennia, and many speculate that Neanderthals may also have used a plant-based stimulant to enhance their moods. Virtually all cultures have had some method to brew or distill a local plant into alcohol or eat or chew other plants to achieve some mind-altering state. Throughout history, psychoactive substances have been used for a wide range of purposes: recreational, medicinal, and ceremonial. Today, life is no different. Wine is used in many religious services, alcohol is a common substance for relaxation and enjoyment, and marijuana and narcotics are smoked or ingested to relieve pain.

The interpretation of drug use is highly subjective. Religious groups, lay organizations, and the various disciplines of medical, behavioral, and social sciences approach drug use in different and sometimes competing ways. This conflict is visible historically by examining the evolution of the dominate paradigms that were thought to explain drug use. In the nineteenth and early twentieth centuries, religious groups dominated the national discourse on drug and alcohol use and judged alcohol, especially drunkenness, to be a threat to the social order. Labeling consumption as willful sinfulness, the remedy was to direct imbibing individuals to churches (the movement was led by Christian temperance organizations) where they could find redemption and cleanse their souls of their vice. This movement had enough power to persuade state and federal governments to ratify the 18th Amendment to the constitution that opened the era of Prohibition, which banned most alcohol production and use until its repeal in 1933.

Having been exposed as a biased, ideological approach rooted in middle class and religious values, the sin "theory" of substance use is now considered a relic of history. It was little more than a value judgment of a behavior that some did not like. Nonetheless, the temperance movements made substance use a topic of national debate by calling attention to the impact of chronic intoxication on individual well-being, family welfare, and even the viability of the economy.

Following the demise of the temperance movement and Prohibition, a Freud-influenced perspective controlled the conversation on drugs and alcohol. This narrative positioned drug and alcohol use less as a sin and more of a shortcoming or defect in character development. For strict Freudians, alcohol use was the result of being stuck at an early stage of development in which children relieve anxiety by putting things such as pacifiers and thumbs in their mouths. In this line of thinking, excessive alcohol use indicated being stuck in the "oral stage" of development to alleviate stress and to feel secure. During this era, alcoholism was viewed as a failure to develop a sound sense of self in which a person could control emotions and engage in mature or adult behavior.

This view, and variations of it, would dominate most lay and scholarly thought for several decades. Alcoholics and drug addicts were of flawed or defective character who needed professionally guided psychotherapy rather than religion to stop consuming psychotropic substances.

Today, the medical model of drug use is the dominant paradigm. Medical schools and funding agencies place strong emphasis on the notion that drug and alcohol use is a disease that users cannot control. The idea is that addicts are born, not made, which means that individuals persistently and habitually consume drugs and alcohol because of a biological predisposition that makes them susceptible to the impact of the drug and affects their brain's ability stop using. Abstinence is the primary treatment in the medical model. The biological explanation of drug dependency suggests that chronic users experience overwhelming desires or compulsions to consume intoxicating drugs. Because of their biological "illness," they are easily hooked and helpless to resist.

While evidence that some genetic and biochemical predispositions may exist among people with alcohol and drug problems more frequently than in nonaddicted people (e.g., the biochemical serum BDNT is associated with cocaine abuse relapse [Sinha 2011]), the evidence is neither fully conclusive nor necessarily causal. In addition to the limited explanatory power of biological factors, there are several arguments against a purely biological causal model of substance abuse. First, the model decontextualizes behavior. There is evidence that environmental stress factors contribute to alcohol and drug abuse with or without the presence of persistent biological factors (Brady and Sonne 1999). Substance abuse frequently occurs as an adaptive reaction to environmental conditions, a process known as self-medication. For example, Hawn's team (2020) found a relationship between PTSD and alcohol use disorder, and Smith's group (2018) demonstrated in a sample of firefighters that alcohol use severity and alcohol use as a coping tool both increase with post-traumatic stress. Second, successful treatments of drug abuse are not medical. Psychosocial treatments, which focus on psychological decision-making, emotion management, and navigating social relationships, are more effective than medical treatments such as taking Antabuse or naltrexone. Third, genetic and other biological markers of drug abuse are not shared by all people with a substance use disorder.

In short, there may be different pathways into substance dependency where some cases are facilitated by individual physiological responses to alcohol and drugs, and others are not. As many drug and alcohol counselors say, anyone can drink themselves into alcoholism.

Because the interpretation of drugs and alcohol varies from socially acceptable and legitimate to illegal and shameful, certain terms must be clarified and set into a sociological context. Consuming drugs, including legal substances like alcohol, caffeine, and tobacco, are subject to situational rules relative to time and place. It may be socially acceptable to drink wine in a religious ceremony in a Roman Catholic church or a synagogue, but it would be considered deviant in a Baptist church or mosque. At a rock concert where marijuana is passed around illegally, not taking a "hit" might be considered deviant by the people at the venue. The context of behavior determines its deviancy.

Given the subjective nature of substance use, the terms **use**, **abuse**, **addiction**, and **dependency** require clarification. These concepts can mean different things to different people.

Drug Use

Drug use is a broad ubiquitous term that refers to any consumption of any chemical substance that has some mental or behavioral effect. Most people are drug users—having coffee in the morning "to get started" or a glass of wine at dinner. The term does not imply amount, frequency, type of drug consumed, or the consequences of taking the drug.

Drug Abuse

Drug abuse, however, has different meanings and is more complicated. One definition states that **drug abuse** refers to any use of an illegal substance or illegal use of a legal drug. Since heroin is illegal in all US jurisdictions, any use of heroin is unlawful and therefore abuse. Similarly, smoking cigarettes and drinking alcoholic beverages by teenagers are considered abuse because the law prohibits their use of a legal substance. In addition, abuse is the use of a substance for reasons other than its intended purpose. Recreational use of pain medications or sniffing glue are examples of this definition.

A different approach contends that abuse is defined by the consequences of substance use (Fuqua 1978). Negative outcomes related to personal health (heart or respiratory disease, for example), relationships (abandoning parental roles), or social obligations and expectations (underperforming at work or in school) become the defining characteristics of drug abuse. In this perspective, people who use psychoactive drugs safely and judiciously without undesirable personal or social consequences are not necessarily abusing drugs, but when use starts to interfere with well-being, daily functioning, and social relationships, the use is redefined as abuse.

Dependency and Addiction

Though related and somewhat overlapping, addiction and psychological dependency are two different processes. Addiction refers to the physiological changes at the cellular level in which the body's cells have changed to adjust to and accommodate the chemical. When the altered cells no longer receive the drug, they have molecular reactions called withdrawal, which in some cases is severe, and craving, a strong and often uncontrollable desire to consume more of the substance. Addiction, therefore, is a physiological reaction to addictive drugs such as heroin, methamphetamines, and nicotine.

Psychological dependency refers to using a substance to satisfy an emotional or behavioral need. Continued use stems not from physiological craving but from the emotional satisfaction that the drug creates. Let's look at the examples of cocaine and alcohol. Although cocaine acts on the brain, it is not necessarily addictive. Instead, a user can easily become habitually dependent on the emotions generated by the way cocaine affects dopamine levels and brain physiology. Cocaine binds to dopamine transporter proteins, which keeps the dopamine in the synapses longer. As the dopamine accumulates in the synapses, it magnifies the signal to the receiving neurons. This amplification is the euphoria that cocaine users experience. Feelings of power and perceived performance enhancement are common reactions, and a user can become more talkative, gregarious, and the "life of the party." Cocaine can act as an emotional crutch to compensate for perceived personal weaknesses or to raise confidence and sociability.

Alcohol is a chemical depressant that acts on the brain to create euphoric feelings in which users can detach from stress and anxiety and be released from the inhibitions that may hinder certain behaviors. Alcohol affects memory, making it easy to temporarily disengage from life's troubles, feel happy, and unwind from stress. Expressions and witticisms such as entertainer W. C. Fields' famous line from almost a century ago, "Reality is an illusion that occurs due to the lack of alcohol," frame alcohol as a method for dealing with personal troubles.

Both cocaine and alcohol create a "feel good" state that becomes highly desirable or even necessary to escape perceived personal shortcomings, daily hassles, or the dreariness of life. If intoxication is paired with positive outcomes, the behavior will likely be repeated, and the user can become psychologically dependent on them to relieve unpleasant emotional states.

Prevalence

Drug and alcohol use is not uncommon, and the National Institute of Drug Abuse annually reports reasonably reliable data on the prevalence and incidence rates for most psychoactive chemicals. Measuring abuse and dependency, however, is another matter. Drug addicts and alcoholics are difficult to locate and count, and denial is a common psychological reaction to questions about substance abuse. Despite these limitations, we have a good idea of the frequency of drug abuse in the United States, though we must assume the counts and estimates are likely to be conservative.

Children's substance use is particularly high. Table 10.1 shows that lifetime prevalence and past year and passed month incidence rates of both illicit drugs and alcohol use among 8th, 10th, and 12th Graders increased between 2017 and 2020. Of note is the rise in alcohol use incidence and daily and binge drinking rates among all three groups from 2019 to 2020. These increases are perhaps a function of COVID-19 stress. During that same time, however, illicit drug use declined for 10th and 12th Graders and slightly increased among the youngest group.

Chart 10.1 shows the percentage of adults who have engaged in binge and heavy drinking in the last month. (These data are pre-COVID.) To put these percentages

TABLE 10.1 Illicit Drug and Alcohol Use Among 8th, 10th, and 12th Graders, 2017–2020

Drug	Time Period	2017	2018	2019	2020
8th Graders					
Illicit drugs	Lifetime	18.2	18.7	20.4	21.3
	Past year	12.9	13.4	14.8	15.6
	Past month	7.0	7.3	8.5	8.7
Alcohol	Lifetime	23.1	23.5	24.5	25.6
	Past year	18.2	18.7	19.3	20.5
	Past month	8.0	8.2	7.9	9.9
	Daily	0.2	0.1	0.2	0.4
	5+Drinks in a row	3.7	3.7	3.8	4.5
10th Graders					
Illicit drugs	Lifetime	34.3	36.3	37.5	37.3
	Past year	27.8	29.9	31.0	30.4
	Past month	17.2	18.3	19.8	18.2
Alcohol	Lifetime	42.2	42.2	43.1	46.4
	Past year	37.7	37.8	37.7	40.7
	Past month	19.7	18.6	18.4	20.3
	Daily	0.6	0.5	0.6	1.0
	5+Drinks in a row	9.8	8.7	8.5	9.6

(Continued)

TABLE 10.1   Illicit Drug and Alcohol Use Among 8th, 10th, and 12th Graders, 2017–2020 *(Continued)*

Drug	Time Period	2017	2018	2019	2020
12th Graders					
Illicit drugs	Lifetime	48.9	47.8	47.4	46.6
	Past year	39.9	38.8	38.0	36.8
	Past month	24.9	24.0	23.7	22.2
Alcohol	Lifetime	61.5	58.5	58.5	61.5
	Past year	55.7	53.3	52.1	55.3
	Past month	33.2	30.2	29.3	33.6
	Daily	1.6	1.21	1.7	2.7
	5+Drinks in a row	16.6	13.8	14.4	16.8

Source: Johnston, et al. (2022).

CHART 10.1   Percent of Adults Who Engaged in Binge and Heavy Drinking in Last Month, 2018

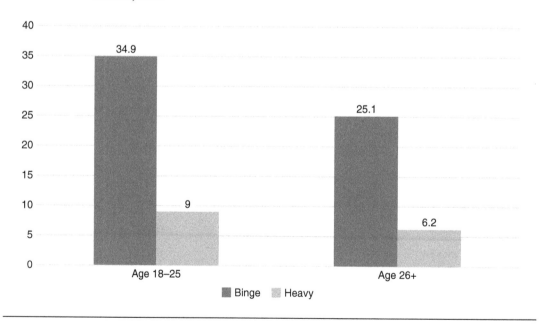

Source: Substance Abuse and Mental Health Services Administration (2019a).

into perspective, about 11.9 million young adults (34.9 percent) and 54 million adults over 25 (9 percent) have engaged in binge drinking in the previous 30 days, and 3.1 million 18- to 25-year-olds and 13.4 million aged 26 and over were heavy drinkers during the same period.

The prevalence of illicit drugs is also alarming. According to national data (SAMHSA 2019c), 19.4 percent of the US population used an illicit drug in the past year (Table 10.2). Chart 10.2 shows the breakdown by age groups.

Substance Abuse Disorder

Given the variability in defining drug abuse and the blurry divisions between psychological dependency and physical addiction, DSM-V redefined pathological substance abuse. Heavy consumption is a necessary but not sufficient cause of disordered use, and a diagnosis of a substance use disorder (SUD) is now "based a pathological pattern of behavior relative to the substance" (American Psychiatric Association 2013: 483).

Despite the difficulties in defining and measuring SUD, the Substance Abuse and Mental Health Services Administration (SAMHSA 2019c) estimates that 19.7 million people aged 12 and over have an SUD. Of these, 14.8 million or 75 percent are alcohol use disorder. Men are almost twice as likely to be diagnosed with an SUD.

The DSM-V sets 11 criteria to form the threshold for identifying an SUD. As you see in Table 10.3, the criteria are grouped around four concepts: Impaired control, social impairment, risky use, and pharmacological criteria.

The criteria for SUD are largely behavioral and specified by the consequences of recurrent substance use. As with other sociological situations, as noted earlier, something is as real as its consequences, and SUDs are in large measure defined by the effects of the substances on users themselves and others around them. Therefore, the deviant-ness of substance abuse lies in the social relativity of the act of consuming drugs.

Many theories attempt to explain drug use, abuse, and dependency. One sociology textbook on drug use describes 13 groups of theories originating from biology, psychology, and sociology, and many of these clusters have subtheories

TABLE 10.2 Frequency of Past Year Illicit Drug Use, 2018

Age Group	%	N (in Millions)
12 and over	19.4	53.2
12–17	16.7	4.2
18–25	38.7	13.2
26 and over	16.7	35.9

Source: Substance Abuse and Mental Health Services Administration (2019a).

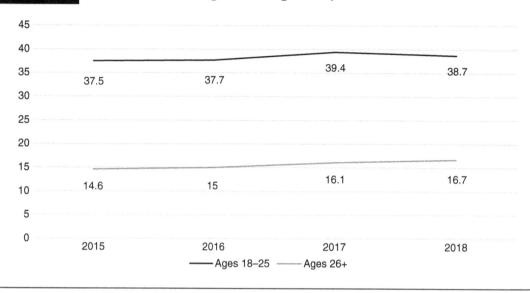

CHART 10.2 Past Year Illicit Drug Use among Adults, 2015–2018

Source: Substance Abuse and Mental Health Services Administration (2019a).

within them (Faupel et al. 2014). This array of theories does not indicate academic confusion about drug use; rather, it points to the fact that drug use is a complex, multidimensional behavior that has biological, psychological, and sociological attributes.

Framing SUDs as a function of stress, which has been shown to be a strong predictor of substance abuse, is one approach that integrates biology, psychology, and sociology by combining learning theory and psychoanalytic thought from psychology with social stress theory from sociology and biology. Stress, as we saw in Chapter 3, causes the body to produce cortisol, and if a person is under chronic stress, the increased levels of cortisol can have damaging effects on various physiological systems. One of those negative effects is that cortisol inhibits normal functioning of the prefrontal cortex. This area of the brain is the location of our executive functioning, high-level cognitive reasoning where impulse control, maintaining attention, interpreting reality, solving problems, and predicting the consequences of our own behavior occur.

The prefrontal cortex also controls dopamine, the neurotransmitter that causes us to seek pleasurable stimuli. If this brain region is not functioning properly, dopamine levels increase and push individuals to engage in behaviors such as drug and alcohol use, overeating, and gambling that stimulate this part of the brain.

When individuals are highly stressed and this biological chain reaction occurs, individuals are likely to find stimulation in ways that have become conditioned. Whereas some may eat too much or gamble, others may consume drugs and

TABLE 10.3 DSM-V Criteria for Substance Abuse Disorder

Criteria	
Impaired Control	
1	Takes substance in larger amounts or over a longer time than initially planned
2	Difficulty decreasing or discontinuing use
3	Spends a lot of time acquiring, using, and recovering from the drug's effects; daily activities are centered around the substance
4	Strong desires to use the drug
Social Impairment	
5	Substance use interferes with performing role expectations at home, school, or work
6	Persistent interpersonal problems caused by substance use
7	Abandons previously important recreational, social, or occupational activities
Risky Use	
8	Repeatedly uses the substance in unsafe or dangerous situations
9	Continues to use the substance despite knowing the physical, psychological, or social dangers of persistent use
Pharmacological Criteria	
10	Tolerance: the body requires increased amounts of the substance to reach the desired effects
11	Withdrawal: physical and mental effects experienced after stopping use of a drug or reducing the dosage of a drug

Source: American Psychiatric Association (2013: 483–484).

alcohol, depending on which behaviors were reinforced in their interpersonal and social background. The behavior creates a sense of relief or euphoria that cognitively and emotionally distances individuals from stress and satisfies the brain's reaction to cortisol. Drugs and alcohol, therefore, act as a negative reinforcer, which is a behavior that is repeated because it terminates a negative or unpleasant condition.

Heavy drinking is frequently associated with stressful social relationships. While biological factors may influence consumption continuance, they are not accountable for initial drinking or early binge drinking. Intimate relationships, for example, have a strong impact on binge drinking (Holway et al. 2017). A romantic partner's binge drinking and depression increase the likelihood of an individual's own binging and depression. Among young adults, the effect is stronger for men; women whose male partner is depressed are less likely to binge drink than men with depressed female partners.

The goal of taking a drug is to change one's state of mind and feel good. Many people take drugs recreationally to enjoy themselves or to help relax, but drug-dependent users, those who may meet the DSM criteria for an SUD, repeatedly consume psychoactive drugs for more complex reasons. Why people drink or drug too much is often rooted in environmental stress and how they process those stressors psychodynamically. People may overconsume to cope with early childhood trauma, self-esteem problems, relational difficulties, or general dissatisfaction with life. All these conditions may operate at a subconscious level that may require psychotherapy to identify and manage or change.

One way to think about drugs and alcohol is that they function as a person's **transitional object** (TO). TOs are objects that we endow with magical qualities to relieve stress. We all have had a transitional object. Most young children have a special stuffed animal or blanket that they use to feel comfortable or to fall asleep. These objects help them feel secure and reduce anxiety. Adults have TOs as well (though they are often called "comfort objects" for adults). Examples may be pets, a lucky charm, memorabilia from childhood, or a comfort food. Baseball players may have a special "enchanted" bat, and a person may have lucky clothing saved for job interviews or important work meetings. All these things cause "feel good" moments, which means that they reduce anxiety. Drugs and alcohol can serve the same purpose, and chronic abusers will interact with their substance of choice in much the same way as children relate to their teddy bears.

Intimate Partner Violence

Intimate Partner Violence (IPV) is a serious social problem that affects millions of people throughout the population. IPV is defined as physical violence, sexual violence, stalking, or psychological harm by a current or former partner, spouse or dating partner. Because of the extent and the social and economic costs of this type of violence, IPV is considered a social problem. IPV is also a public health problem because of the scale of physical and psychological injuries it causes.

According to Centers for Disease Control (CDC) figures, in their lifetime, about one in four women and one in 10 men experience sexual or physical violence and/or stalking that results in worries for personal safety, PTSD symptoms, injury, or needing victim services such as counseling. Half of female murder victims are the result of IPV as are one in 13 male homicides (Smith et al. 2017).

IPV affects women in all ethnoracial groups, albeit at different rates. Almost half of American Indian women, 45 percent of African Americans, 37.3 percent Whites, and 18.3 percent of Asian American and Pacific Islanders have experienced IPV victimization (Smith et al. 2017). The higher rates among American Indians and African Americans may be a function of their overrepresentation in poverty, which is a strong predictor of IPV. While no social class position is free of IPV, it occurs significantly more frequently as income and wealth decrease.

IPV also occurs regardless of sexual orientation. One study found that physical, sexual, and stalking abuse is higher among gay and bisexual men (26 percent and 37.3 percent, respectively) than heterosexual men (29 percent), and higher as well among lesbian women (43.8 percent) and bisexual women (61.1 percent) than heterosexual women (35 percent) (Walters et al. 2013).

Causes of Intimate Partner Violence

Since the large majority of IPV is perpetrated by males in relationships with women, the focus here is on heterosexual relationships.

IPV is a complex, multilayered phenomenon that occurs in the context of four levels of social factors. Figure 10.1 outlines these dynamics.

Sociocultural Factors

The sociocultural context of gender and violence is critical in understanding how and why domestic violence occurs. In cultures such as India, the Democratic Republic of Congo, Turkey, and Columbia where patriarchy remains a strong and central feature of social organization and ideology and public violence is common, rates of IPV are high when compared to low IPV countries such as Spain,

FIGURE 10.1 Four Levels of Analyzing IPV

LEVEL ONE: SOCIOCULTURAL FACTORS
Misogyny and Sexism
Sex Role Stereotyping
Acceptance of Violence

LEVEL TWO: SOCIAL STRUCTURAL FACTORS
Economic Stress – Unemployment and Underemployment
Community Denial of the Problem
Police and Judicial Policies and Practices

LEVEL THREE: FAMILY FACTORS
Traditional Sex Roles
Recurrent Marital Stress
Conflicts over Core Areas of Marital Life
Poor Communication Practices

LEVEL FOUR: INDIVIDUAL QUALITIES

Offender	*Victim*
Self-Esteem Issues	Self-Esteem Issues
Low Stress Tolerance	Low Stress Tolerance
Family History of Violence	Family History of Violence
Alcohol Abuse	Fear and Anxiety

Switzerland, Chile, and Slovenia where community violence and male-dominant beliefs are not strong cultural features.

Patriarchal social systems and ideology, sometimes collectively called male hegemony, provide the ecological context in which IPV is imbedded. Male hegemony refers to stereotypical attributes of maleness, defined as masculine strength, domination, aggression, and power, and the larger context of gender inequality in which social rewards and power are held primarily by men. This definition is applied to all levels of social relationships including familial and interpersonal. For some men, male hegemony allows what Connell and Messerschmidt (2005: 840) call "toxic practices" that can include violence to establish and maintain gender dominance.

Men who lack access to conventional social arenas such as sports, business, and other competitive venues that permit them to express their notion of traditional masculinity may find themselves frustrated and devalued in the eyes of other men or women who hold to traditional gender roles. Violence against women can become one of the outlets they choose to vent that frustration and establish male hegemony and entitlement in their lives (Corbally 2015). This, in part, helps explain why men in lower income levels are more likely to commit IPV. IPV, keep in mind, occurs in all social classes, but is disproportionately high among the poor and working class.

Social Structural Factors

Except for low income and the number of young children in the family, demographic factors such as household size and urban–rural residence are not predictive of IPV. Empowering women educationally, economically, and socially, however, have protective functions against IPV (Jewkes 2002).

Collective responses to IPV are also critical in promoting or slowing violence against women. In many places, police officers and courts are reluctant to enforce laws prohibiting IPV. Not enforcing the law sends the message to perpetrators that they are engaging in legitimate behavior and have the freedom to act without consequence.

Family Factors

Family and couple dynamics affect the likelihood of IPV. Couples who often argue and whose relationships are unstable and conflicted are more vulnerable to IPV. Gender role conflicts, such as when women veer from traditional female roles or challenge masculine ideology, are also associated with violence (Jewkes 2002). Violence is often implemented as a strategy in relationship conflict management to enforce male hegemony.

Individual Factors

Two important variables at the individual level are predictive of perpetrating IPV: experience with violence and alcohol consumption. People who commit IPV are more likely to have a history of familial violence. Either they saw their parents engage in violence and/or they were beaten themselves. Family violence creates anger and teaches the lesson that violence is a legitimate means to solve problems and get what you want.

The empirical links between IPV and alcohol use are well established both in the United States and many other countries. Alcohol reduces inhibitions and clouds judgment, making it easier to side-step social prohibitions on violence. While alcohol use, especially heavy drinking, increases the risk of IPV, it is important to realize that alcohol is not necessarily the cause of the violence (Caetano et al. 2001). IPV can occur without any alcohol. As Caetano and colleagues state (2001: 63), "alcohol's role in partner violence may be explained by the expectation that alcohol will have a disinhibitory effect on behavior. It is also possible that some people consciously use alcohol as an excuse for violent behavior...."

Mental illness is also not necessarily a causal factor. Although male perpetrators of domestic violence are not often considered mentally ill, their behavior may be a consequence of intense psychological distress. Male perpetrators may be confused about their identities and expectations and may have anger management problems because of having witnessed or experienced childhood violence. When alcohol use is connected to IPV, it may be a method of compensating for this distress.

The accumulation of these factors, however, does not constitute a mental illness. In fact, neither psychologists nor sociologists consider violent behavior as a mental illness (Umberson et al. 2002). Whereas psychologists tend to see violence as a symptom of an underlying disorder, sociologists see violence as a deviant behavior designed to realize a goal. Data analyzed by Umberson's research group suggest that violence is best understood as an expression of psychological distress. In their comparison of violent and nonviolent men, the former group tended to repress their emotions and avoid or withdraw from troublesome situations and relationships. This coping strategy may be effective in the short-term; however, in the long-run, avoidance and repression cause tension to build up and may be later expressed in an act of violence.

Victimization

Victimization of IPV does have mental health implications, however. Both women and men who experience IPV have increased risk of depression, anxiety, chronic fear, and PTSD, though the process in which they occur may differ slightly between male and female victims.

The experience of IPV can have a profound effect on psychological well-being among women. Violence by a relationship partner creates severe psychological consequences that frequently evolve into chronic clinical depression, anxiety, and PTSD. All forms of IPV are associated with PTSD: physical violence, sexual assault, psychological violence, and stalking (Basile et al. 2004). Other studies have found IPV associated with suicidality, substance abuse, and low self-esteem (Ruback and Thompson 2001). Given the frequency of violence against women, IPV contributes significantly to their high rate of depression and PTSD.

For some men, however, their reaction to IPV victimization involves the disconnect between their victimization with their ideas of masculinity (Brooks et al. 2020). These men may hide or deny their victimization to protect their perception of manhood. Admitting to victimization conflicts with traditional masculinity; therefore, the social pressure to conceal the experience can add another layer of psychological burden in addition to the emotional problems, such as depression, PTSD, and anxiety, derived from the violence,.

Terrorism and Mental Health

Terroristic Actors

The question of the mental constitution of people who put a bomb on a bus of innocent people or bomb a gathering of innocents watching a sporting event has been debated for decades. While the answer seems simple, the evidence does not necessarily support the conclusion that terrorists are mentally ill.

Researchers have tried to get into the minds of terrorists, but the task is difficult because there is relatively little reliable data on terrorists' psychological characteristics. Terrorists are not often caught. Many die in the execution of their schemes, and those who survive and capture offer little information. If they cooperate with their captors, they are afraid of reprisals by their comrades and feel disloyal to their causes and fellow combatants. They may also believe that clinicians and researchers are feeding their enemy's intelligence operatives and are part of the culture that they are fighting (Hudson 1999).

Before looking at mental health issues, a working definition of terrorism is needed. Enders and Sandler's (2012) definition states that terrorism is the premeditated use or threat to use violence to obtain a political or social objective. Terrorism is the intimidation of an audience larger beyond the actual victims. People who engage in terroristic acts do not necessarily attack the police and military of their opponents; instead, they promote their agenda through disruption of normal social activity and by generating fear among the public (the "audience"). This definition identifies terrorism as a tool of warfare.

The social context in which terrorism occurs is critical in understanding the mind of the terrorist and distinguishes between types of terroristic actors and their motivations. Data suggest a psychological difference between individuals working within a group or movement and those acting in isolation, the so-called "lone wolves." Psychologist Franco Ferracuti (1982) articulated that difference: "there is no such thing as an isolated terrorist—that's a mental case."

Clinical evidence suggests that "lone wolves" who operate unaccompanied rather than within a religious, political, or social movement usually are experiencing emotional or adjustment problems. They are psychologically disturbed individuals whose actions are functions of their mental constitutions rather than a commitment to a revolutionary group or an organized movement. Much has been written about individuals such as the "Unabomber," Ted Kaczynski, who rebelled against modern society by sending homemade bombs to scientists, corporate executives, and computer stores, killing three and seriously injuring over 20 others. Once captured, Kaczynski was diagnosed by most psychiatrists and psychologists with paranoid schizophrenia, schizoidal disorder, or schizotypal personality disorder. These types of diagnoses are typical to lone actors, not those who are acting on behalf or in promotion of ideologies and causes sponsored by religious or political groups such as the Irish Republican Army in Northern Ireland, al Qaeda, and Boko Haram in Nigeria, among many others.

Most clinicians and researchers have concluded that terrorists are not mentally ill, a position largely held by intelligence agencies and law enforcement (Hudson 1999). In fact, research shows that perhaps their most outstanding quality is their normalness. Having shifted their focus away from the stereotype of the "crazed" loner who espouses sentiments of hate, federal intelligence agencies now look for other motivations and patterns of behavior that would suggest or predict terroristic threatening or violence (Hudson 1999).

Taylor (1988) discerned the differences between terrorists and sociopaths. He contended that the behaviors of sociopaths (and presumably people with other serious mental illness) are motivated by personal aims rather than goals created in the context of a social movement. Terror leaders, Taylor argued, prefer not to recruit "crazy people" because their psychopathologies make them unreliable and less controllable. Terror groups need secretive and discreet members who can follow orders, think clearly, and hide "in plain sight." A mentally ill person may have difficulty with these expectations and endanger the group.

Individuals join terror groups for many different reasons and come from all social classes and ages. Left-wing groups tend to have more women and highly educated members. Right-wing organizations tend to have younger and less educated members from lower social strata. Some groups, such as Palestinian organizations, have rank-and-file members from the lower classes who are led by higher status individuals. Many of the poor participants are bored, unemployed youths who seek adventure or to support a cause. Higher educated members are more likely motivated by political or religious principles. They are often idealistic and intellectual but lack outlets for creativity or feel guilty for the plight of others' poverty or other problems (Hudson 1999).

One factor that connects people with these diverse social characteristics is a profound feeling of alienation from and disenchantment with society. They often feel lost as individuals and lack social connections to meaningful social groups and opportunities that could provide a stable social identity.

When people feel estranged from themselves and others, powerless, and isolated from enriching social connections, they often search for alternatives. Membership in an organization that creates a sense of belongingness and social importance, therefore, is highly attractive and fills psychological voids. The group seeks to deliver social ties and networks that enrich self-esteem and belongingness and connects people who have lived similar lives and shared experiences. Members of terror groups convince recruits and members of a worldview that will deliver meaning and a sense of personal power to their lives.

Those who belong to terror groups tend to share similar cognitive characteristics. They hold hostile attitudes toward certain groups and are vulnerable to authoritarian and rigid beliefs of right and wrong. Members trend toward closemindedness and dogmatic thinking and become convinced that terroristic social action is a conventional or normative behavior. That is, terrorism and its consequences are justified as means to a legitimate end. Believing that terrorism is justifiable also serves as a mechanism for relieving the guilt and shame they may feel after an attack.

While all these factors, along with opportunity, expose these individuals to risk of "radicalization" and recruitment into a quasi-military political or religious organization, there is no pattern of psychopathology in this profile. While they may be angry, feel despair and confusion, and need meaning in their lives, angst and alienation do not constitute mental illness. Box 10.1 describes a case study as an example of this theory.

Though most terrorists may not have experienced a mental illness, recent reports have revealed that many of the September 11, 2001, attackers had histories of depression and suicidal ideations and behavior (Lankford 2018). Most likely this new information reveals patterns within terrorist movements in which recruiting depressed and suicidal individuals for suicide missions is a strategy to execute the plans of the leaders and the movement. Many suicide bombers are known to have

Box 10.1 Psychosocial Profile of the Boston Marathon Bombers

Once two brothers, Tamerlan and Dzhokhar Tsarnaev, were identified as the bombers of the Boston Marathon in 2013, the media began to accumulate information about them and their lives so that now we have a reasonably good understanding of their psychosocial histories and perhaps their vulnerability to "radicalization." Although it appears that they acted together and not as a unit of an organization, they were part of the larger movement of religious activists who sought to protect the faith, as they saw it, through terroristic violence. Though it appears they acted alone, they do not satisfy the definition of the "lone wolf" and better represent the alienated and disenchanted "type." They believed they were soldiers of their religion; therefore, their violence was legitimated. There was little evidence of mental illness.

We know a great deal about the brothers' background and state of mind from various media sources and Gessen's (2015) book. Here is a summary of the brothers' biographies.

Family Background

1. The family was of ethnic Chechnyan origin, though they did not live there very long. Chechnya and nearby Dagestan, where they spent much of their time, are relatively poor regions of the Russia Federation plagued with violence and sectarian conflict.
2. The family fled the region to escape the conflict, moving numerous times until settling in the United States. For a while the siblings were separated—some lived in Russia and some in the United States.
3. The brothers' father was a mechanic in Russia, but later got a law degree, though it is believed he never practiced law. This credential was not accepted in the United States. He primarily repaired cars in parking lots and on the side of the street. The family was always facing economic difficulty.

4. Their mother tried several occupations before becoming a beautician, a job she lost during the Great Recession. Previously secular, she became deeply religious as her troubles mounted.
5. The parents separated and eventually divorced and returned to Dagestan.

Tamerlan Tsarnev

1. Tamerlan is the elder brother and had trouble finding his place in the United States. He struggled to get a good job and sold (and used) drugs. He failed in his economic endeavors and received public relief.
2. At first, he seemed to direct his aggression through conventional violence—boxing and mixed martial arts—which were legitimate paths to success in Russia. He achieved initial success, but eventually failed.
3. Later, however, his violence became nonlegitimate. He punched out a high schooler for holding hands with his sister (an honor beating) and was later charged with domestic violence for hitting his girlfriend.
4. He became very angry and confrontational with others, taking offense at anything not consistent with his views and beliefs.
5. He was once asked to leave a mosque for shouting at a speaker for promoting American holidays such as Thanksgiving and Martin Luther King Day, and on another occasion at his mosque, he staged a walkout following raising his voice.
6. He read about and believed conspiracy theories such as the US Army was responsible for 9/11. Accepting unfounded conspiracy theories about Jews, he became anti-Semitic. He developed his ethnic and religious identity in a return trip to Dagestan.
7. Known to dominate others, Tamerlan often made his brother and his friends exercise and read from a prayer book.

Dzhokhar Tsarnev

1. The younger brother was opposite his elder brother in temperament. Often described as "normal," he was a relaxed and aspiring individual. Violence was not part of his character.
2. Dzhokhar was not a loner. He was popular in his high school and captain of his school's wrestling team.
3. In high school, not long after his troubles began, he became a "stoner," smoking marijuana regularly. He later sold marijuana to cover living expenses.
4. He went to college on a small scholarship, doing well at first. He later began to struggle academically, however, and his grades fell. His social network grew smaller, and his friends were mostly students who smoked a lot of marijuana and did not study.
5. He incurred debt, especially to his university.
6. Somewhere along the way, he became religious.

Themes

1. Both brothers became disenchanted but in their own way. Tamerlan was angry, marginalized, and alienated from his surroundings and most other people in his life. He externalized his alienation through violence. Dzhokhar internalized his angst and lack of community identity by using marijuana to detach from his social world.
2. Both felt alienation and dislocation from not having strong familial and cultural roots. The break-up of the family, the father's abandonment, continuous economic failures, and debt were strong stressors that tested and overloaded the brothers' coping abilities. They felt marginalized—"strangers in a strange land."

(Continued)

Box 10.1 Psychosocial Profile of the Boston Marathon Bombers *(Continued)*

3. The void was filled by religion. Religion became the glue to hold them together, providing meaningfulness and reducing confusion. Religion also delivered relief from guilt and shame. Other disaffected coreligionists offered attractive messages that made sense to them: the sources of their troubles were western culture and its people and values. The west was presented as the enemy in a war for righteousness.

acted under duress or the promise of economic gains for their families. Therefore, preying on depressed people may be an effective means for recruiting individuals to complete a task that "sane" members or recruits would not do.

Stereotyping is a concern when studying the psychological well-being of people who commit acts of terror. As seen earlier, prejudice can affect diagnostics, and in this case, there is a temptation to apply a simplistic and overgeneralized belief that people whose political causes and strategies are perceived as unjust or brutal are deranged and inhumane and therefore mentally ill. The line between terrorist and freedom fighter is one of perspective, a point that has relevance for considering the mental well-being of people we call terrorists. There is a tendency to pin people with pejorative labels when they are considered an enemy (Johnson et al. 2017).

Victims of Terrorism

Direct and indirect exposure to terroristic violence has negative mental health outcomes among people in targeted areas. Anxiety, depression, and PTSD are common outcomes. While the connection between terroristic violence and mental health outcomes seems obvious, there are several social and psychological factors that influence this relationship.

Most terroristic violence occurs in nonwestern, industrializing countries, but most of the research on the effects of victimization has been conducted in middle- and high-income countries such as the United States, France, and Israel. Johnson and colleagues (2017) have written of a stereotype, which has proven untrue, that suggests that people in developing economies are more resilient and less emotionally vulnerable to attacks. To the contrary, Norris and associates (2002) found that survivors of disasters and violence in poorer countries experience longer-lasting physical and psychological problems after the event because these countries have fewer resources to help individuals, families, and communities cope with trauma and the emotional aftermath.

Studies have been conducted after terror attacks in the United States for several years. North (1999), for example, found that 45 percent of survivors of the bombing of the Murrah Federal Building in Oklahoma City in 1995 experienced post-disaster psychiatric disorders. Over a third of these diagnoses were PTSD.

Researchers have been particularly interested in the mental health consequences after the September 11, 2001, attacks against the United States. These studies have found that about 7.5 percent of adults living in Manhattan and near the World Trade Center continued to have PTSD symptoms one month after the attack (Galea et al. 2002). Galea's team (2003) later found that PTSD and depression symptoms began to decline at six months post-attack. Other studies found mental health effects at the one-year mark and even two-years after the attack. PTSD and depression were the most common complaints (Adams and Boscarino 2005; Adams et al. 2006). A study of Manhattan residents at two years post-attack found that other factors were involved in the long-lasting psychological consequences. They learned that the direct effects of 9/11 had ended at two years but that indirect effects persisted. Individuals, for example, with poorer physical health were prone to panic attacks. In addition, residents of New York City who had direct exposure to the violence were more likely to experience negative life events and lifestyle changes, such as alcohol dependency, after 9/11. High exposure to terroristic violence can lead to an increase in other life problems such as divorce, which, in turn, predispose people to psychological distress (Adams et al. 2006).

Indirect exposure to violence also has a psychological impact. Seeing the attacks on television, for example, can cause widespread "communal bereavement" that can last for months (Tsai and Venkataramani 2015). Two studies demonstrate this effect. Nixon and Pallavi (2005) studied Midwestern college students, none of whom had been diagnosed with mental disorder or were in therapy, and found that even at such a distance, the 9/11 attacks disrupted the sample's emotional well-being. Another study, this one of Hispanic immigrants, identified mental health symptoms after 9/11: 14 percent showed clinical-level symptoms of PTSD. Those immigrants who had previous exposure to natural disasters and war violence had elevated odds of developing PTSD (Pantin et al. 2003).

Natural and Human-Made Disasters

Disasters are time-specific events that destroy or disrupt the built-environment and social systems. They are natural disasters such as earthquakes and storms and human-made technological disasters such as the Chernobyl, Ukraine nuclear accident and the Bhopal, India chemical plant disaster. Epidemics are events that can produce catastrophic consequences. As seen in historic pandemics such as the bubonic plagues of the fourteenth and seventeenth centuries and the Spanish Flu of 1918 millions of people died, and social systems collapsed or struggled to maintain themselves.

The effects of disasters and epidemics extend beyond the immediate damage they cause to buildings, physical health, and social systems. They also have a strong impact on mental health.

Disasters

Natural and human-made disasters often occur quickly and without warning. They can take lives, shatter homes and livelihoods, and create extraordinarily high levels of stress, which, in some cases, individuals must confront after their material resources have been exhausted or even destroyed. Stress generated by direct and indirect exposure to these catastrophic events increases a person's risk of experiencing psychological distress and full-blown anxiety and depression.

Social impact assessments, which often include a mental health component, are often conducted after a disaster. These studies have provided excellent data to indicate that these events trigger mental health problems. Here are a few examples. Researchers investigating the Deepwater Horizon oil spill in the Gulf of Mexico in 2010 discovered that exposure to the oil predicted stress and negative mental health outcomes (Gill et al. 2012). The stress was higher for those who lost their incomes because of the catastrophe. According to Morris and associates (2013), one year after the spill, among individuals who were exposed to the oil but retained their incomes, 63 percent showed signs of depression and 65 percent for anxiety. For those without incomes, the rates rose to 83 percent (depression) and 85 percent (anxiety). The disaster not only impacted residents and those who rely on the Gulf for their livelihoods. Due to their work restoring the Gulf and coast to ecological health, environmental clean-up workers showed a significantly high prevalence of both depression and post-traumatic stress (Kwok et al. 2017).

Natural disasters such as hurricanes can have long-lasting psychological effects. La Greca and colleagues (1996) found that over half of third and fifth graders in Dade County, Florida had moderate to severe PTSD reactions to Hurricane Andrew three months after the storm. Twelve percent of that group reported serious symptoms after 10 months. Similarly, the psychological impact of Hurricane Katrina was felt long after the storm. Low-income individuals were especially affected. The prevalence of severe mental illness doubled among this group a year after Katrina and about half still experienced symptoms of post-traumatic stress (Rhodes et al. 2010). Groups who were more impacted by Katrina included women, single individuals, young adults, parents of young children, and African Americans (Rhodes et al. 2010).

Similar findings on the impact of disasters are found in studies outside the United States. For instance, 11 years after the Chernobyl nuclear accident, people directly affected by the disaster were still likely to express psychological distress (Havenaar et al. 1996). A later study on Chernobyl discovered high rates of depression for first responders and clean-up workers 25 years after the accident. The more exposure to radiation, the greater the likelihood of depression and PTSD (Bromet et al. 2011). Others whose mental health was affected by the Chernobyl disaster included individuals who had pre-natal radiation exposure and, out of concern for their children's health, mothers with young children at the time of the accident. Epidemiologically, compared to neighboring areas, the Chernobyl region has higher rates of clinical and subclinical depression and anxiety in its general population (Bromet et al. 2011).

The effects of disasters are disproportionately distributed in society. Disasters tend to have a larger impact on the psychological health of women, parents, ethnoracial minorities, and the poor. The stress derived by disasters also can overwhelm those who already have suffered negative life events or traumas or who have a history of psychological disorders (Norris et al. 2002). For example, the psychological impact of the Deepwater Horizon oil spill was more severe for people who five years earlier were most affected by Hurricane Katrina. The cumulative adversities of the two disasters significantly increased the risk of anxiety, depression, and post-traumatic stress following the spill (Osofsky et al. 2011). For some people, especially those in socially vulnerable groups, disasters can create heavy workloads or job loss, cause family disruptions and displacement, deplete finances and other resources, and expose individuals to bureaucratic hassles (Werner and Locke 2012).

Pandemics

The effects of severe epidemics on mental health have been noted in the past, but the 2020 coronavirus pandemic has yielded the best data on the effects of epidemics on mental health. In fact, by the end of 2020, the first full year of the pandemic, more mental health research had been conducted on the psychological sequelae of the coronavirus epidemic than the sum of similar research on H1N1 (the swine flu) and Ebola combined (Maalouf et al. 2021). This epidemic has provided the opportunity to study the psychosocial responses to the disease in good detail, and while we do not yet know the long-term effects of the pandemic, several studies have documented the impact of the crisis in its first year.

COVID-19 (Coronavirus-2019), the disease caused by the Severe Acute Respiratory Syndrome-Coronavirus-2 (SARS-CoV-2), socially impacted everyone on Earth. Its unprecedented reach elicited a global response unparalleled in human history. All social systems were disrupted to various degrees, hundreds of thousands of jobs were lost, families were disrupted, and the loss of life was of historic proportions. In the hardest hit areas, the pandemic exhausted health care systems, and housing and food insecurity problems emerged for countless people and families. The mental health consequences of COVID-19 have been more severe than from any other health crisis in the last century, and health care services reached urgent levels of need.

Could mental health problems have been anticipated? Earlier twenty-first-century epidemics that required quarantines should have prepared countries for the impact that an epidemic can have emotional and behavioral health. The pandemics of SARS in 2003, H1N1 flu in 2009, and Middle East Respiratory Syndrome (MERS) in 2015 had a far smaller reach compared to 2020s novel coronavirus global threat, but these epidemics demonstrated how strong the emotional and behavioral impact of isolation could be.

Studies found that the psychological impact of epidemics and quarantines are important to identify and manage. Health care workers in hospitals that treated SARS patients had a higher probability of developing alcohol and drug dependencies compared to hospital employees that did not treat patients. For many, the substance abuse problems lasted up to three years after the epidemic passed (Wu et al. 2008). Similarly, people who were quarantined due to the MERS epidemic experienced increased feelings of anger and anxiety during their seclusion. For many, these emotions lasted several months after the epidemic ended (Jeong et al. 2016).

Following the H1N1 flu epidemic of 2009, researchers studied parents and children in the United States, Canada, and Mexico who were isolated and quarantined and learned that PTSD symptoms occurred up to six months after quarantines were lifted. Almost a third of isolated children and a quarter of their parents met the clinical threshold for PTSD (Sprang and Silman 2013).

Regarding COVID-19, research has demonstrated that quarantine had a heavy impact on psychological well-being. Among these studies, two groups, the Kaiser Foundation and the CDC in conjunction with the US Census, tracked mental health patterns during the COVID pandemic with two ongoing surveys. The Kaiser Foundation reported that in March 2020, 32 percent of adults in the United States reported that their mental health had been negatively impacted because of worry and stress over coronavirus. By mid-July that figure had increased to over half (53%). COVID affected other indicators of well-being as well: just over one-third reported trouble sleeping, 32 percent had difficulty eating, and 12 percent stated their alcohol and substance abuse had risen (Panchal et al. 2021). The CDC's study, called the Household Pulse Survey, reported the effects of sheltering in place. Of those who followed governmental and health leaders' recommendations to avoid contact with others, 47 percent experienced negative mental health effects, compared to 37 percent who did not shelter in place. Similar to Kaiser's data, the CDC (2020b) also found increases in psychological distress as the pandemic forged on. Chart 10.3 shows the rise in self-reported symptoms of anxiety and depression over the course of the summer of 2020. Anxiety was more prominent than depression, most likely because of dread of getting sick and worries about income, housing, employment, and other tangible resources that were threatened or lost. Note the steady increase in both anxiety and depression. By July of 2020, about four in 10 adults were experiencing symptoms of at least one disorder. The CDC also reported that mental distress increased among individuals 65 years of age and older and among women with young children. Individuals who lost their jobs were vulnerable to depression, anxiety, low self-esteem, substance abuse, and suicide.

Similar findings have been found throughout the world. Studies in China (Duan et al. 2020), Nepal (Shrestha et al. 2020), Pakistan (Amin et al. 2020), Australia (Neill et al. 2020), and Italy (Ravaldi et al. 2020), among other places demonstrated negative psychological effects on children, adolescents, and adults. In some places, alcohol consumption increased, and in others, anxiety and depressive symptoms rose in conjunction with the pandemic. As in the United States, older individuals, women, especially those with children, people previously diagnosed with a psychiatric disorder, and front-line medical care workers were more likely affected.

Worrying about acquiring COVID and the losses of friends, loved ones, and incomes were not the only causes of psychological distress during the pandemic. The public health measures necessary to control infection also caused stress responses. There are only two mechanisms to control the pace and scale of viral infections: vaccines and interrupting infection patterns, which means social distancing. Given the vast interconnections among people both locally and globally, keeping distant from other people proved nearly impossible for many people. Others refused to obey distancing recommendations. Containment of this easily contracted virus quickly became unmanageable.

CHART 10.3 Average Percentage of Adults Reporting Symptoms of Anxiety or Depression During the COVID-19 Pandemic, May–July 2020

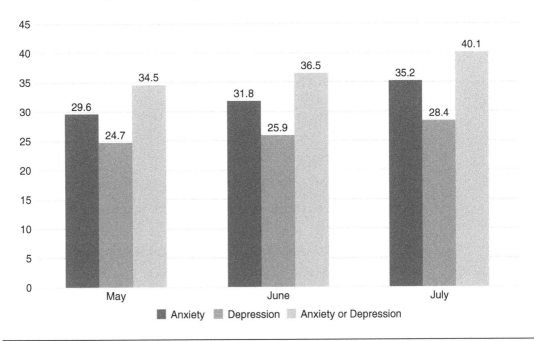

Source: CDC Household Pulse Survey (2020b).

Part of the problem of social distancing is its effects on the human psyche. Social isolation can be detrimental to emotional well-being. Research has shown that the physical health risks of isolation and loneliness are like the effects of smoking cigarettes and obesity (House 2001; Cornwell and Waite 2009). Loneliness has objective and subjective components. Objective loneliness refers to living arrangements and social contacts and engagement. Subjective or perceived loneliness implies the evaluation of those objective conditions. Objective loneliness does not influence mental health if an individual is able to tolerate and adapt to isolation but if the objective conditions are perceived as unsatisfactory or intolerable (subjective loneliness), then mental health is likely to suffer (Cornwell and Waite 2009). Perceived loneliness is how people feel about or are satisfied with the closeness or frequency of their relationships and is predictive of future prevalence and severity of depression, along with several physical health problems, because of the increased stress that accompanies loneliness (de Jong Gierveld et al. 2015; Holvast et al. 2015).

The COVID pandemic suddenly caused objective loneliness throughout society, and many people reacted negatively to being socially isolated. COVID upset usual social patterns that fostered social integration, causing people to feel separated and disconnected. When this situation occurred, individuals felt less social trust and a greater sense of threat since other members of their community posed a threat to health and well-being. Bierman and Schieman (2020) found that by March 2020, three months into the epidemic, subjective isolation and community distrust significantly increased, and that both conditions contributed to increased psychological distress.

The psychological costs of virus containment were high during this pandemic, and research identified a two-pronged COVID stress syndrome characterized by the following characteristics (Taylor et al. 2021). The first type included:

1. Anxiety about the dangers of COVID-19 and encountering infected people and surfaces;
2. Anxiety about personal socioeconomic welfare;
3. Xenophobic worries that foreigners are spreading the disease;
4. COVID-related traumatic stress syndrome with symptoms such as nightmares; and
5. Disease-related obsessiveness in seeking reassurance that one is not infected.

The second type of COVID syndrome has three facets:

1. A belief that one has a natural resistance to COVID
2. The threat of the disease has been exaggerated
3. Social distancing is unnecessary

Both types, though contradictory to one another and not occurring within the same person, were linked to increased alcohol and drug use (Box 10.2).

About the Quote

It seems that somewhere someone is experiencing the "darkest of times." These dark times may be historical periods of mass devastation—slavery, the Holocaust, wars—or they may be tragic events that while on a smaller scale are just as catastrophic—serious illness and death of a loved one or a storm or fire that destroys a house. For others, hard times can be chronic conditions like facing persistent discrimination, poverty, or an abusive partner. At any given moment, someone is confronting their "darkest of times." Misery, it seems, stalks humans.

Despite all this tragedy, humans not only survive—they also learn and prosper. People turn misery into beauty using their pain to create art or music, and they make resolutions to avoid being brought down from what they cannot control. They seek solace in the comfort of others and read poetry and sacred texts. Human beings are highly resilient.

Box 10.2 COVID-19 and Substance Abuse Disorders

The link between mental and physical health is well established. Casual observations tell us that having a cold often leads to a bad mood or to wallow in self-pity that almost appears as depression. Examples of more serious comorbid states are the relationships between depression and heart disease and gastrointestinal problems. Being sick can make you depressed and being depressed can make you sick. The association between chronic conditions and mental health are associated with factors such as persistent stress, which affects the immune system and disrupts sleep, exercise, and healthy dietary habits.

Infectious diseases similarly can have comorbid ties to mental health conditions. One example was found in the COVID-19 pandemic by Nora Volkow, the Director of the National Institute on Drug Abuse and her research team (Volkow 2020; Wang et al. 2020). The group studied the electronic health records of over 73 million patients at 360 US hospitals to identify individuals who were diagnosed with a substance abuse disorder (SUD) and COVID-19. The analysis found that people with SUD diagnoses were at higher risk of acquiring the coronavirus—15.6 percent of the people with an SUD diagnosis had COVID-19, a rate that far exceeded the general population. Both a recent diagnosis (within the last year) and a lifetime SUD increased the odds of getting COVID-19.

The rates varied by the type of substance used. ("x" means "times," so "tobacco 8.2x" means that someone diagnosed with a tobacco use disorder was 8.2 times more likely to get COVID-19 than someone not diagnosed with an SUD.)

Substance Abuse Diagnosis	Last Year	Lifetime
Opioid	10.2x	2.4x
Tobacco (including vaping)	8.2x	1.3x

(Continued)

Substance Abuse Diagnosis	Last Year	Lifetime
Alcohol	7.5x	1.4x
Cocaine	6.5x	1.6x
Cannabis	5.3x	—

Source: Volkow (2020).

A substance abuse disorder was also associated with more severe cases of COVID-19. Compared to 30 percent of nonabusers, about 41 percent of people with any SUD required hospitalization to treat the infection. In addition, almost 10 percent of individuals with any SUD died from the virus, which was half again higher than those without a history of substance abuse (6.6 percent). Substance abuse weakens the body, making a user more vulnerable to infections. Plus, drug abusers need to interact with other users and dealers to obtain their substances, increasing their risk of exposure (Volkow 2020).

These patterns were not generalizable to all groups. In general, COVID-19 hit African Americans particularly hard in comparison to Whites, a trend that can be seen among drug abusers. Although African Americans and Whites abuse opioids at about the same rate, opioid-abusing Blacks were disproportionately more likely to get COVID-19 (Wang et al. 2020). Social and economic disparities among social class and ethnoracial groups are associated with higher probabilities of kidney disease, hypertension, cardiovascular disease, and diabetes, conditions that can affect the chances of infection and severity of infection. Unfortunately, COVID-19 has proven to be a good case study in the intersection of social dynamics, psychological well-being, and physical health.

Resiliency has been studied extensively, and while individual qualities such as temperament account for some people's ability to handle a disaster or stress in general, social environmental factors help most of us "to turn on the light," as dear old Professor Dumbledore counsels.

In a large study of New Yorkers after 9/11, Bonanno and colleagues (2007) found a strong relationship between resiliency and socio-contextual conditions. These researchers operationalized resilience as having no or one PTSD symptom and no or low levels of depression and substance use. Statistical analysis indicated resilience was predicted by male gender, being older (those 65 and over were three times more resilient than 18- to 24-year-olds), low level of trauma exposure, not having a change in income, social support, overall good health, and having few other stressors.

More recently, a study of the resiliency of pregnant women during the COVID-19 pandemic found that social distancing was particularly stressful for them (Farewell et al. 2020). About 12 percent of a sample of expecting women developed depressive symptomatology and 60 percent reported moderate or severe anxiety. Approximately 40 percent felt loneliness. Other than a fear of becoming ill with COVID, stress for this group stemmed from pandemic-related uncertainties in securing perinatal care, inconsistent messages from various information sources, and a reduced supportive network. These women, however, demonstrated strong resiliency by assuming more control over their health, relying on virtual communication platforms and partners for support, going outdoors, keeping structure and routines in their lives, and expressing gratitude for the joys of everyday life. Maintaining control in and over their lives, minimizing chaos, and relying on significant others reduced the impact of pandemic stress.

Mastery over one's life circumstances, material recourses, and strong support from others, those things that foster good mental health, are also what help us survive hard times. Dumbledore's "light" is the support and cooperativeness of other people.

DISCUSSION QUESTION

1. It seems like violence is an individual or psychological behavior; however, it can be framed as a social phenomenon. Violence tends to follow social patterns. What social structural factors create conditions that promote such anger and distress that individuals find it difficult to cope and then turn to violence?

KEY TERMS

Drug Abuse 221
Drug Addiction 221
Drug Dependency 221
Social Problem 214
Transitional Object 228

CHAPTER 11

The Career of Mental Health Patients

> If you are afraid to tell your own story, stigma wins.
>
> —Pete Early (2014)

Learning Objectives

After reading this chapter, students will be able to:

1. Interpret the notion of a moral career path of mental health patients.
2. Analyze the three models of mental health care utilization.
3. Illustrate the ways in which demographic macro-factors influence help-seeking behavior.
4. Recognize the various expressions of mental illness stigma.

Introduction

The gap between need and treatment for mental health problems is quite large among most social groups. Seeking psychological or psychiatric care, however, is not the same as going to a physician to treat an illness or an injury. The decision to obtain help for mental health troubles is more complex and typically involves a dynamic process of trying to make sense of distressing feelings and asking for help within a social context of friends, family members, and social values about mental illness. Some may seek therapy on their own, while others may be pressured or even coerced into outpatient treatment or the hospital. To complicate the matter further, many potential mental health patients, people who may qualify for a diagnosis, do not ask for help because they believe that nothing is wrong with them. Sociologists have discovered that the process to seek mental health care is usually not made in social isolation and involves more than a simple, linear rationale of "if it hurts, fix it."

The Career of a Mental Health Patient

The term **moral career** is often used metaphorically in sociology to describe the experience of having mental health symptoms and engaging the treatment system. It refers to the sequence of events and changing attitudes that occur as individuals and those in their social networks process and make sense of the experience. Undergoing treatment often implies a change in status because of the moral values attached to being labeled mentally ill, which often happens simply by seeing a mental health professional. The moral career of mental health patients has two primary aspects: changes in how individuals see themselves and differences in relationships with other people.

The concept of career began with Erving Goffman's famous book, *Asylums* (1961), in which he described how patients progress through varying perspectives and statuses over time. For Goffman, this progression is the consequence of the socially constructed meanings of being a psychiatric patient. The moral career of a mental health patient is primarily shaped by others' standards of evaluating or judging mental illness, patients' self-definitions and assessments, which are influenced by the attitudes of other people, and how patients manage these evaluations.

The key questions in the study of the moral career of mental health patients focus on identity. How do symptoms of a disorder such as depression affect how people feel about and understand themselves? What does it mean to take psychotropic medications to improve one's personality and mood? How do others' opinions and general social values about mental health affect how people see themselves?

Research has demonstrated that these factors affect individuals as they progress through their mental health careers. Many people, for instance, have trouble taking medications such as antidepressants because it implies a fundamental shortcoming in their personhood and a diminished social status. They may conceal taking these medicines because of how other people may judge them. Seeing a therapist often follows the same course—patients may feel that few other people should know they are in treatment so that they can maintain a higher socially desirable presentation of themselves.

The Pathway of the Moral Career

The career of psychological and psychiatric patients follows distinct patterns. David Karp's important book, *Speaking of Sadness* (1996), outlines the process in which individuals who have been diagnosed with depression come to terms with their depression and what it means to have a psychiatric disorder. We will base our understanding of the career process on his research.

Karp interviewed 50 adults who had been diagnosed with depression and had received treatment. Some had been hospitalized, while others had been treated with therapy and medicines on an out-patient basis. He was particularly interested in patients who adopted a medical conception of their depression and were taking medications. Strikingly, Karp found that all the people in his study followed the same path, which he described as a career. Each person experienced critical and similar "turning points" as they moved from one phase of their career to another. He described these steps as (1) experiencing confusing emotions, (2) feeling that something is wrong, (3) experiencing some sort of crisis, and (4) coming to terms with an illness identity.

Inchoate Feelings

Karp termed the first phase of the moral career of person experiencing depression as **inchoate feelings**. The word "inchoate" means incoherent, unorganized, or not fully formed. Inchoate feelings, therefore, are emotions that are confusing, ambiguous, and perhaps unrecognized. They are emotions that cannot yet be labeled with a word, which implies that they are not well understood. People experiencing depression, according to Karp, begin their depressive career unable to make sense of the feelings that they cannot label. These emotions are not necessarily viewed as abnormal because individuals may have no baseline of "normalcy" for comparison. For some, these feelings have always been present. Others, however, can identify when the feelings began. What they have in common is that experiencing depression starts with nebulous emotional distress. It may take the form of not being excited after a major accomplishment and then wondering "why am I not happy about this?" or as a lack of pleasure in life in general.

Feeling That Something Is Really Wrong

At some point, people with depression eventually conclude that something is wrong with them. This implies a significant transformation in their perception of themselves because now they start to think that they are somehow internally flawed. At this point, people experiencing depressive feelings must adjust their identities to include the possibility of having a fault because their own sense of personhood is at stake. As Karp says, "it is hard to accept a damaged self" (1996: 62). They must consider that something is not right, though they do not yet know what it is.

Another challenge in this phase is deciding whether to tell others about these feelings and their fear that something is wrong. People worry about how others will interpret personal revelations of depressive or other symptoms. The hesitation to reveal their emotions is due to the dread that others may react negatively.

This phase ends when individuals are no longer able to fully control their emotions or behavior. They realize that they "possess a self that is working badly in every situation" (1996: 64), which means that life is becoming difficult, and they sense their troubles are connected to their depressive symptoms. At this juncture, depressive individuals may feel the need to seek professional help to sort out their problems. Receiving a diagnosis from a mental health professional usually has a strong impact on identity. Patients of a psychologist, psychiatrist, or other mental health professional are now faced with the possibility that the problem is within themselves and beyond their ability to control (Karp 1996).

Crisis Stage

The third phase of Karp's patient career sequence is the crisis stage. Everyone in Karp's study could specify an exact moment or a series of events that moved them from recognizing that something was wrong to realizing that they may be sick. At the crisis point, people turn to professionals, or as Karp says, to "the therapeutic world of hospitals, experts, and medicines" (1996: 65). The diagnosis becomes both real and serious, but it also affords the possibility of hope, and that effective treatment will be possible.

At this time, an important element in the career path of psychiatric patients takes place: how do people feel about taking medications? People have strong psychological reactions to psychotropic medications, and this topic will be discussed in more detail later in the chapter.

Coming to Terms

Last is coming to grips with an illness identity. Once individuals with depressive symptoms enter treatment, including hospitalization, they must reconstruct their past in terms of their current lives. They may look for explanations of their condition and attempt to select a theory that makes sense to them. Coping with their symptoms and their illness diagnosis becomes part of their identities. They must decide if they are a "person" or a "depressed person." Many people experiencing depression resist defining themselves as an ill person whereas others embrace their depression and use it to give them a unique insight into themselves and other people. These people believe that their depression affords them an outlook on life that is deeper and more empathetic toward the needs of others. For them, being depressed is a gift. For others, depression is accepted as a flaw in their character or physiology. It is an unwanted condition but one that they cannot seem to shake.

Variations in Karp's Model

Karp's model describes depression. He only interviewed people diagnosed with that affective condition, and though everyone in his study group followed this career sequence, this model cannot be uniformly applied to people with other conditions. For example, the moral career of schizophrenia works slightly differently. Whereas depression can improve or even go away, the course of schizophrenia always tracks downwards, and symptoms worsen over time. Schizophrenia brings about a metaphorical fracturing of the self where personality, language, and perception become scrambled and nonsensical. People with schizophrenia often do not see themselves as sick, and because the symptoms of schizophrenia eventually result in what is often described as a fragmented self that is characterized by hallucinations, delusions, disorganized thinking, and disconnected speech, it is difficult for people with schizophrenia to think about the self in a measured, reflexive, and rational way. Consequently, people with schizophrenia oftentimes have trouble forming insight and personal awareness, especially at latter stages of the disorder.

Another possible variation from this career model stems from cultural differences in the ways in which depressive symptoms are manifested, defined, interpreted, and labeled (Conner et al. 2010). Many depressed African Americans believe that their emotions are a function of their social position in the hierarchy, which differs from a strictly medical model approach that many other people accept when confronting depression. They often believe that their life circumstances explain their depression and are reluctant to accept a medicalized version of their inchoate feelings because it does not represent the African American experience. Therefore, they seek medical treatment only as a last resort (Conner et al. 2010).

This finding does not necessarily contradict Karp's understanding of depression. He is interested in how many people handle the *idea* that they have a medical condition that prescriptions can resolve and how the notion of having a medical condition of the self affects identity. African Americans are leery of these medications because the pills do not solve the problems of poverty and discrimination. While African Americans may follow the career path set forth by Karp, their definitions of the source of their feelings likely differ from most Whites, and they may come to different conclusions about their condition.

The Decision to Take Psychiatric Medications

For physical complaints, people rarely question taking medicines, especially common ones. No one ponders on or has an existential crisis filling prescriptions for amoxicillin to combat an infection, lisinopril to control hypertension, or albuterol to relieve asthma. But a prescription of fluoxetine (Prozac) or sertraline (Zoloft) for depression usually leads to questions about identity and how we understand ourselves as a person taking medications to treat a damaged self. Patients' decisions to take medications for psychological problems differ from decisions to take other medicines. As Karp says in reference to anti-depressants, "Pill-taking is a social act" (2007: 127).

After *Speaking of Sadness*, Karp wrote a second book called *Is It Me or My Meds?* that explored the dynamics of taking psychotropic medicines. His main purpose was to investigate the experience of taking psychiatric medications, and he made several important discoveries. At the core of his study was understanding how individuals come to accept a biomedical version of their emotions and life circumstances. Not everyone who enters psychiatric treatment believes that they have a "brain problem," but to take the medications that psychiatrists prescribe implies embracing the idea that something physiological is wrong.

Karp (2007) found that people who take antidepressants move through a series of life experiences that either strengthen or weaken their belief in a medicalized explanation of their complaints. This process of what he called a commitment to drugs has four stages: desperation, experimentation, engagement, and marriage.

Desperation

At the beginning of the medication phase of the moral career of mental health patients, some individuals resist the notion of drugs, though most are open to taking them. They are not worried about identity issues or do not foresee taking them for a long period of time. As Karp (2007: 74) says, most "tread slowly and gingerly" at the beginning but are desperate to end their pain. They enter the culture of medication because of the urgency to resolve the troubles of their lives.

Experimentation

Once practitioners initiate a patient to psychotropic medications, there is usually a period of experimentation that includes trying different drugs and varying dosages until a good combination is found. Patients must be willing to undergo this period of experimentation, which requires a particular ideological perspective: that their condition is due to problem in the production or absorption of neurotransmitters (Karp 2007). People allow these experiments because there is an expectation of a cure; however, they will eventually realize that the drugs are not perfect, often do not work, and are not a magical remedy.

There are few parallels to the experimentation phase in nonpsychiatric medications. Sometimes blood pressure medications are changed over time because of side effects or ineffectiveness. Autoimmune disorders often require multiple attempts at finding the correct medication, and for some people with asthma, it may take a few changes in prescriptions to find the best treatment. For these conditions, however, changes in medications happen far less often as they do in psychiatry, where dosages and medications can change in every appointment early in treatment. The willingness to allow a physician to do this requires patients to be optimistic and believe that the medicines will work.

Engagement

Karp believed this third stage to be a critical point in which patients must decide to stay with their medication. It is not a decision made lightly. People have what Karp called "commitment phobia." Doctors and other people in the patient's social network may exert pressure to continue their prescribed medication, but the patients may feel that the medicines are not working or providing the cure they expected. If they stay on the medication, they may feel the need to maintain autonomy and control by making their own conclusions about dosage. They may quit and later restart taking the medications though they believe that eventually they will stop them altogether. But by continuing with the medicine patients

> *had decided that their drug relationship, with all its flaws, was worth retaining. At that point, [patients] became more deeply engaged with pharmacological treatments and thus more active in their own care.* (Karp 2007: 85)

The key word in this quote is "relationship." Individuals taking psychiatric medicines related to these treatments in an emotional and social way unlike drugs in most other medical areas. People "relate" to them and process how the medications are impacting the meaning of themselves and their quality of life.

Marriage

In this final stage, the medications become part of people's everyday lives and routines. Some of the people in the study described themselves as having "given up" and "surrendered" in making a long-term commitment to taking antidepressants. They are now "married" to the medications and the idea that biological causes are the roots of their problems.

The issue at hand is authenticity. Karp titled his book as an interesting question: Is it me or my meds? That question reflects the existential struggle that engulfs many people who take antidepressants. If the medications have an effect, is the resulting "person" the true self finally coming out because of help from the pills? Or is the new person a fake or an inauthentic self that really is the pill and not the true person? While some people feel liberated on antidepressants, other may feel a sense of powerlessness because they must rely on medications to have a genuine sense of who they are. The question Karp raises is a good one: is the personality on antidepressants the real person or one shaped and manipulated by a drug?

If individuals on these medications believe that the medical model correctly explains their emotions, thoughts, and behaviors, then their true self is indeed faulty and requires chemicals to keep it bolstered and together. It also implies that individuals have no control over themselves—that they can ignore social and psychological components and influences over the kind of person they are. By taking pills, Karp argues, it is not individuals but society through its institution of biological health care that is responsible for solving personal problems. Relying on others to solve our problems conflicts with the expectation of self-reliance, which is a core value in American culture. This conflict in values adds to the dilemma and existential struggles that come with taking antidepressants.

Other research has reached similar conclusions as Karp. Buus (2014) found that many people on antidepressants have trouble conforming to treatment regimens, and many, over half in some studies, stopped taking them within 12 weeks of the initial dose. According to Buus, people on antidepressants go through two stages. First, the basic restitution stage, in which patients believed they were taking control of their symptoms by taking the drugs. Later, however, their perspective on their health changed, and they attempted to self-regulate their antidepressants. Buus called this period "the frustration stage" in which individuals attempted to resist conforming to the mental health authority. Antidepressants are not always effective, and many people become frustrated that their symptoms persist while they are taking the pills. At that point, they often search for means other than medications to manage their problems.

The Decision to Seek Help

The decision to seek assistance from a mental health professional is largely a sociological act. Some people may make that first appointment without consultation with or pressure from others. They may not want others to know they need help, and the desire to maintain social appearances may be important. Those who pursue psychological or psychiatric treatment solely on their own volition, however, are believed to be the minority among initial mental health patients. Experiencing symptoms, though the strongest predictor of service utilization, is not sufficient to explain people's entries into treatment. Micro factors such as attitudes of significant others and macro factors like ethnorace, gender, and economic status impact the decision to begin treatment. In addition, others are ordered into care by authority agents such as judges or employers.

Because of the complexities of seeking mental health care, there are several theories about mental health care utilization, and three will be reviewed here: the **Health Beliefs Model**, the **Socio-Behavioral Model**, and **Network-Episode theory**.

The Health Beliefs Model

The Health Beliefs Model, or the HBM, is a classical socio-cognitive approach to health care utilization. This theory contends that individuals will initiate mental health services when they believe that their symptoms are having serious consequences for daily living. People must expect that treatments will be effective, however, before making that first call to a therapist (McCaul and Mullens 2003). The HBM assumes that people who have symptoms often feel a sense of vulnerability and become susceptible to "cues to action"—the severity of the symptoms, media messages about getting help, or having a friend who benefitted from therapy or hospitalization, for instance. These cues trigger the decision to act to relieve troubling behavior or emotions (Poss 2001). The theory assumes that seeking care is a rational decision based on relieving pain and suffering.

The HBM, however, was intended to explain health care utilization for physical problems and has limited application to mental health (McAlpine and Boyer 2008). Consequently, there are several criticisms of the model in a mental health context. While some theorists have attempted to include more social dynamics into the approach, the model remains largely a cognitive assessment theory, and several factors known to affect the decision to seek mental health care are excluded from the HBM. For example, because of negative values toward therapy, the idea of seeking mental health care can elicit emotional reactions such as fear and shame that can prevent someone from obtaining assistance. The approach also does not consider cultural differences in perceptions of health problems, the role of social networks and social support in decision-making, socioeconomic factors (such as insurance or income), or policy issues like the availability of services, culturally sensitive programs and providers, and affordability (Poss 2001).

Another problem with the HBM in relation to mental health is that individuals may not process their mental health conditions as the HBM presents. It is possible that mental health patients may not have coherent beliefs about their conditions that parallels how people perceive their physical health. With physical health problems, people can assess their symptoms and separate them from their sense of self so that they can make the decision to get treatment (Helman 2007). With psychiatric symptoms, however, it is the self itself that is experiencing the symptoms, and the ability to distinguish symptoms from the self is difficult. This process interferes with the ability to make decisions about their own care (Frank and Glied 2006). To illustrate this point, a qualitative study of 20 individuals diagnosed with schizophrenia reported that those receiving in-patient care did not identify their experiences as an illness and, therefore, did not have health beliefs pertaining to schizophrenia. Instead, psychotic episodes were understood as episodes or states of altered functioning, not as periods of disease (Kinderman et al. 2006).

The Socio-Behavioral Model

The Socio-Behavioral Model (SBM) dates to the 1960s and was initially devised by Andersen (1995) to explain families' use of health services. The model has three core components that influence utilization: need, predisposing factors, and enabling factors.

The need component refers to the social construction of illness; that is, the perception that something is wrong and what, if anything, should be done to remedy the problem. Need can also be a function of others' evaluation of an individual's well-being—a friend or relative can point out troubling behavior. Need is the recognition by oneself or others to consider whether services are necessary and how to access them (Pescosolido et al. 2013).

Predisposing factors are the social structural characteristics that influence accessing care. Research has long demonstrated that utilizing mental health is affected by gender, social class, occupation, ethnorace, and education. Predisposing factors also include health beliefs and coping abilities and resources that are affected by social status (Thoits 2011b).

The enabling component of the SBM refers to factors that facilitate or bar access to services. Examples include having insurance and transportation and the availability of services.

Similar to the HBM, Andersen's SBM was not developed to account for mental health service utilization; however, researchers have applied it for that purpose despite its shortcomings in dealing with conditions specific to mental health. One contribution of the SBM is its inclusion of enabling factors, or the means of getting treatment. Andersen's (1995) revision of the model, for example, stressed how organizational policies of the health care industry, insurance companies, and the state affect mental health care utilization.

Network-Episode Model

Symptoms and individual decision-making are not the only factors involved in entering mental health care, and in response to the traditional HBM and SBM approaches, Pescosolido (1992) developed the Network-Episode Model (NEM). The NEM focuses on the social network component of mental health utilization rather than individual cognitive processing. In the NEM, people are rational actors, as the HBM and SBM suggest, but their behavior occurs within the context of people in their social networks (friends, relatives, colleagues) who push and pull them into (or away from) mental health treatment. As Pescosolido contends, the pathway to care, and hence the decision to seek treatment, is swayed by the power and influence of others by means of advice, persuasion, or direct pressure. Informal social networks provide important resources that link or inhibits the link of individuals to mental health care. In addition to advice, networks provide information, affirm and validate problems, offer emotional support, and share attitudes about how to define and respond to health problems (Abbott et al. 2012).

Therefore, the decision to get help is a dialectic complex of the interplay of others' opinions and interpretations of a person's mental health and the person's own understanding of their behavior and what should be done. These networks not only influence whether people use mental health services but also when care is sought. In some cases, people in a person's network may reject or deny the existence of problematic behaviors or emotions (Pescosolido et al. 2013). For example, people who make excuses for their spouses' drinking or deny its impact (telling the boss their spouse has the flu when, in fact, they are hungover, for instance) are enabling the behavior and therefore, not pushing the spouse into treatment. In other cases, however, they can take steps to coerce or even force someone involuntarily into therapy or the hospital such as when spouses tell their partners to either get help or the relationship will end.

When an individual is feeling that something is not right, they often activate their social networks to help them manage their symptoms and situations, and they do so strategically (Perry and Pescosolido 2015). People typically seek out those in their social sphere whom they see as most able to give them support and advice. Often, they target friends or relatives who have experience in the mental health system. Not only does feedback from others influence health care assistance, others' opinions and supportiveness also affect the outcomes of the treatment. People who have a strong network of helpful and sympathetic friends and kin, tend to have more positive outcomes once they enter treatment; those who have a less supportive network are more dissatisfied with the services they received (Perry and Pescosolido 2015). Similarly, people who were pressured or coerced into treatment were less open to the recommendations or suggestions proffered by therapists, were often late to appointments or missed them altogether, and had more negative attitudes about treatment (Rogers 1993).

Numerous studies have provided empirical evidence that health care access is linked to interactions with social networks. Horwitz (1977) found that before entering psychiatric treatment, individuals consulted four members of their social networks. Vogel's research group (2007) learned that about 75 percent of the people they studied had someone who recommended seeking help and that over 90 percent knew someone who had received mental health assistance. Many people, especially those with depression symptoms, often rely on the advice of friends and relatives who have received help for mental health issues.

One last example comes from Pescosolido's (1998) research team. They discovered that diagnoses intersected with social networks in how people experienced their entry into care. Individuals with bipolar disorder, for example, often come into conflict with the people around them. People in their social networks frequently have difficulty persuading symptomatic friends and relatives that their symptoms are real. To illustrate the point, people with bipolar disorder often describe the "mania" phase of the condition as a euphoric time in which their sociability and accomplishments are high. Many people with bipolar disorder also report enhanced creativity and increased confidence during the manic phase. Thus, friends and relatives may be unable to convince them that something is wrong, which leads to conflicts in their relationships.

Deciding on mental health care is often made in consultation with other people and not solely on perception of pain and individual choice (Thoits 2011a). Entering care, furthermore, is not always completely voluntary. Partners, spouses, friends, and employers can exert considerable pressure on individuals to get help (for example, see Box 11.1 on interventions). Plus, getting treatment can be involuntary. Judges, for instance, as a condition for parole or probation, often mandate therapy for sex offenders and other violent perpetrators. Counseling for substance abuse is commonly required for individuals after DUI charges. Both formal (judges and employers) as well as informal (friends, spouses, relatives) networks play critical roles for people entering mental health treatment.

Box 11.1 Do Interventions Help People Enter Rehab?

You may have heard of family and friends of alcoholics or drug addicts getting together to confront their loved ones about their substance abuse. These structured confrontations are called interventions. Professionally they are known as a Johnson Intervention, named after Vernon Johnson (1920–1999) who originated the concept (Johnson 1986). Johnson was an Episcopal priest and scholar who studied alcoholism with a particular focus on recovery for he himself was a recovering alcoholic. Dr. Johnson believed that an alcoholic did not need to "hit rock bottom" before entering rehab. Instead, friends and family could bring the "bottom" to the abusers to show how their substance abuse was affecting those who cared for them.

Interventions are emotionally trying affairs. Participants take turns to explain how their loved one's substance abuse has hurt them and state their conditions for continuing their relationships in the future. Interventions involve carefully selecting who is involved, planning, and even rehearsing. Demonstrating anger or placing blame are not a part of an intervention. The goals of an intervention are to show abusers that they are surrounded by people who care for them and want them to stop abusing drugs and alcohol and enter a rehab program. Trained professional interventionists offer their services to organize and prepare the confronting group on best practices for getting their loved one into treatment.

Are interventions effective for moving abusers into treatment and eventually sobriety? The answer is yes. Several studies have shown that if conducted properly, Johnson Interventions are quite successful. In one study of 60 alcoholics who were the target of a Johnson Intervention found that 54, or 90 percent, entered treatment and that 45 of them completed a residential program. After six months, 26 (43 percent) had remained sober (Logan 1983). In another, Liepman and associates (1989) trained 24 social networks (friends and family members) of alcoholics in the techniques of intervention. Of those 24, seven confronted their loved one, and six of them sought

(Continued)

> Box 11.1 Do Interventions Help People Enter Rehab? *(Continued)*
>
> treatment or detox programs. Those six individuals abstained from substances for much longer than the nonconfronted group.
>
> The findings of these studies are not surprising given the influence that social networks have on the decision to enter therapy and change behavior. People in one's social network can instill the motivations to change that a person alone cannot easily do. This social dynamic that propels individuals to seek drug and alcohol therapy is just as powerful for other psychiatric and psychological problems such as depression and anxiety. The Johnson Intervention, therefore, is a good lesson in the NEM of mental health care utilization.

Demographic Effects on Mental Health Care Utilization

Part of the structural influence exerted through social networks occurs through the effects of demographic and sociocultural characteristics. Gender, sexual identity, ethnoracial group, and social class position affect whether individuals seek care for distress and mental illness and color the way social networks influence utilization of services.

Gender

The scholarly literature on gender and service utilization shows that women are more likely to receive treatment for psychological problems than men (Pescosolido et al. 2013). These differences reflect gendered social norms that direct women to recognize, report, and discuss symptoms and men to act with stoicism and self-reliance when confronting problems. Men receive less care for depression, substance abuse, and stressful life events, and these differences transcend age, national origin, and ethnoracial boundaries (Addis and Mahalik 2003).

These variations, however, may depend on the setting. While women utilize care in the general health sector (individual psychotherapy, for instance), there are no differences in specialty mental health care (Leaf and Bruce 1987). If all possible sources of mental health specialty care are considered, men in some cases exceed women in seeking mental health treatment. Examples of specialty care are mental health services at the Veteran's Administration hospitals for military-related conditions such as PTSD and attending Alcoholics Anonymous (AA) meetings.

Why are men less likely to enter conventional psychological or psychiatric treatment but are equally likely as women to be in specialized treatment? Addis and Mahalik (2003) were interested in this question and developed a model to explain this phenomenon. They argued that men were reluctant to enter therapy because it conflicts with their perception of traditional masculinity. Treatment for emotional and behavioral problems contradict and even threaten self-reliance and autonomy, the core components of the masculine persona. Not all men, however, subscribe to these perceptions in the same way; consequently, the answer is not so simple.

Addis and Mahalik said men were more likely to get assistance if certain conditions, which they framed around five questions, were met.

First, is the problem normal? Drinking is often an important part of the expectations of male behavior and identity. When their drinking becomes problematic, men are more likely to seek help if the problem are an outgrowth of their experience as men; that is, if the problem is shared by other men. Getting help for drinking problems is a legitimate remedy because it a masculine behavior that is out of control. It is no surprise then that according to Alcoholics Anonymous (2015), over six in ten AA participants are men. Knowing that they are likely to encounter other men at an AA meeting may contribute to their willingness to start attending, engage 12-Step programs, and accept the emotional support of others.

Next, is the problem a central part of the self? Addis and Mahalik contend that if the problem resides outside the self, meaning the issue is not perceived to lie within the individual's identity or personality, then men are more willing to seek mental health services. An example is accepting treatment or participating in AA to control problem drinking. If alcoholism is believed caused by a disease, which is common among AA participants (Kurtz 2002) rather than a personality problem or as strategy for coping with life's unpleasantness, men are more willing to get help.

Third, is reciprocity possible? Men tend to follow reciprocity rules. If, for instance, a man helps his neighbor build a backyard swing set, then the man with the swing set tends to feel obligated to repay the courtesy. How can men reciprocate asking for help for a mental health problem? The answer may lie in the modality of treatment. Men tend to do well in group counseling where they can reciprocate the help and insight that other members of the group offer them. PTSD, sex offender, and substance abuse treatment groups are often effective for men because they can help each other in a way that fits their perception of masculinity.

How will others react to seeking help? Maintaining a masculine posture is important in many men's perception of masculine culture. Men are less likely to seek help if they believe other men in their social networks will belittle or criticize mental health treatment.

Lastly, what is there to lose by seeking therapy? Seeking help can challenge central facets of masculinity. If others in their social networks pressure them to get help, some men may feel out of control or that they have less autonomy. Therapy may imply dependency or failure as men, and the fear is that those in their social network will perceive them as weak and thus reject them.

Sexual Minorities

Sexual minorities have a higher lifetime prevalence of psychological distress and mental health problems compared to sexual majority individuals (Plöderl and Tremblay 2015; Bostwick et al. 2010). Depression, anxiety, suicidality, and substance abuse rates are higher across all subgroups of the sexual minority community than among heterosexual groups, and people who identify as bisexual experience more distress than other sexual minority groups. These elevated rates stem largely from experiences of discrimination and victimization, internal homophobia, expectations that others will reject them, and concealing their sexual orientation (Hsieh 2014). One example of health disparity by sexual orientation is that lesbian and bisexual women have a higher probability of a lifetime substance abuse disorder: 60 percent compared to 24 percent of heterosexual women (McCabe et al. 2013). Identity, rather than behavior, accounts for many differences in health within sexual minorities. Individuals with a bisexual identity have the highest odds of any mood or anxiety disorder, and almost half of women with a lesbian identity report any lifetime mood disorder compared to 19 percent of women reporting only same-sex behavior (Bostwick et al. 2010).

Because of their relatively high rates of psychological distress and disorders, accessibility to services is of significant concern within the LGBTQ community. Studies have reported that most community members in need do not receive services. Part of this disparity can be explained by members of the LGBTQ community sensing that providers are not sufficiently knowledgeable about the issues that confront their community. In one Australian study, half of the bisexual respondents reported that they would be hesitant to report their sexuality to a therapist (Taylor et al. 2021). Many perceived that heterosexual therapists' lack of knowledge and unfavorable attitudes would create barriers to providing quality care.

A large-scale study of over 33,000 American college students found that students identifying with a sexual minority group were more likely to utilize mental health services than heterosexual students (Dunbar et al. 2017). The study included students who identified as lesbian, gay, bisexual, queer, and questioning (LGBQQ). These students reported seeking mental health assistance, but that they were more likely to use off-campus services compared to their heterosexual counterparts. The LGBQQ students reported campus discrimination, harassment, and a hostile campus environment toward their community, which may have contributed to their decision to receive services away from their colleges and universities. In addition, these students sought services recommended by others in their community. These therapists would be known to be more accepting, knowledgeable, and understanding of the stress of "coming out," and sympathetic to the difficulties in coping with an often-unaccepting society-at-large.

Ethnorace

Accessing mental health services can attenuate the negative impact of discrimination. As with any health condition, addressing symptoms early is more likely to bring them to a quicker resolve and prevent them from festering into a more serious problem. Emotions such as anger, worry, hopelessness, and sadness are strong affective states that can devolve into full-blown conditions if not addressed.

But ethnoracial minorities do not utilize mental health services at the level one would expect, given their rates of full-blown disorders (Aneshensel et al. 2019). Chart 11.1 shows that among people experiencing psychological problems, Whites are more likely to receive services from a mental health professional than other ethnoracial groups. Where almost half of Whites in need of assistance receive help,

CHAPTER 11 The Career of Mental Health Patients   259

CHART 11.1   **Percent of Ethnoracial Groups Receiving Mental Health Services**

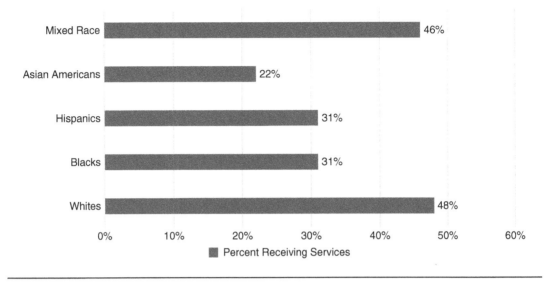

Source: Substance Abuse and Mental Health Services Administration (2015).

less than a third of African Americans and Hispanics access care. Most notable is that only about one in five Asian Americans receive mental health treatment.

What explains these differences? For ethnoracial minorities, seeking help for psychosocial problems is not always an easy option. For some groups, cultural perceptions may preclude services because mental health problems are not believed to require medical or professional care, especially from someone outside the family (Breslau et al. 2017). For many Asian American groups, mental health problems are considered personal failures, not medical or psychological symptoms. As such, medical or therapeutic attention is irrelevant for many Asian peoples. Social **stigma**, bringing shame on the family's name and reputation, and saving face may prevent many Asian Americans from seeking care.

Particularly for immigrants, language barriers and cultural assimilation influence utilization of mental health care. For many Hispanic and Asian peoples, care providers fluent in their languages are not often available. Chinese Americans, for example, are more likely to seek services if they are US citizens, native born, speak English, are not first generation American, and are more assimilated into mainstream American culture (Zhu 2019).

Cultural mistrust of the medical system accounts for some of the underutilization of mental health services. Stemming from a history of neglect and exploitation in medical care and research and treatment that ignores the social causes of illness and distress, African Americans have reason to mistrust the health care system. In mental health, therapists and counselors who discount African American cultural dynamics in identity and psychological well-being are sending a message that to "get well," therapy patients must conform to cultural practices other than their own. When culturally responsive interventions are offered, African Americans increase their willingness to request mental health services (Brooks and Hopkins 2017).

Residential patterns account for some utilization differentials. Segregated and economically disadvantaged neighborhoods influence access and utilization of mental health services (Dinwiddie et al. 2013). Services and clinical practices are often not proximally accessible, and transportation to care centers or private practices can be costly and difficult to arrange. Living in segregated neighborhoods, consequently, influences the type of care that is used. African Americans and Hispanics are more likely to see nonpsychiatrists and general doctors for their mental health concerns (Dinwiddie et al. 2013). Rural areas are grossly underserved, and rural minorities have particularly few options for psychosocial services. They are more likely to talk to their primary care physicians about emotional or behavioral troubles. To compound the problem, rural minorities are less likely than Whites to have a primary care physician (Kozhimannil and Henning-Smith 2018).

Social Class

In discussing utilization patterns, Pescosolido and Boyer (2017: 418) contend that "Perhaps the most intriguing of social selection factors and the most problematic to study is social class." Dating back to the middle twentieth century, social class influences on utilization of mental health services have been a topic of research interest. The relationship between class and service usage is difficult to specify because of the complexities in defining social class and its intersections with ethnorace and gender.

It is not necessarily the case that middle- and upper-class people receive more mental health care, but class position affects the type of treatment received. Individuals with more income typically receive outpatient and "high-end" services, including private hospitals and clinics and expensive talk therapies with clinical psychologists. Less educated individuals receive care from general medical providers or state hospitals (Howard 1996; Wells et al. 1986). Some organizations and clinics provide lower cost services on a sliding scale based on income, but in general, people with lower incomes are less likely to receive high-quality care (Wang et al. 2005).

Some studies, however, have found that income does not predict differences in utilization but that the availability of insurance is the key factor in seeking help. Insurance allows poorer individuals access to care they could not otherwise afford. Expansions in Medicare and Medicaid, for instance, have increased accessibility to low-income earners.

Stigma

An important part of the career of mental health patients is how others treat them when their status as having mental health issues becomes known. As we saw earlier, lay theories of mental illness and the labeling process exert significant influence on how mental health patients understand themselves and therapy and treatment. In general, public attitudes toward mental health patients are negative, and patients are keenly aware of the hostile stereotypes that have been imposed on them by others (Link et al. 1987). Those stereotypes are based on the notion that mental illness is a stigma. Consequently, people with mental illness are forced to struggle with two problems: their own symptoms as well as society's misunderstandings of their condition (Rüsch et al. 2005).

Stigma is a core concept in sociology and is defined as a physical or social attribute that devalues individuals' social identity and disqualifies them from complete social acceptance (Goffman 1963). This attribute is one that is interpreted in such a way that disgraces the individual. Because the characteristic or "mark" carries high social valence, stigma becomes a person's "master status," the attribute that takes priority over all others in the formation of a person's social identity and has the most influence during interactions with others.

Stigma is derived from expectations of what life, and people, should be. Goffman contended that stigma is first grounded in the gap between "virtual social identity" and "actual social identity." Virtual identity is the socially shared idea of what a persona should be, whereas actual identity is what a person really is. Where there is a discrepancy between the two identities, stigma occurs, and interactions between stigmatizer and the stigmatized change.

Stigma, therefore, is a discrediting mark that is assigned to individuals and groups and distinguishes them from those who conform to the ideal or virtual social identity. **Stigmatization**, consequently, is the social process by which a person migrates from "a whole and usual person to a tainted discounted one" (Goffman 1963: 3). The qualities that stray from the ideal are negatively labeled to ensure that persons with those qualities are marginalized, and once defined as alien, stigmatized persons can be kept at a safe distance from the core culture.

Goffman argued that individuals who are targets of stigma are first perceived as people who would have been received "normally" in ordinary social interactions, meaning that stigmatizers would have treated the person with the attribute as if there were no distinguishing characteristic. Once that attribute is identified and known, however, the person with the attribute is discredited and treated differentially.

Stigmatization is one method for creating an "us" and "them" hierarchy in society (Link and Phelan 2001). The distinguishing characteristic is stereotyped and identifies an individual as a member of a group whose "place" in society is subordinate and whose social entitlements are restricted. These "outsiders" are, by definition, rule-breakers; they have violated the norms and values of the groups who have the most influence in creating them. Therefore, to comprehend a stigma, the power dynamics in which the stigma occurs must also be understood (Link and Phelan 2001). Empowered groups invent and perpetuate the rules of social exclusion and marginalization, and as Parker and Aggleton aptly state, stigma "always has a history which influences when it appears and the form it takes" (2003: 17).

Stigma in Everyday Life

Central to this "history" is the role of moral experiences in defining a characteristic as discreditable and how that mark becomes embedded in the moral life of individuals with mental illness. While stigma may exist as a cultural abstraction or ideology, it occurs in people's immediate social milieu, the place where daily life and moral experiences play out. For Yang and colleagues (2007), these local worlds are social arenas with high stakes, where status, money, relationships, life chances, work, and health are won and lost. Everyday life provides the social location for what matters most in the lives of ordinary people and defines individuals' and groups' moral experiences.

Yang and associates' theory, which stems from Goffman (1963), contends that stigma is a moral issue because the stigmatized attribute threatens what really matters most: it violates norms and values that are important in the conduct of everyday life. Focusing on "lived or social experiences" (2007: 1528) identifies not only that which is of the upmost importance, but also that which most threatens life's essentials—the mainstream values of work, family, religion, and the general order of society. Stigma constitutes the "existential and moral experience that one is being threatened" (2007: 1528). In this sense, it is a response to a menace and the unknown; it threatens the loss or attenuation of what is most at stake in life. Stigmatization, therefore, includes discriminatory behavior to protect what is perceived to be of most value in the course of daily living. It is a discrimination based less on exploitation and more on the fear that the stigmatized attribute disrupts or threatens the most fundamental sense of "normality" (Furr 2014).

If a characteristic of a person or group is stigmatized because it is threatening to the moral sentiments of a group, then what danger does mental illness pose? If the idea driving stigma is to keep the "bad" separated from the "good," what is inherently "bad" about mental illness? Why is mental illness strongly stigmatized?

Yang and his colleagues (2007) cite two situations of how mental health stigma threatens norms and values in everyday life. First, consider mental illness stigma in China. As in other cultures, mentally ill people in that country are often stigmatized as different, dangerous, and unpredictable. What values are threatened by mental illness in that East Asian culture?

In China, the family is considered the basic unit of culture. Kinship ties are critical for everyday life, and families provide much of an individual's social and personal identities. Therefore, when someone does well, the entire family benefits, but when a relative makes a mistake or is somehow flawed, the whole family is shamed. In that context, mental illness casts an unfavorable light on a family's credibility, reliability, and marital and business suitability. One mentally ill family member "taints" the full kinship group.

In the United States, the individual is the basic unit of culture, and the core values of American society center on the idea of individualism. Individual freedom, the exercise of free will and choice, and self-reliance gained through personal initiative, achievement, and ability are the central tenets of American culture. Mental illness, however, sits in direct conflict with these values because it fosters dependency on others, including the society-at-large. Mentally ill people, consequently, are stigmatized because they are unable to fulfill those mainstream and most cherished values (Yang et al. 2007). The cornerstone values of culture are threatened by the perceived dependency brought about by mentally illness.

How Stigmatization Affects People With Mental Illness

The social reaction to mental illness takes many forms and operates at different levels of social behavior. Stigmatic attitudes permeate beliefs about mental illness. That mentally ill people are dirty, ignorant, and weak are longstanding beliefs, but the most serious attitude is that mentally ill people, especially those with schizophrenia, are dangerous and unpredictable (Phelan and Link 1998).

In the (relatively) enlightened age of the twenty-first century, it is tempting to believe that mental illness stigma has abated and increases in utilizing mental health services could be seen as evidence of declining stigma. A decline in stigma, however, may not be the case. Research has not detected a decline in stigma. To the contrary, the prevalence of stigma may be rising. Phelan and associates' (2000) study showed that from 1950 to 1996, stigmatic beliefs about mental illness rose dramatically, especially targeting people with psychosis. Compared to those in the first panel, study participants in 1996 were about two and a half times more likely to say that people with a psychosis disorder were subject to violent behavior. McGinty and colleagues' (2016) study of media stories that mention stigma or discrimination against the mentally ill as problems increased 28 percent from 2004 to 2014. Pescosolido and associates (2010) found that stigma remains high despite the public's general belief that mental illness is largely due to biological conditions. This finding means that stigma has increased despite beliefs that if disorders are biological, then individuals are not responsible for their conditions.

Stigma has stayed high for schizophrenia and drug dependency, while the stigma against depression, though it persists, may have relaxed to some degree. The fear of mentally ill people's perceived dangerousness remains and is perhaps core to stigma and the basis of discrimination against people with mental illness (Mossakowski et al. 2011).

Following Link, Phelan, and Hatzenbuehler's (2018) outline, stigma emerges and affects individuals with mental illness in several ways.

Status Loss

Mental illness stigma, by definition, lowers social status. Targets of stigmatization experience decreased social standing in virtually all aspects of social life. Their social esteem or value is lowered and expectations of their ability to conform to social demands and perform their roles competently are reduced. Just as Goffman stated, people with mental health stigma are discredited and stained as if they have become polluted in some way. Once a person's status has been diminished, discriminatory behavior is likely to ensue.

Individual Discrimination

Stigmatization is often visible as **individual discriminatory behavior.** Expressions of individual discrimination can include hostile language, bullying, lack of sympathy or understanding by others, harassment, and physical assault.

Derogatory comments and terms, for instance, are highly stigmatizing and quite hurtful. Referring to psychiatric hospitals as "looney bins" or "nut houses" are expressions of derogatory stigmatization, and stigma is revealed in how individuals with mental illness are labeled. A study of teenagers in England showed that these children had 250 words for mentally ill people. "Disturbed," "nuts," "confused," "psycho," and "spastic" were the most common (Rose et al. 2007).

Other examples of individual discrimination include employers who are reluctant to hire people if believed to have mental health problems (Brohan et al. 2012). Similarly, landlords are known to refuse to rent property to individuals whom they suspect are dangerous or threatening because of their perception of mental illness (Link et al. 2018).

Interactional Discrimination

This form of stigma-based discrimination emerges through interpersonal interaction. There is no discriminatory event. Instead, **interactional discrimination** is about the process of social exchanges and emerges as an individual socially engages a person who has a mental health problem (Link et al. 2018). During these interactions, dynamics change or are different than they would be if the other person were not discredited by the stigma. Several things can unfold during these interactions. Stigmatizers may discount the other person's ideas or feelings or minimize their legitimacy, and their body language may change to indicate discomfort. For example, stigmatizers may maintain more distance from a person they believe to be mentally ill or changing the tone of their voice.

There is an interesting stigma paradox when comparing the experiences of individuals with more severe diagnoses such as bipolar disorder and less severe affective disorders after their initial diagnosis (Perry 2011). For people with more severe and visible symptoms, the diagnosis triggers beneficial social support from relatives and close friends in the early stages of their patient careers. In contrast to their core social network, the diagnosis simultaneously provokes discriminatory and rejecting reactions from people more peripheral to them.

Interactional discrimination is subtle and nuanced, but the stigmatized person can usually detect these behaviors and feel the emotional pain of being treated in a prejudiced manner.

Structural Discrimination

Structural discrimination stems from the way society is organized and includes institutional practices that disadvantage mentally ill persons (Link et al. 2018). One example is the inadequate funding allotted for mental health care (Rüsch et al. 2005).

Another example comes from research that has shown that people with schizophrenia are more likely to receive poor medical care for physical health complaints, including heart disease, than nonmentally ill people (Hippisley-Cox et al. 2007; Rathore et al. 2008).

One significant structural differential action against people with mental illness lies in the distribution of civil rights. As many as one-half of states in the United States levy at least one legal restriction on those labeled mentally ill. As you can see in Table 11.1, states impose several legal restrictions on people who are considered mentally ill or incompetent. Several states have laws to restrict individuals' voting privileges, jury duty participation, and running for office. Some states also regulate marriage and family by having laws that allow a spouse's mental illness serve as grounds for divorce and to terminate parental rights. Of particular note is the difference between "mental illness" and "incompetence." Incompetence refers to a measurable standard of assessing individuals' behavior to determine if they are capable of acting in a responsible manner. Competency laws are generally socially responsible precautions for assessing a person's ability to act in a safe and rational way. Whereas incompetence is a state of disability, "mental illness" is a more suspicious and questionable term in that it reflects a label rather than any measurable evaluation of actual ability. Anyone with any diagnosis could be determined to be mentally ill, regardless of how benign that diagnosis is, and have their rights challenged (Corrigan et al. 2004). As Corrigan and colleagues make clear, "It is sobering to think that legislatures seem to be restricting rights based on a vague notion (or label) of mental illness rather than demonstration that individuals are incompetent or unable to perform in a manner that would qualify them for the civil right" (2004: 483).

Another structural condition indicative of mental illness stigma is the high rate of incarceration of mentally ill people. Seriously mentally ill people are about three times more likely to be found in jails and prisons than in psychiatric hospitals. Two states, Arizona and Nevada, have almost 10 times more mentally ill individuals in jail than in hospitals. About 40 percent of seriously mentally ill individuals will be jailed at least once in their lives (Torrey et al. 2010).

Box 11.2 The Unfortunate Case of Senator Thomas Eagleton

In 1972, the Democratic Party selected South Dakota senator George McGovern as its nominee to run for president against the incumbent Richard Nixon. Before this election became infamous because of the Watergate Scandal, which forced Nixon to resign from office in 1974, it was steeped in drama and conflict, and one of the controversies was the selection of Missouri Senator Thomas Eagleton as McGovern's running mate.

Eagleton was a rising star in the Democratic Party. The youngest attorney general in Missouri's history at age 31, he later won elections as the state's lieutenant governor and, in 1968, as US senator.

(Continued)

Box 11.2 The Unfortunate Case of Senator Thomas Eagleton *(Continued)*

Eagleton was a devout Catholic and vocal opponent of the Viet Nam war.

Eagleton's pick to run with McGovern was decided rather quickly (under an hour). At the time, vetting backgrounds of nominees was based on the honor system rather than complex and detailed background checks, interviews, and reviews of the candidate's writings, which is today's protocol. Since neither Eagleton nor anyone else offered any significant reason not to choose the Missourian, he was put on the ticket to help McGovern with the Catholic and blue-collar votes, groups that were strong Eagleton supporters.

The honeymoon with the Missouri senator did not last long. A few days after the Democratic Convention, an anonymous phone caller told the McGovern campaign that Eagleton was hiding an undisclosed medical history. When McGovern asked Eagleton about it, Eagleton informed him that on three occasions in the 1960s, he had voluntarily entered a psychiatric facility for "nervous exhaustion." During two of those hospitalization, he received electroshock therapy.

The information quickly leaked to the media, and soon the nation knew that Eagleton had likely experienced depression. At first, both candidates publicly resisted the notion that Eagleton's mental health was of any consequence. Nevertheless, the pressure mounted on McGovern to remove Eagleton from the ticket, and within three weeks of the Democratic convention, Eagleton was gone and replaced by Sargent Shriver, a former Ambassador, founder of the Peace Corps, and a member of John and Robert Kennedy's family.

Why was the pressure to dismiss Eagleton from the ticket so strong?

The early 1970s was a period steeped in social conflict and divisions. The Cold War was at a peak, and riots and demonstrations protesting the unpopular war in Viet Nam were occurring regularly throughout the country. Fear of the Soviet Union was high, and a key component in choosing a president was finding the right person to "have a finger on the button"; that is, to have the mettle to launch a full-scale nuclear war.

Eagleton was a victim of the stigma of mental illness. People were afraid that the senator did not have the correct mindset or the emotional stability to protect the country from a nuclear attack. Since no president had launched a nuclear strike during the Cold War, it was not known who could or could not do it, but it was assumed that Eagleton was incapable because he had experienced bouts of depression. Though he had the courage to take on highly controversial subjects (speaking against the war was not always popular) and to lead a public life, it was assumed that he did not have the ability to handle the nuclear arsenal responsibly. He simply was not to be trusted with weapons capable of destroying life on the planet, or so it was believed.

Afterward, Eagleton continued his career in public service competently and energetically. He was elected to two more terms as Senator before retiring in 1980. Then he worked as an attorney and a professor and led several philanthropic and social causes before passing away in 2007 at age 77. Thomas Eagleton, by all accounts, was a highly competent and accomplished person who was wise enough to know when he needed help with his problems. Public misunderstandings about his situation, however, cast him in a light of fear, unpredictability, and instability.

TABLE 11.1 The Number of States That Restrict Civil Rights for People With Mental Illness, 1989, 1999, 2014

	1989	1999	2014
Voting			
Mental Illness[1]	19	19	19
Incompetence[2]	11	12	17
Holding an Elected Office			
Mental Illness	16	19	17
Incompetence	6	6	11
Serving on a Jury			
Mental Illness	16	17	10
Incompetence	6	6	9
Limits on Child Custody			
Mental Illness	20	21	19
Incompetence	1	1	2
Limits on Rights to Remain Married			
Mental Illness	26	21	27
Incompetence	1	1	0

[1] Mental Illness refers to any psychiatric condition.
[2] Incompetence refers to a legal standard of ability to act in responsible ways, according to community expectations.

Source: Hemmens et al. (2002); Corrigan et al. (2004); Walker et al. (2016). Walker et al. (2016) provides a state-by-state listing of restrictions.

Self-Labeling

For many people, mental illness stigma comes from within one's own self, or as Link and Phelan say, it is discrimination that operates through the stigmatized individual. When a person is aware of the negative public beliefs and stereotypes about mental illness, they run the risk of internalizing and believing them, a process known as **self-labeling**. Individuals who believe those labels and then start to show symptoms of psychological distress or a full-blown disorder may accept the idea that the negative images apply to themselves. Self-application of the stigma can lead to feeling shame and self-devaluation and leading a life of secrecy and withdrawal (Corrigan 1998).

About the Quote

The stigmatization of mental illness elicits feelings of shame and humiliation and a sense of failure as a human being. When people feel the symptoms of psychological troubles, they react very differently than when they have bodily pains. It is true that some people ignore body pains. They do this because they do not understand the pain, or they are in denial that something could be wrong, or perhaps because they are depressed and do not have the emotional wherewithal to take care of themselves. People with terminal diseases such as some cancers often become reflexive and think about their lives and get angry about their disease. But a broken body is not the same as a broken self.

Because mental disorders and symptoms are stigmatized, people often try to conceal their condition, especially if they are or have been in treatment. They are attempting to avoid being discredited, as Goffman says, by the taint of stigma. People in the general public who believe that mental illness has biological origins still adhere to beliefs that mentally ill people are dangerous, threatening, and unpredictable. No other health condition challenges or defies social values more mental illness. Consequently, people are affected by possible societal reactions when they feel symptoms and receive a diagnosis. They often think about the symbolic meanings of their diagnosis and what it means to be in treatment and on medication.

Stigma worsens psychological conditions. It surfaces as a source of anxiety that compounds the symptoms of their disorder and another problem to hide, which also aggravates psychological conditions.

As Box 11.2 demonstrates, stigma is a sociological phenomenon, rather than a psychological one, because of the interplay between power dynamics, broad-level or macro social values, and social norms that govern interpersonal interaction. Therefore, ending stigma requires change in the general society. Organizations in the United States, England, Canada, and Australia have implemented large-scale media programs to attempt to reduce stigma; unfortunately, they are not particularly effective, and some have made the problem worse by concretizing stereotypes (National Academies of Sciences, Engineering, and Medicine 2016).

Perhaps changing society from the bottom up would be more effective. Organizations such as NAMI, the National Alliance on Mental Illness, promote a more grassroots strategy to reduce stigma and its impact (Greenstein 2017). NAMI has a 9-point approach:

1. Talk openly about mental health
2. Educate yourself and others about mental illness
3. Be conscious of language
4. Encourage equality between physical and mental illness
5. Show compassion for those with mental illness
6. Choose empowerment over shame

7. Be honest about treatment
8. Let the media know when they are being stigmatizing
9. Do not harbor self-stigma.

The idea of NAMI's strategy is to treat stigma as any other discriminatory behavior. It does not matter if symptoms are a function of biological factors or are reactions to social conditions and stress, stigmatizing mental illness is a "blame the victim" stance similar to racism, sexism, homophobia, and ageism, and if people are afraid to tell their story, prejudice and discrimination will persist.

Research bears this out. When confronting stigma, people who employ strategies such as deflection, which means to minimize mental illness stereotypes and distance oneself from the stereotype, and challenging others through education and activism, experience improved self-esteem and fewer depressive symptoms (Marcussen et al. 2021).

DISCUSSION QUESTIONS

1. Here is a thought experiment to consider: could neglecting to consider the effects of discrimination on psychological well-being constitute an example of "gaslighting" or "blaming the victim"? (Gaslighting is a psychological manipulation to make psychologically sound people believe they are "crazy.") How can sociological knowledge about prejudice and discrimination inform mental health professionals about the psychological conditions of their clients?

2. Consider the case of Senator Thomas Eagleton described in Box 11.2. Given the strength of stigma during that time, what choices did he have? Would this series of events happen today? Why or why not?

KEY TERMS

Health Beliefs Model 252
Inchoate Feelings 247
Individual Discriminatory Behavior 264
Interactional Discrimination 264
Moral Career 246
Network-Episode Theory 252
Self-labeling 267
Socio-Behavioral Model 252
Stigma 259
Stigmatization 261
Structural Discrimination 264

CHAPTER 12

The Medicalization of Social and Psychological Problems

Learning Objectives

After reading this chapter, students will be able to:

1. Articulate the basic assumptions of the medical model of mental illness.
2. Assess sociology's intersection with biological factors associated with mental illness.
3. Analyze psychiatry as a social role.
4. Describe medicalization and its relevance for understanding mental health and illness.

> If the doors of perception were cleansed everything would appear to man as it is, Infinite. For man has closed himself up, till he sees all things thro' narrow chinks of his cavern.
>
> —William Blake (1793)

Introduction

The medical model of psychopathology is ever-present. According to government statistics reported by Harvard Health Publishing (Wehrwein 2020), the rate of antidepressant use by people 12 and older in the United States increased by almost 400 percent between 1988 and 2008. About 10 percent of Americans take

Prozac, Zoloft, Wellbutrin, or similar medications. Harvard also reported that nearly a quarter of women between the ages of 40 and 60 take an antidepressant. About 14 percent of non-Hispanic Whites, compared to four percent of Blacks and three percent of Mexican Americans, are on antidepressants. Interestingly, fewer than a third of people who take antidepressants have seen a mental health professional in the past year (Wehrwein 2020).

While a medical theory of psychological problems has been around for millennia, it has never been more popularly accepted. It is likely that many people believe that mental illness is solely due to biology because they *wish* it were true. A biological answer is a neat, tidy, and easy explanation for deviant behavior, and it is much simpler to comprehend than a complex theory of multiple and interacting factors. Plus, it fits with dominant cultural values of individualism and implies no social or political responsibility toward those in disadvantaged groups, neighborhoods, work environments, or families.

Unfortunately, the biological approach fails to fully explain mental disorders. Psychological and psychiatric problems do not often fit categorical classifications, as shown in an earlier chapter. The boundaries separating disorders are often described as "fuzzy," and there are no biomarkers that identify with any certainty any of the diagnoses found in the DSM.

Therefore, we can conclude that medical theories are as much a sociological phenomenon as they are biological. This chapter differs from others in this text because it focuses on the sociology *of* medicine, rather sociology *in* medicine (see Chapter 1). In this chapter, we will review the medical model of explaining psychological complaints and look at how sociology engages biological data and approaches. We will also look at the acceptance of medical theory as a sociological phenomenon.

The Medical Model

The biological perspective, also known as the medical model, treats mental illness and psychological distress as if they were medical diseases. In this view, those experiencing psychological symptoms are sick in the same way someone with influenza or cancer is sick. Mental symptoms are thought to cluster together as a discrete disorder, and the medical response to a mental condition follows the same linear pattern as any other physiological condition: identify symptoms, assign a diagnosis, and prescribe a treatment. The medical model assumes that behaviors, emotions, and cognitions that meet certain diagnostic criteria are expressions of something wrong in the body.

Though the medical model has been unfolding for hundreds of years, it has never been as powerful or influential as it is today. The bulk of research funds from the National Institute of Mental Health supports biomedical research, leaving mental health research in community and clinical psychology, social psychiatry, sociology, and other fields, largely unfunded. About 17 percent of adult Americans fill prescriptions for psychotropic medications (Moore and Mattison 2017), and estimates indicate that around $50 billion are spent on these drugs each year.

The medical model, as Wheaton (2001: 222) says, rests on "the implicit belief that if we just drill down far enough in biology and genetics, we will explain most of the variance in most behavior." The Holy Grail of the medical model is the identification of a biomarker that predicts abnormal behavior. Indeed, we have generated considerable knowledge about the physiology of some psychiatric disorders. Because of the advances that bio-psychiatric research has made, and the hope bestowed on medical remedies, we have truly entered what many call "The Biological Revolution" in the treatment of mental illness.

The modern medical perspective started with the development of Thorazine in the 1950s and accelerated with three achievements: (1) evidence from twin and adoption studies that show high **concordance rates** of psychopathology for twins raised together and separately, (2) following Thorazine, the development of additional pharmaceutical interventions that target specific symptoms such as anxiety and depression, and (3) technological inventions for sophisticated brain imaging and genome mapping (Schwartz and Corcoran 2017). These applications typically fall into three research areas: brain structure, neurotransmitter activity, and genetics. Let's briefly summarize the major findings of these areas and assess their contribution to understanding mental illness.

Brain Studies

A major direction of psychiatric research focuses on the connection between brain structure and psychopathology. Through imaging, studies seek to identify brain irregularities or abnormalities that distinguish individuals diagnosed with a mental disorder from those who have no diagnosis. These studies have produced interesting findings, especially relating to schizophrenia. One study, for example, found that schizophrenia is associated with alterations in regional brain volumes, meaning the size of different parts of the brain (Brugger and Howes 2017). People with schizophrenia were shown to have greater variability of the temporal cortex, thalamus, and other brain regions. Other studies have identified similar differences (Brambilla and Tansella 2007).

This research is highly suggestive of "the answer" to mental illness; however, caution is recommended. These brain structural differences are only statistical averages between those with and those without schizophrenia. It is not possible to look at any one brain scan and identify schizophrenia or any other specific mental illness (Schwartz and Corcoran 2017). In addition, the brain anomalies may not be the cause of mental illness; instead, they may stem from some other health issue. Brugger and Howes note that brain structure differences may be secondary to certain medications, recreational substance use, or other health conditions.

Neurotransmitters

With the success of Thorazine in managing and reducing delusions and hallucinations, the focus on **neurotransmitters** rapidly accelerated. Because Thorazine lowers the presence of dopamine in the brain, high levels of which are associated

CHAPTER 12   The Medicalization of Social and Psychological Problems

with schizophrenia, researchers were encouraged to study other neurotransmitters and their impact on mental health.

Neurotransmitters are a group of chemicals that serve as messengers in the nerve **synapses**, the space between **neurons**, or nerve cells. At the end of each neuron are **vesicles,** which are sacs that hold neurotransmitters such as **serotonin** until they are triggered to release them when a nerve signal reaches the neuron. Receptors in the next neuron receive the neurotransmitter and continue moving the signal down the nerve pathway. To help remember how this works, think of the nerve signal as a message being relayed from one neuron to another. The neurons, however, are too far apart (the synapses) for a direct passage of a message, so the messages are placed on boats (neurotransmitters) kept in a marina (the vesicles) to sail to the next neuron. The boats not only carry the message but also unlock the gates (the receptors) to the next carrier (neuron).

There are billions of synapses in your body, and these transmissions are occurring constantly and are responsible for innumerable biological actions. For example, about 90% of your body's serotonin, a primary target of psychotropic medications, is found in your gastrointestinal tract. In the brain, neurotransmitters are believed to be connected to memory formations, cognitions, motivation, emotions, pleasure, and arousal, and an excess or depletion of a key neurotransmitter may have implications for psychological wellbeing. There are many neurotransmitters in the brain, but norepinephrine, dopamine, and serotonin are the most studied.

Serotonin is perhaps the most well-known because of the proliferation of medications that attempt to regulate its presence in the brain. **Selective serotonin reuptake inhibitors** (SSRIs) are the most prescribed drugs for depression. There are several different SSRI medications, but you probably recognize several of the more familiar trade names such as Prozac, Paxil, and Zoloft.

In the serotonin theory of depression, to continue the boat metaphor, there are not enough boats to carry the messages. Some boats of serotonin are launched but they do not make it to the other side and are reabsorbed into the marina. SSRIs are based on the theory that brain synapses have insufficient serotonin, which makes for irregular connections between neurons. SSRIs block the reabsorption of serotonin, theoretically leaving more serotonin in the vesicle, which in turn improves communication from one nerve ending to another. SSRIs have achieved some degree of success in relieving symptoms of depression.

Considerable criticism of SSRIs' effectiveness and viability has been proffered, however. Little evidence can be demonstrated to show a cause-and-effect pattern, and many have criticized this theory for being drawn from a treatment. As Marcia Angell, a physician and former editor-in-chief of the *New England Journal of Medicine* has stated, "Instead of developing a drug to treat an abnormality, an abnormality was postulated to fit a drug" (2011: 3). The idea is that because SSRIs sometime work, that "proves" the theory, which is false logic. Daniel Carlat, also a physician, continues, "By this logic, one could argue that the cause of all pain conditions is a deficiency of opiates, since narcotic pain medications activate opiate receptors in the brain" (2010: 7).

To add to the controversy, in his book *The Emperor's New Drugs*, Irving Kirsch (2010) used the Freedom of Information Act to obtain FDA reviews of all placebo-controlled clinical trials of six popular antidepressants. Both negative and positive results were collected. Kirsch found that in the 42 studies, findings were mostly negative, which means that the SSRIs did not significantly reduce depression symptoms. Placebos, however, were 82 percent as effective as the drugs. As Kirsch learned, trials' negative results are hidden; the FDA does not release those studies because they are considered proprietary. The data also suggested that medications not considered anti-depressants such as synthetic thyroid hormone, opiates, sedatives, stimulants, and some herbal remedies, relieved depressive symptoms at roughly the same rate as the antidepressants.

While medications that target specific neurotransmitters are effective for select individuals and conditions such as schizophrenia and bipolar disorder, they are not universally ameliorative and should be avoided by some people, most notably children, according to many clinicians. Research on the efficacy of psychotropic medications, especially for affective disorders, continues, and evidence is available to support both "pro" and "con" positions. Anecdotally, practitioners often think of SSRI effectiveness in thirds: they are beneficial in relieving symptoms for a third, have no effect for a third, and elicit negative side effects among the last third who must stop taking them.

In general, neurotransmitter theory is not necessarily causative, and focusing on a singular neurotransmitter is overly simplistic to explain complex conditions such as mental disorders.

Genetics

Genetics has also become an important area of research. Studies in this field have generally followed two streams: concordance rates among twins and identifying specific genes that are found in diagnosed individuals. For decades, researchers have conducted studies of identical twins with at least one parent with schizophrenia, bipolar disorder, or major depression. Studies compare twins raised together and apart and calculate their chances of developing one of their parents' disorders. Among twins, the concordance rate for schizophrenia, the presence of the same traits in both individuals, is about 50 percent (Fischer 1971), about 40 percent for major depression (Sullivan et al. 2000), and roughly 40–45 percent for bipolar disorder (Barnett and Smoller 2009). **Heritability**, which means the likelihood of developing the same condition as a parent, is found as high as 80 percent in bipolar disorder and schizophrenia (Orrù and Carta 2018; Barnett and Smoller 2009).

Identification of genes that cluster among people with various diagnoses also points toward genetics as root causes of mental illness. Research has identified genes that occur in association with depression (Lavebratt et al. 2010), bipolar (Escamilla and Zavala 2008), and schizophrenia (Gejman et al. 2010). Despite this evidence, researchers have confirmed that explanations relying on single genes do not account for differences in human traits. In addition, data strongly indicate that the genetic expressions that are associated with schizophrenia may reside in tissues outside the brain (Gejman et al. 2010). There is also a possibility that an autoimmune mechanism, perhaps in response to a virus, may compromise the brain and cause schizophrenia.

Identifying genes only locates them—it does not define how the gene may actually cause a disorder. Finding how a functional mutation leads to a disease phenotype is the direction of much genetic work (Schwartz and Corcoran 2017).

There are other limitations of a genetics approach. The monozygotic twin studies that show the likelihood that half of identical twins of one schizophrenic parent will develop the condition also means that half will not, which should not happen in people whose DNA is virtually the same. Genetics do not account for the nonschizophrenic half of the twin pairs, which implies that other forces are at work. We know that even identical twins raised in the same household do not necessarily have identical social and psychological life experiences. Studies that include genetic and environmental variables have found that social factors can reduce or even eliminate genetic effects. Social variables are often stronger predictors of alcohol abuse than genes (Pescosolido et al. 2008), and social factors mediate apparent genetically determined cases of depression among women. Both findings suggest that twin studies may "overstate the strength of genetic influences" (Horwitz et al. 2003: 111).

In summary, what we have learned from medical model research is that no single biological marker fully explains human behavior, whether disordered or not. The research is highly suggestive, but there is no singular mechanism that indicates a linear causal effect. Instead, the likely answer lies in an interaction of many factors, both biological and environmental, that produces pathology. Plus, it is possible that there are multiple pathways to mental illness, especially affective disorders such as depression, which in some people may begin with biology but for others may be rooted in social relationships and the context of environmental factors.

The Intersection of Sociology and Biology

The social and behavioral sciences have identified environmental variables that associate with or influence the course of mental illness. Just as sociologists need to consider the role that biological factors may play in mental illness; biologists conceive ways to include environmental dynamics in their theories. To move closer to a better understanding of mental illness, we should see how sociology and biology intersect and can inform each other's knowledge.

Schwartz and Corcoran have shown four ways in which sociologists deal with biological data. First, they refer to the separatists, those sociologists who say that the field should not study schizophrenia because of the strong data that indicate its biological foundation. Instead, sociologists should concern themselves with mental phenomena that have sociological origins, such as psychological distress (stress, worries, tensions) and disenchantments. This group of sociologists concede that some conditions are biological, and their study should be left to the biomedical researchers.

Schwartz and Corcoran do not agree with this stance. Ceding these conditions means accepting heritability as the cause of these "biological" conditions. If schizophrenia is 70–80 percent heritable, then what about the remaining 20–30 percent? Sociology may contribute to explaining those cases. Similarly, with depression, where there is a considerable variation in people both with and without the identifying genes, sociological factors may explain that variance and identify those most likely to experience depression.

Their second approach is active participation in research conducted within the medical model, or sociology *in* medicine. Sociologists can identify environmental factors that contribute to the cause of disorders and interact with biological vulnerability. As Schwartz and Corcoran write, for many cases of mental illness, biology may be a necessary causal factor, but perhaps not a sufficient one. If that is the case, sociology can play an important role in supporting biological research in understanding the expression of genes or the conditions in which brain structure may be impacted by exposure to stress or other environmental stimuli.

Co-optation is the next way sociology can deal with biological advancements. In this stance, sociology uses biological data to support sociological theories. We know that social dynamics influence the body; therefore, if mental illness has a biological base, then sociology can shed light on how those bodily characteristics are formed or expressed. Schwartz and Corcoran cite established research that demonstrates that jobs in which people have less control over their labor are related to both heart disease and depression. Perhaps this social condition stimulates both physiological ailments. In addition, other disorders that may have a biological foundation often occur in social patterns, such as alcohol abuse, which occurs more frequently among men. Social factors may articulate a way to explain these patterns.

The fourth approach, in Schwartz and Corcoran's phrasing, is "counter-revolution," or using sociology to critique the biological perspective. The medical model is not without criticism and raises more questions than it answers. As Schwartz and Corcoran remind us, all behavior has biological, psychological, and social dimensions, but why are some singled out as biologically unidimensional? Essentially, sociology warns us of bio-reductionism and taking so-called symptomatic behaviors, thoughts, and emotions out of their psychosocial context. The medical model cannot answer questions such as why rates of disorders increase, who benefits from defining a behavior in strict biological terms, what are the consequences of labeling a person with a disorder, why do some disorders occur more frequently in some geographic areas and social groups than others, and at what point is a behavior considered disordered.

Psychiatry as a Medical Specialty

Psychiatry is a practice specialty in medicine. A medical or osteopath doctoral degree and a license to practice medicine are required. After med-school, prospective psychiatrists complete a four-year supervised residency in psychiatry during which they learn to diagnose patients and prescribe treatments. Residencies usually take place in teaching hospitals, psychiatric hospitals, and other clinical settings. Some may devote another year to a Fellowship in which they conduct research or perform specialized teaching and clinical activities.

Psychiatric training strongly emphasizes brain anatomy and chemistry, DSM-based diagnoses, and pharmacological treatments. While there are variations internationally, few if any psychiatry programs in the US teach psychotherapy techniques (talk therapy) as they did in the past. After completing the residency, most psychiatrists elect to take a written and oral examination offered by the American Board of Psychiatry and Neurology. Passing this exam entitles them to become "board certified," a certification that must be renewed every 10 years. Board certification is offered in many subspecialties such as child or geriatric psychiatry, addictions, forensic psychiatry, and sleep medicine, among several others.

Owing to their extensive training and perceived social importance, physicians in general enjoy high occupational and social prestige. All medical specializations, however, are not judged equally, and a stable hierarchy of prestige among medical specialties exists in the minds of both the general public and medical professionals. One study asked laypersons to rank 10 medical specializations on their prestige, and its findings demonstrated the usual pattern: surgeons, cardiologists, and neurologists ranked highest, but psychiatrists, radiologists, and dermatologists placed lowest (Rosoff and Leone 1991). Of note is that many respondents in the study did not know that psychiatrists were physicians. Rosoff and Leone suggested that psychiatrists were rated poorly because they held low social value or importance to laypersons compared to other medical subfields.

Two studies of medical professionals and students gathered similar results. In one study, Australian medical students ranked psychiatry 12th of 19 subfields, scoring higher than only one clinical area, rural medicine, and several nonclinical fields such as medical administration, public health medicine, pathology, and rehabilitation medicine (Creed et al. 2010). In the second research, Hindhede and Larsen (2020) reported comparable findings in a study of physicians, nurses, and medical and nursing students who were asked to rate 17 specializations. The top three were neurosurgery, surgery, and cardiology, and the bottom three were general medicine, psychiatry, and dermatology.

Several factors may explain the differences. Hindhede and Larsen (2020) concluded that characteristics of a specialization influence its prestige. Table 12.1 shows the factors they contend account for the differences in status. If these factors do constitute the rubric for evaluating prestige among medical subfields, then psychiatry would score lower in comparison to other fields of medicine regardless of the benefits they may provide their patients. Psychiatry employs less sophisticated practice techniques compared to surgery, cardiology, and neurology and does not operate on critical organs. Since psychiatry is not generally invasive, except for electroshock therapy, which is not commonly performed, its focus on the brain is not weighed the same as neurosurgeons who conduct brain surgery.

Occupational status is important in the medical profession. Prestige is associated with power and authority relations, which are often crucial in medical practice, most notably in life and death situations or executing surgical procedures. Doctors give orders to nurses and medical technicians, occupational relationships defined by authority differences, and a similar relationship can exist among physicians based on the immediacy and urgency of decisions. Because of the nature of their practice, psychiatrists are not usually part of life and death decisions and do not have expertise in highly sophisticated techniques that are central to surgery and cardiovascular medicine.

TABLE 12.1 Factors That Account for Prestige Differences in Medical Specialties

High Prestige	Low Prestige
High Technological Sophistication	Less Technological Sophistication
Immediate and Invasive Treatment Procedures	Less Visible Treatment Procedures
Focus on Vital Organs in the Upper Body	Focus is on Lower Body Organs or No Specific Bodily Location

Source: Adapted from Hindhede and Larsen (2020).

Psychiatry has undergone a rudimentary and paradigmatic change since 1980 when DSM-III formalized the medical model's foundation in the field. Prior to DSM-III, psychiatry focused on the uniqueness of patients' emotional, behavioral, and cognitive abilities and resources rather than the diagnosis of an illness. Many psychiatrists resisted prescribing medications, preferring to engage patients in talk therapies (Horwitz 2002; Smith 2014). During that time, it was axiomatic in mainstream psychiatry that individuals had their own psychosocial histories, personalities, experiences, and interpretations of those experiences, and the psychiatrist's goal was to understand the nature of each person's suffering and what psychological pain meant to them (Smith 2011).

After the "biological conquest of psychiatry," as Smith calls the transition (2011: 355), the focus on the individual receded in favor of a diagnostic model in which patients who had the same symptoms became essentially interchangeable. Two additional consequences of that transition were that patients saw their psychiatrists less often but took more medications (Kessler et al. 2003). This change in practice standards represented a fundamental shift in addressing mental health problems.

Psychiatry has been subject to severe criticism in the last several decades, and critics have been quick to dismiss the benefits that contemporary psychiatry offers. There is no question that biology plays a role in many cases of mental disorders. While the actual biological agents are not clear, pharmaceutical treatments are helpful for many people, especially those diagnosed with psychotic and bipolar disorders. These medications are very powerful and must be prescribed with great care, which requires specialized training in their use. Psychiatrists undergo that rigorous training, and they have the experience to monitor patients' progress, assess side effects of the medications, and adjust doses and medications in patients' best interests. Medications work for many people, and that requires medical professionals who understand their chemistry and best practices for prescribing them.

The DSM

In the early 1980s, I took a course in abnormal psychology from a psychology professor who on the first day of class held a DSM-III above his head and pronounced, "behold the greatest work of fiction in the English language!" He was a clinician and radical behaviorist who had no truck for **Kraepelinian biological**

psychiatry, which had come to dominate the DSM by that time. (German psychiatrist Emil Kraepelin (1856–1926) sought to establish psychiatry as a clinical science and devised the modern theory of psychiatry that all psychological disorders are diseases caused by "natural disease entities" (Hoff 2015.) He created classifications to distinguish several disorders, most notably separating schizophrenia from bipolar depression.) My professor also disapproved of the classification system presented in the DSM and the way it shaped the perception and understanding of mental illness.

The Diagnostic and Statistical Manual of Mental Disorders, published by the American Psychiatric Association (APA), has exerted significant power over the mental health industry of researchers, clinicians, insurance companies, and pharmaceutical manufacturers, and society in general, and its influence is spreading around the globe. As the handbook of mental conditions, the DSM specifies and labels the conditions judged pathological. Therefore, by providing each condition a name, the DSM provides the language of defining and reifying these conditions as mental illness.

There have been five major editions of the "bible" of psychiatry and two subeditions (III-R and IV-TR) since the DSM was first published in 1952.

A quick history of the DSM demonstrates the controversy that my professor described and provides good examples the social construction of mental illness. Long before DSM-I, the first American effort to classify mental illnesses came not from psychiatry but from the US Census. In the early nineteenth century, the census counted and sorted cases of mental disease to assess treatment facilities rather than to enumerate how many cases fell into specific categories (Kawa and Giordano 2012). Later, in 1918, the Bureau of the Census, in partnership with two medical organizations, one of which was the American Medico-Psychological Association (now the American Psychiatric Association), created a standardized nomenclature of psychiatric conditions that would become the forerunner of the DSM. This book, called the *Statistical Manual for the Use of Institutions for the Insane*, focused on psychotic conditions since most psychiatrists in those days worked in asylums and with severely disturbed individuals. Because of the debilitated condition of most of their patients, the psychiatrists assumed a Kraepelinian theoretical position and argued that the 22 diagnostic categories they created had a somatic, or biological, origin. Nine editions of this manual followed in the 1920s and 1930s (Kawa and Giordano 2012).

Sigmund Freud's work ascended into prominence in American and European psychiatry after World War I. His writings and clinical techniques challenged the Kraepelinian framework by emphasizing how social-environmental stressors caused milder psychological disturbances. Psychiatrists began to treat individuals with these conditions in addition to the severely disturbed "madhouse" residents. Changes in the practice of psychiatry forced the field to redefine mental illness to include those with mild to medium symptoms. At this point, mental illness was conceived as a continuum of symptoms rather than as discrete entities of illness. Freud's psychodynamic theories gained legitimacy when in 1946 they were named the leading school of thought by the American Board of Psychiatry (Kawa and Giordano 2012), and the first two editions of DSM reflected this dynamic. The APA increased the number of diagnoses in DSM-II to accommodate the new but less severe conditions that were treated by psychiatry.

A key watershed moment in the history of the DSM, and indeed all psychiatry, was the release of version III. DSM-III added scores of new diagnoses and started the process of eliminating Freudian concepts and theory from psychiatry. Freudian concepts like neurosis were no longer relevant in the new psychiatric paradigm. DSM-III made many changes in nomenclature to create a stronger medical presentation of psychological problems. For example, the APA changed DSM-II's "Specific Learning Disturbance" to five different "Specific Developmental Disorders" in DSM-III. Another instance was relabeling and reconceptualizing "Phobic Neurosis" to five classes of "Phobic Disorders." The latter edition also created subtypes of broad diagnostic categories. One instance of that shift is how schizophrenia was represented. DSM-II had 14 categories under the heading of schizophrenia, but DSM-III had 18. DSM-III added several other new "disorders" including PTSD, Attention Deficit Disorder, pathological gambling, and seven classes of "psychosexual dysfunction" (Kawa and Giordano 2012). Critics contended that these changes were based on shifts in perception rather than data and questioned whether the new "disorders" were true illnesses rather than deviant behavioral patterns, normative responses to the environment, ideographic or individual differences, or the result of moral judgments.

Over the years, many criticisms have been levied against the DSM. One is the steady increase in disorders identified in the DSM over the five main editions, as shown in Table 12.2. From 1952 to 2013 the number of disorders almost tripled. Is this a question of discoveries of new mental disorders or changes in the perception of a behavior or affective state? Critics assume the latter.

Relatedly, another criticism is that the categories listed in DSM lack validity. As already discussed, evidence does not necessarily support discrete disorders as presented in DSM, which may contribute to the DSM's historical shifts in definitions of mental health.

Part of the validity criticism is the diagnostic variability found in some disorders. Using Major Depressive Disorder as an example, the DSM states that five clinically significant symptoms must be present every day or nearly every day for two weeks.

TABLE 12.2 Increase in the Number of Disorders Recognized by the DSM

DSM Volume	Year of Publication	Number of Diagnoses
I	1952	106
II	1968	182
III	1980	292
IV	1994	297
V	2013	298

Source: Suris et al. (2016). Licensed under CC BY 4.0. https://creativecommons.org/licenses/by/4.0/

Since there are nine symptom criteria listed, the DSM allows for different combinations of symptoms to be labeled Major Depressive Disorder. The criteria for this disorder are shown in Table 12.3 and includes one of two affective states (either depressed mood or loss of interest or pleasure) plus four of the seven remaining criteria. As you can deduce, there is no single diagnostic criteria for Major Depressive Disorder. How many are there? Finding the answer poses an interesting mathematical puzzle as well as a theoretical and clinical problem. The solution to the math part is that there are 105 different combinations of symptoms that comprise a single diagnosis of Major Depressive Disorder.

The theoretical and clinical problems, however, are more complicated. Having so many combinations seem to challenge the notion of a solitary "disease" condition. Nosologically, which refers to the classification of medical conditions, Major Depressive Disorder as it appears in the DSM raises definitional and operational questions. Can it be assumed that someone who has the body-related criteria of weight and sleep changes, and psychomotor agitation or retardation is experiencing the same condition as someone not experiencing those symptoms? Of the 105 different combinations of symptoms, how do we determine epistemologically what depression really is? These are not questions about an individual's pain and distress, but about the process of how the disorder is conceptualized and constructed. That there are so many "appearances" of Major Depressive Disorder calls to mind Spector and Kitsuse's (1987) sociological notion that social issues are phenomena "created through collective definition rather than as conditions that objectively exist" (Kirk and Kutchins 1992: 13).

TABLE 12.3 Diagnostic Criteria for Major Depressive Disorder in DSM-V

Five (or more) of the following symptoms must have been present for 2 weeks and represent a change from previous functioning: symptom 1 or 2 must be present.

1. Depressed mood most of the day, nearly every day as defined by self-reported emotions such as sadness, emptiness, hopelessness; others may observe and report these emotions
2. Noticeably diminished interest or pleasure in all or most all activities most of the day nearly every day; indicated by either subjective account or observation
3. Significant unintentional weight loss or gain or changes in appetite
4. Insomnia or hypersomnia
5. Psychomotor agitation or retardation
6. Fatigue or loss of energy
7. Feelings of worthlessness or excessive or inappropriate guilt
8. Diminished ability to concentrate; indecisiveness
9. Recurrent thoughts of death and suicide ideations

In addition, the symptoms must be of clinical significance and cause disruptions to social relationships and usual activities at work and school.

The symptoms are not attributed to another medical condition or other psychiatric condition such as schizophrenia, among others listed by DSM.

Source: DSM-V (2013: 160–161).

Others have criticized the increase in disorders listed in DSM-V and have accused the DSM of lowering the threshold of several diagnostic categories. By easing the criteria for making a diagnosis, the DSM has increased the likelihood of someone being labeled with a disorder. Psychiatrist Allen Frances (2012) has expressed such concerns. He fears that the reach of the DSM has greatly expanded, and he cites the following examples: (1) normal grieving could become Major Depressive Disorder, (2) older individuals, most of whom tend to have occasional but minor lapses in memory, could be misdiagnosed with Mild Neurocognitive Disorder, and (3) excessive eating 12 times in three months could be redefined from gluttony to Binge Eating Disorder. He lists other examples as well. To illustrate Francis' point, here is the quote from DSM-V (2013: 161) that raises his concern about normal bereavement becoming a diagnosis of Major Depression Disorder:

Responses to a significant loss (e.g. bereavement...) may include the feelings of intense sadness, rumination about the loss, insomnia, poor appetite, and weight loss...which may resemble a depressive episode. Although such symptoms may be understandable or considered appropriate to the loss, the presence of a major depressive episode in addition to the normal response to a significant loss should also be carefully considered. This decision inevitably requires the exercise of clinical judgment based on the individual's history and the cultural norms for the expression of distress in the context of loss.

In the absence of objective criteria in the diagnostic process, psychiatrists must rely on patients' narratives to describe their own emotional, cognitive, and behavioral histories and worries (Lane 2020). During this autobiographical narration, psychiatrists observe and interpret the stories they hear. Instead of decoding this narrative with a theory of psychology such as psychodynamics, cognitive theory, or behaviorism, they dissect the person's statements into individual symptoms that are organized into categorical DSM disorders. Arthur Kleinman (1988: 7) states that "disease refers to the way practitioners recast illness in terms of their theoretical models of pathology.... A psychiatric diagnosis is an interpretation of a person's experience."

When troubles arise, people try to find explanations and meaning, to make sense of what is happening. Many, as Karp described in Chapter 11, turn to physicians and accept physicians' interpretive rationale and course of treatment. The constructs of the medical model have become highly pervasive throughout society, and people actively seek out a diagnosis to explain their problems. Since the process is largely subjective, it is also symbolic, which accounts for why some diagnoses are more sought after than others.

There is a moral hierarchy of diagnoses as people search for validation of their emotions and thoughts (Lane 2020). When someone receives a diagnosis, they may search for a community with which to share experiences and that provides advocacy and support. These communities also offer a narrative to explain their difficulties and differences. Higher status diagnoses may have a celebrity who talks about the condition publicly, making it part of entertainment and offering an audience the opportunity to feel better and to reassure themselves that they do in fact have an illness. Public support provides an important reification of the diagnosis, which means accepting a subjective diagnosis as real though that diagnosis was a result of a subjective interpretation of a personal narrative (Lane 2020).

Despite its detractors, the DSM has important utility among the mental health professions. First it allows psychiatrists, psychologists, social workers, and other therapists to have a common language to describe and discuss cases. When one professional uses the term "major depression," for instance, others have a shared understanding of what that means. The DSM, therefore, provides an important reliability function in that it creates consistency in definitions and vocabulary among mental health professionals. A second important utility of the DSM is that it facilitates insurance coverage of mental health services. With the DSM's system of code numbers assigned to disorders, service providers can easily report to an insurance company the nature of the treatment covered by patients' policies.

The insurance function, however, is a double-edged sword and feeds into the labeling process. For insurance to cover treatment, the provider is required to assign a DSM code, which means that the patient must be diagnosed with a mental illness. Therefore, someone experiencing severe life-long psychotic symptoms of hallucinations and wild delusions receives the same general label of being mentally disordered as a six-year-old child having anxiety about leaving home to start kindergarten or first grade. Although the disorders are not equivalent, both cases are "disordered" in the eyes of the DSM and the insurance company.

Hospitalization

Psychiatric hospitalization has undergone drastic changes historically, as Box 12.1 demonstrates. Having evolved from the old asylum system, hospitals today operate very differently in terms of how individuals are admitted and treated. In years past, hospitals were practically a place of residence for severely mentally ill people. Charitable organizations who ran the hospitals would provide long-term basic residence for people who could not care for themselves and had no family willing or able to house them. Today, taking residence in a psychiatric hospital is a rare occurrence. Those who do stay in the hospital for weeks or even months do so because of severe illness and because they pose a threat to the safety of themselves or others. Otherwise, these individuals are expected to find other places to live, which they may do with the help of social workers who are skilled in assessing needs and matching those needs with an appropriate group home or other facility. Most people with chronic mental illness, however, must fend for themselves.

By most accounts, the average length of stay in a psychiatric hospital is less than a week. Glick and colleagues (2011) report a mean of five to six days. The average hospitalization among severely disordered individuals is longer at a mean of 10 days (Lee et al. 2012). Malone and associates' (2004) study learned that hospital stays vary by diagnosis and the state of the person when admitted and concluded that calculating the median, as opposed to the mean, is a better way to describe hospital stays. Malone's group found that many patients stay in the hospital less than a week,

Box 12.1 The Story of *Titicut Follies*

Titicut Follies is a 1967 documentary by Frederick Wiseman and John Marshall. To be straightforward, it is astonishing. There is nothing like it. Wiseman and Marshall wanted to make a film about conditions in the Bridgewater (Massachusetts) State Hospital that housed people deemed criminally insane (they had committed crimes but were found insane and therefore not housed in a regular prison), and to their surprise, the authorities allowed them complete and unhindered access to all patients, staff, and facilities. The filmmakers were free to go where they wanted and to film anything they saw. The final product had no dialog, narration, musical score, or scripting. It is a collection of actual images from their time inside the hospital edited to create a storyline that provides visual continuity and a structure to the film. Nothing is staged—everything shown in the film is actual live footage of everyday life at Bridgewater.

What Wiseman and Marshall filmed was so dramatic and at times horrific that their documentary led to numerous lawsuits against the staff on behalf of patients and to the eventual closure of the hospital. A judge barred the film from public screening and ordered the filmmakers to destroy copies to protect the privacy of staff and patients. In time, however, doctors, lawyers, and mental health professionals could view the film. In 1991, a judge released the film to the public, and PBS aired it in 1992. By then all the patients had died, so privacy was no longer a legal concern. The film also had an enormous impact on legal conceptions of privacy and censorship (it is the only film censured for a reason other than obscenity).

For our story, *Titicut Follies* (named for the hospital's talent show; Titicut is the Wampanoag language name for the nearby Taunton River) allows rare insight into the conditions of what was presumed to be a typical state-run psychiatric hospital in the mid-twentieth century. Bridgewater State Hospital was a dreary place. For example, the all-male patients did not have access to toilet facilities in their cells, only having a bucket in their rooms overnight, which they carried with them to empty when their doors were opened in the morning. They were kept unclothed much of the time and treated with little respect by the staff who were often shown abusing them. There was evidence of ritualistic harassment, and in one of the film's most disturbing scenes, a guard berates a patient so relentlessly about cleaning his room that the poor man eventually has a psychotic break—and it is all captured on film.

Medical and psychiatric care was, at best, poor. Some of the patients appeared to receive talk therapy with a physician, but in one session the physician seemed more focused on the patient's sexual interests (for lack of a better word) than dealing with the underlying causes of his sexual behavior, which apparently is what landed him in prison. Another patient was force-fed with a funnel and rubber hose. The physician was smoking a cigarette while feeding him, and the ashes of the cigarette fell into the patient's food.

The film also shows a man in the late stages of schizophrenia. This patient believes himself to be a religious figure, holding his arms in a way that Jesus Christ is often portrayed as if giving a blessing. He speaks rapidly in mostly nonsensical rhythmic gibberish. His personality and cognition have collapsed and fragmented into disjointed pieces. This is an unusual sight now because of the success of medications in altering and slowing the course of schizophrenia.

One interesting element of the film portrays Garfinkel's (1956) concept of the degradation ceremony, which refers to the communicative and ritualistic process of changing a person's identity from a higher to a lower status or position. By shaming a person in front of an audience and in a structural context, the "system" reduces a person's place in the social order. Courts do this when finding people guilty of a crime and sentencing them to jail, which reduces their status and identity to "criminal." It also happened in Bridgewater during this era. Patients were forced to remove their clothes and go naked in front of guards and fellow patients, and in one episode, a patient, who happened to be African American, was required to get on his knees when talking to a guard.

> The key "treatment" of this hospital was to coerce patients to conform to hospital rules. This facility was hospital-centered, not patient-centered. The rules of the institution were more important than the welfare of the patients. Hospital culture was focused on maintaining the system and its dictates and authority. All relationships between patients and staff were about conformity and maintaining status differences. Bridgewater resembled Goffman's description of a "total institution," which is an organization that has near complete control over employees' or residents' behavior, thoughts, and even emotions. Patients were completely enclosed and cut off from the outside world so that everything experienced by patients was filtered by the institution.
>
> In the aftermath of *Titicut Follies*, hospital reform became a key point of discussion. Hospitals were reorganized and reconfigured to become more responsible to patients and civil in their interactions. Bridgewater eventually reopened but continued to have problems, and in 2017, management of the hospital was contracted to a private company.

but that more severely distressed people will stay over two weeks, resulting in a median hospitalization of 15 days.

Stays have largely declined because of rising costs, limits imposed by insurance policies, and medications that have reduced the need for longer-term residency. In 2018 dollars, the national average daily cost for inpatient treatment was about $2,400. In some areas, however, the cost could be much higher. Inpatient care at some hospitals topped $5,300 (Kaiser Family Foundation 2018). Insurance policies often limit the number of days of covered inpatient care. Medicare, for example, has a limit of 190 days in a person's lifetime, and many private policies cap coverage at seven days per year. For many people with severe and debilitating mental illness, anti-psychotic medications have lowered the need for long-term hospital care, though it has not necessarily diminished their need for residential assistance. The medications slow the course of schizophrenia and allow patients to maintain a degree of self-reliance and self-care for longer periods of time.

Treatment practices have had to adapt to these structural changes. The typical hospital experience now is acute care. Therapy has been relegated to outpatient modalities because the cost has made it prohibitive in inpatient settings. Plus, the framework of treatment has changed so that hospitalization is not viewed as therapeutically necessary for chronic conditions unless patients pose a threat to themselves or others. In this context, hospitalization is designed around safety, stabilization, and crisis management, and the emphasis is on transitioning back to the community (Glick et al. 2011). This process requires psychiatrists, psychologists, and social workers to make a diagnostic assessment within 24 hours of admission, which may satisfy hospital regulations but contradicts the realities of mental health and illness. A significant amount of time is required to evaluate a person's well-being, drug use, physical health, life history, and to explore comorbid conditions that may be difficult to assess in brief assessment interviews (Glick et al. 2011). Box 12.2 describes a famous 1970s study on hospital diagnostic practices.

Box 12.2 On Being Sane in Insane Places

Since psychiatry relies on patients' narratives to inform diagnoses, the process of determining how to label and then treat patients is highly subjective, which means it is also interpretive and subject to error. This process, therefore, begs the question of how to separate disordered from nondisordered people. In 1973, Daniel Rosenhan, a psychologist at Stanford University, sought to study that question and devised and implemented one of the most famous studies of psychiatric practice.

He began his paper, which was published in the prestigious journal *Science*, with this quote: "If sanity and insanity exist, how shall we know them?" (1973: 250). He wanted to investigate how mental hospitals sorted people into sane and insane categories, given that all they had to use for data was patients' own stories.

His study involved planting eight pseudopatients, including himself, in psychiatric hospitals. The hospitals ranged in type from underfunded rural government facilities to high-priced private hospitals, and the pseudopatients were educated, mostly professional people who, in his words, were "older and established" (251). Rosenhan interviewed the seven other participants and pronounced them "sane" prior to the study. The group included a psychology graduate student, a psychiatrist, a painter, three psychologists, and a homemaker. Five were men and three were women.

The group was instructed to act normally at the admissions appointment except to say that they heard the words "empty," "hollow," and "thud" in a same-sex voice. To protect themselves from stigma (and maybe a lawsuit), they changed their names, vocations, and employment locations, but everything else in their life histories was accurate. In the course of the experiment, all eight were admitted to 12 hospitals; none were turned away. One was diagnosed with bipolar disorder and the others with schizophrenia.

If that is not interesting enough, none of the pseudopatients were "outed" by hospital staff during the course of their stay. In fact, the length of hospitalization ranged from seven to 52 days. The average stay was 19 days, and all were discharged "in remission."

While in the hospital, the pseudopatients acted normally; they did not try to feign mental illness, and here is where the story gets fascinating. Because all the participants were acting normally, which included saying they no longer heard the voices, their behavior was understood through the lens of having been diagnosed. Staff interpreted the "patients'" behavior as indicators of the disorders they were assigned. In one example, the confederates kept diaries of their experiences in the hospital, and staff overseeing three of them wrote in their medical charts that the patients' writing was pathological. Addressing the behavior of one, a nurse charted daily: "Patient engages in writing behavior." As Rosenhan says in the study (253):

> Given that the patient is in the hospital, he must be psychologically disturbed. And given that he is disturbed, continuous writing must be a behavioral manifestation of the disturbance, perhaps a subset of the compulsive behaviors that are sometimes corrected with schizophrenia.

In other words, everything the pseudopatients did was a sign of their disorder.

In another study reported in the same paper, Rosenhan worked with administrators at a research hospital to conduct an experiment in which staff, including psychiatrists and psychologists, were notified that in three months, one or more pseudopatients would attempt to be admitted to the hospital. Each staff member was asked to rate all patients who presented themselves for admission to the facility on the likelihood that the patient was a fake.

In all, 193 patients who were admitted were scored, and the findings are quite telling. Of the 193, 41 were identified as pseudopatients by at least one member of the staff, and 23 were judged fake by at least one psychiatrist. Nineteen were suspected by a psychiatrist and another member of the staff. Here is the catch: Rosenhan sent no pseudopatients to the hospital during that time!

Rosenhan's point was that diagnostics are subjective. His views were in line with the "anti-psychiatry movement" which challenged the validity of psychiatric diagnoses. The movement was led by famous psychiatrists and scholars such as R. D. Laing, Thomas Szasz, David Cooper, Michel Foucault, and Erving Goffman, among many others. Some in this movement questioned the existence of mental illness, saying that the construction of psychiatric terminology is a social and political act of defining deviant behavior, much of which can be explained within a nonpsychiatric paradigm. Others questioned psychiatry's methods and standards and their relationship to pharmaceutical companies. Their reliance on medications is suspicious to people in this social movement because of the lack of evidence to warrant their usage.

One last note about Rosenhan's first study. While no staff member could identify any of the pseudopatients as fakes, the "real" patients easily spotted them.

Medicalization

When there is compelling evidence to suggest that bio-medical factors play only part of the development and course of mental illness, why is the medical model so influential in contemporary society compared to sociological and even psychological theories? Mental illness, as well as many other areas of deviant behavior, as well as normal life cycle processes (menopause, for example) has become subject to medical jurisdiction through a process known as **medicalization.**

Medicalization occurs when a presumably nonmedical problem becomes defined in medical terms. The concept stems from social constructionism, which, as we learned in Chapter 3, contends that all knowledge, including the scientific, is a social product developed through social interaction, interpretation, and negotiation. In social constructionism, social interpretations define the subjective nature of knowledge as right or wrong, real or unreal. In the case of medicine, we construct the meanings of illness and normality. When, for example, do we say that normal grieving becomes depression? That conclusion is reached through interpretation and negotiation—mental health professionals and lay people alike make a subjective judgment when the line from normalcy to pathology has been crossed. In the absence of objective biological data, psychiatry relies on the personal narratives of patients and their own subjective interpretations to reach a diagnosis, which implies that diagnoses are negotiated or even debated (Lane 2020).

According to Peter Conrad (1992), medicalization occurs when:

- A problem is defined and described in medical terms with medical language;
- A medical perspective is used to understand a problem;
- Medical procedures are used to intervene and respond to that problem.

Medicalization assumes that deviance, psychological problems in this case, has a medical genesis, even if those origins cannot be fully or even partially identified. Defining personal and social problems in medical terms is a sociocultural process that involves the intersection of several social forces that are often unrelated to formal medicine. These forces include individualism, technology, pharmaceutical industry practices, managed care, and secularization.

A biological approach is consistent with an individualistic culture that assumes that everyone is responsible for their well-being, their accomplishments and failures, and their behavior. This set of values awards self-reliance and independence and also makes it difficult to see how the social environment creates barriers to individual achievement and negatively impact emotions and behavior. It is not uncommon to see media programs making fun of social explanations of ill behavior: saying that people committed a crime because "they weren't held enough as a baby." Persistent withholding of parental affection is often in the background of adult narcissism, depression, and anger, emotions often connected to criminal behavior. As we have seen in other chapters, poverty, neighborhood violence, and discrimination can generate stress sufficient to have significant negative impacts on psychological wellbeing. Values of individualism, however, interfere with the ability to understand and accept these dynamics as contributing to psychological symptoms.

Relatedly, the focus on individualism conforms to the techno-scientific paradigm that provides solutions to life's problems. Today, so many health problems can be corrected by medical science that it is assumed that science can stop our personal problems as well. Therefore, many people have come to expect solutions to their troubles from a pill. In this paradigm, because problems lie within the individual, they can be resolved by a bio-medical, chemical treatment.

The pharmaceutical industry plays into this mindset. Notorious for "disease mongering," which is a strategy to make healthy people believe they are sick, "big pharma" markets prescription medicines directly to consumers and creates separate and distinct diseases out of normal functioning, risk conditions (obesity is often called a disease but in the large majority of cases it is a risk factor for cardiovascular, kidney and liver diseases, and some cancers, among others), and conditions that are secondary to other illness. Erectile dysfunction, for example, is in the DSM as a discrete psychiatric disorder, and drug companies heavily market chemical remedies for it. But is it a stand-alone ailment? While any man can have sexual problems of this type, and most will experience it at least once, erectile dysfunction is usually a consequence of normal aging, drinking too much, smoking, medications including antidepressants, diabetes, atherosclerosis, hypertension, cardiovascular disease, depression, obesity, and several other antecedents (Larkin and Wood 2018). Situational factors can affect sexual arousal as can anxiety or fear. Conditions once thought of as risk factors are now treated as disorders, and everyday occurrences such as boredom and shyness have been reinvented as attention deficit disorder and social phobia, respectively (Wolinsky 2005).

Managed care also contributes to medicalization. Defining depression and other disorders as brain diseases legitimates treatment based on pills rather than on more expensive psychotherapy (Barker 2008). Many insurance policies only cover psychotherapy if provided by a contracted agency, and in many of those cases the number of sessions is limited. Appointments with psychiatrists, however, are far less frequent than traditional talk therapies and only take a few minutes after the initial meeting. Follow-up appointments with psychiatrists are usually "med checks" in which the physician asks about changes in symptoms and any notable side effects. For managed care, psychiatric treatment comes at a lower price than weekly hour-long sessions with a licensed clinical psychologist.

As societies move away from relying on religious or sacred explanations of health and behavior, they tend to develop more medicalized ideas on mental illness. Medicalization is also a function of westernization. Societies that have more characteristics of the western democracies are more likely to promote medicalized definitions of nonmedical problems. Western notions of rationalism and secular ideologies and technologies displace traditional lore as sources of knowledge and produce medicalization. For example, a sample of Nepalese schoolteachers were shown a vignette portraying an individual who was acting in deviant ways (Furr 2004). The participants in the study were then asked if the character in the vignette was mentally ill. Those Nepalis who had more affinities with western culture (e.g., they listened to western music, spoke English, subscribed to values of women's equality, and were less rigid about caste differences), were more likely to say the character in the story was mentally ill. Those who adhered more to traditional culture attributed the behavior in the vignette to other, nonmedical, causes.

Medicalization Occurs in Degrees

Since medicalization is a process, it is not an either/or situation—it occurs in degrees. Some conditions are fully medicalized and are treated by physicians or under their supervision. Epilepsy, for example, was once in the realm of psychiatric investigation, but the condition, which was judged to be punishment for offending the Goddess of the Moon in ancient times, is now seen as a neurological disorder that can have psychological consequences such as depression. Schizophrenia is approaching being fully medicalized. Both lay and professional thought adheres to the notion that schizophrenia has biological origins, and psychiatrists usually have primary treatment responsibility for people with this disorder. Schizophrenia, however, is often perceived differently than the disease model presents. For example, the disorder has been subject to criticisms by social constructionists who say that schizophrenia only exists as a linguistic device to label a set of symptoms that have no clear origin or identifiable physiological markers. Scholars in Japan, a few other countries in East Asia, and the Netherlands have moved to reclassify schizophrenia to reflect scientific evidence that describes the condition as a syndrome rather than as a disease.

Medicalization does not always begin in medicine. PTSD's path to coming under the domain of physicians and hospitals, for example, began with a group of Vietnam veterans who worked with psychiatrists to create a diagnosis and institutionalize the disorder in DSM-III (Scott 1990).

Addictions, on the other hand, are partly medicalized. The medical model theory of the origins of addictions is not fully adopted by all mental health practitioners, and medical treatments are few and not particularly successful. Sexual addiction is an example of a condition that is minimally medicalized. Despite a literature that argues sex addiction is disordered behavior, the APA has resisted entering it into the DSM. While every version of the DSM has identified a number of sexual behaviors and frequencies of certain sexual acts as pathological, the notion of sex addiction has not been fully accepted as a legitimate disorder. Many mental health scholars are critical of the APA for specifying any sexual behavior as pathological, arguing against the organization's authority to regulate morality. From a sociological point of view, that sexual behaviors are listed in the DSM is an indicator of the social construction of mental illness and an attempt to pathologize behaviors that are morally deviant, according to one perspective of sexual morality, and not an actual medical condition.

Levels of Medicalization

According to Conrad (2007), the medicalization process occurs on three levels. **Conceptual medicalization** refers to the language of conceiving a condition as medical. It takes the form of a medical vocabulary used to define nonmedical things. One example is to say that depression is caused by a "chemical imbalance." If taken literally, chemical imbalance is a confusing reference to what chemicals (neurotransmitters?) are out of balance, which itself is an imprecise term, especially when it is not possible to assess the volume of neurotransmitters. Second, the phrase "chemical imbalance" is shorthand for "brain disease." It implies that depression and other disorders are the result of a single biogenic cause that can be rectified by a taking another chemical. Generally, the conceptual medicalization discourse is constructed and disseminated by universities, scholarly research and clinical journals, professional conferences, and institutional or organizational reports (Halfmann 2012). Because of television programming, commercials, and the internet, lay people are adopting medical lingo to analyze their own health and the health of their friends and family members (Barker 2008).

The words that are used to label problems are important, but their meanings are not always clear. The terms **disorder**, **disease**, and **syndrome** are frequently used and often interchangeably; however, that is incorrect as they are not synonyms.

A disorder, which is the term often used in reference to psychological and psychiatric problems, is a disturbance or interruption of normal functioning that interferes with a person's customary activities and feelings of wellbeing.

A disease is a condition in which identifiable symptoms can be attributed to a specific cause. Diseases have a defined set of symptoms and produce consistent physiological changes (Calvo et al. 2003).

A syndrome refers to an observable and correlated set of symptoms or physical markers that constitute a specific condition for which a direct cause is not understood. There are hundreds of syndromes, some of which are very serious and can cause death. Reye's syndrome, for example, is a collection of serious symptoms that usually occur in children who took aspirin to treat fever while recovering from viral infections like the flu or chicken pox. The syndrome causes swelling in the liver and brain. Fortunately, Reye's syndrome is rare, but if not treated, it is fatal.

In some cases, "syndrome" is misused or confusing. One example is Down syndrome, a condition characterized by several physical and mental developmental delays. Down syndrome, however, is not really a syndrome because its cause, an extra copy of chromosome 21, has been identified.

In other cases, syndromes can be related to diseases. Lyme disease is one such condition. Lyme disease is caused by the *Borrelia burgdorferi* bacterium spread by ticks. Unfortunately, some people continue to suffer symptoms after the antibiotic treatment has eradicated the bacterium. At that point, their problem becomes known as "post-treatment Lyme disease syndrome."

Other syndromes are less serious. For an example, see Box 12.3.

Box 12.3 Is Birth Order a Psychiatric Condition?

The effect of birth order has long interested psychologists, and from their studies they have classified a personality pattern among middle children that has become known as "middle child syndrome."

Some research has concluded that birth order affects personality. Oldest children are often more direct, authoritarian, and have a greater sense of power because parents typically set high expectations for them and assign them more responsibilities. They tend to feel superior because they have control over younger siblings, and they can be less agreeable and more independent. Youngest children are often raised more leniently. Parents, who are now more experienced (and tired), typically are easier on the youngest. By the third or fourth child, parents often have higher incomes and more resources to offer younger children, so many of these children grow up with less pressure and more opportunities and material comforts. Since they are more likely to get what they want, youngest siblings may feel indulged or entitled. Sometimes, however, they feel neglected and can become a "lost child."

Middle children are, well, caught in the middle. For a while they are the youngest child, the "baby" of the family, and receive the most attention. When the new sibling arrives, however, they lose that status and may experience an emotional loss and compensate by engaging in more attention-seeking behavior. Middle children tend to need more friendships, but they are skilled at solving problems and are often highly competitive. Over half of US presidents have been middle children, and middle-born children are over-represented among Olympic athletes.

Should middle kids have their own syndrome? Because of their changing family status, "middles" may develop strong anger or feel unloved. Their competitiveness stems from having to compete for parental attention with older siblings who were frequently cast in the role of co-parents and younger siblings who were dependent and pampered. Because they can feel left out or excluded, they may act out those feelings in a way that draws attention to themselves to get others to notice them, and they may develop symptoms of depression associated with their position in the family (Kotin 1995).

Birth order probably does not cause significant personality differences. One recent large study by Rohrer and colleagues (2015) found no relationship between birth order and the so-called Big 5 personality traits: extraversion, emotional stability, agreeableness, conscientiousness, and openness to experiences. Studies such as this provide evidence that birth order does not constitute a real syndrome. Officially, according to the American Psychiatric Association, middle child syndrome is a hypothetical construct which means that it is a conjectured process not directly observable or grounded in empirical data (MacCorquodale and Meehl 1948). Birth order, therefore, is not medicalized.

Syndromes are often stigmatized because in the absence of a known causal agent, patients often find that physicians and lay people do not believe their ailments are real—the symptoms are "all in your head." People experiencing conditions such as fibromyalgia and chronic fatigue syndrome have been subject to dismissal because it was believed that the symptoms were psychological and not physiological.

Based on these definitions, should psychiatric conditions, including schizophrenia, bipolar disorders, and depression, be classified as syndromes and disorders not diseases? They are clusters of symptoms with no known cause, and, as we saw in an earlier chapter, those symptoms often overlap.

Clarifying these terms helps us to understand why in 2002 the Japanese Society of Psychiatry and Neurology (JSPN) changed the name of schizophrenia from *Seishin Bunretsu Byo*, which translates to "mind-split disease," to *Togo Shitcho Sho* or "integration disorder" (Sato 2006). Patients' families, organized as the National Federation of Families with Mentally Ill in Japan, had lobbied the JSPN to reframe the condition because of the stigma related to *Seishin Bunretsu Byo* in the hope that clinical treatment would improve. The families and supportive physicians argued that the original term was ambiguous.

The name change was not a superficial effort to pacify families; it represented a shift in thinking in Japan that schizophrenia did not fit the traditional Kraepelinian disease concept. The shift, therefore, moved the cluster of symptoms previously known as schizophrenia away from having certain biological origins to a vulnerability-stress model. The name change caught on. Within seven months, 78% of cases had been renamed and seven of ten patients were told of the change.

Unlike the traditional view that schizophrenia is an untreatable disease characterized by a poor prognosis of continuous decline and personality decay, *Togo Shitcho Sho* takes into consideration research that suggests that the condition is treatable and that some patients can recover. Combining pharmacotherapy and appropriate psychosocial interventions implies that the condition can be remedied, and that recovery is possible with the appropriate combination of advanced pharmacotherapy and psychosocial intervention (Sato 2006). A similar consumer-led movement is happening in the Netherlands, and in South Korea schizophrenia has been renamed "attunement disorder" (Maruta and Matsumota 2019). Schizophrenia in these societies has become less medicalized. The disorder remains under the domain of physicians, but its framework has shifted to increase the role of psychosocial factors in its course and treatment.

Institutional medicalization takes place when physicians or other authorities such as administrators direct nonmedical personnel to maintain a medical rubric for treatment. The institution itself controls the medicalization narrative and installs it as treatment policy regardless of whether individuals' problems are biophysical or not. An example would be a drug and alcohol rehabilitation center that bases its treatment protocols on a medical model of addiction rather than a psychosocial model that emphasizes clients' relationships and environmental stressors that could be behind the substance abuse.

Interactional medicalization evolves from interaction between physician and patient during which the physician uses medical language and treatment plans to address a nonmedical problem. For instance, a physician may treat a person's unhappy family life by prescribing a tranquilizer, as was the case of "mother's little helpers" described in Chapter 7. Medicalization can also occur during interactions among lay persons. People, especially those with authority, who subscribe to the chemical imbalance narrative can persuade another person to accept this perspective to explain their substance abuse, violent behavior, or difficulty concentrating.

Medicalization is a method of social control—it is a means to control knowledge and social responses to problems—but it is not always promoted by medical professionals. Medical claims-taking, as Conrad (1992) describes it, does not automatically originate with, or necessarily involve physicians. For example, medical responses to alcoholism and opiate addiction were neither conceived of nor promoted by physicians. In a sense, these definitions were thrust upon formal medicine by lay and nonmedical counseling groups. Relatedly, attempts to medicalize family members of alcoholics by labeling them co-dependents, enablers, and adult children of alcoholics were not adopted by formal medicine and are not in the DSM. For many mental health professionals, these labels are useful only as descriptions of behavioral patterns, not disordered behavior.

As mentioned earlier, medicalization is a process and should not be treated as a categorical or static state (Halfmann 2012). Seeing medicalization as a category poses two problems. First, it suggests that some threshold is crossed where the problem migrates from nonmedicalized to medicalized. It is not always clear when that happens, and rare is the case when a problem switches quickly and thoroughly to a new medical definition. Second, the medicalization process ebbs and flows. Recall that African Americans' perspective on PTSD often rejects a medicalized definition in favor of a viewpoint that describes PTSD symptoms as normal responses to severe trauma. Saying that a problem is medicalized assumes that all groups and perspectives share the definition. Medicalization is generally a function of the power to control the medical discourse, but it does not imply that it is always accepted throughout a society.

Demedicalization

On some occasions, problems lose their medicalized definition and are either no longer considered a medical condition or a problem, a process known as **demedicalization**. One example in American psychiatry is homosexuality. Prior to 1973, the APA constructed homosexuality as a pathology and listed it in DSM-I and II among the disorders. Sweeping social changes, however, brought about the APA's decision to reconstruct homosexuality as nonpathological. The Gay Rights Movement began following the Stonewall Inn riots in New York City in 1969, and the APA was targeted by protests and demonstrations against the homosexual pathology label and the stigma that attended it. Academic panels criticized the APA's position, and a generational change within the APA saw younger physicians questioning the "old guard" who had long ignored the research that argued against homosexuality as a pathology.

After a lengthy debate, the APA board of trustees voted to removed homosexuality from the list of disorders. APA members in opposition to the change, however, forced the board to hold a membership-wide referendum. Of the approximately

10,000 APA members, 58 percent voted in favor of the board's recommendation to remove homosexuality from the DSM (Drescher 2015). Homosexuality had been reconstructed as a "noncondition" and thereby demedicalized by agreement rather than any clinical or physiological data. The demedicalization of homosexuality is another lesson in the social construction of reality.

About the Quote

First, please excuse the archaic sexist language of this chapter's quote. It was written in the 1790s as part of Blake's famous poem *The Marriage of Heaven and Hell*. Blake was a radical thinker writing during the time of the American and French Revolutions. He was questioning the blind authority dominant institutions, and the powerful people who ran them, enjoyed and how they controlled people's thoughts and behaviors. Blake was devoted to human rights, a novel concept at the time. He was part of the Romantic Movement that was championed by the leading philosophers and artists of his day who promoted human rights and individual freedoms, as they were understood then.

We can draw several ideas about mental health from Blake's statement. He is warning us about robotic conformity and closing ourselves off from other viewpoints. If we wed ourselves to established thought reinforced by authoritarians who enforce conformity, we limit our ability to see new ideas and perspectives. We are trapped in an intellectual "cavern" with only the narrow lights of tolerated dogma to guide us. But if we cleanse ourselves from strict ideology, the world of ideas becomes unlimited. We can engage in critical thinking that takes us beyond the official explanations of things.

I encourage you to read *Brain on Fire* by Susannah Cahalan (2012). This bestseller is an extraordinary memoir of the month-long collapse of the author's physical and mental health in which she was struck by several catastrophic physical symptoms including seizures, nausea, unusual muscular movements, slurred speech, memory loss, nightmares, and loss of appetite, as well as psychiatric symptoms such as episodes of mania, anxiety, paranoia, delusions, and hallucinations. Her symptoms came on rather suddenly. During her illness, a vast number of medical tests including MRIs, EEGs, and numerous tests on blood samples were conducted, all proving negative and offering no clue as to what was causing her increasingly debilitating illness. Because there were no signs of a bio-medical cause, she was diagnosed with several mental illnesses including bipolar disorder, schizoaffective disorder, and psychosis. Her symptoms were first assumed to be due to drinking too much and work stress. Eventually one physician, a neurologist, identified the true cause of her illness, which was revealed as a rare autoimmune disorder that caused her body to attack her brain.

Sociologically what is interesting about her story is that it was assumed that her deviant behavior (the symptoms) was a mental illness. You may recall from Chapter 1 that many sociologists define mental illness as deviant behavior not otherwise explained, and *Brain on Fire* is a good example of that idea. Because a medical explanation was not available, she was diagnosed as mentally ill and literally threatened with spending her life under psychiatric care. She sums up this notion in the following passage (Cahalan 2012: 151):

If it took so long for one of the best hospitals in the world to get to this step [her correct diagnosis], how many other people were going untreated, diagnosed with mental illness or condemned to a life in a nursing home or a psychiatric ward?

The idea is that when physicians did not know what else to do, they said Cahalan was mentally ill, which was attributed to her lifestyle, and prescribed several anti-psychotic medications, which had no effect. These physicians were only seeing things through their narrow caverns, to use Blake's metaphor.

Think about this for a minute. Prevailing social forces led to her mental illness diagnoses. Using Blake's language, what were those social forces that rendered their perceptions as less than infinite? How did those forces slow the process of reaching the true diagnosis? This case reveals how uncertain some mental illness diagnoses can be.

DISCUSSION QUESTIONS

1. Think about the name changes from DSM-II to DSM-III. What is the effect of replacing the term "disturbance" with "disorder" on society in general, psychiatrists, and patients?

2. The Rosenhan study is among the most famous in clinical psychology in the way it challenges how diagnoses are made and become reified. He did this work in the early 1970s. Could this study be replicated today? Probably not. What limitations would make this study almost impossible to conduct now? Are there any conditions in which the study could be conducted?

3. Patient narratives are critical data in forming psychological and psychiatric diagnoses. How might a patient's construction of reality influence a mental health care provider's interpretation and subsequent diagnosis? Similarly, how can a broader social narrative of individualism affect a clinician's interpretations?

KEY TERMS

Conceptual Medicalization 290
Concordance Rates 272
Demedicalization 293
Disease 290
Disorder 290
Heritability 274
Institutional Medicalization 292

Interactional Medicalization 292
Kraepelinian Biological Psychiatry 279
Medicalization 287
Neurons 273
Neurotransmitters 272

Selective Serotonin Reuptake Inhibitors 273
Serotonin 273
Synapses 273
Syndrome 290
Vesicles 273

CHAPTER

13

International Mental Health

Learning Objectives

After reading this chapter, students will be able to:

1. Explain the variations in global prevalence rates of mental illness.
2. Discuss the impact of industrialization and westernization on mental health in developing countries.
3. Outline the unique problems affecting mental health in developing countries.
4. Demonstrate differences in perceptions of mental illness around the globe.

> " We must be very clear…that 'culture' or 'social processes' are features not only of 'other' societies, but also of our own. "
>
> —Ellen Corin (1994)

Introduction

Mental illness exists in all cultures. Comparative analyses, however, reveal great variations in prevalence and broad differences in societies' perception of psychological well-being. Global mental health has become an important field of study in sociology because it allows us, first, to bring attention to mental illness in countries often overwhelmed by other health and socio-economic problems, and second, to identify the ways sociocultural factors affect psychological well-being, which are often easier to see in others' cultures than in one's own.

Culture influences mental health and illness in several ways. First, culture affects people's perceptions and experiences of symptoms and the manners in which discomfort is expressed. Second, culture plays a strong role in determining a society's explanatory system of mental illness and treatment modalities. Not all cultures accept how the western world understands and responds to psychiatric symptoms. Third, culture also influences how people cope with their symptoms and seek help (Kirmayer and Swartz 2014). Because culture has such a strong effect on mental health and its definitions, Summerfield (2012) contends that the whole notion of psychiatric disorders is culture bound, making the application of one culture's ideas of mental disorder difficult if not impossible to pertain to another.

Cultures define and respond to mental illness in diverse ways. In some places, mental illness is a low national health priority, despite appearing to be a serious problem. Not responding to mental illness with urgency is not necessarily due to lack of caring, but because of insufficient resources in light of more pressing health conditions. In comparison to the "Big Three" infectious diseases that continue to plague developing countries—HIV, malaria, and tuberculosis—mental illness carries little political and public health value. Infectious disease is not the only source of health problems in many poorer countries. Malnutrition, unclean or insufficient water, and violence pose immediate and serious health risks in many parts of the world. Although, as we will see, mental health is a major source of DALYs (refer to Chapter 4 to recall our discussion of this term) in both developing and developed areas, countries with limited resources must think in terms of setting national-level epidemiological triage protocols that focus on perceived greater threats to population health. Challenges to public health, such as food and water security, safety, waste disposal, vector control (mosquitos for malaria, for example), and poverty are often at the center of a country's plans for improving quality of life. For many low-resource countries, mental health programs are considered luxuries they cannot afford. Consequently, mental illness, which is a serious problem in many of these countries, is largely invisible in the shade of infectious diseases and other health problems that threaten the lives of millions of people.

Stigma also remains a barrier to creating mental health programs in many developing countries. Beliefs that mental illness is shameful, a consequence of "bad" behavior, or due to supernatural causes remain strong in many cultures. These views hinder acceptance of mental illness as legitimate disorders in a medical context and serious personal problems in the humane sense.

In this chapter, we will explore mental health conditions around the globe. We will review variations in prevalence and compare how different countries respond to mental illness. While the chapter covers high-income areas such as western Europe, it will pay more attention to mental well-being in developing countries whose mental health profile is often hidden behind more immediate social and health needs.

Global Prevalence

Until the World Health Organization's large-scale study, the **World Mental Health survey initiative (WMH),** began in the early 2000s, most international mental health knowledge came from comparing studies conducted in assorted places at different times and using different measures of mental health. Since these studies were not coordinated, cross-national comparative analyses were uncommon.

Researchers had to piece together these studies to identify patterns and risk factors among countries. Thus, cross-national comparisons were often not reliable.

Collecting International Data

Collecting data on mental health worldwide is no easy task. Survey techniques of general populations, as discussed in Chapter 4, provide the best data on prevalence, risk factors, and outcomes of mental illness, but they are not without complications. The advantages and disadvantages of survey techniques for collecting international mental health data are summarized in Table 13.1.

The primary advantage of survey methods is that they allow researchers to gather information on many variables from large random samples of individuals. From these data, researchers can determine the frequency and severity of symptoms and the social factors that are associated with those symptoms. **Probability sampling** techniques allow researchers to estimate the characteristics of the entire population from which the sample is drawn with relatively low rates of error. Survey techniques can capture the distribution of symptoms in the population in addition to those known by mental health professionals during their clinical practice.

Survey methods, however, are not without disadvantages and potential error. For example, survey respondents may experience a lapse in memory or misunderstand a question. Respondents may answer questions out of order or not follow instructions properly, and they may hesitate to respond to questions that could be embarrassing or cast themselves in a negative light. Another problem is **sampling error** that may occur when the characteristics of a sample do not truly reflect the population from which research subjects are selected. These problems can occur in all survey data collection.

TABLE 13.1 Advantages and Disadvantages of Using Surveys to Study Cross-National Mental Health

Advantages	Disadvantages
Large random samples allow generalizing from the sample to the population	Western measures of disorders may not fit nonwestern conceptions of mental illness
Researchers can estimate prevalence beyond cases seen by mental health professionals	DSM criteria may not be consistent with other cultures' definitions
Surveys can include many variables	Respondents' unfamiliarity with survey methods
Symptoms can be correlated with risk and outcome factors	Cannot diagnose with survey data; limited to tabulating symptoms
Cross-cultural studies can be standardized for comparative analyses	Surveys are expensive and require highly a trained staff and access to local areas

Conducting surveys on international mental health has obstacles beyond those common to survey data collection in general. Cross-national mental health surveys are capital and labor intensive. They are expensive and require substantial expertise in sampling, questionnaire construction, and data analysis. This method demands a team with high-level training in statistics, fluency in languages, translation experience, excellent interviewing skills, and, for sampling purposes, knowledge of a country's geography and population. International surveys also require access to in-country "gatekeepers," people who can facilitate the implementation of the study. Gatekeepers handle governmental or bureaucratic regulations and permissions for conducting research in their country, serve as a liaison between the researcher and the local staff, and may provide validation to the project so that participants recognize the legitimacy of the study.

Additional limitations and problems in international survey research include translation errors, cultural stigma (which may be stronger in some poorer, preindustrial countries) that may lead to an individual's reluctance to report symptoms, a population's lack of experience completing surveys, and unfamiliarity and discomfort in revealing personal information such as psychiatric symptoms during interviews with strangers (Gureje et al. 2008).

Another problem is discrepancies between cultures' perceptions of mental illness, which can introduce a subtle bias into data. Survey techniques that estimate international mental health typically rely upon measures of disorders created by western researchers. As we saw in Chapter 4, there are numerous measures of disorders that are suitable for use in a survey. But one thing they have in common is that they were designed for western conceptions of the disorders. Definitions and experiences of disorders vary cross-culturally; therefore, a western measure may not capture another culture's actual prevalence of a condition.

Relatedly, a western designed survey instrument may not detect disorders that are unique to an area outside Europe and North America. As shall be seen in this chapter, disorders vary by culture, and disorders not present in the culture of the researchers may be overlooked where it exists if the researcher relies solely on definitions created by western perceptions of mental illness.

On a similar note, many studies operationalize disorders in line with DSM specifications, which represents a cultural bias in defining mental health and may misrepresent the degree of severity of mental health problems in a country. On the other hand, using the DSM standards has certain advantages. While it is inappropriate to diagnose someone without a clinical assessment, the DSM criteria allow researchers to (1) present clusters or patterns of symptoms in a standardized way and (2) communicate those findings with the shared language of DSM terminology. A country's prevalence rate of depression, for instance, should not be construed to represent the actual rate of clinical depression; prevalence identifies the number of people who reported having the DSM symptoms of depressive disorder. The presence of symptoms may or may not indicate clinical depression. For example, if a survey finds that a country has a major depressive disorder prevalence rate of 10 percent, it does not necessarily mean that 10 percent of that population has full-blown depression. It is more accurate to report that 10 percent has symptoms consistent with clinical depression. Remember that major depression, or any disorder, is only diagnosed by a trained mental health professional via a clinical assessment. For simplicity, however, studies report their findings with DSM language, and readers should be cautious as to the conclusions drawn from the findings.

These disadvantages and limitation can create data that may not represent the actual or real behavior of the sample. They are biases or inaccuracies that stem from the procedures of data collection and are collectively known as **process errors**.

Because of these limitations and problems, there are few cross-cultural survey studies at the national level, apart from WHO's WMH study. Collecting data from multiple countries, the WHO's recent and ambitious project allows us to see national variations in prevalence among several indicators of mental well-being (see Box 13.1 for details of the WMH). The data discussed in this section originated from WMH data.

Box 13.1 The World Mental Health Survey

The WHO's WMH survey initiative is the first major attempt to create a standardized international mental health data set. Data were collected from 29 countries: Argentina, Brazil, Colombia, Mexico, Peru, the United States, Nigeria, South Africa, Lebanon, Iraq, Israel, Saudi Arabia, Belgium, Bulgaria, France, Germany, Italy, Netherlands, Northern Ireland, Poland, Portugal, Romania, Spain, Ukraine, Nepal, Australia, China and Hong Kong, Japan, and New Zealand. The participants ranged from low-income to high-income countries.

Collecting high-quality cross-cultural data on mental health is a most challenging enterprise. One difficult task was to create a measurement tool that would work across cultures and then translate it into numerous languages. The WHO called upon several of the world's leading experts in mental health epidemiology, including sociologist Ronald Kessler who was appointed a co-director of the WMH, to create an instrument called the Composite International Diagnostic Interview (CIDI) to meet this challenge. The CIDI was rigorously pretested and translated into the languages of the host countries using the most meticulous translation techniques. Care was taken to keep the intent of the CIDI intact while making linguistic adjustments appropriate for each cultural setting. Consistency was the key. In each location, correctly wording the same questions was necessary so the national samples would yield data with the highest possible reliability and validity.

The CIDI sought to identify prevalence of a range of disorders including anxiety disorders such as PTSD and generalized anxiety disorder, mood disorders (bipolar disorder and major depressive disorder), impulse control disorders (including ADHD and conduct disorders), and substance use disorders. In sum, the CIDI measured 25 disorders in addition to suicidality, assessed 30-day psychological distress and functioning, and measured treatment utilization. Data on risk factors and socio-demographic variables were also collected (Kessler and Üstün 2004).

Implementing the CIDI to a global population was daunting. Via a collaboration between Harvard University, the University of Michigan, the WHO, and teams from the participating countries, the surveys used a complex sampling process to identify individuals to invite to participate in the study. To create a probability sample, a sampling frame is required. A sampling frame is a list that identifies all population elements (potential cases) and allows researchers to use a random selection technique to select cases. Two sampling frames were developed in each country. First, lists of individuals were drawn from national registries, voter registration lists, postal addresses, and household telephone directories. A second, consisting of geographical areas, was created. This latter technique is called multistage cluster sampling. It involves randomly selecting from political or geographical divisions (or "clusters") of a country in stages, moving from large to small, until a sample of households is randomly picked for inclusion in the study. The WMH used both techniques to create a random sample, which means that everyone in each country had an equal chance of inclusion in the study (see Kessler et al. 2018 for a more detailed description of the WMH sampling strategy). In Brazil and China, participants were selected only from a few urban areas that did not represent the national population, and this was clearly stated.

The WHO's research strategy was successful. Surveys delivered robust data on prevalence of disorders and found that disability due to mental disorders is high around the world. Perhaps more interesting were the cross-national differences in prevalence. Researchers also identified how historical events and broad social values affect mental health. For example, the WMH found that Iraq, a country whose population has been uprooted by war and civil unrest for many years had high rates of depressive symptoms and general anxiety disorders in comparison to other nations. Iraq also provides a case in point on how values affect psychological well-being. A country where 99 percent of the people subscribe to Islam, a religion that strictly prohibits alcoholic beverages, Iraq, despite its immense social stressors, has among the lowest prevalence of alcohol use and dependency and alcohol use disorder in the world.

The WMH survey is a remarkable project that has delivered a most thorough comparative assessment of global mental health. It has spawned a new interest in international mental health and comparative mental health epidemiology while alerting the world that mental health problems are widespread and devastate the lives of countless people (Kessler et al. 2018).

Key Findings of the World Mental Health Surveys

The WMH study found significant variation in prevalence among the participating countries. Statisticians concluded that the differences in mental health prevalence among countries were attributed to sociocultural factors rather than process errors (Scott et al. 2018). The patterns are consistent and checks on the veracity of the research process revealed little bias in the results. Consequently, the WMH studies are considered highly reliable.

In its study of countries in North and South America, Africa, Asia, Australia, and Europe, the WMH discovered that the rate of psychopathology was highest among high-income countries such as the United States and France, followed by middle-income countries like Romania and Brazil. The lowest rates were found in poor to lower/middle-income nations such as Nigeria and Peru. Table 13.2 shows the rates for each group and the highest and lowest countries within them.

Of the conditions investigated by the WMH, major depressive disorder occurred most frequently. The lifetime prevalence rate among high-income countries was 12.6 percent of the population compared to 9.2 in the middle-income group. For low-income countries, however, the rate was only 7.1 percent (Bromet et al. 2018).

Several countries had particularly elevated lifetime rates of depression. France had the highest at 21 percent. Other countries with lifetime prevalence rates well above the global average were Netherlands (17.9), the United States and Brazil (16.9), Portugal (16.7), New Zealand and Northern Ireland (16.3), and Ukraine (14.6). Countries with the lowest lifetime rates were primarily in the low- and

TABLE 13.2 Percentage of DALYs and YLDs Attributed to Neuropsychiatric Conditions by Region (2010)

Region	DALYs (%)	YLDs (%)
World	10.4	28.2
High-Income Asia Pacific	14.8	32.8
Western Europe	19.0	29.3
Australasia	6.8	25.3
High-Income North America	12.5	32.9
Central Europe	13.1	28.0
Southern Latin America	14.7	34.0
Eastern Europe	4.3	27.3
East Asia	11.5	27.3
Tropical Latin America	11.7	30.1
Central Latin America	5.9	24.2
Southeast Asia	13.7	25.6
Central Asia	18.7	32.5
Andean Latin America	14.2	30.9
North Africa and Middle East	7.6	26.2
Caribbean	9.4	27.0
South Asia	11.5	30.5
Oceania	16.2	33.5
Southern sub-Saharan Africa	6.7	25.1
Eastern sub-Saharan Africa	15.6	34.1
Central sub-Saharan Africa	17.0	27.8
Western sub-Saharan Africa	4.8	22.2

Source: Kohn (2014: 28), used with permission.

middle-income categories. Romania (2.9), Poland (3.0), Nigeria (3.1), and the Beijing and Shanghai samples from China (3.5) had the fewest people meeting the DSM criteria for major depressive disorder. Note that the Beijing-Shanghai study groups do not necessarily reflect the patterns of mental health throughout that country. For example, the rate of depression in Shenzhen, which is near Hong Kong, was 6.1

percent or approximately 90 percent higher than that of Beijing-Shanghai (Bromet et al. 2018).

When looking at depression by gender, the global pattern follows the trends found in the United States—women are almost twice as likely as men to experience depressive symptoms during their lifetimes. In the global sample, about 13.5 percent of women reported symptoms that met the DSM standards for major depressive disorder during their lifetimes, compared to 7.5 percent of men. Some countries had particularly elevated rates of depression among women. France, for instance, had the highest rate at 26.6 percent.

The Burden of Psychiatric Disorders

The WMH studies show conclusively that the burden of mental health disorders around the globe is the same or larger than that of chronic physical conditions such as arthritis, cancer, cardiovascular diseases, diabetes, neurological disorders (such as Parkinson's Disease or cerebrovascular accident (stroke)), and respiratory diseases (Chatterji et al. 2013b). The burden of mental disorders can be felt at all levels of society.

Even the wealth of a country can be affected by mental disorders. Mental illness causes significant losses in economic productivity through absenteeism and preventing individuals from working at peak performance levels. Because of the high levels of mental illness, the WMH studies concluded that mental disorders result in substantial reductions in population-level earnings. Mental conditions translated into a 0.4 percent reduction in the income of the poorest countries, 0.2 percent of countries in the upper/middle-income group, and 1.0 percent in high-wealth nations. As a point of reference, one percent of income in a high-income country is equivalent to over $61 billion in lost income (Levinson et al. 2013).

To show the source of the loss of productivity caused by neuropsychiatric disorders, see Table 13.2, which reports the DALYs and YLDs attributed to neuropsychiatric conditions. Of note in these figures are the particularly low rates in both categories in Eastern Europe, Australasia, Central Latin America, and southern and western sub-Saharan Africa. The highest percentages for DALYs are found in western Europe, Central Asia, and central sub-Saharan Africa. YLDs are highest in eastern sub-Saharan Africa, southern Latin America, and Oceania.

The WHO primarily focused on assessing the burden of mental health problems on individuals and families. Using a tool called the WHODAS (the WHO Disability Assessment Schedule), researchers at the WMH measured individual difficulties in everyday functioning over the last month. The WHODAS assessed individuals' ability for self-care, social engagement, mental and physical functioning, and family functioning.

Individuals reporting symptoms of mental illness were more likely to report functional limitations than individuals with a physical condition (Chatterji et al. 2013a). Mental disorders correlated with social and cognitive disability, discrimination victimization, and family stress. Mobility was the only assessed area that physical disorders caused more dysfunction than psychiatrically impaired individuals. Bipolar disorders were the most disabling of all conditions studied, and the level of disability caused by bipolar disorders was comparable to neurological diseases. PTSD and anxiety disorders were also severely disabling, followed by major depressive disorder.

Data from the WHODAS found significant differences in mental illness burden among the three categories of countries. Social and cognitive dysfunctions were most significant in high-income countries, and PTSD and bipolar disorders caused the most impairment. But individuals in upper/middle income nations who reported symptoms stated that stigma and discrimination were the most common burdens in their experience. Panic disorder and bipolar disorders caused the most impairment in these countries. Among lower income countries, drug abuse was the most disabling condition, and the most severe burden in these countries was stigma and discrimination. In these states, the rate of disability caused by drug abuse was double that of physical disorders (Chatterji et al. 2013a).

Depression is the most common mental disorder internationally, and the impact of depression on the lives of individuals and their families was about the same as that of physical health conditions. The degree that depression disrupts individual's role performances also follows the pattern of income distribution among countries. People with depressive symptoms in low-income countries were least impaired and those in the higher-resource locations were most impaired. In low-income areas, 43.9 percent of people experiencing symptoms of depression met the WMH criteria for role disruption but in middle- and high-income countries, the rates were 53.7 and 63.9 percent, respectively. The highest rates of severe impairment were found in Northern Ireland, where almost three of four people with depressive symptoms experienced role disruptions, and Australia (71 percent). Samples reporting the lowest rates of role impairment were in Beijing-Shanghai (26 percent) and Nigeria (22.3 percent) (Bromet et al. 2018).

How disorders cause impairment depended on the region where a person experienced symptoms (Chatterji et al. 2013a). The availability of services, public awareness of mental illness, early diagnoses, and cultural values influence the patterns of dysfunctionality caused by mental health problems. One example to highlight this point comes from within China. In that country, migrants relocating from rural areas to the cities tend to have more psychological distress than nonmigrants. The levels of distress, however, are lower for migrants in the eastern part of the country than in the west where services are less available (Cheng et al. 2013).

What Accounts for the Differences Among Income Groups?

The dissimilarities among high-, middle-, and low-income countries are among the more interesting findings of the WHO project. Scott and colleagues (2018) provide one theoretical explanation for this pattern. They contend that lower-income cultures possess protective qualities against mental illness whereas value orientations in wealthier countries promote more psychopathology. According to this theory, for example, less westernized societies may have more opportunity for community engagement and may share a greater sense of communality or collectivism with other people in their villages and neighborhoods. Extended families remain very influential to individual growth and emotional development in nonwestern cultures. Individuals receive a lot of emotional and material support from their kin. These types of social capital, though largely nonmaterial, are important for emotional well-being. They offer protection from stress, give individuals a sense of identity, community, and involvement, and help keep individuals free from loneliness or feeling isolated.

Western, materially rich countries, however, have a different value orientation that may promote or exacerbate psychological distress. Accessibility to material goods is a part of affluent cultures, and the ability to acquire things, according to the theory, breeds a sense of entitlement and undermines motivation. Not everyone can afford to acquire the things they desire, however, and when expectations and outcomes do not match, as is often the case, emotional well-being is subverted (Scott et al. 2018). The association between subjective social status and mental disorder is not as strong in poorer countries than in wealthier ones. In addition, nonwestern cultures place less emphasis on individual achievement and status, which makes individuals less vulnerable to social comparisons with others that can result in emotional distress (Scott et al. 2018).

Social Change and Mental Health in Developing Countries

Traditionally organized agricultural economies are transitioning toward industrialization, which has a dramatic and rapid impact on their social organization and culture. Industrialization often serves as the vanguard of social changes that many believe improves the quality of life for a population. Virtually all aspects of life are transformed by economic modernization, which usually requires adopting features of western cultural and social systems such as bureaucratization and western style labor markets. These developments, however, often come at the expense of traditional psychosocial mechanisms that previously provided the social controls and support that promoted psychological well-being.

Mental illness, particularly depression, is less common in nonwestern precapitalist societies than in western cultures (Lee 2002), but as researchers have shown, mental health problems increase in rate and severity as countries become more westernized. Rapid modernization disrupts traditional family organization, communities, and political stability and replaces them with cultural incongruencies that may have significant negative impact on mental health. The old ways are often cast aside as a society modernizes.

Modernization represents more than economic and technological advancement; it also includes foreign norms and values that reorient interpersonal relationships and intrapersonal psychological dynamics. Development thus alters how people see themselves and relate to other people around them. For example, ideas and personal desires and goals differ in traditional and capitalistic societies (Furr 2004). Individuals in changing societies must adjust to new social conditions, opportunities, and expectations that likely requires emotional and identity changes.

The psychological impact of modernization is not equally distributed in a population (Lambo 1978). The effects of modernization vary based on context or situation.

Some individuals, for instance, may see an improvement in their mental well-being because economic and social development improves their quality of life. Lambo reminds us of the pervasive stereotypes of prewesternized village life as a paradise free of emotional distress and discord. For some, village life may be stressful, especially as changes in land use patterns and the transition to a consumer economy make traditional subsistence agriculture an artifact of the past and out of step with the new society.

In a study of Nepalese school teachers, Furr (2005) found that higher adoption of western cultural values, including liberal and western-influenced views on social diversity such as support of discontinuing the caste system and gender political equality, were associated with fewer symptoms of depression. Stacy Pigg (1995) contended that in Nepal economic and social development is perceived to be progressive, but traditionalism is seen as backward facing. Possessing values consistent with the direction the country seems to be headed may have a psychological pay-off. Progressive mindedness, in the Nepalese context, may imply congruency between self and society and an agreement among values the new culture emphasizes and the values an individual may hold. Those maintaining older and more conventional values are aware that traditional culture is increasingly losing stature in the new Nepal. Old values reinforcing caste and gender divisions in society may be understood as backwards, even among those who hold those values. Perhaps being socially backward is internalized and interpreted as personal backwardness, resulting in depressive symptoms.

As in Nepal, psychological problems are likely to occur where modernization has created stressful incongruities (Dressler 1985). Those who do well in the new economies may establish a social identity in which they feel empowered and successful. Stress is reduced when lifestyle aspirations match social status in the context of modernization. Just as mental health problems are disproportionately found among the poor and working classes in most westernized industrial societies, it is possible that as industrialization generates a new urbanized working class, psychological problems will expand with that social class and become the primary source of psychiatric distress in those countries (Higginbotham and Connor 1989). Table 13.3 suggests that as countries become wealthier through industrialization and development, as indicated by national income, the rates of psychiatric disorders increase.

The dynamics of employment and unemployment in the context of modernization may indeed play a role in mental health in developing countries. In a study of Latin America, Almeida-Filho (1998) found support for this idea. First, rural to urban migration in Latin America was not associated with mental illness in this sample, but having a regular, stable job in the formal labor market did not protect individuals against psychological disorders. Almeida-Filho also found that regular employment was a risk factor for men for developing psychological problems, but not for women. Lastly, housewives with no employment outside the home had higher rates of psychiatric symptoms in every diagnostic category. For Almeida-Filho, these findings suggest that in studying modernization researchers must include the meanings attributed to nonagricultural employment and unemployment and how these perceptions vary by the experiences of social groups.

TABLE 13.3 The WMH Survey's Highest and Lowest Countries in Lifetime Prevalence of Selected Disorders by Income Group (Percent of Population With Disorder)

Disorder	Low- and Lower/Middle-Income	Upper/Middle-Income	High-Income	United States	All Countries
Major Depressive Disorder	Iraq 53.0 Nigeria 18.2	Lebanon 43.5 Mexico 29.5	N. Ireland 47.3 Japan 28.0	37.8	10.6
Group Prevalence	7.1	9.2	12.6		
Bipolar Depressive Disorder	Colombia 2.6 Nigeria 0.1	Lebanon 2.4 Bulgaria 0.3	United States 4.4 Poland 0.6	4.4*	1.9
Group Prevalence	1.0	1.6	2.5		
General Anxiety Disorder	Iraq 3.7 Nigeria 0.1	Brazil 3.7 Romania 0.8	New Zealand 6.2 Poland 0.7	5.7	2.7
Group Prevalence	1.1	2.1	3.7		
Specific Phobias	Colombia 12.5 Iraq 5.9	Brazil 12.5 Romania 3.8	United States 12.5 Japan & Poland 3.4	12.5*	7.4
Group Prevalence	5.7	8.0	8.1		
PTSD	Ukraine 4.8 Peru 0.7	Lebanon 3.4 Romania 1.2	N. Ireland 8.8 Japan 1.3	6.9	3.9
Group Prevalence	2.1	2.3	5.0		
Alcohol Use Disorder**	Ukraine 13.7 Iraq 0.7	S. Africa 11.5 Lebanon 1.6	Australia 22.7 Italy 1.3	13.8	8.6
Group Prevalence	4.4	4.7	7.7		
Drug Use Disorders	Colombia 1.7 Iraq 0.2	S. Africa 4.0 Bulgaria 0.2	United States 8.4 Japan 0.3	8.4*	3.5
Group Prevalence	0.6	1.7	3.0		

(Continued)

TABLE 13.3 The WMH Survey's Highest and Lowest Countries in Lifetime Prevalence of Selected Disorders by Income Group (Percent of Population With Disorder) *(Continued)*

	Low- and Lower/Middle-Income	Upper/Middle-Income	High-Income	United States	All Countries
Psychotic Experiences	Colombia 7.5 Iraq 1.2	Brazil 14.9 Romania 1.0	Netherlands 10.8 Germany 2.8	8.6	5.8
Group Prevalence	3.2	7.2	6.8		

*United States had the highest prevalence.
**WHO also collected data on alcohol and drug use and dependence.

Source: Scott et al. (2018) (only full country data are included; city data are not included).

Problems in Developing Countries

Several ongoing social problems in developing countries impact mental health. These conditions are not necessarily specific to low- and middle-countries, but the influence they exert on mental well-being is strong because of their rapidity, intensity, or chronicity. In this section, we will review several problems—urbanization, poverty, and violence—that are important to completing the picture of the mental health profile of countries outside the sphere of western culture or have yet to develop a fully industrial or postindustrial economy.

Urbanization and Poverty

The degree of urbanization that took the United States a century to accomplish, has occurred in a third to half the time in countries such as Korea, China, India, Egypt, and Nigeria as rural migrants leave their villages in search of better economic opportunities, a more "modern" lifestyle, and improved social services such as medical care. In 1900, the largest cities were all in Europe and the United States, and their populations ranged from 6.5 million to 1.4 million: London, New York City, Paris, Berlin, Vienna, Chicago, Tokyo, Manchester, St. Petersburg (Russia), and Philadelphia were the 10 biggest cities that year. By 2021, only Tokyo remained in the top ten. According to one organization, the ten largest cities, with populations ranging from over 37 million to over 19 million are Tokyo, Delhi, Shanghai, Sao Paulo, Mexico City, Cairo, Dhaka, Mumbai, Beijing, and Osaka (World Population Review 2021). Other "mega-cities" with populations around 15 million have arisen in the Democratic Republic of Congo, Pakistan, Turkey, and the Philippines. (There are numerous rankings of cities by population because of differences in estimating populations, but they all conclude that the largest cities are not only much larger than in times past, but they are situated in nonwestern, industrializing countries.)

The world now has 32 cities with populations over 10 million and another 13 with populations from 8 to 10 million. In cities outside the west and Japan, population growth has outstripped cities' infrastructure to supply clean water and provide adequate sanitation, housing, employment, and transportation. For some, life has improved with the economic opportunities cities provide, but for many, the consequences of living in these huge urban centers have been harsh.

Rapid urbanization affects the mental health of a city's population (Harpham 1994). Urban growth is primarily a function of rural to urban internal migration and is incongruent with village life. Living in these cities changes the pace of everyday activities and forces individuals to conform to the demands of the wage-based labor market, which they did not do in the villages.

Because of the transience of urban populations and difficulty reaching residents for study, assessing the prevalence of mental health problems among residents, especially those who are poor, in these large mega-cities is often difficult. Nonetheless, several studies give us a glimpse at the severity of the problem. One study of 22–35-year-old residents of newly urbanized areas of Khartoum, Sudan found that four in ten reported at least one psychiatric symptom and that 16.6 percent met the criteria for a clinical diagnosis (Rahim and Cederblad 1989). Depression and anxiety were the most common disorders. Interestingly, no gender differences were found in this sample. Rahim and Cederblad also reported that these rates were much higher than those found in rural Sudan. Xiao and colleagues (2021) found a similar rate of depression (20 percent) among internal migrants in urban China. In Bahia, Brazil, 12 percent of the population met the standards for depression (Almeida-Filho et al. 2004).

Once individuals move to the cities, several factors have an impact on their mental health. Many newly arrived residents can find work, but a lot of those jobs pay poor wages, have low status, and demand long hours of difficult or emotionally draining labor. Migrants often live in make-shift housing in slums or on the streets, and many suffer psychologically because family ties and community support from their villages are diminished or no longer available (Khan and Kraemer 2014). As migrants lose traditional village and family supports, the cities have failed to provide supportive alternatives, leaving many urban residents without a sense of identity and belongingness (Sijuwade 1995). Many residents discover living in large urban places more impersonal, competitive, and harder than in the villages, and find themselves less happy and more dissatisfied with life (Cheng et al. 2013). Illiteracy, impoverishment, and being widowed or divorced were the main predictors of urban depression in the Brazil study (Almeida-Filho et al. 2004), and to cope both economically and emotionally, many urban migrants turn to crime, prostitution, and alcohol and drugs (Srivastava 2009; Sijuwade 1995).

Macro-level social forces specific to China have affected the mental health of that country's urban population. In 1978, to handle China's fast-growing population, the government instituted a strict one-child per family policy. As intended, the law drastically reduced China's birth and growth rates; however, an unexpected outcome of the one-child mandate was that children developed fewer social skills and became less resilient and more distrustful of others. Dissatisfaction with their jobs and life in general is common among this generation. These "only children" receive less social support than prior generations because their kinship groups are smaller, and the pressure to support their elders is greater since they have no siblings with whom to share that burden (Xiao et al. 2021).

New generation Chinese urban migrants, those born after 1980 and who grew up in the one-child culture, have been shown to have more psychological distress than first generation rural to urban migrants. Though they are more educated and their better understanding of their legal rights helps them negotiate the complicated Chinese bureaucracy, they have been more negatively affected by migration, experiencing more psychological distress than migrants who relocated to the cities prior to 1980. New generation migrants have fewer family connections and must rely on nonkin individuals and impersonal social agencies when they need support. China's industrial economy, work conditions, job availability, and rapidly growing urban centers have created pressures on individuals in terms of work demands, housing, and social relationships. Consequently, these new generation urbanites experience more workplace distress and job instability than first generation urban migrants (Xiao et al. 2021; Cheng et al. 2013).

Internal rural to urban migrants provide the cheap labor necessary to fuel the burgeoning economies of most developing countries. The wealth produced by this migration, however, has not been used to offset the social and psychological costs of having a large labor supply available to work in the factories.

The psychosocial problems of urbanization are not limited to the cities. The small towns and villages that migrants leave behind also experience mental health problems stemming from changes in land use and ownership and population depletion. Corporate interests enter many areas where land is dedicated to subsistence agriculture. Often with government support, large tracts of land are bought and converted to cash crops, leaving the traditional farmers without land and their traditional way of life. At the same time, younger people are fleeing the villages to find a new life in the cities. These forces affect the psychosocial welfare in rural areas. Elders are left without material and social support, and many young people have no economic opportunities. In many villages around the world, drug and alcohol use has increased dramatically, and many young women turn to sex work to get money.

Women's Health in Developing Countries

The effects of poverty in developing countries are not only about money and poor living conditions but also insecurity, vulnerability, and feeling safe. The consequences of these feelings of vulnerability affect women more than men (Patel and Kleinman 2003). Women are more likely to be undernourished, work low paying jobs, subject to both intimate partner violence and political violence (rape as terrorism or retribution), and are at risk to sex trafficking. Because they are associated with insecurity and trauma, these social forces take a heavy toll on individual women's mental well-being.

Women are more at risk of poverty than men and carry more of the adversity that stems from poverty. Impoverished women are 2.5 times more likely to experience negative mental health outcomes in places as diverse as Scandinavia, India, and Chile (Okpaku et al. 2014). In developing countries, by definition, more people are poor, making these problems more pressing in those countries.

Poverty brings higher risk of injurious social dynamics that target women. One example is that food insecure individuals, who are disproportionately women, are more likely to experience higher rates of depression, anxiety, and other symptoms of mental disorders than people who are food secure (Weaver and Hadley 2009).

Another illustration of the relationship between poverty and vulnerability among women is sexual violence. In the Asia-Pacific region, one in four men admitted to having raped a woman at least once. In Papua New Guinea, 23 percent of these men said they were teenagers at the time of the assault, and in Cambodia, 16 percent of self-reporting rapists committed the crime as a teenager (Fula et al 2013). Sexual assault causes several comorbid conditions for women: chronic pain syndrome, sexually transmitted diseases and HIV/AIDS, PTSD, depression, suicidal thoughts and behavior, substance abuse, and lower life satisfaction.

There is great variability in women's suicide prevalence around the world, and suicide follows different patterns in many developing countries than in wealthier states. In North America and Europe, the ratio of men to women completing suicide is 3.9:1. In Asia, however, the ratio is 1.1:1. In China, women are more likely than men to succeed in taking their own lives (Devries et al. 2011). Suicide rates for women in Africa are relatively low, but they are comparatively high in South America. Indigenous women in Peru, for example, are at particularly high risk of suicide. The cause has been attributed to a history of colonialism, chronic oppression, and trauma (Walters and Simoni 2002).

Exposure to childhood violence is estimated to account for 11 percent of global suicides among women (Andrews et al. 2004). Forced sex is a particular problem for girls and women. In low- and middle-income countries, about one in ten girls experience their first sexual encounter by force. The rate is higher in Nigeria, Uganda, and Zambia. Women experiencing forced sex initiation (FSI) are at risk for psychological problems including suicide. Compared to youths who are not exposed to FSI, these girls and young women typically experience shame and guilt and receive little health care. Severe stigma is common because the FSI is often the result of being forced into prostitution by family members, local thugs who coerce them, or abductors (Nguyen et al. 2019). FSI disgraces the family, tarnishes women's integrity, and diminishes women's social value.

Children's Health in Developing Countries

Children also are subject to social forces that have a negative impact on their mental health. One study estimated that over 14 percent of children in Sub-Saharan Africa have significant psychological problems, and one in ten could be diagnosed with a specific disorder. Interestingly, the rates did not vary among boys and girls or by place of residence (urban vs. rural) (Cortina 2012). In southern Africa, risk factors were primarily poverty-related conditions, but also included family disruptions such as divorce and abandonment and young maternal age (Cortina 2012). In a study conducted in Bangladesh, 25 percent of adolescents reported depressive symptoms that met the threshold of clinical depression (Khan et al. 2020). In that country, the primary risk factor also was poverty, especially living in Dhaka's massive slums. When compared to urban but nonslum dwelling and rural youths, teenagers living in slums were associated with serious behavioral problems and

PTSD (Mullick and Goodman 2005). Adolescents in that south Asian country were more likely to experience lower life satisfaction as well (Khan et al. 2020).

In general, children in poor countries, especially in areas of persistent civil war and social unrest, are at psychological and physical risk compared to children in more wealthy countries. Because of the circumstances of their social environments, these children are prone to **developmental attrition**, aggressive and antisocial behavior, and substance abuse (Desjarlais et al. 1996). Developmental attrition is the failure to reach normal development milestones of height, weight, and cognitive ability in each year of childhood. Children who are suffering from poverty, malnutrition, and an unstable and fearful social climate typically fail to reach expected physiological milestones, which can cause or exacerbate emotional and behavioral difficulties (Desjarlais et al. 1996).

War

In many poor countries, war and militarized political conflict seem ever-present. In areas such as northern Nigeria, terror groups attack villages and kidnap young girls without penalty. Armed militant groups terrorize parts of eastern India, and conflicts in Sudan, Syria, Iraq, Israel-Palestine, Afghanistan, Congo, and Yemen seem endless. Heavily armed paramilitary soldiers working for drug cartels plague the populations of Mexico and the Philippines. These conflicts cause much unhappiness and pathology among everyday people as well as among the combatants. Conducting research in war zones is not safe for researchers and participants, but a few studies have been conducted to show the mental health injuries that occur in conflicted countries. Two examples, from Nepal and Nigeria, show the extent of these collateral damages of war.

During the Nepalese Civil War (1996–2006), war crimes and civil rights abuses were committed by both the insurgents and the government. Bombings, executions, massacres, and kidnappings were all too frequent, and the mental health of those subjected to these traumas suffered. Women, however, carried the higher mental health burden. The risk of developing a mental disorder, especially depression, increased with greater exposure to traumatic events (Axinn et al. 2013).

A currently on-going humanitarian crisis, the Boko Haram insurgency in Nigeria, has caused a significant mental health crisis in the region (Adeboye 2021). This group routinely raids villages and cities, assassinates local leaders and critics, and attacks schools, colleges, and churches. It received worldwide condemnation in 2014 when the bandits, as they are known locally, kidnapped 276 girls from their boarding school to sell them as sex slaves or coerce them into other sexual abuses. Boko Haram has disrupted everyday life throughout northeastern Nigeria and caused a severe mental health crisis. It is estimated that in affected areas as many as 75 percent of residents are functionally impaired because of a psychological disorder (Kaiser et al. 2020). Many people are burdened by obsessive thinking about their problems, sadness, fear, anxiety, and anger. Men, in this study, demonstrated higher rates of disorders than women perhaps because the political violence interfered with their expectations and ability to care for their families (Kaiser et al. 2020). Since they were unable to meet their gender responsibilities and felt out of control of their lives, men's status loss resulted in shame, anxiety, and depression.

An extreme example of the severe negativity of the emotional climate in some countries is that of the child soldier. In some war torn areas, children are kidnapped and indoctrinated into becoming fighters in support of some cause or paramilitary force. They are given a brief training before their leaders deploy them into action, often against fully trained and equipped government forces (Jayatunge and Somasundaram 2014). Many are killed. For those who survive, physical and psychological traumas and social and cognitive developmental delays are common. The children are likely to experience somatization complaints, depression, PTSD, sad moods, suicidal thoughts, chronic fear, and reactive psychosis. They also have trouble forming attachments with other people, feel apathetic toward life, distrust other people, and become oppositional and impulsive.

Not all child soldiers are conscripted against their will. Some join voluntarily to fight for a particular cause or group. These youngsters, many of whom have experienced a lifetime of trauma and exposure to war, have few familial or community ties to provide a sense of safety and belongingness. Acting out of hopelessness and desperation, child volunteers turn to a fighting group to provide that acceptance because they are convinced that "the enemy" is the source of their alienation. They fight to protect themselves, relieve their deprivation, and battle the inequality and injustices they perceive as causing their social and personal miseries. They also may join for the adventure, because of an attraction to military paraphernalia, or out of identification with a hero (Jayatunge and Somasundaram 2014).

Whether these children join the military group voluntarily or by coercion, their psychosocial outcomes are the same: depression, anxiety, PTSD, and functional impairments due to psychopathology.

Perceptions of Mental Health Around the Globe

Lacking a standard definition, mental health is defined differently throughout the world. If we view psychopathology through a multicultural lens, we must conclude that labeling something as mental illness is a matter of perspective. What is mental illness in one culture is perhaps not a disorder in another. In many cases, a condition found in one culture may not even exist elsewhere. Psychiatrist Derek Summerfield (2013) is convinced that global mental health is a *faux* concept because perceptions of mental health and illness are both variable and contextual, making the use of a single definition of mental health impractical. Summerfield views the application of a single paradigm to all cultural systems as a form of medical colonialism. To a degree, he has a point. The presentation of a western bio-medical system of mental medicine to other cultures ignores the social context in which psychiatric problems may arise.

To illustrate this point, Summerfield (2013) describes a region of Cambodia where many people, mostly poor Khmer farmers and their families, occasionally tread upon landmines leftover from the Vietnam War of the 1960s and early 1970s. Survivors of mine explosions suffer severe injuries and require surgeries, amputations, prostheses, and rehabilitative care. Summerfield found that much of the medical care that landmine victims need is provided by a nongovernmental organization (NGO) called The Trauma Care International Foundation (TCIF). The

TCIF specializes in emergency and trauma medicine and works in Cambodia to help mine victims gain access to expensive and highly skilled medical care.

The Khmer have a term that Summerfield translated as "fall of heart or mind" to describe amputees who are slow to recover from their surgeries or adapt to prostheses and feel a strong sense of hopelessness. Western mental health professionals might describe these individuals as clinically depressed, but is that an accurate portrayal of their condition? Summerfield says no and prefers to describe their condition as "social suffering." These farmers are trapped in a problematic social situation. Their predicament implies a loss of their livelihood, social discrimination, family disorganization, and poverty. The NGO's ingenious antidote in these cases of "depression" is the gift of a cow, which provides both income and social status, and resolves the social suffering. As Summerfield says, the cow is both antidepressant and painkiller. Western medicine, to Summerfield, may provide remedies to the injuries to landmine victims' bodies, but it does not understand victims' emotional problems or how they might be treated.

Culture-Bound Syndromes

One way to see the shortcomings of a single definition of mental health and illness is to study disorders that exist outside the western cultural sphere. The DSM primarily addresses conditions that are labeled as mental disorders in most western cultures, but there are many other "illnesses" that are excluded by the DSM or treated as peripheral. Some conditions are specific to certain cultures and are known as **culture-bound syndromes.** Culture-bound syndromes are clusters of symptoms that are common in some cultures but nonexistent in others. While real in the culture in which they are found, they may seem unusual or even weird to outsiders. In the culture in which the symptoms occur, the conditions are considered legitimate illnesses or afflictions and have local names and a conventionally accepted discourse on etiology and treatment. Box 13.2 lists several culture-bound disorders.

Note in Box 13.2 that the inclusion of dissociative identity disorder is among those labeled culture bound. This disorder, in which a person presents with two or more separate identities or personalities, appears confined to western culture. Each personality has its own biography, traits, and preferences. With this disorder, known in the past as multiple personality disorder, one identity often has no knowledge of other identities. This results in the individual having no memory of their actions while an "other" was in control. Other symptoms include hallucinations, a sense of detachment from one's own emotions, and the absence of an integrated sense of identity.

Three dissociative disorders are specified by the DSM—dissociative identity, dissociative amnesia, and depersonalization disorder—and generally occur as a response to chronic and severe trauma such as physical, sexual, and emotional abuse. Individuals experiencing dissociative identity symptoms control the memories of the trauma by repressing thoughts and emotions to the point that they disconnect with reality and replace reality with an alternate identity and personality. Dissociative identity disorder is not common but is unique to western cultures.

Box 13.2 Culture Bound Syndromes

Culture bound psychiatric syndromes (CBSs) are found throughout the world. They are localized conceptions of aberrant behavior that come in many forms. Here are a few examples of CBSs from different parts of the world.

Dhat: India and Sri Lanka
Individuals in South Asia presenting symptoms of weakness, fatigue, sexual dysfunction, loss of virility and vitality due to the loss of valuable body fluid through urine or discharge of semen may be experiencing *dhat*. In western psychology, *dhat* appears as akin to an anxiety disorder.

Dissociative Identity Disorder: Anglo-America
This disorder is considered a culture-specific syndrome because it primarily occurs in persons holding a "modern" or western set of cultural schemas. A schema is a cognitive framework used to interpret information. Dissociative Identity Disorder involves the presence of two or more identities where at least two recurrently take control of the person's behavior. It was formerly known as Multiple Personality Disorder.

Ghost Sickness: American Indians
Forms of Ghost Sickness are reported around the globe and among American Indians. The syndrome occurs when the spirit of a deceased person attaches to a living person and drains their energy. The Navajo people believe this illness manifests from incorrectly performed burial rituals. In other cultures, the disorder stems from thinking about the deceased persons too much or trying to communicate with them. Symptoms include weakness, dizziness, fainting, anxiety, nightmares, confusion, and loss of appetite.

Koro (Japan) and *Suo-yang* (China): East Asia
This disorder is unique to east Asia and presents as a panic anxiety state in which people believe their genitals are shrinking. Death is believed imminent. Afflicted men have the desire to grasp their penis and woman their vulva and nipples to prevent them from retracting into their body. Koro seems to occur in epidemics of widespread fears of losing the ability to procreate and rumors of genitals being stolen by female fox spirits (China) and mass poisonings (Singapore and Thailand).

Ode ori: Nigeria
The chief complaints of *ode ori* are sensations of parasites crawling in the head and body, noises in the ears, heart palpitations, feelings of heat in the head, and paranoid fears of malevolent attacks by evil spirits. *Ode ori* is believed caused by enemies who deploy spirits to afflict victims or by self-induced drug abuse.

Taijin Kyofusho: Japan and Korea
In Japan and Korea, maintaining the integrity of the social group is a prime cultural goal. When individuals feel an intense anxiety that something about them causes displeasure to others, they may be experiencing what is known in those countries as *taijin kyofusho* or TKS. TKS is a culturally specific form of social phobia that presents as a severe dread of doing something that is embarrassing for oneself, which, in turn, causes offense to a social collective. When experiencing TKS, an individual feels extreme self-consciousness about physical appearance or functioning and of offending others by blushing, emitting offensive odors, and inappropriate staring or facial expressions. Strong feelings of shame are typical in this disorder.

"Wild Man" Madness: Kuma and other groups of the New Guinea highlands
"Wild man" madness is unique to the highlands of New Guinea. The disorder happens almost exclusively to young men. Young women have been known to develop symptoms, but they are considered rare. The disorder includes aggressiveness in which young men engage in eccentric and manic behavior that includes running crazily and threatening others with weapons. Victims of the disorder also become deaf and lose the ability to communicate. As they run around madly, they often scream incomprehensibly.

Sources: Balhara (2011), Herdt (1986), Makanjuola (1987), Mattelaer and Jilek (2007), Paniagua (2000), and Vriends et al. (2013).

One disorder of particular interest in the United States occurs primarily among women from Puerto Rico. *Ataque de nervios* is a condition that includes screaming uncontrollably paired with attacks of crying, trembling, and verbal or physical aggression. Fainting or seizure-like episodes and suicidal thoughts may sometimes accompany these symptoms (Guarnaccia et al. 1993). The signs of *ataque de nervios* are often treated as normative forms of expressing deep sadness and strong anger in stressful social situations and typically follow stressors such as divorce or other serious disruptions to married life. Contrary to expectations that *ataque de nervios* would be more prominent in Hispanic homelands and cultural enclaves, a study led by Guarnaccia et al. 2010 found that the disorder is associated with increased acculturation in the United States. Hispanics, especially Puerto Ricans, who were US (mainland) born and spoke more English were more likely to report experiencing *ataque de nervios*. The answer to this puzzle may lie in the fact that social stressors such as discrimination and the loss of family support increase in intensity for Latinos and Latinas the longer they stay in the United States. These factors may heighten vulnerability to stress, which later emerges as culturally specific forms of expressing that stress (Guarnaccia et al. 2010).

While DSM-V acknowledges cultural influences in creating and defining culture-specific disorders, some western psychiatrists have attempted to fit culture-bound conditions into DSM, or western-recognized, disorder categories, saying they are simply folk descriptions of "real" medical disorders. The current DSM, however, states its interest in discovering how social, cultural, and biological contexts interact to shape illnesses and social responses to them. This is an interesting point because it therefore must suggest that the disorders in the DSM are also subject to social and cultural ideas of what is and what is not deviant and disordered. To be legitimate, the field of ethno-psychiatry must apply its cultural relativistic analysis to western definitions of disorder as well as those from other cultures.

Cultural Diversity in Treatments

Western treatment programs are not widely available in low- and middle-income countries. These countries constitute 80 percent of the world's population but have access to only 20 percent of the world's mental health resources (Patel and Prince 2010). Consequently, many people, especially those with severe illness, do not receive treatment. The treatment gap in Sub-Saharan Africa, for example, is estimated in excess of 90 percent (Patel and Prince 2010). Institutions such as hospitals provide care for some people with severe mental illness (Saxena et al. 2007), but many remain untreated.

Treatment gaps are usually measured as utilization of western intervention programs and services offered by psychiatrists and psychologists. Where deprivation and need are highest, these services are less available (Saxena et al. 2007). That, however, does not mean people are not receiving care. Each culture has its own ways of responding to mental health problems through healers learned in their cultural traditions. These healers, who are not western in orientation, enjoy high respect in their communities and are often called upon to respond to mental health problems.

Traditional healing is an umbrella term and is difficult to specify because of great cultural diversity and conflicting characteristics in theory and method (Mutiso et al. 2014). The WHO has attempted to breech those differences and defines traditional medicine as the total knowledge, skills, and practices based on the theories, beliefs, and experiences indigenous to different cultures used in the maintenance of health as well as the prevention, diagnosis, improvement, or treatment of physical and mental illness (World Health Organization 2021).

Traditional mental health practices remain prevalent in low- and middle-income countries and present culturally specific treatments that have developed over centuries and are recognized as legitimate by the culture. These practices include various rituals and remedies very different from practices. Local medicinal remedies are made from locally available plants and herbs. What is central to these practices is that they are consistent with the sensibilities of the culture in which they were developed. In other words, they make sense to people in that culture.

Traditional remedies are diverse and range from herbal treatments to psychotherapy to religious rituals. Surgeries have been performed in some cultures, though they are rarely conducted by traditional healers today. Herbs and other products of the local flora are commonly utilized to treat conditions diagnosed as disordered. In Ghana, traditional healers provide the most accessible and often most preferred modalities of treatment; they use herbal remedies, often paired with spiritual rituals, to help their patients recover from psychological problems.

Relying upon herbal, spiritual, and other informal methods, Ghanaian healers have a systematic technique of diagnosing patients and a prescribed process for treating them. Their diagnoses and treatments combine intricate interactions of their perceptions of physiology and cultural narratives and beliefs that correspond to what some call an African notion of illness (Kpobi et al. 2019; Mbiti 1986).

In southern Africa, the perception of psychological distress differs from how it is understood in western cultures. In the west, which is oriented toward individualism, people think in terms of individual experience and existential confrontations with "reality." The focus of mental health treatment, therefore, is person-centered and strives to help individuals adapt to cultural and social circumstances, opportunities, and stressors.

In southern Africa cultures such as in Namibia, culture and personal identity are collectively oriented. The individual is embedded in kinship and community groups. As Gade (2011) states, people exist through others. The source of distress in these cultures is not perceived as a question of individual adjustment or pathology but as incongruency with values of ancestor reverence and *ubuntu*, or the interconnectedness with others. Traditional treatment in sub-Saharan Africa focuses on realigning individuals with these values and expectations and helps troubled people reestablish their social links to their kinship clan and communities. Doing so often requires religious rituals to regain the protection of their ancestors, which they are believed to have lost, hence their symptoms. The goal of traditional intervention is to reestablish the spirit of *ubuntu* within individuals (Bartholomew 2016).

Religious therapies, therefore, are common traditional practices in sub-Saharan Africa and other collective-based cultures. Spiritual practices are based on beliefs about the "other" world of gods, demons, and ancestors and are designed to bring inner peace and a sense of harmony between a person and the otherworld (Mutiso et al. 2014). These rituals include having the healer recite prayers and advise patients to engage in prayer, exorcisms, and singing sacred songs that have healing powers (Okonji et al. 2008).

The importance of spiritual rituals in treating psychological problems, however, is not based solely on religious precepts and contacting the spirit world. Religious knowledge also provides cores social values and behavioral expectations that serve as guides for individuals to restore their sense of self, gain control of their emotions, and to improve their thinking. Spiritual rituals align patients with their cultures and help people find their way through their problems.

Talk therapies are not exclusive to western mental health practices. In eastern Africa, especially in modern Tanzania and Kenya, traditional healers have a long history of engaging in treatment modalities westerners would recognize as psychotherapy. Dating back centuries and sometimes accompanied by herbal and spiritual interventions, talk therapies are common practices in that region and are similar to those practiced in the west. Healers explore individual psychodynamics and engage in family and group therapy (Ndetei 2007).

Okonji and colleagues (2008) engaged Kenyan traditional health practitioners (THPs) in focus groups to learn more about their approach to treating mental illness. The study learned that THPs have a sophisticated system for understanding the origins of mental illness and the types of treatments that are indicated for each problem. First, THPs believe that mental illnesses have ideographic origins. Some are caused by stressful life events such as the death of loved ones, family and relationship problems, injuries, poverty, and food insecurity. Kenyan healers stated that anxiety is caused by a rapid beating of the heart, severe headaches, poor blood circulation, and a weak brain. Heredity, alcohol abuse, the influence of ancestors, and supernatural possession cause other complaints. Regarding supernatural causes, Okonji's research group found that many THPs and their cultures believe that demons can occur if insects infest the head or if parents act improperly. Other disorders originate when one person bewitches another during a quarrel or acts with pride or showing off. Treatments, Okonji's team found, were specific to the disorder and often varied among THPs.

Traditional therapies in Africa and elsewhere are known to be successful in treating common disorders such as depression and anxiety. A study of indigenous people in the Indian state of Nagaland found that almost 60 percent of people who sought help for affective complaints and substance abuse from traditional healers reported positive outcomes, which meant that the problem had been alleviated. One important difference in these results was found, however. Compared to urban residents, people living in rural areas were two times more likely to report positive results (Longkumar 2019). Perhaps urban residents adhered less to traditional values, thus making the treatment of THPs less meaningful. Studies generally concur that traditional methods administered to people with psychotic disorders are not particularly helpful and may lead other to health problems. Some of the less successful techniques revealed in the Kenyan study were scratching the abdomen and using animal horns to suck out the "contents" of the abdomen and cutting arms and legs to apply herbs (Okonji et al. 2008).

At present, the global trend is to integrate traditional and western theories and practices, especially in rapidly developing places like India and China. These countries and others with blooming urbanization and industrialization are introducing western diagnoses and medical vocabularies, therapies, and medicines to their people as part of their modernization agendas. Box 13.3 describes a program in Uganda that focuses on training local healers to utilize western medicines for severe mental illness. Research suggests that the merging of the two systems provides the best treatment protocols, particularly for psychosis and schizophrenic disorders (Bartholomew 2016; Abbo 2011).

The advent of western psychiatric intervention, however, has proven to be a mixed bag. On the one hand, pharmaceutical interventions are far more effective than remedies administered by traditional healing practitioners for treating psychotic disorders. On the other hand, western modalities are criticized for not fitting into nonwestern cultures.

The mental health of the Maori in New Zealand provides a good example of how western practices are at odds with an indigenous culture. The Maori, the first people of modern-day New Zealand, are now a sociocultural group underrepresented in the country's authority system and are economically disadvantaged. Though their rates of hospitalization for affective disorders are about the same as non-Maoris, the Maoris have a higher rate of hospitalization for schizophrenia, alcohol abuse, and personality disorders, and they are more likely to be psychiatrically disabled than New Zealanders of European origin. The frequency of hospitalizations indicates that

Box 13.3 Blending Traditional Folk Beliefs with Western Treatments in Uganda

One example of how to bridge cultural differences comes from Uganda, a country with high rates of mental illness but low access to care. Estimates suggest that over a third of Ugandans have a mental illness (Molodynski et al. 2017). The majority of Ugandans believe mental illness stems from magical or supernatural origins.

Folk healers provide most mental health care in the country. Their treatments, especially for serious psychiatric problems, at best are ineffective, at worst they are dangerous. It is known that some folk healers have wrought mutilations on people to treat their severe psychological problems. To improve treatments, a team of Ugandan mental health professionals, supported by a Canadian grant in 2014, sought to reduce the country's reliance on traditional healing by coopting the folk healers, some of whom described themselves as witch doctors, into working with, instead of at odds with western-trained mental health practitioners. The team trained 500 THPs and elders to recognize mental illness and to refer them to hospitals where patients could receive treatments other than traditional remedies (Sathya 2014). The trained local healers served as cultural interpreters for local people. The intent was not to convert people to a western conception of mental illness, but to incorporate the foreign western ways of thinking into their own traditions. Because of their high esteem in their villages, the local healers legitimated western treatments, particularly medications. In a sense, they explained the "magic" contained within the pills and merged western practices with local sensibilities.

Maoris are using western mental health services, but most agree that the treatments are not effective (Sachdev 2001).

For the Maori, the concept of mental health differs from Europeans'. Among the Maori, mental health is related to tribal land ownership and controlling one's own affairs, which includes health management (Sachdev 2001). Removing them from their traditional lands and disrupting their economic and social systems undercut the foundations of their mental health. Disempowerment and the disruption of their traditional culture have forced the Maori to rely on western mental health treatments.

Western-based mental health systems, however, fail to consider Maori culture. Sachdev (2001) identified several interconnected ways in which this occurs. First, western practitioners and Maori have difficulty communicating with each other during mental health treatment sessions. The Maori emphasize body language more and verbalizations less than Europeans, and Westerners have difficulty interpreting these gestures. One example is eye contact. For Maori, looking at someone in the eye is a function of authority. Someone perceived as lower in status is not expected to look at a higher status person in the eye as a form of deference to their authority. This behavior could be interpreted as low self-esteem by western therapists.

Second, the Maori show deference to authority in ways than hinder western mental health intervention. They believe that healers possess great power and prestige, therefore they approach doctors cautiously out of respect and awe. Because of this interactive dynamic, Maori patients make few demands of health care workers, making Maori appear more passive in therapeutic relationships. Whereas in the West, patients are expected to be active in and responsible for their own treatment and recovery, Maori patients are hesitant to express themselves and are likely to defer to mental health professionals. Being more collective in orientation, Maori prefer to deliberate options and seek the opinion of others before making up their minds about important decisions. In their culture, decisions are reached after discussions with kin and people of similar status, not individually. Consequently, the one-on-one mental health consultation is a foreign style of solving a problem. Family-centeredness directs the Maori to make decisions with family members and involve them in treatments. Western health practitioners find this practice meddlesome and intrusive (Sachdev 2001).

About the Quote

This quote from Ellen Corin, a Canadian scholar, addresses an important issue in conducting cross-cultural studies in mental health: researchers and practitioners often interpret the behavior of people in other cultures differently than that of people in their own culture. What lies at the heart of this mismatch in perception?

Corin explains that the less cross-cultural experience we have, the more we remain within the boundaries of our own culture's ways of thinking, living, and behaving. Limited exposure to others means that our home culture becomes transparent and invisible. We tend to see our cultural dynamics, expectations, and lifestyles as what she calls a "natural order" to life (1994: 119). It is always easier to see cultural influences on behavior in foreign settings than in our own, where the rules governing how we live and interpret the world are frequently imperceptible to us.

This process has implications for the study of mental health. If we see our cultural systems as natural, then other cultures must be unnatural. Not understanding other cultures' perceptions of mental well-being subjects practitioners and researchers to making subjective judgments about the "others." Oftentimes western mental health professionals with western assumptions about mental health will apply those beliefs to people who may have different perceptions of mental health. This discrepancy in understanding can lead to conflict and treatment plans that make no sense to the patient. Local health care professionals may also have a very different idea than their western counterparts about what constitutes a mental illness and how to treat it. As Corin states, illness is not a mirror of the disease process; it is subject to cultural interpretation.

Westerners often see mental health problems in their home cultures in individualistic terms. This perception fails to include social forces and cultural processes in understanding mental well-being. But when thinking about mental health in foreign places, there is a tendency to see individual problems as connected to the social system and culture. This way of thinking, as Corin states, is "unsupported ethnocentrism" (1994: 119).

DISCUSSION QUESTIONS

1. What steps would you take to make a cross-cultural survey sensitive to cultural differences in definitions and perceptions of mental illness?

2. How would you frame western psychological and psychiatric practices as traditional healing? In addition to the one listed in Box 13.2, are there other western-recognized disorders that may be culture-bound to the west?

3. How could you argue that a western-trained psychiatrist and a pastoral care counselor are traditional healers?

4. Describe situations in your own culture in which the idea of "social suffering" is a better term to represent mental health conditions than psychiatric concepts. Why is it harder to see "social suffering" in another culture than your own?

5. The idea of culture-bound conditions is important beyond being a simple anthropological factoid. They tell us that mental well-being, both nondisordered and disordered, has great cultural variation, which anthropologists of mental health have long taught us. By defining a syndrome as culture-bound also introduces an element of power in diagnosing. Why are the disorders in the DSM not considered culture-specific while those listed as culture-bound are not listed in the DSM, except as a parenthetical aside at the end of the book? Why are conditions that occur among mainstream Americans in their culture presented as basic disorders but those that occur elsewhere are listed separately?

KEY TERMS

Culture-bound Syndromes 314
Developmental Attrition 312
Probability Sampling 298

Process Errors 300
Sampling Error 298

World Mental Health Survey
Initiative (WMH) 297

CHAPTER 14

Mental Health Policy and the Law

> Proposals that promise the most grandiose consequences often legitimate the most unsatisfactory developments. And one grows wary about taking reform programs at face value; arrangements designed for the best of motives may have disastrous results.
>
> —David Rothman (1971)

Learning Objectives

After reading this chapter, students will be able to:

1. Assess the flow of policy changes and how political ideologies can impact mental health programs and funding.
2. Describe how people with mental illness interact with law enforcement and the judicial system.

Introduction

We generally do not think of mental health as an arena in which factional partisan politics play out. Nonetheless, our collective responses to mental illness are frequently mired in politics and subject to party rhetoric. Public debates on mental health policy are usually not about best therapeutic practices or which theory provides the most answers for preventing mental illness and providing for the mentally ill. When politicos discuss (and argue) mental health policy, the discussions are about political philosophies regarding the federal government versus states, the president versus Congress, interest groups versus government, and civil liberties versus the need for treatment. While we will not review the political arguments directly, keep in mind that all the policies, laws, and governmental practices that will be discussed are the result of political wrangling and philosophy.

At the policy level, mental health is a highly politicized topic and the target of many changes and orientations throughout the years. Several factors may account for the way mental health is treated by the political and legal system. The lack of a sound definition of mental illness obstructs efforts to create a comprehensive **public policy** and impedes public agreement on the degree that individuals are responsible for their behavior. This latter idea separates mental health from physical health in terms of governmental and corporate actions. Stigma, therefore, is a key element in understanding mental health policy and contributes to the public sphere's lack of a consistent course of action or guiding principles to respond to mental illness. Another issue is that mental health is a low governmental priority compared to other problems that are politically more pressing. When budget reductions are necessary or the political ideology in power calls for reduced public spending, mental health programs are usually among the first funding cuts.

This chapter will focus primarily on public policy enacted by governmental action. In general, the government involves itself in three primary areas: direct management of services, funding treatment programs and research, and specifying how criminal law pertains to mental illness.

Mental Health Policy in the United States

The term "public policy" refers to the complex of laws, guidelines, and practices enacted by government. Public policy also includes the system by which these norms and values are executed. Mental health public policy, therefore, is the system of laws and governmental actions that organize and regulate a collective response to mental illness and allocate resources to fund programs designed to meet policies' objectives. Policy also includes the values and beliefs that underlie governmental actions.

In this section, we will review the major policies put in place by state and federal government that have formed our system of mental health care. The government has played a major role in shaping mental health care in the United States especially in aiding lower income and vulnerable individuals and families. As you recall from the history of mental illness presented in Chapter 2, governments have been involved in providing the tools of care for centuries primarily through financial support and management of asylums and hospitals. In the last several decades, government's role has greatly expanded. In addition to continuing to support hospitals, government programs fund a wide range of services, create policies that determine how American society approaches mental illness, and influences the research that studies the cause and treatment of mental illness.

Public-Based Mental Health Programs

The public sponsors a wide range of mental health initiatives through direct and indirect support of facilities, clinics, and programs. At times the government takes the lead to create and maintain a mental health care system. Two examples are hospitals operated by the Veterans Administration (VA) and the states. Indirect support mostly comes via **block grant** funding. Block grants are federal funds awarded to state, territorial, or local governments to implement programs in their areas that meet the purpose of the grants and the needs of the local population. In recent years, the block grant system has become a major mechanism the government utilizes to support programs.

Veterans Administration Hospitals

The Veterans Health Administration operates the largest health care system in the United States. The system manages 171 VA hospitals, known as Medical Centers, and 1,112 outpatient clinics, for a total of 1,293 health care facilities. Medical services are provided to over nine million enrollees. The VA's budget is about $68 billion annually. Over 367,000 full-time health care professionals and support staff are employed by the VA (Veterans Administration 2021a).

The VA first studied mental health problems in 1941, and in the last several decades behavioral care has become a high priority. In 2020 alone, 1.7 million military veterans utilized mental health services at Veteran Administration hospitals and clinics (Veterans Administration 2021b). Services are available for inpatient, outpatient, and residential programs. Among the service-related problems addressed by VA psychiatrists, psychologists, and social workers are PTSD, substance abuse, women's stress disorders, behavioral health care for returning veterans, and vocational rehabilitation needs. The most common mental health problems for veterans are PTSD, depression, and the consequences of traumatic brain injury.

According to the Committee to Evaluate the Department of Veterans Affairs Mental Health Services (2018), the VA's mental health services receive mixed reviews. While the VA outperforms the private sector on several quality measures assessing medication treatment for mental disorders, other facets of care have received less than stellar reviews. One complaint is that patients report that treatment programs are "cookbook," which suggests that following a prescribed treatment regimen is emphasized over individualized care. Relatedly, many veterans told researchers that patient preferences for treatment were not routinely considered. Other problems included long periods between appointments, which affected patient retention and completion of treatment plans. These criticisms are likely a consequence of the bureaucratic organization of the VA system. Following a treatment script may be more efficient for the system but does not provide the flexibility to address each veteran's problems ideographically.

State Hospitals

In 1854, Congress presented a bill to President Franklin Pearce that would establish a national system for mental health care. Pearce, however, vetoed the bill because he believed the responsibility for providing mental health care was an obligation of the states not the federal government. As a result of his decision, the states were forced to establish and financially support a network of hospitals to house and treat their mentally ill residents.

For over a century following Pearce's decision, state psychiatric hospitals constituted the primary public treatment system for mental health disorders (Foley and Sharfstein 1983). On any given day in 1950, 322 state psychiatric hospitals treated over 500,000 patients, and as late as 1981, state mental health agencies dedicated 63 percent of their budgets to those facilities (Parks and Radke 2014).

Today, the state hospitals are no longer the centerpiece of publicly supported mental health care. By 2012, systematic closures had reduced the number of hospitals to 207, and together they only treated 50,000 individuals on a typical day. Just 23 percent of state mental health budgets went to support the hospitals (Parks and Radke 2014).

The characteristics of the patients in state hospitals also has changed. Compared to the past when state hospital patients were primarily severely mentally ill individuals suffering from schizophrenia, other psychotic disorders, and bipolar disorders, hospitals now are seeing a different treatment group. Nationally, 1999 to 2014 saw a 76 percent increase in forensic patients (sex offenders and people who had other committed crimes) (Wik et al. 2017). Whereas in 1983 when only 7.6 percent of state hospital budgets were dedicated to forensic patients, by 2012, 36 percent of their budgets were committed to patients who had committed serious crimes. In a few states, over 90 percent of their hospitals' budget went to patients ordered into psychiatric care because of a sex offense or other criminal misconduct (Parks and Radke 2014). As the numbers suggest, the trend was not even in all states. In many, the change was dramatic between 1999 and 2014. For example, Arkansas had an increase of 2,475 percent, and Minnesota's was 517 percent. Nebraska's forensic patient share rose almost 300 percent, and rates in Nevada, Wisconsin, Texas, and West Virginia each rose over 170 percent. A handful of states—New Mexico, Oklahoma, and Washington and the District of Columbia—had a decline in forensic patients during this period. For many states, individuals found incompetent to stand trial or who required competency evaluations or restorative services accounted for most of their increase (Wik et al. 2017). As a side note, New Hampshire has no forensic patients because all mentally ill individuals convicted of a crime are sent to a unit within the state prison. Its state psychiatric hospital does not admit forensic patients.

This change in practice and policy has prompted mental health professionals in state hospitals to alter their training and treatment agendas to meet the needs and new demands. With a large forensic patient population, hospitals have re-oriented their procedures and campuses to accommodate more security measures, and staff has adjusted to more corrections-type duties added to their job descriptions. Psychiatrists, psychologists, and social workers must be skilled in assessing the potential for future violence among individuals who have already been violent. Because of this potential, hospital treatment programs typically allow patients less autonomy than in times past. Clinically, however, patients are expected to become more autonomous individuals and are encouraged to make better decisions about their lives and engage in their own treatment plans (Papapietro 2019).

Community Mental Health

Although community mental health started in a few states in the 1950s, the Kennedy administration extended the concept to the nation in the early 1960s. Kennedy was acutely aware of the rising national need to address mental health problems, and the community mental health program was established to respond to them.

The origin of the administration's recognition for national action came shortly after World War II when several factors spurred a fast-rising national awareness and interest in mental health. First, from 1942 to 1945, about 12 percent of all men screened for induction to military service were rejected for neurological or psychiatric reasons. This figure accounted for 40 percent of all 4F decisions (4F is the status assigned to individuals who are medically unfit for service). In addition, 37 percent of all personnel who were discharged for reasons of disability were due to neuropsychiatric conditions. Because of mental illness, over two million men were disqualified from military service during the national emergency (Rochefort 1997). The large number of psychiatric rejections and discharges increased the public's awareness of mental illness and indicated that mental health problems were more widespread than previously believed.

A second way in which the war affected the public's response to mental illness was a set of new treatments that emerged to handle the high caseload within the military. Innovative techniques and therapies such as hypnosis and sedation proved successful in helping service personnel, including those suffering from psychosis. With the recognition of the impact of social environmental pressures, new treatment modalities such as group therapy also proved effective (Mechanic 1989).

Lastly, post-war mental health awareness was affected by individuals who did not participate in the war. Many conscientious objectors were assigned to work in psychiatric hospitals during the war years. At their assignments they found patients living in broken-down and second-rate facilities and being treated poorly and ineffectively. After the war, many of these men wielded significant influence in leading a movement to reform American mental health hospitals. They inspired numerous newspaper and magazine exposés that called attention to the deplorable state of hospitals throughout the country (Rochefort 1997). Works by scholars such as sociologist Erving Goffman's *Asylums* and creative writers like Ken Kesey, who wrote the famous and influential 1962 novel *One Flew Over the Cuckoo's Nest*, also contributed to changes in perceptions of psychiatric care and the living conditions in hospitals.

The reaction to the military's experience with mental illness among troops and the general citizenry was swift. Just after the War, Congress passed the **National Mental Health Act** (NMHA) in 1946. This bill allotted funds to increase training for mental health professionals and research into causes and treatments of mental illness. These funds would be distributed through the National Institute of Mental Health (NIMH), which was created in 1949. The NMHA also provided monies for states to create outpatient treatment centers, which provided the germ of the idea of community mental health (Grob 1991).

The NMHA represents a particularly important shift in national policy because of its contribution to deinstitutionalization. Changes in treatment modalities, especially the invention of antipsychotic medicines and the medicinal control of syphilis, were largely responsible for moving patients out of hospitals, but policy changes also played a significant role (Watson et al. 2017). The NMHA required the states to distribute money to mental health programs but did not allow the states to use the money to support hospitals. This policy change had two implications. First, the national government was asserting control over the nation's mental wellbeing and second, through the NMHA, the federal government was signaling a transference from hospital-centered care to community-based programs and services.

Other federal policies supported the ideological reorientation and contributed to ending the historical reliance on large institutions to warehouse and treat mentally ill people. Psychiatric hospitals' census reached their peak in 1955 with about 560,000 patients. Over the next 10 years, hospital counts declined about 1.5 percent each year. But in 1965, that decline accelerated to about 10 percent annually (Gronfein 1985). This change was largely due to new policies such as President Johnson's new social insurance programs Medicare and Medicaid, which supported mental health care. As an illustration of the impact of these programs, within three years of Medicare's onset, 37,000 fewer elderly people were housed in state psychiatric hospitals. By 1974, 85,000 were in nursing homes instead of large institutions (Frank and Glied 2006; Watson et al. 2017).

As these social forces reframed perceptions of mental health care, new ideas were evolving to improve treatments. Many notable psychiatrists wanted to steer mental health care away from state hospitals to a community-based practice model. In light of the success of medications such as Thorazine, a reliance on large hospitals was no longer as urgent as in years past. Physicians generally believed that formerly hospitalized patients could be better treated if services were available in the communities where patients were living. In addition, patients' rights to have a voice in their treatment and to challenge involuntary hospitalizations were a strong consideration in deinstitutionalization.

The cornerstone legislation that resulted from these social movements was the Kennedy administration's creation of the community mental health system. The **Community Mental Health Act** of 1963 was a paradigm-changing legislation that many deemed revolutionary. The Act established comprehensive **community mental health centers** (CMHCs) throughout the nation. Seen as cost friendly for taxpayers and private payers and more effective for patients, CMHCs offered a wide range of services designed for all residents of a community but specifically targeted indigent and low-income individuals and families through sliding fee scales. The centers were situated near public transportation and easily accessible, and services were provided by a mix of government agencies, private nonprofit groups, and for-profit organizations. These groups offered an assortment of services such as individual and group therapy, diagnostic services, access to psychiatrists for medications, substance abuse treatment, halfway houses, life skills develop classes, and family support programs.

Originally completely funded by the federal government, subsequent national budgets gradually withdrew financial support, which meant that CMHCs had to cut services or find new sources of revenues to fulfill their mission. A key turning point in funding CMHCs occurred during the late 1970s and early 1980s. During the Carter administration, Congress passed the **Mental Health Systems Act** (MHSA) of 1980. MHSA called for continued funding of national mental health programs including community mental health. Ronald Reagan, however, defeated Carter in 1980, and a Congress friendly to the new president's position repealed the MHSA. Funding for community mental health declined rapidly.

Reagan's stance on mental health was not unpredictable. As governor of California, he supported the **Lanterman-Petris-Short Act** (LPS) of 1967, which essentially abolished involuntary hospitalization in that state and forced institutions to move patients out of hospitals and into group homes, which became a large industry in California. The law also made it difficult to admit mentally ill patients into state hospitals. By reducing the number of patients in hospitals, the LPS freed the money that had been dedicated to the institutions. That money, however, was not diverted to other mental health programs in California or in the many states that followed California's model. These policy changes and budget cuts to state mental health agencies had many ramifications. For example, many scholars attribute the rise of mentally ill people becoming homeless in the 1980s to this policy.

Funding for Mental Health Services and Research

Until CMHCs became a nation-wide program in the 1960s, mental health policy was primarily the responsibility of state governors and their mental health directors. States paid for most of the publicly supported care, which was primarily situated in state hospitals, as President Pearce had planned a hundred years earlier. Today, however, funding and policy decisions are more diffused. State Medicaid directors, the Social Security Commissioner, federal Medicare and Medicaid administrators, and human resource directors in corporations have the most influence in what services are made available to the public and how they are financially supported (Frank and Glied 2006).

From private psychotherapy to state psychiatric hospitals, there are numerous forms of mental health service delivery and ways to pay for them. Chart 14.1 shows the distribution of funding sources for all mental health services in 2009. Roughly two-thirds of all mental health services are funded by public payers, and one-third was paid by private sources including client self-pay and insurance, which is largely provided and subsidized by employers. Public funding primarily stems from direct support of hospitals and programs via Medicare and Medicaid, the latter of which is the largest single funding source. Grants to support specific programs account for

CHART 14.1 US Mental Health Funding Sources, 2009

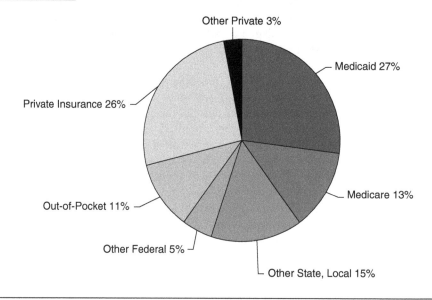

Source: Pew Charitable Trust (2015).

much of the remainder of government spending. The ratio of federal to private spending has not changed significantly the last three decades but differs substantially from physical medical health and surgical (med-surg) funding, which is largely paid by private resources such as insurance (Pew Charitable Trust 2015).

Paying for programs created by legislative actions is a seemingly constant struggle. Programs are generally initiated in response to a need, but in subsequent years their funding is often challenged as the excitement about the program wanes, the need eases, or other problems that require legislative attention and resource allocations arise and take precedence. Community mental health programs are a case in point. Initially well-funded by the federal government, community mental health centers lost the bulk of their support and now must rely on grants and fees to continue providing their services.

The distribution of funding sources also varies over time in ways that may be unrelated to legislative decisions. For instance, population size affects Medicare spending. With the bulk of the Baby Boomer cohort entering retirement and receiving Medicare benefits, the share of behavioral health spending from that program has increased. In the future as the number of people eligible for Medicare diminishes, Medicare's share of spending should decline. A second demographic effect is that as more people live in poverty, demands on Medicaid increase.

Another factor affecting costs is the medication patent system. Drug patents last 20 years but up to 10 years can be spent on clinical trials and testing after a patent is awarded. Consequently, pharmaceutical companies have fewer than 20 years to market a drug and recoup research costs before the patents expire. As patents on widely prescribed medicines end, less expensive generics replace them, resulting in lower costs (Mark et al. 2014). Drug companies, therefore, are constantly searching for new drugs to replace those with expired patents, which can drive up costs for consumers and insurance programs.

Legislation can impact coverage directly, as in the case of the **Affordable Care Act** (ACA) in 2010, which sought to increase the number of people covered by health insurance. The ACA caused an increase in mental health spending in the private sector because of expanded coverage. Prior to the Act's passage, younger people were least likely to be insured and most likely to take advantage of the opportunities created by the law. For example, more private and insurance money was spent after the ACA on the treatment of substance use disorders, which are more common among younger people (Mark et al. 2014).

Federal budgets often reflect officials' perceptions of public need. For example, between 2017 and 2020 budget items targeting the opioid epidemic, serious mental illness, and criminal justice and juvenile justice systems were increased. The 2020 budget dedicated $1.5 billion for state opioid response grants and $800 million for opioid research. An additional $26.7 million were set aside for training grants to address substance use disorders, and suicide prevention programs also received budget increases. Financial support programs that help lower income people with serious mental illness including Medicaid, Social Security Disability Insurance, food stamps, and housing assistance received less funding. The Substance Abuse and Mental Health Services Administration's (SAMHSA) budget was also cut, and the Screening, Brief Intervention and Referral to Treatment Program minority fellowships at SAMHSA were eliminated.

Given the amount of money dedicated to mental illness, mental health has the attention of the federal government. But is the money well spent? Many critics charge that as financial investments in mental health care increase, the prevalence of mental health problems either does not change or rises. Ross and colleagues (2012) conducted a study on this question. Analyzing government expenditures from 1995 through 2005 and comparing them to suicide rates, these researchers found that increases in state allocations for mental health had a small but not statistically significant effect on suicide rates. More interestingly, they found that policies and public welfare spending aimed at enhancing income growth and financial support for low-income families had a much stronger impact on suicide prevention, especially for men. From this study, we can conclude that while suicide prevention programs are necessary and largely successful, targeting the root causes of many suicide attempts may be a better use of public resources.

When studying the effects of public expenditures on mental health beyond suicide prevention, government investments in the population's mental health have shown to be worthwhile. Public expenditures dedicated to mental health care improve the subjective quality of life for people with mental health problems, in particular depression and substance abuse. Mental health spending also affects objective measures such as education, the criminal justice system, and the labor market. Taking an economics perspective, McDaid and colleagues (2019) found that public spending on mental health generates a high economic return. They concluded that each dollar spent on mental health generates a $1.80 to $3.30 return. These returns are found in increased education and greater employment opportunities, which result in higher incomes. In addition, mental health services reduce the demand on the criminal justice system.

Because of the economic retrenchment caused by the Great Recession, states cut over $4.5 billion dollars from their mental health budgets between 2009 and 2013. Workforce development, acute inpatient services, long-term inpatient care, and clinic services were most affected by the budget cuts. At the same time, however, there was an increase in demand for these services in state supported hospitals, emergency rooms, crisis centers, and community mental health centers (Honberg et al. 2011).

As states were still recovering from these funding reductions the COVID pandemic struck, which not only affected state revenues but increased the need for mental health services. In response to the crisis, in spring of 2021, the federal government offered states and territories about $2.5 billion in funding targeting mental illness and substance abuse. Most of the money was earmarked for substance abuse prevention and treatment block grants, and the remainder was dedicated to support community mental health services via grants to local authorities to support programs. Box 14.1 shows an announcement for programs to apply for money to support mental health programs during the COVID-19 pandemic.

Box 14.1 An Example of a Funding Application for Community Mental Health Centers

Here is an abbreviated announcement CMHCs to apply for grants to provide mental health services during the COVID-19 pandemic in 2021. This "Funding Opportunity Announcement" (FOA) was accessed in May 2021 on a website maintained by the Substance Abuse and Mental Health Services Administration (SAMHSA) at the US Department of Health and Human Services. These grant monies enabled CMHCs to address increases in demand for mental health and substance abuse services during the pandemic. Though this is a shortened version of the full FOA, it gives you an idea of the language of these announcements and the basic stipulations they require. It also indicates the competitive nature for funding CMHCs.

Note that funding for this program lasts up to two years. Many programs operated by CMHCs run on **"soft money,"** revenue sources that have planned termination dates. Staff working in these programs also have a planned termination date unless they can secure additional funding.

Community Mental Health Centers (CMHCs) Grant Program
Short Title: CMHCs

Modified Announcement
Applicants are required to ensure their application is error-free by the due date and time. Applications will be returned to address errors but all applications must be error-free and submitted by the deadline to be considered. Please closely review Appendix A, especially 5.1 and 5.2, for more information.

Funding Opportunity Announcement (FOA) Information

Posted on Grants.gov: Tuesday, April 6, 2021

Application Due Date: Friday, May 21, 2021

Intergovernmental Review: Applicants must comply with E.O. 12372 if their state(s) participates. Review process recommendations from the State Single Point of Contact (SPOC) are due no later than 60 days after application deadline.

Public Health System Impact Statement (PHSIS)/ Single State Agency Coordination: Applicants must send the PHSIS to appropriate State and local health agencies by application deadline. Comments from Single State Agency are due no later than 60 days after application deadline.

Description

The Substance Abuse and Mental Health Services Administration (SAMHSA), Center for Mental Health Services (CMHS), is accepting applications for fiscal year (FY) 2021 Community Mental Health Centers (Short Title: CMHCs) grant program. The purpose of this program is to enable community mental health centers to support and restore the delivery of clinical services that were impacted by the COVID-19 pandemic and effectively address the needs of individuals with serious emotional disturbance (SED), serious mental illness (SMI), and individuals with SMI or SED and substance use disorders, referred to as co-occurring disorder (COD). SAMHSA recognizes the needs of individuals with behavioral health conditions, including minority populations and economically disadvantaged communities, have not been met during the pandemic and that CMHCs staff and other caregivers have been impacted.

Eligibility

Community Mental Health Centers, including state and local government-operated Community Mental Health Centers, as defined by Section 1913 (c) of the Public Health Services Act.

Applicants must provide documentation of certification or licensure as a CMHC from their state and/or accreditation from a nationally recognized accreditation organization in Attachment 1. Applicants who do not provide this documentation will be screened-out and not reviewed.

Award Information

Funding Mechanism: Grant

Anticipated Total Available Funding: $825,000,000

Anticipated Number of Awards: 165 to 825

Anticipated Award Amount

From $500,000 to $2,500,000 per year

Length of Project: Up to two years

Cost Sharing/Match Required: No

Proposed budgets cannot exceed from $500,000 to $2,500,000 in total costs (direct and indirect) in any year of the proposed project.

Research Funding

The federal government also supports most of the funded research conducted by scientists in the United States. Through the NIMH, which has a budget of around $1.5 billion, scholars have access to funding for developing new ideas and discoveries about mental illness. This support, however, has ideological underpinnings.

For the last several decades, the NIMH has moved toward prioritizing biomedical research, leaving psychosocial proposals largely under-supported (Teachman et al. 2019). Aligning itself with psychiatric-oriented and pharmaceutical interventions is a decision that minimizes the role of nonmedical psychological and sociological researchers in understanding mental illness. Government support and endorsement of biological sciences in mental health hinders our ability to see the links between human environments, social factors, and behaviors that form and define mental illness and disorders (Teachman et al. 2019).

The NIMH has further entrenched itself in biomedical research in the last decade in changes in its direction from funding clinical trials of new medications toward an emphasis on collecting neurobiological data associated with observable disorders (Goldfried 2016). The NIMH recognized that clinical trials of drugs that were linked to DSM categories may have helped relieve symptoms among some people with certain disorders, they contributed little to developing theories about the causes of those disorders. Now the NIMH is looking for neurobiological indicators of disorders without organizing symptoms within DSM boundaries or definitions. The new NIMH approach is more consistent with earlier research that shows that symptoms do not necessarily cluster according to DSM boundaries. This orientation, however, remains psychiatry-centered and has left many clinical psychologists concerned that biologically reductionistic theories will come to dominate their field. Future generations of clinical therapists may have more understanding of the body, but less knowledge about interpersonal relationships, social environments, individuals' coping skills, and clinical skills in fostering individual growth among therapy patients (Goldfried 2016).

Parity

A funding problem that has persisted for several years is **parity** in the support provided to behavioral health and medical-surgical care. Insurance products have not always provided coverage for mental health and addiction treatments. At the root of the problem were the high costs of treating mental illness compared to med-surg care and that outcomes of psychiatric and psychological interventions are more difficult to measure, which means that insurance companies could not determine if the treatments they were paying for were effective. Between 1946 and the mid-1960s, most people who were in talk therapy, or psychotherapy, were treated by psychoanalytic treatment, a Freudian approach that typically required years of therapy but had few if any measurable outcomes to assess its effectiveness. Because the duration of psychoanalysis is usually long, it is very expensive. The technique requires extensive sessions for the analyst to form a deep understanding of the ideographic nature of each individual client.

The first significant broad-based coverage of mental health treatment began in 1961 when President Kennedy required federal government insurance issuers to provide behavioral health benefits to government employees. As more companies made these benefits available to the public, the lack of parity between behavioral health and med-surg coverage was evident, and a movement began in the 1970s to influence policymakers to require equity in how the two types of benefits were constructed. The **Mental Health Parity and Addiction Equity Act** of 2008 (MHPAEA) was the first major step toward parity and was designed to end discriminatory health care practices against individuals with mental health or addiction problems. The MHPAEA required insurance products not only to include behavioral health benefits but also to ensure that access and funding schedules were the same as those for med-surg benefits. For example, co-pays and maximum treatments were expected to be equal.

Despite the mandates set by the MHPAEA, disparity has persisted. Berry and colleagues (2015) compared insurance policies offered in two states in 2013 and 2014 and found that while most products provided parity in mental health and med-surg benefits, one in four did not. In these cases, there were significant inconsistencies in funding rates, out-of-pocket expenses, the process in which authorization for services is given, and limits on treatment.

Because of these problems, additional regulations were passed to assure compliance with MHPAEA. Among them were the Affordable Care Act, which required parity, and in 2021, federal rules were initiated to require companies to create a detailed analysis of how their products conform to parity expectations.

From the discussion thus far in this chapter, you can seed that crafting mental health policies is subject to intense political debates. Box 14.2 shows an example of policy-making "gone wrong."

Box 14.2 Politics and Mental Health

In 2002, George W. Bush launched the New Freedom Conference that was charged with addressing the President's goal of eliminating disparity in mental health care. Bush recognized that social factors such as stigma, unfair treatment limitations and financial restraints, and fragmented services created barriers to effective treatment. He tasked the conference with creating a plan to address these barriers and create new standards for publicly supported mental health programs. The conference generated 19 recommendations for improving services in the nation:

1. Advance and implement a national campaign to reduce the stigma of seeking care and a national strategy for suicide prevention.
2. Address mental health with the same urgency as physical health.
3. Develop an individualized plan of care for every adult with a serious mental illness and child with a serious emotional disturbance.
4. Involve consumers and families in orienting the mental health system and facilitating recovery.
5. Align federal programs to improve access and accountability for mental health services.
6. Create a Comprehensive State Mental Health Plan.
7. Protect and enhance the rights of people with mental illnesses.
8. Improve access to culturally competent mental health care.
9. Improve access to quality care in rural areas.
10. Promote children's mental health.
11. Improve and expand school mental health programs.
12. Screen for mental health comorbidity with substance use disorders and integrate services.
13. Screen for mental disorders across the life cycle in primary health care settings and connect to services when warranted.
14. Accelerate research to promote prevention, resilience, and recovery.

(Continued)

Box 14.2 Politics and Mental Health *(Continued)*

15. Advance evidence-based practices and disseminate research through public-private partnerships.
16. Improve and expand the workforce providing evidence-based mental health services.
17. Develop the knowledge base in four understudied areas: mental health disparities, long-term effects of medications, trauma, and acute care.
18. Use health technology and telehealth to improve access and coordination of mental health care, especially in remote areas and among underserved populations.
19. Develop and implement integrated electronic health records and personal information systems.

While a good idea on the surface, the details of the New Freedom initiative were criticized across the political spectrum, and the mental health community was divided; some lauded the plan while others deemed it short-sighted and redundant, comparing it to a similar plan created earlier by the Carter administration. One criticism from mental health professionals was that the plan overly relied on psychotropic medications and ignored other needs of many seriously ill people.

When Bush was governor of Texas, the state created a prototype program on which the New Freedom initiative was based. That program was accused of allowing pharmaceutical companies power in designing and operating the state's mental health plan, and that charge was born out. The details of the program showed that the treatment plans relied heavily on expensive patented (not generic) medicines whose benefits were questionable and side effects were potentially life-threatening (Lenzer 2004).

The problems surfaced when a whistleblower reported that people associated with the program in Texas had received kickbacks from the pharmaceutical companies. Officials overseeing the medication plan, the Texas Medication Algorithm Project, were being paid by drug companies to switch many patients from low-cost psychotropic drugs to new medicines that were 10 times more expensive and known to have serious side effects. One company was accused of pressuring the state to prescribe a drug off-label, which means to prescribe an FDA-approved drug for an unapproved use.

The whistleblower was told to stop the investigation into the government's actions. He was later fired from his job.

Mental Health and the Law

The law has a twofold interest regarding mental health. First, the law works to protect and maintain social order, the populace, and property. Its second interest is the protection of mentally ill individuals. Based on this premise, laws related to mental illness follow two directions: to allow mentally ill defendants to use their illness as an excuse for criminal behavior, and to allow the state to suspend the civil rights of individuals whose illness poses a threat to themselves and others.

What Is Insanity?

The term "**insanity**" is not used often in this text because it is neither a psychiatric nor sociological term. Insanity refers to a legal status of defendants who may have a mental defect that compromises their ability to be responsible and accountable for their behavior.

Insanity is an important concept in law because it can be used as a legal defense of a criminal behavior. The law holds a degree of tolerance for individuals who commit an offense while psychologically incapacitated, but as a defense strategy, insanity is not frequently used nor is it often effective. The insanity defense is employed in less than one percent of all arrests and is successful in about 25 percent of those cases (Perlin 1996). It is also highly controversial because many of the most horrifying and news-worthy crimes are committed by people whose mental well-being is questionable. Adding to the problem is that there is no national standard in the United States for declaring a person insane. States and the federal government have their own definitions and operationalizations of insanity.

Three questions lie at the heart of insanity defense. Will offenders benefit from punishment? Did offenders have control of their actions at the time of their crimes? Also, when the offense occurred, were defenders able to understand or comprehend criminal intent? This last question is often the most debated because it requires defendants to prove (a) they could not distinguish society's standards of right and wrong, (b) they will not repeat the offense, or (c) they did not comprehend the consequences of their actions.

Four Types of Insanity Defense

Different types of insanity defense strategies are allowed by state and federal law in the United States. Insanity pleas and defenses are accepted in courts in all jurisdictions except Idaho, Kansas, Montana, and Utah, and they follow one of the following four sets of standards.

The M'Naghten Rule. Sometimes known as the "right-wrong" test, the **M'Naghten defense** dates to 1843 England and the case of Daniel M'Naghten who attempted to murder Robert Peel, the British Prime Minister, but killed Peel's assistant instead. M'Naghten attacked the prime minister because he believed that Peel was trying to kill him and that he was acting to save his own life. M'Naghten's counsel argued their client was psychotic and experiencing paranoid delusions. The court accepted this explanation of M'Naghten's behavior and found him innocent by reason of insanity. As a precedent-setting case, excusing individuals from criminal responsibility because of psychiatric impairment came to be known as the M'Naghten Rule.

The M'Naghten defense is based on the cognitive abilities of defendants and whether they were aware of their actions. For success, clients must be influenced and impaired by a verifiable mental defect, schizophrenia for example, and that they did not comprehend the nature of their criminal act as right or wrong. One indication that might establish defendants' perception of right or wrong is their behavior following the criminal incident. Perpetrators who call police or medical personnel to respond to their own criminal act are functioning cognitively differently than those who flee and attempt to avoid detection or capture. The former, it could be argued, did not perceive their behavior as wrong and exposed themselves to arrest, whereas those who resist capture are assumed to know that their behavior violated social standards of right and wrong.

The M'Naghten rule, or a modified version of it, is used by about half of the US states.

Impulse Insanity Defense. Often known as the **irresistible impulse insanity defense**, this strategy is not recognized by most US states or federal law. With its emphasis on cognitive awareness, it resembles the M'Naghten rule. In addition to the cognitive standard, the impulse insanity defense also allows for defendants to contend that they may have understood their behavior to be wrong but that they could not control their impulse to commit the act. This rule is considered laxer than M'Naghten, and therefore it is usually more successful when applied in a court of law.

Substantial Capacity Test. Prior to the 1980s, the **substantial capacity test** was recognized by about half of the states and the US federal government. In this defense, defendants must have a mental defect, lack substantial capacity to understand right from wrong, and cannot appreciate the criminality of their behavior or conform to society's expectations under the law. Also known as the Model Penal Code rule, it is used in 20 states in the United States.

The word "substantial" is key. This defense allows for defendants to argue they have a substantial, but not total, loss in capability to understand the law and right from wrong. Because the word "appreciate" is used to operationalize insanity in this case, this defense allows defendants to enter their emotional state, character, or personality traits as evidence of their insanity.

The substantial capacity test, however, was sharply criticized after it was successfully used in defense of John Hinckley who attempted to assassinate President Reagan and three others in 1981. Since the shooting was witnessed on national television, Hinckley's guilt was not in question. The explanations of his behavior, on the other hand, were contentious. His attorneys argued an insanity defense based on his inability to resist an impulse to shoot the president. Rather than arguing that Hinckley suffered from a mental deficiency that affected his cognitive ability to determine right from wrong, a M'Naghten strategy, his defense focused on the claim that he had a flawed personality centered on obsessiveness, which obfuscated his ability to control his behavior. Hinckley was found guilty by reason of insanity and sentenced to institutional care in a psychiatric hospital.

The verdict was met with considerable enmity and resentment from officials and the public, and mounting social pressure led Congress to pass the **Insanity Defense Reform Act** in 1984, which initiated several changes in the rules of putting forward an insanity defense. The new law forced the burden of proof of insanity on the defense where previously the government had to establish insanity (the burden of proof still falls on the government in 11 states). It also restricted expert witnesses' testimonies. Witnesses for both the defense and prosecution were no longer allowed to testify as to the sanity of a defendant; they could only report their assessment of the defendant's mental faculties. The law also created a verdict of "guilty by reason of insanity" (Bonnie et al. 2008). The act led to the federal government and many states to drop the substantial capacity test in favor of the more restrictive M'Naghten rule, and it was at that time that Idaho, Montana, and Utah abandoned the insanity plea altogether.

The Durham Rule. The last insanity defense is called the **Durham Rule**. This is an uncommon defense used only in New Hampshire. Under Durham, a criminal act is excused if it is a product of a mental defect or disease. No medical diagnosis of mental illness or disorder is necessary, however. The Durham Rule is very broad in that it allows all mental health problems to be considered in explaining a criminal act. Despite its wide-ranging scope, the defense is usually successful only in the most serious cases of psychopathology in which clear and convincing evidence in given to show that the mental problem caused the criminal act.

Implications of Insanity Verdicts. Having been found insane does not mean that defendants are exonerated from their crimes and released back into society. The common outcome of a guilty verdict is that the person is found guilty by reason of insanity and rather than sentenced to a prison for the general criminal population, the defendant is assigned to a secured medical facility designed to house and support mentally ill persons.

Proving insanity is not often a cut-and-dry process. Judges and juries often must sort through conflicting and subjective assessments by mental health professionals called by the prosecution and the defense. Via mass media and political rhetoric, social pressure in high profile cases can affect how those reports are interpreted, as the case of Reagan's assassination attempt demonstrated.

Social forces centered around insanity cases also influence how mentally ill persons are treated even if they are not part of the case. A noteworthy study from Germany (Angermeyer and Matschinger 1996) explored how insanity defenses shape stereotypes of mentally ill persons by studying a high-profile case where media coverage was extensive. These researchers studied the aftermath of an assassination attempt on a prominent German politician by a schizophrenically ill attacker and found that people maintained more social distance from severely mentally ill persons than before the attack. Two years afterward, people maintained more social distance from people with a psychotic disorder than before the assassination attempt. Interestingly, no differences were found in attitudes and behaviors toward people with depression.

The ethnorace and gender of defendants also influence whether they are deemed mentally incapacitated. Dirks-Linhorst (2014) researched all not guilty by reason of insanity (NGRI) acquittals in Missouri over a 30-year period and found stark differences between men and women defendants. Women NGRI acquittees differed from men along the following lines:

- Women were more likely married.
- Women were less likely diagnosed with schizophrenia, but more likely had a diagnosis of depression.

- Men had more substance use and diagnoses of substance use disorder.
- Women were more likely diagnosed with borderline personality disorder.
- Women were more likely charged with murder and arson (22 percent of women's NGRIs were in murder cases).
- Men had higher probabilities of charges of burglary, sex offenses, and robbery.
- Men were more likely to have had a prior felony offense.
- African American women acquittees tended to be younger and more likely diagnosed with schizophrenia.

The different characteristics and outcomes of women who were acquitted by reason of insanity reflect differences in how judges (all such cases were decided by judges in Missouri) perceived defendants by their gender. It is possible that the judges believed that women would benefit from therapy and rehabilitation rather than confinement and that women posed less of a risk to society than men (Dirks-Linhorst 2014).

Insanity rules have come under criticism from scholars who contend that focusing on cognitive and intellectual functioning is contrary to how moral decisions are really made. Contemporary neuroscientific and behavioral studies have identified the significance of emotions in making decisions. The argument is that moral decisions are not made solely by cognitive neuropsychological processes. Rather, emotions are core elements in decision making and often guide cognitive brain functions. Emotions are motivational states that facilitate how a person thinks about environmental stimuli. They help individuals prioritize and organize behavior to meet the demands of a situation or environmental context (Coppola 2019). As Coppola states, it is old-fashioned and outdated to believe that emotions are simple responses that stem from primitive parts of the brain, namely the limbic system and the amygdala, whereas cognition is situated in the more complex prefrontal cortex.

Brain scientists now know that emotions are also connected to neocortical, orbitofrontal cortex, and ventromedial prefrontal cortex regions of the brain (Coppola 2019). Cognitive functions such as decision-making, learning and memory are no longer believed separate from emotions. Cognitions are, instead, bonded with emotions and cannot function independently (Johnston and Olson 2015).

Considering this understanding, many scholars believe that insanity rules of defense that are solely grounded in the evaluation of cognitive functioning and are dismissive of emotional functioning are shortsighted in terms of the physiology of mental illness and psychosocial determinants of behavior.

Civil Commitment

Civil commitment is a legal intervention in which the state can suspend the civil rights of an individual if a judge or other legal authority determines that person poses a risk of danger to self and others. All states have standards for determining grounds for involuntary holding a person. In general, the primary criterion is an imminent risk of violence.

No national data exist on how many people are subject to involuntary psychiatric holds; however, two studies have examined statistics on the state level. In Virginia, civil commitment orders numbered 13,176 in 2015, which was about a seven percent increase from 2010 (Allen and Bonnie 2015). Counting civil commitments in eight states (California, Texas, Virginia, Florida, Massachusetts, Colorado, Connecticut, and Vermont), Lee and Cohen (2019) reported just under one-half million people were detained on emergency orders annually in 2013, 2014, and 2015. Extrapolating those numbers to the national population, Lee and Cohen estimated that roughly 1.4 million people each year are held in involuntary custodial care each year. We can conclude that civil commitments are not uncommon judicial practices.

Essentially, a civil commitment is the suspension of an individual's civil rights. By judicial decision that must follow the US constitution's tenets on due process, individuals who have a severe mental illness and meet a state's criteria for confinement may be coerced into temporary hospitalization. No state allows the courts to confine a person involuntarily solely on the grounds of having a mental disorder. Three other criteria are used for legal confinement, however, and the states vary in which of these are legal in their jurisdictions: inability of individuals to provide their basic needs, the need to force treatment to prevent further deterioration, and dangerousness to self or others. States also set different rules for the initial period of court-ordered commitment. Some are 14 days, others up to six months; however, the law requires that individuals have the right to a court hearing within 10 days of their commitment. States allow for different people to initiate a civil commitment: any adult may do so in some states but only a physician has that authority in others. Family members, mental health program administrators, and social workers can initiate commitment proceedings under some state laws.

Of the three commitment criteria, the perception of dangerousness is the most important. Imminent violence has only recently served as the core criterion for civil commitment, which represents an ideological change in American policy over the last century (Markowitz 2011). Prior to the early 1900s, civil commitment rules were not as stringent as today's laws and proceedings. In those days, family members and civil authorities could have individuals confined against their will because of any mental state. The primary grounds for justifying involuntary commitment in those days were curative care, control, and relieving the stress a mentally ill person places on families and communities (Markowitz 2011). In the middle to late 1800s, however, several individuals filed lawsuits challenging their involuntary confinement, which led states to tighten their rules and establish more judicially sound protocols in hopes of reducing wrongful commitments.

In 1951, the NIMH issued guidelines to regulate confinements. The **Draft Act Governing Hospitalization of the Mentally Ill** specified that physicians must be involved in deciding if a person's mental health and behavior warrant coerced confinement and hospitalization. The rules also allowed law enforcement officials to initiate detention and emergency treatment. However, the guidelines stated that individuals must be medically certified as mentally ill and that they have the right to a hearing for confinement to continue past the immediate emergency, which is usually 72 hours. After another series of lawsuits claiming unlawful detainment, the guidelines evolved further so that by 1980, the primary stipulation for forced psychiatric confinement was perceived risk of imminent violence to self and others (SAMHSA 2019b).

Clearly civil commitments have a long history of controversy. The "pros" and "cons" of involuntary hospitalization pit arguments of need for treatment against civil liberties. The argument in favor of hospitalization is a utilitarian one that contends that treatment of potentially violent persons protects the public and the individual from violence (Catalano and McConnell 1996). This position is parallel to quarantining people with infectious diseases, and some research supports this position. Catalano and McConnell (1996) found that on the day after the incidence of involuntary confinement increased in San Francisco, fewer assault and battery charges were reported in the city. The study suggests that the quarantine hypothesis is effective in reducing assaults by people with serious mental illness.

On the "con" side, the argument is that legal and psychiatric procedures are not sufficient to predict violent behavior and therefore states should not suspend a person's rights and civil freedoms. Furthermore, forced detention stigmatizes people with mental illness and subjects them to additional civil commitments. Phelan and Link (1998) reported that stigma against mentally ill persons increased dramatically between 1950 and 1996 because of a rise in people thinking that mental illness is associated with violence. These authors attribute this relationship between stigma and violent attributes of mental illness to changes in the law that stipulate dangerousness as the primary criterion for civil commitment.

An unintentional consequence of the dangerousness criterion of involuntary hospitalization is that it provides access to care for some mentally ill persons, but not others (Testa and West 2010). For seriously mentally ill persons, hospitalization often provides their initial access to treatment. Committing a crime allows those individuals to receive care whereas the majority of severely ill people who are not dangerous do not have that opportunity. Unfortunately, the nondangerous group may have to wait for their conditions to devolve further before care is provided for them.

The dangerousness criterion also has the effect of further marginalizing severely mentally ill persons. Because of deinstitutionalization and the strict rules on involuntary hospitalization, seriously ill individuals are often restricted to unsafe and difficult living circumstances. Many are forced into homelessness or dwell in substandard housing, while many others are arrested and jailed. Controlling for circumstances, people with mental illness are more likely to be arrested than nonmentally ill. Jail, ironically, may provide services that were not available in the community (Testa and West 2010).

Another issue with the dispensation of civil commitment concerns the relationship between ethnorace and involuntary confinement. Public perceptions hold that African Americans and Hispanics are more disposed to violence than Whites. Studies also suggest that clinicians tend to expect violence from non-Whites and underestimate Whites' violence even though Whites' and non-Whites' rates of violence are similar (Hicks 2004). Compared to Whites, African Americans are more likely to be brought to emergency rooms by the police, and Blacks seeking care in emergency rooms are more likely involuntarily committed (Perlin and Cucolo 2017).

Although Whites and Blacks experience psychotic disorders and schizophrenia at roughly the same rates when controlling for social class, Blacks are more likely to be subject to involuntary hospitalizations. Perlin and Cucolo (2017) provide four reasons for this difference in treatment. First, Blacks are more likely to be misdiagnosed and over diagnosed with schizophrenia and other psychotic disorders. Second, Blacks' behavior is more likely to interpreted as violent than similar behavior by Whites. Third, Blacks often receive their initial treatment for psychosis later than Whites, which means that Blacks often present more severe symptoms at emergency rooms. Lastly, African Americans are also more likely to be delivered to hospitals by the police, which may influence whether they are involuntarily confined since law enforcement officers are typically called when an alleged crime has been committed.

Consequently, Blacks are disproportionately placed in involuntary hospitalization. Forensic mental health evaluators are less likely to deem African Americans responsible for their behavior than Whites even when comparing individuals in comparable social class positions and with similar criminal record (Perry et al. 2013). Although people are usually more sympathetic toward individuals who have little control over their illness, the deviant or criminal label is particularly powerful when White forensic psychiatrists are evaluating African American and Hispanic defendants (Corrigan et al. 2003). This dynamic may explain why in forensic settings, Blacks are diagnosed with schizophrenia at a rate of three to four times that of Whites (Blow et al. 2004).

Gender stereotypes further influence determinants of dangerousness (Perlin and Cucolo 2017). Stereotypes of women as weak and passive may encourage others to see their behavior as less dangerous and threatening. Women, believed to be more emotional than men, as discussed in Chapter 7, are also thought to have a better chance of benefiting from treatment. Women's behavior is usually interpreted as less threatening. Consequently, women are less likely ordered into civil confinement.

Criminalization of the Mentally Ill

Mentally ill individuals have a higher chance of being arrested, but that does not mean they are more violent. They are arrested because their mental illness places them in positions and situations in which arrest is probable, a dynamic often called the **criminalization of mental illness**. It is widely believed that mentally ill people have proportionately higher arrest rates because deinstitutionalization has released people who are inherently violent and unable to follow social rules to live on the streets and run amok.

This scenario is partially true. Following their release from institutions, mentally ill people receive few compensatory or parallel services to what they obtained in the hospitals.

In addition to being cut adrift from services and a place to live, they are met with stigma against mental illness, especially fears of violence. Stereotypical expectations that mentally disturbed people are unpredictable and dangerous lead people to be less tolerant of mentally ill individuals and more willing to call the police when perceived to be threatened.

Police, however, often have little choice in making an arrest. Treatment centers or residential facilities that will perhaps accept severely mentally ill offenders are often not available (Watson and Angell 2007). Substance abuse facilities commonly refuse to accept abusers who have a dual diagnosis, and emergency rooms may be unwilling to accept mental illness cases because they are not sufficiently sick or dangerous enough for a civil commitment. With nowhere else to take them, police officers, therefore, must arrest and jail mentally ill offenders (Hiday and Ray 2017).

After the arrest, the criminal justice system acts more swiftly to incarcerate mentally ill people than those who are not disordered (Hiday and Ray 2017). When they are released, most go to poor and socially disorganized neighborhoods with few material or social resources. With no place to go and nothing to do, mentally ill people are subject to further arrests for what are sometimes called nuisance crimes such as disorderly conduct, trespassing, and shoplifting.

Research by Hiday and Wales (2011; 2013) shows that most people with severe mental illness who encounter the police and criminal justice system fall into one of five categories or types, which are shown in Table 14.1.

TABLE 14.1 Five Patterns of Offender Groups Among Severely Mentally Ill

"Illness Only Group"	
Fits the stereotype of "crazed madman"	Severely mentally ill
Small in number, but most noticed	Low capacity for judgment
Commits serious crimes	Not amenable to treatment

"No-Place-to-Go Group"	
Marginal and Poor	Minor "nuisance" offenses: e.g., loitering
Behaviors not considered criminal if enacted by nondisordered persons	Services could improve their situation

"Survival Group"	
Also marginal and poor	Commit survival crimes: e.g., shoplifting food
Would benefit from services	

"Substance Abuse Group"	
Severely mental ill and co-morbid with substance abuse	Have few personal resources
Regular users of detox facilities, hospitals, services emergency shelters, jails	Seldom receive adequate treatment or social

"Criminal Thinking Group"	
Not suitable for diversion programs or likely to benefit from treatment	Diagnoses: Sociopathy and personality disorders; but legally not insane

Source: Hiday and Wales (2011; 2013).

Illness Only Group

This group describes the stereotype of the crazed maniacal psychotic who is out of control and commits serious crimes. Although small in number, they are highly noticed and routinely portrayed in crime drama television shows and movies, which may add to the perception that most severely mental ill people fit this description. For those in this group, mental illness is causative—their mental illness causes their crimes. Subject to hallucinations and delusions, these individuals have a low capacity for judgment, have trouble regulating their behavior and emotions, and do not respond well to treatment.

No-Place-to-Go Group

Severely mentally ill persons in this group are poor and live on society's margins. They commit relatively minor nuisance crimes such as loitering in shopping malls and trespassing on the properties of fast-food restaurants. These people, having nothing to do, are often found in public areas and thought to be menacing. Most of their crimes are trivial and would not warrant an arrest if perpetrated by a non-disordered person. People in this category would benefit from appropriate services and treatment programs.

Survival Group

People in this group are also marginal and poor and commit survival crimes: shoplifting food, clothing, and health care items. Stealing is their only means for acquiring those things that are necessary for living. This group would also be responsive to services.

Substance Abuse Group

People in this offender group are diagnosed with severe mental illness and a substance abuse problem. Without suitable treatment resources, they drift from one facility to another. Their comorbidity makes them regular clients of local detox facilities, hospitals, emergency shelters, and jails; however, they seldom receive services adequate to resolve their substance abuse or deal with their mental illness.

Criminal Thinking Group

The last group includes individuals who are not suitable for diversion or treatment programs. These individuals are diagnosed with sociopathy and personality disorders, conditions that are usually resistant to treatment. These disorders are associated with higher rates of criminal behavior, but in most jurisdictions, especially those that are guided by stricter M'Naghten Rules, they are not grounds for insanity rulings. They may be highly disordered individuals and their conditions may impact their moral judgments, but legally they are not insane.

There are three key takeaways to the five types of mentally ill arrestees. First, offenders with severe mental illness are not one dimensional. There are significant differences among them. Second, severe mental illness is neither necessary nor sufficient to account for law-breaking behavior by most persons with mental illness. And third, of all offenses committed by people with mental disorders, the illness itself is accounts for a small minority of cases (Hiday and Wales 2013). The largest group of severely mentally ill people commit no crimes, and those individuals have stable housing, social and personal supports in place, and access to quality health care.

About the Quote

James Hillman (Hillman and Ventura 1993: 3) once wrote, "We've had a hundred years of analysis, and people are getting more and more sensitive, and the world is getting worse and worse." The same could be said about public policy. Rothman's quote points to the frustration of the seemingly endless stream of "great new ideas" that are touted to care for the mentally ill in America. Politicians often come up with programs that claim to be the next "big thing," but the enthusiasm seems to fizzle out after the initial excitement wanes. Sometimes, as in the case in the New Freedom conference, they end in scandal or, as Rothman states, disaster.

Despite all the mental health training, research, treatments, and governmental initiatives, mental health problems persist and seem to worsen as time marches on. All these interventions have one thing in common: they fail to address the fundamental causes of psychological distress. One theme of this textbook is that too often our society takes a reductionistic approach to mental illness. Mental illness is solely viewed as an individual problem caused by characteristics of the person. Sociologists argue that while that may be the origins of mental illness among some people, it is not true for all. Failing to address macro-level and social contextual conditions and their role in creating mental health problems, other interventions are not likely to result in a change in the rate of mental illness in society.

DISCUSSION QUESTIONS

1. Because the physiology of the brain is such that cognitive processes and emotions are inseparable, what are the possible implications for insanity defense rules? Is the M'Naghten Rule sufficiently comprehensive? How would a new insanity rule look if emotions were considered in assessing a defendant's mental capacity to bear responsibility for a crime?

2. How are insanity pleas and involuntary commitments political? What ways are political interests and ideologies expressed in these two legal actions?

3. Is perceived danger to self and others sufficient grounds for mandating mental health treatment? Given current policy, how could differences between civil rights matters and the need for treatment be reconciled? Should changes in the policy be made? Why or why not?

KEY TERMS

Affordable Care Act 331
Block Grant 325
Civil Commitment 340
Community Mental Health Act 328
Community Mental Health Centers 328
Draft Act Governing Hospitalization of the Mentally Ill 341
Durham Rule 339
Insanity 337
Insanity Defense Reform Act 338
Irresistible Impulse Insanity Defense 338
Lanterman-Petris-Short Act 329
M'Naghten Defense 337
Mental Health Parity and Addiction Equity Act 334
Mental Health Systems Act 329
National Mental Health Act 328
Parity 334
Public Policy 324
Soft money 332
Substantial Capacity Test 338

Epilogue

Rather than a quote to start this last unit of the text, let me recount a famous story by sociologist Irving Zola. His tale is about a cardiologist commenting on heart disease, but it is fitting for mental health as well.

You know, sometimes it feels like this. There I am standing by the shore of a swiftly flowing river, and I hear the cry of a drowning man. So, I jump into the river, put my arms around him, pull him to shore and apply artificial respiration. Just when he begins to breathe, there is another cry for help. So, I jump into the river, reach him, pull him to shore, apply artificial respiration, and then just as he begins to breathe, another cry for help. So back in the river again, reaching, pulling, applying, breathing, and then another yell. Again and again, without end, goes the sequence. You know, I am so busy jumping in, pulling them to shore, applying artificial respiration, that I have no time to see who is upstream pushing them all in (cited in McKinlay 1975/2019).

Zola's story is a great allegory for describing how sociologists think of the fundamental causes of mental illness. Our society spends voluminous resources dealing with the immediacy of mental illness, but we rarely take the time to look beyond individual cases to see what social connections they may have. As we have shown in this text, the social context of mental illness underlies all aspects of mental illness. Something "upstream" is indeed throwing people into the river of psychological pain.

Our core values of individualism guide us to reduce mental illness to psychological or biological factors. In this way of thinking, people are responsible for their own well-being; so if there is a problem, it is due to the individual's own constitution or life choices. Thinking in this way makes it impossible to see that social forces such as inequality, discrimination, gendered relations and status differentials, and neighborhood conditions affect mental health. Furthermore, it is hard to believe that people rationally choose to be mentally ill or that physiology alone explains mental problems, especially given the volumes of data that point us to connecting individuals' psychological well-being to the social conditions of their lives.

The social patterns of mental illness that we have described in this text are hardly serendipitous. They exist because somewhere "upstream," social conditions are generating disproportionally more risk among some groups and individuals than others. These people are being "pushed in" somewhere up the river long before they appear to therapists, psychiatrists, or the criminal justice system. As we have discussed, stress accumulates over time, but little is done about the conditions that instigate that stress. Poverty, sexism, racism, and insecure neighborhoods are just a few of the macro-level antecedents to psychological distress and illness.

We have focused on how the social environment creates long-term and severe stressors that can lead to emotional, cognitive, and behavioral problems among individuals. For many people, their psychological problems are a consequence of their social environments failing to protect them or provide an emotionally sound and cognitively stimulating atmosphere in which they can prosper mentally.

Sociological factors cannot explain all psychological problems, however. There are many pathways into distress and mental illness. It's possible that biological factors account for some cases of anxiety and depression and probably most bipolar disorders and schizophrenia diagnoses. Even in these cases social factors play a role in the progression of the disorders. The failure to provide safe treatment venues for severely mentally ill people, for example, is an indication of the collective's unwillingness to help treat and protect the most vulnerable. Jail is not an adequate substitution for therapeutic and restorative residential care.

After reading this text, you may see more clearly why defining mental illness is difficult. Defining something that exists but has few identifiable features that exactly separate it from a "normal" state is indeed a challenge. In some ways, the best people can say is that they know mental illness when they see it. What they are seeing, however, is a function of a social dynamic of perceived normalcy, which itself is influenced by cultural values and norms and ethnorace, gender, age, and social class. These filters alter the rules of classifying mental illness because they affect how people understand what is normal and acceptable. In the end, the sociological approach that mental illness is deviant behavior not otherwise explained remains a sound way to approach the phenomenon. This perspective allows us to understand that variances in diagnostics are rooted in social processes. Furthermore, labeling as an illness behavior that may not be framed as normal also comes into focus. When individuals deviate and do not conform to some behavioral standard, it is easier to label that behavior as an illness rather than to confront social dynamics that may precede the behavior.

In short, in the absence of biological markers that confirm diagnoses, social dynamics rise to the surface of the diagnostic process. Without conclusive biological data, presuming that abnormal behavior is an illness is a value judgment rooted in individualism, power politics of psychopharmacology, and the lack of willingness to change the fundamental cause of many cases of psychological problems—inequality, abusive behavior toward others, alienation, and exploitation.

The social structure creates barriers that prevent individuals from acquiring mental health. First, the lack of control over one's life is a significant point of origin of many psychological problems. Inequality makes mastery of one's own environment, a key dimension of mental well-being, difficult to achieve. When a person makes little money in an insecure job or is over-managed at work, for example, self-determination is less likely. Second, social resources are important for promoting mental health. Emotional and tangible resources are affected by status position in the social organization. Neighborhoods are important sources of social capital, but when disadvantaged neighborhoods are ignored by society-at-large, then young people are left to their own devices to find personal power, self-esteem, and a sense of belongingness. Many times, their only avenues to these mental health essentials are through associating with other alienated individuals and engaging in violence and drug use. Sometimes they simply give up because they cannot see how education will benefit them and conventional jobs are not available. These children fail to utilize their talents and their psychological well-being suffers. Even in high income neighborhoods, some children, while they may have materially and socially privileged parents and social networks, also face alienation. Their privilege may evolve into narcissism because they are led to believe they are entitled to social advantages. Their families may be so overly involved in acquiring wealth and enhancing their public personas that they neglect their children's emotional and developmental needs. Narcissistic adults do not usually make good parents. Third, access to mental health services is critical. While many disadvantaged people can receive mental health services, there are limits. Insurance inequality plays a role, and services for severely disturbed people are insufficient. Homelessness and crime could be greatly reduced if society provided care for people who are most in need. Lastly, social perceptions of mentally ill people tell us that people who are "diagnosable" are threatening, untrustworthy, violent, and unpredictable, when they are not. Stigma is rooted in perceptions of challenges to what is considered normal. These beliefs affect distressed individuals' willingness to discuss their problems or even admit to themselves that they have a problem. Stigma, by definition, is a hostile social environment for people who are having psychological troubles.

Sociologists would say that identifying the sources of what Summerfield called "social suffering" in Chapter 13 is just as important as specifying a gene or neurotransmitter associated with mental illness. The sociological question as to why our society prefers to focus on individual factors rather social ones is an important one.

Social experience is of immense significance for understanding the mental health of individuals and groups (Turner and Lloyd 1995), and not attending to that experience is an indication of the failure to employ the sociological imagination. Having read this text, it is my hope that your ability to connect the substance of a person's life to the attributes of their social context is heightened and that your curiosity is ignited to learn more.

One way to begin thinking about this is to ask this simple question: Do people *have* a mental disorder, or *are* they mentally disordered? The nuanced change in the verb is important. Saying people have a disorder is in step with the medical model discourse. It suggests something that was acquired. In this thinking, there must be a discrete objectified something that a person gets, as in one gets depression.

The second way of thinking, however, is that people's mental health is a function of their continuous interaction with their surroundings. In this view, mental health is a consequence of a dynamic exchange with the social environment. People *become* mentally ill as opposed to *having* an illness. Mental illness unfolds in response to persistent stress that leaves people feeling out of control, unsure of themselves, powerless, and alienated. For some, there may be an interaction with biological presets that cause these stressors to manifest in certain ways. And for others, the biological factors may react to the environmental stress. What we know for certain, is that for every person who sees themselves as psychologically impaired, there is a narrative of suffering amid relationships that in some way is attached to the pain.

For all, however, mental illness is an ascribed status bestowed by agents of society. This status is subject to social rules, social definitions of deviance, and social responses.

Let's close with this metaphor. Imagine that you are an ichthyologist interested in studying the behavior of a particular species of fish. You sail into the ocean, catch a specimen of that fish, put it in aquarium, and record its behavior. But you soon notice that in this artificial environment, it does not do much. It swims around, eats when fed, but that's about it. From these observations, you cannot conclude anything significant about the true nature of this species.

The solution to this methodological problem lies in engaging the fish in its natural environment. To get more reliable and valid observations of the fish's behavior, you conclude that you must (literally) dive into the fish's natural habitat to study its relationship with other fish (predators, for example), the conditions of the water (temperature and pollutants), the behavior of the ocean (waves and tides), the food supply, and how it engages other fish of the same species (mating and protection). The ocean is the environmental context in which the fish lives. It is the dynamic between that environment and the fish that explains much of its behavior.

It is not terribly different in studying people. To thoroughly understand everyone's emotions, thoughts, and behavior, we should analyze their social surroundings and how they intersect with the individual. We must see a person's place in the social order and in history and what meaning that has for their psychological development. What that "ocean" does *to* and *for* us is vital to mental health.

Given the extraordinary stress that people are experiencing in the twenty-first century, the sociological imagination has never been more important.

Appendix 1: Glossary of Diagnostic Categories

Many conventionally recognized diagnostic labels have been used throughout this text to describe psychiatric symptoms. The intention of this glossary is not to replicate the DSM, but rather to give short descriptors of the terms so they make sense in the context in which they were used in the text. If you want to learn more, I encourage you to study further the conditions that interest you.

Agoraphobia

Agoraphobia is a type of anxiety disorder in which the individual fears places or situations that might cause panic and feelings of being trapped or helpless. In its extreme, the fear can prevent people from leaving home or even a room within their home.

Antisocial Personality Disorder (Sociopathy)

Less than four percent of people in the United States are believed to be sociopathic. This group, however, is frequently in the public eye because their behavior is often newsworthy. This disorder is characterized by antagonistic behavior in which little concern for the welfare of others is displayed. People with these traits are often known as sociopaths. They show no regard for right and wrong and are indifferent to the well-being of others. They rarely express guilt or remorse for their actions, which are often violent. Typically, sociopaths are impulsive law-breakers and have great difficulty conforming to normative social expectations.

Many sociopaths are high functioning individuals who are intelligent and charming. They use these qualities to manipulate, deceive, and take advantage of others. So-called low functioning sociopaths do not have these qualities. They are more likely to engage in coercion, intimidation, and violence to get what they want.

The cause of sociopathy is a much debated question. The psychological profile of sociopaths generally includes being victims of physical and sexual abuse and physical or emotional abandonment by their families. Most spent time in foster care or institutions for children. Violence is a central component in the lives of sociopathic people. There is also reason to believe that these life narratives may intersect with brain injuries and genetic predispositions to impulsivity. No gene has been associated with sociopathy; however, because it is common for adult sociopaths to have a near life-long history of violent and unconventional behavior, a genetic component is implied.

Anxiety

Anxiety is a common disorder that presents as excessive worry or fear that lasts six months or longer. Symptoms of generalized anxiety disorder include feeling restless or tense, being easily tired, difficulty concentrating, irritability, muscle tension and aches, difficulty controlling worries, sleep disturbances, and restlessness.

Avoidant Personality Disorder

This disorder, which occurs in about 1 percent of the US population, is characterized by extreme feelings of inadequacy and sensitivity to negative criticism. Friendships and intimate relationships are difficult for these individuals, as they are chronically isolated, emotionally and physically, from others.

Bipolar Disorder

Formerly known as manic-depression, bipolar disorders are a class of mental illness in which individuals experience shifts in mood and activity levels. The ability to concentrate and carry out activities of daily living is impaired. People diagnosed with bipolar disorder undergo dramatic mood changes, swinging from periods of energized elation, which can appear as irritability and/or high productivity and sociability, to periods of depression where they feel sad, hopeless, and apathetic.

The symptoms and severity of bipolar disorder, which affects about 2.5 percent of the US population, varies, but the condition usually worsens over time, especially if left untreated. The course of the disorder is also different in each person. Some people have frequent "ups and downs," whereas others may go years between episodes. Severe cases of bipolar episodes may include hallucinations and delusions, which is why there is occasional confusion in bipolar and schizophrenia diagnoses. Medications have proven to lessen the severity of the condition. Psychotherapy is also an effective intervention.

Borderline Personality Disorder

Borderline personality disorder (BPD) is chronic and persistent disorder in which a person experiences unstable moods and self-concept. People with BPD tend to see the world as extremes of good and bad and are quick to change their perceptions of other people around them. This process, known as splitting, is common to BPD in part because intense anger is one of the core traits of the borderline personality. They can suddenly change their relationships to other people, things, or ideas as they become enraged about some aspect of the target. Consequently, social relationships with other people are often unstable.

Specific symptoms of BPD include fear of abandonment and taking extreme action to avoid rejection. A history of emotionally intense relationships is common. At one moment's notice another person can shift from being idealized to being demonized. Self-identity is unstable, and paranoia is frequent. Risky behaviors, such as gambling, reckless sex, fighting, and drug abuse are also common. People with BPD are at risk for suicide.

Conduct Disorder

"Conduct disorder" is a term usually applied to children who persistently engage in antisocial behavior. These children ignore conventional social expectations of behavior and have difficulty with authority. Gross irresponsibility, lying, delinquency, stealing, violence against others and animals are common examples of the profile of a child labeled as conduct disordered. These behaviors are typically functions of chronic abuse, trauma, and other social problems. In some cases, physiological problems such as a damaged frontal lobe play a role in forming these behavioral patterns. Conduct disorder is the childhood form of antisocial personality disorder.

Dependent Personality Disorder

Dependent personality disorder is an anxiety-based condition in which people feel helpless and submissive. They believe they are not able to take care of themselves and therefore develop a strong reliance on other people to provide for them. They fear criticism, abandonment, and separation especially by those on whom they are dependent. The simplest of decisions is wrought with anxiety because of the lack of confidence in caring for themselves.

Depression

Perhaps the most frequently occurring mental health problem, depression affects people of all ages and can have serious consequences including suicide. Though there are several forms of depression, major depressive disorder is the most assigned diagnosis. Several symptoms encompass depression. These include long-lasting feelings of sadness, hopelessness, irritability, and guilt, loss of interest or pleasure in normal or usual activities, sleep and eating disturbances, fatigue, restlessness, trouble concentrating, thoughts about death, and psychosomatic complaints such as headaches and upset stomach.

To be diagnosed, these symptoms must have lasted at least two weeks and not fall within the bounds of socially expected reactions to grieving or a substantial loss.

Eating Disorders

Eating disorders are somewhat common and serious conditions that can be life-threatening. They present as severe and irregular eating behavior and distressed thoughts and emotions centered on body weight and shape. Symptoms of eating disorders include extreme thinness, odd eating behavior, fear of gaining weight, obsessiveness with being thin, and a distorted perception of one's body shape. Bulimia, anorexia nervosa, and binge-eating are the most common forms of eating disorders.

Exhibitionism

Exhibitionism is a form of paraphilia, which itself is a controversial term used to label perceived deviations from conventional sexual norms. Exhibitionism is defined as the urge, fantasy, or behavior of exposing genitals to unsuspecting strangers and becoming sexually aroused while doing so. Males are far more likely to commit exhibitionistic acts.

Frotteurism

One of eight paraphilias listed in DSM-V, frotteurism is touching or rubbing one's genitals against the body of a nonconsenting and often unaware person in a sexual manner. Such touching behavior stimulates sexual arousal and gratification. The condition is considered rare.

Impulse Control Disorders (ICD)

Impulse control disorders are a group of disorders characterized by excessive urges and harmful behaviors. ICDs are common conditions and include behaviors such as gambling, fire starting, stealing, and buying, among others that are judged as compulsive and pathological. For these behaviors to be classified as an ICD, a person must have difficulty resisting the impulses that lead to negative social, legal, and financial consequences.

Narcissistic Personality Disorder

Individuals with this chronic condition have a highly exaggerated sense of self-worth and entitlement, require excessive admiration, and take advantage of others to get what they want. At the same time, they can easily feel slighted or criticized. Narcissists typically have underlying feelings of shame and vulnerability.

Obsessive-Compulsive Personality Disorder

This personality disorder is characterized by a rigid focus on order, perfectionism, and self-control. Many people exhibiting these behaviors present as organized and successful; however, their preoccupation with rules, order, process, and organization eventually interfere with completing assignments and everyday tasks, which causes frustration among friends, family, and coworkers. Estimates suggest that two to eight percent of the population may meet the criteria for this disorder.

Oppositional Defiant Disorder

Oppositional defiant disorder is a pattern of behavior among children who are chronically argumentative, uncooperative, angry, and irritable. These children cannot easily control their tempers and frequently act vindictively. Children are labeled with this condition when their behavior interferes with normative role expectations in school, social activities, and family life.

Panic Disorder

A panic attack is a sudden and unexpected episode of intense fear that produces often severe physical reactions. Because they are unanticipated, panic attacks are often terrifying and often lead people to think they are having a heart attack or "going crazy." Physical symptoms include heart palpitations or accelerated heart rate, sweating, trembling, shortness of breath. Cognitive and emotional symptoms include feeling out of control, or a sensing an imminent catastrophe.

Personality Disorders

Personality disorders are a class of 10 mental health conditions in which a fixed or persistent pattern of cognitions, emotions, and behavior become dominant in a person's personality and cause distress or impairment. These patterns are rigid and negatively affect perceptions and interactions with other people. People with personality disorders usually have troubles in relationships, school, and work.

The disorder is often characterized by a dominant personality trait that forms the central hub of a person's personality. Examples include paranoia, histrionics, anger, and antisocial behavior.

Diagnosing personality disorders is sometimes subjective because individuals labeled with such a disorder often refuse to accept that anything is wrong with them. People with narcissistic personality disorder, for instance, are often successful occupationally and publicly admired, though their personal "backstage" behavior causes stress in other people.

Phobia-Related Disorders

A phobia is an intense fear of—or aversion to—specific objects or situations. Although it can be realistic to be anxious in some circumstances, the fear people with phobias feel is out of proportion to the actual danger caused by the situation or object.

Phobias typically include an irrational or excessive worry about encountering the feared object or situation and will take action to avoid them. The phobic reaction is usually quick to emerge and presents as severe anxiety.

There are different types of phobias. Specific or simple phobias elicit anxious responses when encountering a specific object or situation. An example of a simple phobia is the fear of snakes or spiders. Social anxiety/phobia is a general anxiety that arises from social encounters or performances. People experiencing social phobia fear being negatively evaluated by others and adjust to their fears by avoiding social contact.

Post-Traumatic Stress Disorder (PTSD)

Post-traumatic stress disorder is a stress reaction that exceeds a typical stress response. It usually follows direct or indirect exposure to personal assault, disasters, accidents, war, and other forms of violence. Symptoms include sleep disruptions, nightmares, unpleasant or even frightening mental "replays" of the traumatizing event, feeling alienated and detached, and being easily startled. PTSD is a common disorder and amenable to treatment.

Reactive Psychosis

Reactive psychosis (also known as brief psychotic disorder in DSM-V) is a sudden onset of psychotic behavior. Reactive psychosis is usually associated with severe trauma and takes the form of delusions, hallucinations, confused speech, and disorganized or catatonic behavior. The symptoms typically last a month or less but can persist for a longer period of time.

Schizophrenia

Schizophrenia is a complex and serious mental illness. It generally includes hallucinations, delusions, disorganized thinking and speech, and bizarre and agitated behavior. People with schizophrenia experience diminished ability to engage in conventional social behavior, and behavior in social roles in usually impaired. Facial expressions typically are often unchanging, and personal hygiene is frequently neglected. Social withdrawal is common.

The onset of schizophrenia usually occurs between ages 18 and 25, and symptoms worsen over time. There are different types or patterns of symptoms within the schizophrenia umbrella of disorders. Although schizophrenia is not common, the prevalence rate is below one percent, the disorder is among the top 15 causes of disability. Lifetime treatment is required.

Schizoaffective Disorder

Schizoaffective disorder has symptoms of schizophrenia and mood disorders. Symptoms include delusions, hallucination, incoherent communication, unusual behavior, depressive mood paired with times of mania, impaired social behavior, and difficulty with personal hygiene. The course of this disorder varies by person but is chronic and can cause severe impairment in performing social roles. The condition is rare and can be managed with medications and therapy.

Schizoid Personality Disorder

Schizoid personality disorder is a condition typified by avoidance of other people and limited emotional expression. People labeled schizoidal prefer being alone and do not enjoy interactions with others. They often appear to be emotionless loners who present as cold, detached, and without affect. Though they are not psychotic in that they speak sensibly and are in touch with reality, individuals experiencing this uncommon condition find work and self-reliance difficult.

Schizotypal Personality Disorder

Schizotypal personality disorder is a persistent pattern of behavior in which people avoid others, preferring to be alone, possess a flat affect, and occasionally have unusual communication and behavioral patterns. Symptoms of this disorder include strange beliefs and magical thinking (the belief that one's thought can control material objects), distorted perceptions, and eccentric or odd appearances. Demonstrating high social anxieties and often paranoia, they have few friends. With a prevalence rate of about four percent, schizotypal personality disorder is more common than schizophrenia.

Substance Abuse Disorders

Substance abuse disorders (SADs) are conditions in which the recurrent use of a drug, including alcohol and tobacco, causes significant health problems, disability, and impaired role performance. SADs frequently coexist with other disorders such as depression, anxiety, and personality disorders.

People with an SAD usually become focused on their drug behavior. They become obsessed about acquiring and taking the drug, spend large amounts of money on getting their supplies, rearrange their social relationships around drug-taking, deny the harm the drug is doing to their lives and bodies, and having difficulty stopping their drug use.

People diagnosed with an SAD may also experience physiological changes related to the chemistry of the drugs they abuse. They may become tolerant to the drug, which means that their bodies have learned to accept certain dose levels and larger amounts of the drug are needed to get high. For many abusers, their body develops cravings, which means that the cells in their bodies have adapted to the drug. When this happens, the abuser finds it increasingly hard to go without the chemical. When the abuser tries to stop taking the drug, the body exhibits symptoms of withdrawal, which for some substances, can be dangerous.

Appendix 2: Glossary of Key Terms

Acute Stress. Short durations of stress as compared to chronic stressors. Acute stress is the initial impact of a stressor event such as losing a job. If a new job in acquired soon after losing the first, the stress is short-term. Acute stressors have relatively less impact on mental health than chronic stress.

Affordable Care Act. A significant bill toward health care reform passed during the Obama administration 2010. The bill sought to increase the number of people covered by health insurance.

Agency. The belief in one's ability to control their own behavior to fulfill goals and complete tasks and overseeing one's life situation. Agency is based on self-efficacy and the opposite of fatalism.

Alienation. A cognitive-emotional state that occurs when people are denied power over their own labor activities and the rewards of their labor. Alienation is a material and emotional condition of powerlessness and is associated with psychological distress. It is an important term in authority relations theory.

Allostatic Load. The accumulation of wear and tear on the body caused by accumulation of wear and tear on the body caused by the inefficient switching on-and-off of physiological responses to stress. It is believed responsible for the emotional and cognitive distress disproportionately found among the poor and working classes.

Altruistic Suicide. A type of suicide based on Durkheim's theory of suicide. Altruistic suicide is said to occur when people take their own life to benefit their social group's welfare. Durkheim's theory stated that altruistic suicide results when people's identity is strongly merged with the social group. Suicide bombers who believe their actions promote their people's cause is an example.

Ambient Stressors. Chronic, unpleasant, uncontrollable, and unmanageable environmental conditions such as overcrowding, noise, odors, and pollution. Ambient conditions can raise stress levels and can be associated with psychological distress.

Anomic Suicide. One of Durkheim's types of suicidal behavior that occurs when norms and values in one's society or social world collapse, producing confusion and a lack of direction. Durkheim believed that social breakdowns interfered with people's ability to be socially integrated into their groups, which he theorized as the main predictor of mental health. An example is the death of a spouse that creates social changes that makes social life confusing and meaningless for the widowed survivor.

Ascribed Status. Position in the social order, or status, that bestowed or assigned by a social agent.

Attribution Theory. Contends that people assign attributes and biases to explain the causes of their social situations and buffer the stress. This theory, for example, contends that higher class people, who by social measures are successful, see their prosperity because of their own efforts, which facilitates their feeling greater self-efficacy and optimism and managing stress.

Authoritarian Personality. A personality style that compensates for personal insecurities and anxieties by blindly relying on other people and an external dogma to define what is real and provide a sense of order. Authoritarians are at concurrently submissive to an ideology and authority and dominant over weaker social groups whom they find threatening.

Authority Relations Theory. A social relational approach to understanding how stratification systems work. This theory holds that a person's position within society's authority structures is the primary determinant of income, material resources, and life chances. The theory accounts for the relationships people have with each other in the social environment. Mental health is affected by a person's relationship to authority in society.

Avoidance. Deliberately not engaging in interactions with others to minimize anxiety. For example, it is a common psychological response to acts of discrimination and includes feelings of numbness, blunted sensations, and a denial of the impact and meaning of the discriminatory event.

Block Grants. Federal funds awarded to state, territorial, or local governments to implement programs in their areas that meet the purpose of the grants and the needs of the local population.

Caste. A closed stratification where social mobility is rarely allowed. Socio-economic standing is determined solely by the social circumstances at birth. In a caste system, status is assigned not achieved.

Chronic Stressors. Long periods of stress in response to environment conditions. Chronic stress has a more serious impact on mental health than acute stress. If someone loses a job and has few resources to withstand a long period of employment, tension and conflict will last longer and have greater implications for mental health.

Civil Commitment. A legal intervention in which the state can suspend the civil rights of an individual if that person poses a risk of danger to self and others. All states have standards for determining grounds for involuntary holding a person.

Class. A group of people found at similar levels of the social hierarchy. Social classes are divisions rooted in economic factors such as occupation, education, income, and authority. These qualities intersect with gender, ethnorace, age, and other social markers of identity. The intersectionality of statuses leads to people having different life experiences and access to mental health.

Community Mental Health Act. Major law passed in 1963 that established the national system of community mental health centers. These centers offered comprehensive services and were intended to fill treatment gaps created by deinstitutionalization.

Community Mental Health Centers. A national network of comprehensive treatment facilities designed to replace hospitals and asylums as the primary centers for mental illness care. These centers offer a wide range of services designed for all residents of a community but specifically targeted indigent and low-income individuals and families through sliding fee scales.

Conceptual Medicalization. The language of conceiving a condition as medical. It takes the form of a medical vocabulary used to define nonmedical things.

Concordance Rate. The presence of the same traits in twins. The concordance rate for schizophrenia, for example, is about 50 percent.

Correspondence Bias. The belief that behavior reflects a deep-seated and unique attribute. For example, some people believe that women are essentially and inherently emotional.

Cortisol. A naturally occurring steroid that is produced when the body is aroused and the hypothalamic-pituitary-adrenal axis is activated. Cortisol levels are often studied as indicators of stress. Extended exposure to cortisol can impact the immune system and has been implicated in psychological distress.

Critical Theory. A theory associated with the Frankfort School of sociology that seeks to explain how social structures and processes prohibit people from exercising their true humanness. According to this perspective, society's rules are not designed to protect people as much as they are to protect wealth, property, and privileged groups. Rules are restrictive and cause people to repress their true aspirations, emotions, and sexuality. Society, through its demands for conformity, restrict expression and prohibits people from living a happy and psychologically healthy life.

Cry of Pain/Entrapment Model. A theory used to explain suicide among farmers. This theory states that social isolation leads to feelings of defeat and entrapment. When individuals are unable to cope with stress, they start to feel there is no safe exit.

Culture-bound Syndrome. Clusters of symptoms that are common in some cultures but nonexistent in others. In the culture in which the symptoms occur, the conditions are considered legitimate illnesses or afflictions.

Degeneracy Theory. An antiquated nineteenth-century theory that contended that mental illness was due to a genetic or family trait that caused individuals to regress and become unable to cope physically and psychologically with social and technological advances.

Deinstitutionalization. The process in the second half of the twentieth century in which patients were released from long-term hospital care. After centuries of policies and medical practices that contended that mentally ill people should be removed from everyday society, perceptions of best practices for treating mentally ill people shifted to community care. Deinstitutionalization came about because of new medications that relaxed the symptoms of psychotic disorders and changes in ideology about the state's ability to deny individuals civil liberties without due process of law.

Demedicalization. The process by which problems lose their medicalized definition and are no longer considered a medical condition.

Developmental Attrition. The failure to reach normal development milestones of height, weight, and cognitive ability in each year of childhood.

Diagnostic and Statistical Manual **(DSM).** The collection or archive of all the psychiatric disorders recognized by the American Psychiatric Association.

Disability-Adjusted Life Years (DALYs). A calculated number that represents the years of healthy life lost to illness. DALYs are the sum of years of life lost due to premature mortality and years lost due to disability or experiencing a degree of disability but are living with the health condition or its consequences.

Disease. A condition in which identifiable symptoms can be attributed to a specific cause. Diseases have a defined set of symptoms and produce consistent physiological changes.

Disorder. A disturbance or interruption of normal functioning that interferes with a person's customary activities and feelings of wellbeing.

Distress. The subjective state that results from having difficulty coping with a stressor. Distress refers to a dysfunctional or destructive cognitive, behavioral, or emotional response to stress and stressors.

Double Jeopardy. A situation in which a person is a target of discrimination based on two statuses.

Draft Act Governing Hospitalization of the Mentally Ill. A policy that required physicians to certify an individual as mentally ill before judges could order civil commitment. The rule also allowed law enforcement officials to initiate detention and emergency treatment.

Drug Abuse. Refers to any use of an illegal substance or illegal use of a legal drug. Abuse is also said to occur if the substance leads to undesirable personal, interpersonal, or social outcomes.

Drug Addiction. The physiological changes at the cellular level in which the body's cells have changed to adjust to and accommodate a chemical. When addicted, a person may experience physiological cravings and withdrawals.

Drug Dependency. Repetitive use of a drug to satisfy an emotional or behavioral need. Continued use stems not from physiological craving but from the emotional satisfaction that the drug creates.

Drug Use. A broad term that refers to any consumption of any chemical substance that has some mental or behavioral effect.

Durham Rule. A legal defense used only in New Hampshire. Under Durham, a criminal act is excused if it is a product of a mental defect or disease. No medical diagnosis of mental illness or disorder is necessary. The Durham Rule is very broad in that it allows all mental health problems to be considered in explaining a criminal act.

Egoistic Suicide. One of Durkheim's types of suicidal behavior in which an individual finds it difficult to integrate into society. Surrounding social norms and values are intact, but the individual feels disconnected and unable to fit in. Examples include cases of "loner" suicides-homicides.

Emotional Labor. The management of one's own emotions to create a publicly observable facial and bodily display within the context of employment. The goal of emotional labor is to produce the proper state of mind in others, though the display may contradict the laborer's actual emotions.

Epidemiology. A comprehensive discipline that studies the social origins of and patterns in the distribution of health and illness. The main concepts of epidemiology are risk, prevalence, incidence, and disability-adjusted life years.

Essentialism. The belief that classes of people have foundational, physiological differences that guide and direct the psychological and behavioral orientation of individuals in those groups. The term is often used in gender studies to describe the biological deterministic idea that males and females have inherently different temperaments, abilities, values, emotions, and social position.

Ethnic Density Hypothesis. A theory that states that living in ethnoracially homogeneous neighborhoods improves mental health and lowers the risk of depression when compared to persons living in neighborhoods with fewer people of their own ethnorace.

Ethnicity. A cultural group, people who share a distinct language, customs and rituals, national origins, and identity.

Ethnorace. Groups that are socially recognized as possessing a distinct ethnic-specific identity and/or may share certain physical characteristics such as skin color that are socially relevant for identity and lived experience.

Eugenics. An attempt to alter a population's genetic base by involuntarily sterilizing or killing persons with mental illness. It is sometimes considered an application of degeneracy theory.

Exploitation. A condition that occurs when a group has exclusionary control over others' behavior and the authority to appropriate the wealth generated by the people who produce it. It is an important concept in authority relations theory.

Familism. A sense of embeddedness in family relationships. Familism is strong when families provide social support, a sense of identity and purpose, and loving relationships.

Fatalism. The belief that life circumstances are out of one's control and in the hands of external forces. Fatalism is acquiescing, passively accepting things as they are. Fatalism is a subjective aspect of social class.

"Fight or Flight." The set of physical changes that occur when the body is alerted to dangerous and threatening situations. The activation of "fight or flight" responses is a natural process, but people exposed to chronic stress experience a prolonged physiological reaction, which has been linked to mental health problems.

Four Humors Theory. A theoretical invention of ancient Greeks physicians and perhaps the first coherent theory of physical and mental illness. The theory contended that the four humors—blood, yellow bile, black, bile, and phlegm—represented the four elements that composed all earthly matter, including the human body, and had qualities that affected physical and mental well-being. Four humors theory rejected the then common notion that supernatural phenomenon caused mental illness.

Gemeinschaft. Term created by Ferdinand Töennies to describe societies and communities where residents live more communally and possess a universal sense of solidarity. The population in these communities is less diverse socially and culturally and are typically rural, follow traditional rules of conduct, and share core values.

Gender. The social, psychological, political, and economic implications of sex.

Germ Theory. The belief that all conditions of ill health, including mental illness, are the result of a pathogen. Germ theory is a perspective that emerged from advances in biological sciences in the nineteenth century that discovered the bacterial and viral causes of many infectious diseases.

Gesellschaft. A term created by Ferdinand Töennies to describe socially complex communities and societies where residents are urban and socially heterogeneous. Individuals in these societies engage in rational self-interest and impersonal behavior. *Gesellschaft* emerges when many people live close together and are organized in governmental and industrial bureaucracies that stress efficiency and a complex division of labor and tend to erode the traditional bonds of family, kinship, and religion found in *gemeinschaft* communities.

Hassles. Stressors that occur in everyday life that disturb a person's routines. They are relatively minor events that emerge from the habits of daily life at home, work, school, and neighborhoods.

Health Beliefs Model. A classical socio-cognitive approach to health care utilization. This theory contends that individuals will seek mental health services when they believe that their symptoms are having serious consequences for daily living.

Health Disparities. Differences in the distribution of preventable ill health and opportunities for good health that are caused by social inequality.

Helicoptering. A parenting style in which parents are over-involved in their children's lives and intrusively and manipulatively control their children's behaviors. Helicoptering often causes anxiety among children.

Heritability. The likelihood of children developing the same condition as one parent. The heritability rate for bipolar disorder is about 80%, for example.

Hypothalamic-Pituitary-Adrenal Axis (HPA). The primary stress response system in the body. The HPA axis is a neuroendocrine system that alters the functioning of various tissues to mobilize the body to respond to a stressor.

Hysteria. A term derived from a Greek word meaning uterus. It is the basis of the theory that the uterus was the center of women's emotions and caused a health condition called hysteria in which women, not men, experienced uncontrolled emotions.

Identity Denial. The process of refusing membership in groups with which a person identifies. Mixed race individuals often encounter resistance to identifying with the group of their parents. Physical and psychological stress responses to identity denial are common.

Identity Diffusion. The loss of the ability to form healthy and stable self-definitions. A failure to commit to values, goals, or relationships and a painful sense of personal incoherence are typical expressions of identity diffusion.

Identity Integration. An unfragmented sense of self where all aspects of personality and ability are consolidated into a solitary whole.

Inchoate Feelings. Karp's term for the first phase of the moral career of experiencing depression. Inchoate feelings are emotions that are confusing, ambiguous, perhaps unrecognized, and not yet labeled with a word. They are emotions not well understood.

Incidence. The number of new cases in a specific time, usually within the last year or 30 days. New cases are important to count because they indicate trends and changes in existing patterns in the occurrence of a disorder and can help determine factors that may cause a particular condition.

Individual Discriminatory Behavior. Individual reaction to the stigma of mental illness expressed as hostile language, bullying, lack of sympathy or understanding, harassment, physical assault, and other forms of discrimination.

Insanity. A legal status for defendants who have a mental defect that compromises their ability to be responsible and accountable for their behavior.

Insanity Defense Reform Act. Bill passed in 1984 to toughen standards for insanity defenses. The law changed court procedures and returned federal courts to tougher M'Naghten rules.

Institutional Medicalization. A form of medicalization that evolves when physicians or other authorities such as administrators direct nonmedical personnel to maintain a medical rubric for treating a psychological condition. The institution itself controls the medicalization narrative and installs it as treatment policy regardless of whether individuals' problems are biophysical or not.

Interactional Discrimination. The process of social exchanges that occurs when an individual socially engages a person who has a mental health problem. During these interactions, dynamics change or are different than they would be if the other person were not discredited by the stigma.

Interactional Medicalization. A form of medicalization that evolves from interaction between physician and patient during which the physician uses medical language and treatment plans to address a nonmedical problem. For instance, a physician may treat a person's unhappy family life by prescribing a tranquilizer.

Intrusion. A psychological term that describes when an environmental event "gets into one's head" in the form of nightmares, repetitious behavior, and invasive thoughts and images. Intrusive thoughts often occur after racist encounters.

Irresistible Impulse Insanity Defense. A legal strategy that allows defendants to contend that they may have understood their behavior to be wrong but that they could not control their impulse to commit the act. The defense is not recognized by most US states or federal law.

Kraepelinian Biological Psychiatry. Named for German psychiatrist Emil Kraepelin who sought to establish psychiatry as a clinical science and devised the modern theory of psychiatry that all psychological disorders are physiological diseases. Kraepelin created classifications to distinguish several disorders, most notably separating schizophrenia from bipolar depression.

Labeling Theory. An approach that attempts to understand why some people are identified as deviants and the consequences of that social designation. Labeling assumes that mental illness is a form of behavior that violates conventional social expectations. When norms are broken, society reacts by tagging deviants with a label to identify and make sense of them. Those assigned a label, in turn, often respond to their ascribed social status by conforming to their deviant role.

Lanterman-Petris-Short Act. Bill passed in California by Governor Ronald Reagan in 1967 that essentially abolished involuntary hospitalization and forced institutions to move patients out of hospitals and into group homes. The law also made it difficult to admit mentally ill patients into state hospitals.

Launching. The time in the life course in which people leave their families of origin and forming intimate relationships, establish families of their own, and find their place in the community and the economy. This period of early adulthood is often a time of psychological distress and the onset of mental illness.

Life Course Studies. The study of how people's lives evolve over time. Life course researchers investigate how institutional rules and social structural conditions, including history, affect human development from birth until death.

Looking-glass self. Cooley's idea that a person's sense of self develops through social interaction. According to Cooley, interacting with others is like looking into a mirror and interpreting what is seen, and individuals base their understanding of themselves on how they interpret the "reflection" of their appearance.

M'Naghten Defense. Sometimes known as the "right-wrong" test. It is a legal strategy allowed in many US states that allows mentally ill defendants to argue that their cognitive capabilities undermine their ability to comprehend if their behavior is right wrong.

Medical Model. A theory of mental illness that presumes that psychological problems are symptoms of an underlying bio-medical disorder.

Medicalization. The process in which a presumably nonmedical problem becomes defined in medical terms. The concept stems from social constructionism.

Mental Health Parity and Addiction Equity Act. Passed in 2008 as a first major step toward parity and an end to discriminatory health care practices against individuals with mental.

Mental Health Systems Act. Bill passed during the Carter administration in 1980 to continue funding for national mental health programs including community mental health. Soon overturned by the Reagan administration later that year.

Minority Stress Model. The theoretical argument that social disadvantages translate into health disparities. The main idea is that lower and stigmatized social status exposes minority groups to more stressful life circumstances and fewer social and economic resources to manage them.

Model Minority. A stereotype label assigned to Asian American minority groups because of the perception that they are ideal immigrants. It is a harmful concept because it assumes that individuals in these groups have no problems or are subject to mental illness.

Modified Labeling Theory (MLT). A more recent approach to Labeling Theory that provides detailed insights into how labeling affects mental health. Proposed by Link and colleagues (1989), MLT illustrates a series of five steps in the labeling process that details how a deviant label reinforces and continues psychiatric symptoms. These steps are (1) stereotyped beliefs about mental illness, (2) internalization of those beliefs, response in which individuals attempt to cope with the label and societal reactions by concealing their symptoms, withdrawing, or deflecting others away from the label, (3) the consequences of the label, (4) the consequences of the labeling process such as alienating others and inattentiveness to self-care, and (5) vulnerability. MLT does not explain the onset of symptoms but contends that old symptoms can worsen, and new symptoms emerge because of the labeling process.

Moral Career. The experience of having mental health symptoms and engaging the treatment system. It refers to the sequence of events and changing attitudes that occur as individuals and those in their social networks process and make sense of the experience.

Moral Treatment. A social movement that attempted to reform the asylums that brutalized mentally ill persons. The aim of moral treatment was to create more humane practices and develop techniques that were more curative and personalized to fit the needs of patients.

Multistage Cluster Sampling. A technique for drawing random samples from large and dispersed populations. It involves randomly selecting from political or geographical divisions (or "clusters") in stages, moving from large to small, until a sample of households and individuals is randomly selected for inclusion in a study.

National Mental Health Act. Major bill passed in 1946 that allotted funds to increase training for mental health professionals and research into causes and treatments of mental illness. The law also provided monies for states to create outpatient treatment centers, which provided the basis of community mental health.

Network-Episode Model. A theory of mental health care utilization that focuses on the ways a person's social network influences the decision to seek care.

Neuron. A nerve cell.

Neurotransmitters. A group of chemicals that serve as messengers in nerve synapses.

Normative Theory. A theory that contends that cultural beliefs govern the norms of emotional expression. These norms specify the appropriate type, intensity, duration, and target of subjective feelings. This theory suggests that gender norms intersect with emotion norms to produce a set of rules that guide normative masculine and feminine emotions. One example is the social norm that anger is a male emotion.

Parity. The movement to create equality between coverage for physical illness care and mental health care in insurance products. Parity suggests that mental health treatments should have the same co-pays, allowed visits, and access to professionals as found in medical, nonmental illness insurance policies.

Population Elements. All potential cases in a population for drawing a sample in a research study.

Prevalence. The number of cases of a disorder in a specified population and time. It is all people with a disorder at any given time. Two timeframes for prevalence are common: over a person's lifetime and the number of people with symptoms or diagnoses in the last year.

Probability Sampling. A set of sampling techniques using random selection processes. Probability sampling allows researchers to estimate the characteristics of the entire population from which the sample is drawn with relatively low rates of error.

Problematic Social Media Use (PSMU). The excessive use of and infatuation with social media. PSMU typically causes impairment in social relationships, schoolwork, employment, and other social activities. Anxiety is often connected PSMU.

Process Errors. Biases or inaccuracies that stem from the procedures of data collection.

Pseudo-Depression. A condition sometimes occurring among the elderly. The term describes older adults who do not complain of melancholia, hopelessness, or somatic symptoms, but present with cognitive and memory deficits. The condition often leads to inaccurate diagnoses of a dementia disorder.

Psychogenic Causes. Psychological causes of mental illness. Cicero of ancient Rome was among the first to propose that psychosocial, emotional, and cognitive disturbances could be the source of mental illness.

Public Policy. The complex of laws, guidelines, and practices enacted by government. Public policy also includes the system by which these norms and values are executed.

Race. A controversial term used to represent biological classes or categories within the human species. Racial differences in people are largely superficial, except in situations of predispositions to certain diseases. For example, Whites have a higher likelihood of cystic fibrosis and African Americans have a heightened risk for sickle cell anemia. Race has no correlation with mental illness.

Random Sample. A sampling technique in which each element has an equal chance of being selected.

Reductionism. The intellectual process of employing one theory or perspective to explain all phenomena. The idea is that all phenomena are reduced to a single causal or explanatory factor.

Reference Grouping. The process of comparing oneself to people in other social groups. Individuals use reference groups as standards for evaluating themselves and their behavior. Reference grouping can have negative effects on psychological well-being when people compare themselves to others higher up the social hierarchy. They may feel inadequate low self-worth, and even depressed.

Relative Deprivation Hypothesis. A subjective aspect of social class in which individuals evaluate themselves along class lines. The realities of inequality, for example, appear in various forms of social comparisons as people without money reference their life situations against wealthier individuals.

Residential Segregation Hypothesis. A theory that holds that living in neighborhoods with a high proportion of residents from their own ethnoracial group increases the risk of psychological symptoms. The theory argues that mental health problems arise because of ethnoracial isolation.

Restricted Emotionality. The tendency to inhibit emotional expressions and unwillingness to express intimate feelings.

Risk. The likelihood of acquiring or developing a disease or disorder. Risk is important to assess because it predicts future quality of life and the demands for services and treatments.

Sampling Errors. The differences between the characteristics of a sample and those of the population from which research subjects are selected.

Sampling Frame. A list that identifies all population elements

Selective Serotonin Reuptake Inhibitor (SSRI). A class of medication that is believed to regulate serotonin's presence in the brain. SSRIs block the reabsorption of serotonin, theoretically leaving more serotonin in the vesicles, which is theorized to improve communication from one nerve ending to another.

Self-efficacy. The belief in one's ability to control their own behavior to fulfill goals and complete tasks and overseeing one's life situation. Low self-efficacy has been shown to correlate with psychological distress.

Self-labeling. Occurs when a person is aware of the negative public beliefs and stereotypes about mental illness and believes and internals them. Individuals who believe those labels usually start to show symptoms of psychological distress.

Serotonin. Perhaps the most well-known neurotransmitter. In the serotonin theory of depression, synapses in the brain have insufficient amounts of serotonin that cause irregular connections between neurons and negatively affect emotions.

Sex. The biological difference in human males, females, and intersex individuals. Sexual differences are primarily based on physiological differences in reproductive organs and chromosome composition.

Social Causation Model. A theory that states social conditions of class create more hardships and stress for those in lower social strata, causing a greater burden of mental health problems for lower status individuals. It is contrary to social drift and selection theories of the relationship between mental health and social class. Greater life struggles and deprivations among lower levels of authority and income are believed to cause a greater burden of chronic stress. The stressful conditions of deprivations brought on by living in disadvantaged and under-resourced families and neighborhoods cause the higher rates of psychological impairments found in lower social class positions.

Social Constructionism. A sociological theory of mental health and illness that contends that the definitions of what is and what is not mental illness are based on cultural perceptions and social interactions. Mental illness is "socially constructed" in that it is subject to norms and values that govern appropriate and expected social behavior. In this view, reality is subjective and a product of social dynamics and only exists as people assign meanings to things, name them, and develop a narrative about them. If society does not accept something as real, then it truly does not exist.

Social Darwinism. A theory proposed by nineteenth-century scholar Herbert Spencer, that promotes the idea that societies evolve like organisms and that what differentiates the rich and powerful from the poor and powerless is strength and fitness. Spencer, not Darwin, coined the phrase "survival of the fittest" to represent the idea that society should do nothing to help mentally ill and other disadvantaged people because their disadvantages were part of a natural selection process that was extracting them from the social organism. The mentally ill, for example, are organically unable to adapt to the environment and should not receive assistance or be allowed to reproduce.

Social Drift Theory. A theory of the relationship between social class and mental health that contends that mental illness causes a person to "drift" downward in class position. It is related to the social section hypothesis and refers to intragenerational mobility. For example, a person reaches a certain socio-economic level but cannot maintain it because of a psychological impairment.

Social Forces. External patterns of behavior, emotions, and thinking typical to a society or group that coerce or direct individuals to act in certain ways. Outside the scope of individual people, social forces take the form of social structures and cultural norms and values that influence action and thinking. Social forces are the activities of the social environment that act upon individuals and to which they must respond.

Social Mobility. In a class stratification system, the ability to move up or down in socio-economic standing.

Social Problem. Any social condition that interrupts or damages usual social functioning for large numbers of people. This condition must be recognized or labeled as a problem by an authority agent.

Social Selection. Similar to social drift theory and describes downward intergenerational mobility caused by mental illness. A psychological impairment impedes individuals' ability to maintain their parents' class position.

Socialization. The process by which people learn how to function in society. Socialization occurs throughout life as individuals learn and adjust to new social expectations and people.

Socio-Behavioral Model. A theory of health care utilization based on three core components that influence utilization: need, predisposing factors, and enabling factors.

Sociological Imagination. Term coined by sociologist C. Wright Mills that refers to the ability to analyze the conditions of one's life in the context of broader society.

Sociology in Medicine. A branch of sociology that employs sociological theory and method to solve medical questions such as who is more or less likely to suffer from mental health problems and what causes social patterns in mental illness. The study of health disparities is an example of sociology in medicine.

Sociology of Medicine. A branch of sociology that employs sociological theory and method to study the medical system as a social institution and how a society defines what is health and what is ill-health.

Somatic Depression. Sometimes occurs during late adulthood when individuals complain of changes in sleep patterns, appetite, weight, energy levels, and sexual functioning rather than communicating their feelings of sadness or hopelessness.

Somatogenic Theories. Theories that contend that mental illnesses are rooted in physiological dysfunctions. Brain injuries, "chemical imbalances," and genetics are frequently cited as causes of abnormal behavior.

Status-Based Identity. Refers to the subjective meanings and values people attach to understanding their own socioeconomic position and incorporating them into their social identity.

Stigma. A physical or social attribute, or "mark," that devalues individuals' or groups' social identity and disqualifies them from complete social acceptance. This attribute is one that is interpreted in such a way that disgraces the individual.

Stigma Consciousness. Expectations of being devalued, discriminated against, or stereotyped; usually results in stress reactions among members of ethnoracial minorities.

Stigmatization. The social process by which a person or group is assigned a stigma.

Stratification. The process by which people are organized into a hierarchical system of classes. A stratification system includes the ideologies and mechanisms for distributing wealth, power, prestige, and material resources. Where people are located in this hierarchy has considerable influence on their quality of life and physical and psychological well-being.

Stress. An important concept in the sociology of mental health that has two meanings. First, stress refers to a force enacted against a person. In this usage, "stress" and "stressor" are roughly equivalent. Such pressure is caused by an environmental event or change that is perceived as a threat and requires a social or psychological adjustment by an individual. Second, stress is the physiological response to a threat or socio-environmental demand that taxes a person's usual coping ability.

Stress Theory. A theory that connects structural conditions to individual responses by attempting to explain how a person's social location creates stress that can translate into symptoms of psychological distress and mental illness. It is a major theoretical paradigm that integrates sociological phenomena to biological outcomes.

Stressors. Conditions that threaten, challenge, or constrain individuals' attempts to achieve well-being. They are external events or conditions that place pressure on mental and physiological well-being and usual functioning. Examples of stressors are unemployment, persistent threat of violence, and conflicted relationships.

Structural Discrimination. An expression of stigmatization derived from the way society is organized and includes institutional practices that disadvantage mentally ill persons.

Structural Strain Theory. A theory that contends that macro social forces create pressures or barriers for psychological well-being. Mental health problems evolve from macro-level forces such as discrimination and poverty impede healthy emotional and cognitive development. These barriers block opportunities and stymie individuals' aspirations, creating feelings of frustration, loneliness, and disappointment. Probably the oldest sociological theory of mental health.

Structural Theory of Emotions. A theory that contends that status and social power influence emotions. During a social interaction, people in the higher status positions will have a different emotional position than the person in the lower position. Having more power leads a person to more positive feelings, whereas those in lower positions will have more negative emotions.

Sub-threshold Symptoms. Symptoms that are present but not at the level necessary to be assigned a DSM diagnosis. The symptoms are of such severity that daily functioning is impaired.

Subjective Aspects of Class. The cognitive and emotional aspects of class status. They reflect the ways in which class standing affects identity, self-esteem, and perspective.

Substantial Capacity Test. Once a legal defense recognized by about half of the states and the US federal government but was changed after the assassination attempt on Ronald Reagan. This defense allows for defendants to argue they have a substantial, but not total, loss in capacity to understand the law and right from wrong and enter their emotional state, character, or personality traits as evidence of their insanity. The defense is still recognized in some US states.

Supernaturalism. A theory that suggests mental illness is the result of supernatural phenomena such as curses, possessions, or demonic control. The theory was found throughout the world and remains present in some cultures.

Synapse. The space between neurons, or nerve cells.

Syndrome. An observable and correlated set of symptoms or physical markers that constitute a specific condition for which a direct cause is not understood.

Thorazine. The first successful antipsychotic drug for treating schizophrenia and the manic phase of bipolar disorder. Thorazine, though not a cure, allowed patients to control their symptoms and avoid institutional care.

Transitional Object. Objects that individuals endow with magical qualities to relieve stress. Examples include a young child's favorite stuffed animal or alcohol for an adult.

Trepanation. An ancient form of brain surgery dating back 7,000 years that involved drilling holes in the head to relieve pressure caused by the build-up of blood after a head trauma or to release demons that possessed the individual and caused them to act in bizarre or deviant ways.

True Prevalence. The sum of people with symptoms who are seeking treatment and those who are not.

Typification. The creation of social types or entities that have their own identity and role expectations.

Vesicle. Sacs located in neurons that hold neurotransmitters until a nerve signal reaches the neuron.

World Mental Health Survey Initiative (WMH). A major research project undertaken by the World Health Organization to create a standardized international data set on mental health.

Bibliography

Aaseth, Jan, Grethe Emilie Roer, Lars Lien, and Geir Bjørklund. 2019. "Is There a Relationship between PTSD and Complicated Obesity? A Review of the Literature." *Biomedicine & Pharmacotherapy* 117:108834. doi: 10.1016/j.biopha.2019.108834.

Abbo, Catherine. 2011. "Profiles and Outcome of Traditional Healing Practices for Severe Mental Illnesses in Two Districts of Eastern Uganda." *Global Health Action* 4(1):7117. doi: 10.3402/gha.v4i0.7117.

Abbott, Katherine M., Janet Prvu Bettger, Alexandra Hanlon, and Karen B. Hirschman. 2012. "Factors Associated with Health Discussion Network Size and Composition among Elderly Recipients of Long-Term Services and Supports." *Health Communication* 27(8):784–93. doi: 10.1080/10410236.2011.640975.

Adams, Richard E., and Joseph A. Boscarino. 2005. "Stress and Well-Being in the Aftermath of the World Trade Center Attack: The Continuing Effects of a Communitywide Disaster." *Journal of Community Psychology* 33(2):175–90. doi: 10.1002/jcop.20030.

Adams, Richard E., Joseph A. Boscarino, and Sandro Galea. 2006. "Social and Psychological Resources and Health Outcomes after the World Trade Center Disaster." *Social Science & Medicine* 62(1):176–88. doi: 10.1016/j.socscimed.2005.05.008.

Addis, Michael E., and James R. Mahalik. 2003. "Men, Masculinity, and the Contexts of Help Seeking." *American Psychologist* 58(1):5–14. doi: 10.1037/0003-066X.58.1.5.

Adeboye, Adewale Olusola. 2021. "Addressing the Boko Haram-Induced Mental Health Burden in Nigeria." *Health and Human Rights* 23(1):71–73.

Adewuya, Abiodun O., and Roger O. A. Makanjuola. 2008. "Lay Beliefs Regarding Causes of Mental Illness in Nigeria: Pattern and Correlates." *Social Psychiatry and Psychiatric Epidemiology* 43(4):336–41. doi: 10.1007/s00127-007-0305-x.

Adkison, Sarah E., Kerry Grohman, Craig R. Colder, Kenneth Leonard, Toni Orrange-Torchia, Ellen Peterson, and Rina D. Eiden. 2013. "Impact of Fathers' Alcohol Problems on the Development of Effortful Control in Early Adolescence." *Journal of Studies on Alcohol and Drugs* 74(5):674–83. doi: 10.15288/jsad.2013.74.674.

Adorno, Theodor W., Else Frenkel-Brunswik, Daniel J. Levinson, Nevitt Sanford, and Peter Eli Gordon. 2019. *The Authoritarian Personality*. London; New York, NY: Verso.

Afifi, Tracie O., Douglas A. Brownridge, Brian J. Cox, and Jitender Sareen. 2006. "Physical Punishment, Childhood Abuse and Psychiatric Disorders." *Child Abuse & Neglect* 30(10):1093–1103. doi: 10.1016/j.chiabu.2006.04.006.

Africa, Jei, and Majose Carrasco. 2011. *Asian-American and Pacific Islander Mental Health: Report from a NAMI Listening Session*. National Alliance on Mental Illness.

Ahonen, Marke. 2019. "Ancient Philosophers on Mental Illness." *History of Psychiatry* 30(1):3–18. doi: 10.1177/0957154X18803508.

Akyeampong, Emanuel E. 2015. "A Historical Overview of Psychiatry in Africa." Pp. 24–49 in *The Culture of Mental Illness and Psychiatric Practice in Africa*, edited by Emanuael E. Akyeampong, Arthur Kleinman, and Allen G. Hill. Bloomington, IN: Indiana University Press.

Albee, George W. 1996. "Introduction to the Special Issue on Social Darwinism." *The Journal of Primary* 17(1):3–16.

Albuja, Analia F., Sarah E. Gaither, Diana T. Sanchez, Brenda Straka, and Rebecca Cipollina. 2019. "Psychophysiological Stress Responses to Bicultural and Biracial Identity Denial." *Journal of Social Issues* 75(4):1165–91. doi: 10.1111/josi.12347.

Alcoholics Anonymous. 2015. *2014 A.A. Membership Survey Reveals Current Trends.*

Alegria, Analucia A., Carlos Blanco, Nancy M. Petry, Andrew E. Skodol, Shang-Min Liu, Bridget Grant, and Deborah Hasin. 2013. "Sex Differences in Antisocial Personality Disorder: Results from the National Epidemiological Survey on Alcohol and Related Conditions." *Personality Disorders: Theory, Research, and Treatment* 4(3):214–22. doi: 10.1037/a0031681.

Allen, A. A., and J. K. Bonnie. 2015. *Annual Statistical Report Adult Civil Commitment Proceedings in Virginia FY 2015.* University of Virginia Institute of Law, Psychiatry, and Public Policy.

Almeida-Filho, Naomar. 1998. "Becoming Modern after All These Years: Social Change and Mental Health in Latin America." *Culture, Medicine and Psychiatry,* 22:285–316.

Almeida-Filho, Naomar, Ines Lessa, Lucélia Magalhães, Maria Jenny Araújo, Estela Aquino, Sherman A. James, and Ichiro Kawachi. 2004. "Social Inequality and Depressive Disorders in Bahia, Brazil: Interactions of Gender, Ethnicity, and Social Class." *Social Science & Medicine* 59(7): 1339–53. doi: 10.1016/j.socscimed.2003.11.037.

Altemeyer, Bob. 1998. "The Other Authoritarian Personality." Pp. 48–92 in *Advances in Experimental Social Psychology.* Vol. 30, edited by Mark P. Zanna. San Diego, CA: Academic Press.

Amad, Ali, and Pierre Thomas. 2011. "Histoire de la maladie mentale dans le Moyen-Orient médiéval." *Annales Médico-psychologiques, Revue Psychiatrique* 169(6):373–76. doi: 10.1016/j.amp. 2010.06.023.

Amato, Paul R., and Bruce Keith. 1991. "Parental Divorce and the Well-Being of Children: A Meta-Analysis." *Psychological Bulletin,* 110:26–46.

American Academy of Child & Adolescent Psychiatry. 2019. *Alcohol Use in Families.*

American Psychiatric Association. 1952. *Diagnostic and Statistical Manual of Mental Disorders. I.* Washington, DC: American Psychiatric Association.

American Psychiatric Association. 1968. *Diagnostic and Statistical Manual of Mental Disorders. II.* Washington, DC: American Psychiatric Association.

American Psychiatric Association. 1980. *Diagnostic and Statistical Manual of Mental Disorders. III.* Washington, DC: American Psychiatric Association.

American Psychiatric Association. 2000. *Diagnostic and Statistical Manual of Mental Disorders.* 4th ed. Washington, DC: American Psychiatric Association.

American Psychiatric Association. 2013. *Diagnostic and Statistical Manual of Mental Disorders.* 5th ed. Washington, DC: American Psychiatric Association.

Amin, Faridah, Salman Sharif, Rabeeya Saeed, Noureen Durrani, and Daniyal Jilani. 2020. "COVID-19 Pandemic-Knowledge, Perception, Anxiety and Depression among Frontline Doctors of Pakistan." *BMC Psychiatry* 20(1):459. doi: 10.1186/s12888-020-02864-x.

Andersen, Ronald M. 1995. "Revisiting the Behavioral Model and Access to Medical Care: Does It Matter?" *Journal of Health and Social Behavior* 36(1):1. doi: 10.2307/2137284.

Andreassen, Cecilie Schou, Torbjørn Torsheim, and Ståle Pallesen. 2014. "Predictors of Use of Social Network Sites at Work—A Specific Type of Cyberloafing." *Journal of Computer-Mediated Communication* 19(4):906–21. doi: 10.1111/jcc4. 12085.

Andrews, Gavin, Justine Corry, Tim Slade, Cathy Issakidis, and Heather Swantson. 2004. "Child Sexual Abuse." Pp. 1851–1940 in *Comparative Quantification of Health Risks: Global and Regional Burden of Disease Attributable to Selected Major Risk Factors.* Vol. 1, edited by M. Ezzati, A. D. Lopez, A. Rodgers, and C. J. L. Murray. Geneva: World Health Organization.

Aneshensel, Carol S. 1992. "Social Stress: Theory and Research." *Annual Review of Sociology* 18(18): 15–38.

Aneshensel, Carol S., Jenna van Draanen, Helene Riess, and Alice P. Villatoro. 2019. "Newcomers and Old Timers: An Erroneous Assumption in Mental Health Services Research." *Journal of Health and Social Behavior* 60(4):453–73. doi: 10.1177/002 2146519887475.

Aneshensel, Carol S., Jo C. Phelan, and Alex Bierman. 2013. "The Sociology of Mental Health:

Surveying the Field." Pp. 1–19 in *Handbook of the Sociology of Mental Health*, edited by Carol S. Aneshensel, Jo C. Phelan, and Alex Bierman. New York, NY: Springer.

Aneshensel, Carol S., and Clea A. Sucoff. 1996. "The Neighborhood Context of Adolescent Mental Health." *Journal of Health and Social Behavior* 37(4):293–310.

Angell, Marcia. 2011. "The Epidemic of Mental Illness: Why?" The New York Review of Books, June 23.

Angermeyer, Matthias C., and Herbert Matschinger. 1996. "The Effect of Violent Attacks by Schizophrenic Persons on the Attitude of the Public towards the Mentally Ill." *Social Science & Medicine* 43(12):1721–28. doi: 10.1016/S0277-9536(96)00065-2.

Angst, Jules. 2010. "Biological Research into Depression: A Clinician's Commentary." *World Psychiatry* 9(3):163–64. doi: 10.1002/j.2051-5545.2010.tb00300.x.

Ansfield, Matthew E. 2007. "Smiling When Distressed: When a Smile Is a Frown Turned Upside Down." *Personality and Social Psychology Bulletin* 33(6):763–75. doi: 10.1177/0146167206297398.

Arani, Mohammad, Esmaeil Fakharian, and Fahimeh Sarbandi. 2012. "Ancient Legacy of Cranial Surgery." *Archives of Trauma Research* 1(2):72–74. doi: 10.5812/atr.6556.

Arboleda-Florez, Julio, and Heather Stuart. 2012. "From Sin to Science: Fighting the Stigmatization of Mental Illness." *Canadian Journal of Psychiatry* 57(8):457–63.

Aseltine, Robert H. 1996. "Pathways Linking Parental Divorce with Adolescent Depression." *Journal of Health and Social Behavior* 37(2):133. doi: 10.2307/2137269.

Auerbach, Judith D. 1988. *In the Business of Child Care: Employer Initiatives and Working Women*. New York, NY: Praeger.

Auerbach, Judith D., and Anne E. Figert. 1995. "Women's Health Research: Public Policy and Sociology." *Journal of Health and Social Behavior* 35:115. doi: 10.2307/2626960.

Austin, D. Mark, L. Allen Furr, and Michael Spine. 2002. "The Effects of Neighborhood Conditions on Perceptions of Safety." *Journal of Criminal Justice* 30(5):417–27. doi: 10.1016/S0047-2352(02)00148-4.

Axinn, William G., Dirgha J. Ghimire, Nathalie E. Williams, and Kate M. Scott. 2013. "Gender, Traumatic Events, and Mental Health Disorders in a Rural Asian Setting." *Journal of Health and Social Behavior* 54(4):444–61. doi: 10.1177/0022146513501518.

Ayano, Getinet, Getachew Tesfaw, and Shegaye Shumet. 2019. "The Prevalence of Schizophrenia and Other Psychotic Disorders among Homeless People: A Systematic Review and Meta-Analysis." *BMC Psychiatry* 19(1):370. doi: 10.1186/s12888-019-2361-7.

Bachman, Jerald G., Patrick M. O'Malley, Peter Freedman-Doan, Kali H. Trzesniewski, and M. Brent Donnellan. 2011. "Adolescent Self-Esteem: Differences by Race/Ethnicity, Gender, and Age." *Self and Identity* 10(4):445–73. doi: 10.1080/15298861003794538.

Baiden, Philip, and Savarra K. Tadeo. 2020. "Investigating the Association between Bullying Victimization and Suicidal Ideation among Adolescents: Evidence from the 2017 Youth Risk Behavior Survey." *Child Abuse & Neglect* 102:104417. doi: 10.1016/j.chiabu.2020.104417.

Balhara, Yatan Pal Singh. 2011. "Culture-bound Syndrome: Has it Found its Right Niche?" *Indian Journal of Psychological Medicine*, 33(2):210–215.

Ballenger, James F., Suzanne R. Best, Thomas J. Metzler, David A. Wasserman, David C. Mohr, Akiva Liberman, Kevin Delucchi, Daniel S. Weiss, Jeffrey A. Fagan, Angela E. Waldrop, and Charles R. Marmar. 2011. "Patterns and Predictors of Alcohol Use in Male and Female Urban Police Officers: Alcohol Use among Urban Police Officers." *The American Journal on Addictions* 20(1):21–29. doi: 10.1111/j.1521-0391.2010.00092.x.

Bandura, Albert. 1997. *Self-Efficacy: The Exercise of Control*. New York, NY: W.H. Freeman.

Bao, Yuhua, John Fisher, and James Studnicki. 2008. "Racial Differences in Behavioral Inpatient Diagnosis: Examining the Mechanisms Using the 2004 Florida Inpatient Discharge Data." *The*

Journal of Behavioral Health Services & Research 35(3):347–57. doi: 10.1007/s11414-008-9116-4.

Barker, Kristin K. 2008. "Electronic Support Groups, Patient-Consumers, and Medicalization: The Case of Contested Illness." *Journal of Health and Social Behavior* 49(1):20–36. doi: 10.1177/002214650804900103.

Barnes, Grace M., John W. Welte, Joseph H. Hoffman, and Marie-Cecile O. Tidwell. 2010. "Comparisons of Gambling and Alcohol Use among College Students and Noncollege Young People in the United States." *Journal of American College Health* 58(5):443–52. doi: 10.1080/07448480903540499.

Barnett, Jennifer H., and Jordan W. Smoller. 2009. "The Genetics of Bipolar Disorder." *Neuroscience* 164(1):331–43. doi: 10.1016/j.neuroscience.2009.03.080.

Barrett, Lisa Feldman, and Eliza Bliss-Moreau. 2009. "She's Emotional. He's Having a Bad Day: Attributional Explanations for Emotion Stereotypes." *Emotion* 9(5):649–58. doi: 10.1037/a0016821.

Barry, Christopher T., Chloe L. Sidoti, Shanelle M. Briggs, Shari R. Reiter, and Rebecca A. Lindsey. 2017. "Adolescent Social Media Use and Mental Health from Adolescent and Parent Perspectives." *Journal of Adolescence* 61:1–11. doi: 10.1016/j.adolescence.2017.08.005.

Bartholomew, Theodore T. 2016. "Mental Health in Namibia: Connecting Discourses on Psychological Distress, Western Treatments and Traditional Healing." *Psychology and Developing Societies* 28(1):101–25. doi: 10.1177/0971333615622909.

Basile, Kathleen C., Ileana Arias, Sujata Desai, and Martie P. Thompson. 2004. "The Differential Association of Intimate Partner Physical, Sexual, Psychological, and Stalking Violence and Posttraumatic Stress Symptoms in a Nationally Representative Sample of Women." *Journal of Traumatic Stress* 17(5):413–21. doi: 10.1023/B:JOTS.0000048954.50232.d8.

Baumann, Eleen A., Richard G. Mitchell, and Caroline Hodges Persell. 1989. *Encountering Society: Student Resource Manual to Accompany Understanding Society by Caroline Hodges Persell*. 3rd ed. New York, NY: Harper and Row.

Beck, Aaron T. 1961. "An Inventory for Measuring Depression." *Archives of General Psychiatry* 4(6):561. doi: 10.1001/archpsyc.1961.01710120031004.

Beck, Aaron T., Robert A. Steer, and Gregory K. Brown. 1996. *Beck Depression Inventory: Second Edition Manual*. San Antonio, TX: The Psychological Corporation.

Becker, Dana. 2000. "When She Was Bad: Borderline Personality Disorder in a Posttraumatic Age." *American Journal of Orthopsychiatry* 70(4):422–32. doi: 10.1037/h0087769.

Becker, Dana, and Sharon Lamb. 1994. "Sex Bias in the Diagnosis of Borderline Personality Disorder and Posttraumatic Stress Disorder." *Professional Psychology: Research and Practice* 25(1):55–61. doi: 10.1037/0735-7028.25.1.55.

Beller, Emily, and Michael Hout. 2006. "Intergenerational Social Mobility: The United States in Comparative Perspective." *The Future of Children* 16(2):9–361.

Bener, Abdulbari, and Suhaila Ghuloum. 2011. "Gender Differences in the Knowledge, Attitude and Practice towards Mental Health Illness in a Rapidly Developing Arab Society." *International Journal of Social Psychiatry* 57(5):480–86. doi: 10.1177/0020764010374415.

Bergeman, C. S., and K. A. Wallace. 1999. "Resiliency in Later Life." Pp. 207–25 in *Life Span Perspectives on Health and Illness*, edited by Thomas V. Merluzzi, Thomas L. Whitman, and Robert D. White. Mahwah, NJ: Erlbaum.

Berndt, Ernst R., Stan N. Finkelstein, Paul E. Greenberg, Robert H. Howland, Alison Keith, A. John Rush, James Russell, and Martin B. Keller. 1998. "Workplace Performance Effects from Chronic Depression and Its Treatment." *Journal of Health Economics* 17(5):511–35. doi: 10.1016/S0167-6296(97)00043-X.

Berry, Kelsey N., Haiden A. Huskamp, Howard H. Goldman, and Colleen L. Barry. 2015. "A Tale of Two States: Do Consumers See Mental Health Insurance Parity When Shopping on State Exchanges?" *Psychiatric Services* 66(6):565–67. doi: 10.1176/appi.ps.201400582.

Bertolote, Jose. 2008. "The Roots of the Concept of Mental Health." *World Psychiatry* 7(2):113–16.

Bertram, Lars, and Rudolph E. Tanzi. 2008. "Thirty Years of Alzheimer's Disease Genetics: The Implications of Systematic Meta-Analyses." *Nature Reviews Neuroscience* 9(10):768–78. doi: 10.1038/nrn2494.

Bickerstaff, Karen, and Gordon Walker. 2001. "Public Understandings of Air Pollution: The 'Localisation' of Environmental Risk." *Global Environmental Change* 11(2):133–45. doi: 10.1016/S0959-3780(00)00063-7.

Bierman, Alex, and Scott Schieman. 2020. "Social Estrangement and Psychological Distress before and during the COVID-19 Pandemic: Patterns of Change in Canadian Workers." *Journal of Health and Social Behavior* 61(4):398–417. doi: 10.1177/0022146520970190.

Blake, William. 1793. *The Marriage of Heaven and Hell*. Project Gutenberg.

Blashill, Aaron J., and Sabine Wilhelm. 2014. "Body Image Distortions, Weight, and Depression in Adolescent Boys: Longitudinal Trajectories into Adulthood." *Psychology of Men & Masculinity* 15(4):445–51. doi: 10.1037/a0034618.

Blow, Frederic C., John E. Zeber, John F. McCarthy, Marcia Valenstein, Leah Gillon, and C. Raymond Bingham. 2004. "Ethnicity and Diagnostic Patterns in Veterans with Psychoses." *Social Psychiatry and Psychiatric Epidemiology* 39(10):841–51. doi: 10.1007/s00127-004-0824-7.

Bonanno, George A., Sandro Galea, Angela Bucciarelli, and David Vlahov. 2007. "What Predicts Psychological Resilience after Disaster? The Role of Demographics, Resources, and Life Stress." *Journal of Consulting and Clinical Psychology* 75(5):671–82. doi: 10.1037/0022-006X.75.5.671.

Bonnie, Richard J., John Calvin Jeffries, and Peter W. Low. 2008. *A Case Study in the Insanity Defense: The Trial of John W. Hinckley, Jr*. 3rd ed. New York, NY: Foundation Press ; Thomson/West.

Bornstein, Marc H., Diane L. Putnick, Maria A. Gartstein, Chun-Shin Hahn, Nancy Auestad, and Deborah L. O'Connor. 2015. "Infant Temperament: Stability by Age, Gender, Birth Order, Term Status, and Socioeconomic Status." *Child Development* 86(3):844–63. doi: 10.1111/cdev.12367.

Bostwick, Wendy B., Carol J. Boyd, Tonda L. Hughes, and Sean Esteban McCabe. 2010. "Dimensions of Sexual Orientation and the Prevalence of Mood and Anxiety Disorders in the United States." *American Journal of Public Health* 100(3):468–75. doi: 10.2105/AJPH.2008.152942.

Bourdieu, Pierre. 2002. *Distinction: A Social Critique of the Judgement of Taste*. Cambridge, MA: Harvard University Press.

Boyd, Carol. 2002. "Customer Violence and Employee Health and Safety." *Work, Employment and Society* 16(1):151–69. doi: 10.1177/09500170222119290.

Bradley-Geist, Jill C., and Julie Olson-Buchanan. 2014. "Helicopter Parents: An Examination of the Correlates of over-Parenting of College Students." *Education + Training* 56(4):314–28. doi: 10.1108/ET-10-2012-0096.

Brady, Kathleen T., and Susan C. Sonne. 1999. "The Role of Stress in Alcohol Use, Alcoholism Treatment, and Relapse." *Alcohol Research & Health: The Journal of the National Institute on Alcohol Abuse and Alcoholism* 23(4):263–71.

Brambilla, Paolo, and Michele Tansella. 2007. "Can Neuroimaging Studies Help Us in Understanding the Biological Causes of Schizophrenia?" *International Review of Psychiatry* 19(4):313–14. doi: 10.1080/09540260701507954.

Braun, Jerome. 1982. "Pressuring Institutions and Flat Personalities." *International Journal of Social Psychiatry* 29(4):313–17.

Breitner, J., K. A. Gau, B. L. Welsh, et al. 1990. "Alzheimer's Disease in the National Academy of Sciences Registry of Aging Twin Veterans." *Dementia* 1:297–303.

Breslau, Joshua, Matthew Cefalu, Eunice C. Wong, M. Audrey Burnam, Gerald P. Hunter, Karen R. Florez, and Rebecca L. Collins. 2017. "Racial/Ethnic Differences in Perception of Need for Mental Health Treatment in a US National Sample." *Social Psychiatry and Psychiatric Epidemiology* 52(8):929–37. doi: 10.1007/s00127-017-1400-2.

Breslau, Joshua, Kenneth S. Kendler, Maxwell Su, Sergio Gaxiola-Aguilar, and Ronald C. Kessler. 2005. "Lifetime Risk and Persistence of Psychiatric Disorders across Ethnic Groups in the United

States." *Psychological Medicine* 35(3):317–27. doi: 10.1017/S0033291704003514.

Bridewell, Will B., and Edward C. Chang. 1997. "Distinguishing between Anxiety, Depression, and Hostility: Relations to Anger-in, Anger-out, and Anger Control." *Personality and Individual Differences* 22(4):587–90. doi: 10.1016/S0191-8869(96)00224-3.

Brody, Leslie R. 2000. "The Socialization of Gender Differences in Emotional Experience: Display Rules, Infant Temperament, and Differentiation." Pp. 24–47 in *Gender and Emotion: Social Psychological Perspectives, Studies in Emotion and Social Interaction*, edited by Agneta H. Fischer. Cambridge: Cambridge University Press.

Brody, Leslie R., and Judith A. Hall. 2008. "Gender and Emotion in Context." Pp. 395–408 in *Handbook of Emotions*, edited by Michael Lewis, Jeannette M. Haviland-Jones, and Lisa Feldman Barrett. New York, NY: Guilford Press.

Brody, Gene H., Joshua C. Gray, Tianyi Yu, Allan W. Barton, Steven R.H. Beach, Adrianna Galván, James MacKillop, Michael Windle, Edith Chen, Gregory E. Miller, and Lawrence H. Sweet. 2017. Protective Prevention Effects on the Association of Poverty With Brain Development. *JAMA Pediatrics*, 171(1):46053. doi:10.1001/jamapediatrics.2016.2988.

Brohan, Elaine, Claire Henderson, Kay Wheat, Estelle Malcolm, Sarah Clement, Elizabeth A. Barley, Mike Slade, and Graham Thornicroft. 2012. "Systematic Review of Beliefs, Behaviours and Influencing Factors Associated with Disclosure of a Mental Health Problem in the Workplace." *BMC Psychiatry* 12(1):11. doi: 10.1186/1471-244X-12-11.

Bromet, E. J., J. M. Havenaar, and L. T. Guey. 2011. "A 25 Year Retrospective Review of the Psychological Consequences of the Chernobyl Accident." *Clinical Oncology* 23(4):297–305. doi: 10.1016/j.clon.2011.01.501.

Bromet, Evelyn J., Laura Helena Andrade, Ronny Bruffaerts, and David R. Williams. 2018. "Major Depressive Disorder." Pp. 41–56 in *Mental Disorders Around the World: Facts and Figures from the WHO World Mental Health Surveys*, edited by Kate M. Scott, Peter DeJonge, Dan J. Stein, and Ronald C. Kessler. Cambridge: Cambridge University Press.

Brooks, Carolyn, Stephanie Martin, Lisa Broda, and Jennifer Poudrier. 2020. "'How Many Silences Are There?' Men's Experience of Victimization in Intimate Partner Relationships." *Journal of Interpersonal Violence* 35(23–24):5390–5413. doi: 10.1177/0886260517719905.

Brooks, Randolph T., and Reginald Hopkins. 2017. "Cultural Mistrust and Health Care Utilization: The Effects of a Culturally Responsive Cognitive Intervention." *Journal of Black Studies* 48(8):816–34. doi: 10.1177/0021934717728454.

Broverman, Inge K., Donald M. Broverman, Frank E. Clarkson, Paul S. Rosenkrantz, and Susan R. Vogel. 1970. "Sex-Role Stereotypes and Clinical Judgments of Mental Health." *Journal of Consulting and Clinical Psychology* 34(1):1–7. doi: 10.1037/h0028797.

Brown, Diane Robinson, and Lawrence E. Gary. 1988. "Unemployment and Psychological Distress among Black American Women." *Sociological Focus* 21(3):209–21. doi: 10.1080/00380237.1988.10570979.

Brown, George W., and Tirril O. Harris. 2012. *Social Origins of Depression: A Study of Psychiatric Disorder in Women*. Abingdon, Oxfordshire; New York, NY: Routledge.

Brown, Phil. 1995. "Naming and Framing: The Social Construction of Diagnosis and Illness." *Journal of Health and Social Behavior* 35:34. doi: 10.2307/2626956.

Brown, Robyn Lewis, and Gabriele Ciciurkaite. 2017. "Understanding the Connection between Social Support and Mental Health." Pp. 207–23 in *A Handbook for the Study of Mental Health: Social Contexts, Theories, and Systems*, edited by Teresa L. Scheid and Eric R. Wright. Cambridge: Cambridge University Press.

Browning, Christopher R., Brian Soller, Margo Gardner, and Jeanne Brooks-Gunn. 2013. "'Feeling Disorder' as a Comparative and Contingent Process: Gender, Neighborhood Conditions, and Adolescent Mental Health." *Journal of Health and Social Behavior* 54(3):296–314. doi: 10.1177/0022146513498510.

Brugger, Stefan P., and Oliver D. Howes. 2017. "Heterogeneity and Homogeneity of Regional Brain Structure in Schizophrenia: A Meta-Analysis." *JAMA Psychiatry* 74(11):1104. doi: 10.1001/jamapsychiatry.2017.2663.

Burns, Jonathan K., Andrew Tomita, and Amy S. Kapadia. 2014. "Income Inequality and Schizophrenia: Increased Schizophrenia Incidence in Countries with High Levels of Income Inequality." *International Journal of Social Psychiatry* 60(2):185–96. doi: 10.1177/0020764013481426.

Busfield, Joan. 2000. "Introduction: Rethinking the Sociology of Mental Health." *Sociology of Health & Illness* 22(5):543–58.

Buus, Niels. 2014. "Adherence to Anti-Depressant Medication: A Medicine-Taking Career." *Social Science & Medicine* 123:105–13. doi: 10.1016/j.socscimed.2014.11.010.

Caetano, Raul, John Schafer, and Carole B. Cunradi. 2001. "Alcohol-Related Intimate Partner Violence among White, Black, and Hispanic Couples in the United States." *Alcohol Research & Health* 25(1):58–65.

Cahalan, Susannah. 2012. *Brain on Fire: My Month of Madness*. 1st Free Press hardcover ed. New York, NY: Free Press.

Calvo, Franz, Bryant T. Karras, Richard Phillips, Ann Marie Kimball, and Fred Wolf. 2003. "Diagnoses, Syndromes, and Diseases: A Knowledge Representation Problem." *AMIA ... Annual Symposium Proceedings. AMIA Symposium* 802.

Campbell, Jacquelyn C., Joan Kub, Ruth Ann Belknap, and Thomas N. Templin. 1997. "Predictors of Depression in Battered Women." *Violence Against Women* 3(3):271–93.

Campbell, Joan M. 1983. "Ambient Stressors." *Environment and Behavior* 15:355–80.

Carlat, Daniel J. 2010. *Unhinged: The Trouble with Psychiatry—A Doctor's Revelations about a Profession in Crisis*. New York, NY: Free Press.

Carr, Deborah. 2011. *Life Course*. 9780199756384-0030.

Cartwright, Samuel. 1851. "Diseases and Peculiarities of the Negro Race."

Castañeda, Carlos. 1968. *The Teachings of Don Juan: A Yaqui Way of Knowledge*. New York, NY: Simon and Schuster.

Catalano, Ralph A., and William McConnell. 1996. "A Time-Series Test of the Quarantine Theory of Involuntary Commitment." *Journal of Health and Social Behavior* 37(4):381. doi: 10.2307/2137264.

Cavanaugh, Ray. 2015. "From Demons to Doctors." *History Today* 65(4):44–45.

Center for Behavioral Health Statistics and Quality. 2017a. *Results from the 2016 National Survey on Drug Use and Health: Detailed Tables*. Rockville, MD: Substance Abuse and Mental Health Services Administration.

Centers for Disease Control and Prevention. 2017. Youth Risk Behavior Surveillance—United States. *MMWR* 67(8), 1–114.

Centers for Disease Control and Prevention. 2019. *Early Release of Selected Estimates Based on Data from the 2018 National Health Interview Survey*.

Centers for Disease Control and Prevention. 2020a. *Healthy People*.

Centers for Disease Control and Prevention. 2020b. *Household Pulse Survey*.

Charland, Louis C. 2002. "Tuke's Healing Discipline: Commentary on Erica Lilleleht's Progress and Power: Exploring the Disciplinary Connections between Moral Treatment and Psychiatric Rehabilitation." *Philosophy, Psychiatry, & Psychology* 9(2):183–86. doi: 10.1353/ppp.2003.0023.

Chatterji, Somnath, Jordi Alonso, Maria V. Petukhova, Gemma Vilagut, Meyer Glantz, and Mohammad Salih Khalaf. 2013a. "Disability Associated with Common Mental and Physical Disorders." Pp. 186–94 in *The Burdens of Mental Disorders: Global Perspectives from the WHO World Mental Health Surveys*, edited by Jordi Alonso, Somnath Chatterji, and Yanling He. Cambridge: Cambridge University Press.

Chatterji, Somnath, Yanling He, and Jordi Alonso. 2013b. "Conclusions and Future Directions." Pp. 244–47 in *The Burdens of Mental Disorders: Global Perspectives from the WHO World Mental Health Surveys*, edited by Jordi Alonso, Somnath

Chatterji, and Yanling He. Cambridge: Cambridge University Press.

Cheadle, Jacob E., and Les B. Whitbeck. 2011. "Alcohol Use Trajectories and Problem Drinking Over the Course of Adolescence: A Study of North American Indigenous Youth and Their Caretakers." *Journal of Health and Social Behavior* 52(2):228–45. doi: 10.1177/0022146510393973.

Cheng, Zhiming, Haining Wang, and Russell Smyth. 2013. "Happiness and Job Satisfaction in Urban China: A Comparative Study of Two Generations of Migrants and Urban Locals." *Urban Studies* 51(10):2160–84. doi: 10.1177/0042098013506042.

Cho, Young-A, Woo-Teak Jeon, Jong-Ja Yu, and Jin-Sup Um. 2005. "Predictors of Depression among North Korean Defectors: A 3-Year Follow-up Study." *Korean Journal of Counseling and Psychotherapy* 17(2):467–84.

Choi, Heejeong, and Nadine F. Marks. 2008. "Marital Conflict, Depressive Symptoms, and Functrional Impairment." *Journal of Marriage and the Family* 70(2):377–90.

Choudhry, Fahad Riaz, Vasudevan Mani, Long Ming, and Tahir Mehmood Khan. 2016. "Beliefs and Perception about Mental Health Issues: A Meta-Synthesis." *Neuropsychiatric Disease and Treatment* 12:2807–18. doi: 10.2147/NDT.S111543.

Christensen, Krista, Marjorie J. Coons, Reghan O. Walsh, Jon G. Meiman, and Elizabeth Neary. 2019. "Childhood Lead Poisoning in Wisconsin." *WMJ* 118(1):16–20.

Chun, Hae-ryoung, Inhyung Cho, Youngeun Choi, and Sung-il Cho. 2020. "Effects of Emotional Labor Factors and Working Environment on the Risk of Depression in Pink-Collar Workers." *International Journal of Environmental Research and Public Health* 17(14):5208. doi: 10.3390/ijerph17145208.

Chung, Angie Y. 2017. "Behind the Myth of the Matriarch and the Flagbearer: How Korean and Chinese American Sons and Daughters Negotiate Gender, Family, and Emotions." *Sociological Forum* 32(1):28–49. doi: 10.1111/socf.12316.

Cisek, Sylwia Z., Claire M. Hart, and Constantine Sedikides. 2008. "Do Narcissists Use Material Possessions as a Primary Buffer against Pain?" *Psychological Inquiry* 19(3–4):205–7. doi: 10.1080/10478400802608848.

Clark, Andrew E., and Andrew J. Oswald. 1996. "Satisfaction and Comparison Income." *Journal of Public Economics* 61(3):359–81. doi: 10.1016/0047-2727(95)01564-7.

Cohen, Ayala. 2009. "Welfare Clients' Volunteering as a Means of Empowerment." *Nonprofit and Voluntary Sector Quarterly* 38(3):522–34. doi: 10.1177/0899764008320196.

Cohen, Sheldon, William J. Doyle, and Andrew Baum. 2006. "Socioeconomic Status Is Associated With Stress Hormones." *Psychosomatic Medicine*, 68(3):414-20. doi: 10.1097/01.psy.0000221236.37158.b9.

Committee to Evaluate the Department of Veterans Affairs Mental Health Services, Board on Health Care Services, Health and Medicine Division, and National Academies of Sciences, Engineering, and Medicine. 2018. *Evaluation of the Department of Veterans Affairs Mental Health Services*. Washington, DC: National Academies Press.

Connell, R. W., and James W. Messerschmidt. 2005. "Hegemonic Masculinity: Rethinking the Concept." *Gender & Society* 19(6):829–59. doi: 10.1177/0891243205278639.

Conner, Kyaien O., Brenda Lee, Vanessa Mayers, Deborah Robinson, Charles F. Reynolds, Steve Albert, and Charlotte Brown. 2010. "Attitudes and Beliefs about Mental Health among African American Older Adults Suffering from Depression." *Journal of Aging Studies* 24(4):266–77. doi: 10.1016/j.jaging.2010.05.007.

Conrad, Peter. 1992. "Medicalization and Social Control." *Annual Review of Sociology* 18:209–32.

Conrad, Peter. 2007. *The Medicalization of Society: On the Transformation of Human Conditions into Treatable Disorders*. Baltimore, MD: Johns Hopkins University Press.

Conwell, Yeates, Kimberly Van Orden, and Eric D. Caine. 2011. "Suicide in Older Adults." *Psychiatric Clinics of North America* 34(2):451–68. doi: 10.1016/j.psc.2011.02.002.

Cooley, Charles Horton. 1902. *Humnan Nature and the Social Order*. New York, NY: Charles Scribner and Sons.

Cooper, M. Lynne, Marcia Russell, Jeremy B. Skinner, Michael R. Frone, and Pamela Mudar. 1992. "Stress and Alcohol Use: Moderating Effects of Gender, Coping, and Alcohol Expectancies." *Journal of Abnormal Psychology* 101(1):139–52. doi: 10.1037/0021-843X.101.1.139.

Coppola, Federica. 2019. "Motus Animi in Mente Insana: An Emotion-Oriented Paradigm of Legal Insanity Informed by the Neuroscience of Moral Judgments and Decision-Making." *Journal of Criminal Law & Criminology* 109(1):1–69.

Corbally, Melissa. 2015. "Accounting for Intimate Partner Violence: A Biographical Analysis of Narrative Strategies Used by Men Experiencing IPV From Their Female Partners." *Journal of Interpersonal Violence* 30(17):3112–32. doi: 10.1177/0886260514554429.

Corin, Ellen. 1994. "The Social and Cultural Matrix of Health and Disease." Pp. 93–132 in *Why Are Some People Health and Others Not?: The Determinants of Health of Populations*, edited by Robert G. Evans, Morris L. Barer, and Theodore R. Marmor. Hawthorne, NY: Aldine De Gruyter.

Cornwell, Erin York. 2014. "Social Resources and Disordered Living Conditions: Evidence from a National Sample of Community-Residing Older Adults." *Research on Aging* 36(4):399–430. doi: 10.1177/0164027513497369.

Cornwell, Erin York, and Linda J. Waite. 2009. "Social Disconnectedness, Perceived Isolation, and Health among Older Adults." *Journal of Health and Social Behavior* 50(1):31–48. doi: 10.1177/002214650905000103.

Corrigan, Patrick W. 1998. "The Impact of Stigma on Severe Mental Illness." *Cognitive and Behavioral Practice* 5(2):201-222.

Corrigan, Patrick W., Fred E. Markowitz, and Amy C. Watson. 2004. "Structural Levels of Mental Illness Stigma and Discrimination." *Schizophrenia Bulletin* 30(3):481–91. doi: 10.1093/oxfordjournals.schbul.a007096.

Corrigan, Patrick, Fred E. Markowitz, Amy Watson, David Rowan, and Mary Ann Kubiak. 2003. "An Attribution Model of Public Discrimination towards Persons with Mental Illness." *Journal of Health and Social Behavior* 44(2):162. doi: 10.2307/1519806.

Cortina, Melissa A. 2012. "Prevalence of Child Mental Health Problems in Sub-Saharan Africa: A Systematic Review." *Archives of Pediatrics & Adolescent Medicine* 166(3):276. doi: 10.1001/archpediatrics.2011.592.

Costello, C. G., and Andrew L. Comrey. 1967. "Scales For Measuring Depression and Anxiety." *The Journal of Psychology* 66(2):303–13. doi: 10.1080/00223980.1967.10544910.

Costello, Lauren Fries, and Sacha Klein. 2019. "Racial/Ethnic Differences in Determinants of Trauma Symptomatology among Children in the U.S. Child Welfare System Exposed to Intimate Partner Violence." *Journal of Family Violence* 34(1):33–45. doi: 10.1007/s10896-018-9976-1.

Cowan, C. S. M., B. L. Callaghan, J. M. Kan, and R. Richardson. 2015. "The Lasting Impact of Early-Life Adversity on Individuals and Their Descendants: Potential Mechanisms and Hope for Intervention: Impact of Early-Life Adversity on Individuals and Their Descendants." *Genes, Brain and Behavior* 15(1):155–68. doi: 10.1111/gbb.12263.

Creed, Peter A., Judy Searle, and Mary E. Rogers. 2010. "Medical Specialty Prestige and Lifestyle Preferences for Medical Students." *Social Science & Medicine* 71(6):1084–88. doi: 10.1016/j.socscimed.2010.06.027.

Crenner, Christopher 2012. "The Tuskegee Syphilis Study and the Scientific Concept of Racial Nervous Resistance." *Journal of the History of Medicine and Allied Sciences* 67(2):244–80. doi: 10.1093/jhmas/jrr003.

Crnic, Keith A., and Cathryn L. Booth. 1991. "Mothers' and Fathers' Perceptions of Daily Hassles of Parenting across Early Childhood." *Journal of Marriage and Family* 53(4):1042. doi: 10.2307/353007.

Crocq, Marc-Antoine, and Louis Crocq. 2000. "From Shell Shock and War Neurosis to Posttraumatic Stress Disorder: A History of Psychotraumatology." *Dialogues in Clinical Neuroscience* 2(1):47–55.

Cui, Ming, Hille Janhonen-Abruquah, Carol A. Darling, Fiorella L. Carlos Chavez, and Päivi Palojoki. 2019. "Helicopter Parenting and Young Adults' Well-Being: A Comparison between United States and Finland." *Cross-Cultural Research* 53(4):410–27. doi: 10.1177/1069397118802253.

Dahrendorf, Ralf. 1959. *Class and Class Conflict in Industrial Society*. Stanford, CA: Stanford University Press.

D'Ambrosio, Conchita, Markus Jäntti, and Anthony Lepinteur. 2020. "Money and Happiness: Income, Wealth and Subjective Well-Being." *Social Indicators Research* 148(1):47–66. doi: 10.1007/s11205-019-02186-w.

D'Andrea, Wendy, Ritu Sharma, Amanda D. Zelechoski, and Joseph Spinazzola. 2011. "Physical Health Problems After Single Trauma Exposure: When Stress Takes Root in the Body." *Journal of the American Psychiatric Nurses Association* 17(6):378–92. doi: 10.1177/1078390311425187.

David, E. J. R. 2008. "A Colonial Mentality Model of Depression for Filipino Americans." *Cultural Diversity and Ethnic Minority Psychology* 14(2):118–27. doi: 10.1037/1099-9809.14.2.118.

DeAngelis, Reed T., and Christopher G. Ellison. 2018. "Aspiration Strain and Mental Health: The Education-Contingent Role of Religion." *Journal for the Scientific Study of Religion* 57(2):341–64. doi: 10.1111/jssr.12520.

Deas-Nesmith, D., and S. McLeod-Bryant. 1992. "Psychiatric Deinstitutionalization and Its Cultural Insensitivity: Consequences and Recommendations for the Future." *Journal of the National Medical Association* 84(12):1036–40.

Deery, Stephen J., Roderick D. Iverson, and Janet T. Walsh. 2010. "Coping Strategies in Call Centres: Work Intensity and the Role of Co-Workers and Supervisors." *British Journal of Industrial Relations* 48(1):181–200. doi: 10.1111/j.1467-8543.2009.00755.x.

deLara, Ellen W. 2019. "Correction to: Consequences of Childhood Bullying on Mental Health and Relationships for Young Adults." *Journal of Child and Family Studies* 28(9):2631. doi: 10.1007/s10826-019-01515-4.

Desai, Pooja R., Kenneth A. Lawson, Jamie C. Barner, and Karen L. Rascati. 2013. "Estimating the Direct and Indirect Costs for Community-Dwelling Patients with Schizophrenia: Schizophrenia-Related Costs for Community-Dwellers." *Journal of Pharmaceutical Health Services Research* 4(4):187–94. doi: 10.1111/jphs.12027.

Desjarlais, Robert R., Leon Eisenberg, Byron Good, and Arthur Kleinman. 1996. *World Mental Health: Problems, Priorities, and Responses in Low-Income Countries*. New York, NY: Oxford Univ. Press.

Destin, Mesmin, and Régine Debrosse. 2017. "Upward Social Mobility and Identity." *Current Opinion in Psychology* 18:99–104. doi: 10.1016/j.copsyc.2017.08.006.

Devries, Karen, Charlotte Watts, Mieko Yoshihama, Ligia Kiss, Lilia Blima Schraiber, Negussie Deyessa, Lori Heise, Julia Durand, Jessie Mbwambo, Henrica Jansen, Yemane Berhane, Mary Ellsberg, and Claudia Garcia-Moreno. 2011. "Violence against Women Is Strongly Associated with Suicide Attempts: Evidence from the WHO Multi-Country Study on Women's Health and Domestic Violence against Women." *Social Science & Medicine* 73(1):79–86. doi: 10.1016/j.socscimed.2011.05.006.

Diaz, Christina J., and Michael Niño. 2019. "Familism and the Hispanic Health Advantage: The Role of Immigrant Status." *Journal of Health and Social Behavior* 60(3):274–90. doi: 10.1177/0022146519869027.

Diez Roux, Ana V., and Christina Mair. 2010. "Neighborhoods and Health: Neighborhoods and Health." *Annals of the New York Academy of Sciences* 1186(1):125–45. doi: 10.1111/j.1749-6632.2009.05333.x.

Dinwiddie, Gniesha Y., Darrell J. Gaskin, Kitty S. Chan, Janette Norrington, and Rachel McCleary. 2013. "Residential Segregation, Geographic Proximity and Type of Services Used: Evidence for Racial/Ethnic Disparities in Mental Health." *Social Science & Medicine* 80:67–75. doi: 10.1016/j.socscimed.2012.11.024.

Dirks-Linhorst, P. Ann. 2014. "Missouri's Not Guilty by Reason of Insanity Acquittees, 1980–2009: Is Gender Important When Comparing

Female and Male Insanity Acquittees and Convicted Offenders?" *Women & Criminal Justice* 24(3):252–77. doi: 10.1080/08974454.2014.890160.

Dix, Dorothea. 1843. *Memorial to the Legislature of Massachusetts*. Boston, MA: Munroe & Francis.

Dohrenwend, Bruce P., Itzhak Levav, Patrick E. Shrout, Andrew E. Schwartz, Guedalia Naveh, Bruce G. Link, Andrew E. Skodol, and Ann Stueve. 1992. "Socioeconomic Status and Psychiatric Disorders: The Causation-Selection Issue." *Science* 255(5047):946–52. doi: 10.1126/science.1546291.

Dohrenwend, Bruce P., Patrick E. Shrout, Gladys Egri, and Frederick S. Mendelsohn. 1980. "Nonspecific Psychological Distress and Other Dimensions of Psychopathology. Measures for Use in the General Population." *Archives of General Psychiatry* 37(11):1229–36. doi: 10.1001/archpsyc.1980.01780240027003.

Douglas, Karen C., and Darlene Fujimoto. 1995. "Asian Pacific Elders. Implications for Health Care Providers." *Clinics in Geriatric Medicine* 11(1):69–82.

Dowd, Jennifer B., Amanda M. Simanek, and Allison E. Aiello. 2009. "Socio-Economic Status, Cortisol and Allostatic Load: A Review of the Literature." *International Journal of Epidemiology* 38(5):1297–1309. doi: 10.1093/ije/dyp277.

Doyle, David Matthew, and Lisa Molix. 2018. "Stigma Consciousness Modulates Cortisol Reactivity to Social Stress in Women: Stigma Consciousness and Cortisol Reactivity." *European Journal of Social Psychology* 48(2):217–24. doi: 10.1002/ejsp.2310.

Drake, Robert E., Jonathan S. Skinner, Gary R. Bond, and Howard H. Goldman. 2009. "Social Security and Mental Illness: Reducing Disability with Supported Employment." *Health Affairs* 28(3):761–70. doi: 10.1377/hlthaff.28.3.761.

Drescher, Jack. 2015. "Out of DSM: Depathologizing Homosexuality." *Behavioral Sciences* 5(4):565–75. doi: 10.3390/bs5040565.

Dressler, William W. 1985. "Psychosomatic Symptoms, Stess, and Modernization: A Model." *Medicine and Psychiatry* 9(3):257–86.

Drew, Elaine M., and Nancy E. Schoenberg. 2011. "Deconstructing Fatalism: Ethnographic Perspectives on Women's Decision Making about Cancer Prevention and Treatment: Deconstructing Fatalism." *Medical Anthropology Quarterly* 25(2):164–82. doi: 10.1111/j.1548-1387.2010.01136.x.

Duan, Li, Xiaojun Shao, Yuan Wang, Yinglin Huang, Junxiao Miao, Xueping Yang, and Gang Zhu. 2020. "An Investigation of Mental Health Status of Children and Adolescents in China during the Outbreak of COVID-19." *Journal of Affective Disorders* 275:112–18. doi: 10.1016/j.jad.2020.06.029.

Dunbar, Michael S., Lisa Sontag-Padilla, Rajeev Ramchand, Rachana Seelam, and Bradley D. Stein. 2017. "Mental Health Service Utilization among Lesbian, Gay, Bisexual, and Questioning or Queer College Students." *Journal of Adolescent Health* 61(3):294–301. doi: 10.1016/j.jadohealth.2017.03.008.

Duncan, Lauren E. 2006. "What Feminist and Political Psychologists Can Learn from Each Other: The Case of Authoritarianism." *Feminism & Psychology* 16(1):58–64. doi: 10.1177/0959-353506060821.

Dupéré, Véronique, Tama Leventhal, and Frank Vitaro. 2012. "Neighborhood Processes, Self-Efficacy, and Adolescent Mental Health." *Journal of Health and Social Behavior* 53(2):183–98. doi: 10.1177/0022146512442676.

Early, Pete. 2014. "My Son Says: 'If You Are Afraid To Tell Your Story, Stigma Wins." *Official Website of Pete Early.* Retrieved October 24, 2021. http://www.peteearley.com/2014/07/14/son-says-afraid-tell-story-stigma-wins/.

Eaton, William W. 2001. *The Sociology of Mental Disorders*. 3rd ed. Westport, CT: Praeger.

Eaton, William W., and Carles Muntaner. 2017. "Socioeconomic Stratification and Mental Disorder." Pp. 239–66 in *A Handbook for the Study of Mental Health: Social Contexts, Theories, and Systems*, edited by Teresa L. Scheid and Eric R. Wright. Cambridge: Cambridge University Press.

Ebert, David D., Claudia Buntrock, Philippe Mortier, Randy Auerbach, Kiona K. Weisel, Ronald C. Kessler, Pim Cuijpers, Jennifer G. Green, Glenn Kiekens, Matthew K. Nock, Koen Demyttenaere, and Ronny Bruffaerts. 2019. "Prediction of Major Depressive Disorder Onset in College Students."

Depression and Anxiety 36(4):294–304. doi: 10.1002/da.22867.

Eder, Donna, Catherine Colleen Evans, and Stephen Parker. 1995. *School Talk: Gender and Adolescent Culture*. New Brunswick, NJ: Rutgers University Press.

Edidin, Jennifer P., Zoe Ganim, Scott J. Hunter, and Niranjan S. Karnik. 2012. "The Mental and Physical Health of Homeless Youth: A Literature Review." *Child Psychiatry & Human Development* 43(3):354–75. doi: 10.1007/s10578-011-0270-1.

Eisenberg, Leon. 1995. "The Social Construction of the Human Brain." *American Journal of Psychiatry* 152(11):1563–1575. doi: 10.1176/ajp.152.11.1563b.

Eldridge, Larry D. 1996. "'Crazy Brained': Mental Illness in Colonial America." *Bulletin of the History of Medicine* 70(3):361–86.

Elliott, Luther, Alexander S. Bennett, Kelly Szott, and Andrew Golub. 2018. "Competing Constructivisms: The Negotiation of PTSD and Related Stigma among Post-9/11 Veterans in New York City." *Culture, Medicine, and Psychiatry* 42(4):778–99. doi: 10.1007/s11013-018-9586-7.

Elliott, Marta. 2013. "Gender Differences in the Determinants of Distress, Alcohol Misuse, and Related Psychiatric Disorders." *Society and Mental Health* 3(2):96–113. doi: 10.1177/2156869312474828.

Ellis, B. Heidi, Helen Z. MacDonald, Alisa K. Lincoln, and Howard J. Cabral. 2008. "Mental Health of Somali Adolescent Refugees: The Role of Trauma, Stress, and Perceived Discrimination." *Journal of Consulting and Clinical Psychology* 76(2):184–93. doi: 10.1037/0022-006X.76.2.184.

Ellis, Trenton, and Breanna Brass. 2018. "Bullying Victimization as a Predictor of Suicidality among South Dakota Adolescents: A Secondary Data Analysis Using the 2015 Youth Risk Behavior Survey." *The Great Plains Sociologist* 27:41.

Emery, Clifton R., Jung Yun Lee, and Chulhee Kang. 2015. "Life after the Pan and the Fire: Depression, Order, Attachment, and the Legacy of Abuse among North Korean Refugee Youth and Adolescent Children of North Korean Refugees." *Child Abuse & Neglect* 45:90–100. doi: 10.1016/j.chiabu.2015.02.002.

Enders, Walter, and Todd Sandler. 2012. *The Political Economy of Terrorism*. Cambridge: Cambridge University Press.

English, Devin, Sharon F. Lambert, Brendesha M. Tynes, Lisa Bowleg, Maria Cecilia Zea, and Lionel C. Howard. 2020. "Daily Multidimensional Racial Discrimination among Black U.S. American Adolescents." *Journal of Applied Developmental Psychology* 66:101068. doi: 10.1016/j.appdev.2019.101068.

Eriksen, Karen, and Victoria E. Kress. 2008. "Gender and Diagnosis: Struggles and Suggestions for Counselors." *Journal of Counseling & Development* 86(2):152–62. doi: 10.1002/j.1556-6678.2008.tb00492.x.

Erikson, Erik H. 1993. *Childhood and Society*. New York, NY: Norton.

Erskine, H. E., T. E. Moffitt, W. E. Copeland, E. J. Costello, A. J. Ferrari, G. Patton, L. Degenhardt, T. Vos, H. A. Whiteford, and J. G. Scott. 2015. "A Heavy Burden on Young Minds: The Global Burden of Mental and Substance Use Disorders in Children and Youth." *Psychological Medicine* 45(7):1551–63. doi: 10.1017/S0033291714002888.

Escamilla, Michael A., and Juan M. Zavala. 2008. "Genetics of Bipolar Disorder." *Dialogues in Clinical Neuroscience* 10(2):141–52.

Espí Forcén, Carlos, and Fernando Espí Forcén. 2014. "Demonic Possessions and Mental Illness: Discussion of Selected Cases in Late Medieval Hagiographical Literature." *Early Science in Medicine* 19(3):258–79. doi: 10.1163/15733823-00193p03.

Evans, Gary W., and Kimberly English. 2002. "The Environment of Poverty: Multiple Stressor Exposure, Psychophysiological Stress, and Socioemotional Adjustment." *Child Development* 73(4):1238–48. doi: 10.1111/1467-8624.00469.

Evans, Gary W., Stephen V. Jacobs, David Dooley, and Ralph Catalano. 1987. "The Interaction of Stressful Life Events and Chronic Strains on Community Mental Health." *American Journal of Community Psychology* 15(1):23–34. doi: 10.1007/BF00919755.

Evans, Gary W., and Pilyoung Kim. 2007. "Childhood Poverty and Health: Cumulative Risk Exposure and Stress Dysregulation." *Psychological Science* 18(11):953–57. doi: 10.1111/j.1467-9280.2007.02008.x.

Evans, Gary W., Nancy M. Wells, and Annie Moch. 2003. "Housing and Mental Health: A Review of the Evidence and a Methodological and Conceptual Critique: Housing and Mental Health." *Journal of Social Issues* 59(3):475–500. doi: 10.1111/1540-4560.00074.

Evans, Sarah E., Corrie Davies, and David DiLillo. 2008. "Exposure to Domestic Violence: A Meta-Analysis of Child and Adolescent Outcomes." *Aggression and Violent Behavior* 13(2):131–40. doi: 10.1016/j.avb.2008.02.005.

Farewell, Charlotte V., Jennifer Jewell, Jessica Walls, and Jenn A. Leiferman. 2020. "A Mixed-Methods Pilot Study of Perinatal Risk and Resilience during COVID-19." *Journal of Primary Care & Community Health* 11:215013272094407. doi: 10.1177/2150132720944074.

Faris, Robert E. L., and H. Warren Dunham. 1939. *Mental Disorders in Urban Areas: An Ecological Study of Schizophrenia and Other Psychoses*. Chicago, IL: University of Chicago Press.

Farreras, Irene G., 2022. "History of Mental Illness." In *Psychology: Noba Textbook Series*, edited by R. Biswas-Diener, and E. Diener. Champaign, IL: DEF Publishers. Retrieved from http://noba.to/65w3s7ex.

Faupel, Charles E., Greg S. Weaver, and Jay Corzine. 2014. *The Sociology of American Drug Use*. 3rd ed. New York, NY: Oxford University Press.

Ferracuti Franco. 1982. "A Sociopsychiatric Interpretation of Terrorism." *The Annals of the American Academy of Political and Social Science*, 463: 129–41.

Finkelhor, David. 1984. *Child Sexual Abuse: New Theory and Research*. New York, NY: Free Press.

Finkelhor, David, Heather Turner, Richard Ormrod, and Sherry L. Hamby. 2009. "Violence, Abuse, and Crime Exposure in a National Sample of Children and Youth." *Pediatrics* 124(5):1411–23. Doi: 10.1542/peds.2009-0467.

Finkelhor, David, and Anne Shattuck. 2012. *Characteristics of Crimes against Juveniles*. Durham, NH: University of New Hampshire.

Fischer, Margit. 1971. "Psychoses in the Offspring of Schizophrenic Monozygotic Twins and Their Normal Co-Twins." *British Journal of Psychiatry* 118(542):43–52. Doi: 10.1192/bjp.118.542.43.

Foley, Henry A., and Steven S. Sharfstein. 1983. *Madness and Government: Who Cares for the Mentally Ill?* Washington, DC: American Psychiatric Press.

Foster, Holly, and John Hagan. 2013. "Maternal and Paternal Imprisonment in the Stress Process." *Social Science Research* 42(3):650–69. Doi: 10.1016/j.ssresearch.2013.01.008.

Foucault, Michel. 1965. *Madness and Civilization: A History of Insanity in the Age of Reason*. New York, NY: Pantheon Books.

Fox, John W. 1990. "Social Class, Mental Illness, and Social Mobility: The Social Selection-Drift Hypothesis for Serious Mental Illness." *Journal of Health and Social Behavior* 31(4):344. Doi: 10.2307/2136818.

Frances, Allen. 2016. "Entrenched Reductionisms: The Bête Noire of Psychiatry." *History of Psychology* 19(1):57–59. Doi: 10.1037/hop0000018.

Frances, Allen J. 2012. *DSM 5 Is Guide Not Bible—Ignore Its Ten Worst Changes: APA Approval of DSM-5 Is a Sad Day for Psychiatry.*

Frank, Richard G., and Sherry Glied. 2006. *Better But Not Well: Mental Health Policy in the United States Since 1950*. Baltimore, MD: Johns Hopkins University Press.

Fraser, John, Susan Clayton, Jessica Sickler, and Anthony Taylor. 2009. "Belonging at the Zoo: Retired Volunteers, Conservation Activism and Collective Identity." *Ageing and Society* 29(3): 351–68. Doi: 10.1017/S0144686X08007915.

Freedenthal, Stacey, and Arlene Rubin Stiffman. 2004. "Suicidal Behavior in Urban American Indian Adolescents: A Comparison with Reservation Youth in a Southwestern State." *Suicide and Life-Threatening Behavior* 34(2):160–71.

Friedan, Betty. 1963. *The Feminine Mystique*. New York, NY: WW Norton and Company.

Frissen, Aleida, Jim van Os, Ritsaert Lieverse, Petra Habets, Ed Gronenschild, and Machteld Marcelis. 2017. "No Evidence of Association between Childhood Urban Environment and Cortical Thinning in Psychotic Disorder." *Plos One* 12(1):e0166651. Doi: 10.1371/journal.pone.0166651.

Fromm, Erich. 1955. *The Sane Society*. Greenwich, CT: Fawcett Premier.

Fromm, Erich. 2010. *The Pathology of Normalcy*. Riverdale, NY: AMHF.

Fula, Emma, Xian Warner, Stephanie Miedema, Rachel Jewkes, Tim Rosselii, and James Lang. 2013. *Why Do Some Men Use Violence Against Women and How Can We Prevent IT? Quantitative Findings from the United Nations Multi-Country Study on Men and Violence in Asia and the Pacific*. Bangkok: UNDP, UNFPA, UN Women, and UNV.

Fullana, Miquel A., Diego Hidalgo-Mazzei, Eduard Vieta, and Joaquim Radua. 2020. "Coping Behaviors Associated with Decreased Anxiety and Depressive Symptoms during the COVID-19 Pandemic and Lockdown." *Journal of Affective Disorders* 275:80–81. doi: 10.1016/j.jad.2020.06.027.

Fuqua, Paul Q. 1978. *Drug Abuse: Investigation and Control*: New York, NY: McGraw-Hill.

Furr, L. Allen. 2002. "Perceptions of Genetics Research As Harmful to Society: Differences among Samples of African-Americans and European-Americans." *Genetic Testing* 6(1):25–30. doi: 10.1089/109065702760093889.

Furr, L. Allen. 2004. "Medicalization in Nepal: A Study of the Influence of Westernization on Defining Deviant and Illness Behavior in a Developing Country." *International Journal of Comparative Sociology* 45(1–2):131–42. doi: 10.1177/0020715204048314.

Furr, L. Allen. 2005. "On the Relationship between Cultural Values and Preferences and Affective Health in Nepal." *International Journal of Social Psychiatry* 51(1):71–82. doi: 10.1177/0020764005053283.

Furr, L. Allen. 2014. "Facial Disfigurement Stigma: A Study of Victims of Domestic Assaults with Fire in India." *Violence Against Women* 20(7):783–98.

Furr, L. Allen, Wayne Usui, and Vicki Hines-Martin. 2003. "Authoritarianism and Attitudes toward Mental Health Services." *American Journal of Orthopsychiatry* 73(4):411–18. doi: 10.1037/0002-9432.73.4.411.

Fuss, Johannes, Peer Briken, and Verena Klein. 2018. "Gender Bias in Clinicians' Pathologization of Atypical Sexuality: A Randomized Controlled Trial with Mental Health Professionals." *Scientific Reports* 8(1):3715. doi: 10.1038/s41598-018-22108-z.

Gade, Christian B. N. 2011. "The Historical Development of the Written Discourses on Ubuntu." *South African Journal of Philosophy* 30: 303–29.

Galea, Sandro, Jennifer Ahern, Heidi Resnick, Dean Kilpatrick, Michael Bucuvalas, Joel Gold, and David Vlahov. 2002. "Psychological Sequelae of the September 11 Terrorist Attacks in New York City." *New England Journal of Medicine* 346(13):982–87. doi: 10.1056/NEJMsa013404.

Galea, Sandro, David Vlahov, Heidi Resnick, Jennifer Ahern, Ezra Susser, Joel Gold, Michael Bucuvalas, and Dean Kilpatrick. 2003. "Trends of Probable Post-Traumatic Stress Disorder in New York City after the September 11 Terrorist Attacks." *American Journal of Epidemiology* 158(6):514–24. doi: 10.1093/aje/kwg187.

Garfinkel, Harold. 1956. "Conditions of Successful Degradation Ceremonies." *American Journal of Sociology* 61(5):420–24.

Gary, Tiffany L., Sarah A. Stark, and Thomas A. LaVeist. 2007. "Neighborhood Characteristics and Mental Health among African Americans and Whites Living in a Racially Integrated Urban Community." *Health & Place* 13(2):569–75. doi: 10.1016/j.healthplace.2006.06.001.

Gayman, Mathew D., and Juan Barragan. 2013. "Multiple Perceived Reasons for Major Discrimination and Depression." *Society and Mental Health* 3(3):203–20. doi: 10.1177/2156869313496438.

Gee, Gilbert C., Andrew Ryan, David J. Laflamme, and Jeanie Holt. 2006. "Self-Reported Discrimination and Mental Health Status among African Descendants, Mexican Americans, and Other Latinos in the New Hampshire REACH 2010 Initiative: The Added Dimension of Immigration."

American Journal of Public Health 96(10): 1821–28. doi: 10.2105/AJPH.2005.080085.

Gejman, Pablo V., Alan R. Sanders, and Jubao Duan. 2010. "The Role of Genetics in the Etiology of Schizophrenia." *Psychiatric Clinics of North America* 33(1):35–66. doi: 10.1016/j.psc.2009.12.003.

George, Susan. 2006. *Religion and Technology in the 21st Century: Faith in the e-World*. Hershey, PA: Information Science Pub.

Gessen, Masha. 2015. *The Brothers: The Road to an American Tragedy*. New York, NY: Riverhead Books.

Gill, Duane A., J. Steven Picou, and Liesel A. Ritchie. 2012. "The Exxon Valdez and BP Oil Spills: A Comparison of Initial Social and Psychological Impacts*." *American Behavioral Scientist* 56(1): 3–23. doi: 10.1177/0002764211408585.

Gilman, Sander L., and James M. Thomas. 2016. *Are Racists Crazy? How Prejudice, Racism, and Antisemitism Became Markers of Insanity*. New York, NY: New York University Press.

Girgus, Joan, Kaite Yang, and Christine Ferri. 2017. "The Gender Difference in Depression: Are Elderly Women at Greater Risk for Depression than Elderly Men?" *Geriatrics* 2(4):35. doi: 10.3390/geriatrics2040035.

Glick, Ilra D., Steven S. Sharfstein, and Harold I. Schwartz. 2011. "Inpatient Psychiatric Care in the 21st Century: The Need for Reform." *Psychiatric Services* 62(1):206–9.

Goffman, Erving. 1961. *Asylums: Essays on the Social Situation of Mental Patients and Other Inmates*. Garden City, NY: Anchor Books.

Goffman, Erving. 1963. *Stigma: Notes on the Management of Spoiled Identity*. New York, NY: Simon and Schuster.

Goldfried, Marvin R. 2016. "On Possible Consequences of National Institute of Mental Health Funding for Psychotherapy Research and Training." *Professional Psychology: Research and Practice* 47(1):77–83. doi: 10.1037/pro0000034.

Goldman, Bruce. 2017. "Two Minds: The Cognitive Differences between Men and Women." *Standford Medicine*.

Goldman, Howard H., and Gerald N. Grob. 2006. "Defining 'Mental Illness' in Mental Health Policy." *Health Affairs* 25(3):737–49. doi: 10.1377/hlthaff.25.3.737.

Gonzalez, Hector M., Mary N. Haan, and Ladson Hinton. 2001. "Acculturation and the Prevalence of Depression in Older Mexican Americans: Baseline Results of the Sacramento Area Latino Study on Aging." *Journal of the American Geriatrics Society* 49(7):948–53. doi: 10.1046/j.1532-5415.2001.49186.x.

Goth, Kirstin, Pamela Foelsch, Susanne Schlüter-Müller, Marc Birkhölzer, Emanuel Jung, Oliver Pick, and Klaus Schmeck. 2012. "Assessment of Identity Development and Identity Diffusion in Adolescence - Theoretical Basis and Psychometric Properties of the Self-Report Questionnaire AIDA." *Child and Adolescent Psychiatry and Mental Health* 6(1):27. doi: 10.1186/1753-2000-6-27.

Gove, Walter R. 1984. "Gender Differences in Mental and Physical Illness: The Effects of Fixed Roles and Nurturant Roles." *Social Science and Medicine* 19(2):77–84.

Greenfield, Emily A., George E. Vaillant, and Nadine F. Marks. 2009. "Do Formal Religious Participation and Spiritual Perceptions Have Independent Linkages with Diverse Dimensions of Psychological Well-Being?" *Journal of Health and Social Behavior* 50(2):196–212. doi: 10.1177/002214650905000206.

Greenstein, Luna. 2017. "9 Ways to Fight Mental Health Stigma."

Greenwald, Mark K., E. W. Cook, and Peter J. Lang. 1989. "Affective Judgment and Psychophysiological Response: Dimensional Covariation in the Evaluation of Pictorial Stimuli." *Journal of Psychophysiology* 3(1):51–64.

Griep, Yannick, Ulla Kinnunen, Jouko Nätti, Nele De Cuyper, Saija Mauno, Anne Mäkikangas, and Hans De Witte. 2016. "The Effects of Unemployment and Perceived Job Insecurity: A Comparison of Their Association with Psychological and Somatic Complaints, Self-Rated Health and Life Satisfaction." *International Archives of Occupational and Environmental Health* 89(1):147–62. doi: 10.1007/s00420-015-1059-5.

Grob, Gerald N. 1991. *From Asylum to Community.* Princeton, NJ: Princeton University Press.

Grollman, Eric Anthony. 2012. "Multiple Forms of Perceived Discrimination and Health among Adolescents and Young Adults." *Journal of Health and Social Behavior* 53(2):199–214. doi: 10.1177/00221 46512444289.

Gronfein, William 1985. "Incentives and Intentions in Mental Health Policy: A Comparison of the Medicaid and Community Mental Health Programs." *Journal of Health and Social Behavior* 26(3):192–206.

Grzywacz, Joseph G., David M. Almeida, Shevaun D. Neupert, and Susan L. Ettner. 2004. "Socioeconomic Status and Health: A Micro-Level Analysis o Exposure and Vulnerability to Daily Stressors." *Journal of Health and Social Behavior* 45(1):1–16. doi: 10.1177/002214650404500101.

Guarnaccia, Peter J., Glorisa Canino, Maritza Rubio-Stipec, and Milagros Bravo. 1993. "The Prevalence of Ataques De Nervios in the Puerto Rico Disaster Study: The Role of Culture in Psychiatric Epidemiology." *The Journal of Nervous and Mental Disease* 181(3):157–65. doi: 10.1097/ 00005053-199303000-00003.

Guarnaccia, Peter J., Roberto Lewis-Fernandez, Igda Martinez Pincay, Patrick Shrout, Jing Guo, Maria Torres, Glorisa Canino, and Margarita Alegria. 2010. "Ataque De Nervios as a Marker of Social and Psychiatric Vulnerability: Results from the NLAAS." *International Journal of Social Psychiatry* 56(3):298–309. doi: 10.1177/00207 64008101636.

Guittar, Nicholas A. 2012. "On and Off the Reservation: A Discussion of the Social, Physical, and Mental Health Indicators of Suicide in the Native American Community: On and Off the Reservation." *Sociology Compass* 6(3):236–43. doi: 10.1111/ j.1751-9020.2011.00445.x.

Gureje, Oye, Olusola Adeyemi, N. Enydah, Nonyenim Enyidah, Michaelk Ekpo, Owoidoho Udofia, Richard Uwakwe, and Abba Wakil. 2008. "Mental Disorders among Adult Nigerians: Risks, Prevalence and Treatment." Pp. 211–37 in *The WHO world Mental Health Surveys: Global Perspectives on the Epidemiology of Mental Disorders*, edited by R. C. Kessler and T. B. Üstün. Cambridge: Cambridge University Press.

Haddock, Geoffrey, Mark P. Zanna, and Victoria M. Esses. 1993. "Assessing the Structure of Prejudicial Attitudes: The Case of Attitudes toward Homosexuals." *Journal of Personality and Social Psychology* 65(6):1105–18. doi: 10.1037/0022-3514.65. 6.1105.

Haggerty, Jim. 2020. *History of Psychotherapy.* https://psychcentral.com/lib/history-of-psychotherapy.

Halfmann, Drew. 2012. "Recognizing Medicalization and Demedicalization: Discourses, Practices, and Identities." *Health* 16(2):186–207. doi: 10.1177/ 1363459311403947.

Halpern, David. 1993. "Minorities and Mental Health." *Social Science & Medicine* 36(5):597–607. doi: 10.1016/0277-9536(93)90056-A.

Hamilton, Jane E., Angela M. Heads, Thomas D. Meyer, Pratikkumar V. Desai, Olaoluwa O. Okusaga, and Raymond Y. Cho. 2018. "Ethnic Differences in the Diagnosis of Schizophrenia and Mood Disorders during Admission to an Academic Safety-Net Psychiatric Hospital." *Psychiatry Research* 267:160–67. doi: 10.1016/j.psychres. 2018.05.043.

Hamilton, M. 1986. "The Hamilton Rating Scale for Depression." Pp. 143–52 in *Assessment of Depression*, edited by Norman Sartorius and Thomas Arthur Ban. Berlin, Heidelberg: Springer Berlin Heidelberg.

Haroz, E. E., M. Ritchey, J. K. Bass, B. A. Kohrt, J. Augustinavicius, L. Michalopoulos, M. D. Burkey, and P. Bolton. 2017. "How Is Depression Experienced around the World? A Systematic Review of Qualitative Literature." *Social Science & Medicine* 183:151–62. doi: 10.1016/j.socscimed. 2016.12.030.

Harpham, Trudy. 1994. "Urbanization and Mental Health in Developing Countries: A Research Role for Social Scientists, Public Health Professionals and Social Psychiatrists." *Social Science & Medicine* 39(2):233–45. doi: 10.1016/0277-9536(94)90332-8.

Harris, Neal. 2019. "Reconstructing Erich Fromm's 'Pathology of Normalcy': Transcending the Recognition-Cognitive Paradigm in the Diagnosis of Social

Pathologies." *Social Science Information* 58(4): 714–33. doi: 10.1177/0539018419881403.

Hartshorn, Kelley J. Sittner, Les B. Whitbeck, and Dan R. Hoyt. 2012. "Exploring the Relationships of Perceived Discrimination, Anger, and Aggression among North American Indigenous Adolescents." *Society and Mental Health* 2(1):53–67. doi: 10.1177/2156869312441185.

Hastings, A. 1991. *With the Tongues of Men and Angels: A Study of Channeling*. Fort Worth, TX: Hold, Rinehart and Winston.

Havenaar, Johan M., W. Van Den Brink, J. Van Den Bout, A. P. Kasyanenko, N. W. Poelijoe, T. Wohlfarth, and L. I. Meijler-Iljina. 1996. "Mental Health Problems in the Gomel Region (Belarus): An Analysis of Risk Factors in an Area Affected by the Chernobyl Disaster." *Psychological Medicine* 26(4):845–55. doi: 10.1017/S0033291700037879.

Hawn, Sage E., Shannon E. Cusack, and Ananda B. Amstadter. 2020. "A Systematic Review of the Self-Medication Hypothesis in the Context of Posttraumatic Stress Disorder and Comorbid Problematic Alcohol Use." *Journal of Traumatic Stress* 33(5):699–708. doi: 10.1002/jts.22521.

He, Hairong, Qingqing Liu, Ning Li, Liyang Guo, Fengjie Gao, Ling Bai, Fan Gao, and Jun Lyu. 2020. "Trends in the Incidence and DALYs of Schizophrenia at the Global, Regional and National Levels: Results from the Global Burden of Disease Study 2017." *Epidemiology and Psychiatric Sciences* 29:e91. doi: 10.1017/S2045796019000891.

Head, Rachel N., and Maxine Seaborn Thompson. 2017. "Discrimination-Related Anger, Religion, and Distress: Differences between African Americans and Caribbean Black Americans." *Society and Mental Health* 7(3):159–74. doi: 10.1177/2156869317711225.

Headey, Bruce, and Mark Wooden. 2004. "The Effects of Wealth and Income on Subjective Well-Being and Ill-Being*." *Economic Record* 80(s1): S24–33. doi: 10.1111/j.1475-4932.2004.00181.x.

Heiden-Rootes, Katie, Ashley Wiegand, Danielle Thomas, Rachel M. Moore, and Kristin A. Ross. 2020. "A National Survey on Depression, Internalized Homophobia, College Religiosity, and Climate of Acceptance on College Campuses for Sexual Minority Adults." *Journal of Homosexuality* 67(4): 435–51. doi: 10.1080/00918369.2018.1550329.

Helman, Cecil G. 2007. *Culture, Health and Illness*. 5th ed. London: Hodder Arnold.

Hemmens, Craig, Milo Miller, Velmer S. Burton, Jr., and Susan Milner. 2002. "The Consequences of Official Labels: An Examination of the Rights Lost by the Mentally Ill and Mentally Incompetent Ten Years Later." *Community Mental Health Journal* 38(2): 129–40.

Hendryx, Michael. 2008. "Mental Health Professional Shortages in Rural Appalachia." *The Journal of Rural Health* 24(2):179–82.

Henry, Tanya Albert. 2019. *Employed Physicians Now Exceed Those Who Own Their Practices*.

Herdt, Gilbert. 1986. "Madness and Sexuality in the New Guinea Highlands." *Social Research* 5(2): 349–67.

Heron, Melonie. 2019. Deaths: Leading Causes for 2017. *National Vital Statistics Reports*. 68 (6). 1–77.

Heslin, Kevin C., Anne Elixhauser, and Claudia A. Steiner. 2015. *Hospitalizations Involving Mental and Substance Use Disorders among Adults, 2012*. H-CUP Statistical Brief #191. Rockville, MD: Agency for Healthcare Research and Quality.

Hicks, James W. 2004. "Ethnicity, Race, and Forensic Psychiatry: Are We Color-Blind?" *The Journal of the American Academy of Psychiatry and the Law* 32(1):21–33.

Hiday, Virginia Aldigé, and Bradley Ray. 2017. "Mental Illness and the Criminal Justice System." Pp. 467–92 in *A Handbook for the Study of Mental Health: Social Contexts, Theories, and Systems*, edited by Teresa L. Scheid and Eric R. Wright. Cambridge: Cambridge University Press.

Hiday, Virginia Aldigé, and Heathcote W. Wales. 2011. "The Criminalization of Mental Illness." Pp. 80–93 in *Applied Research and Evaluation in Community Mental Health Servicers: An Update of Key Research Domains*, edited by Evelyn Vingilis and Stephen A. State. Montreal, QC: McGill-Queen's University Press.

Hiday, Virginia Aldigé, and Heathcote W. Wales. 2013. "Mental Illness and the Law." Pp. 563–84 in

Handbook of the Sociology of Mental Health, edited by Carol S. Aneshensel, Jo C. Phelan, and Alex Bierman. New York, NY: Springer Berlin Heidelberg.

Higginbotham, Nick, and Linda Connor. 1989. "Professional Ideology and the Construction of Western Psychiatry in Southeast Asia." *International Journal of Health Services* 19(1): 63–78. doi: 10.2190/J3A3-BX0E-LJ26-5ABT.

Hill, Terrence D., Catherine E. Ross, and Ronald J. Angel. 2005. "Neighborhood Disorder, Psychophysiological Distress, and Health." *Journal of Health and Social Behavior* 46(2):170–86. doi: 10.1177/002214650504600204.

Hillman, James, and Michael Ventura. 1993. *We've Had a Hundred Years of Psychotherapy and the World's Getting Worse*. San Francisco, CA: Harper.

Hindhede, Anette Lykke, and Kristian Larsen. 2020. "Prestige Hierarchies and Relations of Dominance among Healthcare Professionals." *Professions and Professionalism* 10(2). doi: 10.7577/pp.3447.

Hippisley-Cox, J., C. Parker, C. Coupland, and Y. Vinogradova. 2007. "Inequalities in the Primary Care of Patients with Coronary Heart Disease and Serious Mental Health Problems: A Cross-Sectional Study." *Heart* 93(10):1256–62. doi: 10.1136/hrt.2006.110171.

Hirsch, Jameson K., and Kelly C. Cukrowicz. 2014. "Suicide in Rural Areas: An Updated Review of the Literature." *Journal of Rural Mental Health* 38(2): 65–78. doi: 10.1037/rmh0000018.

Hochschild, Arlie Russell. 1975. "The Sociology of Feeling and Emotion: Selected Possibilities." *Sociological Inquiry* 45(2–3):280–307. doi: 10.1111/j.1475-682X.1975.tb00339.x.

Hochschild, Arlie Russell. 1981. "Attending to, Codifying, and Managing Feelings: Sex Differences in Love." 225–262 in *Feminist Frontiers: Rethinking Sex, Gender, and Society*, edited by Laurel Richardson and Verta Taylor. Reading, MA: Addison-Wesley.

Hochschild, Arlie Russell. 1985. *The Managed Heart: Commercialization of Human Feeling*. Berkeley, CA: University of California Press.

Hoff, Paul. 2015. "The Kraepelinian Tradition." *Dialogues in Clinical Neuroscience* 17(1):31–41.

Holland, Brenna. 2019. "Mad Speculation and Mary Girard: Gender, Capitalism and the Cultural Capital of Madness in the Revolutionary Atlantic." *Journal of the Early Republic* 39(4):647–75.

Hollingshead, August B., and Frederick C. Redlich. 1958. *Social Class and Mental Illness*. New York, NY: Wiley.

Holmes, Thomas H., and Richard H. Rahe. 1967. "The Social Readjustment Rating Scale." *Journal of Psychosomatic Research* 11(2):213–18. doi: 10.1016/0022-3999(67)90010-4.

Holvast, Floor, Huibert Burger, Margot M. W. de Waal, Harm W. J. van Marwijk, Hannie C. Comijs, and Peter F. M. Verhaak. 2015. "Loneliness Is Associated with Poor Prognosis in Late-Life Depression: Longitudinal Analysis of the Netherlands Study of Depression in Older Persons." *Journal of Affective Disorders* 185:1–7. doi: 10.1016/j.jad.2015.06.036.

Holway, Giuseppina Valle, Debra Umberson, and Mieke Beth Thomeer. 2017. "Binge Drinking and Depression: The Influence of Romantic Partners in Young Adulthood." *Society and Mental Health* 7(1): 36–49. doi: 10.1177/2156869316674056.

Honberg, Ron, Sita Diehl, Angela Kimball, Darcy Gruttadaro, and Mike Fitzpatrick. 2011. *State Mental Health Cuts: A National Crisis*. National Alliance on Mental Illness.

Hong, S. I., and Nancy Morrow-Howell. 2010. "Health Outcomes of Experience Corps: A High-Commitment Volunteer Program." *Social Science & Medicine* 71(2):414–20. doi: 10.1016/j.socscimed.2010.04.009.

Hooker, Karen, Sandi Phibbs, Veronica L. Irvin, Carolyn A. Mendez-Luck, Lan N. Doan, Tao Li, Shelbie Turner, and Soyoung Choun. 2018. "Depression among Older Adults in the United States by Disaggregated Race and Ethnicity." *The Gerontologist*. doi: 10.1093/geront/gny159.

Hooker, Karen, Sandi Phibbs, Veronica L. Irvin, Carolyn A. Mendez-Luck, Lan N. Doan, Tao Li, Shelbie Turner, and Soyoung Choun. 2019. "Depression among Older Adults in the United

States by Disaggregated Race and Ethnicity" edited by R. Pruchno. *The Gerontologist* 59(5):886–91. doi: 10.1093/geront/gny159.

Horwitz, Allan V., and Helene Raskin White. 1987. "Gender Role Orientations and Styles of Pathology among Adolescents." *Journal of Health and Social Behavior,* 28:158–70.

Horwitz, Allan V., H. R. White, and S. Howell-White. 1996. "The Use of Multiple Outcomes in Stress Research: A Case Study of Gender Differences in Responses to Marital Dissolution." *Journal of Health and Social Behavior* 37:278–91.

Horwitz, Allan V. 1977. "Pathways into Psychiatric Treatment: Some Differences between Men and Women." *Journal of Health and Social Behavior* 18:169–78.

Horwitz, Allan V. 2002. *Creating Mental Illness.* Chicago, IL: University of Chicago Press.

Horwitz, Allan V., and Teresa L. Scheid. 1999. "Approaches to Mental Health and Illness." Pp. 1–12 in *A Handbook for the Study of Mental Health*, edited by A. V. Horwitz and T. L. Scheid. Cambridge: Cambridge University Press.

Horwitz, Allan V., Tami M. Videon, Mark F. Schmitz, and Diane Davis. 2003. "Rethinking Twins and Environments: Possible Social Sources for Assumed Genetic Influences in Twin Research." *Journal of Health and Social Behavior* 44(2):111. doi: 10.2307/1519802.

House, James S. 2001. "Social Isolation Kills, but How and Why?" *Psychosomatic Medicine* 63(2):273–74.

House, James S. 2002. "Understanding Social Factors and Inequalities in Health: 20th Century Progress and 21st Century Prospects." *Journal of Health and Social Behavior* 43(2):125. doi: 10.2307/3090192.

Houts, Arthur C. 2001. "Harmful Dysfunction and the Search for Value Neutrality in the Definition of Mental Disorder: Response to Wakefield, Part 2." *Behaviour Research and Therapy* 39(9):1099–1132.

Howard, Kenneth I. 1996. "Patterns of Mental Health Service Utilization." *Archives of General Psychiatry* 53(8):696. doi: 10.1001/archpsyc.1996.01830080048009.

Høyersten, Jon Geir. 2007. "Madness in the Old Norse Society. Narratives and Ideas." *Nordic Journal of Psychiatry* 61(5):324–31. doi: 10.1080/08039480701643258.

Hoyt, Lynne A., Emory L. Cowen, JoAnne L. Pedro-Carroll, and Linda J. Alpert-Gillis. 1990. "Anxiety and Depression in Young Children of Divorce." *Journal of Clinical Child Psychology* 19(1):26–32. doi: 10.1207/s15374424jccp1901_4.

Hsieh, Ning. 2014. "Explaining the Mental Health Disparity by Sexual Orientation: The Importance of Social Resources." *Society and Mental Health* 4(2):129–46. doi: 10.1177/2156869314524959.

Hudson, Rex A. 1999. *The Sociology and Psychology of Terrorism: Who Becomes a Terrorist and Why?* Washington, DC: Federal Research Division of the Library of Congress.

Hughes, Diane L., Jon Alexander Watford, and Juan Del Toro. 2016. "A Transactional/Ecological Perspective on Ethnic–Racial Identity, Socialization, and Discrimination." Pp. 1–41 in *Advances in Child Development and Behavior.* Vol. 51. Elsevier.

Hughes, John S. 1992. "Labeling and Treating Black Mental Illness in Alabama, 1861-1910." *The Journal of Southern History* 58(3):435. doi: 10.2307/2210163.

Hughes, Michael, and David H. Demo. 1989. "Self-Perceptions of Black Americans: Self-Esteem and Personal Efficacy." *American Journal of Sociology* 95(1):132–59.

Hughes, Michael, K. Jill Kiecolt, and Verna M. Keith. 2014. "How Racial Identity Moderates the Impact of Financial Stress on Mental Health among African Americans." *Society and Mental Health* 4(1):38–54. doi: 10.1177/2156869313509635.

Hunter, Bronwyn A., Nathaniel Vincent Mohatt, Dana M. Prince, Azure B. Thompson, Samantha L. Matlin, and Jacob Kraemer Tebes. 2017. "Socio-Psychological Mediators of the Relationship between Behavioral Health Stigma and Psychiatric Symptoms." *Social Science & Medicine* 181:177–83. doi: 10.1016/j.socscimed.2017.03.049.

Hyde, Janet Shibley. 2005. "The Gender Similarities Hypothesis." *American Psychologist* 60(6):581–92. doi: 10.1037/0003-066X.60.6.581.

Ishizuka, Patrick. 2019. "Social Class, Gender, and Contemporary Parenting Standards in the United States: Evidence from a National Survey Experiment." *Social Forces* 98(1):31–58. doi: 10.1093/sf/soy107.

Jackson, Bradford E., Gabriela R. Oates, Karan P. Singh, James M. Shikany, Mona N. Fouad, Edward E. Partridge, and Sejong Bae. 2017. "Disparities in Chronic Medical Conditions in the Mid-South." *Ethnicity & Health* 22(2):196–208. doi: 10.1080/13557858.2016.1232805.

Jaffe, D. H. 2017. *Insane Consequences: How the Mental Health Industry Fails the Mentally Ill.* Amherst, NY: Promestheus Books.

Jansz, Jeroen. 2000. "Masculine Identity and Restrictive Emotionality." Pp. 166–86 in *Gender and Emotion: Social Psychological Perspectives.* Ed. by Agneta H. Fischer. Cambridge: Cambridge University Press.

Jauho, Mikko, and Ilpo Helén. 2018. "Symptoms, Signs, and Risk Factors: Epidemiological Reasoning in Coronary Heart Disease and Depression Management." *History of the Human Sciences* 31(1):56–73. doi: 10.1177/0952695117741055.

Jayatunge, Ruwan, and Daya Somasundaram. 2014. "Child Soldiers." Pp. 213–21 in *Essentials of Global Mental Health*, edited by S. O. Okpaku. Cambridge: Cambridge University Press.

Jeon, Bong-Hee, Moon-Doo Kim, Seong-Chui Hong, Na-Ri Kim, Chang-In Lee, Young-Sook Kwak, Joon-Hyuk Park, Jaehwan Chung, Hanul Chong, Eun-Kyung Jwa, Min-Ho Bae, Sanghee Kim, Bora Yoo, Jun-What Lee, Mi-Yeui Hyun, Mi-Jeong Yan, and Kuk-Soo Kim. 2009. "Prevalence and Correlates of Depressive Symptoms among North Korean Defectors Living in South Korea for More than One Year." *Psychiatry Investigation* 6(3):122–30.

Jeong, Hyunsuk, Hyeon Woo Yim, Yeong-Jun Song, Moran Ki, Jung-Ah Min, Juhee Cho, and Jeong-Ho Chae. 2016. "Mental Health Status of People Isolated Due to Middle East Respiratory Syndrome." *Epidemiology and Health* 38:1–7. doi: 10.4178/epih.e2016048.

Jewkes, Rachel. 2002. "Intimate Partner Violence: Causes and Prevention." *The Lancet* 359(9315):1423–29. doi: 10.1016/S0140-6736(02)08357-5.

Jiang, Yongwen, and Jana Earl Hesser. 2012. "Using Disability-Adjusted Life Years to Assess the Burden of Disease and Injury in Rhode Island." *Public Health Reports* 127(3):293–303. doi: 10.1177/003335491212700309.

Johnson, Andrew O., Michael D. Mink, Nusrat Harun, Charity G. Moore, Amy B. Martin, and Kevin J. Bennett. 2008. "Violence and Drug Use in Rural Teens: National Prevalence Estimates From the 2003 Youth Risk Behavior Survey." *Journal of School Health* 78(10):554–61. doi: 10.1111/j.1746-1561.2008.00343.x.

Johnson, Kurt D., Les B. Whitbeck, and Dan R. Hoyt. 2005. "Substance Abuse Disorders among Homeless and Runaway Adolescents." *Journal of Drug Issues* 35(4):799–816. doi: 10.1177/002204260503500407.

Johnson, Robert J., Stevan E. Hobfell, and Isabelle Beulaygue. 2017. "Mental Health and Terrorism." Pp. 357–85 in *A Handbook for the Study of Mental Health: Social Contexts, Theories, and Systems*, edited by Teresa L. Scheid and Eric R. Wright. Cambridge: Cambridge University Press.

Johnson, Vernon E. 1986. *Intervention: How to Help Those Who Don't Want Help.* Minneapolis, MN: The Johnson Institute.

Johnston, Elizabeth, and Leah Olson. 2015. *The Feeling Brain: The Biology and Psychology of Emotions.* W. W. Norton & Company.

Johnston, L. D., Miech, R. A., O'Malley, P. M., Bachman, J. G., Schulenberg, J. E., and Patrick M. E. 2022. Monitoring the Future national survey results on drug use 1975–2021: Overview, key findings on adolescent drug use. Ann Arbor: Institute for Social Research, University of Michigan.

Jones, Marian Moser. 2015. "Creating a Science of Homelessness During the Reagan Era: Creating a Science of Homelessness during the Reagan Era." *Milbank Quarterly* 93(1):139–78. doi: 10.1111/1468-0009.12108.

de Jong Gierveld, Jenny, Norah Keating, and Janet E. Fast. 2015. "Determinants of Loneliness among Older Adults in Canada." *Canadian Journal on Aging/La Revue Canadienne Du Vieillissement* 34(2):125–36. doi: 10.1017/S0714980815000070.

Judd, Fiona K., Henry J. Jackson, Angela Komiti, Greg Murray, Gene Hodgins, and Caitlin Fraser. 2002. "High Prevalence Disorders in Urban and Rural Communities." *The Australian and New Zealand Journal of Psychiatry* 36(1):104–13. doi: 10.1046/j.1440-1614.2002.00986.x.

Juffer, Femmie, and Marinus H. van IJzendoorn. 2005. "Behavior Problems and Mental Health Referrals of International Adoptees: A Meta-Analysis." *JAMA* 293(20):2501. doi: 10.1001/jama.293.20.2501.

Jung, John, and Hari Krishnan Khalsa. 1989. "The Relationship of Daily Hassles, Social Support, and Coping to Depression in Black and White Students." *The Journal of General Psychology* 116(4):407–17. doi: 10.1080/00221309.1989.9921127.

Juruena, Mario F., Filip Eror, Anthony J. Cleare, and Allan H. Young. 2020. "The Role of Early Life Stress in HPA Axis and Anxiety." Pp. 141–53 in *Anxiety Disorders*. Vol. 1191, *Advances in Experimental Medicine and Biology*, edited by Y.-K. Kim. Singapore: Springer Singapore.

Kaiser, Bonnie N., Cynthia Ticao, Jeremy Boglosa, John Minto, Charles Chikwiramadara, Melissa Tucker, and Brandon A. Kohrt. 2020. "Mental Health and Psychosocial Support Needs among People Displaced by Boko Haram in Nigeria." *Global Public Health* 15(3):358–71. doi: 10.1080/17441692.2019.1665082.

Kaiser Family Foundation. 2018. *Hospital Adjusted Expenses per Inpatient Day by Ownership*.

Kaplan, Cynthia, Naomi Tarlow, Jeremy G. Stewart, Blaise Aguirre, Gillian Galen, and Randy P. Auerbach. 2016. "Borderline Personality Disorder in Youth: The Prospective Impact of Child Abuse on Non-Suicidal Self-Injury and Suicidality." *Comprehensive Psychiatry* 71:86–94. doi: 10.1016/j.comppsych.2016.08.016.

Kaplan, Howard B. 1975. *The Sociology of Mental Illness*. New Haven, CT: College and University Press.

Karasek, Robert, and Töres Theorell. 1999. *Healthy Work: Stress, Productivity, and the Reconstruction of Working Life*. New York, NY: Basic Books.

Karp, David A. 2007. *Is It Me or My Meds?* Cambridge, MA: Harvard University Press.

Karp, David Allen. 1996. *Speaking of Sadness: Depression, Disconnection, and the Meanings of Illness*. Oxford: Oxford University Press.

Kawa, Shadia, and James Giordano. 2012. "A Brief Historicity of the Diagnostic and Statistical Manual of Mental Disorders: Issues and Implications for the Future of Psychiatric Canon and Practice." *Philosophy, Ethics, and Humanities in Medicine* 7:2. doi: 10.1186/1747-5341-7-2.

Keeley, Bethany, Lanelle Wright, and Celeste M. Condit. 2009. "Functions of Health Fatalism: Fatalistic Talk as Face Saving, Uncertainty Management, Stress Relief and Sense Making." *Sociology of Health & Illness* 31(5):734–47. doi: 10.1111/j.1467-9566.2009.01164.x.

Keese, Matthias, and Hendrik Schmitz. 2014. "Broke, Ill, and Obese: Is There an Effect of Household Debt on Health?: Broke, Ill, and Obese." *Review of Income and Wealth* 60(3):525–41. doi: 10.1111/roiw.12002.

Keeshin, Brooks R., Jeffrey R. Strawn, Aaron M. Luebbe, Shannon N. Saldaña, Anna M. Wehry, Melissa P. DelBello, and Frank W. Putnam. 2014. "Hospitalized Youth and Child Abuse: A Systematic Examination of Psychiatric Morbidity and Clinical Severity." *Child Abuse & Neglect* 38(1):76–83. doi: 10.1016/j.chiabu.2013.08.013.

Kemp, Simon. 2019. "Mental Disorder and Mysticism in the Late Medieval World." *History of Psychology* 22(2):149–62. doi: 10.1037/hop0000121.

Kemper, Theodore D. 1978. *A Social Interactional Theory of Emotions*. New York, NY: Wiley.

Kessler, Ronald C., Patricia Berglund, Olga Demler, Robert Jin, Doreen Koretz, Kathleen R. Merikangas, A. John Rush, Ellen E. Walters, and Philip S. Wang. 2003. "The Epidemiology of Major Depressive Disorder: Results from the National Comorbidity Survey Replication (NCS-R)." *JAMA* 289(23):3095. doi: 10.1001/jama.289.23.3095.

Kessler, Ronald C., Howard Birnbaum, Olga Demler, Ian R. H. Falloon, Elizabeth Gagnon, Margaret Guyer, Mary J. Howes, Kenneth S. Kendler, Lizheng Shi, Ellen Walters, and Eric Q. Wu. 2005. "The Prevalence and Correlates of Nonaffective Psychosis in the National Comorbidity Survey Replication (NCS-R)." *Biological Psychiatry* 58(8):668–76. doi: 10.1016/j.biopsych.2005.04.034.

Kessler, Ronald C., Steven G. Heeringa, Beth-Ellen Pennell, Nancy A. Sampson, and Alan M. Zaslavesky. 2018. "Methods of the World Mental Health Surveys." Pp. 9–40 in *Mental Disorders Around the World: Facts and Figures from the WHO World Mental Health Surveys*, edited by K. M. Scott, P. De Jong, D. J. Stein, and R. C. Kessler. Cambridge: Cambridge University Press.

Kessler, Ronald C., and Jane D. McLeod. 1984. "Sex Differences in Vulnerability to Undesirable Life Events." *American Sociological Review* 49(5): 620. doi: 10.2307/2095420.

Kessler, Ronald C., Kristin D. Mickelson, and David R. Williams. 1999. "The Prevalence, Distribution, and Mental Health Correlates of Perceived Discrimination in the United States." *Journal of Health and Social Behavior* 40(3):208. doi: 10.2307/2676349.

Kessler, Ronald C., Richard H. Price, and Camille B. Wortman. 1985. "Social Factors in Psychopathology: Stress, Social Support, and Coping Processes." *Annual Review of Psychology* 36:531–72.

Kessler, Ronald C., and T. Bedirhan Üstün. 2004. "The World Mental Health (WMH) Survey Initiative Version of the World Health Organization (WHO) Composite International Diagnostic Interview (CIDI)." *International Journal of Methods in Psychiatric Research* 13(2):93–121. doi: 10.1002/mpr.168.

Khan, Asaduzzaman, Rushdia Ahmed, and Nicola W. Burton. 2020. "Prevalence and Correlates of Depressive Symptoms in Secondary School Children in Dhaka City, Bangladesh." *Ethnicity & Health* 25(1):34–46. doi: 10.1080/13557858.2017.1398313.

Khan, Md. Mobarak Hossain, and Alexander Kraemer. 2014. "Are Rural-Urban Migrants Living in Urban Slums More Vulnerable in Terms of Housing, Health Knowledge, Smoking, Mental Health and General Health?: Vulnerability of Rural-Urban Migrants in Slums." *International Journal of Social Welfare* 23(4):373–83. doi: 10.1111/ijsw.12053.

Khan, Tm, Ma Hassali, H. Tahir, and A. Khan. 2011. "A Pilot Study Evaluating the Stigma and Public Perception about the Causes of Depression and Schizophrenia." *Iranian Journal of Public Health* 40(1):50–56.

Kim, Giyeon, Minjung Kim, Soohyun Park, Daniel E. Jimenez, and David A. Chiriboga. 2018. "Limited English Proficiency and Trajectories of Depressive Symptoms Among Mexican American Older Adults." *The Gerontologist*. doi: 10.1093/geront/gny032.

Kim, Jaehyun, Junhyoung Kim, and Areum Han. 2020. "Leisure Time Physical Activity Mediates the Relationship between Neighborhood Social Cohesion and Mental Health among Older Adults." *Journal of Applied Gerontology* 39(3):292–300. doi: 10.1177/0733464819859199.

Kim, Joongbaeck. 2010. "Neighborhood Disadvantage and Mental Health: The Role of Neighborhood Disorder and Social Relationships." *Social Science Research* 39(2):260–71. doi: 10.1016/j.ssresearch.2009.08.007.

Kim, Yeun-Hee. 2006. "Predictive Factors Affecting Depression and Alcohol Abuse among North Korean Refugees in South Korea." *Mental Health and Social Work* 22:149–80.

Kinavey, Hilary, and Carmen Cool. 2019. "The Broken Lens: How Anti-Fat Bias in Psychotherapy Is Harming Our Clients and What to Do About It." *Women & Therapy* 42(1–2):116–30. doi: 10.1080/02703149.2018.1524070.

Kinderman, Peter, Erika Setzu, Fiona Lobban, and Peter Salmon. 2006. "Illness Beliefs in Schizophrenia." *Social Science & Medicine* 63(7):1900–1911. doi: 10.1016/j.socscimed.2006.04.022.

Kirk, Stuart A., and Herb Kutchins. 1992. *The Selling of DSM: The Rhetoric of Science in Psychiatry.* New York, NY: Aldine De Gruyter.

Kirmayer, Laurence J., and Leslie Swartz. 2014. "Culture and Global Mental Health." Pp. 41–62 in *Global Mental Health: Principles and Practice*, edited by V. Patel, H. Minas, A. Cohen, and M. J. Prince. Oxford: Oxford University Press.

Kirsch, Irving. 2010. *The Emperor's New Drugs: Exploding the Antidepressant Myth.* New York, NY: Basic Books.

Kirschman, Ellen, Mark Kamena, and Joel Fay. 2014. *Counseling Cops: What Clinicians Need to Know.* New York, NY: The Guilford Press.

Kleinman, Arthur. 1988. *Rethinking Psychiatry: From Cultural Category to Personal Experience.* New York, NY: Free Press.

Klerman, Gerald L., and Myrna M. Weissman. 1989. "Increasing Rates of Depression." *JAMA* 261(15): 2229. doi: 10.1001/jama.1989.03420150079041.

Kohn, Melvin L., and Carmi Schooler. 1983. *Work and Personality: An Inquiry into the Impact of Social Stratification.* Norwood, NJ: Ablex Publishing Corporation.

Kohn, Melvin L., Atsushi Naoi, Carrie Schoenbach, Carmi Schooler, and Kazmierz M. Slomcyzynski. 1990. "Position in the Class Structure and Psychological Functioning in the United States, Japan, and Poland." *American Journal of Sociology,* 95(4): 962–1008.

Kohn, Robert. 2014. "Trends, Gaps, and Disparities in Mental Health." in *Essentials of Global Mental Health*, edited by S. O. Okpaku. Cambridge: Cambridge University Press.

Kopp, Sheldon. 1974. *If You Meet the Buddha on the Road, Kill Him!: The Pilgrimage of Psychotherapy Patients.* London: Sheldon Press.

Koss, Kalsea J., E. Mark Cummings, Patrick T. Davies, and Dante Cicchetti. 2017. "Patterns of Adolescent Regulatory Responses during Family Conflict and Mental Health Trajectories." *Journal of Research on Adolescence* 27(1):229–45. doi: 10.1111/jora.12269.

Kotin, Joel. 1995. *Getting Started: An Introduction to Dynamic Psychotherapy.* Northvale, NJ: Aronson.

Kozhimannil, Katy B., and Carrie Henning-Smith. 2018. "Racism and Health in Rural America." *Journal of Health Care for the Poor and Underserved* 29(1):35–43. doi: 10.1353/hpu.2018.0004.

Kpobi, Lily N. A., Leslie Swartz, and Cephas N. Omenyo. 2019. "Traditional Herbalists' Methods of Treating Mental Disorders in Ghana." *Transcultural Psychiatry* 56(1):250–66. doi: 10.1177/1363461518802981.

Kraus, Michael W., Jacinth J. X. Tan, and Melanie B. Tannenbaum. 2013. "The Social Ladder: A Rank-Based Perspective on Social Class." *Psychological Inquiry* 24(2):81–96. doi: 10.1080/1047840X.2013.778803.

Kring, Ann M., and Albert H. Gordon. 1998. "Sex Differences in Emotion: Expression, Experience, and Physiology." *Journal of Personality and Social Psychology* 74(3):686–703. doi: 10.1037/0022-3514.74.3.686.

Kroenke, Kurt, Robert L. Spitzer, and Janet B. W. Williams. 2001. "The PHQ-9: Validity of a Brief Depression Severity Measure." *Journal of General Internal Medicine* 16(9):606–13. doi: 10.1046/j.1525-1497.2001.016009606.x.

Kroll, Jerome. 1973. "A Reappraisal of Psychiatry in the Middle Ages." *Archives of General Psychiatry* 29(2):276. doi: 10.1001/archpsyc.1973.04200020098014.

Kroll, Jerome, and Bernard Bachrach. 1984. "Sin and Mental Illness in the Middle Ages." *Psychological Medicine* 14(3):507–14. doi: 10.1017/S0033291700015105.

Kroska, A., and S. K. Harkness. 2011. "Coping with the Stigma of Mental Illness: Empirically-Grounded Hypotheses from Computer Simulations." *Social Forces* 89(4):1315–39. doi: 10.1093/sf/89.4.1315.

Kulik, Dina M., Stephen Gaetz, Cathy Crowe, and Elizabeth (Lee) Ford-Jones. 2011. "Homeless Youth's Overwhelming Health Burden: A Review of the Literature." *Paediatrics & Child Health* 16(6): e43–47. doi: 10.1093/pch/16.6.e43.

Kumar, Shailesh. 2007. "Burnout in Psychiatrists." *World Psychiatry* 6(3):186–89.

Kurtz, Ernest. 2002. "Alcoholics Anonymous and the Disease Concept of Alcoholism." *Alcoholism Treatment Quarterly* 20(3–4):5–39. doi: 10.1300/J020v20n03_02.

Kutchins, Herb, and Stuart A. Kirk. 1997. *Making Us Crazy: DSM: The Psychiatric Bible and the Creation of Mental Disorders.* New York, NY: Free Press.

Kwok, Richard K., John A. McGrath, Sarah R. Lowe, Lawrence S. Engel, W. Braxton Jackson, Matthew D. Curry, Julianne Payne, Sandro Galea, and Dale P. Sandler. 2017. "Mental Health Indicators Associated with Oil Spill Response and Cleanup: Cross-Sectional Analysis of the GuLF STUDY Cohort." *The Lancet Public Health* 2(12):e560–67. doi: 10.1016/S2468-2667(17)30194-9.

Kyu, Hmwe Hmwe, et al. 2018. "Global, Regional, and National Disability-Adjusted Life-Years (DALYs) for 359 Diseases and Injuries and Healthy Life Expectancy (HALE) for 195 Countries and Territories, 1990–2017: A Systematic Analysis for the Global Burden of Disease Study 2017." *The Lancet* 392(10159):1859–1922. doi: 10.1016/S0140-6736(18)32335-3.

La Greca, Annette M., Wendy K. Silverman, Eric M. Vernberg, and Mitchell J. Prinstein. 1996. "Symptoms of Posttraumatic Stress in Children after Hurricane Andrew: A Prospective Study." *Journal of Consulting and Clinical Psychology* 64(4):712–23. doi: 10.1037/0022-006X.64.4.712.

Lachance-Grzela, Mylène, and Geneviève Bouchard. 2010. "Why Do Women Do the Lion's Share of Housework? A Decade of Research." *Sex Roles* 63(11–12):767–80. doi: 10.1007/s11199-010-9797-z.

Lachs, Mark S., and Karl A. Pillemer. 2015. "Elder Abuse." *New England Journal of Medicine* 373(20):1947–56. doi: 10.1056/NEJMra1404688.

Lam, Jack, Wen Fan, and Phyllis Moen. 2014. "Is Insecurity Worse for Well-Being in Turbulent Times? Mental Health in Context." *Society and Mental Health* 4(1):55–73. doi: 10.1177/2156869313507288.

Lambo, T. A. 1978. "Psychotherapy in Africa." *Human Nature* 1:32–39.

Landrine, Hope. 1988. "Depression and Stereotypes of Women: Preliminary Empirical Analyses of the Gender-Role Hypothesis." *Sex Roles* 19(7–8):527–41. doi: 10.1007/BF00289722.

Lane, Rhiannon. 2020. "Expanding Boundaries in Psychiatry: Uncertainty in the Context of Diagnosis-seeking and Negotiation." *Sociology of Health & Illness* 42(S1):69–83. doi: 10.1111/1467-9566.13044.

Lankford, Adam. 2018. "A Psychological Re-Examination of Mental Health Problems among the 9/11 Terrorists." *Studies in Conflict & Terrorism* 41(11):875–98. doi: 10.1080/1057610X.2017.1348742.

Larkin, Milton, and Hadley Wood. 2018. "Erectile Dysfunction." https://www.clevelandclinicmeded.com/medicalpubs/diseasemanagement/endocrinology/erectile-dysfunction/.

Lasch, Christopher. 1979. *The Culture of Narcissism: American Life in an Age of Diminishing Expectations.* New York, NY: WW Norton.

Lauber, C., L. Falcato, C. Nordt, and W. Rossler. 2003. "Lay Beliefs about Causes of Depression." *Acta Psychiatrica Scandinavica* 108(s418):96–99. doi: 10.1034/j.1600-0447.108.s418.19.x.

Lavebratt, Catharina, Louise K. Sjöholm, Pia Soronen, Tiina Paunio, Marquis P. Vawter, William E. Bunney, Rolf Adolfsson, Yvonne Forsell, Joseph C. Wu, John R. Kelsoe, Timo Partonen, and Martin Schalling. 2010. "CRY2 Is Associated with Depression." *PLoS One* 5(2):e9407. doi: 10.1371/journal.pone.0009407.

Lazarus, R., and S. Folkman. 1984. *Stress Appraisal and Coping.* New York, NY: Springer.

Leaf, Philip J., and Martha Livingston Bruce. 1987. "Gender Differences in the Use of Mental Health-Related Services: A Re-Examination." *Journal of Health and Social Behavior* 28(2):171. doi: 10.2307/2137130.

Leamy, Mary, Victoria Bird, Clair Le Boutillier, Julie Williams, and Mike Slade. 2011. "Conceptual Framework for Personal Recovery in Mental Health: Systematic Review and Narrative Synthesis." *British Journal of Psychiatry* 199(6):445–52. doi: 10.1192/bjp.bp.110.083733.

Leavey, Gerard, and Michael King. 2007. "The Devil Is in the Detail: Partnerships between Psychiatry and Faith-Based Organisations." *British Journal of Psychiatry* 191(2):97–98. doi: 10.1192/bjp.bp.106.034686.

Lee, Barrett A., Kimberly A. Tyler, and James D. Wright. 2010. "The New Homelessness Revisited." *Annual Review of Sociology* 36(1):501–21. doi: 10.1146/annurev-soc-070308-115940.

Lee, Dominic T. S., Joan Kleinman, and Arthur Kleinman. 2007. "Rethinking Depression: An Ethnographic Study of the Experiences of Depression among Chinese:" *Harvard Review of Psychiatry* 15(1):1–8. doi: 10.1080/10673220601183915.

Lee, Gi, and David Cohen. 2019. "How Many People Are Subjected to Involuntary Psychiatric Detention in the U.S.? First Verifiable Population Estimates of Civil Commitment." In Society for

Social Work and Research 23rd Annual Conference, San Francisco, CA.

Lee, Jennifer, and Min Zhou. 2015. *The Asian American Achievement Paradox*. New York, NY: Russell Sage Foundation.

Lee, Sing. 2002. "Socio-Cultural and Global Health Perspectives for the Development of Future Psychiatric Diagnostic Systems." *Psychopathology* 35(2–3):152–57. doi: 10.1159/000065136.

Lee, Stacey J. 2009. *Unraveling the "Model Minority" Stereotype: Listening to Asian American Youth*. 2nd ed. New York, NY: Teachers College Press.

Lee, Sungkyu, Aileen B. Rothbard, and Elizabeth L. Noll. 2012. "Length of Inpatient Stay of Persons with Serious Mental Illness: Effects of Hospital and Regional Characteristics." *Psychiatric Services* 63(9):889–95. doi: 10.1176/appi.ps.201100412.

Lemert, Edwin M. 1967. *Human Deviance, Social Problems, and Social Control*. Englewood Cliffs, NJ: Prentice Hall.

Lenardson, J. D., E. C. Ziller, D. Lambert, M. M. Race, and A. Yousefian. 2010. *Mental Health Problems Have Considerable Impact on Rural Children and Their Families*. Research & Policy Brief. Portland, ME: Muskie School of Public Service, Maine Rural Health Research Center, University of Southern Maine.

Lenzer, Jeanne. 2004. "Bush Plans to Screen Whole US Population for Mental Illness." *BMJ* 328(7454):1458. doi: 10.1136/bmj.328.7454.1458.

Leung, Mei-yung, Isabelle Yee Shan Chan, and Jingyu Yu. 2012. "Preventing Construction Worker Injury Incidents through the Management of Personal Stress and Organizational Stressors." *Accident Analysis & Prevention* 48:156–66. doi: 10.1016/j.aap.2011.03.017.

Levinson, Daphna, Maria V. Petukhova, Michael Schoenbaum, Guilherme Borges, Ronny Bruffaerts, Giovanni de Girolamo, Yanling He, Oye Gureje, Mark A. Oakley Browne, and Ronald C. Kessler. 2013. "Association between Serious Mentakl Illness and Personal Earnings." Pp. 97–109 in *The Burdens of Mental Disorders: Global Perspectives from the WHO World Mental Health Surveys*, edited by J. Alonso, S. Chatterji, and Y. He. Cambridge: Cambridge University Press.

Li, Mengying, Sara B. Johnson, Rashelle J. Musci, and Anne W. Riley. 2017. "Perceived Neighborhood Quality, Family Processes, and Trajectories of Child and Adolescent Externalizing Behaviors in the United States." *Social Science & Medicine* 192:152–61. doi: 10.1016/j.socscimed.2017.07.027.

Liepman, Michael R., Ted D. Nirenberg, and Mary M. Begin. 1989. "Evaluation of a Program Designed to Help Family and Significant Others to Motivate Resistant Alcoholics into Recovery." *The American Journal of Drug and Alcohol Abuse* 15(2):209–21.

Liester, Mitchell B. 1998. "Toward a New Definition of Hallucination." *American Journal of Orthopsychiatry* 68(2):305–12. doi: 10.1037/h0080339.

Limonic, Laura, and Mary Clare Lennon. 2017. "Work and Unemployment as Stressors." in *A Handbook for the Study of Mental Health: Social Contexts, Theories, and Systems*, edited by Teresa L. Scheid and Eric R. Wright. Cambridge: Cambridge University Press.

Lin, Li-Rong, Hui-Lin Zhang, Song-Jie Huang, Yan-Li Zeng, Ya Xi, Xiao-Jing Guo, Gui-Li Liu, Man-Li Tong, Wei-Hong Zheng, Li-Li Liu, and Tian-Ci Yang. 2014. "Psychiatric Manifestations as Primary Symptom of Neurosyphilis among HIV-Negative Patients." *The Journal of Neuropsychiatry and Clinical Neurosciences* 26(3):233–40. doi: 10.1176/appi.neuropsych.13030064.

Link, B. G., and J. C. Phelan. 1996. "Evaluating the Fundamental Cause Explanation for Social Disparities in Health." *American Journal of Public Health* 86:471–73.

Link, Bruce G., Francis T. Cullen, James Frank, and John F. Wozniak. 1987. "The Social Rejection of Former Mental Patients: Understanding Why Labels Matter." *American Journal of Sociology* 92(6):1461–1500. doi: 10.1086/228672.

Link, Bruce G., Francis T. Cullen, Elmer Struening, Patrick E. Shrout, and B. P. Dohrenwend. 1989. "A Modified Labeling Theory Approach to Mental Disorders: An Empirical Assessment." *American Sociological Review* 54(3):400–423.

Link, Bruce G., and Jo C. Phelan. 2001. "Conceptualizing Stigma." *Annual Review of Sociology* 27:368–85.

Link, Bruce G., and Jo C. Phelan. 2013. "Labeling and Stigma." Pp. 525–42 in *Handbook of the Sociology of Mental Health*, edited by C. S. Aneshensel, J. C. Phelan, and A. Bierman. New York, NY: Springer.

Link, Bruce G., Jo C. Phelan, and Mark L. Hatzenbuehler. 2018. "Stigma as a Fundamental Cause of Health." Pp. 53–67 in *Oxford Handbook of Stigma, Discrimination, and Health*, edited by B. Major, J. F. Dovidio, and B. G. Link. Oxford: Oxford University Press.

Link, Bruce G., Jo Jo Phelan, Michaeline Bresnahan, Ann Stueve, and Bernice A. Pescosolido. 1999. "Public Conceptions of Mental Illness: Labels, Causes, Dangerousness, and Social Distance." *American Journal of Public Health* 89(9):1328–33.

Livingston, James D., and Jennifer E. Boyd. 2010. "Correlates and Consequences of Internalized Stigma for People Living with Mental Illness: A Systematic Review and Meta-Analysis." *Social Science & Medicine* 71(12):2150–61. doi: 10.1016/j.socscimed.2010.09.030.

Llena-Nozal, A. 2009. "The Effect of Work Status and Working Conditions on Mental Health in Four OECD Countries." *National Institute Economic Review* 209(1):72–87.

Logan, D. G. 1983. "Getting Alcoholics to Treatment by Social Network Intervention." *Hospital & Community Psychiatry* 34(4):360–61. doi: 10.1176/ps.34.4.360.

Longkumar, Ningsangrenia. 2019. *"Traditional Healing Practices and Perspectives of Mental Health in Nagaland."* Unpublished dissertation, Martin Luther Christian University, Shillong.

Lorber, Judith. 1994. *Paradoxes of Gender*. New Haven, CT: Yale University Press.

Lorenzo-Blanco, Elma I., Alan Meca, Jennifer B. Unger, José Szapocznik, Miguel Ángel Cano, Sabrina E. Des Rosiers, and Seth J. Schwartz. 2019. "Cultural Stress, Emotional Well-Being, and Health Risk Behaviors among Recent Immigrant Latinx Families: The Moderating Role of Perceived Neighborhood Characteristics." *Journal of Youth and Adolescence* 48(1):114–31. doi: 10.1007/s10964-018-0907-5.

Lovibond, P. F., and S. H. Lovibond. 1995. "The Structure of Negative Emotional States: Comparison of the Depression Anxiety Stress Scales (DASS) with the Beck Depression and Anxiety Inventories." *Behaviour Research and Therapy* 33(3):335–43. doi: 10.1016/0005-7967(94)00075-U.

Lutterman, Ted, Robert Shaw, William Fisher, and Ronald Manderscheid. 2017. *Trend in Psychiatric Inpatient Capacity, United States and Each State, 1970-2014.* Assessment #10. Alexandria, VR: National Association of State Mental Health Program Directors.

Lyons Reardon, Maureen, Andrea B. Burns, Robyn Preist, Natalie Sachs-Ericsson, and Alan R. Lang. 2003. "Alcohol Use and Other Psychiatric Disorders in the Formerly Homeless and Never Homeless: Prevalence, Age of Onset, Comorbidity, Temporal Sequencing, and Service Utilization." *Substance Use & Misuse* 38(3–6):601–44. doi: 10.1081/JA-120017387.

Maalouf, Fadi T., Bernadette Mdawar, Lokman I. Meho, and Elie A. Akl. 2021. "Mental Health Research in Response to the COVID-19, Ebola, and H1N1 Outbreaks: A Comparative Bibliometric Analysis." *Journal of Psychiatric Research* 132: 198–206. doi: 10.1016/j.jpsychires.2020.10.018.

MacCorquodale, Kenneth, and Paul E. Meehl. 1948. "On a Distinction between Hypothetical Constructs and Intervening Variables." *Psychological Review* 55(2):95–107. doi: 10.1037/h0056029.

Madison, Guy, and Edward Dutton. 2020. "Sex Differences in Crying." Pp. 1–4 in *Encyclopedia of Evolutionary Psychological Science*, edited by T. K. Shackelford and V. A. Weekes-Shackelford. Cham: Springer International Publishing.

Maher, Winifred B., and Brendan Maher. 1982. "The Ship of Fools: Stultifera Navis or Ignis Fatuus?" *American Psychologist* 37(7):756–61. doi: 10.1037/0003-066X.37.7.756.

Mair, Christina, Ana V. Diez Roux, Theresa L. Osypuk, Stephen R. Rapp, Teresa Seeman, and Karol E. Watson. 2010. "Is Neighborhood Racial/Ethnic Composition Associated with Depressive

Symptoms? The Multi-Ethnic Study of Atherosclerosis." *Social Science & Medicine* 71(3):541–50. doi: 10.1016/j.socscimed.2010.04.014.

Maisel, Eric R. 2013. "The New Definition of a Mental Disorder: Is It an Improvement or Another Brazen Attempt to Name a Non-Existing Thing?" *Psychology Today*, March 23.

Makanjuola, R. O. A. 1987. "'Ode Ori': A Culture-Bound Disorder with Prominent Somatic Features in Yoruba Nigerian Patients." *Acta Psychiatrica Scandinavica* 75(3):231–36. doi: 10.1111/j.1600-0447.1987.tb02781.x.

Malone, Darren, Naomi A. Fineberg, and Tim M. Gale. 2004. "What Is the Usual Length of Stay in a Psychiatric Ward?" *International Journal of Psychiatry in Clinical Practice* 8(1):53–56. doi: 10.1080/13651500310004498.

Maraldi, Everton de Oliveira, and Stanley Krippner. 2019. "Cross-Cultural Research on Anomalous Experiences: Theoretical Issues and Methodological Challenges." *Psychology of Consciousness: Theory, Research, and Practice* 6(3): 306–19. doi: 10.1037/cns0000188.

Marcotte, Dave E., and Virginia Wilcox-Gök. 2001. "Estimating the Employment and Earnings Costs of Mental Illness: Recent Developments in the United States." *Social Science & Medicine* 53(1): 21–27. doi: 10.1016/S0277-9536(00)00312-9.

Marcussen, Kristen, Mary Gallagher, and Christian Ritter. 2021. "Stigma Resistance and Well-Being in the Context of the Mental Illness Identity." *Journal of Health and Social Behavior* 62(1): 19–36. doi: 10.1177/0022146520976624.

Mark, Tami L., Katharine R. Levit, Tracy Yee, and Clifton M. Chow. 2014. "Spending On Mental And Substance Use Disorders Projected To Grow More Slowly Than All Health Spending Through 2020." *Health Affairs* 33(8): 1407.

Markides, Kyriakos S. 1986. "Minority Status, Aging, and Mental Health." *The International Journal of Aging and Human Development* 23(4): 285–300. doi: 10.2190/N0X1-2486-L9NN-JKMQ.

Markowitz, Fred. E. 2011. "Dysfunctional Social Control of Mental Illness: A Commentary on Yoon." *Social Science & Medicine* 72(4):456–59. doi: 10.1016/j.socscimed.2010.11.013.

Maruta, Toshimasa, and Chihiro Matsumoto. 2019. "Renaming Schizophrenia." *Epidemiology and Psychiatric Sciences* 28(3):262–64. doi: 10.1017/S2045796018000598.

Mathers, Colin, Doris Ma Fat, J. T. Boerma, and World Health Organization, eds. 2008. *The Global Burden of Disease: 2004 Update*. Geneva: World Health Organization.

Mattelaer, Johan J. and Wolfgang Jilek. 2007. "Koro—The Psychological Disappearance of the Penis." *The Journal of Sexual Medicine*, 4(5): 1509–15.

Maura, Jessica, and Amy Weisman de Mamani. 2017. "Mental Health Disparities, Treatment Engagement, and Attrition among Racial/Ethnic Minorities with Severe Mental Illness: A Review." *Journal of Clinical Psychology in Medical Settings* 24(3–4):187–210. doi: 10.1007/s10880-017-9510-2.

Mayans, Laura. 2019. "Lead Poisoning in Children." *American Family Physician* 100(1):24–30.

Mayes, Rick, and Allan V. Horwitz. 2005. "DSM-III and the Revolution in the Classification of Mental Illness." *Journal of the History of the Behavioral Sciences* 41(3):249–67. doi: 10.1002/jhbs.20103.

Mbiti, J. S. 1986. *Introduction to African Religion*. London: Heinemann Educational.

McAlpine, Donna D., and Carol A. Boyer. 2008. "Sociological Traditions in the Study of Mental Health Services Utilization." Pp. 355–78 in *Mental Health, Social Mirror*, edited by W. R. Avison, J. D. McLeod, and B. A. Pescosolido. New York, NY: Springer.

McCabe, Sean Esteban, Brady T. West, Tonda L. Hughes, and Carol J. Boyd. 2013. "Sexual Orientation and Substance Abuse Treatment Utilization in the United States: Results from a National Survey." *Journal of Substance Abuse Treatment* 44(1):4–12. doi: 10.1016/j.jsat.2012.01.007.

McCaul, Kevin D., and Amy B. Mullens. 2003. "Affect, Thought and Self-protective Health Behavior: The Case of Worry and Cancer Screening." Pp. 137–68 in *Social Psychological Foundations of Health and Illness*, edited by J. Suls and K. A. Wallston. Malden, MA: Blackwell.

McDaid, David, A.-La Park, and Kristian Wahlbeck. 2019. "The Economic Case for the Prevention of Mental Illness." *Annual Review of Public Health* 40(1):373–89. doi: 10.1146/annurev-publhealth-040617-013629.

McEwen, Bruce S., and Teresa Seeman. 1999. "Protective and Damaging Effects of Mediators of Stress: Elaborating and Testing the Concepts of Allostasis and Allostatic Load." *Annals of the New York Academy of Sciences* 896(1):30–47. doi: 10.1111/j.1749-6632.1999.tb08103.x.

McGinty, Emma E., Alene Kennedy-Hendricks, Seema Choksy, and Colleen L. Barry. 2016. "Trends in News Media Coverage of Mental Illness in the United States: 1995–2014." *Health Affairs* 35(6):1121–29. doi: 10.1377/hlthaff.2016.0011.

McGrath, Ellen, Gwendolyn Puryear Keita, Bonnie R. Strickland, and Nancy Felipe Russo, eds. 1990. *Women and Depression: Risk Factors and Treatment Issues: Final Report of the American Psychological Association's National Task Force on Women and Depression.* Washington, DC: American Psychological Association.

McGrath, J., S. Saha, D. Chant, and J. Welham. 2008. "Schizophrenia: A Concise Overview of Incidence, Prevalence, and Mortality." *Epidemiologic Reviews* 30(1):67–76. doi: 10.1093/epirev/mxn001.

McGuire, Thomas G., and Jeanne Miranda. 2008. "New Evidence Regarding Racial and Ethnic Disparities in Mental Health: Policy Implications." *Health Affairs* 27(2):393–403. doi: 10.1377/hlthaff.27.2.393.

McIntosh, Wendy LiKamWa, Srica Spies, Deborah M. Stone, Colby N. Lokey, Aimeé-Rika T. Trudeau, and Brad Bartholow. 2016. Suicide Rates by Occupational Group—17 States, 2012. *MMWR.* 65(25). Centers for Disease Control.

Mckenna, Matthew T., Catherine M. Michaud, Christopher J. L. Murray, and James L. Marks. 2005. "Assessing the Burden of Disease in the United States Using Disability-Adjusted Life Years." *American Journal of Preventive Medicine* 28(5):415–23. doi: 10.1016/j.amepre.2005.02.009.

McKinlay, John B. 1975. *A Case for Refocusing Upstream: The Political Economy of Illness.* American Heart Association; reprinted in IAPHS Occasional Classics.

McLeod, Jane D. 1991. "Childhood Parental Loss and Adult Depression." *Journal of Health and Social Behavior* 32(3):205–20.

McLeod, Jane D., and Ronald C. Kessler. 1990. "Socioeconomic Status Differences in Vulnerability to Undesirable Life Events." *Journal of Health and Social Behavior* 31(2):162. doi: 10.2307/2137170.

McShane, Kathleen Molly. 2011. "Mental Health in Haiti: A Resident's Perspective." *Academic Psychiatry* 35(1):8–10.

Mechanic David. 1989. "In Sickness and in Wealth. American Hospitals in the Twentieth Century." *Science* 244(4910):1385–86.

Medlow, Sharon, Emily Klineberg, and Kate Steinbeck. 2014. "The Health Diagnoses of Homeless Adolescents: A Systematic Review of the Literature." *Journal of Adolescence* 37(5):531–42. doi: 10.1016/j.adolescence.2014.04.003.

Meijer, Miriam Claude. 1999. *Race and Aesthetics in the Anthropology of Petrus Camper (1722-1789).* Amsterdam: Rodopi.

Merscham, Carrie, James M. Van Leeuwen, and Megan McGuire. 2009. "Mental Health and Substance Abuse Indicators among Homeless Youth in Denver, Colorado." *Child Welfare* 88(2):93–110.

Mersky, Joshua P., Colleen E. Janczewski, and Jenna C. Nitkowski. 2018. "Poor Mental Health among Low-Income Women in the U.S.: The Roles of Adverse Childhood and Adult Experiences." *Social Science & Medicine* 206:14–21. doi: https://doi.org/10.1016/j.socscimed.2018.03.043.

Merton, Robert K. 1948. "The Self-Fulfilling Prophecy." *The Antioch Review* 8(2):193–210.

Meyer, Dixie, Joanne Salas, Stephanie Barkley, and Tony W. Buchanan. 2019. "In Sickness and in Health: Partner's Physical and Mental Health Predicts Cortisol Levels in Couples." *Stress* 22(3):295–302. doi: 10.1080/10253890.2018.1561843.

Miller, Byron, Sunshine M. Rote, and Verna M. Keith. 2013. "Coping with Racial Discrimination:

Assessing the Vulnerability of African Americans and the Mediated Moderation of Psychosocial Resources." *Society and Mental Health* 3(2): 133–50. doi: 10.1177/2156869313483757.

Miller, Lisa, Priya Wickramaratne, Marc J. Gameroff, Mia Sage, Craig E. Tenke, and Myrna M. Weissman. 2012. "Religiosity and Major Depression in Adults at High Risk: A Ten-Year Prospective Study." *American Journal of Psychiatry* 169(1):89–94.

Millon, Theodore. 2004. *Masters of the Mind: Exploring the Story of Mental Illness from Ancient Times to the New Millennium*. Hoboken, NJ: Wiley.

Mirola, William A. 1999. "A Refuge for Some: Gender Differences in the Relationship between Religious Involvement and Depression." *Sociology of Religion* 60(4):419. doi: 10.2307/3712024.

Mirowsky, John. 2011. "Wage Slavery or Creative Work?" *Society and Mental Health* 1(2):73–88. doi: 10.1177/2156869311413141.

Mirowsky, John, and Catherine E. Ross. 1995. "Sex Differences in Distress: Real or Artifact?" *American Sociological Review* 60:449–68.

Mirowsky, John, and Catherine E. Ross. 2003/2017. *Social Causes of Psychological Distress*. 2nd ed. New York, NY: Routledge.

Mirowsky, John, and Catherine E. Ross. 2012. *Social Causes of Psychological Distress*. 2nd ed. New Brunswick, NJ: AldineTransaction.

Mishra, Sandeep, and R. Nicholas Carleton. 2015. "Subjective Relative Deprivation is Associated with Poorer Physical and Mental Health." *Social Science & Medicine* 147:144–49. doi: https://doi.org/10.1016/j.socscimed.2015.10.030.

Mizock, Lauren, and Megan Brubaker. 2019. "Treatment Experiences with Gender and Discrimination among Women with Serious Mental Illness." *Psychological Services*. doi: 10.1037/ser0000346.

Modecki, Kathryn L., Jeannie Minchin, Allen G. Harbaugh, Nancy G. Guerra, and Kevin C. Runions. 2014. "Bullying Prevalence across Contexts: A Meta-Analysis Measuring Cyber and Traditional Bullying." *Journal of Adolescent Health* 55(5):602–11. doi: 10.1016/j.jadohealth.2014.06.007.

Moen, Phyllis, Erin L. Kelly, Eric Tranby, and Qinlei Huang. 2011. "Changing Work, Changing Health: Can Real Work-Time Flexibility Promote Health Behaviors and Well-Being?" *Journal of Health and Social Behavior* 52(4):404–29. doi: 10.1177/0022146511418979.

Molodynski, Andrew, Christina Cusack, and Jurua Nixon. 2017. "Mental Healthcare in Uganda: Desperate Challenges but Real Opportunities." *BJPsych International* 14(4):98–100. doi: 10.1192/s2056474000002129.

Montgomery, S. A., and M. Åsberg. 1979. "A New Depression Scale Designed to be Sensitive to Change." *The British Journal of Psychiatry* 134: 382–89.

Moore, Sarah, Leon Grunberg, and Edward Greenberg. 2006. "Surviving Repeated Waves of Organizational Downsizing: The Recency, Duration, and Order Effects Associated with Different Forms of Layoff Contact." *Anxiety, Stress & Coping* 19(3): 309–29. doi: 10.1080/10615800600901341.

Moore, Thomas J., and Donald R. Mattison. 2017. "Adult Utilization of Psychiatric Drugs and Differences by Sex, Age, and Race." *JAMA Internal Medicine* 177(2):274. doi: 10.1001/jamainternmed.2016.7507.

Morris, J. Glenn, Lynn M. Grattan, Brian M. Mayer, and Jason K. Blackburn. 2013. "Psychological Responses and Resilience of People and Communities Impacted by the Deepwater Horizon Oil Spill." *Transactions of the American Clinical and Climatological Association* 124: 191–201.

Mossakowski, Krysia N. 2009. "The Influence of Past Unemployment Duration on Symptoms of Depression among Young Women and Men in the United States." *American Journal of Public Health* 99(10):1826–32. doi: 10.2105/AJPH.2008.152561.

Mossakowski, Krysia N., Lauren M. Kaplan, and Terrence D. Hill. 2011. "Americans' Attitudes toward Mental Illness and Involuntary Psychiatric Medication." *Society and Mental Health* 1(3): 200–216. doi: 10.1177/2156869311431100.

Mullick, Mohammad Sayadul Islam, and Robert Goodman. 2005. "The Prevalence of Psychiatric Disorders among 5–10 Year Olds in Rural, Urban and Slum Areas in Bangladesh: An Exploratory Study." *Social Psychiatry and Psychiatric Epidemiology* 40(8):663–71. doi: 10.1007/s00127-005-0939-5.

Muntaner, C. 2004. "Socioeconomic Position and Major Mental Disorders." *Epidemiologic Reviews* 26(1):53–62. doi: 10.1093/epirev/mxh001.

Murray, Christopher J. L., and Alan D. Lopez, eds. 1996. *The Global Burden of Disease: A Comprehensive Assessment of Mortality and Disability from Diseases, Injuries, and Risk Factors in 1990 and Projected to 2020; Summary.* Cambridge: Harvard School of Public Health [u.a.].

Murray, Rheana. 2020. What Is Racial Trauma? How Black Therapists Are Helping Patients Cope.

Mutiso, Victoria N., Patrick Galonga, David M. Ndetei, Teddy Gafna, Anne W. Mbwayo, and Lincoln I. Khasakhala. 2014. "Collaboration between Traditional and Western Practioners." Pp. 135–41 in *Essentials of Global Mental Health*, edited by S. O. Okpaku. Cambridge: Cambridge University Press.

Nam, Yunju, Nora Wikoff, and Michael Sherraden. 2015. "Racial and Ethnic Differences in Parenting Stress: Evidence from a Statewide Sample of New Mothers." *Journal of Child and Family Studies* 24(2):278–88. doi: 10.1007/s10826-013-9833-z.

Napoletano, Anthony, Frank J. Elgar, Grace Saul, Melanie Dirks, and Wendy Craig. 2016. "The View from the Bottom: Relative Deprivation and Bullying Victimization in Canadian Adolescents." *Journal of Interpersonal Violence* 31(20):3443–63. doi: 10.1177/0886260515585528.

Nathan, Debbie. 2012. *Sybil Exposed: The Extraordinary Story behind the Famous Multiple Personality Case.* New York, NY: Free Press.

Nathan, Peter E., Mandy Conrad, and Anne Helene Skinstad. 2016. "History of the Concept of Addiction." *Annual Review of Clinical Psychology* 12:29–51. doi: 10.1146/annurev-clinpsy-021815-093546.

National Academies of Sciences, Engineering, and Medicine. 2016. *Ending Discrimination against People with Mental and Substance Use Disorders: The Evidence for Stigma Change.* Washington, D.C.: National Academies Press.

National Institute for Mental Health. 2017. *2017 National Survey on Drug Use and Health: Detailed Tables.*

National Institute for Mental Health. 2022. *Mental Illness.* https://www.nimh.nih.gov/health/statistics/mental-illness. Accessed January 25, 2022.

National Institute of Mental Health. 2017. *Statistics.*

National Institute of Mental Health. 2018. *Schizophrenia.* National Institute on Mental Health.

National Institute on Drug Abuse. 2020. *Sex and Gender Differences in Substance Use.* National Institute on Drug Abuse.

Ndetei, David M. 2007. "Traditional Healers in East Africa." *International Psychiatry* 4(4):85–86. doi: 10.1192/S1749367600005233.

Neill, Erica, Denny Meyer, Wei Lin Toh, Tamsyn Elizabeth Rheenen, Andrea Phillipou, Eric Josiah Tan, and Susan Lee Rossell. 2020. "Alcohol Use in Australia during the Early Days of the COVID-19 Pandemic: Initial Results from the COLLATE project." *Psychiatry and Clinical Neurosciences* 74(10):542–49. doi: 10.1111/pcn.13099.

Nelson, Jason M., and Hannah Harwood. 2011a. "Learning Disabilities and Anxiety: A Meta-Analysis." *Journal of Learning Disabilities* 44(1):3–17. doi: 10.1177/0022219409359939.

Nelson, Jason M., and Hannah R. Harwood. 2011b. "A Meta-Analysis of Parent and Teacher Reports of Depression among Students with Learning Disabilities: Evidence for the Importance of Multi-Informant Assessment: Depression and LD." *Psychology in the Schools* 48(4):371–84. doi: 10.1002/pits.20560.

Neria, Yuval, Priya Wickramaratne, Mark Olfson, Marc J. Gameroff, Daniel J. Pilowsky, Rafael Lantigua, Steven Shea, and Myrna M. Weissman. 2013. "Mental and Physical Health Consequences of the September 11, 2001 (9/11) Attacks in Primary Care: A Longitudinal Study: 9/11 Health Consequences in Primary Care." *Journal of Traumatic Stress* 26(1):45–55. doi: 10.1002/jts.21767.

New Freedom Commission. *Achieving the Promise: Transforming Mental Health Care in America*, Final Report, July 2003.

Nguyen, Kimberly H., Mabel Padilla, Andrés Villaveces, Pragna Patel, Victor Atuchukwu, Dennis Onotu, Rose Apondi, George Aluzimbi, Peter Chipimo, Nzali Kancheya, and Howard Kress. 2019. "Coerced and Forced Sexual Initiation and Its Association with Negative Health Outcomes among Youth: Results from the Nigeria, Uganda, and Zambia Violence against Children Surveys." *Child Abuse & Neglect* 96:104074. doi: 10.1016/j.chiabu.2019.104074.

Nicholi, Armand M. 1970. "The Motorcycle Syndrome." *American Journal of Psychiatry* 126(11):1588–95. doi: 10.1176/ajp.126.11.1588.

Nikelly, Arthur G. 2001. "The Role of Environment in Mental Health: Individual Empowerment through Social Restructuring." *The Journal of Applied Behavioral Science* 37(3):305–23. doi: 10.1177/0021886301373004.

Nisbett, Richard E. 2003. *How Asians and Westerners Think Differently...and Why.* New York, NY: Free Press.

Nixon, Reginald D. V., and Pallavi Nishith. 2005. "September 11 Attacks: Prior Interpersonal Trauma, Dysfunctional Cognitions, and Trauma Response in a Midwestern University Sample." *Violence and Victims* 20(4):471–80. doi: 10.1891/0886-6708.20.4.471.

Noh, Jin-Won, Hyunchun Park, Young Dae Kwon, In Hye Kim, Yo Han Lee, Yoon Jung Kim, and Sin Gon Kim. 2017. "Gender Differences in Suicidal Ideation and Related Factors among North Korean Refugees in South Korea." *Psychiatry Investigation* 14(6):762. doi: 10.4306/pi.2017.14.6.762.

Noh, Samuel, Violet Kaspar, and K. A. S. Wickrama. 2007. "Overt and Subtle Racial Discrimination and Mental Health: Preliminary Findings for Korean Immigrants." *American Journal of Public Health* 97(7):1269–74. doi: 10.2105/AJPH.2005.085316.

Nolen-Hoeksema, Susan, and Lort Hilt. 2006. "Possible Contributors to the Gender Differences in Alcohol Use and Problems." *The Journal of General Psychology* 133(4):357–74. doi: 10.3200/GENP.133.4.357-374.

Noonan, Robert J., John R. Barry, and Hugh C. Davis. 1970. "Personality Determinants in Attitudes towards Visible Disability." *Journal of Personality* 38:1–15.

Norman, Judith. 2004. "Gender Bias in the Diagnosis and Treatment of Depression." *International Journal of Mental Health* 33(2):32–43.

Norris, Fran H., Matthew J. Friedman, Patricia J. Watson, Christopher M. Byrne, Eolia Diaz, and Krzysztof Kaniasty. 2002. "60,000 Disaster Victims Speak: Part I. An Empirical Review of the Empirical Literature, 1981–2001." *Psychiatry: Interpersonal and Biological Processes* 65(3):207–39. doi: 10.1521/psyc.65.3.207.20173.

North, Carol S. 1999. "Psychiatric Disorders among Survivors of the Oklahoma City Bombing." *JAMA* 282(8):755. doi: 10.1001/jama.282.8.755.

Oiamo, Tor H., Isaac N. Luginaah, and Jamie Baxter. 2015. "Cumulative Effects of Noise and Odour Annoyances on Environmental and Health Related Quality of Life." *Social Science & Medicine* 146:191–203. doi: 10.1016/j.socscimed.2015.10.043.

Ojeda, Victoria D., and Thomas G. McGuire. 2006. "Gender and Racial/Ethnic Differences in Use of Outpatient Mental Health and Substance Use Services by Depressed Adults." *Psychiatric Quarterly* 77(3):211–22. doi: 10.1007/s11126-006-9008-9.

Okasha, Ahmed, and Tarek Okasha. 2000. "Notes on Mental Disorders in Pharaonic Egypt." *History of Psychiatry* 11(44):413–24. doi: 10.1177/0957154X0001104406.

O'Keefe, Maura. 1994. "Racial/Ethnic Differences among Battered Women and Their Children." *Journal of Child and Family Studies* 3(3):283–305. doi: 10.1007/BF02234687.

Okonji, Marx, Frank Njenga, David Kiima, James Ayuyo, Pius Kigamwa, Ajit Shah, and Rachel Jenkins. 2008. "Traditional Health Practitioners and Mental Health in Kenya." *International Psychiatry* 5(2):46–48.

Okpaku, Samuel O., Thara Rangaswamy, and Hema Tharoor. 2014. "Women's Mental Health." Pp. 243–50 in *Essentials of Global Mental Health*, edited by S. O. Okpaku. Cambridge: Cambridge University Press.

Olkin, Rhoda, H'Sien Hayward, Melody Schaff Abbene, and Goldie VanHeel. 2019. "The Experiences of Microaggressions against Women with Visible and Invisible Disabilities." *Journal of Social Issues* 75(3):757–85. doi: 10.1111/josi.12342.

Ornelas, India J., and Krista M. Perreira. 2011. "The Role of Migration in the Development of Depressive Symptoms among Latino Immigrant Parents in the USA." *Social Science & Medicine* 73(8):1169–77. doi: 10.1016/j.socscimed.2011.07.002.

Orrù, Germano, and Mauro Giovanni Carta. 2018. "Genetic Variants Involved in Bipolar Disorder, a Rough Road Ahead." *Clinical Practice & Epidemiology in Mental Health* 14(1):37–45. doi: 10.2174/1745017901814010037.

Osofsky, Howard J., Joy D. Osofsky, and Tonya C. Hansel. 2011. "Deepwater Horizon Oil Spill: Mental Health Effects on Residents in Heavily Affected Areas." *Disaster Medicine and Public Health Preparedness* 5(4):280–86. doi: 10.1001/dmp.2011.85.

Owen, Jesse, Karen Tao, and Emil Rodolfa. 2010. "Microaggressions and Women in Short-Term Psychotherapy: Initial Evidence." *The Counseling Psychologist* 38(7):923–46. doi: 10.1177/0011000010376093.

Padilla-Walker, Laura M., and Larry J. Nelson. 2012. "Black Hawk down?: Establishing Helicopter Parenting as a Distinct Construct from Other Forms of Parental Control during Emerging Adulthood." *Journal of Adolescence* 35(5):1177–90. doi: 10.1016/j.adolescence.2012.03.007.

Pal, G. C. 2015. "Social Exclusion and Mental Health: The Unexplored Aftermath of Caste-Based Discrimination and Violence." *Psychology and Developing Societies* 27(2):189–213. doi: 10.1177/0971333615593446.

Panchal, Nirmita, Rabah Kamal, Cynthia Cox, and Rachel Garfield. 2021. *The Implications of COVID-19 for Mental Health and Substance Use*. Kaiser Family Foundation.

Paniagua, Freddy A. 2000. "Culture-Bound Syndromes, Cultural Variations, and Psychopathology." 139-169 in *Handbook of Multicultural Mental Health*. Israel Cuellar and Freddy A. Paniagua, eds. San Diego, CA: Elsevier.

Pantin, Hilda M., Seth J. Schwartz, Guillermo Prado, Daniel J. Feaster, and José Szapocznik. 2003. "Posttraumatic Stress Disorder Symptoms in Hispanic Immigrants after the September 11th Attacks: Severity and Relationship to Previous Traumatic Exposure." *Hispanic Journal of Behavioral Sciences* 25(1):56–72. doi: 10.1177/0739986303251695.

Papapietro, Daniel J. 2019. "Involving Forensic Patients in Treatment Planning Increases Cooperation and May Reduce Violence Risk." *The Journal of the American Academy of Psychiatry and the Law* 47(1):35–41. doi: 10.29158/JAAPL.003815-19.

Parker, Richard, and Peter Aggleton. 2003. "HIV and AIDS-Related Stigma and Discrimination: A Conceptual Framework and Implications for Action." *Social Science and Medicine* 57:13–24.

Parks, Joe, and Alan Q. Radke. 2014. *The Vital Role of State Psychiatric Hospitals*. Alexandria, VR: National Association of State Mental Health Program Directors.

Pasman, Joelle. 2011. "The Consequences of Labeling Mental Illnesses on the Self-Concept: A Review of the Literature and Future Directions." *Social Cosmos* 2:122–27.

Patel, Vikram. 1995. "Explanatory Models of Mental Illness in Sub-Saharan Africa." *Social Science & Medicine* 40(9):1291–98. doi: 10.1016/0277-9536(94)00231-H.

Patel, Vikram, and Arthur Kleinman. 2003. "Poverty and Common Mental Disorders in Developing Countries." *Bulletin of the World Health Organization* 81:609–15.

Patel, Vikram, and Martin Prince. 2010. "Global Mental Health: A New Global Health Field Comes of Age." *JAMA* 303(19):1976. doi: 10.1001/jama.2010.616.

Patten, S. B. 1991. "Are the Brown and Harris 'Vulnerability Factors' Risk Factors for Depression?" *Journal of Psychiatry & Neuroscience: JPN* 16(5):267–71.

Paul, Karsten I., and Klaus Moser. 2009. "Unemployment Impairs Mental Health: Meta-Analyses." *Journal of Vocational Behavior* 74(3): 264–82. doi: 10.1016/j.jvb.2009.01.001.

Pavalko, E. K., and B. Smith. 1999. "The Rhythm of Work: Health Effects of Women Work Dynamics." *Social Forces* 77:1141–62.

Pearce, Lisa D., Jeremy E. Uecker, and Melinda Lundquist Denton. 2019. "Religion and Adolescent Outcomes: How and Under What Conditions Religion Matters." *Annual Review of Sociology* 45(1): 201–22. doi: 10.1146/annurev-soc-073117-041317.

Pearlin, Leonard I. 1989. "The Sociological Study of Stress." *Journal of Health and Social Behavior* 30(3):241. doi: 10.2307/2136956.

Pearlin, Leonard I., and Alex Bierman. 2013. "Current Issues and Future Directions in Research into the Stress Process." Pp. 325–40 in *Handbook of the Sociology of Mental Health*. Carol s. Aneshensel, Jo C. Phelan, and Alex Bierman, eds. New York, NY: Springer.

Pearlin, Leonard I., Scott Schieman, Elena M. Fazio, and Stephen C. Meersman. 2005. "Stress, Health, and the Life Course: Some Conceptual Perspectives." *Journal of Health and Social Behavior* 46(2):205–19. doi: 10.1177/002214650504600206.

Peltier, MacKenzie R., Seandra J. Cosgrove, Kelechi Ohayagha, Kathleen A. Crapanzano, and Glenn N. Jones. 2017. "Do They See Dead People? Cultural Factors and Sensitivity in Screening for Schizophrenia Spectrum Disorders." *Ethnicity & Health* 22(2):119–29. doi: 10.1080/13557858.2016.1196650.

Penner, Francesca, Malgorzata Gambin, and Carla Sharp. 2019. "Childhood Maltreatment and Identity Diffusion among Inpatient Adolescents: The Role of Reflective Function." *Journal of Adolescence* 76:65–74. doi: 10.1016/j.adolescence.2019.08.002.

Pereda, Noemí, Georgina Guilera, Maria Forns, and Juana Gómez-Benito. 2009. "The Prevalence of Child Sexual Abuse in Community and Student Samples: A Meta-Analysis." *Clinical Psychology Review* 29(4):328–38. doi: 10.1016/j.cpr.2009.02.007.

Pérez, Jesús, Ross J. Baldessarini, Juan Undurraga, and José Sánchez-Moreno. 2012. "Origins of Psychiatric Hospitalization in Medieval Spain." *Psychiatric Quarterly* 83(4):419–30. doi: 10.1007/s11126-012-9212-8.

Pérez-Fuentes, Gabriela, Mark Olfson, Laura Villegas, Carmen Morcillo, Shuai Wang, and Carlos Blanco. 2013. "Prevalence and Correlates of Child Sexual Abuse: A National Study." *Comprehensive Psychiatry* 54(1):16–27. doi: 10.1016/j.comppsych.2012.05.010.

Perlin, Michael L. 1996. "The Insanity Defense: Deconstructing the Myths and Reconstructing the Jurisprudence." Pp. 341–59 in *Law, Mental Health, and Mental Disorder*, edited by B. D. Sales and D. W. Shuman. Pacific Grove, CA: Brooks-Cole.

Perlin, Michael L., and Heather Ellis Cucolo. 2017. "'Tolling for the Aching Ones Whose Wounds Cannot Be Nursed': The Marginalization of Racial Minorities and Women in Institutional Mental Disability Law Policing Rape Complaints." *The Journal of Gender, Race, and Justice* 20(3):431–58.

Perry, Brea L. 2011. "The Labeling Paradox: Stigma, the Sick Role, and Social Networks in Mental Illness." *Journal of Health and Social Behavior* 52(4):460–77. doi: 10.1177/0022146511408913.

Perry, Brea L., Matthew Neltner, and Timothy Allen. 2013. "A Paradox of Bias: Racial Differences in Forensic Psychiatric Diagnosis and Determinations of Criminal Responsibility." *Race and Social Problems* 5(4):239–49. doi: 10.1007/s12552-013-9100-3.

Perry, Brea L., and Bernice A. Pescosolido. 2015. "Social Network Activation: The Role of Health Discussion Partners in Recovery from Mental Illness." *Social Science & Medicine* 125:116–28. doi: 10.1016/j.socscimed.2013.12.033.

Perry, Melissa J. 1996. "The Relationship between Social Class and Mental Disorder." *The Journal of Primary Prevention* 17(1):17–30. doi: 10.1007/BF02262736.

Pescosolido, Bernice A. 1992. "Beyond Rational Choice: The Social Dynamics of How People Seek Help." *American Journal of Sociology* 97(4): 1096–1138. doi: 10.1086/229863.

Pescosolido, Bernice A., Carol A. Boyer, and Tait R. Medina. 2013. "The Social Dynamics of Responding to Mental Health Problems." Pp. 505–24 in *Handbook of the Sociology of Mental Health*, edited by C. S. Aneshensel, J. C. Phelan, and A. Bierman. New York, NY: Springer Berlin Heidelberg.

Pescosolido, Bernice A., Carol Brooks Gardner, and Keri M. Lubell. 1998. "How People Get into Mental Health Services: Stories of Choice, Coercion and 'Muddling through' from 'First-Timers'." *Social Science & Medicine* 46(2):275–86. doi: 10.1016/S0277-9536(97)00160-3.

Pescosolido, Bernice A., Jack K. Martin, J. Scott Long, Tait R. Medina, Jo C. Phelan, and Bruce G. Link. 2010. "'A Disease Like Any Other'? A Decade of Change in Public Reactions to Schizophrenia, Depression, and Alcohol Dependence." *American Journal of Psychiatry* 167(11):1321–30. doi: 10.1176/appi.ajp.2010.09121743.

Pescosolido, Bernice A., Jack K. Martin, Sigrun Olafsdottir, J. Scott Long, Karen Kafadar, and Tait R. Medina. 2015. "The Theory of Industrial Society and Cultural Schemata: Does the 'Cultural Myth of Stigma' Underlie the WHO Schizophrenia Paradox?" *American Journal of Sociology* 121(3):783–825. doi: 10.1086/683225.

Pescosolido, Bernice A., Brea L. Perry, J. Scott Long, Jack K. Martin, John I. Nurnberger, Jr., and Victor Hesselbrock. 2008. "Under the Influence of Genetics: How Transdisciplinarity Leads Us to Rethink Social Pathways to Illness." *American Journal of Sociology* 114(S1):S171–201. doi: 10.1086/592209.

Peterson Edwards, Ellen, Kenneth E. Leonard, and Rina Das Eiden. 2001. "Temperament and Behavioral Problems among Infants in Alcoholic Families." *Infant Mental Health Journal* 22(3):374–92. doi: 10.1002/imhj.1007.

Peterson, James L., and Nicholas Zill. 1986. "Marital Disruption, Parent-Child Relationships, and Behavior Problems in Children." *Journal of Marriage and the Family* 48(2):295. doi: 10.2307/352397.

Pew Charitable Trust. 2015. *Mental Health and the Role of the States*. Pew Charitable Trusts and the MacArthur Foundation.

Pew Charitable Trust. 2016. *Demographic Trends and Economic Well-being*. Pew Charitable Trusts and the MacArthur Foundation.

Pfeifer, Samuel. 1994. "Belief in Demons and Exorcism in Psychiatric Patients in Switzerland." *British Journal of Medical Psychology* 67:247–58.

Phelan, Jo C., and Bruce G. Link. 1998. "The Growing Belief that People with Mental Illnesses Are Violent: The Role of the Dangerousness Criterion for Civil Commitment." *Social Psychiatry and Psychiatric Epidemiology* 33(13):S7–12. doi: 10.1007/s001270050204.

Phelan, Jo C., Bruce G. Link, Ann Stueve, and Bernice A. Pescosolido. 2000. "Public Conceptions of Mental Illness in 1950 and 1996: What Is Mental Illness and Is It to Be Feared?" *Journal of Health and Social Behavior* 41(2):188. doi: 10.2307/2676305.

Piechowski, Lisa Drago. 1992. "Mental Health and Women's Multiple Roles." *Families in Society* 73(3):131–39.

Pigg, Stacey L. 1995. "Social Symbolism of Healing in Nepal. 34(1), 17–36.

Piña-Watson, Brandy, Jasmín D. Llamas, Aundrea Garcia, and Abigail Cruz. 2019. "A Multidimensional Developmental Approach to Understanding Intragroup Marginalization and Mental Health among Adolescents and Emerging Adults of Mexican Descent." *Hispanic Journal of Behavioral Sciences* 41(1):42–62. doi: 10.1177/0739986318816392.

Pitti, Ilaria. 2017. "What Does Being an Adult Mean? Comparing Young People's and Adults' Representations of Adulthood." *Journal of Youth Studies* 20(9):1225–41. doi: 10.1080/13676261.2017.1317336.

Plöderl, Martin, and Pierre Tremblay. 2015. "Mental Health of Sexual Minorities. A Systematic Review." *International Review of Psychiatry* 27(5):367–85. doi: 10.3109/09540261.2015.1083949.

Porter, Roy. 2002. *Madness: A Brief History*. Oxford: Oxford University Press.

Poss, Jane E. 2001. "Developing a New Model for Cross-Cultural Research: Synthesizing the Health

Belief Model and the Theory of Reasoned Action." *Advances in Nursing Science Issue* 23(4):1–15.

Powers, Richard E. 1994. "Bureaucrat: A New Disorder." *American Journal of Psychiatry* 151(11):1716.

Pratt L. A., Brody D. J. Depression in the U.S. household population, 2009–2012. NCHS Data Brief. 2014 Dec;(172):1–8.

Pratt, Laura A, and Debra J. Brody 2014. "Depression in the U.S. Household Population, 2009–2012NCHS Data Brief No. 172. Centers for Disease Control. https://www.cdc.gov/nchs/products/databriefs/db172.htm

Prusty, Bhupesh K., Nitish Gulve, Sheila Govind, Gerhard R. F. Krueger, Julia Feichtinger, Lee Larcombe, Richard Aspinall, Dharam V. Ablashi, and Carla T. Toro. 2018. "Active HHV-6 Infection of Cerebellar Purkinje Cells in Mood Disorders." *Frontiers in Microbiology* 9:1955. doi: 10.3389/fmicb.2018.01955.

Przybylski, Andrew K., Kou Murayama, Cody R. DeHaan, and Valerie Gladwell. 2013. "Motivational, Emotional, and Behavioral Correlates of Fear of Missing Out." *Computers in Human Behavior* 29(4):1841–48. doi: 10.1016/j.chb.2013.02.014.

Rabinowitz, Jill A., Terrinieka Powell, Richard Sadler, Beth Reboussin, Kerry Green, Adam Milam, Mieka Smart, Debra Furr-Holden, Amanda Latimore, and Darius Tandon. 2020. "Neighborhood Profiles and Associations with Coping Behaviors among Low-Income Youth." *Journal of Youth and Adolescence* 49(2):494–505. doi: 10.1007/s10964-019-01176-y.

Radloff, Lenore Sawyer. 1977. "The CES-D Scale: A Self Report Depression Scale for Research in the General Population." *Applied Psychological Measurements* 1:385–401.

Rahim, Sheikh Idris A., and Marianne Cederblad. 1989. "Epidemiology of Mental Disorders in Young Adults of a Newly Urbanised Area in Khartoum, Sudan." *British Journal of Psychiatry* 155(1):44–47. doi: 10.1192/bjp.155.1.44.

Ramaiah, A. 2007. *Dalit's Physical and Mental Health: Status, Root Causes and Challenges*. Mumbai: Tata Institute of Social Sciences.

Ramsden, Edmund, and Matthew Smith. 2018. "Remembering the West End: Social Science, Mental Health and the American Urban Environment, 1939–1968." *Urban History* 45(1):128–49. doi: 10.1017/S0963926817000025.

Rasic, Daniel, Jennifer A. Robinson, James Bolton, O. Joseph Bienvenu, and Jitender Sareen. 2011. "Longitudinal Relationships of Religious Worship Attendance and Spirituality with Major Depression, Anxiety Disorders, and Suicidal Ideation and Attempts: Findings from the Baltimore Epidemiologic Catchment Area Study." *Journal of Psychiatric Research* 45(6):848–54. doi: 10.1016/j.jpsychires.2010.11.014.

Rathore, Saif S., Yongfei Wang, Benjamin G. Druss, et al. 2008. "Mental Disorders, Quality of Care, and Outcomes among Older Patients Hospitalized with Heart Failure An Analysis of the National Heart Failure Project." *Archives of General Psychiatry* 65(12):1402–8.

Ravaldi, Claudia, Valdo Ricca, Alyce Wilson, Caroline Homer, and Alfredo Vannacci. 2020. "Previous Psychopathology Predicted Severe COVID-19 Concern, Anxiety, and PTSD Symptoms in Pregnant Women during 'Lockdown' in Italy." *Archives of Women's Mental Health*. doi: 10.1007/s00737-020-01086-0.

Rawlings, Charles E., and Eugene Rossitch. 1994. "The History of Trephination in Africa with a Discussion of Its Current Status and Continuing Practice." *Surgical Neurology* 41:507–13.

Read, Jen'nan Ghazal and Michael O. Emerson. 2005. "Racial Context, Black Immigration and the U.S. Black/White Health Disparity." *Social Forces* 84(1):181–99. doi: 10.1353/sof.2005.0120.

Reifman, Alan, Laura C. Villa, Julie A. Amans, Vasuki Rethinam, and Tiffany Y. Telesca. 2001. "Children of Divorce in the 1990s: A Meta-Analysis." *Journal of Divorce & Remarriage* 36(1–2):27–36. doi: 10.1300/J087v36n01_02.

Reiss, Franziska. 2013. "Socioeconomic Inequalities and Mental Health Problems in Children and Adolescents: A Systematic Review." *Social Science & Medicine* 90:24–31. doi: 10.1016/j.socscimed.2013.04.026.

Repko, Melissa. 2020. *For Grocery Workers, the Need for Mental Health Care May Outlast Coronavirus Pandemic.*

Reynolds, Shirley. 1997. "Psychological Well-Being at Work: Is Prevention Better than Cure?" *Journal of Psychosomatic Research* 43(1):93–102. doi: 10.1016/S0022-3999(97)00023-8.

Rhodes, Jean, Christian Chan, Christina Paxson, Cecilia Elena Rouse, Mary Waters, and Elizabeth Fussell. 2010. "The Impact of Hurricane Katrina on the Mental and Physical Health of Low-Income Parents in New Orleans." *The American Journal of Orthopsychiatry* 80(2):237–47. doi: 10.1111/j.1939-0025.2010.01027.x.

Richards, Misty, and Maureen Sayres Van Niel. 2017. *Mental Health Disparities: Women's Mental Health*. American Psychiatric Association.

Rieker, Patricia P., and Chloe E. Bird. 2000. "Sociological Explanations of Gender Differences in Mental and Physical Health." Pp. 98–113 in *Handbook of Medical Sociology*, 5th Ed. Edited by Chloe E. Bird, Peter Conrad, and Allen M. Fremont. Upper Saddle River, NJ: Prentice Hall.

Riley, Anna L., and Verna M. Keith. 2004. "Work and Housework Conditions and Depressive Symptoms among Married Women: The Importance of Occupational Status." *Women & Health* 38(4):1–17. doi: 10.1300/J013v38n04_01.

Riley, K. P. 1994. "Depression." Pp. 256–68 in *Functional Performance in Older Adults*, edited by B. R. Bonder and M. B. Wagner. Philadelphia, PA: F.A. Davis.

Rochefort, David A. 1997. *From Poorhouses to Homelessness: Policy Analysis and Mental Health Care*. 2nd ed. Westport, CT: Auburn.

Rogers, Anne. 1993. "Coercion and 'Voluntary' Admission: An Examination of Psychiatric Patient Views." *Behavioral Sciences & the Law* 11(3):259–67. doi: 10.1002/bsl.2370110304.

Rohrer, Julia M., Boris Egloff, and Stefan C. Schmukle. 2015. "Examining the Effects of Birth Order on Personality." *Proceedings of the National Academy of Sciences* 112(46):14224–29. doi: 10.1073/pnas.1506451112.

Rose, Chad A., and Brendesha M. Tynes. 2015. "Longitudinal Associations between Cybervictimization and Mental Health among U.S. Adolescents." *Journal of Adolescent Health* 57(3):305–12. doi: 10.1016/j.jadohealth.2015.05.002.

Rose, Diana, Graham Thornicroft, Vanessa Pinfold, and Aliya Kassam. 2007. "250 Labels Used to Stigmatise People with Mental Illness." *BMC Health Services Research* 7:97. doi: 10.1186/1472-6963-7-97.

Rosen, L. D., K. Whaling, S. Rab, L. M. Carrier, and N. A. Cheever. 2013. "Is Facebook Creating 'IDisorders'? The Link between Clinical Symptoms of Psychiatric Disorders and Technology Use, Attitudes and Anxiety." *Computers in Human Behavior* 29(3):1243–54. doi: 10.1016/j.chb.2012.11.012.

Rosenberg, Morris. 1984. "A Symbolic Interactionist View of Psychosis." *Journal of Health and Social Behavior* 25:289–302.

Rosenfield, Sarah, Kelly Kato, and Dena Smith. 2017. "Gender and Mental Health." Pp. 266–80 in *A Handbook for the Study of Mental Health: Social Contexts, Theories, and Systems*, edited by Teresa L. Scheid and Eric R. Wright. Cambridge: Cambridge University Press.

Rosenfield, Sarah, Mary Clare Lennon, and Helene Raskin White. 2005. "The Self and Mental Health: Self-Salience and the Emergence of Internalizing and Externalizing Problems." *Journal of Health and Social Behavior* 46(4):323–40. doi: 10.1177/002214650504600402.

Rosenhan, D. L. 1973. "On Being Sane in Insane Places." *Science* 179(4070):250–58.

Rosmarin, David H., Joseph S. Bigda-Peyton, Sarah J. Kertz, Nasya Smith, Scott L. Rauch, and Thröstur Björgvinsson. 2013. "A Test of Faith in God and Treatment: The Relationship of Belief in God to Psychiatric Treatment Outcomes." *Journal of Affective Disorders* 146(3):441–46. doi: 10.1016/j.jad.2012.08.030.

Rosoff, Stephen M., and Matthew C. Leone. 1991. "The Public Prestige of Medical Specialties: Overviews and Undercurrents." *Social Science & Medicine* 32(3):321–26. doi: 10.1016/0277-9536(91)90110-X.

Ross, Catherine E. 2000. "Neighborhood Disadvantage and Adult Depression." *Journal of Health and Social Behavior* 41(2):177. doi: 10.2307/2676304.

Ross, Catherine E., and John Mirowsky. 2009. "Neighborhood Disorder, Subjective Alienation, and Distress." *Journal of Health and Social Behavior* 50(1):49–64. doi: 10.1177/002214650905000104.

Ross, Justin M., Pavel A. Yakovlev, and Fatima Carson. 2012. "Does State Spending on Mental Health Lower Suicide Rates?" *The Journal of Socio-Economics* 41(4):408–17. doi: 10.1016/j.socec.2010.10.005.

Rothman, David J. 1971. *The Discovery of the Asylum: Social Order and Disorder in the New Republic*. Boston, MA: Little, Brown, and Company.

Rousseau, Sofie, and Miri Scharf. 2018. "Why People Helicopter Parent? An Actor–Partner Interdependence Study of Maternal and Paternal Prevention/Promotion Focus and Interpersonal/Self-Regret." *Journal of Social and Personal Relationships* 35(7):919–35. doi: 10.1177/0265407517700514.

Rowling, J. K. 2000. *Harry Potter and the Prisoner of Azkaban*. 1. publ., [53. Nachdr.]. London: Bloomsbury.

Ruback, Richard Barry, and Martie P. Thompson. 2001. *Social and Psychological Consequences of Violent Victimization*. Thousand Oaks, CA: SAGE.

Ruggeri, M., M. Leese, G. Thornicroft, G. Bisoffi, and M. Tansella. 2000. "Definition and Prevalence of Severe and Persistent Mental Illness." *The British Journal of Psychiatry: The Journal of Mental Science* 177:149–55. doi: 10.1192/bjp.177.2.149.

Rüsch, Nicolas, Matthias C. Angermeyer, and Patrick W. Corrigan. 2005. "Mental Illness Stigma: Concepts, Consequences, and Initiatives to Reduce Stigma." *European Psychiatry* 20(8):529–39. doi: 10.1016/j.eurpsy.2005.04.004.

Russell, D., and J. Taylor. 2009. "Living Alone and Depressive Symptoms: The Influence of Gender, Physical Disability, and Social Support among Hispanic and Non-Hispanic Older Adults." *The Journals of Gerontology Series B: Psychological Sciences and Social Sciences* 64B(1):95–104. doi: 10.1093/geronb/gbn002.

Rutter, D. R., and P. J. Fielding. 1988. "Sources of Occupational Stress: An Examination of British Prison Officers." *Work & Stress* 2(4):291–99. doi: 10.1080/02678378808257490.

Sachdev, Perminder S. 2001. "The Impact of Colonialism on the Mental Health of the New Zealand Maori: A Historical and Contemporary Perspective." Pp. 15–45 in *Colonialism and Psychiatry*, edited by D. Bhugra and R. Littlewood. New Delhi: Oxford University Press.

Sackville-West, Vita. 1936. *Saint Joan of Arc*. New York, NY: Doubleday.

Sanders Thompson, Vetta L. 1996. "Perceived Experiences of Racism as Stressful Life Events." *Community Mental Health Journal* 32(3):223–33. doi: 10.1007/BF02249424.

Sarhan, Walid. 2018. "The Contribution of Arab Islamic Civilization to Mental Health." *The Arab Journal of Psychiatry* 29(1):57–66. doi: 10.12816/0046445.

Sassi, Maria Michela. 2013. "Mental Illness, Moral Error, and Responsibility in Late Plato." in *Mental Disorders in the Classical World*, edited by W. V. Harris. BRILL.

Sathya, Chethan. 2014. "Uganda's Witch Doctors Tackle Mental Illness." *Toronto Star*, April 26.

Sato, Mitsumoto. 2006. "Renaming Schizophrenia: A Japanese Perspective." *World Psychiatry* 5(1):53–55.

Satre, Jean-Paul. 1943. *Being and Nothingness*. New York, NY: Philosophical Library.

Saxena, Shekhar, Graham Thornicroft, Martin Knapp, and Harvey Whiteford. 2007. "Resources for Mental Health: Scarcity, Inequity, and Inefficiency." *The Lancet* 370(9590):878–89. doi: 10.1016/S0140-6736(07)61239-2.

Schiamberg, Lawrence B., James Oehmke, Zhenmei Zhang, Gia E. Barboza, Robert J. Griffore, Levente Von Heydrich, Lori A. Post, Robin P. Weatherill, and Teresa Mastin. 2012. "Physical Abuse of Older Adults in Nursing Homes: A Random Sample Survey of Adults with an Elderly Family Member in a Nursing Home." *Journal of Elder Abuse & Neglect* 24(1):65–83. doi: 10.1080/08946566.2011.608056.

Schinnar, Arie P., Aileen B. Rothbard, Rebekah Kanter, and Yoon Soo Jung. 1990. "An Empirical Literature Review of Definitions of Severe and Persistent Mental Illness." *The American Journal of Psychiatry* 147(12):1602–8. doi: 10.1176/ajp.147.12.1602.

Schnittker, Jason. 2013. "Public Beliefs about Mental Illness." Pp. 75–94 in *Handbook of the*

Sociology of Mental Health. New York, NY: Springer.

Schnittker, Jason, Jeremy Freese, and Brian Powell. 2000. "Nature, Nurture, Neither, Nor: Black-White Differences in Beliefs about the Causes and Appropriate Treatment of Mental Illness." *Social Forces* 78(3):1101. doi: 10.2307/3005943.

Schonfeld, Lawrence., and Larry W. Dupree. 1991. "Antecedents of Drinking for Early- and Late-Onset Elderly Alcohol Abusers." *Journal of Studies on Alcohol* 52(6):587–92. doi: 10.15288/jsa.1991.52.587.

Schroeder, Shawnda M., and Mandi-Leigh Peterson. 2018. "Identifying Variability in Patient Characteristics and Prevalence of Emergency Department Utilization for Mental Health Diagnoses in Rural and Urban Communities: Rural-Urban Utilization of ED for Mental Health." *The Journal of Rural Health* 34(4):369–76. doi: 10.1111/jrh.12282.

Schwartz, Sharon, and Cheryl Corcoran. 2017. "Biological Approaches to Psychiatric Disorders: A Sociological Approach." Pp. 98–125 in *A Handbook for the Study of Mental Health: Social Contexts, Theories, and Systems*, edited by Teresa L. Scheid and Eric R. Wright. Cambridge: Cambridge University Press.

Schwartz, Sharon, and Ilan H. Meyer. 2010. "Reflections on the Stress Model: A Response to Turner." *Social Science & Medicine* 70(8):1121–22. doi: 10.1016/j.socscimed.2009.11.038.

Scott, Kate M., Dan J. Stein, Peter De Jonge, and Ronald C. Kessler. 2018. "Discussion." Pp. 324–36 in *Mental Disorders around the World: Facts and Figures from the WHO World Mental Health Surveys*, edited by K. M. Scott, D. J. Stein, P. De Jong, and R. C. Kessler. Cambridge: Cambridge University Press.

Scott, Wilbur J. 1990. "PTSD in DSM-III: A Case in the Politics of Diagnosis and Disease." *Social Problems* 37(3):294–310. doi: 10.2307/800744.

Scull, Andrew. 2015. *Madness in Civilization: A Cultural History of Insanity, from the Bible to Freud, from the Madhouse to Modern Medicine*. Princeton, NJ: Princeton University Press.

Seeskin, Kenneth. 2008. "Plato and the Origin of Mental Health." *International Journal of Law and Psychiatry* 31(6):487–94. doi: 10.1016/j.ijlp.2008.09.004.

Selekman, J. 2012. "People of Jewish Heritage." Pp. 338–56 in *Transcultural Health Care: A Culturally Competent Approach*, edited by L. D. Purnell. Philadelphia, PA: FA Davis.

Sennett, Richard, and Jonathan Cobb. 1972. *The Hidden Injuries of Class*. New York, NY: Alfred A. Knopf.

Serido, Joyce, David M. Almeida, and Elaine Wethington. 2004. "Chronic Stressors and Daily Hassles: Unique and Interactive Relationships with Psychological Distress." *Journal of Health and Social Behavior* 45(1):17–33. doi: 10.1177/002214650404500102.

Shensa, Ariel, César G. Escobar-Viera, Jaime E. Sidani, Nicholas D. Bowman, Michael P. Marshal, and Brian A. Primack. 2017. "Problematic Social Media Use and Depressive Symptoms among U.S. Young Adults: A Nationally-Representative Study." *Social Science & Medicine* 182:150–57. doi: 10.1016/j.socscimed.2017.03.061.

Sherman, Jennifer, and Elizabeth Harris. 2012. "Social Class and Parenting: Classic Debates and New Understandings: Social Class and Parenting." *Sociology Compass* 6(1):60–71. doi: 10.1111/j.1751-9020.2011.00430.x.

Shilling, Chris. 2012. *The Body and Social Theory*. 3rd ed. Los Angeles, CA: SAGE.

Shin, Hwajin, and In-Jin Yoon. 2018. "Acculturative Stress as a Mental Health Predictor of North Korean Refugees in South Korea." *Asian and Pacific Migration Journal* 27(3):299–322. doi: 10.1177/0117196818794680.

Shrestha, Dhan Bahadur, Bikash Bikram Thapa, Nagendra Katuwal, Bikal Shrestha, Chiranjibi Pant, Bina Basnet, Pankaj Mandal, Amol Gurung, Ankita Agrawal, and Ramhari Rouniyar. 2020. "Psychological Distress in Nepalese Residents during COVID-19 Pandemic: A Community Level Survey." *BMC Psychiatry* 20(1):491. doi: 10.1186/s12888-020-02904-6.

Siegrist, Johannes. 1996. "Adverse Health Effects of High-Effort/Low-Reward Conditions." *Journal of Occupational Health Psychology* 1(1):27–41. doi: 10.1037/1076-8998.1.1.27.

Sijuwade, Philip O. 1995. "Urbanization and Mental Health Problems in Nigeria: Implications for Social Policy." *International Review of Modern Sociology* 25(1):43–54.

Simandan, Dragos. 2018. "Rethinking the Health Consequences of Social Class and Social Mobility." *Social Science & Medicine* 200:258–61. doi: 10.1016/j.socscimed.2017.11.037.

Simon, Robin W. 2002. "Revisiting the Relationships among Gender, Marital Status, and Mental Health." *American Journal of Sociology* 107: 1065–96.

Simon, Robin W. 2014. "Sociological Scholarship on Gender Differences in Emotion and Emotional Well-Being in the United States: A Snapshot of the Field." *Emotion Review* 6(3):196–201. doi: 10.1177/1754073914522865.

Simon, Robin W., Donna Eder, and Cathy Evans. 1992. "The Development of Feeling Norms Underlying Romantic Love among Adolescent Females." *Social Psychology Quarterly* 55(1):29. doi: 10.2307/2786684.

Simon, Robin W., and Leda E. Nath. 2004. "Gender and Emotion in the United States: Do Men and Women Differ in Self-Reports of Feelings and Expressive Behavior?" *American Journal of Sociology* 109(5):1137–76. doi: 10.1086/382111.

Sinha, Rajita. 2011. "New Findings on Biological Factors Predicting Addiction Relapse Vulnerability." *Current Psychiatry Reports* 13(5):398–405. doi: 10.1007/s11920-011-0224-0.

Skopp, Nancy A. 2018. *"Do Gender Stereotypes Influence Mental Health Diagnosis and Treatment in the Military?"* Psychological Health Center of Excellence.

Smaje, Chris. 2000. "Race, Ethnicity and Health." Pp. 114–28 in *Handbook of Medical Sociology*, edited by C. E. Bird, P. Conrad, and A. Fremont. Upper Saddle River, NJ: Prentice Hall.

Smedley, Audrey, and Brian D. Smedley. 2012. *Race in North America: Origin and Evolution of a Worldview*. New York, NY: Westview Press.

Smith, Deborah. 2008. "The Four Temperaments."

Smith, Dena T. 2014. "The Diminished Resistance to Medicalization in Psychiatry: Psychoanalysis Meets the Medical Model of Mental Illness." *Society and Mental Health*, 4:2: 75-91.

Smith, Dena T. 2011. "A Sociological Alternative to the Psychiatric Conceptualization of Mental Suffering: Medicalization of Mental Suffering." *Sociology Compass* 5(5):351–63. doi: 10.1111/j.1751-9020.2011.00369.x.

Smith, James Patrick, and Gillian C. Smith. 2010. "Long-Term Economic Costs of Psychological Problems during Childhood." *Social Science & Medicine* 71(1):110–15. doi: 10.1016/j.socscimed.2010.02.046.

Smith, Lia J., Matthew W. Gallagher, Jana K. Tran, and Anka A. Vujanovic. 2018. "Posttraumatic Stress, Alcohol Use, and Alcohol Use Reasons in Firefighters: The Role of Sleep Disturbance." *Comprehensive Psychiatry* 87:64–71. doi: 10.1016/j.comppsych.2018.09.001.

Smith, S. G., J. Chen, K. C. Basile, L. K. Gilbert, M. T. Merrick, N. Patel, M. Walling, and A. Jain. 2017. *The National Intimate Partner and Sexual Violence Survey (NISVS): 2010-2012 State Report*. Atlanta, GA: National Center for Injury Prevention and Control, Centers for Disease Control and Prevention.

Snedker, Karen A., and Jerald R. Herting. 2016. "Adolescent Mental Health: Neighborhood Stress and Emotional Distress." *Youth & Society* 48(5): 695–719. doi: 10.1177/0044118X13512335.

Social Security Administration. 2018. *National Beneficiary Survey: Disability Statistics, 2015*. Washington, DC: Office of Research Demonstration and Employment Support.

Spain, Austin James. 2018. *"Models of Moral Treatment: British Lunatic Asylums in the Mid-19th Century."* Thesis, Auburn University, Auburn, Alabama.

Spector, Malcolm, and John I. Kitsuse. 1987. *Constructing Social Problems*. Hawthorne, NY: Aldine De Gruyter.

Spence, S. J. A. 1992. "Problems That Patients Feel Are Appropriate to Discuss with Their GPs." *Journal of the Royal Society of Medicine* 85:669–73.

Sprang, Ginny, and Miriam Silman. 2013. "Posttraumatic Stress Disorder in Parents and

Youth After Health-Related Disasters." *Disaster Medicine and Public Health Preparedness* 7(1): 105–10. doi: 10.1017/dmp.2013.22.

Springer, Kristen W., Jennifer Sheridan, Daphne Kuo, and Molly Carnes. 2007. "Long-Term Physical and Mental Health Consequences of Childhood Physical Abuse: Results from a Large Population-Based Sample of Men and Women." *Child Abuse & Neglect* 31(5): 517–30. doi: 10.1016/j.chiabu.2007.01.003.

Srivastava, Kalpana. 2009. "Urbanization and Mental Health." *Industrial Psychiatry Journal* 18(2):75. doi: 10.4103/0972-6748.64028.

Srole, L., T. S. Langer, and S. Michael. 1963. *Life Stress and Mental Health: The Midtown Manhattan Study.* New York, NY: Free Press.

Stark, C. R., V. Riordan, and R. O'Connor. 2011. "A Conceptual Model of Suicide in Rural Areas." *Rural and Remote Health* 11(2):1622.

Sternthal, Michelle J., David R. Williams, Marc A. Musick, and Anna C. Buck. 2010. "Depression, Anxiety, and Religious Life: A Search for Mediators." *Journal of Health and Social Behavior* 51(3): 343–59. doi: 10.1177/0022146510378237.

Stewart, Hannah, John Paul Jameson, and Lisa Curtin. 2015. "The Relationship between Stigma and Self-Reported Willingness to Use Mental Health Services among Rural and Urban Older Adults." *Psychological Services* 12(2):141–48. doi: 10.1037/a0038651.

Straus, Murray A., Richard J. Gelles, and Suzanne K. Steinmetz. 1980. *Behind Closed Doors: Violence in the American Family.* 1st ed. Garden City, NY: Anchor Press/Doubleday.

Straus, Robert. 1957. "The Nature and Status of Medical Sociology." *American Sociological Review* 22(2):200. doi: 10.2307/2088858.

Substance Abuse and Mental Health Services Administration (SAMHSA). 2007. *Results from the 2006 National Survey on Drug Use and Health: National Findings.* NSDUH Series H-32, DHHS Publication No. SMA 07-4293. Rockville, MD: Substance Abuse and Mental Health Services Administration.

Substance Abuse and Mental Health Services Administration (SAMHSA). 2015. *Racial/Ethnic Differences in Mental Health Service Use among Adults.* HHS Publication No. SMA-15-4906. Rockville, MD: Substance Abuse and Mental Health Services Administration.

Substance Abuse and Mental Health Services Administration (SAMHSA). 2019a. *Adolescent Depression.* Center for Behavioral Health Statistics and Quality, National Survey of Drug Use and Health.

Substance Abuse and Mental Health Services Administration (SAMHSA). 2019b. *Civil Commitment and the Mental Health Care Continuum: Historical Trends and Principles for Law and Practice.* Rockville, MD: Office of the Chief Medical Officer, Substance Abuse and Mental Health Services Administration.

Substance Abuse and Mental Health Services Administration (SAMHSA). 2019c. *Key Substance Use and Mental Health Indicators in the United States: Results from the 2018 National Survey on Drug Use and Health.* PEP19-5068. U.S. Department of Health and Human; Services Substance Abuse and Mental Health Services Administration.

Sullivan, Patrick F., Michael C. Neale, and Kenneth S. Kendler. 2000. "Genetic Epidemiology of Major Depression: Review and Meta-Analysis." *American Journal of Psychiatry* 157(10):1552–62. doi: 10.1176/appi.ajp.157.10.1552.

Summerfield, Derek. 2012. "Afterword: Against 'Global Mental Health.'" *Transcultural Psychiatry* 49(3–4):519–30. doi: 10.1177/1363461512454701.

Summerfield, Derek. 2013. "'Global Mental Health' Is an Oxymoron and Medical Imperialism." *BMJ* 346:f3509. doi: 10.1136/bmj.f3509.

Surís, Alina, Ryan Holliday, and Carol North. 2016. "The Evolution of the Classification of Psychiatric Disorders." *Behavioral Sciences* 6(1):5. doi: 10.3390/bs6010005.

Sweet, Elizabeth, Arijit Nandi, Emma K. Adam, and Thomas W. McDade. 2013. "The High Price of Debt: Household Financial Debt and Its Impact on Mental and Physical Health." *Social Science & Medicine* 91:94–100. doi: 10.1016/j.socscimed.2013.05.009.

Szymanski, Dawn M., and Rachel F. Carretta. 2020. "Religious-Based Sexual Stigma and Psychological

Health: Roles of Internalization, Religious Struggle, and Religiosity." *Journal of Homosexuality* 67(8):1062–80. doi: 10.1080/00918369.2019.1601439.

Takizawa, Ryu, Barbara Maughan, and Louise Arseneault. 2014. "Adult Health Outcomes of Childhood Bullying Victimization: Evidence From a Five-Decade Longitudinal British Birth Cohort." *American Journal of Psychiatry* 171(7):777–84. doi: 10.1176/appi.ajp.2014.13101401.

Tartaglia, Sophia. 2019. "Who Was Mother's Little Helper?"

Tasca, Cecilia, Mariangela Rapetti, Mauro Giovanni Carta, and Bianca Fadda. 2012. "Women and Hysteria in the History of Mental Health." *Clinical Practice & Epidemiology in Mental Health* 8(1):110–19. doi: 10.2174/1745017901208010110.

Tausig, Mark, Sree Subedi, Janaerdan Subedee, James Ross, Chris L. Broughton, Robin Singh, Robin J. Blangero, and S. Williams-Blangero. 2000. "Mental Illness in Jiri, Nepal." *Contributions to Nepalese Sociology (The Jiri Issue)* 200–215.

Taylor, Julia, Jennifer Power, and Elizabeth Smith. 2021. "Bisexuals' Experiences of Mental Health Services: Findings from the Who I Am Study." *Sexuality Research and Social Policy* 18(1):27–38. doi: 10.1007/s13178-020-00440-2.

Taylor, Maxwell. 1988. *The Terrorist*. London: Brassey's.

Taylor, Steven, Michelle M. Paluszek, Geoffrey S. Rachor, Dean McKay, and Gordon J. G. Asmundson. 2021. "Substance Use and Abuse, COVID-19-Related Distress, and Disregard for Social Distancing: A Network Analysis." *Addictive Behaviors* 114:106754. doi: 10.1016/j.addbeh.2020.106754.

Teachman, Bethany A., Dean McKay, Deanna M. Barch, Mitchell J. Prinstein, Steven D. Hollon, and Dianne L. Chambless. 2019. "How Psychosocial Research Can Help the National Institute of Mental Health Achieve Its Grand Challenge to Reduce the Burden of Mental Illnesses and Psychological Disorders." *American Psychologist* 74(4):415–31. doi: 10.1037/amp0000361.

Tearne, Jessica E., Karina L. Allen, Carly E. Herbison, David Lawrence, Andrew J. O. Whitehouse, Michael G. Sawyer, and Monique Robinson. 2015. "The Association between Prenatal Environment and Children's Mental Health Trajectories from 2 to 14 Years." *European Child & Adolescent Psychiatry* 24(9):1015–24. doi: 10.1007/s00787-014-0651-7.

Testa, Megan, and Sara G. West. 2010. "Civil Commitment in the United States." *Psychiatry* 7(10):30–40.

The Onion. 2000. "More U.S. Children Being Diagnosed with Youthful Tendency Disoder." *The Onion*, September 27.

Thoits, Peggy A. 1991. "On Merging Identity Theory and Stress Research." *Social Psychology Quarterly* 54:101–12.

Thoits, Peggy A. 2003. "Personal Agency in the Accumulation of Multiple Role Identities." Pp. 179–94 in *Advances in Identity Theory and Research*, edited by P. J. Burke, T. J. Owens, R. T. Serpe, and P. A. Thoits. New York, NY: Kluwer Academic Publishers.

Thoits, Peggy A. 2010. "Stress and Health: Major Findings and Policy Implications." *Journal of Health and Social Behavior* 51:S41–53.

Thoits, Peggy A. 2017. "Sociological Approaches to Mental Illness." Pp. 126–44 in *A Handbook for the Study of Mental Health: Social Contexts, Theories, and Systems*, edited by Teresa L. Scheid and Eric R. Wright. Cambridge: Cambridge University Press.

Thoits, Peggy A. 1983. "Dimensions of Life Events That Influence Psychological Distress: An Evaluation and Synthesis of the Literature." Pp. 33–103 in *Psychological Stress: Trends in Theory and Research*. Howard B. Kaplan. New York, NY: Academic Press.

Thoits, Peggy A. 2011a. "Resisting the Stigma of Mental Illness." *Social Psychology Quarterly* 74:6–28.

Thoits, Peggy A. 2011b. "Perceived Social Support and the Voluntary, Mixed, or Pressured Use of Mental Health Services." *Society and Mental Health* 1(1):4–19.

Thomas, William I., and Dorothy Swaine Thomas. 1928. *The Child in America: Behavior Problems and Programs*. New York, NY: Knopf.

Thompson, Melissa. 2010. "Race, Gender, and the Social Construction of Mental Illness in the

Criminal Justice System." *Sociological Perspectives* 53(1):99–125. doi: 10.1525/sop.2010.53.1.99.

Töennies, Ferdinand. 1887. *Community and Society*. East Lansing, MI: Michigan State University Press.

Torrey, E. Fuller, Aaron D. Kennard, Don Eslinger, Richard Lamb, and James Pavle. 2010. *More Mentally Ill Persons Are in Jails and Prisons Than Hospitals: A Survey of the States*. Treatment Advocacy Center.

Tsai, Alexander C., and Atheendar S. Venkataramani. 2015. "Communal Bereavement and Resilience in the Aftermath of a Terrorist Event: Evidence from a Natural Experiment." *Social Science & Medicine* 146:155–63. doi: 10.1016/j.socscimed.2015.10.050.

Tsai, Jeanne L., Jennifer Y. Louie, Eva E. Chen, and Yukiko Uchida. 2007. Learning What Feelings to Desire: Socialization of Ideal Affect Through Children's Storybooks. *Personality and Social Psychology Bulletin*. 33(1): 17–30. doi: 10.1177/0146167206292749.

Turner, Heather A., Anne Shattuck, Sherry Hamby, and David Finkelhor. 2013. "Community Disorder, Victimization Exposure, and Mental Health in a National Sample of Youth." *Journal of Health and Social Behavior* 54(2):258–75. doi: 10.1177/0022146513479384.

Turner, R. Jay, and Donald A. Lloyd. 1995. "Lifetime Traumas and Mental Health: The Significance of Cumulative Adversity." *Journal of Health and Social Behavior* 36(4):360. doi: 10.2307/2137325.

Twenge, Jean M. 2011. "Generational Differences in Mental Health: Are Children and Adolescents Suffering More, or Less?" *American Journal of Orthopsychiatry* 81(4):469–72. doi: 10.1111/j.1939-0025.2011.01115.x.

Ullrich, Simone, David P. Farrington, and Jeremy W. Coid. 2007. "Dimensions of DSM-IV Personality Disorders and Life-Success." *Journal of Personality Disorders* 21(6):657–63. doi: 10.1521/pedi.2007.21.6.657.

Umberson, Debra, and Meichu D. Chen. 1994. "Effects of a Parent's Death on Adult Children: Relationship Salience and Reaction to Loss." *American Sociological Review* 59(1):152. doi: 10.2307/2096138.

Umberson, Debra, Kristi Williams, and Kristin Anderson. 2002. "Violent Behavior: A Measure of Emotional Upset?" *Journal of Health and Social Behavior* 43(2):189–206.

Umeh, Uchenna. 2019. *Mental Illness in Black Community, 1700–2019: A Short History*. https://www.blackpast.org/african-american-history/mental-illness-in-black-community-1700-2019-a-short-history/.

Underwood, Lynn G., and Jeanne A. Teresi. 2002. "The Daily Spiritual Experience Scale: Development, Theoretical Description, Reliability, Exploratory Factor Analysis, and Preliminary Construct Validity Using Health-Related Data." *Annals of Behavioral Medicine* 24(1):22–33. doi: 10.1207/S15324796ABM2401_04.

U.S. Department of Health and Human Services. 2020. *Facts about Bullying*.

Vaghela, Preeti, and Koji Ueno. 2017. "Racial-Ethnic Identity Pairings and Mental Health of Second-Generation Asian Adolescents." *Sociological Perspectives* 60(4):834–52. doi: 10.1177/0731121416683159.

Valiant, G. E., and C. O. Valiant. 1990. "Natural History of Male Psychological Health, XII: A 45-Year Study of Predictors of Successful Aging at Age 65." *American Journal of Psychiatry* 147(1):31–37. doi: 10.1176/ajp.147.1.31.

Valois, Robert F., Keith J. Zullig, and Amy A. Hunter. 2015. "Association between Adolescent Suicide Ideation, Suicide Attempts and Emotional Self-Efficacy." *Journal of Child and Family Studies* 24(2):237–48. doi: 10.1007/s10826-013-9829-8.

Vargas, Edward D., Melina Juárez, Gabriel R. Sanchez, and Maria Livaudais. 2019. "Latinos' Connections to Immigrants: How Knowing a Deportee Impacts Latino Health." *Journal of Ethnic and Migration Studies* 45(15):2971–88. doi: 10.1080/1369183X.2018.1447365.

Veterans Administration. 2021a. *Veterans Health Administration*. Veterans Administration.

Veterans Administration. 2021b. *Mental Health Services*. Veterans Administration.

Vilsaint, Corrie L., Amanda NeMoyer, Mirko Fillbrunn, Ekaterina Sadikova, Ronald C. Kessler,

Nancy A. Sampson, Kiara Alvarez, Jennifer Greif Green, Katie A. McLaughlin, Ruijia Chen, David R. Williams, James S. Jackson, and Margarita Alegría. 2019. "Racial/Ethnic Differences in 12-Month Prevalence and Persistence of Mood, Anxiety, and Substance Use Disorders: Variation by Nativity and Socioeconomic Status." *Comprehensive Psychiatry* 89:52–60. doi: 10.1016/j.comppsych.2018.12.008.

Vogel, David L., Nathaniel G. Wade, Stephen R. Wester, Lisa Larson, and Ashley H. Hackler. 2007. "Seeking Help from a Mental Health Professional: The Influence of One's Social Network." *Journal of Clinical Psychology* 63(3):233–45. doi: 10.1002/jclp.20345.

Volkow, Nora D. 2020. *New Evidence on Substance Use Disorders and COVID-19 Susceptibility.* National Institute on Drug Abuse.

Vriends, N., M.C. Pfaltz, P. Novianti, and J. Hadiyono. 2013. "Taijin Kyofusho and Social Anxiety and Their Clinical Relevance in Indonesia and Switzerland." *Frontiers in Psychology* 4, 3.

Wakefield, Jerome C., and Mark F. Schmitz. 2010. "The Measurement of Mental Disorder." Pp. 20–45 in *A Handbook for the Study of Mental Health.* Cambridge: Cambridge University Press.

Walker, William D., Robert C. Rowe, and Vernon L. Quinsey. 1993. "Authoritarianism and Sexual Aggression." *Journal of Personality and Social Psychology* 65:1036–45.

Walker, Andrea M., Michael S. Klein, Craig Hemmens, Mary K. Stohr, and Velmer S. Burton. 2016 "The Consequences of Official Labels: An Examination of the Rights Lost by the Mentally Ill and Mentally Incompetent Since 1989." *Community Mental Health Journal*, 52(3):272-280.

Wall Street Journal. 2013. *Ariel Castro's Full Courtroom Statement.*

Wallerstein, Judith S. 1984. "Children of Divorce: Preliminary Report of a Ten Year Follow-up of Young Children." *American Journal of Orthopsychiatry* 54:444–58.

Wallerstein, Judith S., and Joan B. Kelly. 1976. "The Effects of Parental Divorce: Experiences of the Child in Later Latency." *American Journal of Orthopsychiatry* 46:256–69.

Wallerstein, Judith S., and Joan B. Kelly. 1980. *Surviving the Breakup: How Children and Parents Cope with Divorce.* New York, NY: Basic Books.

Walls, Melissa L., and Les B. Whitbeck. 2011. "Distress among Indigenous North Americans: Generalized and Culturally Relevant Stressors." *Society and Mental Health* 1(2):124–36. doi: 10.1177/2156869311414919.

Walters, Karina L., and Jane M. Simoni. 2002. "Reconceptualizing Native Women's Health: An 'Indigenist' Stress-Coping Model." *American Journal of Public Health* 92(4):520–24. doi: 10.2105/AJPH.92.4.520.

Walters, M. L., J. Chen, and M. J. Breiding. 2013. *The National Intimate Partner and Sexual Violence Survey (NISVS): 2010 Findings on Victimization by Sexual Orientation.* Atlanta, GA: National Center for Injury Prevention and Control, Centers for Disease Control and Prevention.

Wandersman, Abraham, and Maury Nation. 1998. "Urban Neighborhoods and Mental Health: Psychological Contributions to Understanding Toxicity, Resilience, and Interventions." *American Psychologist* 53(6):647–56. doi: 10.1037/0003-066X.53.6.647.

Wang, Jian Li. 2004. "Rural-Urban Differences in the Prevalence of Major Depression and Associated Impairment." *Social Psychiatry and Psychiatric Epidemiology* 39(1):19–25. doi: 10.1007/s00127-004-0698-8.

Wang, Liang, Tiejian Wu, James L. Anderson, and James E. Florence. 2011. "Prevalence and Risk Factors of Maternal Depression during the First Three Years of Child Rearing." *Journal of Women's Health* 20(5):711–18. doi: 10.1089/jwh.2010.2232.

Wang, Philip S., Michael Lane, Mark Olfson, Harold A. Pincus, Kenneth B. Wells, and Ronald C. Kessler. 2005. "Twelve-Month Use of Mental Health Services in the United States: Results from the National Comorbidity Survey Replication." *Archives of General Psychiatry* 62(6):629. doi: 10.1001/archpsyc.62.6.629.

Wang, Quan Qiu, David C. Kaelber, Rong Xu, and Nora D. Volkow. 2020. "COVID-19 Risk and Outcomes in Patients with Substance Use Disorders: Analyses from Electronic Health Records in the

United States." *Molecular Psychiatry.* doi: 10.1038/s41380-020-00880-7.

Wang, Zhen, Sabra S. Inslicht, Thomas J. Metzler, Clare Henn-Haase, Shannon E. McCaslin, Huiqi Tong, Thomas C. Neylan, and Charles R. Marmar. 2010. "A Prospective Study of Predictors of Depression Symptoms in Police." *Psychiatry Research* 175(3):211–16. doi: 10.1016/j.psychres.2008.11.010.

Warikoo, Natasha, Mark Chin, Nicole Zillmer, and Suniya Luthar. 2020. "The Influence of Parent Expectations and Parent-Child Relationships on Mental Health in Asian American and White American Families." *Sociological Forum* 35(2):275–96. doi: 10.1111/socf.12583.

Watson, Amy C., and Beth Angell. 2007. "Applying Procedural Justice Theory to Law Enforcement's Response to Persons with Mental Illness." *Psychiatric Services* 58(6):787–93. doi: 10.1176/ps.2007.58.6.787.

Watson, Dennis P. 2012. "The Evolving Understanding of Recovery: What Does the Sociology of Mental Health Have to Offer?" *Humanity & Society* 36(4):290–308. doi: 10.1177/0160597612458904.

Watson, Dennis P., Erin L. Adams, and Joanna R. Jackson. 2017. "Mental Health Policy in the United States: Critical Reflection and Future Directions for Sociological Research." Pp. 573–90 in *A Handbook for the Study of Mental Health: Social Contexts, Theories, and Systems*, edited by Teresa L. Scheid and Eric R. Wright. Cambridge: Cambridge University Press.

Weaver, Lesley Jo, and Craig Hadley. 2009. "Moving Beyond Hunger and Nutrition: A Systematic Review of the Evidence Linking Food Insecurity and Mental Health in Developing Countries." *Ecology of Food and Nutrition* 48(4):263–84. doi: 10.1080/03670240903001167.

Wehrwein, Peter. 2020. *Astounding Increase in Antidepressant Use by Americans.*

Weiner, Dora B. 2008. "The Madman in the Light of Reason Enlightenment Psychiatry." Pp. 255–77 in *History of Psychiatry and Medical Psychology*, edited by E. R. Wallace and J. Gach. Boston, MA: Springer.

Wells, Kenneth B., Willard G. Manning, Naihua Duan, Joseph P. Newhouse, and John E. Ware Jr 1986. "Sociodemographic Factors and the Use of Outpatient Mental Health Services." *Medical Care* 24(1):75–85.

Werner, Danilea, and Chris Locke. 2012. *One Year After: Community Response and Use of Mental Health Services.* Auburn, AL: Auburn University.

Wheaton, Blair. 1980. "The Sociogenesis of Psychological Disorder: An Attributional Theory." *Journal of Health and Social Behavior* 21(2):100. doi: 10.2307/2136730.

Wheaton, Blair. 1983. "Stress, Personal Coping Resources, and Psychiatric Symptoms: An Investigation of Interactive Models." *Journal of Health and Social Behavior* 24(3):208. doi: 10.2307/2136572.

Wheaton, Blair. 1990. "Life Transitions, Role Histories, and Mental Health." *American Sociological Review* 55:209–23.

Wheaton, Blair. 2001. "The Role of Sociology in the Study of Mental Health and the Role of Mental Health in the Study of Sociology." *Journal of Health and Social Behavior* 42(3):221–34.

Wheaton, Blair, and Philippa Clarke. 2003. "Space Meets Time: Integrating Temporal and Contextual Influences on Mental Health in Early Adulthood." *American Sociological Review* 68(5):680–706.

Wheaton, Blair, and Shirin Montazer. 2010. "Stressors, Stress, and Distress." Pp. 171–99 in *A Handbook for the Study of Mental Health: Social Contexts, Theories, and Systems*, edited by A. V. Horwitz and T. L. Scheid. Cambridge: Cambridge University Press.

Wheaton, Blair and Shirin Montazer, 2017. "Studying Stress in the 21st Century: An Update on Stress Concepts and Research," Pp. 180–206 in *A Handbook for the Study of Mental Health: Social Contexts, Theories, and Systems*, 3rd ed., edited by Theresa L. Scheid and Eric R. Wright. Cambridge: Cambridge University Press.

Wheaton, Blair, Marisa Young, Shirin Montazer, and Katie Stuart-Lahman. 2013. "Social Stress in the Twenty-First Century." Pp. 299–324 in *Handbook of the Sociology of Mental Health*, edited by C. S. Aneshensel, J. C. Phelan, and A. Bierman. New York, NY: Springer.

Whitaker, Robert. 2002. *Mad in America: Bad Science, Bad Medicine, and the Enduring Mistreatment of the Mentally Ill*. New York, NY: Basic Books.

Whitbeck, Les B., Barbara J. McMorris, Dan R. Hoyt, Jerry D. Stubben, and Teresa LaFromboise. 2002. "Perceived Discrimination, Traditional Practices, and Depressive Symptoms among American Indians in the Upper Midwest." *Journal of Health and Social Behavior* 43(4):400. doi: 10.2307/3090234.

Whitley, Bernard E., Jr 1999. "Right-Wing Authoritarianism, Social Dominance Orientation, and Prejudice." *Journal of Personality and Social Psychology* 77(1):126–34.

Wik, Amanda, Vera Hollen, and William H. Fisher. 2017. *Forensic Patients in State Psychiatric Hospitals: 1999-2016*. Alexandria, VR: National Association of State Mental Health Program Directors.

Wilkinson, Richard G. 2005. *The Impact of Inequality: How to Make Sick Societies Healthier*. New York, NY: New Press: Distributed by W.W. Norton.

Wilkinson, Richard G., and Kate E. Pickett. 2017. "The Enemy between Us: The Psychological and Social Costs of Inequality: Costs of Inequality." *European Journal of Social Psychology* 47(1):11–24. doi: 10.1002/ejsp.2275.

Williams, David R., Hector M. González, Harold Neighbors, Randolph Nesse, Jamie M. Abelson, Julie Sweetman, and James S. Jackson. 2007. "Prevalence and Distribution of Major Depressive Disorder in African Americans, Caribbean Blacks, and Non-Hispanic Whites: Results From the National Survey of American Life." *Archives of General Psychiatry* 64(3):305. doi: 10.1001/archpsyc.64.3.305.

Williams, David R., Harold W. Neighbors, and James S. Jackson. 2003. "Racial/Ethnic Discrimination and Health: Findings from Community Studies." *American Journal of Public Health* 93(2):200–208. doi: 10.2105/AJPH.93.2.200.

Williams, JMG, L. Pollock, and C. van Heeringen. 2001. "Psychological Aspects of the Suicidal Process." Pp. 76–94 in *Understanding Suicidal Behaviour: The Suicidal Process Approach to Research, Treatment and Prevention*. Chichester: Wiley.

Williford, Amanda P., Susan D. Calkins, and Susan P. Keane. 2007. "Predicting Change in Parenting Stress across Early Childhood: Child and Maternal Factors." *Journal of Abnormal Child Psychology* 35(2):251–63. doi: 10.1007/s10802-006-9082-3.

Wilson, John. 2012. "Volunteerism Research: A Review Essay." *Nonprofit and Voluntary Sector Quarterly* 41(2):176–212. doi: 10.1177/0899764011434558.

Winsper, Catherine, Suzet Tanya Lereya, Steven Marwaha, Andrew Thompson, Julie Eyden, and Swaran P. Singh. 2016. "The Aetiological and Psychopathological Validity of Borderline Personality Disorder in Youth: A Systematic Review and Meta-Analysis." *Clinical Psychology Review* 44:13–24. doi: 10.1016/j.cpr.2015.12.001.

Winterson, Jeanette. 2011. *Why Be Happy When You Can Be Normal?* New York, NY: Grove Press.

Wodtke, Geoffrey T. 2016. "Social Class and Income Inequality in the United States: Ownership, Authority, and Personal Income Distribution from 1980 to 2010." *American Journal of Sociology* 121(5):1375–1415. doi: 10.1086/684273.

Wolff, Joshua R., Heather L. Himes, Sabrina D. Soares, and Ellen Miller Kwon. 2016. "Sexual Minority Students in Non-Affirming Religious Higher Education: Mental Health, Outness, and Identity." *Psychology of Sexual Orientation and Gender Diversity* 3(2):201–12. doi: 10.1037/sgd0000162.

Wolinsky, Howard. 2005. "Disease Mongering and Drug Marketing. Does the Pharmaceutical Industry Manufacture Diseases as Well as Drugs?" *EMBO Reports* 6(7):612–14. doi: 10.1038/sj.embor.7400476.

Woods, Mary B., and Michael Woods. 2014. *Ancient Medical Technology: From Herbs to Scalpels*. Brookfield, CT: Twenty-First Century Books.

Woods, Megan, Rob Macklin, Sarah Dawkins, and Angela Martin. 2019. "Mental Illness, Social Suffering and Structural Antagonism in the Labour Process." *Work, Employment and Society* 33(6):948–65. doi: 10.1177/0950017019866650.

World Health Organization. 2002. *Gender and Mental Health*.

World Health Organization. 2011. *Alcohol Use Disorders Identification Test*.

World Health Organization. 2020. *Health Statistics and Information Systems. Metrics: Disability-Adjusted Life Year (DALY)*.

World Health Organization. 2021. *Traditional, Complementary and Integrative Medicine*.

World Health Organization. 2004b. *Promoting Mental Health: Concepts, Emerging Evidence, Practice (Summary Report)*. Geneva: World Health Organization.

World Population Review. 2021. *World City Populations 2021*.

Wright, Erik Olin. 1979. *Class Structure and Income Determination*. New York, NY: Academic.

Wright, Erik Olin. 2002. "Basic Income, Stakeholder Grants, and Class Analysis." Presented at the The Real Utopias Project conference on "Rethinking Redistribution," University of Wisconsin.

Wu, Eric Q., Lizheng Shi, Howard Birnbaum, Teresa Hudson, and Ronald Kessler. 2006. "Annual Prevalence of Diagnosed Schizophrenia in the USA: A Claims Data Analysis Approach." *Psychological Medicine* 36(11):1535–40. doi: 10.1017/S0033291706008191.

Wu, Ping, Xinhua Liu, Yunyun Fang, Bin Fan, Cordelia J. Fuller, Zhiqiang Guan, Zhongling Yao, Junhui Kong, Jin Lu, and Iva J. Litvak. 2008. "Alcohol Abuse/Dependence Symptoms among Hospital Employees Exposed to a SARS Outbreak: Table 1." *Alcohol and Alcoholism* 43(6):706–12. doi: 10.1093/alcalc/agn073.

Xiao, Yang, Siyu Miao, and Chinmoy Sarkar. 2021. "Social Ties, Spatial Migration Paradigm, and Mental Health among Two Generations of Migrants in China." *Population, Space and Place* 27(2). doi: 10.1002/psp.2389.

Xur, Honghong. 2016. "An Indigenous Perspective on Chinese Depression." *Trauma and Acute Care* 1, 6.

Yang, Lawrence Hsin, Arthur Kleinman, Bruce G. Link, Jo C. Phelan, Sing Lee, and Byron Good. 2007. "Culture and Stigma: Adding Moral Experience to Stigma Theory." *Social Science & Medicine* 64(7):1524–35. doi: 10.1016/j.socscimed.2006.11.013.

Yesavage, Jerome A., T. L. Brink, Terence L. Rose, Owen Lum, Virginia Huang, Michael Adey, and Otto Leirer. 2011. "Geriatric Depression Scale."

Yonker, Julie E., Chelsea A. Schnabelrauch, and Laura G. DeHaan. 2012. "The Relationship between Spirituality and Religiosity on Psychological Outcomes in Adolescents and Emerging Adults: A Meta-Analytic Review." *Journal of Adolescence* 35(2):299–314. doi: 10.1016/j.adolescence.2011.08.010.

York Cornwell, Erin, and Alyssa W. Goldman. 2020. "Neighborhood Disorder and Distress in Real Time: Evidence from a Smartphone-Based Study of Older Adults." *Journal of Health and Social Behavior* 61(4):523–41. doi: 10.1177/0022146520967660.

Young, Marisa, and Blair Wheaton. 2013. "The Impact of Neighborhood Composition on Work-Family Conflict and Distress." *Journal of Health and Social Behavior* 54(4):481–97. doi: 10.1177/0022146513504761.

Young, Susan, Jessica Bramham, Katie Gray, and Esther Rose. 2008. "The Experience of Receiving a Diagnosis and Treatment of ADHD in Adulthood: A Qualitative Study of Clinically Referred Patients Using Interpretative Phenomeno-logical Analysis." *Journal of Attention Disorders* 11(4):493–503. doi: 10.1177/1087054707305172.

Yuen, Hon Keung, Peng Huang, Jerry K. Burik, and Thomas G. Smith. 2008. "Impact of Participating in Volunteer Activities for Residents Living in Long-Term-Care Facilities." *American Journal of Occupational Therapy* 62(1):71–76. doi: 10.5014/ajot.62.1.71.

Yunus, Raudah Mohd, Noran Naqiah Hairi, and Wan Yuen Choo. 2019. "Consequences of Elder Abuse and Neglect: A Systematic Review of Observational Studies." *Trauma, Violence, & Abuse* 20(2):197–213. doi: 10.1177/1524838017692798.

Zanarini, Mary C., Lynne Yong, Francis R. Frankenburg, et al. 2002. "Severity of Reported

Childhood Sexual Abuse and Its Relationship to Severity of Borderline Psychopathology and Psychosocial Impairment among Borderline Inpatients." *The Journal of Nervous and Mental Disease* 190(6):381–87.

Zhu, Lin. 2019. "Complementary and Alternative Medical Service Use for Mental Health Problems among Chinese Americans: The Roles of Acculturation-Related Factors." *Society and Mental Health* 9(3):366–87. doi: 10.1177/2156869318804304.

Zigmond, A. S., and R. P. Snaith. 1983. "The Hospital Anxiety and Depression Scale." *Acta Psychiatrica Scandinavica* 67(6):361–70. doi: 10.1111/j.1600-0447.1983.tb09716.x.

Zung, William W. K. 1965. "A Self-Rating Depression Scale." *Archives of General Psychiatry* 12:63–70.

Index

A

Abstinence, 220
Academic disciplines, 2
Acquired immunodeficiency syndrome (AIDS), 11
Actual social identity, 261
Acute stressors, 64
Addis, Michael E., 256–257
Adolescents, homelessness, 218
Adorno, Theodor W., 65, 66
Adrenocorticotropic hormones (ACTH), 60
Adulthood, life course studies
    alcohol abuse, 191
    dementia, 188–189
    depression, 189–190
    early, 186–187
    elder abuse, 191
    late, 188
    middle, 187–188
    suicide, 190–191
    U-shape curve, 186
Adverse childhood experience (ACE), 106–107
Affordable Care Act (ACA), 331
Afifi, Tracie O., 176
Agency, 111–112
Aggleton, Peter, 261
Agoraphobia, 352
Agricultural economy, 32
Alcohol abuse, 191
Alcoholics Anonymous (AA), 256, 257
Alienation, 52, 102, 115–116
Allostatic load, 105
Almeida-Filho, Naomar, 306
Altruistic suicide, 57, 57 (chart)
Alzheimer's disease (AD), 188–189
Amad, Ali, 32
Ambient stressors, 63
American Academy of Child and Adolescent Psychiatry, 174
American history, mental illness, 38–40
American Indians and Native Alaskans (AINA), 129–130
American Psychiatric Association (APA), 4, 5, 279, 293–294
Andersen, Ronald M., 253
Aneshensel, Carol, 15
Angelicus, Bartholomeus, 31
Angell, Marcia, 273
Angel, Ronald J., 199
Anger, 175
Angst, Jules, 141
Anomic suicide, 57, 57 (chart)
Anomie, 52
Ansfield, Matthew E., 148
Anti-psychiatry movement, 5
Antisocial personality disorder (Sociopathy), 352
Anxiety, 352–353
Any mental illness (AMI), 88–89, 90 (table)
Ariel Castro, 56 (box)
Asclepiades, 25, 25 (box)–26 (box), 28
Ascribed status, 8
Aseltine, Robert H., 174
Asian cultures, 3
Attribution theory, 112
Authoritarianism, 115–116, 208
Authoritarian personality, 66–67
Authority relations theory, 101, 101 (figure)
Avoidance, 127
Avoidant personality disorder, 353

B

Bachrach, Bernard, 31
Barrett, Lisa Feldman, 148, 149
Barry, Christopher T., 185
Beck Depression Inventory (BDI), 83, 84 (box)–87 (box)
Becker, Dana, 146
Beijing-Shanghai study groups, 302–303
Bertolote, José, 21

Index

Bierman, Alex, 242
Biological reductionism, 18
Bio-medical disorder, 7
Bio–psycho–social factors, 50
Bipolar disorder, 353
Bizarre behavior, 5
Blake, William, 294, 295
Bliss-Moreau, Eliza, 148, 149
Block grant funding, 325
Bloodletting, 25
Bodin, Jean, 34–35
Bonanno, George A., 244
Borderline personality disorder (BPD), 176, 353
Borrelia burgdorferi bacterium, 291
Boston Marathon Bombers, 234 (box)–236 (box)
Boyer, Carol A., 260
Brant, Sebastian, 33 (box)
Braun, Jerome, 207 (box)
Brody, Leslie R., 106, 148
Brown, George, 156, 158–160
Brown, Robyn Lewis, 65
Brubaker, Megan, 149
Buddhism, 17
Bullying, 184–185
Bureaucrat, 206, 206 (box)–208 (box)
Bush, George W., 335 (box)–336 (box)

C

Caetano, Raul, 231
Cahalan, Susannah, 294
Camper, Petrus, 121
Carlat, Daniel J., 273
Carr, Deborah, 164
Cartwright, Samuel, 132
Castañeda, Carlos, 6 (box)
Caste
 delusion, 99 (box)
 in India, 97, 98
 stratification ideology, 98 (box)–99 (box)
 wealth and power, unequal distribution, 98
Catalano, Ralph A., 342
Catastrophes and traumas, Stress Theory, 63–64
Celsus, 25, 27
Center of Epidemiologic Studies—Depression (CES-D), 83, 84 (box)–87 (box)
Centers for Disease Control (CDC), 228

Chaplin, Charlie, 216
Chaucer, 33
Chemical imbalance, 290
Childhood disruptions
 early traumas, 177–178
 family violence, 174–175
 healthy socialization process, 172
 learning disabilities (LD), 172
 life course disruptions, 178
 life transition timing and sequencing, 178
 loss of parenting, 173–174
 material deprivation, 177
 physical abuse, 176–177
 sexual abuse, 175–176
Children's health, developing countries, 311–312
Chinese bureaucracy, 310
Chinese culture, 4
Chinese Exclusion Act, 136
Chronic stressors, 61, 64–65
Chung, Angie Y., 137
Cicero, 25, 27
Ciciurkaite, Gabriele, 65
Civil commitment, 340–343
Civil rights activism, 45
Civil Rights and Women's movements, 44
Class-based anxiety, 113
CMHCs. *See* Community Mental Health Centers (CMHCs)
Cobb, Jonathan, 111
Coherent theory, 24
Communities and organizations
 bureaucrat, 206, 206 (box)–208 (box)
 compensation, 208
 employment, 206
 macrolevel economics, 209
 neighborhoods. *See* Neighborhoods
 social forces, 194
 time at work, 205
 urban and rural residence, 195–198
 voluntary organizations. *See* Voluntary organizations
 workplace stress, 208
Community Mental Health Act, 328
Community Mental Health Centers (CMHCs), 328–329, 332 (box)
Community mental health services, 2

Competency laws, 265
Composite International Diagnostic Interview (CIDI), 300 (box)
Conceptual medicalization, 290
Conduct disorder, 354
Confucians, 28
Connell, R. W., 230
Conrad, Peter, 287, 290, 293
Cooley, Charles, 169–172, 169 (box)
Cooper, David, 287 (box)
Corcoran, Cheryl, 275–276
Corin, Ellen, 320
Corrigan, Patrick W., 265
Corticotropin-releasing hormone (CRF), 60
Cortisol, 60
Costello-Comrey Depression and Anxiety Scales, 89 (box)
COVID-19, 94–95, 100, 131, 136, 165, 239–242, 241 (chart), 332
  substance abuse disorders (SUD), 243 (box)
Cowan, C. S. M., 64
CRF. *See* Corticotropin-releasing hormone (CRF)
Criminalization of mental illness
  criminal justice system, 344
  criminal thinking group, 345–346
  deinstitutionalization, 343
  illness only group, 345
  no-place-to-go group, 345
  patterns, 344, 344 (table)
  substance abuse group, 345
  survival group, 345
Criminal justice system, 344
Criminal thinking group, 345–346
Critical Theory
  authoritarian personality, 66–67
  The Frankfurt School, 65–66
  GLBTQ communities, 67
  normalcy state, 66
Cry of Pain/Entrapment model, 197
Cucolo, Heather Ellis, 343
Cukrowicz, Kelly C., 197
Cultural diversity, 6, 127, 135
  Maori culture, 320
  religious therapies, 317
  spiritual practices, 317–318
  traditional health practitioners (THPs), 318
  traditional remedies, 317
  treatment gaps, 316
  western treatments, Uganda, 319, 319 (box)
Cultural mistrust, 259
Cultural Revolution, 44
Culture-bound syndromes (CBSs), 314, 315 (box), 316
Culture/ethnic group, 2
The Culture of Narcissism, 67
Cynicism, 16

D

Daily hassles, 61, 63
Dalits, 98 (box)–99 (box)
Darwin, Charles, 42
Darwin's theory of evolution, 42
Das Narrenschiff, 33 (box)
da Vinci, 33
DeAngelis, Reed T., 211
Degeneracy theory, 42
Deinstitutionalization, 44–46, 53, 342, 343
  homelessness, 217
Delusions, 25 (box)–26 (box)
Demedicalization, psychiatry, 293–294
Dementia, 188–189
Demo, David H., 171
Dendy, Walter, 44
Dependent personality disorder, 354
Depersonalization, 16, 314
Depression, 304, 354
  adolescent, 90, 91 (table), 181, 182 (chart), 183 (chart)
  adulthood, life course studies, 90, 91 (table), 189–190
  childhood abuse, 160, 160 (box)–161 (box)
  children care, 158–159
  confiding relationship, 157–158
  parental loss, 156–157
  race and ethnicity, 128–129, 128 (chart)
  symptoms, 3
  unemployment, 159
  vulnerability factors, 156–160
Descartes, 33, 34
Developmental attrition, 312

Dhat, 315 (box)
Diagnostic and Statistical Manual of Mental
    Disorders (DSM), 4, 5
  American Psychiatric Association (APA), 279
  culture-bound syndromes (CBSs), 314, 315 (box),
      316
  DSM-III, 280
  DSM-V, 225, 226 (table)–227 (table), 281, 281 (table)
  insurance function, 283
  Kraepelinian biological psychiatry, 278–279
  number of disorders, 280, 280 (table)
Diaz, Christina J., 134
Dirks-Linhorst, P. Ann., 339
Disability-adjusted life years (DALYs), 74, 180, 301,
    302 (table)
  causes, 75, 76 (table)–80 (table)
  culture-bound syndromes (CBSs), 314, 315 (box),
      316
  in Rhode Island, 80, 82 (table)
  US men and women, 80, 81 (table)
  World Health Organization (WHO) calculation,
      75, 75 (box), 77 (table)–78 (table)
  years lost to disability (YLD), 75, 78, 82 (table)
  years of life lost (YLL), 75, 80
Disasters, 215–216
  direct and indirect exposure, 238
  effects of, 238–239
  natural and human-made, 237–242
  pandemics, 239–242, 241 (chart)
  social impact assessments, 238
Disease, 290
Disenchantment, 52
Disorder, 290
Dissociative amnesia, 314
Dissociative identity disorder, 314, 315 (box)
Dix, Dorothea, 40
Double jeopardy, 134
Dowd, Jennifer B., 105
Down syndrome, 290–291
Doyle, David Matthew, 60
Draft Act Governing Hospitalization of the
    Mentally Ill, 341
Drug abuse, 221–222
Drugs and alcohol, 219–221, 223 (table)–224 (table)
Drug use, 221, 225 (table), 226 (chart)
Du Bois, W.E.B., 123

Dumbledore, Albus, 244
Dunham, H. Warren, 103
Dupéré, Véronique, 200
Dupree, Larry W., 191
Durham Rule, 339
Durkheim, 52, 57, 209–211
Dysaethesia aethiopica, 132

E
Eagleton, Thomas, 265 (box)–266 (box)
Early civilizations, 23–24
Eating disorders, 354
Eaton, William W., 106, 107
Ebert, David D., 92
Economic development, 3
Economic inequality, 57
Economic marginality, 15
Economic modernization, 305
Eder, Donna, 150
Education, 119
Education and mental health, 108, 109 (box)–110
    (box)
Egoistic suicide, 57, 57 (chart)
Egyptian culture, 23
Eldridge, Larry D., 38
Elliot, Luther, 68
Ellison, Christopher G., 211
Emotional distress, 2
Emotional labor, 16
Emotions, 154, 247
  anger, 150
  beach ball metaphor, 154 (box)–155 (box)
  confiding relationship, 157–158
  men's emotionality, 148
  normative theory, 149–150
  social situations, 149
  structural theory of emotions, 150
  women's emotionality, 149
Enders, Walter, 232
Enlightenment
  period, 35–37
  race and ethnicity, 121
Epidemiology
  disability-adjusted life years (DALYs), 74, 75–78,
      75 (box), 76 (table)–78 (table), 80, 81 (table)–
      82 (table)

incidence, 74–75
prevalence, 74
risk, 74
Erectile dysfunction, 288
Erikson, Erik, 178 (box), 180, 188
　developmental stages, 179 (box)–180 (box)
Essentialism, 142–143, 151
Ethnic density hypothesis, 202
Ethnorace, 123–124, 258–260, 259 (chart)
Ethnoracial groups, 124–127, 125 (chart), 134
Eugenics, 42
Exhibitionism, 355

F

Familism, 134
Family violence, 174–175
Faris, Robert E. L., 103
Farmer suicide, 196–197
Fatalism, 111–112
Fear, 175
Ferracuti, Franco, 232
Fields, W.C., 222
Fight or flight responses, Stress Theory, 59
Forced sex initiation (FSI), 311
Foster, Holly, 157
Foucault, Michel, 33 (box), 36, 287 (box)
Four Humors Theory, 24–25, 24 (table)
Frances, Allen J., 282
Freedom of Information Act, 273–274
Freud, Sigmund, 44, 65, 279
Friedan, Betty, 162
Fromm, Erich, 65, 66, 94
Frotteurism, 355
FSI. *See* Forced sex initiation (FSI)
Funding
　Affordable Care Act (ACA), 331
　Community Mental Health Centers (CMHCs) Grant Program, 332 (box)
　COVID pandemic, 332
　federal budgets, 331
　financial support programs, 331
　Funding Opportunity Announcement (FOA) Information, 332 (box)–333 (box)
　medication patent system, 330
　parity, 334–335
　public expenditures, 329, 331
　research, 333–334
　US Mental Health sources, 329, 330 (chart)
Funding Opportunity Announcement (FOA) Information, 332 (box)–333 (box)
Furr, L. Allen, 306
Fuss, Johannes, 147

G

Gade, Christian B. N., 317
Galen, 25, 27–28, 31
Galileo, 33
Galt, John, 131
Garfinkel, Harold, 284
Gelles, Richard, 215
Gemeinschaft, 195, 198
Gender, 140, 141, 211, 256–257. *See also* Emotions
　adolescent differences, patterns, 144, 144 (table)
　bias, 145–147
　correspondence bias, 148, 149
　cost of caring, 153
　cross-cultural lines, 145
　depression, vulnerability factors, 156–160
　essentialism, 142–143
　feminized, 146–147
　lifetime prevalence, 144, 145 (chart)
　masculine and feminine, 152
　men's emotionality, 148
　men's vulnerability, alcohol abuse, 155–156
　mental health for men, 153–154
　mental health for women, 152–153
　past year prevalence, 144, 146 (chart)
　restrictive emotionality, 149
　social characteristics, 146
　social expectations, 152
　social roles, 151–152
　stereotypes, 147–148, 147 (box), 343
　women's emotionality, 149
Gender inequality, 230
Germ theory, 42–43
Gesellschaft, 195, 198
Gessen, Masha, 234 (box)
Ghost sickness, 315 (box)
Gilman, Sander L., 138
Glick, Ilra D., 283

Global prevalence
  Beijing-Shanghai study groups, 302–303
  clinical depression, 299
  cross-national mental health surveys, 299
  DALYs and YLDs, 301, 302 (table)
  data collection, 298
  gatekeepers, 299
  income groups, 304–305
  international surveys, 299
  probability sampling, 298
  process errors, 300
  psychiatric disorders, 303–304
  sampling error, 298
  survey methods, 298, 298 (table)
  World Mental Health survey initiative (WMH), 297, 300 (box)–301 (box), 301
Goffman, Erving, 246, 261, 262, 263, 268, 287 (box), 327
Goldman, Alyssa W., 200
Great Confinement, 36, 41
Grecian treatments, 25
Greenfield, Emily A., 210
Greenwald, Mark K., 148
Grzywacz, Joseph G., 63
Guarnaccia, Peter J., 316
Guittar, Nicholas A., 129

H
Hagan, John, 157
Hall, Judith A., 148
Hallucinations, 25 (box)–26 (box)
Harkness, S. K., 54–55
Harmonic convergences, 18
Harris, Tirril, 156, 158–160
Harvard Health Publishing, 270
Harwood, Hannah R., 172
Hatzenbuehler, Mark L., 263
Hawn, Sage E., 220
Health Beliefs Model (HBM), 252–253
Health disparities, 3
Healthy socialization process, 172
Helicoptering, 183–184
Herd immunity, 129
Heritability, 274
Hiday, Virginia Aldigé, 344
The Hidden Injuries of Class, 111
Hillman, James, 346
Hill, Terrence D., 199

Hinckley, John, 338
Hindhede, Anette Lykke, 277
Hippocrates' theory, 24, 25
Hirsch, Jameson K., 197
Hobbes, 33
Hochschild, Arlie Russell, 16
Holmes, Thomas H., 61, 62 (figure)
Homelessness
  adolescents, 218
  cause-and-effect relationship, 219
  deinstitutionalization, 217
  Great Depression, 216
  New Homelessness, 217
  skid row bums, 216
Horkheimer, Max, 65
Horwitz, Allan V., 4, 5, 8, 254
Houts, Arthur C., 5, 7
Hoyt, Lynne A., 173
Hughes, Michael, K., 171, 209
Human immunodeficiency virus (HIV), 11
Hume, David, 121
Hyde, Janet Shibley, 141
Hypothalamic–pituitary–adrenal axis (HPA), 60, 61
Hysteria, 23

I
Identity denial, Stress Theory, 60
Identity diffusion, socialization, 170
Identity integration, socialization, 170
Illness only group, 345
Illusions, 25 (box)–26 (box)
Impulse control disorders (ICD), 355
Impulse insanity defense, 338
Individual discriminatory behavior, 264
Individualism, 14–15, 18, 37 (box), 262
  medicalization, 288
Informal social networks, 254
Insanity, 121, 122 (box)
  cognitive neuropsychological process, 340
  defense, 337
  Durham Rule, 339
  implications, 339
  impulse insanity defense, 338
  M'Naghten Rule, 337–338
  social forces, 339
  substantial capacity test, 338–339
  types, 337

Insanity Defense Reform Act, 338
Institutional medicalization, 292
Insurance policies, 288
Intellectual developments, nineteenth century, 42–43
Intensive parenting, 137
Interactional discrimination, 264
Interactional medicalization, 292–293
International mental health
   global prevalence. *See* Global prevalence
   malnutrition, 297
   social change. *See* Social change
   stigma, 297
Intimate partner violence (IPV)
   causes of, 229
   Centers for Disease Control (CDC), 228
   definition, 228
   family factors, 230
   individual factors, 230–231
   levels, 229, 229 (figure)
   sexual orientation, 229
   social structural factors, 230
   sociocultural factors, 229–230
Intrusion, 127
Irresistible impulse insanity defense, 338

J

Jackson, Bradford E., 60–61
Japanese Society of Psychiatry and Neurology (JSPN), 292
Johnson, Kurt D., 218
Johnson, Lyndon, 116
Johnson, Robert J., 236
Johnson, Vernon E., 255 (box)
Juan, Don, 26 (box)
Juffer, Femmie, 83
Jung, John, 63

K

Kaczynski, Ted, 232
Kaplan, Howard B., 3
Karp, David A., 246–251, 282. *See also* Moral career
   model variations, 248–249
Keith, Verna M., 159, 209
Kelly, Joan B., 173
Kempe, Henry, 215

Kemper, Theodore D., 150
Kesey, Ken, 327
Khalsa, Hari Krishnan, 63
Khan, Tm, 50
Kiecolt, Jill, 209
Kirk, Stuart A., 55
Kirsch, Irving, 273–274
Kitsuse, John I., 281
Kleinman, Arthur, 282
Kohn, Melvin L., 114
Kopp, Sheldon, 71
Koro, 315 (box)
Kraepelin, Emil, 279
Kraepelinian biological psychiatry, 278–279
Kraepelinian disease concept, 292
Kroll, Jerome, 31
Kroska, A., 54–55
Kutchins, Herb, 55
Kyu, Hmwe Hmwe, 78

L

Labeling Theory
   criticisms, 55, 56 (box)
   deinstitutionalization movement, 53
   Modified Labeling Theory (MLT), 54–55
   and power, 55
   self-fulfilling prophecy, 54
   social authority agents, 53
La Greca, Annette M., 238
Laing, R.D., 287 (box)
Lam, Jack, 209
Lanterman-Petris-Short Act (LPS), 329
Larsen, Kristian, 277
Lasch, Christopher, 14, 67, 71
Lay theories, 49
   lay beliefs, causality, 50–52
   mental health awareness movement, 50
   stigma, 260–261
Lead poisoning, 12
Learning disabilities (LD), 172
Lee, Barrett A., 217
Lee, Jennifer, 137
Lee, Nathaniel, 37, 37 (box)
Lee, Stacey, 136
Leone, Matthew C., 277

Index

Lesbian, gay, bisexual, queer, and questioning (LGBQQ), 258
Life course studies
  adolescent depression, 181, 182 (chart), 183 (chart)
  adulthood, 186–191
  bullying, 184–185
  childhood disruptions. *See* Childhood disruptions
  Great Depression, 164–165
  helicopter parents, 183–184
  historical events and social circumstances, 165
  launching stage, 166
  problematic social media use (PSMU), 185, 186
  self-efficacy, 165–166
  socialization, 167–172
  social media use (SMU), 185–186
  social relationships, 165–166
  socio-historical changes, 182
  trust development, children, 180–181
Lifetime prevalence, 306, 307 (table)–308 (table)
Link, Bruce G., 54, 55, 263, 342
Locke, John, 41
Lopez, Alan, 75, 78
Lorenzo-Blanco, Elma I., 202
Lyme disease, 291

M

Macro-level social forces, 309
Madness and Civilization, 33 (box)
Mahalik, James R., 256–257
Maher, Brendan, 33 (box)
Maher, Winifred B., 33 (box)
Maisel, Eric R., 5
Maladaptive biopsychosocial stress responses, 105
Malone, Darren, 283
Mania, 27, 255
Maori culture, 320
Marcuse, Herbert, 65
Marshall, John, 284
Marx, Karl, 52, 65
Masochism, 148
Maternal incarceration, 157
Mayes, Rick, 4
McConnell, William, 342
McDaid, David, 331
McGinty, Emma E., 263

McGovern, George, 265 (box)–266 (box)
McGrath, Ellen, 157
McLeod, Jane D., 156, 160
Measurement issues
  Beck Depression Inventory (BDI), 83, 84 (box)–87 (box)
  benefits, 88
  Center of Epidemiologic Studies—Depression (CES-D), 83, 84 (box)–87 (box)
  in cross-cultural settings, 87, 89 (box)
  depression measures, 83, 88 (table)
  DSM criteria, 83–84
  epidemic proportions, 84
  incidence, 81–82
  meta-analysis, 83
  physical health morbidity, 82
  reliability and validity, 80
  survey-based measures, 84
  true prevalence, 83, 87
Medicalization
  birth order, 291 (box)
  in degrees, 289–290
  erectile dysfunction, 288
  health and behavior, 289
  individualism, 288
  institutional medicalization, 292
  insurance policies, 288
  interactional medicalization, 292–293
  levels of, 290–291
  life cycle process, 287
  self-reliance, 288
  social constructionism, 287
  social control, 293
  social forces, 295
  sociocultural process, 287–288
Medical model, 7
  brain studies, 272
  concordance rates, 272
  genetics, 274–275
  National Institute of Mental Health, 271
  neurotransmitters, 272–274
  psychiatry. *See* Psychiatry
  psychological symptoms, 271
  social and behavioral sciences, 275–276
Medicare and Medicaid expenditures, 92–93
Medlow, Sharon, 218

Melancholy, 27
Men's emotionality, 148
Men's vulnerability, alcohol abuse, 155–156
Mental disorder, 5
    academic attainment, 9
    ascribed status, 8
    distress symptoms, 8
    human behavior, 9
    intra-personal stress, 10
    social construction, psychiatric illness, 10–12
Mental health policy and law
    civil commitment, 340–343
    community mental health, 327–329
    criminal behavior, 336
    criminalization of mental illness, 343–346, 344 (table)
    funding. *See* Funding
    insanity, 337–340
    politics, 335 (box)–336 (box)
    public-based mental health programs, 325
    public policy, 324
    State Hospitals, 326–327
    stigma, 324
    in United States, 324–325
    Veterans Administration Hospitals, 325–326
Mental health statistics, 125
Mental Health Systems Act (MHSA), 329
MERS. *See* Middle East Respiratory Syndrome (MERS)
Merton, Robert, 54
Mesopotamians, 23
Messerschmidt, James W., 230
Meyer, Dixie, 60
Michelangelo, 33
Middle Ages
    agricultural economy, 32
    Arabic and Islamic cultures, 31
    Early Middle Ages, 30
    Late Middle Ages, 30
    maristans, 31
    psychotherapy, 31
    public health, 29
    religious minorities, 29
    Roman Catholic Church, 29
    Ship of Fools, 33 (box)

Middle East Respiratory Syndrome (MERS), 239
Mills, C. Wright, 12–13, 165
Minority stress model, 128
Mirola, William A., 211
Mirowsky, John, 15, 115, 116, 151, 205–206
Mizock, Lauren, 149
M'Naghten Rule, 337–338, 345
Modecki, Kathryn L., 185
Model minority, 136, 137 (table)
Modified Labeling Theory (MLT)
    beliefs, 54
    consequences, 54–55
    internalization, 54
    response, 54
    vulnerability, 55
Molix, Lisa, 60
Montazer, Shirin, 63
Moral career
    crisis stage, 248
    desperation, 249–250
    engagement, 250–251
    experimentation, 250
    inchoate feelings, 247
    marriage, 251
    mental health patient, 246
    mental health professional, 247
    pathway of, 246–247
Moral treatment, 40–41
Morris, J. Glenn, 238
Morton, Samuel George, 121
Motorcycle Syndrome, 69, 69 (box)–70 (box), 71
Multiple personality disorder (MPD), 46
Muntaner, Carles, 106, 107
Murray, Christopher J. L., 75
Murray, Rheana, 78

N

Narcissism, 14
Narcissistic personality disorder, 355
Nath, Leda E., 150
National Alliance on Mental Illness (NAMI), 268–269
National Institute for Mental Health (NIMH), 4, 88–90, 271, 328, 333, 334
National Institute of Drug Abuse, 222

Index

National Mental Health Act (NMHA), 328
Natural disasters, 63
Neighborhoods, 349
    characteristics, 199, 199 (chart)
    character/personality, 198
    consequences of, 204 (box)–205 (box)
    qualities, 199
    self-efficacy, 200–201
    social diversity, 202–204
    types, 201, 202 (chart)
Nelson, Jason M., 172
Network-Episode Model (NEM), 253–255
Neurotransmitters
    neurons, 273
    selective serotonin reuptake inhibitors (SSRIs), 273
    serotonin, 273
    synapses, 273
    Thorazine, 272–273
    vesicles, 273
New age health practices, 17
Nicholi, Armand, 69 (box)–70 (box)
Niño, Michael, 134
Nisbett, Richard E., 28
Nixon, Reginald D. V., 237
Nongovernmental organization (NGO), 313
No-place-to-go group, 345
Norman, Judith, 146–147
Normative theory, 149–150
Norris, Fran H., 236
North Korean Refugees, 160 (box)–161 (box)
Not guilty by reason of insanity (NGRI), 339–340

O

Obsessive-compulsive personality disorder, 355
Ode ori, 315 (box)
Okonji, Marx, 318
Oppositional defiant disorder, 355–356
Ornelas, India J., 135
Owen, Jesse, 148

P

Pal, G.C., 99 (box)
Pallavi, Nishith, 237
Pan-Asian ethnic identity, 136
Pandemics, 239–242, 241 (chart)

Panic disorder, 356
Parental divorce, 173–174
Parenting behaviors, social class, 113–114
Parker, Richard, 261
Patriarchal social systems, 230
Patten, S. B., 156–159
Pearce, Franklin, 326
Pearlin, Leonard I., 58, 172, 177
Penner, Francesca, 170
Pereda, Noemí, 175
Perlin, Michael L., 343
Perreira, Krista M., 135
Personality disorders, 356
    social class, 115
Pescosolido, Bernice A., 51, 253, 260, 263
Pfeifer, Samuel, 51
Phelan, Jo C., 263, 342
Phobia-related disorders, 356
Phobic Disorders, 280
Phobic Neurosis, 280
Phrenitis, 27
Physical abuse, 176–177
Pigg, Stacey L., 306
Pinel, Philippe, 40, 41
Plato, 24
Porter, Roy, 37
Post-traumatic stress disorder (PTSD), 68, 231, 357
    racial trauma, 133
Poverty, 3, 112–113, 177, 200, 215, 311, 348
    race and ethnicity, 128–129, 128 (chart)
    urbanization, 308–310
Powell, T. O., 133
Power, 55
    authority inequalities, 120
Prehistory, mental illness
    healing powers, 22
    immaterial and impersonal force, 22
    protracted sleep, 23
    solidarity law, 23
    supernaturalism, 22
    trepanation, 22
Problematic social media use (PSMU), 185, 186
Pseudo-depression, 190
Psychiatry, 2
    biological conquest, 278
    demedicalization, 293–294

Diagnostic and Statistical Manual of Mental Disorders (DSM), 278–283, 280 (table), 281 (table)
hospitalization, 283, 284 (box)–285 (box), 285, 286 (box)–287 (box)
medicalization, 287–293
occupational status, 277
prestige differences, 277, 278 (table)
US teach psychotherapy techniques, 276–277
Psychogenic theories, 21, 27
Psychological distress, 2, 3
Psychological problems, 2, 3
Psychological/psychiatric care, 245
Psycho-therapeia, 44

R

Rabinowitz, Jill A., 201
Race and ethnicity, 348
    African Americans, 130–133
    American Indians and Native Alaskans (AINA), 129–130
    Asian Americans, 135–138, 137 (table)
    characteristics, 123
    cultural group, 120
    depression, 128–129, 128 (chart)
    discrimination, 126–128
    Enlightenment, 121
    ethnorace, 123–124
    ethnoracial groups, 124–127, 125 (chart)
    Hispanics, 133–135
    minority stress model, 128
    polygenism ideology, 121
    poverty status, 128–129, 128 (chart)
    power and authority inequalities, 120
    racialized events, 119
    sub-threshold conditions, 125
    syphilis and insanity, 121, 122 (box)
Rahe, Richard H., 61, 62 (figure)
Ramaiah, A., 99 (box)
Reactive psychosis, 357
Reagan, Ronald, 329, 338
Reardon, Lyons, 217
Redlich, Frederick, 103
Reductionism, 49
Reference grouping, 110
Reich, Wilhelm, 65
Relative deprivation hypothesis, 110
Religiosity, 210
Religious-based social discrimination, 211
The Renaissance, 33–35
Residential segregation hypothesis, 203
Resiliency, 244
Rico, Puerto, 316
Riley, Anna L., 159
Rohrer, Julia M., 291
Rosenberg, Morris, 18
Rosenhan, D. L., 286 (box)–287 (box)
Rosoff, Stephen M., 277
Ross, Catherine E., 15, 115, 116, 151, 199, 331
Rothman, David J., 346
Rousseau, Sofie, 184
Rural mental health care services, 197–198
Rush, Benjamin, 38, 39, 40, 121

S

Sachdev, Perminder S., 320
Sandler, Todd, 232
Sartre, Jean-Paul, 166, 172
Scharf, Miri, 184
Schieman, Scott, 242
Schinnar, Arie P., 4, 81
Schizoaffective disorder, 357
Schizoid personality disorder, 357–358
Schizophrenia, 357
Schizotypal personality disorder, 358
Schnittker, Jason, 50, 51
Schonfeld, Lawrence, 191
Schooler, Carmi, 114
Schwartz, Sharon, 275–276
Scientific racism, 120–121
Scott, Kate M., 304
Selective serotonin reuptake inhibitors (SSRIs), 273
Self-actualization, 14
Self-defeating identity, 111
Self-efficacy, 108, 112
    life course studies, 165–166
    neighborhoods, 200–201
    socialization, 171, 172, 177
    voluntary organizations, 209

Self-esteem, 201
  socialization, 171, 175, 177
  voluntary organizations, 209
Self-fulfilling prophecy, 54
Self-gratification, 14
Self-labeling, stigma, 267
Self-reflection, 17 (box)
Selye, Hans, 59, 61
Sennett, Richard, 111
Serious mental illness (SMI), 88–89
Severe Acute Respiratory Syndrome-Coronavirus-2 (SARS-CoV-2), 239
Sex, 140
  physical differences, 141
  psychological differences, 141
Sexism, 348
Sexual abuse, 175–176
Sexual minorities, 257–258
Shensa, Ariel, 186
Ship of Fools, 33 (box)
Simon, Robin W., 150
Smedley, Audrey, 124
Smedley, Brian D., 124
SMI. *See* Serious mental illness (SMI)
Smith, Dena T., 278
Smith, Lia J., 221
SMU. *See* Social media use (SMU)
Social causation model, 105, 108
Social change
  children's health, developing countries, 311–312
  cultural diversity, treatments, 316–320
  culture-bound syndromes (CBSs), 314, 315 (box), 316
  economic modernization, 305
  lifetime prevalence, 306, 307 (table)–308 (table)
  perceptions of, 313–314
  psychological impact, 305
  rapid modernization, 305
  social suffering, 314
  stress, 306
  urbanization and poverty, 308–310
  war, 312–313
  western culture, 308
  women's health, developing countries, 310–311
Social class, 260
  alienation, 102
  authority relations theory, 101, 101 (figure)
  caste, 97–100
  causality, 103–106
  characteristics, 97, 100
  complications, 102
  exploitation, 102
  manic depressive insanity, 103
  meritocracy, 99, 100
  parenting behaviors, 113–114
  personality disorders, 115
  position and psychological distress, 115–116
  social forces, 100
  social inequality, 102–103
  social mobility, 98, 100
  socio-economics, 100
  stratification, 96–102
  and stress, 106–108
  structure, 102
  subjective aspects of class, 108–112
Social Constructionism
  depressive symptoms, 68
  medicalization, 287
  Motorcycle Syndrome, 69, 69 (box)–70 (box), 71
  post-traumatic stress disorder (PTSD), 68
  psychiatric illness, 10–12
  typification, 69
Social control, medicalization, 293
Social costs, 92–93
Social Darwinism, 42, 43
Social diversity, 202–204
Social dynamics, 252
Social esteem, 263
Social exclusion, 99 (box)
Social forces, 19
  communities and organizations, 194
  cultural factors, 14–15
  interaction factors, 16–17
  medicalization, 295
  patterned activities, 13
  psychological distress, 13
  self-reflection, 17 (box)
  social class, 100
  social structural factors, 15–16
  sociological imagination, 12
Social inequality, 3, 102–103, 126
Socialization
  delayed gratification, 167
  identity diffusion, 170
  identity integration, 170
  looking-glass self, 169–170, 169 (box)

primary, 167
secondary, 167
self-efficacy, 171, 172, 177
self-esteem, 171, 175, 177
social mirror, 169, 171
Twenty Statements Test (TST), 168, 168 (box)
Social media use (SMU), 185–186
Social mirror, 169, 171
Social mobility, 98, 100
Social organizational structure, 98 (box)
Social patterns, 88–92, 90 (table), 91 (table), 142
Social problem
  definition, 214, 215
  dependency and addiction, 222
  drug abuse, 221–222
  drugs and alcohol, 219–221
  drug use, 221
  homelessness, 216–219
  intimate partner violence (IPV). See Intimate partner violence (IPV)
  prevalence, 222–225, 223 (table)–224 (table), 224 (chart), 225 (table), 226 (chart)
  substance abuse disorder (SUD), 225, 226 (table)–227 (table), 227–228, 243 (box)
  terrorism. See Terrorism
  victimization, 231–232
Social Readjustment Rating Scale, 61, 62 (figure)
Social Security Disability Insurance, 92
Social Security program, 92
Social selection, 104
Social selection-drift hypothesis, 104, 108
Social stigma, 259
Social structure, 349
Social suffering, 350
Social support, Stress Theory, 65
Socio-Behavioral Model (SBM), 253
Socio-cultural systems, 2, 10
Sociological imagination, 12, 351
The Sociological Imagination, 12
Sociological theory
  Critical Theory, 65–67
  Labeling Theory, 53–55
  lay theories, 49–52
  Social Constructionism, 68–70
  Stress Theory. *See* Stress theory
  Structural Strain Theory, 55–58

Sociology in medicine, 3, 271
Sociology of medicine, 2, 271
Soft money, 332 (box)
Somatic depression, 190
Somatogenic theories, 21, 24
Soranus, 25, 27
Spector, Malcolm, 281
Spencer, Herbert, 43
Srole, L., 114
SSI. *See* Supplemental Security Income (SSI)
SSRIs. *See* Selective serotonin reuptake inhibitors (SSRIs)
Stark, C. R., 197
Status-based identity, 111
Steinmetz, Suzanne, 215
Sternthal, Michelle J., 210
Stigma, 350
  actual social identity, 261
  consciousness, 60
  in everyday life, 262–263
  individual discriminatory behavior, 264
  interactional discrimination, 264
  international mental health, 297
  lay theories, 260–261
  mental health policy and law, 324
  restrict civil rights, 265, 267 (table)
  self-labeling, 267
  status loss, 263
  stereotypes, 261
  structural discrimination, 264–265
  virtual social identity, 261
Stigmatization, 261, 263, 268
Stratification, 96
  caste and class, 97–100
  ideologies, 98 (box)–99 (box)
  intersectionality, 97
  in United States, 100
Straus, Murray, 215
Stressors, 58–59
Stress Theory, 120
  acute stressors, 64
  adrenocorticotropic hormones (ACTH), 60
  ambient stressors, 63
  catastrophes and traumas, 63–64
  chronic stressors, 61, 64–65
  corticotropin-releasing hormone (CRF), 60

cortisol, 60
daily hassles, 61, 63
distress, 58–59
fight or flight responses, 59
hypothalamic–pituitary–adrenal axis (HPA), 60, 61
identity denial, 60
individuals' social situation and context, 58
personality strengths, 65
and social class, 106–108
social location and psychopathology rates, 58
Social Readjustment Rating Scale, 61, 62 (figure)
social support, 65
stigma consciousness, 60
stressor, 58–59
Structural discrimination, 264–265
Structural inequalities, 3
Structural Strain Theory
　economic inequality, 57
　limitation, 58
　macro social forces, 55–56
　social patterns, 57
　suicidal behavior, 57
Structural theory of emotions, 150
Subjective aspects of class
　education and mental health, 108, 109 (box)–110 (box)
　fatalism, 111–112
　reference grouping, 110
　relative deprivation hypothesis, 110
　status-based identity, 111
　upper-class, 112–113
Substance Abuse and Mental Health Services Administration's (SAMHSA) budget, 331, 332 (box)
Substance abuse disorder (SADs), 358
　COVID-19, 243 (box)
　social problem, 225, 226 (table)–227 (table), 227–228, 243 (box)
Substantial capacity test, 338–339
Suicide
　adulthood, life course studies, 190–191
　behavior, 57
　farmer, 196–197
Summerfield, Derek, 297, 313, 314
Suo-yang, 315 (box)
Supernaturalism, 21–23
Supplemental Security Income (SSI), 92

Survival group, 345
Syndrome, 290
Syphilis, 121, 122 (box)
Szasz, Thomas, 287 (box)

T

Taijin Kyofusho, 315 (box)
Talk therapies, 44–45
Taoists, 28
Taylor, Maxwell, 233
TCIF. *See* The Trauma Care International Foundation (TCIF)
The Teachings of Don Juan, 6 (box)
Teresi, Jeanne A., 210
Terrorism
　Boston Marathon Bombers, 234 (box)–236 (box)
　communal bereavement, 237
　radicalization, 234
　stereotyping, 236
　terroristic actors, 232–236
　victims of, 236
Thoits, Peggy A., 53, 58
Thomas, Dorothy Swaine, 123
Thomas, James M., 138
Thomas, Pierre, 32
Thomas, William I., 123
Thompson, Melissa, 69
Thorazine, 45, 272–273
THPs. *See* Traditional health practitioners (THPs)
Titicut Follies, 284 (box)–285 (box)
Töennies, Ferdinand, 195
Traditional health practitioners (THPs), 318
Transitional object (TO), 228
The Trauma Care International Foundation (TCIF), 313–314
Trepanation, 22
True prevalence, measurement issues, 83, 87
Trust development, children, 180–181
Tsai, Jeanne L., 3
Tsarnev, Dzhokhar, 234, 234 (box)–235 (box)
Tsarnev, Tamerlan, 234, 234 (box)–235 (box)
Tuke, William, 40
Tuskegee Syphilis Study, 122
Twentieth century, mental illness
　Civil Rights and Women's movements, 44
　Cultural Revolution, 44
　de-institutionalization, 44–46

pharmaceuticals and institutions, 45–46
psychotherapy models, 43
talk therapies, 44–45
Twenty Statements Test (TST), 168, 168 (box)
Typification, 69

U
Umberson, Debra, 231
Underwood, Lynn G., 210
Union of Soviet Socialist Republics (USSR), 10
United States, mental health policy and law, 324–325
community mental health, 327–329
funding. *See* Funding
public-based mental health programs, 325
State Hospitals, 326–327
Veterans Administration Hospitals, 325–326
US Mental Health sources, 329, 330 (chart)

V
Valiant, C. O., 189
Valiant, G. E., 189
Valois, Robert F., 172
van IJzendoorn, Marinus H., 83
Vargas, Edward D., 135
Veterans Health Administration, 325
Victimization, social problem, 231–232
Virtual social identity, 261
Vogel, David L., 254
Voluntary organizations
empowerment, 209
religion and mental health, 209–211
self-efficacy, 209
self-esteem, 209

W
Wales, Heathcote W., 344
Wallerstein, Judith S., 173–174

Wandering uterus, 27
Wang, Zhen, 158
Warikoo, Natasha, 137
Weber, Max, 52, 65, 206 (box)
Western treatments, Uganda, 319, 319 (box)
Weyer, Johann, 34
Wheaton, Blair, 16–17, 63, 203, 272
Whitaker, Robert, 46
Wild man madness, 315 (box)
Williford, Amanda P., 158
Winterson, Jeanette, 212
Wiseman, Frederick, 284
Women's emotionality, 149
Women's health, developing countries, 310–311
Woods, Megan, 206
World Health Organization (WHO), 4
disability-adjusted life years (DALYs) calculation, 75, 75 (box), 77 (table)–78 (table)
World Mental Health survey initiative (WMH), 297, 300 (box)–301 (box), 301
Wright, Erik Olin, 101, 101 (figure)

X
Xiao, Yang, 309

Y
Yang, Lawrence Hsin, 262
Yaqui culture, 6 (box), 7–8
Years lost to disability (YLD), 75, 78, 82 (table), 301, 302 (table)
Years of life lost (YLL), 75, 80
Yoga, 17
York Cornwell, Erin, 200
York Retreat, 40–41
Young, Marisa, 203

Z
Zhou, Min, 137
Zola, Irving, 348

Ingram Content Group UK Ltd.
Milton Keynes UK
UKHW031859110523
421606UK00010B/409